T0192122

Lecture Notes in Computer Science

Lecture Notes in Artificial Intelligence   13856

Founding Editor

Jörg Siekmann

Series Editors

Randy Goebel, *University of Alberta, Edmonton, Canada*
Wolfgang Wahlster, *DFKI, Berlin, Germany*
Zhi-Hua Zhou, *Nanjing University, Nanjing, China*

The series Lecture Notes in Artificial Intelligence (LNAI) was established in 1988 as a topical subseries of LNCS devoted to artificial intelligence.

The series publishes state-of-the-art research results at a high level. As with the LNCS mother series, the mission of the series is to serve the international R & D community by providing an invaluable service, mainly focused on the publication of conference and workshop proceedings and postproceedings.

Katsutoshi Yada · Yasufumi Takama ·
Koji Mineshima · Ken Satoh
Editors

New Frontiers in Artificial Intelligence

JSAI-isAI 2021 Workshops, JURISIN,
LENLS18, SCIDOCA, Kansei-AI, AI-BIZ
Yokohama, Japan, November 13–15, 2021
Revised Selected Papers

 Springer

Editors
Katsutoshi Yada ⓘD
Kansai University
Suita, Japan

Yasufumi Takama ⓘD
Tokyo Metropolitan University
Tokyo, Japan

Koji Mineshima ⓘD
Keio University
Tokyo, Japan

Ken Satoh ⓘD
National Institute of Informatics
Tokyo, Japan

ISSN 0302-9743　　　　　　　　ISSN 1611-3349　(electronic)
Lecture Notes in Artificial Intelligence
ISBN 978-3-031-36189-0　　　　ISBN 978-3-031-36190-6　(eBook)
https://doi.org/10.1007/978-3-031-36190-6

LNCS Sublibrary: SL7 – Artificial Intelligence

This Springer imprint is published by the registered company Springer Nature Switzerland AG
The registered company address is: Gewerbestrasse 11, 6330 Cham, Switzerland

Preface

JSAI (The Japanese Society for Artificial Intelligence) is a premier academic society that focuses on artificial intelligence in Japan and was established in 1986. The JSAI-isAI (JSAI International Symposium on Artificial Intelligence) 2021 was the 13th international symposium on AI supported by the JSAI. JSAI-isAI 2021 was successfully held entirely online from November 13th to 15th. JSAI-isAI 2021 included five workshops. 85 papers were submitted and 72 papers were selected for presentation at the workshops. This volume, New Frontiers in Artificial Intelligence: JSAI-isAI 2021 Workshops, is the post-proceedings of JSAI-isAI 2021. From the five workshops (JURISIN 2021, LENLS18, SCIDOCA2021, Kansei-AI 2021, and AI-Biz 2021) 26 papers were carefully selected and revised according to the comments of the workshop program committees. This has resulted in an excellent selection of papers that are representative of some of the topics of AI research both in Japan and in other parts of the world.

The fifteenth International Workshop on Juris-Informatics (JURISIN 2021) was held with the support of JSAI in association with JSAI International Symposia on AI (JSAI-isAI 2021). Juris-informatics was organized to discuss legal issues from the perspective of information science. Compared with conventional AI and law, this workshop covers a wide range of topics, including any theories and technologies which are not directly related to juris-informatics but have the potential to contribute to this domain.

LENLS 18 was the eighteenth event in the series, and it focused on the formal and theoretical aspects of natural language. LENLS (Logic and Engineering of Natural Language Semantics) is an annual international workshop recognised internationally in the formal syntax-semantics-pragmatics community. It brings together for discussion and interdisciplinary communication researchers working on formal theories of natural language syntax, semantics and pragmatics, (formal) philosophy, artificial intelligence and computational linguistics.

The Fifth International Workshop on SCIentific DOCument Analysis (SCI-DOCA2021) is an annual international workshop focusing on various aspects and perspectives of scientific document analysis for their efficient use and exploration. It gathers together researchers and experts who are aiming at scientific document analysis from various perspectives, and invites technical paper presentations and system demonstrations that cover any aspects of scientific document analysis.

Kansei-AI 2021 was the international workshop on Artificial Affective (Kansei) Intelligence. The scope of this workshop was research in science and engineering related to value judgements made through the five senses, such as image processing, tactile engineering, acoustics, machine learning, sensitivity engineering, and natural language processing.

AI-Biz 2021 (Artificial Intelligence of and for Business) was the fifth workshop hosted by the SIG-BI (Business Informatics) special interest group of JSAI and we believe the workshop was successful, addressing very wide fields of business and AI technology including human capital, industry classifications, capturing mercurial customers, variable selection, organizational performance, traffic congestion, visualization of R&D projects, credit risk, ecocars, stock price prediction, and so on.

It is our great pleasure to be able to share some highlights of these fascinating workshops in this volume. We hope this book will introduce readers to the state-of-the-art research outcomes of JSAI-isAI 2021, and motivate them to participate in future JSAI-isAI events.

October 2022

Katsutoshi Yada
Yasufumi Takama
Koji Mineshima
Ken Satoh

Organization

JURISIN 2021

Workshop Co-chairs

Yasuhiro Ogawa   Nagoya University, Japan
Makoto Nakamura   Niigata Institute of Technology, Japan

Program Committee

Thomas Ågotnes   University of Bergen, Norway
Michał Araszkiewicz   Jagiellonian University, Poland
Ryuta Arisaka   Kyoto University, Japan
Marina De Vos   University of Bath, UK
Jürgen Dix   Clausthal University of Technology, Germany
Kripabandhu Ghosh   Indian Institute of Science Education and
                            Research (IISER) Kolkata, India
Saptarshi Ghosh   Indian Institute of Technology Kharagpur, India
Randy Goebel   University of Alberta, Canada
Guido Governatori   CSIRO, Australia
Tokuyasu Kakuta   Chuo University, Japan
Yoshinobu Kano   Shizuoka University, Japan
Takehiko Kasahara   Toin Univ. of Yokohama, Japan
Mi-Young Kim   U. of Alberta, Canada
Nguyen Le Minh   Japan Advanced Institute of Science and
                            Technology, Japan
Makoto Nakamura   Niigata Institute of Technology, Japan
Yoshiaki Nishigai   Chiba University, Japan
Tomoumi Nishimura   Osaka University, Japan
Katsumi Nitta   National Institute of Advanced Industrial Science
                            and Technology, Japan
Yasuhiro Ogawa   Nagoya University, Japan
Monica Palmirani   CIRSFID, Italy
Ginevra Peruginelli   ITTIG-CNR, Italy
Juliano Rabelo   AMII, Canada
Seiichiro Sakurai   Meiji Gakuin University, Japan
Ken Satoh   National Institute of Informatics and
                            SOKENDAI, Japan

Akira Shimazu	JAIST, Japan
Kazuko Takahashi	Kwansei Gakuin University, Japan
Satoshi Tojo	JAIST, Japan
Katsuhiko Toyama	Nagoya University, Japan
Yueh-Hsuan Weng	Tohoku University, Japan
Masaharu Yoshioka	Hokkaido University, Japan

Additional Reviewers

Lorenzo Bacci
Hiroaki Yamada

LENLS 18

Workshop Chair

Alastair Butler	Hirosaki University, Japan

Workshop Co-chairs

Daisuke Bekki	Ochanomizu University, Japan
Elin McCready	Aoyama Gakuin University, Japan
Koji Mineshima	Keio University, Japan

Program Committee

Richard Dietz	University of Tokyo, Japan
Patrick D. Elliott	Massachusetts Institute of Technology, USA
Naoya Fujikawa	University of Tokyo, Japan
Yurie Hara	Hokkaido University, Japan
Robert Henderson	University of Arizona, Japan
Hitomi Hirayama	Kyushu Institute of Technology, Japan
Magdalena Kaufmann	University of Connecticut, Japan
Kristina Liefke	Ruhr University Bochum, Germany
Yoshiki Mori	University of Tokyo, Japan
David Y. Oshima	Nagoya University, Japan
Katsuhiko Sano	Hokkaido University, Japan
Osamu Sawada	Kobe University, Japan
Ribeka Tanaka	Ochanomizu University, Japan
Wataru Uegaki	University of Edinburgh, UK

Katsuhiko Yabushita   Naruto University of Education, Japan
Tomoyuki Yamada   Hokkaido University, Japan
Shunsuke Yatabe   Kyoto University, Japan
Kei Yoshimoto   Tohoku University, Japan

SCIDOCA2021

Workshop Chair

Le-Minh Nguyen   Japan Advanced Institute of Science and
                             Technology, Japan

Workshop Advisors

Yuji Matsumoto   AIP-RIKEN, Japan
Ken Satoh   NII, Japan

Program Committee

Nguyen Le Minh   Japan Advanced Institute of Science and
                             Technology, Japan
Noriki Nishida   RIKEN Center for Advanced Intelligence Project,
                             Japan
Vu Tran   Institute of Statistical Mathematics, Japan
Yusuke Miyao   University of Tokyo, Japan
Yuji Matsumoto   RIKEN Center for Advanced Intelligence Project,
                             Japan
Yoshinobu Kano   Shizuoka University, Japan
Akiko Aizawa   National Institute of Informatics, Japan
Ken Satoh   National Institute of Informatics and
                             SOKENDAI, Japan
Junichiro Mori   University of Tokyo, Japan
Kentaro Inui   Tohoku University, Japan

Kansei-AI2021

Workshop Chair

Koichi Yamagata   University of Electro-Communications, Japan

Workshop Co-chair

Yuji Nozaki   University of Electro-Communications, Japan

Program Committee

Koichi Yamagata   University of Electro-Communications, Japan
Yuji Nozaki   University of Electro-Communications, Japan

AI-Biz2021

Workshop Chair

Takao Terano   Chiba University of Commerce, Japan

Workshop Co-chairs

Setsuya Kurahashi   University of Tsukuba, Japan
Hiroshi Takahashi   Keio University, Japan

Program Committee

Chang-Won Ahn   VAIV Company, South Korea
Ernesto Carella   University of Oxford, UK
Reiko Hishiyama   Waseda University, Japan
Manabu Ichikawa   Shibaura Institute of Technology, Japan
Yoko Ishino   Yamaguchi University, Japan
Hajime Kita   Kyoto University, Japan
Hajime Mizuyama   Aoyama Gakuin University, Japan
Matthias Raddant   Kiel University, Germany
Chathura Rajapaksha   University of Kelaniya, Sri Lanka
Masakazu Takahashi   Yamaguchi University, Japan
Shingo Takahashi   Waseda University, Japan
Alfred Taudes   Vienna University, Austria
Takashi Yamada   Yamaguchi University, Japan
Chao Yang   Hunan University, China

Sponsored By

The Japanese Society for Artificial Intelligence (JSAI)

Contents

SCIDOCA 2021

KANSEIAI 2021

AI-Biz 2021

JURISIN 2021

Fifteenth International Workshop on Juris-informatics (JURISIN 2021)

Yasuhiro Ogawa[1] and Makoto Nakamura[2]

[1] Nagoya University, Japan
[2] Niigata Institute of Technology, Japan

1 The Workshop

Juris-informatics is a new research area that studies legal issues from the perspective of informatics. This workshop aims to discuss the fundamental and practical issues among people from various backgrounds such as law, social science, information and intelligent technology, logic and philosophy, including the conventional AI and law area. JURISIN 2021 is the 15th International Workshop on Juris-informatics, which is held in association with the Thirteenth International Symposia on AI by the Japanese Society of Artificial Intelligence (JSAI-isAI).

In JURISIN 2021, we invited two lecturers. Yasutomo Kimura of Otaru University of Commerce gave a lecture titled "Shared Tasks on Japanese Local Assembly Minutes Dataset," and Mayu Watanabe of Rikkyo University gave a lecture titled "Expanding Access to Justice with Technology -Online Dispute Resolution and its Policy Development-."

Furthermore, we have a special session on the project "Advanced Reasoning Support for Judicial Judgment by Artificial Intelligence." This project aims to develop a system that supports advanced reasoning and analyzes argumentation for juridical judgment.

2 Papers

This year, we have twenty-two submissions. Three program committee members reviewed each paper, and as a result, twenty-one papers were selected for a presentation at the workshop, but six papers were withdrawn due to the double acceptance for JURISIN 2021 and JURIX 2021. Papers cover various fields of juris-informatics such as logical inference, legal documents processing, and legal issues of applications of AI.

After JURISIN 2021, according to reviewers' comments and discussion during the workshop, authors revised their papers and submitted them for the post-proceedings. Each paper was reviewed again, and we selected six excellent papers included in this volume.

Acknowledgements. We thank all the Steering Committee, Advisory Committee, and Program Committee of JURISIN 2021, all authors who submitted papers, and all the members of the Organizing Committee of JSAI-isAI.

Prediction Model for Drunk Driving Sentencing: Applying TextCNN to Chinese Judgement Texts

Hsuan-Lei Shao[1] ⓘ, Yu-Ying Huang[2], and Sieh-Chuen Huang[3](✉) ⓘ

[1] Department of East Asian Studies, National Taiwan Normal University, Taipei, Taiwan
hlshao@ntnu.edu.tw
[2] Graduate Institute of Interdisciplinary Legal Studies, National Taiwan University, Taipei, Taiwan
r08a41001@ntu.edu.tw
[3] College of Law, National Taiwan University, Taipei, Taiwan
schhuang@ntu.edu.tw

Abstract. Drunk driving cases often arouse public concern in Taiwanese society. According to 2013 amended Paragraph 1 of Article 185–3, the Taiwan Criminal Code, a drunk person may face up to a maximum sentence of two years in prison if his/her exhalation contains alcohol of 0.25 mg per liter or more, or blood alcohol concentration is 0.05% or more. The huge volume of "drunk driving" cases becomes a considerable workload for the court and therefore it may be worthwhile developing an automatic sentencing supportive system. This research attempts to train a deep-learning model to predict sentences by inputting the section of "recidivist/facts of the judgement." The TextCNN (Convolutional Neural Networks) model reached a 73% accuracy rate in four-category sentencing prediction. This research suggests that adopting two kinds of pre-processing methods and a well-trained model directly to unstructured judgement texts without word segmentation can result in a good performance. It opens the possibility of applying different machine learning techniques to legal texts.

Keywords: Text-classification · sentencing system · drunk driving · convolutional neural network · deep learning · TextCNN

1 Introduction

Drunk driving (referred to as "the criminal offense of driving under the influence (DUI)" in Article 185–3[1] of the Taiwan Criminal Code) is a topic of considerable importance in Taiwanese society. The DUI cases exhibit the following features: 1. High volume of cases,

---

[1] Taiwan Criminal Code Article 185–3 has three paragraphs. This article involves only the first paragraph, which provides that:*A person who drives a motor vehicle in any one of the following circumstances shall be sentenced to imprisonment for not more than two years; in addition thereto, a fine of not more than two hundred thousand dollars may be imposed:.1. The person's exhalation contains alcohol of 0.25 mg per liter or more, or the person's blood alcohol concentration is 0.05% or more..2. There are circumstances other than those stipulated in the preceding subparagraph which may prove that the person has consumed alcohol or other similar substances which prevent the person from driving safely.3. The person uses drugs, narcotics*

© Springer Nature Switzerland AG 2023
K. Yada et al. (Eds.): JSAI-isAI 2021 Workshops, LNAI 13856, pp. 3–15, 2023.
https://doi.org/10.1007/978-3-031-36190-6_1

exceeding thousands of cases per year; 2. Culturally, Taiwanese are unusually highly aversive to drunk driving. 3. Jurisprudentially, whether and how to see crimes constituted by abstract endangerment[2] of legal interests without harms or without victims are issues worth discussing [8]. Taiwan has made several law amendments in recent years, mainly in the direction of "increasing penalties and relaxing the definition of drunk driving". Criminal law has been repeatedly amended to increase the term of imprisonment, which also shows society's deep anxiety of drunk driving. However, the number of cases of drunk driving remains high, resulting in courts having to repeatedly and extensively determine the penalty of drunk driving.

Therefore, one of the purposes of the study is to construct a model to predict the length of a drunk driving sentence. This automated process is expected to alleviate the labor costs incurred by a large number of "drunk driving" cases. In addition, this study will provide a different approach to deal with text data.

2   Literature Review and Research Design

There has been a couple of studies on drunk driving in the field of empirical legal studies, discussing whether it is possible to reduce the number of drunk driving cases by increasing sentences. In the case of Chile, raising the penalty may have a short-term deterrent effect, but the long-term caseload will gradually return to its original level [1]. The other approach is to study sentencing factors. For example, the study in Colorado, U.S. involves the use of criminal record and blood alcohol levels as the benchmark [2]. This is also the present system in Taiwan. The two methods mainly focused on designing a legal regime, while the goal of the former is "reducing drunk driving cases", and the latter concentrates on "fair judgments." On the other hand, the large number of cases on the front line indicates a burden of extensive practical working hours.

In Taiwan, the statutory penalty for drunk driving is less than two years of punishment, but depending on the individual case, there may be room for an increase or decrease in sentences. This research assumes that, based on the principle of equality, judges should make decisions based on "certain rules" in de jure, and implement a fair proportion of punishments corresponding to crimes, which are consistent with the principle of fairness and in accordance with the expectations of society. At the same time, even if a judge has a special preference or makes a "special disposition" for any specific reason in a case, "numerous cases" themselves have a comparable existence of "collective rationality" [3]. Therefore, under the premise of sufficient samples, the "sentencing" in court judgments may be computed and a model may be established. As indicated in the *"Reference Manual for Sentencing Factors That Should Be Taken into Account in Criminal Cases"* published by the Judicial Yuan, which is advising the court

---

or other similar substances that prevent the person from driving safely. The second paragraph of this Article stipulates DUI causing death or serious injury. The third paragraph increases penalties for recidivists. For the full contents of the Taiwan Criminal Code, *see* https://law.moj.gov.tw/ENG/LawClass/LawAll.aspx?pcode=C0000001 (last visited: March 13, 2022).

[2] The term "abstract endangerment" is the common term in German criminal legal doctrine. This means offences in which harm is not mentioned explicitly. Abstract endangerment offences need clear justification because the reference to harm is vague.

to implement the appropriate considerations for driving under the influence (DUI), it lists 19 indicators such as alcohol concentration, motor vehicle size, and time of driving, etc. [4]. However, it is not clear whether or to what extent judges follow those "guidelines" to do sentencing.

In the field of computer science, using the convolution neural network (CNN) method to classify images has been a common approach. The CNN algorithm has laid a milestone in the image-classification competitions, performing very well with the datasets like the CIFAR-10. Following this trend, researchers have attempted to apply this algorithm to the task of text-classification. For example, some used TextCNN on the sentiment analysis of specific texts [5, 6]. In addition, TextCNN also performs competitively with other types of texts through delicate combination of different algorithms [7].

By comparison, there are few studies applying TextCNN on Chinese texts. One of the papers analyzed Chinese medical intents and set a benchmark accuracy of 47.3% on 36 subtypes of intent classification using TextCNN. This reveals that applying TextCNN to Chinese texts is still a difficult mission [9]. From this starting point, our research attempted to make some progress. More specifically, we will construct a drunk driving sentencing model based on legal texts. This is not the first attempt to apply machine learning to Chinese legal texts. For example, the authors had used MLP (multilayer perceptron) on child custody decisions which were carefully labelled by human and resulted an accuracy of 98.8% [17]. In contrast to this approach, the article suggests another one abbreviating some steps of human processing with the assistance of deep learning and forms an end-to-end solution. It is possible to adopt more advanced models such as the RNN series (BERT, transformers and etc.) in the future. In summary, the purpose of the study is to decide a sentencing result for a case after the machine reads its relevant circumstances (facts) without human labelling (Fig. 1).

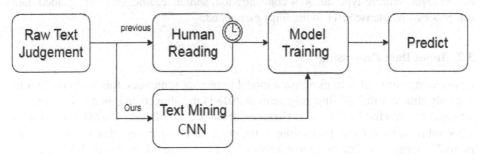

Fig. 1. Research structure

3 Data Source and Processing

3.1 Data Source

As drunk driving is an issue with many citizens concern, in 2019, the Central News Agency (CNA) in Taiwan collected 490,000 judgments from 2000 to 2019 and completed a special report [11]. The report pointed out that the number of "the DUI vehicular injury and homicide cases" has been decreasing since year 2000 and "simple drunk driving cases" (which did not cause harms to persons) started decreasing after the amendments of the Criminal Code in 2013. CNA also released the abovementioned dataset to the public to stimulate further studies. We used this dataset to construct a prediction model. Before introducing the model, it is necessary to describe how this dataset was established by CNA. First, through inputting "alcohol" to query the full text of criminal judgments in district courts, as the initial collection standard, there were about 590,000 cases found. Then, through the arrangement and combination of relevant words, such as "185–3 of the Criminal Code," "driving under influence," "the person's exhalation contains alcohol of 0.25 mg per liter or more," and "taking alcohol," it gave approximately 510,000 results. After eliminating cases that are not relevant to "drunk driving" (e.g., cases regarding alcohol lamps), there were 490,000 judgments left.

Next, the CAN data was divided into three parts: the DUI homicide (consisting of 2,807 cases), the DUI injury (5,202 cases), and simple drunk driving (488,603 cases). This categorization is necessary because the Criminal Code provided quite different sentences respectively. Therefore, cases with "death" or "injury" appearing in the operative provisions [10] (main text) of the judgments were excluded [11]. The remaining 488,603 judgments were then labeled according to judgment date, jurisdiction, whether it is a recidivist, whether the punishment may be commuted to a fine, perpetrators' education level, vehicle type, alcohol concentration, sentence, fine, etc. For detailed data pre-processing, please refer to the links mentioned.

3.2 Input Data Processing

Considering our goal is to establish a model to predict sentences, this study decides to use only simple drunk driving judgments in 2018 in the abovementioned CNA's dataset, which accounted for 46,231 cases. However, about one out of every 10,000 cases showed error values caused by text-encoding or file errors and hence were discarded, resulting in 46,228 cases left. The average number of words contained for those 46,228 cases is 1,823, while the standard deviation was 545 words in Chinese. The median was 1,817 words. The word counts for judgements can be as few as 644 words for the shortest one, but as many as 9,251 words for the longest one.

We do not input full texts of judgments to train the model because the answers (sentences) are included. And after this study is completed, we will construct a system/interface where users can enter any facts to get predictive result of sentencing. Therefore, the next step of our data processing is to extract the texts of "facts" to be the data for training. A typical simple drunk driving judgment contains four sections as other judgments: the title (including the case number, the parties and their lawyers), operative provisions, facts and reasons (including parties' arguments, the facts recognized and reasons articulated by the court) and miscellaneous items (the judgment date and the names of the judge and clerk) [10]. We only picked up the third sections "Facts and Reasons" to be *inputs 1,* which contains the following sentences. By pruning the judgment texts, we can ensure that the model will not acquire the answer (sentencing) directly from the training data.

[Facts and Reasons: 1. At 0:00 a.m. on September 7, 2017 (the intent of soliciting a summary judgment for execution is recorded from 12:00 p.m. on September 6, to 1:00 a.m. on the next day), after drinking beer in the residence of a friend in Manzhou Township and Xinglu Road, Pingtong County, the concentration of alcohol in the defendant's breath has reached more than 0.25 mg per liter. The defendant rode a motorcycle with the plate number 000-000 on the road with the intent of unsafe driving. At 1:55 on the same day, when passing through the 33th lane of Hengxi Road, Hengchun Town, Pingdong County, the police found that the back light of the defendant's motorcycle did not turn on so stopped the defendant. At 2:02 on the same day, the alcohol concentration in the exhaust of the defendant reached 0.57 mg per liter, 2. Dong OO, the defendant, has admitted his behavior in the process of police inquiry and investigation. The police officers' investigation report, the alcohol test record, the vehicle details report, and the notification sheet of a violation of road traffic management issued by the Pingdong County Government Police Bureau all indicate that the confessions of the defendant is consistent to the truth.]—inputs 1 for the model 1.

It should be noted that sentencing is not only based on the crime fact but also the defendant's background such as the age (Article 63 of the Taiwan Criminal Code), motivation, life style, personality, etc. (Article 57) and recidivism (Article 47). However, these sentencing factors are not easy to be identified by using a single word and hence difficult to automatize text-encoding. The only exception may be the recidivism as the judge in Taiwan always clearly states whether the defendant is a "recidivist" by using string comparison of a single phrase "recidivist (累犯)" in operative provisions. In our sample, there are 15,352 cases in which the defendant is a recidivist (representing by 1 in this feature), around one third of the whole samples. And this new feature of recidivism along with "Facts and Reasons" become another training dataset: *inputs 2.* The purpose of creating *inputs 2* is to compare with the pure *inputs 1* to see whether the model will perform better by adding more information.

Nevertheless, some judgments contain only texts regarding procedure without "Facts and Reasons." These usually are appeal decisions or procedure decisions, which are usually quite short in length. Therefore, we decided to collect judgments consisting of more than 250 Chinese words to ensure there is enough fact information for machine learning. After the above data preprocessing, the total number of effective samples was reduced to 33,129, with an average of 468 words, a standard deviation of 235 words, and the third quartile of 522 words. The comparison of samples before and after processing is shown in the Table 1. The reason of categorizing sentence into four types will be elaborated in the next section.

Table 1. Comparison of sample quantities before and after processing

Sentence-Four Classifications	Original sample size	Sample size after processing
≤2 months	15,263 (33.0%)	10,998 (33.2%)
>2 months, ≤3 months	13,948 (30.2%)	10,921 (33.0%)
>3 months, ≤6 months	15,359 (33.2%)	9,926 (30.0%)
>6 months	1,551 (3.4%)	1,284 (3.8%)
Total samples	46,228 (100%)	33,129 (100%)

3.3 Choosing Classification Method

Different from previous literature considering sentence prediction to be a regression task, we treat it as a classification question and categorize our output (sentence) into four types based on the observation of sentencing. First, in our dataset before processing (46,228 samples of drunk driving judgments that occurred in 2018), the minimum sentence is a month and the maximum sentence is 2 years. And the average sentence was 102.7 days with a standard deviation of 46.1 days. Nonetheless, the imprisonment declared by Taiwanese court is always counted by months as a unit, not by days, which means sentence will not be 40 days or 1.33 months. Therefore, viewing sentencing as a continuous value and a regression task is not always appropriate. The second reason is the highly asymmetric distribution of the data. As indicated in the histogram distribution diagram (Fig. 2), the distribution of sentence is very skewed. As long as the defendant is guilty, the judge can declare the imprisonment to be less than 2 years according to Paragraph 1 of Article 185–3 of the Taiwan Criminal Code. But in reality, 96% of judgments impose sentence less than 6 months. Although it is not completely impossible to do regression analysis on asymmetric data through some kind of transformation (preprocessing) [16], the skewness of our samples is too extreme (1.47) to proceed. Therefore, we regard the sentence of simple drunk driving as a classification question, not a regression one.

Next, we decide to split the whole dataset into four sets to classify under the following two considerations. First, as shown in Fig. 2, two months and three months will be the primary breakpoints because the cases between 1–2 months, 2–3 months, and more than 3 months have almost the same share (one third of all samples). From the legal viewpoint, another proper breakpoint is 6 months. According to Paragraph 1 of Article 41 of the Taiwan Criminal Code, if the sentence is more than six months, there is no possibility for the punishment to be commuted to a fine, so judges are usually careful with sentencing more than 6 months. Therefore, this article divides the outputs to be four types pursuant to the breakpoints of "two months, three months and six months" so that the number of samples in each group will be roughly equal except the last one (see Table 1).

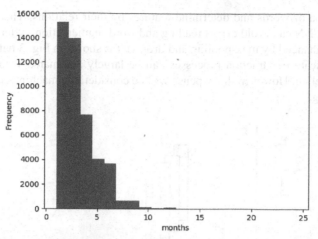

Fig. 2. Drunk driving sentencing histogram diagram (The X-axis is the term of the sentence (months), and the Y-axis is the sample size (number of cases).)

4 Model Training and the Result

After data processing, the Convolutional Neural Networks (CNN) is applied to calculate sentences and make prediction to unknown cases.

4.1 Model Training

Convolutional Neural Networks (CNN) has been commonly applied to analyze visual imagery. It extracts features of images by subsampling groups of pixels contained in an image as filters or kernels as the basis to compute new features. As the kernels slide over an image as the input map, corresponding feature tiles would be extracted to form a convoluted feature matrix summarizing the image characteristics. After performing transformation and pooling to obtain a full connected layer, a softmax activation function will then be applied to determine the classification labels the model is trying to predict [12]. Image recognition is currently one of the hot topics in artificial intelligence, and has been developed into the fields of real-time object detection [13]. Instead of rule-based image recognition, a CNN model uses kernels to extract features, thus saving the use of manual labor to describe features [14]. So this paper will explore whether the CNN/ TextCNN can be adopted to legal texts including word vectors to extract text features and classify successfully.

The size of the selected kernel is 5. For example, when the judgment text is "不能安全駕駛動力交通工具" (unable to drive vehicle safely), it will be broken down into a combination of (combined word vectors) "不能安全駕" and "能安全駕駛" and "安全駕駛動" and "全駕駛動力", etc. In short, kernels read fives words as a n-gram at the same time in TextCNN, as well as read n*n pixels graph in CNN. Then can establish connections between the previous and the latter series, which can further be used to extract the meaning and characteristics of sequential data. Compared with the bag-of-words model [15] used in the previous literature, the CNN algorithm extracts feature of all combination of words and determine features by their relations. Therefore, with a good design, CNN can avoid expert reading and word segmentation. Afterward, feature weights are enhanced by max-pooling and dropout (as shown in Fig. 3 below). In other words, these feature extraction processes can be largely automated without the need for expert labeling. However, the expense will be considerable machine computing and model building.

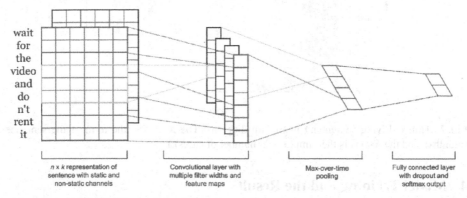

Fig. 3. Processing of Text Convolutional Neural Networks [14]

Every sample for CNN needs to be in the same size. In our case, we have to input the "Facts and Reasons" of judgments with the same number of words. Given that the mean of word numbers is 468 and more than 75% of samples are under 600 words, after consideration, the standard for the number of words adopted here is 600. In the case that judgment is longer, the first 600 words will be chosen and the rest will be discarded. While the judgment is shorter, "0" will be added to make the word number counted for 600. The input for the model is the 600 words of every sample (which is equivalent to n in the Fig. 3) and its word vector (128 dimensions, which is equivalent to k in the Fig. 3). Through convolutional layers and fully connected layers, the output will be born, consisting of four categories. The accuracy rate will be derived from comparing the model prediction with the ground truth (real sentencing).

The Fig. 4 shows that the model of *inputs 1* has become stable after 900 times iterations without significant improvements afterwards. The model of *inputs 2* stopped at the 1700th iteration. Also it is clear that the accuracy curve of *inputs 2* (with recidivist feature) usually performs better than *inputs 1* (without recidivist feature) and finally reaches higher rates than *inputs 1*.

The same situation appears on the loss curve (Fig. 5). Both loss of *inputs 1* and *inputs 2* converges fast and goes stable after 600 times iterations. *Inputs 1* stops at the 900th iteration while *inputs 2* keeps converges until 1700th iteration and reaches lower rates than *inputs 1*.

4.2 Presentation of Model Results

In the total 33,129 samples, we choose 80% for training, 10% for validation, and 10% for testing (comprising 3,312 samples). The confusion matrix of *inputs 1 test set* is as

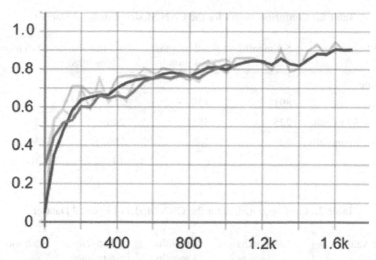

Fig. 4. Accuracy processing curve (dark orange line: validation set of *inputs 1*; light orange line: training set of *inputs 1*, dark red line: validation set of *inputs 2*; light red line: training set of *inputs 2*)

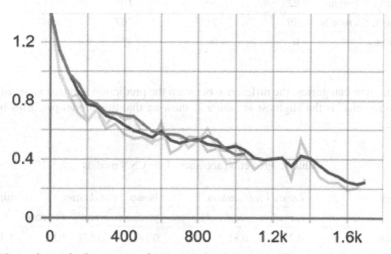

Fig. 5. Loss change in the process of convergence (dark orange line: validation set of *inputs 1*; light orange line: training set of *inputs 1*, dark red line: validation set of *inputs 2*; light red line: training set of *inputs 2*)

Table 2. The accuracy is 71%. And *inputs 2 test set* is shown in Table 3. The accuracy is 73%. Through comparing these two results, it is found that adding a key attribute (recidivism) can improve the performance of the CNN model up to two percent.

The precision, recall, and F1-score are also slightly more than 0.7 as shown in Table 4. Compared to the 25% baseline of the original four categories, approximately 71% of hits was met in our model of *inputs 1* and 73.31% in *inputs 2*. It is also worth noting that

Table 2. Confusion matrix for the CNN Model of *inputs 1* Dataset

Predictive Value, n = 3312	≤2 months	>2 months, ≤3 months	>3 months, ≤6 months	>6 months
Actual Value				
≤2 months	891	138	71	1
>2 months, ≤3 months	225	555	240	2
>3 months, ≤6 months	62	182	790	36
>6 months	0	0	19	100

Table 3. Confusion matrix for the CNN Model of *inputs 2* Dataset

Predicitve Value, n = 3312	≤2 months	>2 months, ≤3 months	>3 months, ≤6 months	>6 months
Actual Value				
≤2 months	962	125	14	0
>2 months, ≤3 months	227	599	195	1
>3 months, ≤6 months	49	211	767	43
>6 months	0	0	19	100

among the four categories, the difference between the prediction and true value of "less than two months" is the slightest at *inputs 2*, showing that this model performs best in this part.

Table 4. Prediction accuracy of the CNN models

Sentences	Inputs 1 test dataset			Inputs 2 test dataset			support
	precision	recall	f1-score	precision	recall	f1-score	
≤2 months	0.76	0.81	0.78	0.78	0.87	**0.82**	1,101
>2 months, ≤3 months	0.63	0.54	0.59	0.64	0.59	0.61	1,022
>3 months, ≤6 months	0.71	0.74	0.72	0.77	0.72	0.74	1,070
>6 months	0.72	0.84	**0.78**	0.69	0.84	0.76	119
Macro avg	0.70	0.73	0.72	0.72	0.75	0.73	3,312
Weighted avg	0.70	0.71	**0.70**	0.73	0.73	**0.73**	3,312

5 Discussion and Conclusion

This article applied TextCNN to simple drunk driving judgment texts directly to predict a sentence outcome. The model uses a large number of features, which are comprised of enormous combinations of 5 words in the texts. Compared to previous research which defined the feature by experts' opinions, features in our study are extremely huge in number. Furthermore, the kernel size (5) also made computational work intensive. In other words, deep learning methods utilizing models such as CNN can almost all information of the texts and gradually approach to correct values through gradient operations. For example, in the input item, "the defendant has made a confession in the interrogation and investigation", the words *confession in the interrogation* can be found in the CNN algorithm, which makes it a feature that can be extracted without human efforts. This TextCNN model has a 71% accuracy rate in four-category sentencing prediction and further reaches 73% accuracy rate when provided with additional "recidivist" feature. From the point of model evaluate of the drunk-driving sentencing in Chinese Character, this is the state-of-art of this topic.

As mentioned previously, there has been no research adopting deep-learning method to court judgements in Taiwan yet. This paper is a preliminary study and we claim 71% accuracy as a benchmark temporarily. By offering background information of the defendant, in our research, whether the defendant is a recidivist, the accuracy can be improved to 73%. Of course, it is not difficult to understand that given more useful information, the model can perform better. But how much *inputs 2* can work in the real world is doubtful. This also relates to the user interface that we design based on the TextCNN model of *inputs 1*, not *inputs 2*.

Let's imagine a scenario that the user of sentence prediction system is a layman, not a prosecutor, lawyer or judge. This user may not get access to complete information regarding the crime facts as well as the defendant himself/herself, such as whether the defendant is a recidivist. If a sentence prediction system requires the user to input all features that defined by experts in advance, the user may feel confused about whether he/she should check the box regarding which he/she is lack of information. Meanwhile, our TextCNN model (*inputs 1*) does not contain experts-defined features, and therefore our prediction system only requires the user to input a few words or sentences related to crime facts. There are no check boxes and the user will not be forced to input the facts or background information that he/she does not know. We consider this design is more friendly to non-expert users who do not have comprehensive information as prosecutors or judges.

However, this research has its limits. First of all, the defect of the CNA's dataset was inevitable. For example, there were judgments garbled so that legal terms cannot be accurately identified. Fortunately, this limitation does not have a fatal impact on our research. The main reason is that most of the flawed judgments (such as judgments that are too short) are simply discarded through our data processing rule (which requires judgments to consist of more than 250 words). The number of remaining judgments is still substantial enough for computation. Another question is whether the model based on "simple drunk driving judgments" can be applied to other types of crimes. Because the deep learning (TextCNN) in relatively a data-driven method, the model in one crime might not fit other types of crimes very well. In short, artificial intelligence is more likely to play a role in a single task of legal data analysis.

Overall, this study demonstrates the potential of applying deep learning techniques to legal prediction, which saves human labor and reaches a promising accuracy rate. Because of the huge number of "simple drunk driving cases" and its routineness, it may be worth considering establishing a decision-making support system to provide advice for sentencing. On another note, due to the resource constraints of this study, we did not attempt many extractions of expert-appointing features except for recidivism. Text -mining also can be a way to reduce human intervention too. Compared with the CNN, it only depends on the degree of domain knowledge of the data by the researchers themselves. The CNN is more able to analyze the data without requiring researchers themselves, but with the aid of algorithm to map the corresponding knowledge. If more labor investment is possible, combining human-defining features with the current model may improve the performance of prediction, as we have shown by comparing *inputs 1* and *inputs 2*. The rapid development of algorithms is expected to enhance more efficient information extraction.

Acknowledgment. Hsuan-Lei Shao, "Knowledge Graph of China Studies: Knowledge Extraction, Graph Database, Knowledge Generation" (MOST 110–2628-H-003–002-MY4, Ministry of Science and Technology) in Taiwan.

Sieh-Chuen Huang, "Digital Court, Legal Tech, and Access to Justice" (MOST 110–2423-H-002–003, Ministry of Science and Technology) in Taiwan.

References

1. García-Echalar, A., Rau, T.: The effects of increasing penalties in drunk driving laws-evidence from Chile. Int. J. Environ. Res. Public Health **17**(21), 8103 (2020). https://doi.org/10.3390/ijerph17218103
2. Lange, T.J., Greene, E.: How judges sentence DUI offenders: an experimental study. Am. J. Drug Alcohol Abuse **16**(1–2), 125–133 (1990). https://doi.org/10.3109/00952999009001577
3. DiMaggio, P.J., Powell, W.W.: The iron cage revisited: institutional isomorphism and collective rationality in organizational fields. Am. Sociol. Rev. **48**(2), 147–160 (1983). https://doi.org/10.2307/2095101
4. Judicial Yuan, Reference Manual for Sentencing Factors That Should Be Taken into Account in Criminal Cases, 7–11 (2018)
5. Dong, M., Li, Y., Tang, X., Xu, J., Bi, S., Cai, Y.: Variable convolution and pooling convolutional neural network for text sentiment classification. IEEE Access **8**, 16174–16186 (2020)
6. Xuanyuan, M., Xiao, L., Duan, M.: Sentiment classification algorithm based on multi-modal social media text information. IEEE Access **9**, 33410–33418 (2021)
7. Guo, B., Zhang, C., Liu, J., Ma, X.: Improving text classification with weighted word embeddings via a multi-channel TextCNN model. Neurocomput. (Amsterdam) **363**, 366–374 (2019). https://doi.org/10.1016/j.neucom.2019.07.052
8. Ten Voorde, J.: Prohibiting remote harms: on endangerment. Citizensh. Control. Utrecht L. Rev. **10**, 163 (2014)
9. Chen, N., Su, X., Liu, T., Hao, Q., Wei, M.: A benchmark dataset and case study for Chinese medical question intent classification. BMC Med. Inform. Decis. Mak. **20**(3), 1–7 (2020)

10. Aletras,N., Tsarapatsanis, D., Preoţiuc-Pietro, D., Lampos, V.: Predicting judicial decisions of the european court of human rights: a natural language processing perspective. Peer J. Comput. Sci. **2**, e93 (2016). https://doi.org/10.7717/peerj-cs.93
11. Ke, H.: Outline of drunk driving in Taiwan seen from 490,000 judgments, CNA English News (2019). https://www.cna.com.tw/project/20190719-drunkdriving/epilogue.html. Accessed 10 Aug 2021
12. Krizhevsky, A., Sutskever, I., Hinton, G.E.: Imagenet classification with deep convolutional neural networks. In: Advances in Neural Information Processing Systems, pp. 1097–1105 (2012)
13. Ren, S., He, K., Girshick, R., Sun, J.: Faster r-cnn: towards real-time object detection with region proposal networks. In: Advances in Neural Information Processing Systems, pp. 91–99 (2015). Because the CNN research cycle is progressing rapidly, this paper only cites hotspot literature more than 10,000 times
14. Kim, Y.: Convolutional neural networks for sentence classification. arXiv preprint arXiv:1408.5882 (2014)
15. Huang, S., Shao, H.: Applying natural language processing and text mining to classifying child custody cases and predicting outcomes. Nat. Taiwan Univ. Law J. **49**(1), 195–224 (2020)
16. Kumar, U.A.: Comparison of neural networks and regression analysis: a new insight. Expert Syst. Appl. **29**(2), 424–430 (2005)
17. Huang, S., Shao, H.: Predicting family court cases by machine learning: an application of legal informatics. Taiwan Law Rev. **270**, 86–96 (2017). https://doi.org/10.3966/102559312 017110270006

User-Guided Machine Understanding
of Legal Documents

Kevin Purnell[✉] and Rolf Schwitter

School of Computing, Macquarie University, Sydney, Australia
kevin.purnell@hdr.mq.edu.au

Abstract. We present a novel approach to gaining a machine understanding of a legal document and then modelling the logic of that document in an integrated process. This paper describes a smart editor that
uses a declarative language to represent both the ontology and logic
models of a legal document. A document is incrementally elaborated in
a fixed sequence of steps beginning with an ontology discovery step that
identifies the explicit and implicit artefacts and applicable constraints.
This information is used to generate code representations paired with
words and icons which provide the foundation required for modelling the
legal logic. The pairing with words and icons achieves a formal correspondence that allows logic modelling via either a textual or a graphical
means. Similarly, this mechanism also supports both verbal and visual
user feedback, enhancing user understanding. The tree of rules produced
during this process is embedded in the original legal document, which
can then be used as a smart contract on a modified blockchain. The integrated use of a declarative language auto-generated from a smart user
interface for modelling both the ontology and the logic of a legal document, provides a simplicity and agility that enables domain experts to
create and test custom smart contracts.

Keywords: Answer Set Programming · Declarative Language · Legal
Logic · Logic Modelling · Ontology · Smart Contract · Verbalisation ·
Visualisation

1 Introduction

This research investigates the potential of declarative programming to advance
what can be achieved with smart contracts; that is, distributed programs embedded in a blockchain and executed according to a predefined mining protocol
[17]. The risk, understandability and cost problems being encountered with the
current compiled imperative language approach [2] creates a clear opportunity
for an application that allows domain experts to create, test and deploy their
own smart contacts while also reducing errors and security flaws. Such a system needs to be oriented towards users with low technical skills and moderate
domain expertise; therefore it requires an advanced smart user interface (UI)
which includes a natural language component and visual and verbal feedback
[27]. An overlooked area is the acquisition of a machine understanding; that is,

© Springer Nature Switzerland AG 2023
K. Yada et al. (Eds.): JSAI-isAI 2021 Workshops, LNAI 13856, pp. 16–32, 2023.
https://doi.org/10.1007/978-3-031-36190-6_2

the process by which the ontology of a legal document is discovered. Most papers discussing legal ontologies address all inclusive domain ontologies [28]; however, ontology concepts such as, 'what exists' and how are these 'related', also structure single documents and need to be dealt with as a prerequisite to modelling the embedded logic. The mathematical concept of "domain of discourse" is a useful simplifier, because the modeller only needs to consider the world of the document. Current approaches hard code this ontology as assumptions, which makes creation of custom smart contracts problematic, something which cannot be overcome by using pretested code libraries [7].

The term "smart contract" implies an underlying legal contract; however, smart contracts can have wider scope; for example, one of our use cases, a "Will and Testament", is not a legal contract (no offer or acceptance [1]). It can, however, be implemented as a smart contract because there is a future electronic transfer of assets (inheritance) controlled by external events (death of the testator). This paper addresses the issue of implementing legal contracts and other legal/normative documents as smart contracts where possible, because some types of legal reasoning (abductive, by analogy, by principle, by precedent [21]) are problematic for computers. Our focus on contract and contract-like legal documents and our current avoidance of legislation, limits the complexity we encounter. Consequently, this paper deals with only those parts of documents that are 'amenable' to implementation as smart contracts; that is, the parts that use deductive logic where the performance can be electronic (e.g., transfer of money and assets). Our use of a non-monotonic declarative language allows for the expression of defeasible and deontic concepts.

We investigate a declarative approach that: 1) fits into existing processes; 2) enables domain experts to create and test 'amenable' smart contracts; 3) enables a flexible evolutionary approach; and 4) auto-generates an executable declarative program that becomes the smart contract. We have identified an approach that starts with an existing legal document in electronic form, then understands that document via a guided question-answer dialogue. This step generates an ontology that guides the creation of representations. The recent availability of mature non-monotonic declarative languages in the knowledge representation and reasoning domain (e.g., Answer Set Programming, ASP) [3] provides an ability to model with and reason over these representations. Our approach pairs ASP representations with text and visual representations, which then allows user manipulation of ASP and feedback via these representations.

We investigate using rapid prototyping, and seek to demonstrate some advanced features that are difficult to achieve with the compiled imperative language approach [6]. Our prototype, the Smart Document Editor (SDE editor), is built using the HTML/CSS/JavaScript stack, with clingo [8] as the ASP solver.

Why Answer Set Programming. There are a number of reasons for starting with ASP as the first knowledge representation and reasoning language evaluated in our editor, including its status as the most mature of the applicable declarative languages, and the availability of a WebAssembly (WASM) compile [18,19]. ASP has some useful features: 1) achieving formal correspondence between text, icons and ASP representations is straightforward; 2) an ASP representation is declarative so it can be easily structured to facilitate translation to English and visual rendering; 3) ASP allows for reasoning over its knowledge; 4) ASP has formal semantics; 5) ASP allows rule trees to be built up in building block style; and, 6) ASP as we use it (without functions) always provides an answer (not Turing complete). Furthermore, the logic embedded in many amenable legal documents is not complex and conforms to closed world assumption (CWA) logic; that is, if something is not known to be true, then it is treated as false, opening up the possibility for using non-monotonic modelling constructs. ASP's research roots include logic programming, knowledge representation and constraint satisfaction. Brewka et al. [3] note that the close connection to non-monotonic logics provides ASP with the power to model default negation, deal with incomplete information, encode domain and problem-specific knowledge, defaults, and preferences in an intuitive and natural way [3], although Batsakis et al. [20] demonstrate that ASP is less efficient and less concise than some alternatives when computing deontic modalities. Finally, ASP exhibits 'elaboration tolerance', important because our approach involves frequent automatic assembly of ASP programs.

Related Research. Initial efforts at representing legal logic with logic programs [25,29] were redirected towards non-monotonic languages [33–36] after Herrestad [31] pointed out the limitations of pure first order logic when dealing with legal concepts. The modelling of contracts on top of an ontology [30] has previously been investigated, with Choudhury et al. [11] using a supplied domain specific ontology to assist with smart contract auto-generation. Ontology discovery from text is also well established [12] and has a well-developed toolset [13]; however, discovery from a dialogue with a domain expert stepping through placeholders is novel. ASP is frequently applied to difficult problems like configuration and scheduling [14]; however, there is a recent example of using ASP to represent both the ontology and to model business processes [24]. Other suitable declarative languages with efficient solvers exist, including ASPIC+(TOAST), Defeasible Logic (SPINdle) [37], and Defeasible Deontic Logic (Turnip) [38]. Batsakis et al. [20] compare ASP against ASPIC+ and DL. The visualisation of ASP execution results (called answer sets) has been investigated [15], but there are few attempts to visualise the modelling process, the closest being partial visual specification with ASPIDE [9]. The verbalisation builds on previous work [39]. Our focus on using a sophisticated smart user-interface (UI) to auto-generate executable declarative code on top of an ontology, and the tightly integrated exhaustive rule-by-rule testing with visual and verbal feedback are novel.

2   Overview of the Smart Document Editor (SDE)

Traditionally, most legal documents were paper forms filled out and signed by hand, and this format is retained in the electronic documents used by word processors and document automation systems [5]. The SDE editor adds the ability to first understand the implied world, then model and test the logic embedded in these legal documents. The SDE editor takes an existing legal document (see Fig. 1) and allows it to be incrementally developed into a smart contract. This workflow consists of a fixed sequence of steps that can be split into two main phases: 1) machine understanding of the legal document; and 2) smart contract creation. Machine understanding of the legal document involves three steps: (i) modelling the ontology (ontology discovery); (ii) modelling the legal logic (modelling logic); and (iii) validating that this model matches the user's understanding (model validation). Smart contract creation involves two steps: i) entering actual data (instantiation); and ii) testing that the output is what is expected (program verification). The final product is the initial legal document completed with actual information, with a tested ASP program embedded as markup. Contracts that are legally binding and both human and machine readable are known as Ricardian contracts [10]. This paper discusses techniques used for 'machine understanding of the legal document' parts (i) and (ii) and briefly describes (iii). Techniques used for 'smart contract creation' part (i); the creation of a smart contract by instantiating the logic model are covered in [22].

3   Ontology Discovery Process

Auto-generation of ASP programs requires a systematic approach that includes a representation grammar and a controlled vocabulary. The representation grammar specifies how ASP is used to represent things, relations, events, properties or constraints (artefacts) referred to or inferred by a legal document. A subset of ASP is used, which allows programs that conform to the definition of an "extended logic program" [4]. The controlled vocabulary aligns terminology and icons with common usage for the domain, which facilitates interpretation by domain experts, and simplifies ASP to English translation and graphical rendering. We use a structured controlled vocabulary [23] which also holds subsumption relations and a representative icon against each term. The grammar and the controlled vocabulary both conform to an ontology framework built into the SDE editor. An understanding of an unprocessed legal document begins with an ontology discovery process which steps a user through placeholders (e.g., "_____" see Fig. 1) in the document in sequential order, requesting input at each step (see Fig. 2). Guidance is provided by restricting selections to terms supplied by the controlled vocabulary, and by a prediction feature that guesses the correct term to use (see Fig. 2). This dialogue unfolds differently depending on the selections made, so that a picture of the data element is built up in five different objects: 1) an ASP representation specification (like a class declaration) used to generate the executable forms of ASP; 2) a visual representation (icon); 3) a text representation (word); 4) an in-memory representation; and 5) an instantiation placeholder (IPH) (red and olive underlined words in Fig. 2) which transforms the original placeholder and embeds a specification for the data required for instantiation. Artefacts not explicitly revealed via a placeholder can be added via other means, so that at the conclusion of this step a visual model is built up on the right side of the SDE editor screen (see Fig. 3). A formal correspondence between the first three objects is achieved, allowing ASP code to be manipulated via icons or text. Other details like constraints, properties, and identifiers can also be ascertained; where: 1) 'things' are tangible objects like people or assets; 2) 'relations' are associative tables which relate two or more 'things'; 3) 'events' are actions caused by, or impacting 'things'; 4) 'constraints' are limitations on the values of the foreign keys of 'artefacts'; 5) 'properties' describe features of 'artefacts'; and, 6) 'identifiers' name an instance of an 'artefact' or 'property', where 'artefact' names are assigned from the controlled vocabulary, while 'property' names are free form. Some aspects of the ontology can be displayed (and re-hidden) as shown in the left pane of Fig. 4, which shows the agents (short arrow points from the agent) and experiencers (pointed to by the long arrow) of all events. Events (i.e. "die") which do not have agents, are shown without associated lines, but are positioned next to their experiencers.

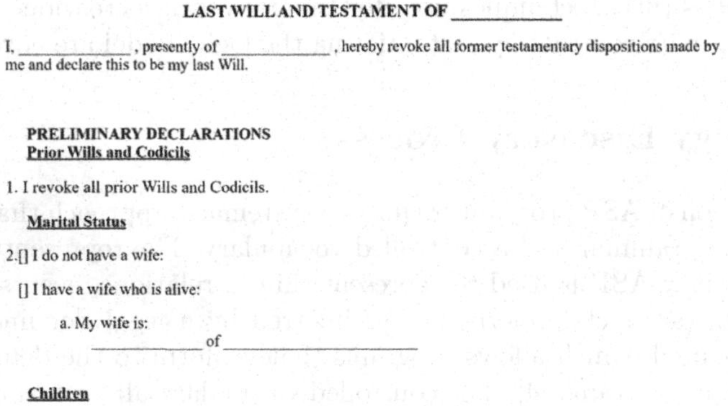

LAST WILL AND TESTAMENT OF _____

I, _____ , presently of _____ , hereby revoke all former testamentary dispositions made by me and declare this to be my last Will.

PRELIMINARY DECLARATIONS
Prior Wills and Codicils

1. I revoke all prior Wills and Codicils.

Marital Status

2.[] I do not have a wife:

[] I have a wife who is alive:

a. My wife is:

_____ of _____

Children

Fig. 1. The SDE editor starts with an existing Legal Document.

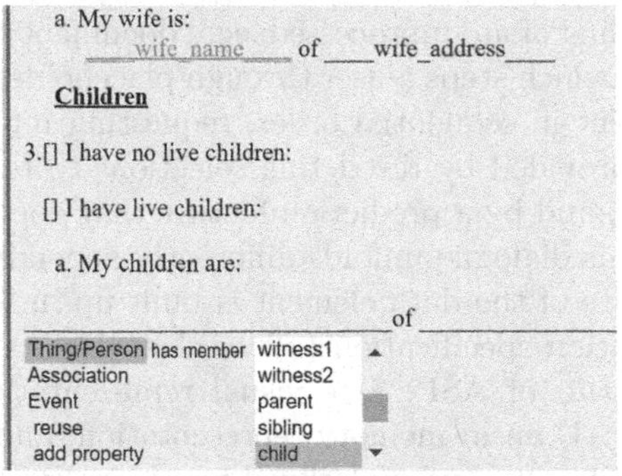

a. My wife is:
_____wife_name_____ of _____wife_address_____

Children

3.[] I have no live children:

[] I have live children:

a. My children are:

_____ of _____

Thing/Person has member	witness1	▲
Association	witness2	
Event	parent	
reuse	sibling	
add property	child	▼

Fig. 2. Ontology Discovery Dialogue (predicting that 'child' is the correct term).

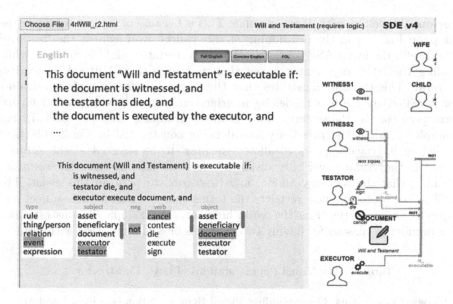

Fig. 3. SDE editor modelling the rule "is_executable" with text input.

4 Modelling and Testing the Logic Model

Modelling with Text. The lower left pane of Fig. 3 shows a rule being generated by text input with a partial verbalisation from the ASP rule shown in the top left pane. The syntax of ASP and the ASP representations chosen allow rules to be constructed in a building block fashion by adding representations one-by-one to a rule head. The lower left pane of Fig. 3 shows a fourth literal being added to a rule named "is_executable". This literal specifies that, if the 'testator' has 'not' 'cancelled' the 'document' (Will), then the value of this literal will be 'true', allowing the rule to also evaluate to 'true'. The remaining rules comprising the smart contract, are built atop this rule, so that the resulting smart contract will never execute if the testator cancels the contract. In the lower left pane, the words in the scrolling lists are determined during ontology discovery. The correspondence between the ontology and English is that the names of 'things' can be subjects or objects, while the names of 'events' are always verbs. The scrolling lists (lower left pane of Fig. 3) are then placed in subject, verb, object (SVO) order across the screen, in the case of events; so that selection creates a SVO sentence which also happens to create a 'cancel' event as an ASP representation.

Modelling with Graphics. Rules are created graphically by double clicking the mouse in an empty area of the canvas (right panel Fig. 3), then typing in a name. Arrows are drawn by dragging the mouse between two icons. Dragging the mouse (while holding 'ctrl') between the icon corresponding to the term 'cancel' and the bar labelled "is_executable" produces identical ASP code to the previous 'Modelling with Text' example. This is because of the ontology (see the left pane Fig. 4) and the positioning of the 'cancel' icon against the 'testator' icon; prefill the event ASP representation with 'testator' and 'document', while holding the 'ctrl' key creates a negation as failure (NAF) literal, instead of a literal. This example illustrates that the visual interface reveals constraints not revealed via the text modelling interface, and that there is another formal correspondence at the sentence, and 'graphics grouping' level (see Sect. 5). For example; consider the rule body literal being constructed in Fig. 3. The text modelling interface appears to allow 'executor' to be selected as the subject; however, the visual panel only displays a 'cancel' icon against the 'testator'; meaning that the ontology allows only 'testators' to perform this event. The SDE editor prototype now restricts the terms that can occupy the subject and object positions of the transitive verb; however, this example demonstrates one of a number of reasons for having two channels of communication with users.

Table 1. The Visual Representations of Logic Constructors.

Logic Constructors	Corresponding Visual Representation (see Figs. 3 and 4)
rule head	bar (can be red or green)
AND	blue arrow meeting a bar
OR[1]	2 bars with an "OR" in the centre (see Fig. 4)
expression	blue box attached to bar
aggregate	blue box attached to bar + keyword ("SUM | COUNT")
NAF	red arrow meeting bar +"NOT"
NOT	a "-" in front of an atom identifier (not shown)
many-to-many	the 'allocate' icon (see Fig. 4)

[1] Note that this "OR" is an inclusive disjunction in the body of a rule.

In Fig. 3, the larger icons represent 'things' and 'relations', while 'events' are displayed as smaller overlayed icons; for example, the pen (sign) overlayed on the icon representing the testator. The bars represent rule heads; highlighted so that rules that generate an answer set are coloured 'green' (see Fig. 4), and rules that do not generate an answer set are coloured 'red'. The arrows touching the bars represent rule body literals, while blue boxes attached to a bar represent either expressions or aggregations. Red arrows labelled with the reserved word "NOT" represent 'negation as failure' (NAF) literals (see Fig. 3), while a "-" in front of an atom represents strong negation. Disjunction is handled in the body of a rule only, and is achieved by having two or more rules with the same head identifier which the system groups together with the reserved word "OR". These correspondences are summarised in Table 1.

Introduction to Testing. The right pane of Fig. 4 displays the visual result of a partially complete logic modelling and testing session, where the rule "is-executable" is being tested. In the scenario being tested, only the 'cancel' event has not happened (shown as a grey dashed line with text "NOT" in Fig. 4). The answer set for the rule "is-executable" in this test scenario verbalises as:

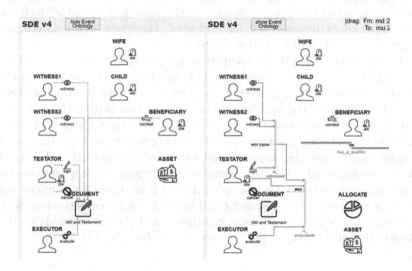

Fig. 4. SDE editor visual panel: 1) left: event relationships view; 2) right: logic view.

```
This document "Will and Testament" is executable if:
    the document is witnessed, and
    the testator has died, and
    the document is executed by the executor, but
    the document is not cancelled by the testator.
```

This example provides a glimpse of how the SDE editor allows rules to be tested as they are built, how a tree of tested rules can be built on top of one another, and how the system verbalises each rule. The verbalisation during testing is a verbalisation of the answer set of the rule, rather than the rule itself as during modelling; however, it is displayed in the same top left pane in Fig. 3. Testing couples this visual and verbal feedback with a mechanism that automatically creates the exhaustive set of scenarios for a rule, and steps the user through them. For combinations of events without an answer set, the rule head remains coloured red and no verbalisation appears, while for combinations with an answer set (as shown in Fig. 4), the rule head turns green and a verbalisation appears.

5 Formal Correspondence

The system achieves three formal correspondences: 1) icon ≡ text term ≡ ASP representation; 2) a graphics group ≡ an English sentence ≡ an ASP literal; and 3) the graphic for a rule ≡ a complete verbalisation ≡ an ASP rule. In this section we work though the creation of the rule "is_executable" to illustrate the correspondence between the text selected, the graphics displayed and the auto-generated ASP representation (Table 2).

This rule determines if the conditions for the execution of the "Will and Testament" have been met. These are: 1) it has been signed by the testator; 2) it has been witnessed by 2 different witnesses in the same location at the same time as the signing by the testator; 3) the testator has died; 4) the executor has wound-up the estate and executed the 'Will'; 5) the testator has not cancelled the 'Will'. We choose to package the rules we create according to when they occur, so that signing and witnessing are packaged into rule "is_witnessed", while the later events are packaged into rule "is_executable" which now has only four conditions. This simplifies both textual and graphical modelling, eases user understanding, and makes exhaustive testing practical. Literal 4 (under construction) will add the absence of a 'cancel' event as a condition, and this corresponds to the red line from the 'cancel' icon to the "is_executable" bar (see Fig. 3).

Table 2. Formal Correspondence between ASP, Text and Graphics Representations.

ASP item	Text Displayed (see Fig. 3)	Graphics Displayed (see Fig. 3)
rule head:-	This document .. is executable if:	bar labelled "is_executable"
body literal 1,	is witnessed, and	blue arrow from rule "is_witnessed" to rule "is_executable" (the rule)
body literal 2,	testator die, and	blue arrow from the 'die' icon (on the 'testator' icon) to the rule
body literal 3,	executor execute document, and	blue arrow from 'execute' icon (on the 'executor' icon) to the rule
body literal 4	testator not cancel document	red arrow from the 'cancel' icon (on the 'testator' icon) to the rule

6 ASP Representations

Implementing the integrated ontology and logic models, and both text and graphical input and feedback, requires carefully crafted ASP representations.

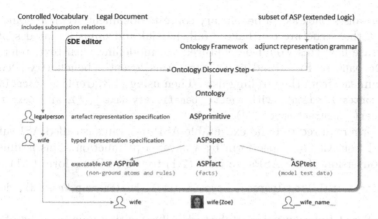

Fig. 5. Derivation of ASP, Visual, and Text Representations in the SDE editor.[2] (Note that the photo is computer generated.)

The ASP representations for artefacts and heads of ASP rules, use a grammar (partially shown below) built upon the ASP 'classical literal' [16]. The system unfolds this grammar systematically through intermediate forms (see Fig. 5).

(1.1) thing(<thingId>[,<typeId>],<key>[,<prop>[,<prop>]])
(1.2) relation(<relationId>,<key>,<key>[,<prop>[,<prop>]])
(1.3) event(<eventId>,<time>[,<agent>],<expnr>[,<modfr>][,<prop>[,<prop>]])
(1.4) ruleh(<rulehId>[,<term>[,<term>]])

ASP terms are structured <termId>(<placeholderId>,<data>), except for terms postfixed "Id" which have one parameter. An ASP representation example is:

(2.1) thing(thingId(legalperson), typeId(wife), key(_wife_name_, "Zoe"), dob(...[3] ('key' is replaced with 'name' because placeholder identifiers are exposed to the user.)

Replacing "Zoe" with "" in (2.1) provides the ASPspec form (see Fig. 5) which is the output of the ontology discovery step. This form provides the well-defined foundation required to support logic modelling. In the grammar, keys "<key>" are only created for 'things,' so that the two "<key>" in (1.2) are foreign keys, and "<agent>", "<expnr>", and "<modfr>" in (1.3) are labelled forms of foreign keys. This structure allows a 'relation' to represent the relating of 'things'; and an 'event' to represent something caused by a 'thing', and happening to a different 'thing'. The representation grammar chosen, preserves information required for verbalisation; for example, in (1.3) "<eventId>" is a verb, while "<agent>" is the subject, and "<expnr>" is the object; so that the ASP auto-generated for the sentence "a beneficiary contests the Will" is;

event(eventId(contest), time(_contest_time_,""), agent(_beneficiary_name_, ""),
    experiencer(_document_name_, "Will"))

which verbalises back as: "a beneficiary contests document 'Will' at some time". Note that this structure can handle full, partial and uninstantiated sentences. To illustrate how this would be captured via modelling with text, refer to the lower left pane of Fig. 3 and select the terms 'event', 'beneficiary', 'contest', and 'document' from the scrolling lists. Then using (1.3), replace <eventId> with eventId(contest), <agent> with agent(_beneficiary_name_,""), and <expnr> with experiencer(_document_name_,"").

The form required to build executable ASP programs is called ASPrule. It is generated from the ASPspec form by a JavaScript function. This is illustrated by the conversion of the ASPspec form (2.1) to the ASPrule form (3.1):

(3.1) thing(thingId(legalperson), typeId(wife), key(Wname_p,Wname_d), dob(...

The JavaScript function pairs artefact identifiers with a unique string of capital letters which are then substituted to create ASP variables with unique identifiers. Examples are: (wife, W), (witness, WI), and (die, D). The postfixes are: 1) "_p" for placeholder identifiers (see below); and 2) "_d" for data. These ASP variables need to be unique in order to: 1) allow placeholder identifiers to bind user input data to ASPfacts; and 2) to support the use of foreign keys in 'relations' and 'events'. In (1.1) above, the ASP term <thingId> identifies the type of the artefact and the ASP term <key> identifies the instance of that type of artefact. As all ASP terms have identifiers, a unique data identifier called a placeholder identifier <placeholderId> can be created by concatenating the artefact and term identifiers. Placeholder identifiers are what an IPH displays on screen (see top of Fig. 2) and are the binding mechanism between instantiation data and ASP representations. Users of this system have already experienced the use of "_____" as a placeholder, so a modified placeholder of the form "__xxxx__" is a small step, allowing pre- and postfixing with "__", to give the form shown in (2.1). The use of 'typing' (e.g., typeId(wife)) reduces the number of representations for artefacts with many varieties (e.g., differentiating between people with different roles). Another aspect is the implementation of constraints via this typing mechanism. The grammar unfolds incrementally so that a more primitive representation can limit the ASPspec forms that can be generated. For example; the event "die" can be constrained to use "legalperson" 'things' only.

The ASPfact form (2.1) is the form used to instantiate executable ASP programs. ASPfacts are generated by duplicating the ASPspec form and adding the data by matching via unique placeholder identifiers. There can be many ASPfacts for each ASPspec; for example, eight beneficiaries are represented by eight ASPfacts of type 'beneficiary'. The sole purpose of the ASPtest form is to generate one ASPfact for each placeholder identifier as test data for model validation, such that the numeric literals execute.

To record expressions and aggregates, the SDE editor uses ASP's 'built-in atom' [16] via an interface that recognises reserved words; for example, the blue rectangle with text "NOT EQUAL" in Fig. 4. Some situations require two or more things to be related at instantiation; for example, the allocation of assets to beneficiaries. The construct 'relation' ('allocate' icon in Fig. 4), embeds machinery that inserts a triple (key1,key2,property) into the ASP code.

7   Evidence of Usability

The purpose of this section is to provide evidence of the usability of the Smart Document Editor (SDE) by the targeted user group (i.e. paralegals).

Ontology Discovery. There are three features of the smart document editor (SDE) that reduce the knowledge and skill required of a user: 1) use of familiar existing legal documents as a starting point; 2) a smart list feature which assembles and presents all correct entries for a given placeholder; 3) a 'guess' feature which often correctly guesses the correct entry for a given placeholder. The following discussion establishes that for domain experts, using the SDE to fill in a legal document is easier than filling in the document by hand.

The Starting Document: The editor is designed to use existing documents (see Fig. 1) which ensures that domain experts are familiar with both the form and the function of these documents. The SDE detects the type of any legal document loaded, then loads the appropriate structured controlled vocabulary (SCV) so that the list of undefined terms displayed is short and relevant. As the user defines terms by moving though the placeholders, this undefined term list shrinks while the number of associated icons displayed rises (see Fig. 4). The SDE simplifies the processing of large complex documents, because it skips between placeholders, and refers to lists in one line (as a set).

Smart List Feature: It is reasonable to expect that a domain expert will know how to fill out an existing legal document, so in effect the SDE simply provides a smart assist to the user. Our insight is that the process of stepping through placeholders can be managed to simultaneously yield most of the ontological information. The SDE moves from placeholder to placeholder and displays only valid options in two lists in a form "x (type) has member y (term)". In the example shown in Fig. 2, one double mouse click will select the text string (term) the user wishes to use to represent the set of "child". This one double click triggers the creation of the five objects (see page 5) at this instant. The names of actual children are selected during a later instantiation step.

Simple AI Assist: The SDE also has a "guess" mechanism which scans text adjacent to the placeholder (before and after), and reacts if a word in the SCV or any other identifying word pattern is detected. In Fig. 2, this guess mechanism has detected the word "child" in the text preceding this placeholder, and knows that child is a "Thing/Person" from the SCV. Capture of both the type and the term is achieved with one double mouse click, if a correct guess is made. This simple text scanning mechanism has potential for further development.

Artefacts without Placeholders or SCV Entries: The user can add a custom term if it does not exist in the SCV, while two screens are provided [32] to allow users to explicitly define events and their agents and experiencers if no placeholder is present. In addition, artefacts not captured by the above two mechanisms, can be added from a tool bar [32]. The above input mechanisms use the same techniques as placeholder capture and are intuitive for users.

Modelling Legal Logic and Model Validation. Modelling the legal logic in a document can be done with either the text interface or by manipulating graphics, and modelling with either method will automatically generate the other representation. The text interface; however, is similar to that used during Ontology Discovery (see Fig. 3), so is likely to be preferred by a novice.

The more challenging part of logic modelling is knowing which components to package together into a rule. Being a domain expert assists in this process, because the user will know what steps are taken at what time during the life cycle of the Will, and this information is required to model the Will effectively. For example, the first events that occur are the signing and witnessing of the Will by the testator and two different witnesses respectively at the same time and location. Consequently, these are the obvious events to package into the rule 'is_witnessed'. The second obvious grouping is if the document 'is_witnessed', and the testator has died, and the testator has not cancelled the document, and the executor has executed the document, then the document 'is executable'. This example illustrates the ability of the SDE to reflect the normal thinking processes of domain experts, which simplifies use of the SDE for logic modelling.

Another simplifying aspect is the close coupled rule-by-rule approach to model validation. A newly created rule can be immediately tested by the user using an automated scenario generator that presents all possible scenarios one-by-one with visual and verbal feedback for each scenario. This feature allows the user to be taught to experiment with constructing and testing a rule in one step, and to build up a tested rule base. Being able to scroll the canvas horizontally allows the tested rule base to be moved left out of view while the current rule is constructed then tested. Experience suggests this iterative approach scales well.

The ability to model using text or graphics, with system feedback in both text and graphics, provides confidence that the learning curve for domain experts is low. Our training estimate for paralegals is that providing a brief description of how the system interacts with users and then working through a number of examples, will suffice.

8   Evaluation and Future Work

Our work demonstrates most of the requirements of a system that enables the modelling of the ontology and logic of an amenable legal document by a domain expert. We contrast this system with systems that use the compiled imperative language approach in Fig. 6. We have demonstrated: 1) a system usable by domain experts; 2) ontology modelling by text; 3) logic modelling by both text and graphics; 3) user feedback via both restricted English and graphics; 4) highly modular construction with guided exhaustive testing at individual rule and at the global level; and, 6) a formal correspondence between graphics, restricted English and the ASP rules.

	Criteria	Compiled Language Approach	Our Approach
1	Use by domain experts (DEs)	Standard smart contracts (SCs) only	✓ DEs can build both standard and custom SCs
2	Understandability	No verbal feedback	✓ Visual and verbal feedback for each rule
3	Ease of testing	Limited decomposition	✓ DEs build & test by rule, with visual and verbal feedback
4	Agility	Custom SCs need programming	✓ DEs can build & test custom SCs
5	Cost	Any programming is costly	✓ DEs can build custom SCs at no extra cost

Fig. 6. Summary of Key Advantages.

The advantages of our approach are most apparent in testing, custom smart contract creation, and in understandability. Using a declarative language allows a model of both the ontology and the legal logic to be built by a domain expert. This different development methodology then allows testing to be split between model validation and program verification, a division that eases testing for domain experts. Furthermore, we found that the visualisation of logic naturally guides the creation of a highly modular tree of connected rules, providing the decomposition necessary to accommodate understanding by domain experts. This granularity allows the user to focus on creating and testing one rule at a time which we accommodate with a tight testing feedback loop. These simplifications allow exhaustive testing of the logic model by domain experts. Unlike a compiled imperative language approach like Solidity, our method does not require a different approach to create a custom smart contract. Finally, the understandability advantage is amplified by providing both visual and verbal feedback to users, with the verbalisation feature being difficult to duplicate.

Future work involves: 1) A user evaluation of our prototype by our target audience [26]; 2) applying our approach to a wider range of legal documents; 3) experimenting with different representation grammars; 4) converting more code to ASP (meta-programming in ASP); 5) improving verbalisation; 6) describing the model validation and program verification techniques used; and 7) comparing the use and expressive power of alternative declarative languages with ASP.

9   Conclusion

We have presented a novel approach that allows domain experts to model both the ontology and logic of amenable legal documents. The key innovations that enable this system are the use of an advanced user interface to auto-generate the underlying formal representations, the use of a representation grammar and automatic rewriting of that grammar into representation specifications and then executable ASP, and the three formal correspondences achieved. The advantages observed are that the system allows domain experts to perform all the modelling and testing activities required, with further advantages in the areas of understandability, agility and the ability to model custom legal documents. A declarative approach allowing this level of modelling by domain experts has significant economic implications, because it provides a practical pathway to formally verified user-defined custom smart contracts.

References

1. Working with Contracts, Practical assistance for small business managers (2019). https://treasury.gov.au/sites/default/files/2019-03/WorkingWithContractsGuide.pdf
2. Levi, S., Lipton, A.: An introduction to smart contracts and their potential and inherent limitations. Forum on Corporate Governance (2018). https://corpgov.law.harvard.edu/2018/05/26/an-introduction-to-smart-contracts-and-their-potential-and-inherent-limitations/
3. Brewka, G., Eiter, T., Truszczynski, M.: Answer set programming at a glance. Commun. ACM **54**(12), 92–103 (2011)
4. Eiter, T., Ianni, G., Krennwallner, T.: Answer set programming: a primer. In: Tessaris, S., et al. (eds.) Reasoning Web 2009. LNCS, vol. 5689, pp. 40–110. Springer, Heidelberg (2009). https://doi.org/10.1007/978-3-642-03754-2_2
5. Thompson Reuters: HighQ Document Automation (2021). https://legal.thomsonreuters.com/en/products/highq/document-automation
6. Solidity. https://docs.soliditylang.org/en/v0.8.9/
7. OpenZeppelin. Build Secure Smart Contracts in Solidity. https://openzeppelin.com/contracts/
8. Potassco. clingo and gringo (2021). http://potassco.org/clingo/
9. Febbraro, O., et al.: ASPIDE: integrated development environment for answer set programming. University of Calabria. (2021) https://www.mat.unical.it/ricca/aspide/index.html
10. Grigg I.: The Ricardian contract. In: Proceedings of First IEEE International Workshop on Electronic Contracting, San Diego, CA, USA, pp. 25–31 (2004). https://doi.org/10.1109/WEC.2004.1319505
11. Choudhury, O., et al.: Auto-generation of smart contracts from domain-specific ontologies and semantic rules (2018). https://doi.org/10.1109/Cybermatics_2018.2018.00183
12. Maedche, A., Staab, S.: The TEXT-TO-ONTO Ontology Learning Environment. Institute AIFB, University of Karlsruhe (2000)
13. Konys, A.: Knowledge Repository of Ontology Learning Tools from Text. Procedia Comput. Sci. **159**, 1614–1628 (2019)
14. Falkner, A., et al.: Industrial applications of answer set programming. KI - Künstliche Intelligenz **32**(2–3), 165–176 (2018)
15. Kloimüllner, C., et al.: Kara: a system for visualising and visual editing of interpretations for answer set programs. In: Proceedings INAP. arXiv:1109.4095. (2011)
16. Calimeri, F., et al.: ASP-core-2 input language format. Theory Pract. Logic Program. **20**(2), 294–309 (2019)
17. Wood, G.: Ethereum: a secure decentralised generalised transaction ledger. EIP-150 Revision (2017). http://www.gavwood.com/paper.pdf
18. Hjort, R.: Formally verifying webassembly with KWasm (2020). https://odr.chalmers.se/handle/20.500.12380/300761

19. Moritz, D.: Clingo WebAssembly (2021). https://github.com/domoritz/clingo-wasm
20. Batsakis, S., et al.: Legal representation and reasoning in practice: a critical comparison. In: JURIX, pp. 31–40 (2018)
21. Stanford Encyclopedia of Philosophy (2021). https://plato.stanford.edu/contents.html
22. Purnell, K., Schwitter, R.: Towards Declarative Smart Contracts. In: Proceedings of The 4th Symposium on Distributed Ledger Technology (2019). https://symposium-dlt.org/SDLT2019-FinalProceedings.pdf
23. Getty Research Institute (2021). https://www.getty.edu/research/publications/electronic_publications/intro_controlled_vocab/what.pdf
24. Giordano, L., Dupré, D.T.: Enriched modeling and reasoning on business processes with ontologies and answer set programming (2018). https://doi.org/10.1007/978-3-319-98651-7_5
25. Sergot, M., et al.: The British nationality act as a logic program. Commun. ACM **29**, 370–386 (1986). https://doi.org/10.1145/5689.5920
26. Norman, D., Nielsen, J.: Nielsen norman group. beyond the NPS: measuring perceived usability with the SUS, NASA-TLX, and the single ease question after tasks and usability tests (2018). https://www.nngroup.com/articles/measuring-perceived-usability/
27. Salik, I., Ashurst, J.V.: Closed loop communication training in medical simulation (2019). https://www.statpearls.com/articlelibrary/viewarticle/63796/
28. Rodrigues, C., et al.: Legal ontologies over time: a systematic mapping study. Expert Syst. Appl. **130**, 12–30 (2019). https://doi.org/10.1016/j.eswa.2019.04.009
29. Bench-Capon, T., et al.: A history of AI and Law in 50 papers: 25 years of the international conference on AI and law. ICAIL 20, 215–319 (2012) https://www.csc.liv.ac.uk/%20tbc/publications/ICAIL25AuthorsVersion.pdf
30. Antoniou, G.: Nonmonotonic rule systems on top of ontology layers. In: Horrocks, I., Hendler, J. (eds.) ISWC 2002. LNCS, vol. 2342, pp. 394–398. Springer, Heidelberg (2002). https://doi.org/10.1007/3-540-48005-6_30
31. Herrestad, H.: Norms and formalization. In: Proceedings of the 3rd International Conference on Artificial Intelligence and Law. ICAIL 1991, pp. 175–184, May 1991. https://doi.org/10.1145/112646.112667
32. SDEv4: Smart Document Editor v4 prototype (2022). http://130.56.246.229
33. Panagiotidi, S., Nieves, J., Vázquez-Salceda, J.: A framework to model norm dynamics in answer set programming. In: CEUR Workshop Proceedings, vol. 494 (2009)
34. De Vos, M., Padget, J., Satoh, K.: Legal modelling and reasoning using institutions. In: Onada, T., Bekki, D., McCready, E. (eds.) JSAI-isAI 2010. LNCS (LNAI), vol. 6797, pp. 129–140. Springer, Heidelberg (2011). https://doi.org/10.1007/978-3-642-25655-4_12
35. Sileno, G., Boer, A., van Engers, T.: A petri net-based notation for normative modeling: evaluation on deontic paradoxes. In: Pagallo, U., Palmirani, M., Casanovas, P., Sartor, G., Villata, S. (eds.) AICOL 2015-2017. LNCS (LNAI), vol. 10791, pp. 89–104. Springer, Cham (2018). https://doi.org/10.1007/978-3-030-00178-0_6
36. Kowalski, R., Satoh, K.: Obligation as optimal goal satisfaction. J. Philos. Log. **47**(4), 579–609 (2017). https://doi.org/10.1007/s10992-017-9440-3
37. Lam, H., Governatori, G., Riveret, R.: On ASPIC+ and defeasible logic (2016). https://doi.org/10.3233/978-1-61499-686-6-359

38. Governatori, G., Casanovas, P., Koker, L.: On the formal representation of the Australian spent conviction scheme (2020). https://doi.org/10.26181/6073968f457d2
39. Schwitter, R.: Specifying and verbalising answer set programs in controlled natural language. Theory Pract. Logic Program. **18**, 691–705 (2018). https://doi.org/10.1017/S1471068418000327

Benchmarks for Indian Legal NLP: A Survey

Prathamesh Kalamkar[1]([✉])([iD]), Janani Venugopalan[1]([iD]), and Vivek Raghavan[2]

[1] Thoughtworks India Pvt. Ltd., Chennai, India
{prathamk,janani.venugopalan}@thoughtworks.com
[2] Ek Step Foundation, Bangalore, India
vivek@ekstep.org
https://ekstep.org/

Abstract. Legal text is significantly different from English text (e.g. Wikipedia, News) used for training most natural language processing (NLP) algorithms. As a result, the state of the art algorithms (e.g. GPT-3, BERT derivatives), need additional effort (e.g. fine-tuning and further pre-training) to achieve optimal performance on legal text. Hence there is a need to create separate NLP data sets and benchmarks for legal text which are challenging and focus on tasks specific to legal systems. This will spur innovation in applications of NLP for legal text and will benefit AI community and legal fraternity. This paper focuses on an empirical review of the existing work in the use of NLP in Indian legal text and proposes ideas to create new benchmarks for Indian Legal NLP.

Keywords: Natural Language Processing · Legal Text Processing · NLP Benchmarks

1 Need for Indian Legal NLP Benchmarks

In NLP, a benchmark is for evaluating the NLP models for a specific task or set of tasks. Some of the famous NLP benchmarks are Stanford Question & Answer Dataset SQuad2.0 by [32], General Language Understanding GLUE by [36] and super GLUE by [35], NIST Open MT. Creation of such benchmarks has proven to be the foundation of progress of NLP in an area with papers and open source the code[1] for the developed solution. Hence creating a challenging benchmark with the right data set can spur innovation in desired fields. While there are some limited official applications of AI and ML techniques in the Indian legal systems[2], there exists several avenues and sub-problems where these techniques can be leveraged to improve the efficiency of repetitive tasks. To spur innovation in processing of the legal text corpora, we identify some NLP benchmarks which focus on Indian Law systems.

Supported by Ek Step Foundation.

[1] https://paperswithcode.com/area/natural-language-processing.
[2] https://indiaai.gov.in/article/ai-is-set-to-reform-justice-delivery-in-india.

© Springer Nature Switzerland AG 2023
K. Yada et al. (Eds.): JSAI-isAI 2021 Workshops, LNAI 13856, pp. 33–48, 2023.
https://doi.org/10.1007/978-3-031-36190-6_3

1. Unique Structure: India has hybrid legal system having elements of civil law, common law, equitable law, and customary and religious laws. Immense religious, ethnic, linguistic, and social diversity in India is also reflected in the law. E.g. there is no uniform civil code. [10] describes how constitution of India is unique in many aspects like Public Interest Litigations, positive discrimination using caste based reservations and judicial independence. This uniqueness required AI models to be trained on Indian law data especially for the tasks where law interpretation is required like in case of automatic charge identification.

2. Indian law uses its own language which is esoteric and latin language based. Many of the terms used are peculiar and not used in general purpose English or in other countries legal language. E.g. Term "7/12" refers to a property document, "Panchnama" refers to procedure during investigation. Such terms occur very frequently in legal language and NLP models should be able to understand their meaning. Hence models pre-trained on general purpose English (like Wikipedia) produce degraded performance on Indian Legal tasks. Hence Indian legal data sets would enable NLP models to learn the legal language. In addition, the data for developing such models is also quite fragmented in the form of police investigation files (First information report (FIR), case files, charge-sheets), legal community created (judgments, petitions, writs, etc.) and government records. Each of above bodies have their own set of terms and language use.

3. Huge Case Pendency: As of July 2021, there were 45 million pending cases[3] in Indian courts. Small improvements in legal processes will lead to significant impact on case pendency. The focus of legal AI in India should be to augment human capacity to improve the operational efficiency and NLP benchmarks should focus on tasks which help this.

Translation of relevant legal tasks to NLP tasks is important in defining where AI can help legal systems. Application of NLP techniques to solve legal tasks needs understanding of the NLP world and legal world. A team of legal and NLP experts need to brainstorm and come up with relevant legal problems which can be solved with NLP. A good benchmark would be valuable for the legal community and at the same time challenging for the machine learning community.

2   How Can NLP Benchmarks Help Innovation in Indian Legal System?

There are legal NLP benchmarks for countries [41] such as China, USA [8] and the EU[4]. So many of the mentioned datasets cannot be directly leveraged for use in the Indian context. In addition, the legal challenges faced by the Indian judiciary are different from those addressed by the current legal NLP datasets. For

---

[3] https://www.news18.com/news/explainers/explained-cji-ramana-says-4-5-crore-cases-pending-heres-what-has-been-fuelling-backlog-3977411.html.

[4] https://github.com/thunlp/LegalPapers.

e.g. US has a federal systems courts which India does not, and Indian judiciary can makes laws which UK does not in the strictest sense.

To the best of our knowledge, there are currently no NLP benchmarks specifically for Indian legal system. As a result, Indian legal specific NLP benchmarks along with relevant data will attract the ML community to solve such unique problems. NLP benchmark will also act as an open evaluation platform for commercial legal NLP solutions providers. Using this platform they can prove the effectiveness of the products and solutions created by them. ML community, startups and researchers will benefit from the knowledge sharing through research papers and open source code thereby helping to solve complex problems in Indian Legal NLP space. As a consequence, for this paper we will focus on the different benchmarks and their creation as opposed to the solutioning of the individual benchmarks.

3   Data Availability

To be able to create Indian legal NLP benchmarks, Indian law specific text data is needed. Using this data, task specific datasets could be created using human annotations. E.g. factoid question and answer benchmark dataset, rhetorical roles. Using Indian law text ensures that the NLP models learn the language used in Indian Law. Thanks to many open data initiatives like National Judicial Data Grid[5] and Crime and Criminal Tracking Network and System [6], a lot of data related to law and crime is publicly available. Additionally some sites[7] provide court judgments along with extra metadata.

3.1   Court Judgments

District courts, high courts and supreme court makes judgments publicly available on their websites (millions of judgement texts). These judgments are in English and contain rich text data for Indian law. Police departments of many states provide recent First Information Reports on their websites (thousands of FIRs). Some of them are in local Indian languages.

3.2   First Investigation Reports

Police departments of many states provide recent First Investigation Reports on their websites[8]. Some of them are in local Indian Languages.

3.3   Indian Laws

Digital repository of all central and state acts[9] provides all the written laws.

---

[5] https://njdg.ecourts.gov.in/njdgnew/index.php.
[6] https://ncrb.gov.in/en/crime-and-criminal-tracking-network-systems-cctns.
[7] https://indiankanoon.org/.
[8] https://www.mhpolice.maharashtra.gov.in/Citizen/MH/PublishedFIRs.aspx.
[9] https://www.indiacode.nic.in/.

4   Indian Legal NLP Benchmark Areas

Mind map Fig. 1 shows the four major NLP areas and their associated NLP benchmarks.

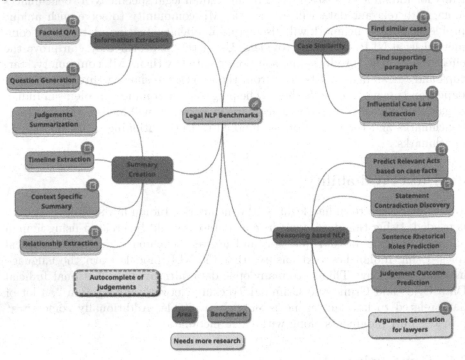

Fig. 1. Indian Legal Bench Marks: An Overview. The main NLP areas are marked in green color. The orange and yellow boxes are the associated NLP benchmarks. The yellow boxes identify NLP benchmarks which are more far-sighted. (Color figure online)

4.1   Information Extraction

Factoid Question & Answers

Description of Task & Value Proposition : Legal community look for certain information that can be framed as some template questions that need to be answered from the case text. Along with the template questions, there would be some context specific questions. E.g. For a criminal case, template questions could be "What was the place of occurrence?" etc. If the case is murder case then along with the template questions the context specific questions could be "What was the murder weapon?" etc. So this can be treated as factoid questions i.e. you are looking for answers which are written explicitly in the text as a span of few contiguous words. Factoid Q/A system will find such answers written in text and highlight the answers in the text. This automatic extraction of answers to such questions would significantly save the human reading time.

Mapping to Standard NLP Tasks & Similar NLP Benchmarks: This benchmark maps to a NLP task called factoid Q/A. This is a widely studied task in NLP and many pretrained NLP models are available which focus on general purpose English language. Given availability of data and many published approaches, this NLP task falls into the easy category. Similar benchmarks exist for open domain tasks like general wikipedia factoid Question & answers (Squad2.0 [32, 33], ComQA [1], Google Natural Questions [17] etc.) But these datasets lack the domain specific legal language which limits use of such benchmarks. There is also a reasoning based legal dataset (JEC-QA [42]) which involves complex questions based on the questions from the National Judicial Examination of China. These questions need prior knowledge of law and reasoning. Hence such datasets from civil law countries and using general English text are not relevant in the context of Indian legal domain. Hence a factoid question and answer dataset using Indian legal text would ensure that the solutions developed work well with Indian legal language.

Dataset to be Collected & Evaluation Metrics: Data needed for this benchmark would be template questions about a given legal text and humans would mark the answers in that text. The person will also create the context specific questions which could be generated by him/her or taken from the automatically generated context specific questions (as mentioned in the next question generation benchmark). The evaluation of this benchmark would be done by matching the answers generated by NLP models with human extracted answers. Evaluation metric could be F1 score using exact match.

Question Generation

Description of Task & Value Proposition: In order to get meaningful insights from answers of questions, it is important to ask the right questions which are context specific. These questions can be of two types: factoid and non-factoid or reasoning based questions. Factoid questions are the questions for which the answers are explicitly stated in text as facts of contiguous text. E.g. Context: "... companion were thieves and therefore took away driving licence of Mohammad Nisar Khan along with some visiting cards and coins...." From this context the generated factoid Question would be "What is the name of the victim?" Reasoning based questions are those for which the answers have to be created using information written in text along with using some logic. E.g. A reasoning based question for the context mentioned before would be , "Did Mohammad Nissar Khan contradict himself when he gave evidence between the district and the high court?" Recent advancements in Neural question generation allow us to create answer-aware questions i.e. given a context and an answer , the question can be generated. Machine generated QA pairs would be compared with the Human generated QA pairs to evaluate the quality of question generation. A lot of time would be saved if the questions are also generated automatically while collecting human annotated data for the creation of the NLP benchmarks such as question answering benchmarks. In many benchmark datasets like Squad [32, 33], the questions are generated by humans by looking at the text and answers are marked in that text.

Mapping to Standard NLP Tasks & Similar NLP Benchmarks: This benchmark maps to a NLP task called question generation and language generation. With recent advancements in question answering, question generation, there are several studies which focus on both factoid and reasoning based question generation. Similar benchmarks exist for selection specific question generation benchmarks such as Sel-QA [14], Wiki-QA [39], and GIGE [20]. They are taken from a curated list of topics from corpora such as wikipedia. They are essentially question-answering benchmarks where the questions are generated based on a selected text, and cover various versions of the questions through human annotations. The questions generated are essentially evaluated for coverage of the text and linguistic correctness. But these datasets lack the domain specific legal language which limits use of such benchmarks. There is also a reasoning based legal dataset (JEC-QA [42]) which involves complex questions based on the questions from the National Judicial Examination of China. However, this is a question answering benchmark and not a question generation one.

Dataset to be Collected & Evaluation Metrics: The text for this task could be collected from judgments, FIR), chargesheets. The humans will mark the QA pairs generated by a baseline model as valid, and also generate additional QA pairs for the same selected piece of text to get as many variations as possible. We can leverage existing tools such as ProphetNET [30], T5 [16] and Squash [15] fine-tune them if needed for legal question generation. There are two main aspects of the evaluation of this benchmark. First one is whether the question generation process has identified the right answers from context to create questions (called as coverage). The second is to check the quality of question text. For coverage of the answers, the generated answers would be compared with human answers to calculate the overlap. The quality of the questions could be checked by checking the grammar of the questions, passing the question through the standard question answering model to check whether the answer matches with the given answer.

4.2   Summary Generation

Judgment Summarization

Description of Task & Value Proposition: The court judgments, especially from high courts and supreme court, tend to be very long. Finding the right context from such long judgment is time consuming and error prone. This benchmark would focus on evaluating various aspects of the summaries created for a given judgment. The summary of high courts and supreme court is often used in establishing precedent. Searching in summaries rather than entire text would help lawyers to establish better arguments for precedence. Summary of judgments from lower courts also help in reducing processing time when case moves to higher court.

Mapping to Standard NLP Tasks & Similar NLP Benchmarks: Summarization of texts is a standard NLP task. There are two types of summaries; extractive and abstractive. Extractive summaries focus on extracting important complete sentences from text to form the summary. Abstractive summaries on the other hand create summaries by constructing new sentences which effectively summarizes the text. While there are no summarization benchmarks that focus on the legal documents, there are many benchmarks that focus on summarizing general English text like wikipedia articles, news articles [24], CNN/dailynews [23], research(ArXiv) articles [13,19], pubmed articles [34]. Similarly, the current state of the art research focuses on comparing the performance of various algorithms on Indian judgments [3]. Bhattacharya et. al [5] created unsupervised extractive summaries incorporating domain knowledge. [26] has created datasets to create extractive & abstractive summaries of supreme court judgements.

Dataset to be Collected & Evaluation Metrics: Since the summaries created by lawyers of the supreme court for judgments from 1950 to 1994 are available in the form of headnotes, this data could be utilized to create the benchmark. The automatic evaluation of summaries created is a complex topic. Recent research [11] proposes that there are four main aspects of summary evaluation: coherence, consistency, fluency & relevance. Many of the existing evaluation metrics like ROUGE, METEOR etc. depend on availability of the human generated summary to compare against. But these metrics do not capture the faithfulness and factuality [21] of the generated summaries. In addition, they do not capture hallucinations, which are defined as generated text not found in the original text or misrepresentations of the original text. The proposed ways to capture hallucinations [21] are either not relevant to the legal context or are computationally expensive. Hence there is a need to formulate better evaluation metrics which can measure faithfulness and factuality efficiently.

Timeline Extraction

Description of Task & Value Proposition: In this use-case scenario we propose the use of NLP to extract timelines from these case documents. We propose a timeline extraction benchmark to be of use to both the legal informatics community and the machine learning (ML) community. Depending on the type of case, each case may have hundreds or even thousands of pages worth documentation. The legal representation and decision making process for each court case is also handled by multiple people. The fact that the cases are often handled by multiple lawyers and judges, extracting the facts of the case according to events which occurred in time can get very challenging. With witness statements, and arguments being recorded several times, this can get even more challenging.

Mapping to Standard NLP Tasks & Similar NLP Benchmarks: This benchmark maps to a NLP task called temporal event extraction. There is a very nascent and growing field in NLP with a few seminal studies. The NLP models for this are also focused on general purpose English language. Some of the different approaches for this task include event extraction and temporal sequence ordering. Event extraction can include tasks such as named entity extraction, relationship extraction, event knowledge extraction, and co-reference handling. Temporal sequence handling can include tasks such as event duration extraction and temporal reference handling. One can leverage existing timeline extraction techniques including event extraction and temporal sequence techniques [28], [9,12,25,40]. Despite the existence of a few companies [18], there exist very few open event, timeline extraction datasets and benchmarks in the ML community e.g.[CoNLL2012 [29], SemEval2015 [22]]. A lot of works rely on text such as WikiPedia and news articles. A major challenge with this is that there exist very few temporal relationships in these datasets or the studies only extract dated events.

Dataset to be Collected & Evaluation Metrics: The training/test data we propose are human extracted events ordered in time. An initial baseline model for extracting timelines and events from a selected text can assist the annotator. The annotator has to add missing information and reorder timelines where necessary. The automatically generated benchmarks are evaluated against the expert created ones using accuracy and degree of overlap metrics.

4.3   Case Similarity

Indian law is common law, which means that precedent set by previous courts to interpret laws must be respected. Hence finding out cases which are similar to a given case becomes important for legal research. This activity is manual and a lot of commercial tools use keyword based or act based similarities. But to be able to search the similar judgments based on longer text like case facts, FIR etc. would make the search more relevant and automated. Following benchmarks focus on these tasks.

Find Similar Cases

Description of Task & Value Proposition: This benchmark deals with finding most relevant cases for given text descriptions about a case. Many existing search engines of Indian legal documents (Indian Kanoon, Legitquest, aironline etc.) focus on searches based on keywords. Searching with text descriptions allows you to look for more detailed information rather than keywords based search. Hence one can input the FIR, charge sheets, case description and search for the judgments which are similar. E.g. case description says, "republic editor Arnab Goswami was arrested in criminal case of suicide. His claims that he was targeted by the state govt and his personal liberty was violated". Then similar cases might be judgments that interpret personal liberty like Maneka Gandhi v. Union of India and Another (1978), Kharak Singh v. State of U.P. and Others etc. The similar cases could come from other high courts or supreme courts. Reduce time needed for manual search of similar cases and provide more meaningful results. Provision of search by larger text instead of just keywords would be very helpful. Many startups are developing such search engines as well. But there is no benchmark about how good the search engines are. Hence this benchmark would provide an objective way of evaluating such products

Mapping to Standard NLP Tasks & Similar NLP Benchmarks: This maps to case2vec where the cases are mapped to vectors in latent space. This mapping of cases to latent vectors is learnt while training. These types of tasks are harder to evaluate and hence hard to improve on. In the Forum of Information Retrieval Evaluation 2019 [2], there is a dataset created which identifies the most similar cases for a given text description of a case from a set of 2914 supreme court judgments. This data is available for 50 text description queries. Chinese AI law competition [38] has created a similar case matching competition (CAIL 2019 - SCM). This competition focuses on finding which 2 supreme court cases are similar in a triplet of cases. But the data is in Chinese language. Other existing benchmarks focus on finding similarity between sentences (Semantic textual similarity benchmark and Microsoft research paraphrase corpus). But these focus on open domain sentences similarity and not on similarity of the entire document. Competition on legal information extraction/entailment [31] focuses on extracting supporting cases for a given new case using Canada cases.

Dataset to be Collected & Evaluation Metrics: The data needed for this benchmark is past judgments and metadata about the case like acts etc. Using this data, triplets of cases (A,B,C) would be made. Legal experts would tag if case A is more similar to B or C. Such triplets need to be created carefully so that cases in a triplet share some common factors and are not random. This is because it is much easier to distinguish between two completely different cases like land case vs. murder case than to find similarity of one murder case to other 2 murder cases. Legal experts are needed for the manual tagging of such triplets and multiple such opinions would be taken for a record. This task can be evaluated by comparing model predictions with the consensus of the legal experts. The score could be the accuracy of the predictions.

Find Supporting Paragraph for New Judgment from an Existing Relevant Judgment

Description of Task & Value Proposition: Many times references of an old judgments which interpret law are used in judgments to follow case precedent. Typically there are multiple paragraphs that support the new decision. So finding the exact paragraph which supports the new judgment can be time consuming. E.g. A review case of visa rejection comes to a judge where the appellant says that the visa was rejected without an interview by the visa officer based on information collected by other people. Judge is writing a judgment where he wants to write "in matters of administrative decisions, the rule of "he who hears must decide" does not apply" . Judge has found an existing relevant judgment based on similarity search. Now the judge wants the exact paragraph from the existing judgment which interprets this. So he searches using query as "in matters of administrative decisions, the rule of "he who hears must decide" does not apply" and gives an existing document. The system returns the paragraph from existing judgment which interprets this law in detail. Time saved to find supporting exact text from existing judgment would enable legal stakeholders to process the decisions faster.

Mapping to Standard NLP Tasks & Similar NLP Benchmarks: This maps to paragraph2vec where similarity between new judgment text and paragraphs from a given judgment are found out. These type of tasks are hard to evaluate and hence hard to improve on. There is an existing similar benchmark by Competition on Legal Information Extraction/Entailment ([31]) which focuses on extracting an entailing paragraph from a relevant case for a new judgment using Canada cases. Creating a similar benchmark for Indian law would be more useful.

Dataset to be Collected & Evaluation Metrics: Data needed for this benchmark would be created using Indian courts judgments. Legal experts would create a triplet (relevant case text, new judgment, paragraph id supporting new judgment). Evaluation of this benchmark would be done by matching the paragraph extracted by humans to paragraphs extracted by model. A custom annotator tool needs to be built to allow such human annotations. The annotator would show the new judgment line and suggest paragraphs based on NLP model output. The answer suggested can be accepted by the expert or he can change it to an appropriate one. This suggestion would reduce the human processing time significantly. The evaluation of this benchmark can be done by comparing if the paragraph id predicted by the model matches the one provided by the expert. F1 score of the match can be used to rank the submissions.

Influential Case Law Extraction

Description of Task & Value Proposition: Some of the judgments have far reaching implications and are commonly cited in multiple judgments. The idea of this benchmark is to objectively identify such influential judgments for each of the legal topics. Many supreme court judgments cite other judgments for interpretation of laws. Such citations can be extracted automatically with NLP techniques and a network of such citations can be created. Using such a network, one can find influential judgments overall and for specific legal topics. The benchmark would provide objective evaluation of influence of a judgment. This would also mean time saving for legal research.

Mapping to Standard NLP Tasks & Similar NLP Benchmarks: This maps to citations extraction and algorithms like pagerank to decide influence once the network of citations is created. These NLP tasks are considered easy because of availability of pretrained models and libraries. There is an existing benchmark that focuses on prediction of case importance for European human rights cases [7]. To the best of our knowledge, there are no benchmarks that focus on establishing influential judgments in specific areas of Indian law.

Dataset to be Collected & Evaluation Metrics. Opinions of multiple legal experts need to be combined to create the curated list of influential cases in specific areas. Since data to be collected involves ranked lists in a given area, complex tools may not be needed for data collection. Experts can use simple tools like MS Excel to create such lists. Many of the existing NLP components like Legal named entity relation extractor can be leveraged for creating structured data for human annotations. Evaluation of this benchmark could be done in a similar way like case similarity benchmark above by matching the model created ranked list of expert created list

4.4 Reasoning Based NLP

Predict Relevant Acts Based on Case Facts

Description of Task & Value Proposition. Predicting the relevant act of the law based on the text description of the fact is an important legal research task. This is done typically by lawyers and police while making the chargesheet. Automating this process can also help layman people who don't understand law. This would help people to collect the right information about the case in a timely manner before they interact with lawyers or police. E.g, A citizen enters text "thieves took away Rs. 10000 and my Mobile last night...." the NLP system would return "Section 378 under Indian Penal Code". It can also return what are the keywords in the input text description that triggered this prediction. In this case keywords could be "took away". Informed with the right section of the law, citizens can make better decisions about documents to be collected, lawyers to contact etc. This will also increase familiarity with law among citizens.

Mapping to Standard NLP Tasks & Similar NLP Benchmarks. This maps to standard tasks of text classification. There is a similar existing benchmark about predicting which specific human rights articles and/or protocols have been violated on European human rights cases [7]. Another similar benchmark in Chinese language is Chinese criminal judgment prediction dataset, C-LJP [37] which is a part of Chinese AI Law Challenge. In the Forum of Information Retrieval Evaluation 2019 [2], there is a dataset created which finds most relevant statutes for 50 text descriptions from 197 Sections of Acts. The description of these 197 sections is also provided. [27] have created Indian Legal Statute Identification data set which has 66K documents and statutes.

Dataset to be Collected & Evaluation Metrics. The labelled data could be created using an unsupervised approach like using pattern matching to extract and hide acts, sections from judgments, FIR or using pretrained models for such extraction. This data can be used to train the NLP model and evaluation. There is no human annotation needed for this benchmark. Evaluation of this benchmark could be done by measuring the accuracy of predicted acts and sections by comparing them with actual acts and section

Statement Contradiction Discovery

Description of Task & Value Proposition. Identification of contradictions in witnesses, accused and victims statements has a lot of impact on the verdict. These contradictions are found out by lawyers, judges and legal research teams. The first step is to identify the statements by multiple people about the same topic. The topic could be specific to cases like arrival time of police, observations about incidence etc. Then these statements can be compared with each other to find out potential contradictions. These contradictions by the NLP model can be validated by humans to accept or reject them. This feedback about acceptance or rejection can be used to improve the model. This task will greatly reduce the time needed for identification of contradictions in case documents which is an important part of legal research.

Mapping to Standard NLP Tasks & Similar NLP Benchmarks. This maps to an NLP task called textual entailment also called natural language inference. Depending on the dataset, these tasks can be of medium to hard complexity. Similar benchmarks focus on finding textual entailment in general English text (The Stanford natural language inference corpus [6], recognizing textual entailment as part of super glue [35]. Another similar benchmark [31] is about finding a specific paragraph from case R that is relevant to a new case such that the paragraph entails decision Q of a new case.

Dataset to be Collected & Evaluation Metrics. Humans with experience in legal research would be needed to annotate if two sentences are contradicting or not. E.g. ("Police reached the site at 5pm", "Police reached the site at 6 pm", "Contradiction"). This benchmark can be evaluated by comparing the human labels with model predictions. Accuracy of such predictions can be used as a metric.

Sentence Rhetorical Roles Prediction

Description of Task & Value Proposition. Although the style of writing a judgment varies by the judge, most of the judgments have an inherent structure. Giving structure to the judgment text is important for many information retrieval and other downstream tasks. Sentence rhetorical roles prediction means identifying what role a sentence is playing in the judgment. The identification of right section of the judgment narrows the text to focus for a given task. E.g. If a person wants to know the final decision then it could be found in the section marked as "Current Court Decision". If someone wants to know the description of the case then it could be found in "Facts" section. The rhetorical roles identification would also help significantly in creating summary of the judgments and semantic search.

Mapping to Standard NLP Tasks & Similar NLP Benchmarks: This would fit into the task of sequential text classification where each sentence is assigned with a rhetorical role. The rhetorical role of a sentence is also dependent on the previous and next sentences. There are some datasets released about this task but there is no benchmark. The dataset published by [4] is very small and noisy in nature.

Dataset to be Collected & Evaluation Metrics The manual annotations at the sentence level about which sentence belongs to what rhetorical role need to be collected. The accuracy of the prediction could be used as evaluation metric

5   Operationalizing Indian Legal NLP Benchmarks

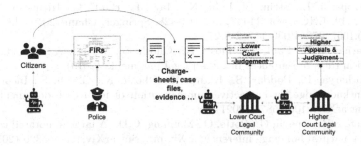

Fig. 2. Indian Legal Bench Marks: The Indian legal Process

Figure 2 shows the Indian legal process, where the citizens file the FIRs with the police, who prepare the charge sheets in conjunction with the legal community. The case then proceeds to trial through several levels of court to the final judgment. In the long run we envision that the AI assisted software would help the stakeholders at each step of the process. The relevant act/document identification engine would help the citizens and police gather the prerequisite documents. Timeline extraction, text summarizing tools can help prepare charge-sheets. The question answering and generation AI, case similarity tools and supporting paragraph identification can help with the trial process. Reasoning tools such as argument generation, judgment auto-complete, and influential case law discovery can also support a seamless and transparent AI driven judiciary. Towards our long-term vision of an efficient and transparent legal system, the benchmarks would serve as the stepping stones which would foster innovation. As the next steps, relevant datasets would be collected (either using humans or automatically from the text based on the benchmark). Baseline NLP models would be created which indicate bare minimum evaluation metric values. Following this the benchmarks would be launched. Since these benchmarks present challenging tasks they will open up more possibilities and applications. All these things would help Indian Legal systems to be more efficient, open and citizen centric.

Acknowledgements. This paper is funded by EkStep Foundation

References

1. Abujabal, A., Saha Roy, R., Yahya, M., Weikum, G.: ComQA: a community-sourced dataset for complex factoid question answering with paraphrase clusters. In: Proceedings of the 2019 Conference of the North American Chapter of the Association for Computational Linguistics: Human Language Technologies. vol. 1 (Long and Short Papers). Association for Computational Linguistics, Minneapolis, Minnesota (Jun 2019). https://doi.org/10.18653/v1/N19-1027, https://aclanthology.org/N19-1027
2. Bhattacharya, P., et al.: Fire 2019 aila track: Artificial intelligence for legal assistance (12 2019). https://doi.org/10.1145/3368567.3368587
3. Bhattacharya, P., Hiware, K., Rajgaria, S., Pochhi, N., Ghosh, K., Ghosh, S.: A comparative study of summarization algorithms applied to legal case judgments. In: Azzopardi, L., Stein, B., Fuhr, N., Mayr, P., Hauff, C., Hiemstra, D. (eds.) ECIR 2019. LNCS, vol. 11437, pp. 413–428. Springer, Cham (2019). https://doi.org/10.1007/978-3-030-15712-8_27
4. Bhattacharya, P., Paul, S., Ghosh, K., Ghosh, S., Wyner, A.: Identification of rhetorical roles of sentences in Indian legal judgments (2019)
5. Bhattacharya, P., Poddar, S., Rudra, K., Ghosh, K., Ghosh, S.: Incorporating domain knowledge for extractive summarization of legal case documents. arXiv preprint arXiv:2106.15876 (2021)
6. Bowman, S.R., Angeli, G., Potts, C., Manning, C.D.: A large annotated corpus for learning natural language inference. arXiv preprint arXiv:1508.05326 (2015)
7. Chalkidis, I., Androutsopoulos, I., Aletras, N.: Neural legal judgment prediction in English (2019)
8. Chalkidis, I., et al.: LexGLUE: a benchmark dataset for legal language understanding in English. arXiv preprint arXiv:2110.00976 (2021)
9. Chieu, H.L., Lee, Y.K.: Query based event extraction along a timeline. In: Proceedings of the 27th Annual International ACM SIGIR Conference on Research and Development in Information Retrieval (2004)
10. Choudhry, S., Khosla, M., Mehta, P.B.: The Oxford Handbook of the Indian Constitution. Oxford University Press, Oxford (2016)
11. Fabbri, A.R., Kryściński, W., McCann, B., Xiong, C., Socher, R., Radev, D.: SummEval: re-evaluating summarization evaluation. Trans. Assoc. Comput. Linguist. **9**(2), 391–409 (2021)
12. Finlaysona, M.A., Cremisini, A., Ocal, M.: Extracting and aligning timelines
13. Gehrke, J., Ginsparg, P., Kleinberg, J.: Overview of the 2003 KDD cup. ACM SIGKDD Explor. Newslett. **5**(2), 149–151 (2003)
14. Jurczyk, T., Zhai, M., Choi, J.D.: SelQA: a new benchmark for selection-based question answering. In: 2016 IEEE 28th International Conference on Tools with Artificial Intelligence (ICTAI) (2016). https://doi.org/10.1109/ICTAI.2016.0128

15. Krishna, K., Iyyer, M.: Generating question-answer hierarchies. arXiv preprint arXiv:1906.02622 (2019)
16. Grover, K., Kaur, K., Tiwari, K., Rupali, Kumar, P.: Deep learning based question generation using T5 transformer. In: Garg, D., Wong, K., Sarangapani, J., Gupta, S.K. (eds.) Advanced Computing. IACC 2020. Communications in Computer and Information Science, vol 1367. Springer, Singapore (2021). https://doi.org/10.1007/978-981-16-0401-0_18
17. Kwiatkowski, T., et al.: Natural questions: a benchmark for question answering research. Trans. Assoc. Comput. Linguist. **7**, 452–466 (2019)
18. Leban, G., Fortuna, B., Brank, J., Grobelnik, M.: Event registry: learning about world events from news. In: Proceedings of the 23rd International Conference on World Wide Web (2014)
19. Leskovec, J., Kleinberg, J., Faloutsos, C.: Graphs over time: densification laws, shrinking diameters and possible explanations. In: Proceedings of the Eleventh ACM SIGKDD International Conference on Knowledge Discovery in Data Mining (2005)
20. Liu, D., et al.: GLGE: a new general language generation evaluation benchmark. arXiv preprint arXiv:2011.11928 (2020)
21. Maynez, J., Narayan, S., Bohnet, B., McDonald, R.: On faithfulness and factuality in abstractive summarization. arXiv preprint arXiv:2005.00661 (2020)
22. Minard, A.L.M., et al.: SemEval-2015 task 4: Timeline: Cross-document event ordering. In: 9th International Workshop on Semantic Evaluation (SemEval 2015) (2015)
23. Nallapati, R., Zhou, B., Gulcehre, C., Xiang, B., et al.: Abstractive text summarization using sequence-to-sequence RNNs and beyond. arXiv preprint arXiv:1602.06023 (2016)
24. Narayan, S., Cohen, S.B., Lapata, M.: Don't give me the details, just the summary! Topic-aware convolutional neural networks for extreme summarization. arXiv preprint arXiv:1808.08745 (2018)
25. Ning, Q., Zhou, B., Feng, Z., Peng, H., Roth, D.: CogCompTime: a tool for understanding time in natural language. In: Proceedings of the 2018 Conference on Empirical Methods in Natural Language Processing: System Demonstrations (2018)
26. Parikh, V., et al.: Aila 2021: Shared task on artificial intelligence for legal assistance. In: Forum for Information Retrieval Evaluation (2021)
27. Paul, S., Goyal, P., Ghosh, S.: LeSICiN: a heterogeneous graph-based approach for automatic legal statute identification from Indian legal documents (2021)
28. Piskorski, J., Zavarella, V., Atkinson, M., Verile, M.: Timelines: entity-centric event extraction from online news. In: Text2Story@ ECIR (2020)
29. Pradhan, S., Moschitti, A., Xue, N., Uryupina, O., Zhang, Y.: CoNLL-2012 shared task: modeling multilingual unrestricted coreference in Ontonotes. In: Joint Conference on EMNLP and CoNLL-Shared Task (2012)
30. Qi, W., et al.: ProphetNet-X: large-scale pre-training models for English, Chinese, multi-lingual, dialog, and code generation. arXiv preprint arXiv:2104.08006 (2021)
31. Rabelo, J., Kim, M.-Y., Goebel, R., Yoshioka, M., Kano, Y., Satoh, K.: COLIEE 2020: methods for legal document retrieval and entailment. In: Okazaki, N., Yada, K., Satoh, K., Mineshima, K. (eds.) JSAI-isAI 2020. LNCS (LNAI), vol. 12758, pp. 196–210. Springer, Cham (2021). https://doi.org/10.1007/978-3-030-79942-7_13
32. Rajpurkar, P., Jia, R., Liang, P.: Know what you don't know: Unanswerable questions for squad (2018)

33. Rajpurkar, P., Zhang, J., Lopyrev, K., Liang, P.: Squad: 100,000+ questions for machine comprehension of text. arXiv preprint arXiv:1606.05250 (2016)
34. Sen, P., Namata, G., Bilgic, M., Getoor, L., Galligher, B., Eliassi-Rad, T.: Collective classification in network data. AI Magazine (Sep 2008) https://doi.org/10.1609/aimag.v29i3.2157, https://ojs.aaai.org/index.php/aimagazine/article/view/2157
35. Wang, A., et al.: SuperGLUE: a stickier benchmark for general-purpose language understanding systems (2020)
36. Wang, A., Singh, A., Michael, J., Hill, F., Levy, O., Bowman, S.R.: GLUE: a multi-task benchmark and analysis platform for natural language understanding (2019)
37. Xiao, C., et al.: CAIL 2018: a large-scale legal dataset for judgment prediction (2018)
38. Xiao, C., et al.: CAIL 2019-SCM: a dataset of similar case matching in legal domain (2019)
39. Yang, Y., Yih, W.T., Meek, C.: WikiQA: a challenge dataset for open-domain question answering. In: Proceedings of the 2015 Conference on Empirical Methods in Natural Language Processing. Association for Computational Linguistics, Lisbon, Portugal (Sep 2015). https://doi.org/10.18653/v1/D15-1237, https://aclanthology.org/D15-1237
40. Yu, M., et al.: Spatiotemporal event detection: a review. Int. J. Digital Earth 13(12), 1339–1365 (2020)
41. Zhong, H., Xiao, C., Tu, C., Zhang, T., Liu, Z., Sun, M.: How does NLP benefit legal system: A summary of legal artificial intelligence. arXiv preprint arXiv:2004.12158 (2020)
42. Zhong, H., Xiao, C., Tu, C., Zhang, T., Liu, Z., Sun, M.: JEC-QA: a legal-domain question answering dataset. In: Proceedings of the AAAI Conference on Artificial Intelligence. vol. 34 (2020)

Computer-Aided Comparative Law
on Meiji Civil Code

Kaito Koyama[1], Tomoya Sano[2], and Yoichi Takenaka[1]([✉]) [iD]

[1] Kansai University, Osaka, Japan
{k183647,takenaka}@kansai-u.ac.jp
[2] Nagoya University, Nagoya, Japan
tomoya@law.nagoya-u.ac.jp

Abstract. We propose the framework to analyze the legislative study
on the Meiji civil code. Comparative law research on the Meiji civil code
and foreign codes has been done manually by legal scholars. In principle,
they have to compare all the combinations of articles from the Meiji civil
code and a foreign code. As the number of the combination is enormous,
comparative law researches have been a slavery task. Therefore, there is
a need to reduce the amount of work by using computers. Our research
aims to support comparative law research by automatically estimating
the reference relation by computer. In order to accomplish this objective,
we defined the problem of estimating the reference articles of foreign
codes. We used the seven types of distance measures used by document
and string comparison. Then, we verified our proposed method by comparing the estimated reference articles of foreign codes with the actual
reference articles. The results based on the Jaccard distance were the
best. In addition, we verified the effectiveness of our method by comparing the results with the studies of jurists. As a result, we found that the
proposed method gives results that agree with actual jurists' knowledge
and can support comparative law by computers.

Keywords: Comparative law · Legal document analysis · AI and
intellectual property

1 Introduction

The study of comparative law has a long history, and comparative law research
has been conducted to draft and evaluate various laws. [1] In recent years, with
globalization and the spread of the Internet, the importance of comparative law
has been increasing. In Japan, comparative law research accompanying the study
of the legislative history of the Japanese Civil Code has been actively conducted.
[2]

The present Japanese Civil Code was drafted based on the Japanese Old
Civil Code (hereafter, the Japanese Old Civil Code referred to as the Old Civil
Code), which imitated the French Civil Code, and was revised many times. [3]

© Springer Nature Switzerland AG 2023
K. Yada et al. (Eds.): JSAI-isAI 2021 Workshops, LNAI 13856, pp. 49–61, 2023.
https://doi.org/10.1007/978-3-031-36190-6_4

In particular, we recognized the Japanese Civil Code at the time of drafting (hereafter, the Japanese Civil Code at the time of drafting referred to as the Meiji Civil Code) as a "fruit of comparative jurisprudence." [4] [5] [6] The drafters drafted the Meiji Civil Code while closely connected with modern codes, such as American and British codes, French codes, and German codes. [7] [8] In addition, they also drafted the Meiji Civil Code with attention to the codes of small countries. The First Proposal of the Meiji Civil Code [9] lists the articles of each country's foreign codes corresponding to each article as "reference." The Meiji Civil Code has 34 reference countries and regions. [10] In addition, the average of "reference" is about 6.5 in each article. [4] Therefore, "reference" could have several meanings. For example, when drafting specific articles of the Meiji Civil Code, there is a possibility that they inherited specific articles of foreign code or parts of them. Alternatively, there is a possibility that the text of foreign code was negatively evaluated and drafted as a unique law. Therefore, we expect comparative law research on the Meiji Civil Code to produce many results, such as contributions to the generalization of the inheritance of foreign laws and the evaluation of foreign laws against the Meiji Civil Code. [2]

Jurists have often conducted comparative law research targeting a single code, operating manually. [11] Comparative law is the comparison of the law of one country with the laws of other countries. When multiple reference codes exist, as in the Meiji Civil Code, it is desirable to conduct comparative law among multiple codes. In addition, principally, they have to compare all the combinations of articles. However, comparative law researches have been a slavery task as the number of the combination is enormous. Therefore, there is a need to reduce the amount of work by using computers.

This study aims to support comparative researches on the legislative history of the Meiji Civil Code. Therefore, we examine the method of estimating the reference articles to a given article of the Meiji Civil Code by computer from the given article of the Meiji Civil Code and all articles of foreign codes. In addition, we evaluate the plausibility of the estimated reference articles.

2   Problem Definition and Modeling

2.1   Reference Relation Estimation Problem

When comparing articles, we need to estimate the reference articles of foreign codes for a specific article of the Meiji Civil Code. In this paper, we define this problem as the reference relation estimation problem. As mentioned in Sect. 1, each article of the Meiji Civil Code has a corresponding article of foreign codes in the form of "reference." [9] Table 1 shows some of the reference relationships. For example, the article 2 of the Meiji Civil Code references the article 11 of the French Civil Code. We aim to discover the article 11 of the French Civil Code as the reference article to the article 2 of the Meiji Civil Code by using a computer. In addition, for a given article of the Meiji Civil Code, when there exist multiple reference articles of the foreign codes, our goal is to discover at least one.

Table 1. A part of the reference relationships

Meiji	French	Belgium	Italian	Spanish	Switzerland
Article 1	Article 8,725	Article 50,743	Article 1,724	Article 29,30	Article 5
Article 2	Article 11	Article 50	Article 3	Article 27	Article 1,5
Article 3	Article 388,488	Article 384,486	Article 240,323	Article 320	Article 16
Article 4	Article 1305	Article 1074	Article 1303	Article 1263	Article 66
Article 5	–	–	–	–	–
Article 6	Article 487,1308	–	–	–	–

2.2   Algorithm for Reference Relation Estimation

In order to automatically estimate the reference articles, we calculate the degree of similarity between a specific article of the Meiji Civil Code and all articles of the target code given as input. Based on the similarity, we can solve the reference relation estimation problem. Given the definition of similarity in this study, i.e., the distance measure, we propose the following algorithm to estimate the reference relationship between two articles.

Input

   x:An article in Meiji Civil Code

   Y:All the articles in the target code

Output

   $Y\prime \subset Y$

Conditions

   Distance $\phi(\ x\ ,\ y\prime\ ) \leq \phi(\ x\ ,\ y\ ), \forall y \in Y\ , \forall y\prime \in Y$

2.3   Finding the Best Distance Measure

In order to solve the reference relation estimation problem, we need to set up a distance measure that matches or is similar to the knowledge that the jurist uses to discover the reference articles. [12] However, it is still unknown the measure representing the jurists' knowledge on a computer. Therefore, we define the problem of finding a measure representing the jurists' knowledge on a computer as finding the best distance measure.

2.4   Definition of Distance

In Sect. 2.3, we have not defined the distance measure. In order to discover a distance measure that is consistent with the knowledge of jurists, it is desired to take a small value when the distance between two given articles is close. Alternatively, it is an enormous value when the distance between the two given articles is far. Therefore, we test the following seven types of similarity measures based on document and string comparison used in the research area of Natural Language Processing(NLP). Moreover, we adapt them to our algorithm.

- Levenshtein distance
- Jarrow distance
- Jarrow-Winkler distance
- Jaccard distance
- Dice distance
- Simpson distance

We treat the Jaccard, Dice, and Simpson distances as distances in the closed interval from 0 to 1 by normalizing the scores of the Jaccard, Dice, and Simpson coefficients. [13, 14]

3   Evaluation Experiment

3.1   Target Codes

When calculating the distance between articles in the proposed method, it is inadequate to calculate between different languages. In other words, the input codes must be in the same language. For example, it is necessary to use the English versions of the Meiji Civil Code and the French Civil Code. Therefore, when calculating the distance between articles in this research, we will use the French version of each code from the viewpoint of linguistic resources. The target codes of our study are the French Civil Code, the Spanish Civil Code, the Belgian Draft Civil Code, and the Italian Civil Code. They have enough reference articles to the Meiji Civil Code and have French versions. In addition, as mentioned in Sect. 1, the Meiji Civil Code was drafted with attention to small countries. [9] Therefore, in addition to the above-mentioned foreign codes, we include the Swiss (Graubünden) Civil Code as a target code. These codes are digitized and arranged. [15] Table 2 shows the number of articles of the target codes and reference articles from the Meiji Civil Code.

3.2   Preprocessing

In comparing the similarity of strings, it is desirable to have the original form of the words. For this reason, we remove stemming and stop words before calculating. Stemming is the processing of returning a word whose form changes due

Table 2. The reference relationships

Codes	Articles	Reference Articles
Meiji Civil Code	1146	
French Civil Code	2283	673
Belgium Draft Civil Code	2411	622
Italian Civil Code	2146	673
Spanish Civil Code	1976	628
Switzerland (Canton des Grisons) Civil Code	335	200

to conjugation or inflection to its original form. For example, in English, when the verb is in the past tense, we often add "ed" to the original form of the verb. When the subject is in the third person singular, we often add "s" to the original form of the verb. For example, "walk" would be "walked" or "walks." By reverting to the original form, we can eliminate the effect of words considered to have the same meaning on the distance calculation. Stop words are the words that frequently exist in a document. For example, stop words in English are articles and numerals such as "a", "the", and "one." In this research, when calculating the distance between two articles, it is required to reduce the influence of stop words as much as possible. Therefore, before calculating the distance between articles, we perform stemming and remove stop words. In addition, we simultaneously remove numbers and symbols such as "1" and "-." For stemming and stop word definition, we used spaCy [24], an open software library of NLP.

3.3 Result

Table 3 shows the calculation results based on the Jaccard distance, the best distance among the distance scale methods used in this paper. In the table, the "Target Code" indicates the foreign codes of the five countries targeted in this paper for comparative law research with the Meiji Civil Code. The "True Positive (TP)" means that the article that the proposed method estimated as a reference article was an actual reference article. The "False Positive (FP)" means that the article that the proposed method estimated as a reference article was not an actual reference article. The "False Negative(FN)" means that the article that the proposed method did not estimate as a reference article was an actual reference article. We verify the effectiveness of the proposed method by considering the percentage of the articles estimated as reference articles and the actual reference articles. Therefore, in this study, we use the recall as an evaluation index. The recall is an indicator to integrate TP, FP, and FN, defined by the following formula.

$$Recall = \frac{TP}{TP + FN}$$

For each foreign code, the recall is 27% for the French Civil Code, 26% for the Belgian Draft Civil Code, 25% for the Italian Civil Code, 20% for the Spanish Civil Code, and 17% for the Swiss (Graubünden) Code.

4 Discussion

We evaluate the validity of our results from two perspectives that are important to consider when conducting comparative law by jurists. [4,16] The first perspective is the macro perspective, which is the overall view of the reference status of foreign codes to the Meiji Civil Code. The second perspective is the micro perspective, which examines the individual articles and the reference articles of the foreign codes in detail. In this chapter, we discuss the effectiveness of the proposed method from these two perspectives.

Table 3. The comparison result based on Jaccard Distance

Target Code	TP	FP	FN	Recall
French	185	961	488	27%
Belgium	163	983	459	26%
Italy	166	980	507	25%
Spanish	126	1020	502	20%
Switzerland (Canton des Grisons)	35	1111	165	18%

4.1 Macro Perspective

We evaluate the effectiveness of the proposed method from a macro perspective in this section. [4,16] The evaluation from the macro perspective in this paper examines the influence of the target codes by using the recall adopted as an evaluation index. The correct estimation by the proposed method means that the sentences of the articles of the Meiji Civil Code and the estimated reference articles of the target codes are similar. In other words, we consider that the articles of the Meiji Civil Code inherited the estimated reference articles of the target codes. Therefore, we use the recall as the indicator of the influence of target codes. Accordingly, we compare the recall with the findings and theories of the actual drafters or jurists of the Meiji Civil Code.

Firstly, we compare our result with a study of Okamatsu [17], a civil law scholar of the Meiji era. The French Civil Code, the Belgian Draft Civil Code, the Italian Civil Code, and the Spanish Civil Code are the French legal system. Their recall is between 20% to 27% each. Okamatsu said, "Old Civil Code is of the French legal system. The Meiji Civil Code constructed 60% of the German Civil Code, 30% of the French Civil Code, 2% of the British Civil Code, and 8% Japanese custom." The mention agrees with our result. Due to this, our proposed method effectively examines the influence of foreign codes and regulations when drafting the Meiji Civil Code.

Secondly, we compare our results with the evaluation of each foreign code in a study of Ume [18,19], one of the drafters of the Meiji Civil Code, and the mention of Ito [11], the prime minister at that time. In the results of this study, the recall of the French Civil Code is 27%. This rate proves that they drafted the Meiji Civil Code referring to foreign codes other than the French Civil Code. The Old Civil Code before the compilation of the Meiji Civil Code was called the Imitation Code. The Old Civil Code modeled the French Civil Code. One of the reasons for the motion against the Old Civil Code was that this Old Civil Code was too similar to the French Civil Code. Therefore, Ito claimed as follows. "Assuming the principle of 'the common of the Western countries,' we should adopt the foreign civil codes that are adaptable to such as Japanese customs and senses as models." [18,20] In addition, Ume evaluated the French Civil Code as follows. "Although scholars admit that the French Civil Code has many 'good provisions that revolutionize the old bad habits,' the compilation style is not good. Moreover, the articles are too detailed. For this reason, the French Civil Code was not the primary model when drafting the Meiji Civil Code." Our results that the recall of the French Civil Code is close to the recall of the other foreign codes agree with their mentions.

The recall of the Belgian Draft Civil Code is 1 point lower than that of the French Civil Code. Ume described the Belgian Draft Civil Code as following. "The Belgian Draft Civil Code, drafted by Laurent, is highly voluminous, consisting of 2411 articles. We can say that it clarifies and supplements the French Civil Code in accordance with the existing case law. However, as with the Old Civil Code, there is much redundancy in the same articles and sentences. Its style is like a textbook." [18,20] Our result of the Belgian Draft Civil Code agrees with his assessment. In addition, the higher recall rate than the French Civil Code in our result indicates that the Belgian Draft Civil Code referred to supplement the gaps in the French Civil Code considering his assessment. In order to examine this consideration in more detail, we need to simultaneously compare and examine the Meiji Civil Code, the French Civil Code, and the Belgian Draft Civil Code. By conducting the comparative study simultaneously, the ratio of the articles in which the French Civil Code and the Belgian Draft Civil Code simultaneously referred to in the Meiji Civil Code will become clear.

The recall of the Italian Civil Code is 2 points lower than that with the French Civil Code. The Italian Civil Code uses the French Civil Code as its mother law. In addition, Ume described the Italian Civil Code as "a great improvement over the imitation law, French law, in many respects." [18,20] The result shows that the recall value of the French Civil Code and the Italian Civil Code are almost the same. It indicates our result agrees with his evaluation. Moreover if we compare the Italian Civil Code and the French Civil Code in detail in each article, we may find novel knowledge. For example, since the Italian Civil Code was enacted later than the French Civil Code, it referred to more recent articles in similar provisions. Alternatively, when the Meiji Civil Code was translated into French, the french translation of the Italian Civil Code was used. Our proposed method shows the possibility of developing into a detailed analysis of individual articles.

The recall of the Spanish Civil Code is 7 point lower than that of the French Civil Code. Ume explained the Spanish Civil Code as follows. "The Spanish Civil Code is positioned in the French legal system. However, there are not a few provisions that rely on the country's customs or directly adopt the provisions of Roman law. In addition, we can evaluate as greatly simplified compared to other countries, and there are quite a few provisions that are worth referring to." [18,20] It is hard to evaluate this editorial from our result correctly. In order to properly exemplify this consideration, we need to simultaneously compare and examine the Meiji Civil Code, French Civil Code, and Spanish Civil Code. Suppose the analysis results show that the ratio of simultaneous reference to the Meiji Civil Code in the French Civil Code and the Spanish Civil Code is low. In that case, it would exemplify the uniqueness of the Spanish Civil Code.

The recall of the Swiss (Graubünden) code is 18%, which is the lowest among the foreign codes included in this study. Ume explained the Spanish Civil Code as follows. "As for Swiss (Graubünden) code, the Graubünden Civil Code has only 518 articles. However, each article is very long and is comparable to 1000 articles. Although the number of articles is small, there are many 'unnecessary redundancies,' and almost unparalleled. It is the German legal system. However, it has its unique points and can be said to be an innovation." [18, 20] The other target codes consist of around 2000 articles. They are twice times much as the content of the Swiss (Graubünden) Code. However, the recall of the Swiss (Graubünden) code is half of the other target codes, despite the smaller number of articles. The result agrees with Ume's assessment. In order to properly exemplify this consideration, we need to simultaneously compare and examine the Meiji Civil Code, the Swiss (Graubünden) Code, and the other codes. It describes the number of "unnecessary redundancies" as extremely high. Suppose a specific article of the Meiji Civil Code referenced a specific article of the Swiss (Graubünden) Code. In that case, the reference articles of the Swiss (Graubünden) Code may have a more substantial influence than the reference articles of other foreign codes at the same time.

We summarize the macro perspective discussions. Our results objectively show that the Meiji Civil Code reflected the claim of Hirobumi Ito [20] to a great extent. In addition, the comparison of our results with Ume's evaluation of the drafters of the Civil Code shows that our proposed method is effective. [18, 20] Our results for the Belgian Draft Civil Code, the Spanish Civil Code, and the Swiss (Graubünden) Code show the possibility of developing to analyze the relationships among the Meiji Civil Code, the French Civil Code, moreover individual foreign codes. In other words, our results show the possibility of development to comparative law among more than two codes in the overall view.

4.2 Micro Perspective

We evaluate the effectiveness of the proposed method from a micro perspective in this section. [4, 16] The evaluation from a micro perspective in this paper is analyzing the individual articles of the Meiji Civil Code and the reference articles. There are two points to evaluate our results from a micro perspective.

Firstly, we show that the proposed method is effective for the analysis between two articles. Suppose the reference articles that the proposed method estimated are the actual reference articles. In that case, the articles of the Meiji Civil Code and the reference articles are similar. In other words, we consider that the article of the Meiji Civil Code took over the reference articles of the foreign codes. For example, the article 765 of the Meiji Civil Code referred to the article 144 of the French Civil Code when drafting. [9] In the proposed method, the distance between these articles is 0. The result suggests that the article of the Meiji Civil Code inherited the article of the French Civil Code. Thus, our proposed method correctly extracts the inherited articles. On the other hand, suppose our proposed method failed to estimate the reference articles. In that case, we consider that they did not directly take over the reference articles. In other words, the articles that our proposed method failed to extract despite the reference articles are worthy of jurists' study. It is one of the reduce the amount of the work by using the computer that we aimed.

Secondly, we show that our proposed method effectively analyzes among the articles of the Meiji Civil Code and the reference articles of foreign codes. Analyzing the Meiji Civil Code and multiple reference articles makes us possible to verify such as Japan and the situation of other countries at that time. Therefore, we propose a method to create a figure that arranges the reference articles around a specific article of the Meiji Civil Code on a plane. In the visualization, we use the multi-dimensional scaling(MDS) and the traveling salesman problem algorithm. [21,22] We perform the visualization as follows.

Step1 Measure the distance between the article of the Meiji Civil Code and the reference articles of the foreign codes.
Step2 Based on step1, extract the reference articles to be visualized.
Step3 Measure the distance between the reference articles extracted in step2.
Step4 Perform MDS on the distance between the reference articles measured in step3.
Step5 Center the relevant article of the Meiji Civil Code, and arrange the reference articles around it based on the distance in step 4.

In step1 and step2, we calculate the distance between the articles based on the Jaccard distance, which has the best recall in our proposed method. In step2, suppose there is more than one reference article of the same foreign code to the article of the Meiji Civil Code. In that case, we extract the one closer reference article to the article of the Meiji Civil Code. In addition, we include the articles of the Old Civil Code in the articles that we arrange. In step5, we arrange reference articles in order counterclockwise based on the traveling salesman problem algorithm.

Figure 1 and 2 show the article 446 and 540 of the Meiji Civil Code. We use Fig. 1 as an example to explain the figures. The vertical and horizontal axes of the figure are the Jaccard distance, which is the distance from the article of the Meiji Civil Code placed center. Most of the articles successfully extracted in our result have a Jaccard distance of around 0.7. Therefore, we draw concentric circles with distances of 0.9, 0.8, and 0.7 to make the relationship between the Meiji Civil Code and the reference articles easier to understand. We place the closest reference article from the article of the Meiji Civil Code where the vertical axis of the diagram is 0, and the horizontal axis is positive. The closest article to the article 446 of the Meiji Civil Code is the article 668 of the First Draft German Civil Code. Figure 1 also shows the article 668 of the First Draft German Civil Code is the closest reference article to the article 446 of the Meiji Civil Code. The other reference articles are arranged counterclockwise from the article 668 of the First Draft German Civil Code based on the traveling salesman problem algorithm. In Fig. 1, the French, Belgian, Italian Civil Code articles are nearby on the left side of the figure. Here, the contexts of the article 446 of the Meiji Civil Code and some reference articles of the foreign codes are as follows.

58   K. Koyama et al.

Meiji Civil Code Article 446
   La caution est obligée à l'exécution de l'obligation du débiteur principal, au cas où celui-ci ne l'exécuterait pas lui-même.
First Draft of the German Civil Code Article 668
   Par le contrat de cautionnement la caution s'oblige envers le créancier d'un tiers à exécuter l'obligation de ce dernier, si celui-ci ne le fait pas. La preuve de l'accomplissement de l'obligation principale incombe à la caution.
French Civil Code Article 2011
   Celui qui se rend caution d'une obligation, se soumet envers le créancier à satisfaire à cette obligation, si le débiteur n'y satisfait pas lui-même.
Belgian Draft Civil Code Article 2090
   Celui qui se rend caution d'une obligation se soumet envers le créancier à satisfaire à cette obligation, si le débiteur n'y satisfait pas lui-même.
Italian Civil Code Article 1898
   Celui, qui se rend caution d'une obligation, se soumet envers le créancier à seftiâfaire à cette obligation, si le débiteur n'y satisfait pas lui-même.

We confirmed that the contexts of the articles of the French, Belgian, and Italian Civil Code are similar. In addition, when we calculated their distance by the proposed method based on Jaccard distance, each article is an exact match with a distance of 0. Therefore, Fig. 1 is a successful example of visualization because these clauses are close to each other.

   Figure 2 shows the result for the article 540 of the Meiji Civil Code. The article 540 of the Meiji Civil Code describes the regulations on contract termination. Civil Code Amendment Reason Statement says that the legislative examples of

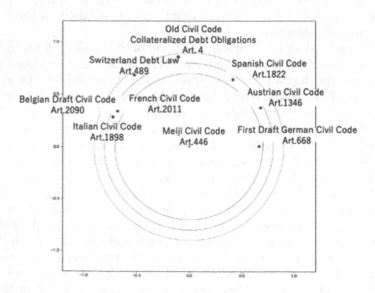

Fig. 1. Meiji Civil Code Article 446

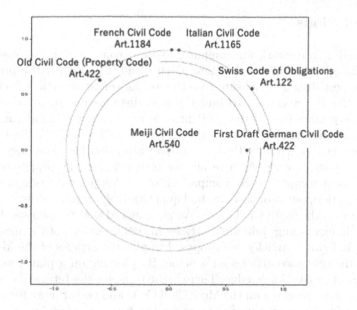

Fig. 2. Meiji Civil Code Article 540

countries regarding the way of the contract termination are distinguished into three types as follows. [23]

1 Judicial Termination (French, Italian, Dutch, Old Civil Code)
2 Termination by notice of intention(German draft Civil Code, Swiss Code of Obligations)
3 Automatic Termination

The Meiji Civil Code follows the principle of termination by notice of intention. In Fig. 2, the closest article to the article of the Meiji Civil Code is the article of the First Draft German Civil Code. The First Draft German Civil Code adopts the termination principle by notice of intention, and the Swiss Code of Obligations does the same. In addition, the French, Italian, and the Old Civil Code, which are statutes that adopt the principle of Judicial Termination, are nearby. Our result is similar to the distinction in the actual articles. Figure 2 is a successful example of expressing the knowledge of legal scholars by our proposed method.

We summarize the discussions from a micro perspective. First, we showed that our proposed method effectively analyzes articles with two individual reference relations. In particular, we showed that our proposed method is effective in finding inherited relations. In addition, we succeeded in reducing the work of jurists by focusing on the articles that fail to extract the reference articles. Next, we proposed a two-dimensional plot of the relationships among a specific Meiji Civil Code article and reference articles in the foreign codes. We showed that the figures of a particular article are similar to jurists' knowledge and that it is effective for analyzing individual articles.

5   Conclusions

We proposed a framework for computer-assisted comparative law research on the legislative history of the Japanese Civil Code. We defined the problem of finding the best distance measure to estimate the reference article from all the articles of the target codes. To find the best distance measure, we compared seven distance measures in the NLP field. As a result, we found the method based on Jaccard distance to have the highest Recall value. We discussed our results from two viewpoints that jurists pay attention to when they conduct comparative law research. As a result, we revealed that the proposed method is effective for a comprehensive comparison of the Meiji Civil Code and foreign codes. In addition, our proposed method quantitatively examines the influence of foreign codes on the Meiji Civil Code. We also showed that the proposed method is effective in examining individual articles in detail. As one of the methods for examining individual articles, we proposed to plot the articles of the Meiji Civil Code and the reference articles on a plane. By plotting on a plane, we express the findings of jurists' knowledge. There is the topic for the future of conducting comparative legal research on the Meiji Civil Code and two or more foreign codes simultaneously. Alternatively, the topic for the future is verifying whether the proposed method is also effective for other codes such as the Meiji Commercial Code. In addition, we need to conduct a comparative law study of the German Civil Code, which is considered the most influential in drafting the Meiji Civil Code. In order to do the research, we need to propose a method of comparative law by a computer that does not depend on language resources.

References

1. Eberle, E.J.: The Method and Role of Comparative Law (2009)
2. Kitagawa, Z.: History and Theory of Japanese Law. NIPPON HYORON SHA CO., LTD., (1968)
3. Kishigami, H.: the beginning of Japanese civil law -Boissonade and legislator's intention-. CHUKYO HOGAKU 30(4), 7–37 (1996)
4. Sano, T.: Analysis of reference foreign codes at the time of drafting the Meiji civil code. Nagoya Univ. Law Politics Conf. 257, 89–108 (2014)
5. Takizawa, T.: The identity of Japanese law from comparative law
6. Hozumi, S.: Lectures on the New Japanese Civil Code : As Material for the Study of Comparative Jurisprudence. Maruzen, 2nd (edn) (1912)
7. Ono, S.: Comparative law and the civil code of japan (1). Hitotsubashi J. law Politics 24, 27–45 (1996)
8. Ono, S.: Comparative law and the civil code of japan (ii). Hitotsubashi J. law Politics 25, 29–52 (1997)
9. Japan Society for the Promotion of Science. The First Proposal of the Meiji Civil Code. Japan Society for the Promotion of Science (1941)
10. Sano, T.: Legal information base for analyzing foreign laws in the drafting process of the Japanese civil code. Nagoya Univ. Law Politics Conf. 263, 37–79 (2015)
11. Hoshino, E.: Impact of French civil code on the Japanese civil code-1-. Jpn. Fr. Law 3, 1–70 (1965)

12. Takenaka, Y., Wakao, T.: Automatic generation of article correspondence tables for the comparison of local government statutes. J. Nat. Lang. Process. **19**(3), 193–212 (2012)
13. Gusfield, D.: Algorithms on strings, trees, and sequences: computer science and computational biology. Cambridge University Press40 W. 20 St. New York, NYUnited States (1997)
14. Niwattanakul, S., Singthongchai, J., Naenudorn, E., Wanapu, S.: Using of Jaccard coefficient for keywords similarity (2013)
15. Sano, T.: A New Stage in the Study of Legislative History : Construction of Information Base for Meiji Civil Code. Shinzansha (2016)
16. Kaise, Y.: Introduction to Comparative Law. NIPPON HYORON SHA CO., LTD., (2019)
17. Wani, A.: The unfinished synthesis of legal comparison and academic theory. law school, pp. 79-79. December 1995
18. Ume, K.: Our New Civil Code and Foreign Civil Code. Code Questioning Conference (1896)
19. Ume, K.: Our New Civil Code and Foreign Civil Code(Part2). Code Questioning Conference (1896)
20. Oka, T.: Impact of foreign law on the process of drafting the Meiji civil code. J. Int. Philos. **4**, 16–33 (2014)
21. Torgerson, W.: Multidimensional scaling: I. theory and method. Psychometrika **17**(4), 401–419 (1952)
22. Laporte, G.: The traveling salesman problem: an overview of exact and approximate algorithms. Eur. J. Oper. Res. **59**(2), 231–247 (1992)
23. Hironaka, T.: Reasons for the revision of the Civil Code (first three volumes). Yuhikaku (1987)
24. Honnibal, M., Montani, I.: spaCy 2: natural language understanding with Bloom embeddings, convolutional neural networks and incremental parsing. To appear (2017)

Topic Modelling for Risk Identification in Data Protection Act Judgements

Aaron Ceross(✉) ⓘ and Andrew Simpson ⓘ

Department of Computer Science, University of Oxford, Wolfson Building, Parks Road, Oxford OX1 3QD, UK
{aaron.ceross,andrew.simpson}@cs.ox.ac.uk

Abstract. Data protection legislation, such as the EU's General Data Protection Regulation (GDPR), obliges data controllers to address risks to personal data. Risk assessment rules for data protection stipulate taking into account instances where the processing of personal data may affect other rights of the individual. It is acknowledged that engineering systems in order to address all risks is challenging and there is a need for prioritisation of risks. Previously decided decisions regarding personal data may provide insight to facilitate this. To this end, we ask: (i) in what context has data protection legislation been invoked in courts? and (ii) what other legal concerns were affected by these cases? To answer these questions, we use structural topic modelling (STM) to extract topics from the case judgements related to the United Kingdom's Data Protection Act, incorporating covariate information related to the case outcomes, such as court type and year. The outputs of the model can be utilised to provide topics which relate to context; they can also examine how the other associated variables relate to the resultant topics. We demonstrate the utility of unsupervised text clustering for context and risk identification in legal texts. In our application, we find that STM provides clear topics and allows for the analysis of trends regarding the topics, clearly showing where data protection issues succeed and fail in courts.

Keywords: natural language processing · machine learning · data protection

1 Introduction

Data controllers are obliged to protect the personal data of data subjects held within their information systems. These obligations are derived from laws which are designed to hold the controllers of information systems accountable for the misuse of the data. The European Union's General Data Protection Regulation (GDPR) [2] provides a framework by which to govern the management of the personal data of individuals. The legislation provides rights for the data subjects (those whose personal data is collected, stored, and processed) and obligations for the data controllers (those that are managing the personal information). The

© Springer Nature Switzerland AG 2023
K. Yada et al. (Eds.): JSAI-isAI 2021 Workshops, LNAI 13856, pp. 62–76, 2023.
https://doi.org/10.1007/978-3-031-36190-6_5

GDPR contains, within Article 25, a duty on data controllers to incorporate a "data protection-by-design" approach (DPbD) to information systems. DPbD is based on the wider concept of "Privacy-by-Design" [11], which argues that seven foundational principles of privacy protection ought to motivate system design choices. Aside from the aspirational aim of the principles, the literature has recognised the challenge in transforming the abstract nature of the principles into actionable system requirements [30, 38].

There are challenges in the implementation of data protection measures in information systems regarding the combination of: (i) a duty to adopt a "data protection-by-design" with (ii) an objective, metrics-driven risk-based approach to personal data management. The lack of specified methodology and established risk metrics makes adoption difficult for practitioners [13], especially as this field has few empirical studies [12]. While the emphasis on risk-based assessment features prominently within the GDPR, the nature, scope, and operation of this risk-based approach is not adequately defined within the regulation itself. The questions addressed by this work are therefore:

1. In what contexts has the Data Protection Act been utilised?
2. What other legal concerns were invoked or affected in these contexts?

We approach these questions utilising natural language processing and unsupervised clustering of text. We aim to extract the context of judicial decisions through topic modelling and assess the resultant topics in respect of the case outcomes. Furthermore, we parse the cases and identify cited legislation. The cited legislation acts as a proxy for other rights aside from those found in the data protection legislation. We then group these cited legislative instruments according to the resultant topics.

We provide a background to data protection obligations and the challenges these pose to the design of information systems in Sect. 2. Section 3 details the collection and description of the data used in this analysis. We describe the methodology in Sect. 4. Section 5 presents the results. A discussion is provided in Sect. 6. We outline future work in the final section.

2 Background

Article 35(1) of the GDPR obliges data controllers to undertake a 'data protection impact assessment' (DPIA) where the processing of personal data has a high risk to the "rights and freedoms of natural persons".[1] The provided guidance on

---

[1] "Where a type of processing in particular using new technologies, and taking into account the **nature, scope, context and purposes of the processing**, is likely to result in a **high risk to the rights and freedoms of natural persons**, the controller shall, prior to the processing, carry out an assessment of the impact of the envisaged processing operations on the protection of personal data. A single assessment may address a set of similar processing operations that present similar high risks." (emphasis added).

this provision in order to assist those responsible for managing personal data states that the 'rights and freedoms' contemplated in Article 33(1) go beyond privacy and may include other rights related to expression and conscience [7].

However, the guidance provides no indication as to the precise methodology which might be employed to determine and evaluate risk, only that it ought to be done in the form of a DPIA — a derivative of 'privacy impact assessments' (PIAs). Both DPIAs and PIAs are qualitative assessments [39,41]. However, there have been increased efforts to incorporate more formal methods into the risk assessment methodologies so as to maximise utility to information system designers [5,26]. In examining the nature and function of DPIAs, Binns [8] argues that the mandatory nature of the DPIA is a form of 'meta-regulation', which functions more accurately as a legal compliance assessment rather than any purported holistic means for system design and management.

Gellert [19] argues that the notion of risk described in Article 33(1) is more about "compliance risk" — with less compliance meaning a higher likelihood of infringing on rights. This definition of risk by the GDPR and supplementary material on this topic by the Article 29 Working Party [6,7] leaves essential elements of risk assessment unaddressed, including the criteria for harm, calculation of likelihood, and selection of appropriate methodologies. It is argued therein that the effect of this is to render the notion of risk in this article "irrelevant", concluding that it only considers severity rather than likelihood, has no means to calculate any notion of risk, and does not identify appropriate sources from data.

Thus, it may be argued that a quantitative approach is necessary for legal analysis to derive these necessary contextual and risk informatics. There has been some work regarding prediction of classification of judicial outcomes. For example, Katz et al. [20] utilised random forests to train a classifier for US Supreme Court cases. Aletras et al. [4] trained an SVM classifier using n-grams and topic in order to predict judgements from the European Court of Human Rights. Šadl and Olsen [33] evaluated the judgements of the Court of Justice of the European Union and the European Court of Human Rights through corpus linguistics and citation network analysis. In their work, the authors focused on determining: (i) the structure of the examined case law; (ii) the language utilised by the court (re-occurring and co-occurring expressions); and (iii) the identification of legal arguments. Ceross and Zhu [14] examined machine learning models for the prediction of data protection case outcomes based on case briefs translated in three languages. The work found that the identified predictive features were different in the three languages evaluated, raising issues regarding the generalisability of data protection risk predictors in a multilingual setting. Nevertheless, these contributions have shown that there is promise in using natural language processing in legal analysis and may suggest a means by which to derive metrics for legal analysis which may inform data protection risk analysis.

3   Data

The GDPR, which replaced the EU's Personal Data Directive [1], is applicable to all member states of the EU. Despite renouncing its membership of the EU, the United Kingdom (UK) mapped the GDPR into its law in 2018 to ensure that the GDPR would remain applicable. While there have been indications from the UK government that there may be changes to data protection legislation (potentially resulting in deviation from the GDPR) [16], the current GDPR rules remain in force in the UK and justifies utilising judgements from the UK courts for our experiment.

In total, there have been three Data Protection Acts in British law: in 1984, 1998, and 2018. A dataset of all judgements related to all of these was constructed using the texts provided by the British and Irish Legal Information Institute (BAILII) website [10]. We input the search string "data protection act" as an exact phrase into the case law search. We limited the search to the (i) Supreme Court/House of Lords; (ii) Court of Appeal; and (iii) the High Court (excluding the Family Division). We excluded the courts of Northern Ireland and Scotland, given the different legal systems in those jurisdictions. This resulted in total of 408 cases. After removing duplicate results, cases that mentioned the Act fewer than five times were removed in order ensure that the cases were truly discussing the Act and not merely mentioning it in passing.

The resulting corpus is comprised of 238 cases, dating from 1999 to 2019. There are also 11 variables in addition to the text of the judgements. These include name of case, court level, citation, judges, the date of the judgement, which party was relying on the DPA, the relevant Data Protection Act, and outcome of the case. The vast majority of the cases (227 (95%)) involve the 1998 version of the DPA, with the older 1984 version having only 6 cases, and only 5 cases invoking the newer 2018 version. This provides uniformity and consistency in the analysis of Sect. 5.

4   Methods

This section describes the methodology used. We describe the theory and construction of the topic modelling approach, as well as methods for increasing coherence in topic models. Additionally, we detail the pre-processing steps of the data in order to input the text into the model.

4.1   Structural Topic Modelling

To address the challenges set out in Sects. 1 and 2, we require a means by which to identify context and quantify the relationship between the different contexts. In this study, we utilise *structural topic modelling* (STM) [31,32], an unsupervised machine learning approach to deriving topics from a text corpora, incorporating the document's covariate information. This allows for the identification of topics within a text corpora and the ability to link this to the document's metadata. In this present work, the variable of interest is decision outcomes.

We briefly describe the details of the STM model. This model is combination of three existing models: (i) the correlated topic model [9]; (ii) the Dirichlet-Multinomial Regression topic model [28]; and (iii) the Sparse Additive Generative model [18].

To summarise the model as proposed by and detailed by Roberts *et al.* [31], a text corpus is composed of documents, $d_1, ..d_n$, where each document is a mixture of k topics $z_1, ..z_k$. Topics are composed of any words, w. The distribution of topics θ_d is drawn from a global distribution. For each w in d (indexed by n), a topic is assigned based on the specific-document distribution over topics $z_{d,n}|\theta_d \sim Multinomial(\theta)$

Based on the topic assigned, the observed word $w_{d,n}$ is drawn over the vocabulary

$$w_{d,n}|z_{d,n}, \beta d, k = z \sim Multinomial(\beta_{d,k=z})$$

Here, $\beta_{d,k=z}$ is the probability of selecting the v-th word in the vocabulary for topic k. However, unlike LDA, topics may be correlated and the prevalence of those topics can be influenced by a set of covariates X through a logistic-normal generalised linear model (GLM) based on document covariates X_d:

$$\theta_d\gamma, \Sigma \sim LogisticNormal(X_d\gamma, \Sigma)$$

This forms the document-specific distribution over words representing each topic (k) using the baseline word distribution (m), the topic specific deviation (κ_k), the covariate group deviation κ_g, and the interaction between the two κ_i.

$$\beta_{d,k} \propto exp(m + \kappa_k + \kappa_{g_d} + \kappa_{i=\kappa_{g_d}})$$

The model utilises a semi-collapsed variational expectation-maximisation (EM) algorithm, whereby the E-step provides the joint optimum of θ while the global parameters, κ, γ and Σ, are inferred during the M-step. Roberts *et al.* [32] note that the theoretical guarantees associated with mean-field variational inference do not hold as the STM prior is not conjugate to the likelihood.

4.2   Determining Topic Numbers

The determination of number of topics for topic modelling is a challenge. There is no set means of selecting an appropriate number of topics, but methods have been proposed. Wallach *et al.* [40] demonstrated that the heldout likelihood may help in determining the number of topics. However this is contrasted with the findings in Chang *et al.* [15], which showed a negative relationship between perplexity and human based evaluations.

In our study we use the method proposed by Mimno *et al.* [27], which focuses on semantic coherence of the model. In that work, the authors found that their proposed metric significantly correlates with human annotator judgement of topic quality. The method determines the number of times words v and v' occur simultaneously in a document, given as $D(v, v')$. For a list of the M most probable words in topic k, the semantic coherence for topic k is given as

$$C_k = \sum_{i=2}^{M} \sum_{j=1}^{i-1} \log \left(\frac{D(v, v') + 1}{D(v_j)} \right)$$

Informed by measures of semantic coherence and exclusivity, we set k to 6 for this study based on a search for topic numbers based on these parameters. In one of the introductory works on STM, Roberts *et al.* [32] combined semantic coherence with exclusivity in order to reduce the possibility of few, yet highly occurring, words dominating topics. In that study, the authors used FREX, a weighted harmonic mean of the word's rank in terms of exclusivity and frequency.

$$FREX_k, v = \left(\frac{\omega}{ECDF(\beta_k, v / \sum_{j=1}^{K} \beta_j, v)} + \frac{1 - \omega}{ECDF(\beta_k, v)} \right)^{-1}$$

Here, ECDF is the empirical cumulative distribution function and ω is the weight.

4.3   Pre-processing of Text

Schofield *et al.* [35] found that aggressive removal of stop-words may heuristically improve the topics returned. In this study, we use the stop word list from the SMART lexicon [34], comprised of 1,149 word tokens. Furthermore, we removed common legal terms (e.g. "court", "evidence", "hearing"), totalling 177 additional word tokens. As we are interested in the themes of the cases and features pertaining to data protection issues, the names of the parties to the case, the legal representation, and the sitting judges or panel were identified from the header notes of each case document and added to the stop word list. In this work we lemmatised the words rather than stemming as the latter has been shown to be less effective than lemmatisation when returning topics that are coherent [36]. We also tagged the word tokens with parts-of-speech in order better refine the topic models as Martin and Johnson [25] found that use of noun-only topic models were efficient. We included both nouns and verbs in order to widen the scope of what may constitute "risk" in the judgements.

5   Results

The results of the model are provided in two parts. In the first part, we describe the outcome of STM and detail the topics. Further information using covariate data is also examined in relation to the provided topics. In the second part, we evaluate the court outcomes in respect of the topics from the model and identify associated cited legislation in these cases.

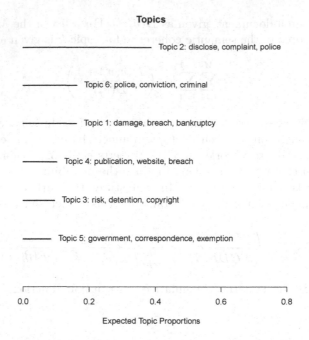

Fig. 1. Topics and the proportions

5.1 Data Protection Case Topics

A topic model provides clusters of documents based on words which are closely associated within the corpus. Figure 1 shows the outcome of the model on the DPA judgements, listing the top three terms of that cluster. Topic 2 is the largest topic proportion, which involves the complaints and the police. Topic 1 groups issues related to damages for breaches. The smallest topic proportion relates to governmental information, particularly correspondence and exemptions.

One of the features of STM is the ability to link covariate information with the topics. We are interested in the change of contexts for the topics over time. Figure 2 illustrates the changes in expected proportion of topics between 1999 and 2019. Topic 2 (disclose, complaint, police), the largest topic, has a decline from 2010. Topic 3 (risk, detention, copyright), which was one of the smallest topics, has a consistent increase. It starts in 1999 with virtually no reference, rising to its modest 20% of topics nearly 20 years later. Topic 1 (damage, breach, bankruptcy), is the most variable, rising and falling in more pronounced manner than the other topics. Topics 6 (police, conviction, criminal) has a constant trend, with no meaningful changes.

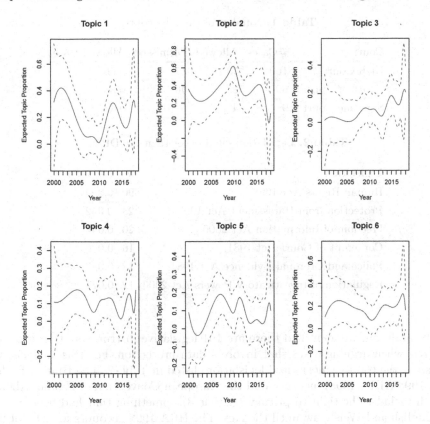

Fig. 2. Topic trends by year

5.2   Court Outcomes by Topic

The 238 cases are divided with 100 (39%) cases overall having an acceptance of the data protection arguments and 138 (65%) dismissing such argument. The acceptance rate by court is shown in Table 1, which shows that the Court of Appeal has the lowest acceptance rate, with the High Court and Supreme Court somewhat higher. In our analysis we do not consider the nature of the appeals or the final outcome of the case, as not all cases related directly to the Data Protect Act; cases for inclusion may have merely raised a point of data protection.

Using the resultant STM for the data protection cases, the association of outcomes with topics may be determined. Figure 3 shows that Topic 1 (damage, breach, bankruptcy) is most associated with arguments for data protection issues being dismissed. Topic 5 (government, correspondence, exemption) is also more strongly related to being dismissed as well. Topic 6 (police, conviction, criminal) is most correlated with being allowed. Topic 2 (disclose, complaint, police) and Topic 3 (risk, detention, copyright) are also more allowed. Topic 4 (publication, website, breach) is only slightly more associated with the 'dismissed' label.

Table 1. Number of cases by court.

Court	#Cases	Allowed	Dismissed	Allowed Rate
High Court	160	73	87	0.46
Court of Appeal	69	25	46	0.33
Supreme Court	9	4	5	0.44

Table 2. Legislation cited other than the DPA.

Legislation	n	Proportion
Human Rights Act 1998	90	0.204
Protection from Harassment Act 1997	23	0.052
Freedom of Information Act 2000	20	0.045
Contempt of Court Act 1981	16	0.036
Police and Criminal Evidence Act 1984	12	0.027
Regulation of Investigatory Powers Act 2000	12	0.027

In addition, we identified there are 161 legislative instruments that are considered when arguing cases that involves data protection. For this analysis, we consider the top five most cited legislation, listed in Table 2. The Human Rights Act 1998 (HRA 1998) incorporated the European Convention of Human Rights, which includes the right to privacy (Article 8), something that had been absent in English and Welsh law until the Act. The HRA 1998 accounts for 20% of the cited legislation, greatly outnumbering all other legislation. This is likely due to data protection issues deeply impinging on privacy concerns and thus necessitating a consideration of the law in this area. A group of legislation addresses issues in justice, related to investigative powers and rules of evidence: (i) the Contempt of Court Act 1981, (ii) the Police and Criminal Evidence Act 1984, and (iii) the Regulation of Investigatory Powers Act 2000. The Protection from Harassment Act 1997 deals with criminal offences related to the physical and mental harassment against individuals.

In Fig. 4 the division between the case outcome becomes more apparent. The HRA is cited nearly equally for both case outcomes. In cases where the Freedom of Information Act 2000 is cited, there are slightly more dismissals of data protection arguments than not. However, where investigatory powers by the state are invoked, arguments for data protection issues are dismissed.

6   Discussion

6.1   Associating Outcomes with Contexts

The context for a decision is fundamental to the application of the law. In this work, there are clear associations with topics to court outcomes, which broadens

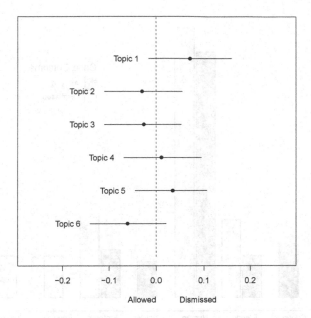

Fig. 3. The point estimate and 80% confidence interval of the mean difference in topic proportions for court decisions allowing or dismissing arguments for data protection issues.

knowledge about how the Data Protection Act has been utilised in the courts of England and Wales. In relation to Question 1 of Sect. 1, we find that the analysis has provided six discrete topics in which data protection cases have fallen within the last 20 years. Through STM, we also have identified the trajectory for each of those topics over time. From the analysis, disclosures, complaints about disclosures and the police (Topics 2 and 6) dominate the subject matter for DPA cases. However, these topics are often have negative outcomes (Fig. 3). This means that arguments provided for data protection issues are dismissed. Regarding Question 2 of Sect. 1, our approach has given some insight into other legal concerns which are involved in these cases. Importantly, we find that the cases tend to be in tension with the use of investigatory powers for criminal matters. This suggests that the courts are less likely to prioritise data protection issues over criminal investigations. From this preliminary experiment, we observe that system designers ought to consider how manage personal data that likely to be requested by authorities. This has implications for not only the types of data that these systems collect, but also how the data is conveyed when requested.

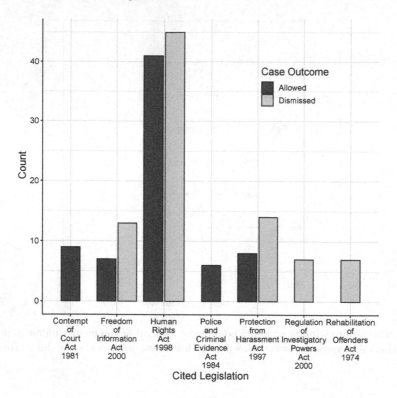

Fig. 4. Count of legislation by case outcome.

6.2   The Utility of STM for Legal Analysis

While there have been a small number of works utilising topic modelling approaches using corpora of legal judgements (e.g. [33]), our use of STM allows for the evaluation of covariate information associated with the texts. Considering the results more widely, this work provides continuing evidence for the use of computational methods, such as natural language processing and wider artificial intelligence, in order to derive novel insights into the law. A quantitative approach to legal scholarship is arguably necessary in order to address the acknowledged limited nature of legal theory [29]. Quantitative approaches allow for more experimentation and may complement more traditional doctrinal analysis, providing a more holistic view of legal informatics. Automated methods, such as the unsupervised clustering used in this work, can be applied across large corpora of texts, providing novel insights on emergent patterns.

6.3   Limitations

There are several limitations that ought to be borne in mind when considering the outcome of this work. The first is that we have analysed the cases without a view of precedent. In many jurisdictions, the lower courts follow the decisions provided by higher courts: cases may be decided in one manner only to be reversed later by a higher court, as a legal doctrine develops. Furthermore, the complexity of issues in court cases may not be captured adequately by topic modelling. The model relies on the use of n-grams which do not capture semantic meaning. Additionally, the issue of stop words and phrases are particularly challenging as legal phrases of interest may incorporate these. Nevertheless, topic modelling has potential to provide broad overviews of contexts in legal corpora, which is valuable to legal informatics.

Other limitations to the use of topic modelling include (i) the lack of labels in the unsupervised approach and (ii) the identification of the requisite number of topics. We selected an unsupervised approach for our experiment due to the lack of ground truth labels. It is therefore difficult to assess the accuracy of the provided topics. However, the use of the coherence measures described in Sect. 4.2 help in this regard. There is utility in future work to annotate the cases in order to evaluate the provided topics.

Additionally, in Sect. 4.2, we address our own approach to the determination of topic numbers. However, it should be noted that this is only one of an array of approaches that may be taken in determining topic numbers. There are intrinsic difficulties and challenges in providing quality topic clustering, as the statistical approaches do not retain semantic meaning [22,23]. There have been studies which have sought to improve semantic meaning [3], although with modest results. There have, however, been improvements when human labelling is incorporated into the topic model approach [21,37]. This approach represents an interesting avenue for future work in computational approaches for legal analysis.

7 Conclusions

In this work, we utilised STM in order to cluster data protection cases in order to derive contexts where the rights are being invoked. STM is an unsupervised text clustering methodology able to associate covariates to the resultant topics, which in this case was the outcome of the case, the year of the case and the court level the case was decided. We find that there is modest but practical utility in the use of STM with legal texts. While this experiment did not assess the utility of these outcomes in the design and development of data protection compliant systems, the topic model in this application may provide designers of information systems an indication of priorities for addressing data protection concerns. In a field with few empirical studies for such prioritisation tasks, this work's results provide some welcome insight. We aim to explore this in future work utilising these results.

There are issues related to the retention of semantic meaning, as the method does not retain it. In future work, we hope to explore transformer models, such as BERT and ROBERTA [17,24], which can retain semantic meaning. These models require little training and may facilitate more effective risk predictors and richer coherence in clusters.

Acknowledgements. The authors would like to thank the anonymous reviewers for their helpful and insightful comments. AC would like to acknowledge and thank the support of the Centre of Doctoral Training in Cyber Security, which is funded by EPSRC grant number (EP/P00881X/1).

References

1. Directive 95/46/EC of the European Parliament and of the Council of 24 October 1995 on the protection of individuals with regard to the processing of personal data and on the free movement of such data. http://eur-lex.europa.eu
2. Regulation on the protection of natural persons with regard to the processing of personal data and on the free movement of such data, and repealing Directive 95/46/EC (General Data Protection Regulation). L119, 4/5/2016, p. 1–88 (2016)
3. Aletras, N., Stevenson, M.: Evaluating topic coherence using distributional semantics. In: Proceedings of the 10th International Conference on Computational Semantics (IWCS 2013)-Long Papers, pp. 13–22 (2013)
4. Aletras, N., Tsarapatsanis, D., Preoţiuc-Pietro, D., Lampos, V.: Predicting judicial decisions of the European court of human rights: a natural language processing perspective. PeerJ Comput. Sci. **2**, e93 (2016)
5. Alshammari, M., Simpson, A.: Towards an effective privacy impact and risk assessment methodology: risk analysis. In: Garcia-Alfaro, J., Herrera-Joancomartí, J., Livraga, G., Rios, R. (eds.) DPM/CBT -2018. LNCS, vol. 11025, pp. 209–224. Springer, Cham (2018). https://doi.org/10.1007/978-3-030-00305-0_16
6. Article 29 Working Party: Statement on the role of a risk-based approach in data protection legal frameworks (2014). Accessed at: https://ec.europa.eu/justice/article-29/documentation/opinion-recommendation/files/2014/wp218_en.pdf
7. Article 29 Working Party: Revised Guidelines on Data Protection Impact Assessment (DPIA) and determining whether processing is "likely to result in a high risk" for the purposes of Regulation 2016/679 (2017). Accessed at: https://ec.europa.eu/newsroom/document.cfm?doc_id=44137
8. Binns, R.: Data protection impact assessments: a meta-regulatory approach. Int. Data Priv. Law **7**(1), 22–35 (2017)
9. Blei, D., Lafferty, J.: Correlated topic models. In: Advances in Neural Information Processing Systems, vol. 18, p. 147 (2006)
10. British and Irish Legal Information Institute (2021): Home page. https://www.bailii.org/. Accessed Jan 2021
11. Cavoukian, A., Taylor, S., Abrams, M.E.: Privacy by design: essential for organizational accountability and strong business practices. Identity Inf. Soc. **3**(2), 405–413 (2010)
12. Ceross, A., Simpson, A.: The use of data protection regulatory actions as a data source for privacy economics. In: Tonetta, S., Schoitsch, E., Bitsch, F. (eds.) SAFECOMP 2017. LNCS, vol. 10489, pp. 350–360. Springer, Cham (2017). https://doi.org/10.1007/978-3-319-66284-8_29
13. Ceross, A., Simpson, A.C.: Rethinking the proposition of privacy engineering. In: Proceedings of the New Security Paradigms Workshop, NSPW 2018, pp. 89–102. ACM, New York (2018)
14. Ceross, A., Zhu, T.: Prediction of monetary penalties for data protection cases in multiple languages. In: Proceedings of the Eighteenth International Conference on Artificial Intelligence and Law, ICAIL 2021, pp. 185–189. Association for Computing Machinery, New York (2021)

15. Chang, J., Gerrish, S., Wang, C., Boyd-Graber, J.L., Blei, D.M.: Reading tea leaves: how humans interpret topic models. In: Advances in Neural Information Processing Systems, pp. 288–296 (2009)
16. Department for Digital, Culture, Media, & Sport: Government response to the consultation on the National Data Strategy (2021). https://www.gov.uk/government/consultations/uk-national-data-strategy-nds-consultation/outcome/government-response-to-the-consultation-on-the-national-data-strategy. Accessed 08 Sept 2021
17. Devlin, J., Chang, M.W., Lee, K., Toutanova, K.: BERT: pre-training of deep bidirectional transformers for language understanding. In: Proceedings of the 2019 Conference of the North American Chapter of the Association for Computational Linguistics: Human Language Technologies, Volume 1 (Long and Short Papers), pp. 4171–4186. Association for Computational Linguistics, Minneapolis, June 2019. https://doi.org/10.18653/v1/N19-1423. https://www.aclweb.org/anthology/N19-1423
18. Eisenstein, J., Ahmed, A., Xing, E.P.: Sparse additive generative models of text. In: Proceedings of the 28th International Conference on Machine Learning, pp. 1041–1048. Citeseer (2011)
19. Gellert, R.: Understanding the notion of risk in the general data protection regulation. Comput. Law Secur. Rev. **34**(2), 279–288 (2018)
20. Katz, D.M., Bommarito, M.J., II., Blackman, J.: A general approach for predicting the behavior of the supreme court of the United States. PLoS ONE **12**(4), e0174698 (2017)
21. Kumar, V., Smith-Renner, A., Findlater, L., Seppi, K., Boyd-Graber, J.: Why didn't you listen to me? Comparing user control of human-in-the-loop topic models. In: Proceedings of the 57th Annual Meeting of the Association for Computational Linguistics, pp. 6323–6330. Association for Computational Linguistics, Florence, July 2019. https://doi.org/10.18653/v1/P19-1637, https://aclanthology.org/P19-1637
22. Lau, J.H., Baldwin, T., Newman, D.: On collocations and topic models. ACM Trans. Speech Lang. Process. (TSLP) **10**(3), 1–14 (2013). https://doi.org/10.1145/2483969.2483972
23. Lau, J.H., Newman, D., Baldwin, T.: Machine reading tea leaves: automatically evaluating topic coherence and topic model quality. In: Proceedings of the 14th Conference of the European Chapter of the Association for Computational Linguistics, pp. 530–539 (2014)
24. Liu, Y., et al.: RoBERTa: a robustly optimized BERT pretraining approach. arXiv preprint: arXiv:1907.11692 (2019)
25. Martin, F., Johnson, M.: More efficient topic modelling through a noun only approach. In: Proceedings of the Australasian Language Technology Association Workshop 2015, pp. 111–115 (2015)
26. Meis, R., Heisel, M.: Supporting privacy impact assessments using problem-based privacy analysis. In: Lorenz, P., Cardoso, J., Maciaszek, L.A., van Sinderen, M. (eds.) Software Technologies, pp. 79–98. Springer International Publishing, Cham (2016)
27. Mimno, D., Wallach, H.M., Talley, E., Leenders, M., McCallum, A.: Optimizing semantic coherence in topic models. In: Proceedings of the Conference on Empirical Methods in Natural Language Processing, EMNLP 2011, pp. 262–272. Association for Computational Linguistics, Stroudsburg (2011)

28. Mimno, D.M., McCallum, A.: Topic models conditioned on arbitrary features with dirichlet-multinomial regression. In: Proceedings of the 24th Conference on Uncertainty in Artificial Intelligence, vol. 24, pp. 411–418. Citeseer (2008)
29. Posner, R.A.: Frontiers of Legal Theory. Hardvard University Press, Cambridge (2001)
30. van Rest, J., Boonstra, D., Everts, M., van Rijn, M., van Paassen, R.: Designing privacy-by-design. In: Preneel, B., Ikonomou, D. (eds.) APF 2012. LNCS, vol. 8319, pp. 55–72. Springer, Heidelberg (2014). https://doi.org/10.1007/978-3-642-54069-1_4
31. Roberts, M.E., Stewart, B.M., Airoldi, E.M.: A model of text for experimentation in the social sciences. J. Am. Stat. Assoc. **111**(515), 988–1003 (2016)
32. Roberts, M.E., et al.: Structural topic models for open-ended survey responses. Am. J. Polit. Sci. **58**(4), 1064–1082 (2014)
33. Šadl, U., Olsen, H.P.: Can quantitative methods complement doctrinal legal studies? Using citation network and corpus linguistic analysis to understand international courts. Leiden J. Int. Law **30**(2), 327–349 (2017)
34. Salton, G., Lesk, M.E.: The smart automatic document retrieval systems-an illustration. Commun. ACM **8**(6), 391–398 (1965). https://doi.org/10.1145/364955.364990
35. Schofield, A., Magnusson, M., Mimno, D.: Pulling out the stops: rethinking stopword removal for topic models. In: Proceedings of the 15th Conference of the European Chapter of the Association for Computational Linguistics: Volume 2, Short Papers, vol. 2, pp. 432–436 (2017)
36. Schofield, A., Mimno, D.: Comparing apples to apple: The effects of stemmers on topic models. Trans. Assoc. Comput. Linguist. **4**, 287–300 (2016)
37. Smith, A., Kumar, V., Boyd-Graber, J., Seppi, K., Findlater, L.: Closing the loop: User-centered design and evaluation of a human-in-the-loop topic modeling system. In: 23rd International Conference on Intelligent User Interfaces, pp. 293–304 (2018)
38. Spiekermann, S.: The challenges of privacy by design. Commun. ACM **55**(7), 38–40 (2012)
39. The Information Commissioner's Office: Data protection impact assessments, March 2018. https://ico.org.uk/media/for-organisations/guide-to-the-general-data-protection-regulation-gdpr/data-protection-impact-assessments-dpias-1-0.pdf
40. Wallach, H.M., Murray, I., Salakhutdinov, R., Mimno, D.: Evaluation methods for topic models. In: Proceedings of the 26th Annual International Conference on Machine Learning, ICML 2009, pp. 1105–1112., ACM, New York (2009)
41. Wright, D.: The state of the art in privacy impact assessment. Comput. Law Secur. Rev. **28**(1), 54–61 (2012)

A Compliance Mechanism for Planning in Privacy Domain Using Policies

Yousef Taheri[✉], Gauvain Bourgne, and Jean-Gabriel Ganascia

Sorbonne Universite, CNRS, LIP6, 75005 Paris, France
{yousef.taheri,gauvain.bourgne,Jean-gabriel.ganascia}@lip6.fr

Abstract. As more and more applications relying on the use and processing of personal data grow, privacy protection is becoming increasingly important. With the enforcement of the GDPR, such applications must guarantee compliance with the obligations set forth. Integrating a compliance checking mechanism with AI methods is helpful to fulfill this requirement. Toward this end, we investigate the GDPR automatic compliance checking using a planning system including personal data and an agent with actions that process data. We propose a modular framework that is capable to generate possible plans (sequence of data processing) to satisfy a given goal state, check the compliance of the plan with GDPR regulatory constraints, and provide explanation of missing obligations in case of a non-compliant. We use Answer Set Programming(ASP) and event calculus formalism to model the planning problem and make use of SPECIAL policy language as an existing work to translate GDPR requirements into ASP.

Keywords: Automatic Compliance Checking · AI planification · Compliance Mechanism · Personal Data Privacy

1 Introduction

AI applications handling personal data is being largely adopted by many companies and data processors to deliver their services to their users. Building trustworthy AI and enhancing liability in society requires tools and techniques to ensure users privacy protection. The European General Data Protection Regulation (GDPR) provides legal requirements concerning personal data processing. Organizations need to take technical measures to evaluate the compliance of personal data processing with GDPR. Compliance mechanism tools help these organizations to fulfill their need for compliance assessment.

Many of the AI products require handling personal data through an automated procedure, therefore, they need to be integrated with compliance mechanisms to operate lawfully. Most of the current works on compliance checking focus on either representing GDPR concepts as Palmirani et al. [12] or building policy pipeline for representing regulatory norms and business policies De Vos et al. [6], Bonatti et al. [4]. These tools are built for assessing the compliance of

K. Yada et al. (Eds.): JSAI-isAI 2021 Workshops, LNAI 13856, pp. 77–92, 2023.
https://doi.org/10.1007/978-3-031-36190-6_6

a business policy, which is used to represent characteristics of a data processing. However, none of them has studied the integration of GDPR compliance checking in planning or an automatic data manipulation setting. Bandara et al. [2] introduces a policy specification and enforcement method in a dynamic environment. They use it for detecting conflicts among policies and do not concern with personal data and privacy protection. De Vos et al. [5] propose a methodology to support legal reasoning using institutions (systems that specify normative behavior of participants) and a corresponding computational model. Given a set of observed actions their method captures the evolution of legal model after each action in a multi-agent setting, but it does not include automatic action generation and also does not deal with privacy domain.

In this paper, we build an agent that is capable to generate a sequence of personal data manipulations that are compliant with GDPR legal constraints. The agent can change the state of the system by performing a data processing *e.g.* transfer, analyze, etc. Each state in the planning domain represents a characteristic of the personal data. The agent is capable to reach a given a target state, by performing a number of processes on personal data called a plan. We are interested in the plan's compliance with GDPR regulatory norms, including the data subject's given consent. Toward this end, we propose a modular framework with the following components.

- **Planning**, Given a goal state, an initial state and a description of the domain, this module generates all possible plans regardless of their compliance.
- **Compliance Engine**, Given a plan, this module checks for its compliance against GDPR regulatory norms, and data subject's given consent. In the case of a non-compliant plan, it explains the missing obligations.

In order to do planning while checking for compliance we need a logical formalism that deals with sequence of actions while keeping track of the world state at each step of execution. Furthermore, since expressivity is essential in the current (and future) work, such formalism should enable modeling complex narratives with multiple events. A useful candidate, is event calculus (cf. Shanahan [15]), a well-known formalism in the planning literature. Event calculus uses an explicit linear representation of time in which fluents hold and events occur. In other words, the linear time-line is used to associate states and events when a change happens in the world. Combined with non-monotonic reasoning, event calculus allows exploring different alternatives as required for planning. Therefore, it eliminates the need for a more expressive or complex formalism based on branching-time, such as situation calculus. We give a more precise description at Sect. 2.2.

We also need to represent GDPR regulatory norms, in order to support compliance checking. To do so, we chose to use the SPECIAL policy language which offers a unified representation of regulatory norms and data subject's given consent to enable compliance checking of business policies.

In a legal setting we deal with a potentially large body of knowledge in the related law and there are usually multiple constraints which need to be verified to assess compliance. In order to implement such a domain we need a formalism that allows on one hand to express both rules and facts, and on the other hand it has to support non-monotonic reasoning (since we would normally encounter situations with incomplete information). Answer Set Programming (ASP) (cf. Lifschitz [10]) is a proper candidate for this purpose. A knowledge representation and reasoning paradigm with an expressive formalism and efficient solvers. ASP is largely used for common sense reasoning, abductive and deductive reasoning and is especially suitable for planning and dealing with incomplete knowledge. ASP is compatible with event calculus and is a practical choice for future developments of our current work. We use Clingo by Gebser et al. [7], as an answer set solver for ASP. Briefly speaking, it is composed of two main steps; (i)The grounder which takes as input the provided knowledge, substitute all variables with the given instances, (ii)The solver which takes the extended knowledge of the previous step as input and extract the answer sets which are basically stable models of the program.

The rest of the paper is organized as follows: Sect. 2 presents both a brief background on SPECIAL policy language and the version of event calculus used to model the planning domain. In Sect. 3 we explain our modular framework and describe how each component is constructed. In Sect. 4 we evaluate our framework on two simple scenarios, and discuss the results. Section 5 presents a brief discussion of the related works. Finally, in Sect. 6 we discuss the conclusions and mention the future works.

2 Backgrounds

2.1 The SPECIAL Policy Language

In order to support automated compliance checking, we need a representation of GDPR requirements in a machine understandable format. Such representation is required to construct the compliance engine in our modular framework (see Fig. 1). There are many works trying to develop an ontology or a policy pipeline to represent GDPR requirements for compliance checking. Here we make use of the SPECIAL, a policy language based on OWL2, that offers a unified representation for consent, business policies, and regulatory obligations.

In the SPECIAL policy language, a personal data processing is formalized as a business policy. The following is an example of a business policy, each attribute describes a characteristic of the personal data handling.

```
1  ObjectIntersectionOf(
2      ObjectSomeValuesFrom(spl:hasData  svd:purchasesAndSpendingHabit)
3      ObjectSomeValuesFrom(spl:hasProcessing svpr:Analyze)
4      ObjectSomeValuesFrom(spl:hasPurposes vpu:Marketing)
5      ObjectSomeValuesFrom(spl:hasRecipient svr:aCompany)
6      ObjectSomeValuesFrom(spl:hasStorage
7          ObjectIntersectionOf(
8          spl:hasLocation svl:EU
9          spl:hasDuration svdu:Indefinitely))
10     ObjectSomeValuesFrom(sbpl:hasDuty getValidConsent)
11     ObjectSomeValuesFrom(sbpl:hasDuty getAccessReqs)
12     ObjectSomeValuesFrom(sbpl:hasDuty getRectifyReqs)
13     ObjectSomeValuesFrom(sbpl:hasDuty getDeleteReqs)
14     ObjectSomeValuesFrom(sbpl:hasLegalBasis A6-1-a-consent)
15 )
```

Listing 1.1. a business policy in SPECIAL

The above attributes for this business policy are described respectively as follows, (i) The category of the personal data used in the processing is *Purchases and Spending Habit*, (ii) the processing category is *analyze*, (iii) The purpose of the processing is *Marketing*, (iv) the recipient of the processing result is *aCompany*, (v) the processing is taking place in a storage located in Europe and the duration of data storage is *Indefinite*, (vi) the duties defined for this processing, for example *getValidConsent* means that the specified software can read the data sources if consent has been given, (vii) the legal basis the processing is *A6-1-a-consent*. The values of these attributes are selected from a suitable vocabulary. SPECIAL uses the W3C's *Data Privacy Vocabularies and Controls Community Group*, (DPVCG) Pandit et al. [13]. We have made use of the same vocabulary for the terms in our framework, which will be presented in Sect. 3

Consent Representation. A consent is represented as a usage policy in SPECIAL and expresses the characteristics of the processing for which the data subject has given his consent. Consent has the same attributes as business policy but, without legal basis and duties. For example, the following policy demonstrates data subject's consent to transfer his *Service Consumption Behavior* data with the purpose *Create Personalized Recommendations*. The recipient is *aCompany*, the storage is located in Europe, and it is valid for a duration of 365 d.

```
1  ObjectIntersectionOf(
2      ObjectSomeValueFrom(has_purpose createPersonalizedRecommendations )
3      ObjectSomeValueFrom(has_data serviceConsumptionBehavior)
4      ObjectSomeValueFrom(has_processing Transfer)
5      ObjectSomeValueFrom(has_recipient aCompany)
6      ObjectSomeValueFrom(has_storage
7          ObjectIntersectionOf(
8              ObjectSomeValueFrom( has_location:EU )
9              DataSomeValueFrom( has_duration DatatypeRestriction(
    xsd:integerxsd:minInclusive "365" xsd:integer))))
```

Listing 1.2. A consent in SPECIAL

A business policy is compliant with data subject's consent, if the business process is a subclass of the given consent.

Regulatory Norms. In the SPECIAL policy language, the GDPR regulative norms in the form of permissions, obligations, and prohibitions are formalized as the constraints that should hold over the different attributes of a business policy. As an example Article 6–1 (lawfulness) the class Art6_1 is formalized as follows, it means that a business process holds the obligation of this article if it has a legal basis from the provided list in Article 6–1.

```
1  ObjectSomeValuesFrom( hasLegalBasis
2      ObjectUnionOf(
3          Art6_1_a_Consent
4          Art6_1_b_Contract
5          Art6_1_c_LegalObligation
6          Art6_1_d_VitalInterest
7          Art6_1_e_PublicInterest
8          Art6_1_f_LegitimateInterest))
```

Obligations are formalized as classes and can be combined by operations ObjectUnionOf or ObjectIntersectOf to form the GDPR obligations at the top level partially. For example, the obligations of Chap. 2 of GDPR (Principles) is modeled is SPECIAL as a union of the obligations of Article 6 (Lawful processing), Article 9 (Sensitive Data), and Article 10 (Criminal Data).

```
1  ObjectUnionOf(
2      Art6_LawfulProcessing
3      Art9_SensitiveData
4      Art10_CriminalData)
```

The above expression means the processing is lawful if either the obligations of Article 6 (Lawful Processing), or Article 9 (Sensitive Data), or Article 10 (Criminal Data), are satisfied.

2.2 Event Calculus

Event Calculus (EC) is a logic based formal language for representing events and their effects. It has first been introduced by Kowalski and Sergot [8]. Various versions of the Event Calculus has been used in the literature. In this work, we use a specific version taken from Berreby et al. [3]. It relies on formal representation of events and states on a discrete set of time points. The dynamic state of the world is represented by a set of properties called fluent that hold or not at any time point. Transition between the states is made by events that occur in time T. These events are characterized by preconditions that must hold for the event to occur and effects that describe how they affect states at $T + 1$. A fluent holds at T if it was initiated by an event occurrence at $T - 1$. A fluent which is true at T continues to hold until the occurrence of an event which terminates it. An event in our framework represents an action which is described in Sect. 3. The axioms of the event calculus is presented below.

```
1  negative(neg(F)) :- effect(E,neg(F)).
2  initiates(E,F,T) :- effect(E,F), occurs(E,T), not negative(F).
3  terminates(E,F,T) :- effect(E,neg(F)), occurs(E,T),time(T).
4  clipped(F,T) :- terminates(E,F,T).
5
6  holds(F,0) :- initially(F).
7  holds(F,T) :- initiates(E,F,T-1), time(T).
8  holds(F,T) :- holds(F,T-1), not clipped(F,T-1), time(T).
9
10 :- occurs(E,T), prec(F,E), not holds(F,T), act(E), time(T).
11 0 {occurs(E, T)} 1 :- act(E), time(T),T<maxtime.
12 :- occurs(E1,T), occurs(E2,T) ,E1!=E2.
```

Listing 1.3. Event calculus axioms

The choice rule `0 {performs(E, T)} 1 :- act(E), time(T),T<maxtime.` is used to exempt the `perform/2` predicate from minimization in ASP, this is the generator part that we use to solve a planning problem. The rule `:- performs(E1,T), performs(E2,T) ,E1!= E2.` means that events can not occur at the same time.

Note that ASP programs are represented as a finite set of rules where the head and body of the rules are composed of atoms which are equivalent to classical FOL(under the form of clauses with universally quantified variables). Variables in ASP are strings that begin with a capital lette, and they are all universally quantified.

3   Modular Framework

We consider an agent that handles personal data processing. We are concerned about the compliance of the agents' actions with GDPR. In order to model both requirements of the planning domain and compliance checking, we built a modular framework with 2 components. The first one is the planning module that contains the specification of storage, and personal data in the system and the agents' actions. Each action describes a transformation on data or changes its storage. Given an initial state and a goal state, this module generates all the possible plans which satisfy the goal. By plan, we refer to a sequence of processing on personal data. The second module (Compliance engine) checks if each plan is compliant with both regulatory norms and data subject's given consent, and can provide explanation of missing obligations in the case of non-compliance. Figure 1 illustrates the structure of the framework.

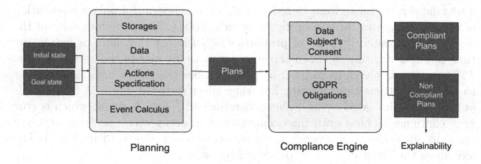

Fig. 1. Modular structure

3.1   A Use Case Model

We describe our framework by implementing it on a use case model. An international company operates in multiple European countries and United States as well. The company has several sectors for providing services to customers. Each sector owns a server for storing personal data. The servers are connected through an internal network and can transmit data among each other. One of the servers is a computing server in which the company analyze customers data for various purposes. The company has also a partner as a data processor which delivers analytic services to the company. Figure 2 illustrates the connection between servers of the company and its partner processor, as well as their location.

In order to provide services, the company needs to analyze customers data and use its result. When a sector requests the outcome of a particular analysis, a sequence of processing should be performed to provide the result to it's corresponding server. We implement our framework in this scenario to design an agent to automatically generate a sequence of data processing to provide the requested output on a data, and check for the compliance of generated sequences.

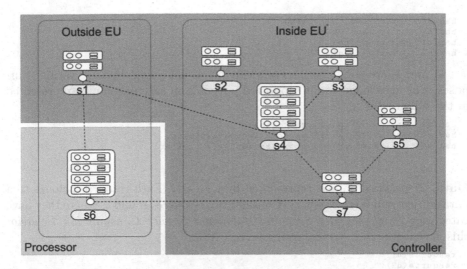

Fig. 2. Connection among servers

3.2 Planning

The key challenge in the design of the planning domain is formalizing actions, states and domain knowledge in a way that enables for both planning and compliance checking. We assign GDPR related attributes to domain objects to use it for compliance checking. We describe the main parts of the planning domain.

Storage. A storage in our framework basically represents anything capable of storing data and processing it. *e.g.* servers, cloud space etc. We use the storage to represent a server in our planning domain. We also use connected/2 predicate to represent that there is a connection between 2 storage. For example, below ASP formalization means that s1, s2, and s3 are storage and there is a connection between s1 and s2, and s1 and s3, meaning that they can transmit data.

```
1  storage(s1).
2  storage(s2).
3  storage(s3).
4  connected(s1,s2).
5  connected(s1,s3).
```

The knowledge about other servers, and the connection between them, has been formalized the same way. In order to assess the compliance of these actions, we need the information about the action itself as well as the other complementary information that are concerned with the GDPR. For example, the below code, shows how we represent the controller of the storage s6 and s7 and the location of s1 and s2.

```
1 has(s6, controller, aProcessor).
2 has(s7, controller, aCompany).
3 has(s1, location, us).
4 has(s2, location, eu).
```

s4 and s6 are computing servers capable of analyzing data for various purposes. The knowledge about supported purposes on each one can be represented in the following way.

```
1 has(s4, analysisPurpose ,marketing).
2 has(s4, analysisPurpose ,personalisedAdvertising).
3 has(s6, analysisPurpose ,optimisationForController).
```

Data. A personal data is represented by a resource. Each resource belongs to a data subject and has a category. Consider two resources d1 and d2 where they have categories *Purchases and Spending Habit* and *Service Consumption Behavior* this is represented in the following way in ASP.

```
1 resource(d1).
2 resource(d2).
3 has(d1, dataCategory, purchasesAndSpendingHabit).
4 has(d2, dataCategory, serviceConsumptionBehavior).
```

When performing actions on resources, they either move to another storage or transform into a new data. We need to represent these data manipulations in our domain. We define the predicate *data* which represents any personal data either a resource or the output of analysis process on this resource with a certain purpose.

```
1 data(D):- resource(D).
2 data( analysisOutput(D,P) ):-  resource(D), purpose(P).
```

If the attributes are static we represent them as facts and if they are dynamic we represent them by fluents. Attributes like storage of the data or the content of a storage are effected by actions.

Actions Specification. The agent action in our domain represents a data processing. It supports transfer and analysis processing of personal data with several purposes. A transfer action in our domain is characterized by the data, its current location, the destination and purpose of the transfer. In order to perform analysis action we require the data, and the storage where the processing is taking place and the purpose of the analysis as well. We formalize the knowledge about agents actions as follows:

```
1 act(transfer(D,A,B,P)):- data(D), storage(A),storage(B), purpose(P),
      connected(A,B), A!=B.
2 act(analyse(D,A,P)):- data(D), storage(A), purpose(P) , has(A,
      analysisPurpose ,P).
```

Each action should be specified by its preconditions and effects. A transfer action changes the storage of the data, or equivalently, it modifies the content of the origin and destination storage. This is captured by the fluent hasData(A ,D) predicate, which represents that storage A has data D.The analysis action transforms the personal data into a new data, which is the output of this analysis. Below, we represent the effects and preconditions of these actions.

```
1 prec( hasData(A,D), transfer(D,A,B,P)):- act(transfer(D,A,B,P)).
2 effect(transfer(D,A,B,P), hasData(B,D)):- act(transfer(D,A,B,P)).
3 effect(transfer(D,A,B,P), neg(hasData(A,D))):- act(transfer(D,A,B,P)).
4
5 prec( hasData(A,D), analyze(D,A,P)):- act(analyze(D,A,P)).
6 effect(analyze(D,A,P), hasData( A, analysisOutput(D,P) )):- act(analyze(D,A,P)).
7 effect(analyze(D,A,P), neg( hasData(A,D) )):- act(analyse(D,A,P)).
```

As an example, we describe the effects and preconditions of analyze action. prec(hasData(A,D), analyze(D,A,P)) means that in order to perform the action, analyze (D,A,P) the fluent hasData(S,D) should hold, meaning that the corresponding data should be present on the corresponding storage. When the action is performed, the data transforms into the output and is represented by analysisOutput(D,P) . The last line effect(analyze(D,A,P), neg(hasData(A,D))) means that after the action is performed, the output data would be replaced by the input data. The predicate neg (hasData(A,D))) indicates the negative effect of the action, which is the input data in no longer on the corresponding storage (see event calculus axioms in Listing 1.3).

3.3   Compliance Engine

This module contains required elements for compliance checking against regulative norms and data subject's consent. For this purpose, it should be fed with legal specifications and formalization of the given consent. Legal specification contains organizational measures, the legal basis of the processing, and the duties defined for processing. The compliance engine has 3 main parts, the first part assigns legal information to actions based on the legal specifications. It then checks for the compliance against regulatory obligations in the next one. In the last part can check the compliance of these actions with the data subject's given consent. Each part is described below.

Actions as Business Policy. An action should be associated with the legal information similar to the attributes of a business policy in SPECIAL (see the example of a business policy in Listing 1.1). The legal information associated with an action should match with the description of a business policy to be compatible with the underlying policy language. The below example shows how a transfer action is associated with the legal information using the format has(Action, GDPR_attribute, Value). For example, the knowledge about legal basis at line 6 or appropriate safeguards for a personal data transfer at line 7 and 8. Notice that only a fragment of the associated attributes are shown below, you can find the complete list in the code repository[1].

```
1 has(transfer(D,A,B,P), dataCategory, X) :- act(transfer(D,A,B,P)), has(D,
     dataCategory, X).
2 has(transfer(D,A,B,P), storage, B):- act(transfer(D,A,B,P)).
3 has(transfer(D,A,B,P), purpose, P):- act(transfer(D,A,B,P)).
4 has(transfer(D,A,B,P), recipient, X):- act(transfer(D,A,B,P)), has(B,
     controller, X).
5 system_legal_basis(art6_1_a_Consent).
6 has(transfer(D,A,B,P), legalBasis, X):- act(transfer(D,A,B,P)),
     system_legal_basis(X).
```

---

[1] https://gitlab.lip6.fr/taheri/planning-compliance-mechanism-policies.git.

```
7  transfer_safeguard(s4, s1, art46_2_e_ApprovedCodeOfConduct).
8  has(transfer(D,A,B,P), measures, X):- act(transfer(D,A,B,P)),
        transfer_safeguard(A,B, X).
```

GDPR Regulatory Obligations. We define necessary predicates and axioms to produce a straightforward translation of the GDPR regulatory obligations encoded in SPECIAL policy language and support for explainability in the case of non-compliance. As an example, the obligation at bottom level, Article 6–1(lawful processing) presented in 2.1, has been translated into ASP using the predicate fulfills/2. This rule means that an action O fulfills the obligations of article 6–1, if it has a legal basis as defined in the list. Note that in, ASP pred(a;b) is equivalent to pred(a) and pred(b).

```
1  art6_1_LegalBasis( art6_1_a_Consent;
2                     art6_1_b_Contract;
3                     art6_1_c_LegalObligation;
4                     art6_1_d_VitalInterest;
5                     art6_1_e_PublicInterest;
6                     art6_1_f_LegitimateInterest).
7  fulfills(O, art6_1_LegalBasis):- has(O, legalBasis, X), art6_1_LegalBasis(X
        ), act(O).
```

Each regulation is named after its reference in the GDPR text, part of the current supported obligations in this module are presented as by the predicate regulation. Where gdpr_Requirements represents the obligations at the top level.

```
1  regulation(art6_1_LegalBasis;
2      art6_lawfulProcessing;
3      art12_22_SubjectRights;
4      chap3_RightsOfDataSubjects;
5      chap2_LawfulProcessing;
6      art9_sensitiveData;
7      gdpr_Requirements).
```

In the SPECIAL policy language, the obligation at the bottom level are nested to form the top level obligation. The regulations are combined using the operators ObjectUnionOf and ObjectIntersectOf. We capture the same semantic by the predicates inUniounOf and inIntersectOf. For example, the Listing 2.1 is translated as follows

```
1  inUnionOf(art6_LawfulProcessing ,chap2_LawfulProcessing ).
2  inUnionOf(art9_SensitiveData, chap2_LawfulProcessing ).
3  inUnionOf(art10_CriminalData, chap2_LawfulProcessing ).
```

The predicate inUnionOf/2 is defined as below. It means that if an action P fulfills the obligation set of $R2$, and $R2$ is in union set of $R1$ then, it also fulfills the obligation of $R1$.

```
1  fulfills(P,R1):- fulfills(P,R2), inUnionOf(R2,R1), act(P).
```

An action is compliant if it fulfills all obligations of the fraction of the GDPR at the top level. A plan contains several actions, and it is possible that only a certain operation violates the compliance of the plan. In this case we are interested to know which missing obligation caused the non-compliance, in order to do so we use the predicate missing/2 in the following ASP rule, it indicates that the obligations of a certain article are missed.

```
1 missing1(P,R,R):- not fulfills(P,R),regulation(R), act(P), occurs(P,_).
2 missing1(P,R1,R2):- not fulfills(P,R2),  upperClass(R3,R2),missing1(P,R1,R3
    ), regulation(R1), regulation(R2).
3 missing(P,R):- missing1(P,R,gdpr_Requirements), not auxiliaryRegulation(R).
```

Data Subject's Consent. Suppose that when collecting personal data, the user has given explicit consent for transferring his *Purchases and Spending Habit* data for the purpose of *marketing*. Based on this consent, the data can only be disclosed to *aCompnay*, and it should be stored only in Europe. We translate this consent using the same format as listing 1.2. Note that SPECIAL also supports time intervals for the validity of the consent, but we do not support it here. In our scenario, the data subject has also given his consent to analyze processing with same attributes.

```
1 has(c2, dataCategory, serviceConsumptionBehavior).
2 has(c2, processing, transfer).
3 has(c2, purpose, marketing).
4 has(c2, recipient, aCompany).
5 has(c2, storageLocation, eu).
```

In our modeling, a processing is compliant with the given consent if it has the same attributes as the action. We check for the compliance of an action with the given consent using the following set of rules. It basically states that valid consent of an operation is satisfied if there is a coherent consent for it; and an action is coherent with a consent if there is no difference between the attributes of the consent and the operation. We capture it by the predicate validConsentSatisfied that is true when there is coherent consent for it.

```
1 non_coherent(P,C):- has(P,A, Z1) , has(C, A, Z2) ,Z1!=Z2, act(P), consent(C
    ).
2 validConsentSatisfied(P):- not non_coherent(P,C), act(P), consent(C).
```

4 Evaluation

Once we have modeled our domain knowledge, the planning module can be used to generate plans by providing an initial state and a goal state. A plan is generated to deliver the result of processing of personal data to the server asking for it. Consider that data $d1$ is initially stored in the server $s1$. We represent this initial state by `initially( hasData(s1,d1))`.

There is a request from server $s4$ for the results of the analysis on data $d1$ with the purpose *marketing*. We represent this request by `requestAnalysis(s4, d7 , marketing)`. This request is then translated into a goal for the system that the output of this analysis should be stored on the storage asking for it.

```
1 holds(goal,T):- holds( hasData(A, analysisOutput(D,P)), T ),
    requestAnalysis(A,D,P).
2 :- not holds(goal, maxtime).
```

After providing the initial state and a goal state, all the possible plans are generated to satisfy the given request. Plans are included in Table 1. Note that all these sequence of actions are generated regardless of their compliance. Each

Table 1. Automatic generated plans.

Plan	Time Step	Actions
1	1	transfer(d1,s2,s3,marketing)
	2	transfer(d1,s3,s4,marketing)
	3	analyse(d1,s4,marketing)
	4	transfer(analyseOut(d1,marketing),s4,s7,marketing)
	5	transfer(analyseOut(d1,marketing),s7,s5,marketing)
2	1	transfer(d1,s2,s1,marketing)
	2	transfer(d1,s1,s4,marketing)
	3	analyse(d1,s4,marketing)
	4	transfer(analyseOut(d1,marketing),s4,s7,marketing)
	5	transfer(analyseOut(d1,marketing),s7,s5,marketing)
3	1	transfer(d1, s2, s3, marketing)
	2	transfer(d1, s3, s4, marketing)
	3	analyse(d1, s4, marketing)
	4	transfer(analyseOut(d1, marketing), s4, s3, marketing)
	5	transfer(analyseOut(d7, marketing), s3, s5, marketing)
4	1	transfer(d1,s2,s1,marketing)
	2	transfer(d1,s1,s4,marketing)
	3	analyse(d1,s4,marketing)
	4	transfer(analyseOut(d1,marketing),s4,s3,marketing)
	5	transfer(analyseOut(d1,marketing),s3,s5,marketing)

plan is a set of actions presented by the predicate perform/2 which indicates the action and the time step in which it can be performed.

Having the plans generated by the previous module, the compliance engine can distinguish the compliant plans with the non-compliant ones and also provide a simple explanation for non-compliance by referring to the missing obligations. A plan is compliant if all the actions in that plan are compliant. Below we show the compliance checking result in two scenarios; Compliance checking with (i) data subject's given consent and (ii) GDPR regulatory norms. In both cases the initial state and the goal state are the same and the same plans are generated by the planning module (shown in Table 1), therefore the compliance engine assess the compliance of the identical plans but with different legal restrictions.

Consent Compliance Checking. In this scenario the customer has given a customized set of consent for various data processing. In particular we suppose that the data subject has given her consent only for internal transfers in EU so the compliance engine distinguish non-compliant plans if they are compatible with data subject's given consent. Table 2 presents the compliance of each plan as well as the explanation of the missing obligations.

Table 2. Automatic compliance checking of plans (Consent).

Plan	Compliance	Explanation
1 and 3	Yes	-
2 and 4	No	`missing(transfer(d1,s2,s1,marketing), art12_22_SubjectRights,)`
		`missing(transfer(d1,s2,s1,marketing), chap3_RightsOfDataSubjects)`
		`missing(transfer(d1,s2,s1,marketing), exceptions_as_per_Art23)`
		`missing(transfer(d1,s2,s1,marketing), chap9_Derogations)`
		`missing(transfer(d1,s2,s1,marketing), gdpr_Requirements)`

All the plans are generated automatically by the personal data managing agent. The process of compliance checking is also done automatically in the second module. Plan 1 and 3 are compliant since they fulfill all the obligation set forth of GDPR as well as the compliance with consent. Plan 2 and 4 are both non-compliant because of the same reason. The action `transfer(d1,s1,s3,marketing)` lacks the obligation of `art12_22_SubjectRights` since the transfer action does not match with the provided consent. When the obligations of a regulation are missed, it also causes that the obligations of the super class regulations to fail. In this case the action `transfer(d1,s2,s1,marketing)` misses the obligations of `chap3_RightsOfDataSubjects`, and `gdpr_Requirements` as they are the top classes of regulations in the policy formalization. Two other regulations have been reported as missed obligations, `exceptions_as_per_Art23` and `chap9_Derogations`, this is because if the obligations of these regulations is fulfilled, it causes the transfer action to comply with GDPR.

Compliance Checking Against GDPR Regulatory Norms. In this scenario we suppose that all the necessary consent is provided, so consent is no more a restricting constraint. We check the compliance of plans against GDPR regulatory norms, in particular obligations of GDPR Chap. 5 (Transfers of personal data to third countries or international organisations).

According to SPECIAL policy language[2] a transfer to a third country is only possible if it is not among the unauthorized transfers by Union law Article 48 (Transfers or disclosures not authorised by Union law) and is equipped with measures to assure a secure data transfer; these measures could be one of the appropriate safeguards as in Article 46 (Transfers subject to appropriate safeguards). Again we aim at checking the compliance of plans shown in Table 1, with the assumption that all the necessary consent is provided but no safety measures exist among the servers outside the EU (third countries) and the servers located in EU. The resulting compliance report is indicated in Table 3

---

[2] link to the documentations: https://specialprivacy.ercim.eu/platform/pilots-polici es-and-the-formalization-of-the-gdpr.

Table 3. Automatic compliance checking of plans (obligations of GDPR Chap. 5)

Plan	Compliance	Explanation
1 and 3	Yes	-
2 and 4	No	`missing(transfer(d1,s2,s1,marketing),chap5_DataTransferToThirdCountry)`
		`missing(transfer(d1,s2,s1,marketing),adequateLevelOfProtection_as_per_Art45)`
		`missing(transfer(d1,s2,s1,marketing),appropriateSafeguards_as_per_Art46)`
		`missing(transfer(d1,s2,s1,marketing),art49_Derogations)`
		`missing(transfer(d1,s2,s1,marketing),chap9_Derogations)`
		`missing(transfer(d1,s2,s1,marketing), gdpr_Requirements)`

As shown in Table 3 plan 2 and 4 are not compliant, since the action `transfer(d1,s2,s1,marketing)` miss the required obligations of GDPR Chap. 5. The principal missed elements are `adequateLevelOfProtection_as_per_Art45`, `appropriateSafeguards_as_per_Art46` or `art49_Derogations`. The transfer action could be compliant if certain regulations among missed ones are satisfied.

5 Related Works

Since the adoption of the GDPR, several tools and techniques have been introduced to facilitate the compliance assessment for data controllers and processors. Some of these methods are in the form of a questionnaire which evaluates the compliance of data processor and controllers e.g. Microsoft Trust Center, Agarwal et al. [1], but these methods do not support automated compliance checking.

Others focus on building an ontological concept of GDPR, e.g. PrOnto a privacy ontology Palmirani et al. [12] which relays on LegalRuleML Palmirani et al. [11] for legal reasoning and compliance checking of business processes. These methods can be used to make a repository of rules based on regulative and constitutive norms (cf. Robaldo et al. [14]). However, they provide a machine-readable representation of GDPR norms suitable for legal reasoning. One of our aims as future work is to integrate use a comprehensive ontology of GDPR norms with a legal reasoning engine.

Another body of works develop policy languages to enable the compliance checking of business processes De Vos et al. [6], Bonatti et al. [4]. The latter is based on the W3C Data Privacy Vocabulary and Controls Community Group (DPVCG) Pandit et al. [13] that is a vocabulary towards interoperability in the context of data privacy. De Vos et al. [6] introduce an ODRL policy pipeline to represent GDPR requirements and business policies. They then translate these representations in answer set programming and use it to check for the compliance of a business policy with GDPR regulatory obligations.

A number of works focus on integrating policies in a dynamic environment. Bandara et al. [2] present a method for transforming both, policy and system behavior specifications into a formal notation that is based on Event Calculus. However, they use it for detecting conflicts in the system. In the privacy domain,

Le Métayer and Rauzy [9] propose a formal framework to specify the notion of control over personal data and to reason about it, but it does not support compliance mechanism with any data protection regulation.

The methodology by De Vos et al. [5] uses a domain-specific language called *InstAL* based on ASP which is fairly similar to event calculus. They use *InstAL* to model events and time-varying properties in the system but not to generate sequences of actions to satisfy a given goal. Instead, they provide the program with the performed actions and are mainly interested in the evolution of the governing norms when an action takes place by an agent. However, in our current work norms are assumed constant and we use them to distinguish compliant and non-compliant plans. Adding support for time-varying norms is considered as a future extension to the current work.

6 Conclusion and Future Work

The goal in the current paper was two-fold (i) designing an AI agent that generates sequence of data processing or plans in order to satisfy a given goal, (ii) compliance checking of these plans with GDPR. In order to fulfill these goals, we presented a framework for planning in the privacy domain and compliance checking with GDPR. We made use of event calculus to formalize agent actions on personal data, and time-varying properties of the system. In order to formalize GDPR obligation set and data subjects consent, we chose SPECIAL policy language. We described how the knowledge of the planning domain and legal knowledge can be represented and combined together in our framework. We presented two scenarios in Sect. 4 and showed how our framework can be used to achieve the mentioned goals.

Our future goal is to design an AI agent with real-time legal and ethical supervisors concerning personal data protection. This work is highly dependent on the legal ontology or the policy language that we use to represent GDPR requirements. In the current paper we use SPECIAL as the underlying policy language, which is a simple machine-readable policy that does not support deontic operations.

Our ongoing work includes using a more comprehensive legal ontology like, PrOnto Palmirani et al. [12] or other policy languages like ODRL based one by De Vos et al. [6], and cover more GDPR articles in the design of the system. The current work assess the compliance in a static manner, i.e., it does not consider the evolution of norms in real-time as in De Vos et al. [5], adding support for more complex legal models is on other aspect of this work which we are trying to improve.

Other future works include developing our framework to implement more complex data processing scenarios cable to handle specific ethical issues concerning data protection an adding support for deontic operators and handle conflicts in real-time.

References

1. Agarwal, S., Steyskal, S., Antunovic, F., Kirrane, S.: Legislative compliance assessment: framework, model and GDPR instantiation. In: Medina, M., Mitrakas, A., Rannenberg, K., Schweighofer, E., Tsouroulas, N. (eds.) APF 2018. LNCS, vol. 11079, pp. 131–149. Springer, Cham (2018). https://doi.org/10.1007/978-3-030-02547-2_8
2. Bandara, A.K., Lupu, E.C., Russo, A.: Using event calculus to formalise policy specification and analysis. In: Proceedings POLICY 2003. IEEE 4th International Workshop on Policies for Distributed Systems and Networks, pp. 26–39. IEEE (2003)
3. Berreby, F., Bourgne, G., Ganascia, J.-G.: A declarative modular framework for representing and applying ethical principles. In: 16th Conference on Autonomous Agents and MultiAgent Systems 2017)
4. Bonatti, P.A., Kirrane, S., Petrova, I.M., Sauro, L.: Machine understandable policies and GDPR compliance checking. KI-Künstliche Intelligenz **34**(3), 303–315 (2020)
5. De Vos, M., Padget, J., Satoh, K.: Legal modelling and reasoning using institutions. In: Onada, T., Bekki, D., McCready, E. (eds.) JSAI-isAI 2010. LNCS (LNAI), vol. 6797, pp. 129–140. Springer, Heidelberg (2011). https://doi.org/10.1007/978-3-642-25655-4_12
6. De Vos, M., Kirrane, S., Padget, J., Satoh, K.: ODRL policy modelling and compliance checking. In: Fodor, P., Montali, M., Calvanese, D., Roman, D. (eds.) RuleML+RR 2019. LNCS, vol. 11784, pp. 36–51. Springer, Cham (2019). https://doi.org/10.1007/978-3-030-31095-0_3
7. Gebser, M., Kaminski, R., Kaufmann, B., Schaub, T.: Clingo= asp+ control: preliminary report. arXiv preprint arXiv:1405.3694 (2014)
8. Kowalski, R., Sergot, M.: A logic-based calculus of events. In: Schmidt, J.W., Thanos, C. (eds.) Foundations of Knowledge base Management, Topics in Information Systems, pp. 23–55. Springer, Berlin (1989)
9. Le Métayer, D., Rauzy, P.: Capacity: an abstract model of control over personal data. In: Proceedings of the Eighth ACM Conference on Data and Application Security and Privacy, pp. 64–75 (2018)
10. Lifschitz, V.: Answer Set Programming. Springer, Cham (2019). https://doi.org/10.1007/978-3-030-24658-7
11. Palmirani, M., Governatori, G., Rotolo, A., Tabet, S., Boley, H., Paschke, A.: LegalRuleML: XML-based rules and norms. In: Olken, F., Palmirani, M., Sottara, D. (eds.) RuleML 2011. LNCS, vol. 7018, pp. 298–312. Springer, Heidelberg (2011). https://doi.org/10.1007/978-3-642-24908-2_30
12. Palmirani, M., Martoni, M., Rossi, A., Bartolini, C., Robaldo, L.: Legal ontology for modelling GDPR concepts and norms. In: Legal Knowledge and Information Systems, pp. 91–100. IOS Press (2018)
13. Pandit, H.J., et al.: Creating a vocabulary for data privacy. In: Panetto, H., Debruyne, C., Hepp, M., Lewis, D., Ardagna, C.A., Meersman, R. (eds.) OTM 2019. LNCS, vol. 11877, pp. 714–730. Springer, Cham (2019). https://doi.org/10.1007/978-3-030-33246-4_44
14. Robaldo, L., Bartolini, C., Palmirani, M., Rossi, A., Martoni, M., Lenzini, G.: Formalizing GDPR provisions in reified i/o logic: the DAPRECO knowledge base. J. Logic Lang. Inf. **29**(4), 401–449 (2020)
15. Shanahan, M.: The event calculus explained. In: Wooldridge, M.J., Veloso, M. (eds.) Artificial Intelligence Today. LNCS (LNAI), vol. 1600, pp. 409–430. Springer, Heidelberg (1999). https://doi.org/10.1007/3-540-48317-9_17

LENLS 18

Logic and Engineering of Natural Language Semantics (LENLS) 18

Alastair Butler

Faculty of Humanities and Social Sciences, Hirosaki University, Bunkyo-cho 1,
Hirosaki-shi, 036-8560, Japan
ajb129@hirosaki-u.ac.jp

Over the three day period of November 13 (Sat), 14 (Sun), and 15 (Mon), 2021, the Eighteenth International Workshop of Logic and Engineering of Natural Language Semantics (LENLS 18) was held as one of the workshops of the Thirteenth JSAI International Symposia on AI (JSAI-isAI 2021) sponsored by the Japan Society for Artificial Intelligence (JSAI). All interactions of the event took place online (via video conferencing platforms) due to the continued COVID-19 pandemic.

LENLS is an annual international workshop focusing on topics from formal approaches to the analysis of natural language and related fields. This year the workshop featured three invited lectures: Maria Aloni (University of Amsterdam) talked about logic and conversation, Michael Wayne Goodman (Nanyang Technological University) talked about meaning representation for computational semantics, and Atsushi Shimojima (Doshisha University) talked about semantic functions of diagrams. In addition there were twenty five presentations of talks selected by the program committee from the abstracts submitted for presentation.

As with previous LENLS workshops, presented papers were rich and varied in content. There were papers focused on formal accounts of specific empirical phenomena, there were papers concerned with broader annotation driven analysis, there were papers with proposals to extend or modify existing formal theories and methods, and there were papers tackling theoretical and foundational questions.

The present volume contains a selection of thirteen papers from the workshop. The remainder of this introduction will briefly indicate the content of the papers selected to appear in the present volume.

In the paper 'Remembering Individuals and Remembering Scenes', Kristina Liefke provides a compositional semantics that accounts for observed differences in interpretation involving intensional transitive verbs that take a direct object noun phrase (paradigmatically: *remember*).

In the paper 'Factivity Variation in Episodic Memory Reports', Kristina Liefke and Markus Werning give a compositional semantics for episodic memory reports that captures observations concerning whether or not factivity inferences arise.

Shun Ihara and Yuta Tatsumi's paper 'The Duality of Negative Attitudes in Japanese Conditionals' provides an analysis of Japanese *nara* conditionals that occur with the noun *mono* 'thing'. The analysis is able to account for new observations that such conditionals induce negativity of the antecedent.

Continuing the theme of detailed analysis for specific natural language data, Osamu Sawada's 'Interpretations of sense-based minimizers in Japanese and English: Direct and indirect sense-based measurements' adopts a multidimensional approach to meaning to explain aspects of meaning for degree adverbs *kasukani* from Japanese and *faintly* from English.

Eri Tanaka and Kenta Mizutani's paper 'Presuppositions and Comparison Classes in Japanese *hodo*-equatives' focuses on the Japanese equative marker *hodo*. The analysis has *hodo* taking a comparison class as one of its arguments to capture differences that arise with norm-related implications in interaction with the focus particle *mo* 'even/also'.

David Y. Oshima's paper 'The Japanese honorific titles *san*, *kun*, and *chan*', provides a theoretically-oriented study of the semantics, pragmatic effects, and usage of the three honorific expressions *san*, *kun*, and *chan* that are typically attached to a name in Japanese.

The theme of considering data from honorifics and honorification is developed further in Elin McCready's paper 'Honorifics, Grounds and Ideologies', with grounds for a greatly expanded yet unspecified machinery for interpretation.

In the paper 'QNP Textual Entailment with Polynomial Event Semantics', Oleg Kiselyov and Haruki Watanabe develop polynomial event semantics, an approach that combines quantification and Neo-Davidsonian event semantics. The theory is applied to parts of the FraCaS textual entailment corpus, a standard benchmark for theories of semantics.

In the paper 'Parsed corpus development with a quick access interface', Alastair Butler describes corpus development with considerations of data format, search, and visualisations of analysis from discourse dependency levels to word sense levels.

Daisuke Bekki's paper 'A Proof-theoretic Analysis of Weak Crossover' is concerned both with a particular language phenomena, weak crossover, and with amending aspects of an existing formal framework, Dependent Type Semantics (DTS), so to provide analysis that is sensitive to syntactic positioning and so able to replicate the observed natural language behaviour.

Continuing the theme of theory enhancement, Julian Grove and Jean-Philippe Bernardy, in their paper 'Probabilistic compositional semantics, purely', propose a general framework for the integration of probabilistic reasoning as side effects using continuations integrated with standard mechanics for formal semantics in the tradition of Montague.

In the paper 'Pluralism for Relativists: a new framework for context dependence', Ahmad Jabbar motivates a new way of dealing with context-sensitive expressions based on relativizing interpretation with respect to either a context of use or a context of assessment so that there is no need to choose between contextualism and relativism.

Employing the framework of game-theoretic pragmatics, Liping Tang, in the paper 'Cheap talk under partial conflicts: a dynamic analysis of pragmatic meaning', provides a systematic analysis of the deviation from literal meaning to pragmatic meaning when interlocutors have partial conflicts.

Acknowledgements. We are deeply grateful to all participants of LENLS 18 who made the event so enjoyable and productive. We are also particularly grateful to JSAI and the organisers of JSAI-isAI 2021, Katsutoshi Yada (Kansai University) and Naoaki Okazaki (Tokyo Institute of Technology), for giving the opportunity to hold the workshop.

Remembering Individuals
and Remembering Scenes

Kristina Liefke[✉]

Department of Philosophy II, Ruhr University Bochum, 44780 Bochum, Germany
kristina.liefke@ruhr-uni-bochum.de
https://www.ruhr-uni-bochum.de/phil-inf/

Abstract. In the object position of certain intensional transitive verbs (paradigmatically: *remember*), DPs are semantically ambiguous between individuals and scenes [= scenes that saliently feature these individuals]. This ambiguity cuts across the familiar intensionality-related distinctions (esp. specific/non-specific, referentially transparent/referentially opaque) and cannot be explained at the level of LF. As a result, it poses a challenge for existing semantics for intensional transitive verbs, esp. for Zimmermann's property-based account, for Stephenson's situation-theoretic account, and for Moltmann's truthmaker-semantic account. My paper provides a uniform compositional semantics for 'individual'- and for 'scene'-interpretations of *remember* DP-reports that explains this ambiguity. To do this, it investigates the situations that feature in the proposition-type complement of *remember*. It finds that, if the referent of the object DP has <u>different</u> properties in these situations, the report receives an individual-interpretation. If the referent has the <u>same</u> properties in all situations, the report can receive an individual-interpretation (next to its scene-interpretation). The resulting semantics captures the intensionality and entailment properties of *remember* DP-reports and predicts the preferred individual-interpretation of strongly quantificational object DPs.

Keywords: Intensional transitive verbs · Objectual attitude reports · Memory reports · Specificity · Substitution-resistance · Semantic ambiguity · Cross-categorial entailments

The paper has profited from discussions with Maria Aloni, Liz Coppock, James Openshaw, Dolf Rami, Florian Schwarz, Markus Werning, and Ede Zimmermann. The research for this paper is supported by the German Research Foundation, DFG, as part of Ede Zimmermann's project Propositionalism in Linguistic Semantics (ZI 683/13-1) and of Kristina Liefke and Markus Werning's project in the research unit FOR 2812: Constructing Scenarios of the Past (grant 397530566). It is further supported by the German Federal Ministry of Education and Research, BMBF (through Kristina Liefke's WISNA professorship).

K. Yada et al. (Eds.): JSAI-isAI 2021 Workshops, LNAI 13856, pp. 97–109, 2023.
https://doi.org/10.1007/978-3-031-36190-6_7

1   Introduction

Remember-reports with a direct object DP (e.g. (1a)) are ambiguous between an 'individual'- and a 'scene'-interpretation. On the former interpretation, these reports assert the remembering agent's relation to an individual object (in (1a): to the gray-haired man from the library; see (1a-i)) [17,20]. On the latter interpretation, they assert the remembering agent's relation to a personally experienced past event or scene that saliently features this individual (in (1a): to a man's pacing up and down the aisles, muttering to himself; see (1a-ii)) [4,21]:

(1)   *Context:* Last month at the library, Anna saw a gray-haired man pacing up and down the aisles, muttering to himself.

   a.   (Today still,) Anna remembers the man.

      i.   Anna remembers a <u>particular individual</u>, viz. the man from the library.

      ii.   Anna remembers a <u>particular event/scene</u> (from the library), viz. a man's pacing up and down the aisles, muttering to himself.

The ambiguity between an individual- and a scene-interpretation is also exemplified by the object DPs in imagination and depiction reports (e.g. (2)). In these reports, the different interpretations (roughly!) coincide with a specific reading (see (2a-i)) respectively with a non-specific reading of the DP (in (2b-i)). The specific reading relates Penny to a particular penguin in the real world (call him 'Pingo'). This reading is even true in scenarios in which Penny is unaware that Pingo is a penguin. The non-specific reading relates Penny to some possibly non-existing object that she conceptualizes as a penguin. The presence *vis-à-vis* absence of a causal connection to the depicted penguin motivates a Goodman-style description of the object DP in (2) as the designator of a penguin *portrait* (in (2a)) respectively as the designator of a penguin *picture* (in (2b)) (see [26], following [10]).

(2)   Penny is {painting, imagining} a penguin.   [26, ex. 3]

   a.   i.   There exists a certain penguin whom Penny is painting. (specific) ($\equiv$ Penny is painting a penguin *portrait.*)

      ii.   Penny is painting a <u>particular individual</u>, viz. a certain penguin.

   b.   i.   Penny is painting some (possibly non-existing) penguin. ($\equiv$ Penny is painting a penguin *picture.*)   (non-specific)

      ii.   Penny is depicting <u>an event or scene</u> that saliently features a/ some penguin.

Since the specific reading of (2) 'anchors' the content of Penny's painting to a particular penguin, viz. to Pingo, it straightforwardly elicits an individual-interpretation (in (2a-ii)). Since the non-specific reading describes the content of Penny's picture or mental image [26], it is best compatible with a scene-interpretation (in (2b-ii)).

The present paper identifies the particularities of the individual/scene-ambiguity from (1), and contrasts it with related ambiguities. To this end, I first show that the ambiguity from (1) is not a scope or a structural ambiguity (unlike (2); Sect. 2). To prepare my semantics for *remember* DP-reports, I then identify other notable semantic properties of these reports (in Sect. 3) and show that these properties remain unexplained by state-of-the-art semantics for intensional transitive verbs (see Sect. 4). Section 5 presents a uniform compositional semantics for *remember* DP-reports that captures the individual/scene-ambiguity of these reports as well as the above properties. The paper closes by showing that my proposed semantics also accounts for the individual/scene-ambiguity of specific readings of the object DP in imagination and depiction reports.

2 Not a 'Classical' Ambiguity

I have started this paper by describing the availability of two interpretations for (1a) as an *ambiguity*. Remarkably however, this availability is neither a consequence of differences in the scope of the intensional transitive verb with respect to the object DP (see Sect. 2.1) nor does it arise from the presence or absence of silent syntactic material (see Sect. 2.2):

2.1 Not a Scope Ambiguity

At a first glance, the individual/scene-ambiguity of the *remember*-report in (1a) appears to be parallel to the well-studied ambiguity of depiction reports like (2) (see e.g. [7,25,26]). However, at a second glance, (1a) differs from (2) in allowing the individual/scene-ambiguity within specific readings of the object DP. This is attested by the use of the definite determiner in (1a) (see the strong preference for (1a) over (3)).

(3)   ?? (Today still,) Anna remembers a man.

Since remembering individuals or scenes presupposes the agent's acquaintance with the memory target (i.e. their personal witnessing, e.g. observing, of the target event or scene of the remembering), the specific reading is the only admissible reading of these reports. This differs from depiction reports (see (2b-i)), which also allow scene-interpretations on unspecific readings of the DP.

Arguably, the observation that the individual/scene-ambiguity holds for specific DPs still leaves open the possibility that this ambiguity is due to the ambiguity of (1a) between a *de re* [= specific, referentially transparent] reading (see (4a)) and a 'fourth' [= specific, referentially opaque] reading (see (4b); due to [23])[1]:

(4)   a.   [the man]$_1$ [λ$_1$ [Anna remembers t_1]]

---

[1] Szabó's analysis is much more sophisticated than is presented here. However, since it cannot be used to explain the individual/scene-ambiguity, I refrain from a more detailed presentation.

b. [[the]$_2$ thing] [λ_2 [Anna remembers [t_2 man]]]

However, this possibility is excluded by the observation that, on both interpretations, *remember*-reports can resist the truth-preserving substitution of their
object DP by a co-referential expression (see [9,19]). For example, in a scenario
in which Anna did not recognize the gray-haired man from the library as the
former President of her alma mater, the content of her remembering could only
be correctly described by (5a), but not by the result, (5c), of replacing the object
DP, i.e. *the gray-haired man*, in (5a) by *the former President of her* [= *Anna's*]
alma mater:

(5)   a. Anna remembers the gray-haired man (from the library).   (**T**)
       b. The gray-haired man (from the library) is
           the former President of Anna's alma mater.   (**T**)

   $\not\Rightarrow$ c. Anna remembers the former President of her alma mater.   (**F**)

To see that the observed substitution-resistance also holds for explicitly 'scenic'
variants of (5a) (see (1a-ii)), consider the result of replacing the object DP by an
explicitly event-/scene-denoting DP (e.g. *a event/scene in which a gray-haired
man was pacing*; see (6a)) or by a gerundive small clause (here: *a gray-haired
man pacing and muttering to himself*).

(6)   a. Anna remembers (a scene [at the library] in which) a gray-
           haired man (was) pacing and muttering to himself.   (**T**)
       b. The gray-haired man (from the library) is
           the former President of Anna's alma mater.   (**T**)

   $\not\Rightarrow$ c. Anna remembers (a scene in which) the former President
           of her alma mater (was) pacing and muttering to himself.   (**F**)

The above shows that the individual/scene-ambiguity of (5a) (see (1a)) can
not only <u>not</u> be explained through the DP's ambiguity between a specific and a
non-specific reading: It is can also not be explained through the DP's ambiguity between a referentially transparent and a referentially opaque reading. The
individual/scene-ambiguity thus cuts across the familiar intensionality-related
distinctions.

2.2 Not a Structural Ambiguity

Notably, the individual/scene-ambiguity in (1) can also not be explained through
a structural ambiguity: To defend a propositional account of the complement
in depiction reports, some researchers have analyzed the complement in these
reports as a non-constituent element of the form DP XP, where XP is a silent,
contextually supplied predicate (see e.g. [2,14,24]). Since the XP can be dropped
in these constructions, this account analyzes (1a) as ambiguous between a report
with a direct object (in (7a)) and a report with a direct object and a gerund XP
predicate (in (7b)). Since the XP is silent, it is printed in grey in (7b):

(7)   a. Anna remembers [_DP_the man].
          ($\equiv$ Anna remembers a <u>particular individual</u>, viz. the man from the
          library.)

      b. Anna remembers [_DP_the man] [_XP_pacing up and down the aisles].
          ($\equiv$ Anna remembers a <u>particular event/scene</u> (from the library), viz.
          a man's pacing up and down the aisles.)

Unfortunately however, this account makes unwarranted predictions about
the admissible readings of reports with temporal modifiers. This analysis projects
that the scene-reading, (7b), of (1a) provides two predicates (i.e. the matrix
predicate, _remember_, and the contextually provided predicate in the verb's complement, i.e. _pace up and down the aisles_) that allow modification by a temporal
adverbial (e.g. _yesterday_; see (8)). However, the low-scope reading of the modifier (on which _yesterday_ modifies the 'lower' predicate, i.e. _pacing up and down
the aisles_; in (8b)) is intuitively unavailable. This is supported by the deviance[2]
of (9), which should be acceptable if _yesterday_ could modify this predicate:

(8)   Anna remembered [the man] [_XP_pacing up and down the aisles] yesterday.

      a. Anna's remembering of the man's pacing happened yesterday. ($\checkmark$)

      b. The man's pacing (which Anna remembers) happened yesterday. ($\bm{X}$)

(9)   #Today, Anna remembers the gray-haired man yesterday.

The availability of a contextually provided predicate is also excluded by the
observation that the DP/XP-sequence cannot provide the antecedent for propositional anaphora. In particular, in (10), the common object of Anna's and John's
remembering can only be referred to by the individual-denoting pronoun _him_,
but not by the more general (and, hence, also event-denoting) pronoun _it_ (see
[3]):

(10)   Anna remembers [_DP_the man] [_XP_pacing up and down the aisles], but John
       has no recollection of him/*it.

---

[2] In some languages (e.g. German; see ($\star$) below), this deviance can be corrected by
converting the modifier _yesterday_ into a temporal preposition:

($\star$)   ✓Heute erinnert sich Anna an den grauhaarigen Mann <u>von</u> gestern.
          [_gloss:_ Today, remembers-REFL Anna to the gray-haired man <u>from</u> yes-
                terday.]
          [_translation:_ Today, Anna remembers the gray-haired man <u>from</u> yesterday.]

However, since this preposition modifies the DP _gray-haired man_ rather than the
silent predicate _pace up and down the aisles_, ($\star$) cannot be used to rectify the predictions of the structural ambiguity-account.

3   Other Properties of 'remember DP'-Reports

The impossibility of explaining the different interpretations of (1a) through a structural or scope ambiguity suggests that these interpretations must have some other source. Before I move on to investigate this source, I first identify two other properties of *remember* DP-reports that will provide useful insights into the semantics of these reports.

3.1   'Individual Only'-Interpretations

My discussion so far has assumed that *remember*-reports with an object DP generally have both an individual- and a scene-interpretation. However, some such reports require that the DP be interpreted as an individual. This is the case when the DP is strongly quantificational (i.e. when it has the form *each/every/all* N; see (11))[3] or when the non-linguistic context suggests the absence of a non-trivial property that is constant across all relevant events or scenes (see (12)):

(11)   *Context:* Last week, Eva visited San Diego Zoo, which is well-known for its emus.

    a. Eva remembers every emu.

      ≡ i. For a certain domain of <u>individuals</u> (viz. the emus in San Diego Zoo), Eva remembers each particular member of this domain (of individuals).

      ≢ ii. For a certain domain of <u>events/scenes</u> (involving the emus in San Diego Zoo), Eva remembers each particular member of this domain (of events/scenes).

(12)   *Context:* Over many years, Oscar has occasionally spotted the same cat in different locations: in his garden, on his neighbor's front porch, and in the fields nearby. Since the time when he first spotted it as a kitten, it has changed in every perceivable way. In particular, it has almost tripled in size and its fur has turned grey, but it has become a lot more trusting.

    a. Oscar remembers the cat.

      ≡ i. Oscar remembers <u>a particular individual</u>, viz. a certain cat.

      ≢ ii. Oscar remembers <u>a particular event/scene</u>, viz. a cat's having a particular property or engaging in a specific activity.

For (12a), the reading in (12a-ii) is excluded by the observation that there is no 'interesting' property (other than 'being a cat') that the target individual has in all events or scenes in which Oscar has encountered it and that now feed into his memory.

---

[3] Since the object DP in *remember*-reports is always specific, this is different from the unavailability of *de dicto*-readings for strong quantificational objects of intensional transitive verbs in [25] (see also [8, pp. 148–149]).

3.2 Cross-Categorial Entailments

Above, I have used explicitly event/scene-denoting DPs or gerund complements to paraphrase a report's scene-interpretation. Because of the felicity of such paraphrases, it is unsurprising that – in the context from (1) – (1a-ii) (copied in (13a)) mutually entails (13b):

(13) a. Anna remembers a <u>particular event/scene</u> (from the library) in which a man was pacing up and down the aisles.

$\Leftarrow\Rightarrow$ b. Anna remembers a man pacing up and down the aisles (at the library).

Interestingly, however, (uni-directional) versions of these entailments can also hold for the report's individual-interpretation, (1a-i). Thus, in the context from (1),[4] it seems impossible that there is a remembering scenario which makes (14a) true, but (14b) false.

(14) a. Anna remembers a man pacing up and down the aisles at the library.

$\overset{c}{\Leftarrow}\Rightarrow$ b. Anna remembers a <u>particular individual</u>, viz. the man from the library.

Even if Anna were unable to recall any other of the man's properties (but his pacing up and down the aisles), her remembering him would still qualify as a truthmaker for (14b). In cases (like (1)) in which the agent has only encountered the individual on a single occasion on which the individual exemplified the properties that are ascribed by the scene-DP/gerund complement, it even seems that the entailment is mutual (s.t. $[\![(1a\text{-ii})/(14a)]\!] \overset{c}{\Leftarrow}\Rightarrow [\![(1a\text{-i})/(14b)]\!]$).

The situation is different for cases (e.g. (12)) in which the agent has encountered the individual on different occasions in which the individual exhibited different properties. Since these cases potentially do not allow any inferences from the individual to its properties, the entailment relation is only uni-directional (see (15)):

(15) a. Oscar remembers a cat sitting on his neighbor's front porch.

$\not\Leftarrow\Rightarrow$ b. Oscar remembers a <u>particular individual</u>, viz. the neighborhood cat.

4 Previous Accounts

Recent work on intensional transitive verbs has provided different semantic accounts of reports containing these verbs. The best-known of these accounts are Zimmermann's property-based semantics [25,26], Stephenson's situation-theoretic semantics [21], and Moltmann's object-based truthmaker semantics

---

[4] To capture the context-dependence of the entailment from (14b) to (14a), I mark the left arrow, $\Leftarrow$, in (14) with a superscript 'c'.

[16]. Respectively, these semantics interpret[5] the object DP in (1a) as the property that is denoted by the DP's restrictor (see (16a)), as the agent's personally experienced situation in which the DP refers (see (16b)), and as the set of situations that exactly verify the attitudinal (here: the mnemonic) object (see the streamlined (16c)). For the verb *remember*, these semantics are compared in (16). There, x, y, z, and u are individual variables (type e). The variables w, σ (σ'), and e range over possible worlds, possible situations (both type s), and events (type v), respectively. P is a variable over individual properties (type $\langle s, \langle e, t \rangle \rangle$); Q is a variable over intensional generalized quantifiers (type $\langle s, \langle \langle s, \langle e, t \rangle \rangle, t \rangle \rangle$).

In (16), the interpretation of the DP object is highlighted in grey. In Moltmann's semantics (see (16c)), *att-obj*(e) is the attitudinal object of Anna's particular remembering event e. $\mathscr{F}_{cont}(att\text{-}obj(e))$ [= the propositional content of this object] is a subset of the set of situations that exactly verify the complement that is associated with the DP object.

(16) $[\![remember]\!]^{@} =$

a. $\lambda Q \lambda z \exists x.\ remember'_@ (z,\ \lambda w \lambda y [Q_w(\lambda w' \lambda u.\ u = y) \wedge y = x]\ )$ \hfill (Zimmermann)

b. $\lambda Q \lambda z \exists x\ \exists \sigma:\ \underline{Q_\sigma(\lambda w \lambda y.\ y = x)} \ .\ remember''_@(z, \sigma)$ \hfill (Stephenson)

c. $\lambda Q \lambda z \exists x \exists e.\ remember'''_@(e, z,\ \mathscr{F}_{cont}(att\text{-}obj(e))) \wedge$ \hfill (Moltmann)
$(\forall \sigma.\ \mathscr{F}_{cont}(att\text{-}obj(e))(\sigma) \to (\lambda \sigma'.\ Q_{\sigma'}(\lambda w \lambda y.\ y = x)))$

The different semantics for *remember* give rise to the different interpretations of (1a) in (18). These interpretations assume the interpretation of proper names (here: *Anna*) and quantificational DPs (*a man*) from (17):

(17)   a. $[\![Anna]\!] = anna$

b. $[\![a\ man]\!] = \lambda w \lambda P (\exists x)[man_w(x) \wedge P_w(x)]$

(18) $[\![Anna\ remembers\ a/the\ man]\!]^{@}$
$\equiv [\![[[a]_1\ thing]\ [\lambda_1.\ [\![Anna]\ [remembers\text{-}in\text{-}@\ [t_1\ man]]]]]\!]$
$\equiv [\![[a]_1\ thing]\!]^{@}(\lambda Q_1.\ ([\![remember]\!]^{@}([\![Q_1]\!]([\![man]\!])))([\![Anna]\!]))$

a. $\exists x.\ remember'_@ (anna,\ \lambda w \lambda y.\ man_w(y) \wedge y = x\ )$ \hfill (Zimmermann)

b. $\exists x.\ \exists \sigma:\ \underline{man_\sigma(x)} \ .\ remember''_@(anna, \sigma)$ \hfill (Stephenson)

c. $\exists x \exists e.\ remember'''_@(e, anna,\ \mathscr{F}_{cont}(att\text{-}obj(e))\ ) \wedge$ \hfill (Moltmann)
$(\forall \sigma.\ \mathscr{F}_{cont}(att\text{-}obj(e))(\sigma) \to (\lambda \sigma'.\ man_{\sigma'}(x)))$

On Zimmermann's account, (1a) thus asserts the obtaining of a binary relation (at @) between Anna and a property (i.e. 'is a man') of a certain individual (see

---

[5] Zimmermann [25, 26] and Moltmann [16] do not apply their accounts to the particular verb *remember*. My comparison of these approaches is based on their semantics for specific readings of depiction verbs (esp. *paint, imagine*).

(18a), which uses de Swart's [22] simplified version of Zimmermann's semantics). Stephenson's account replaces the second relatum of this relation by a situation (i.e. an event or scene) of which it is presupposed that the relevant individual is a man in this situation (see (18b), which uses a different non-logical constant, *remember''*, for the translation of the matrix verb in (18)). Moltmann's account replaces the situation by the exact verifiers (and, respectively, falsifiers) of the sentence that asserts of this individual 'He is a man' (see (18c)).

My presentation of these accounts already suggests that they may be able to capture some of the discussed properties of *remember* DP-reports. This holds for Zimmermann and Moltmann with regard to the referential opacity of the object DPs in these reports (see (5)) and for Stephenson with regard to the entailments between reports with direct object- and with gerundive complements (see (14)). In particular, since they assign the DP an intensional interpretation (in terms of possible worlds/situations) whose restrictor can take scope below *remember*, (18a) and (18c) capture the blocked substitution of co-referential expressions in (5). Since Stephenson interprets direct objects and gerundive complements as situations – and since she assumes that situations are ordered by a Kratzer-style information-ordering, $\leq$ (see [12,15]) –, her semantics captures the intuitive validity of the inferences between individual- respectively scene-denoting DPs and gerund complements in (14).

The above merits notwithstanding, none of the presented semantics seems able to capture the individual/scene-ambiguity from (1). One could try to address this shortcoming by interpreting Stephenson's situations as situations and as representations of individuals, respectively (see, e.g., [1,11,15]). However, since Stephenson's semantics does not capture the dependence of the target situation on the specific remembering event, it is difficult to see how this semantics could explain the contextual equivalence of (14a) and (14b). Similar observations hold for the exact verifiers that are associated with Moltmann's attitudinal objects. As a consequence of these observations, the presented semantics also cannot account for 'individual only'-readings of memory reports. This holds especially since the difference between specific and unspecific readings – which is used to explain a similar observation in [25] – is already excluded by the interpretations of *remember* (see my discussion in Sect. 2).

5   Proposal

To capture the individual/scene-ambiguity, I propose to combine Stephenson's intuition about the situation- [= event- or scene-]argument in *remember* DP-reports with Moltmann's choice of the propositional argument type, $\langle s, t \rangle$. In this type, the 'man pacing'-scene, σ, from (1a-ii) can be straightforwardly represented by its singleton.[6] This representation proceeds through a suitably-typed version, $\lambda \sigma'. \sigma' = \sigma$, of Partee's [18] type-shifter IDENT. To obtain the individual-interpretation in (12a-i), I interpret the DP *the cat* as the set of all relevant (events

---

[6] This possibility assumes a Kratzer-style generalization of possible worlds (type s) to possible situations, events, and scenes (see [12]).

or) scenes in which Oscar has encountered the cat and that now feed into his remembering. In the semantics of the verb *remember* (in (19)), these scenes are identified by a subset selection function, $\mathcal{C}$ (see [6]). This function chooses a subset from a given set of situations (for (12): the set of situations in which said cat exists) in dependence on a parameter, e, for the reported remembering event.

In my interpretation of DP-taking occurrences of *remember* (in (19)), E is a situation-relative existence predicate. '$E_{\sigma'}(y)$' asserts that the individual y exists (or, using my earlier terminology, 'features saliently') in the situation σ'. For an axiomatic specification of E's behavior, the reader is referred to [13, p. 117 ff.].

(19) $[\![\text{remember}_{\text{DP}}]\!]^@$
$$= \lambda \mathcal{Q} \lambda z \exists x \exists e. \, remember_@\big(e, z, \, \mathcal{C}_e(\lambda\sigma. \, \mathcal{Q}_\sigma(\lambda\sigma'\lambda y. \, E_{\sigma'}(y) \wedge y = x))\big)$$

The dependence of $\mathcal{C}$ on e is evidenced by the observation that different remembering events of Oscar's (at different times) – and different remembering events of different agents with the same target (e.g. the cat's indulging in a can of tuna on Oskar's front porch) – typically have different contents. The resulting – unique (!) – interpretation of (12a) *[Oscar remembers the cat]* is given in (20):

(20) $[\![\text{Oscar remembers the cat}]\!]^@$
$$\equiv [\![[[a]_1 \text{ thing}] [\lambda_1. [[\text{Oscar}] [\text{remembers-in-}@ [t_1 \text{ cat}]]]]]\!]$$
$$\equiv [\![[a]_1 \text{ thing}]\!]^@ (\lambda\mathcal{Q}_1. ([\![\text{remember}]\!]^@ ([\![\mathcal{Q}_1]\!]([\![\text{cat}]\!]))) ([\![\text{Oscar}]\!]))$$
$$= \lambda\mathcal{Q}\lambda z\exists x\exists e. \, remember_@\big(e, z, \, \mathcal{C}_e(\lambda\sigma. \, \mathcal{Q}_\sigma(\lambda\sigma'\lambda y. \, E_{\sigma'}(y) \wedge y = x))\big)$$
$$\qquad\qquad (\lambda\sigma\lambda P \exists u. \, cat_\sigma(u) \wedge P_\sigma(u))(oscar)$$
$$\equiv \lambda z\exists x\exists e. \, remember_@\big(e, z, \, \mathcal{C}_e(\lambda\sigma. \, cat_\sigma(x) \wedge E_\sigma(x))\big)(oscar)$$
$$\equiv \exists x\exists e. \, remember_@\big(e, oscar, \, \mathcal{C}_e(\lambda\sigma. \, cat_\sigma(x) \wedge E_\sigma(x))\big)$$

5.1 Capturing the Individual/Scene-Ambiguity

The above interpretation relates Oscar to some subset (viz. Oscar's personally experienced scenes [= situations]) of the set of situations that saliently feature this particular cat. This subset can be a singleton, or it can be a larger [= non-empty, non-singleton] set. The former is the case in contexts in which the agent's remembering is based on a single personally experienced event or scene (in (1): on Anna's unique encounter with the gray-haired man at the library). The latter is the case in contexts in which the agent's remembering is based on multiple personally experienced events or scenes.

In the case of (12a) – given the context from (12) –, the different members will likely not be *qualitatively identical* [= the cat will have different properties in different members] (see [12, p. 667]; [5, p. 136]). As a result, this set triggers an individual-interpretation (see (12a-i)). In the case of (1a) – given the context from (1) –, the singleton will likely contain more information about said man than 'x is a man' (see (1)). As a result, the singleton can also trigger a scene-interpretation, (12a-ii). The same-type interpretation of the object DP in the individual- and the scene-interpretation – and the existence of a partial ordering on sets of situations – facilitates an easy explanation of the inferences from Sect. 3.2.

5.2 Predicting 'Individual Only'-Interpretations

Above, I have focused on cases in which the individual- and the scene-interpretation are – at least in principle – both possible. The two interpretations come apart in cases in which the object DP has a divided reference (e.g. in *every emu*; see (11a) [*Eva remembers every emu*]) or in which the remembering agent has encountered the individual on multiple occasions (on which it exemplified different properties; see (12a)).

The description of the context in (12) suggests that the different members, σ', of $\mathcal{C}_e(\lambda\sigma. cat_\sigma(x) \wedge E_\sigma(x))$ do not share any non-trivial information besides $E_{\sigma'}(c)$ and $cat_{\sigma'}(c)$ (for c the relevant witness of $\exists x$). As a result, there is no non-trivial <u>kind</u> (or class) of situations to which the different members of $\mathcal{C}_e(\lambda\sigma. cat_\sigma(x) \wedge E_\sigma(x))$ belong. This observation also explains the 'individual only'-interpretation of (11a) in the context from (11). The strong favoring of this interpretation suggests that the individual-interpretation is even preferred when the relevant individual(s) share some – but not all – properties.

5.3 Capturing Referential Opacity

My proposed semantics for the verb *remember* in (19) provides an <u>intensional</u> interpretation of the object DPs in memory reports that converts the familiar interpretation of these DPs (i.e. type-$\langle s, \langle\langle s, \langle e, t\rangle\rangle, t\rangle\rangle$ intensional generalized quantifiers, $\mathcal{Q}$) to characteristic functions of sets of situations, $\mathcal{C}_e(\lambda\sigma. \llbracket\text{DP}\rrbracket^\sigma(\lambda\sigma'\lambda y. E_{\sigma'}(y) \wedge y = x))$ (type $\langle s, t\rangle$). Since these sets will be different for the DP *the gray-haired man (from the library)* and the DP *the former President of Anna's alma mater*, they block the substitution in (5):

(21) a. $\exists x \exists e.\, remember_@(e, anna, \mathcal{C}_e(\lambda\sigma. man_\sigma(x) \wedge E_\sigma(x)))$

     b. $\underline{(\exists x)[\exists\sigma.\, man_\sigma(x) \wedge \neg former\text{-}president_\sigma(x)]}$

  $\not\Rightarrow$ c. $\exists x \exists e.\, remember_@(e, anna, \mathcal{C}_e(\lambda\sigma. former\text{-}president_\sigma(x) \wedge E_\sigma(x)))$

Despite this success, the proposed semantics still accounts for the substitutivity of these DPs in the *de re-* [= specific, referentially transparent] reading of (1a) (in (22a)). The interpretation of this reading – and its desired behavior – can be obtained through Quantifier Raising, as usual:

(22) a. $\llbracket[\text{the man}]_1\,[\lambda_1\,[\text{Anna remembers } t_1]]\rrbracket^@$

      $= \exists x.\, man_@(x) \wedge (\exists e.\, remember_@(e, anna, \mathcal{C}_e(\lambda\sigma. E_\sigma(x))))$

     b. $\underline{(\exists x)[\exists\sigma.\, man_\sigma(x) \wedge \neg former\text{-}president_\sigma(x)]}$

  $\Rightarrow$ c. $\exists x.\, former\text{-}president_@(x) \wedge (\exists e.\, remember_@(e, anna, \mathcal{C}_e(\lambda\sigma. E_\sigma(x))))$

6 Outlook

This paper has focused on explaining the individual/scene-ambiguity of DP *remember*-reports. Remarkably, my proposed semantics for these reports – which explains this ambiguity – can also be used to account for the (hitherto neglected) individual/scene-ambiguity of *specific* readings of the object DP in imagination and depiction reports like (2) (see (23)). To force a specific reading of the object DP in (23) (as opposed to (2)), I have raised the DP outside of the scope of the matrix verb.

(23) [A penguin]$_1$ [λ_1 [Penny is painting t_1]]   (see (2a-i))
      $= \exists x.\, penguin_@(x) \wedge \left(\exists e.\, paint_@(e, penny, \mathcal{C}_e(\lambda\sigma.\, E_\sigma(x)))\right)$

    a. Penny is depicting a particular individual, viz. a penguin.

    b. Penny is depicting a particular scene that (saliently) features this individual.

The explanation of this ambiguity is analogous to my explanation of the ambiguity in (1a). In particular, if the referent of the object DP has different properties in the members of $\mathcal{C}_e(\lambda\sigma.\, E_\sigma(x))$, (23) receives an individual-interpretation. If the referent (trivially or non-trivially) has the same properties in all members of $\mathcal{C}_e(\lambda\sigma.\, E_\sigma(x))$, the report can receive a scene-interpretation.

References

1. Armstrong, D.M.: Nominalism and Realism: Volume 1: Universals and Scientific Realism. Cambridge University Press, Cambridge (1978)
2. D'Ambrosio, J., Stoljar, D.: Vendler's puzzle about imagination. Synthese **199**, 12923–12944 (2021). https://doi.org/10.1007/s11229-021-03360-9
3. den Dikken, M., Larson, R., Ludlow, P.: Intensional transitive verbs and abstract clausal complementation. In: Non-Propositional Intentionality, pp. 46–94. Oxford University Press, Oxford and New York (2018)
4. van der Does, J.: A generalized quantifier logic for naked infinitives. Linguist. Philos. **14**(3), 241–294 (1991). https://doi.org/10.1007/BF00627404
5. Fine, K.: Properties, propositions and sets. J. Philos. Log. **6**(1), 135–191 (1977). https://doi.org/10.1007/BF00262054
6. von Fintel, K.: Quantifier domain selection and pseudo-scope. In: Handout of a Talk at the Cornell Conference on Theories of Context Dependency (1999). http://mit.edu/fintel/fintel-1999-cornell-context.pdf
7. Forbes, G.: Objectual attitudes. Linguist. Philos. **23**(2), 141–183 (2000)
8. Forbes, G.: Attitude Problems: An Essay on Linguistic Intensionality. Oxford University Press, Oxford (2006)
9. Frege, G.: Über Sinn und Bedeutung [on Sinn und Bedeutung]. In: Beaney, M. (ed.) The Frege Reader, pp. 151–171. Blackwell, Oxford (1997)
10. Goodman, N.: Languages of Art: An Approach to a Theory of Symbols. Hackett (1969)
11. Kratzer, A.: An investigation of the lumps of thought. Linguist. Philos. **12**(5), 607–653 (1989)

12. Kratzer, A.: Facts: particulars or information units? Linguist. Philos. **5–6**(25), 655–670 (2002)
13. Liefke, K.: A single-type semantics for natural language. Ph.D. thesis, Tilburg University (2014)
14. Liefke, K.: Reasoning with an (experiential) attitude. In: Sakamoto, M., Okazaki, N., Mineshima, K., Satoh, K. (eds.) JSAI-isAI 2019. LNCS (LNAI), vol. 12331, pp. 276–293. Springer, Cham (2020). https://doi.org/10.1007/978-3-030-58790-1_18
15. Liefke, K., Werning, M.: Evidence for single-type semantics: an alternative to e/t-based dual-type semantics. J. Semant. **35**(4), 639–685 (2018)
16. Moltmann, F.: Truthmaker semantics for natural language. Theor. Linguist. **46**(3–4), 159–200 (2020)
17. Openshaw, J.: Remembering objects. Philosophers' Imprint (Accepted). http://www.jamesopenshaw.com/Remembering_objects.pdf
18. Partee, B.: Noun phrase interpretation and type-shifting principles. In: Groenendijk, J., de Jongh, D., Stokhof, M. (eds.) Studies in Discourse Representation Theory and the Theory of Generalized Quantifiers, Dordrecht, pp. 115–143 (1987)
19. Quine, W.V.: Quantifiers and propositional attitudes. J. Philos. **53**, 177–87 (1956)
20. Schwarz, F.: Intensional transitive verbs. In: Gutzmann, D., et al. (ed.) The Wiley Blackwell Companion to Semantics, pp. 1–33. Wiley (2020)
21. Stephenson, T.: Vivid attitudes: centered situations in the semantics of *remember* and *imagine*. Semant. Linguist. Theory (SALT) **20**, 147–160 (2010)
22. de Swart, H.: Scope ambiguities with negative quantifiers. In: von Heusinger, K., Egli, U. (eds.) Reference and Anaphoric Relations. SLAP, vol. 72, pp. 109–132. Springer, Dordrecht (2000). https://doi.org/10.1007/978-94-011-3947-2_6
23. Szabó, Z.G.: Specific, yet opaque. In: Aloni, M., Bastiaanse, H., de Jager, T., Schulz, K. (eds.) Logic, Language and Meaning. LNCS (LNAI), vol. 6042, pp. 32–41. Springer, Heidelberg (2010). https://doi.org/10.1007/978-3-642-14287-1_4
24. Williams, E.S.: Against small clauses. Linguist. Inquiry **14**(2), 287–308 (1983)
25. Zimmermann, T.E.: On the proper treatment of opacity in certain verbs. Nat. Lang. Semant. **1**(2), 149–179 (1993). https://doi.org/10.1007/BF00372561
26. Zimmermann, T.E.: Painting and opacity. In: Freitag, W., Rott, H., Sturm, H., Zinke, A. (eds.) Von Rang und Namen: Philosophical Essays in Honour of Wolfgang Spohn, pp. 427–453. Mentis, Münster (2016)

Factivity Variation in Episodic Memory Reports

Kristina Liefke$^{(\boxtimes)}$ and Markus Werning

Department of Philosophy II, Ruhr University Bochum, 44780 Bochum, Germany
{kristina.liefke,markus.werning}@rub.de
https://www.rub.de/phil-inf/, https://www.rub.de/phil-lang/

Abstract. Recent work in experimental semantics has found that some memory reports fail to give rise to theoretically predicted factivity-inferences (see, e.g., White and Rawlins; de Marneffe et al.). Our paper accounts for one domain of such failures, viz. factivity variation in *episodic* memory reports. The latter are reports like *John remembers a woman dancing* that require the agent's personal experience of a past event or scene. We argue that, in episodic memory reports, the factivity inference is not triggered by the presupposition of the verb *remember* or its complement, but by the veridicality of the underlying experience: if the experience is veridical (as is often the case in perception), the factivity inference arises. If the experience is counterfactual (as is the case in hallucination and dreaming), the inference does not arise. We give a compositional semantics for episodic memory reports that captures this dependence.

Keywords: Episodic memory reports · Experiential attitude reports · Veridicality inferences · Factivity variation · Presupposition · Parasitic attitudes

1 Introduction

The verb *remember* and its cognates (e.g. *recall, recollect, reminisce*) often give rise to factivity inferences.[1] The latter are inferences like (1a) that conclude

The paper has profited from discussions with Kyle Blumberg, Justin D'Ambrosio, Chungmin Lee, and Thomas Ede Zimmermann. Kristina Liefke's contribution is supported by the German Federal Ministry of Education and Research, BMBF (through the WISNA program) and by the German Research Foundation, DFG, as part of the research unit FOR 2812: Constructing Scenarios of the Past (grant 397530566, joint with Markus Werning). Markus Werning's contribution is furthermore supported by FOR 2812 grants no. 419038924, 419040015, and 397530566.

[1] In [48], such inferences are called *veridicality inferences*. We prefer the name *factivity inferences* since it takes seriously the 'backgrounding' of these inferences (for a similar argument, see [14]) and since it allows us to reserve the name *veridicality* for a different (though related) property (see Sect. 4.2).

K. Yada et al. (Eds.): JSAI-isAI 2021 Workshops, LNAI 13856, pp. 110–127, 2023.
https://doi.org/10.1007/978-3-031-36190-6_8

the truth of, e.g., a *that*-clause or gerundival complement (in (1a): *a woman was dancing*) from the truth of a sentence whose matrix verb embeds this complement. Since these inferences project through different entailment-cancelling operators (e.g. through matrix negation, see (1b), and through the scope of a question, see (1c)) – and since they do not contribute at-issue content –, they are often assumed to be presuppositional [14] (see [16,19]). (Below, we use Uegaki's [45] notation for presupposition, $\overset{presup}{\Rightarrow}$):

(1)   a.   John remembers that a woman was dancing.
           $\overset{presup}{\Rightarrow}$ 'A woman was dancing.'

      b.   John does not remember that a woman was dancing.
           $\overset{presup}{\Rightarrow}$ 'A woman was dancing.'

      c.   Does John remember that a woman was dancing?
           $\overset{presup}{\Rightarrow}$ 'A woman was dancing.'

The factivity of the memory report in (1a) is evidenced by the observation that the truth of the complement in (1a) cannot be denied without yielding a contradiction (see the semantic deviance of (2)):

(2)   #John remembers that a was woman dancing, but – in fact – no woman was dancing.

It is also evidenced by the observation that, in contexts in which the speaker explicitly acknowledges their ignorance about the truth of the complement, this acknowledgement cannot be felicitously combined with a sentence that embeds this complement under *remember* (as in (3a); due to [7,8], following [40]):

(3)   a.   #I do not know whether a woman was dancing, but John remembers that a woman was dancing.

      b.   *Contrast:* ✓I do not know whether a woman was dancing, but Mary believes that a woman was dancing.

The factivity of (1a) is further supported by the observation that, in contexts in which the truth of the complement has been established, a speaker can only make a genuine conversational contribution by expressing a knowledge-like attitude towards the content of this complement (see (4a); due to [7]):

(4)   A: A woman was dancing in the park.

      a.   B: ✓I {know, remember} that a woman was dancing in the park.

      b.   B: #I {believe, think} that a woman was dancing in the park.

Analogously to the above, factivity inferences are also valid in some memory reports with gerundival complements (e.g. (5a)). Since these reports require that the agent has personally experienced the event or scene that is described by the complement, we call such reports *episodic memory reports* (following [10,42]).

(5)   *Context:* During last week's picnic in the park, John saw a woman dance.

    a. (Now,) John remembers a/the woman dancing.
        $\overset{\text{presup}}{\Rightarrow}$ 'A woman was dancing (in @).'

The factivity of (5a) is evidenced by the observation that this report likewise passes the tests from (2) to (4) (see (6)–(8)).[2] The possibility of giving these examples a charitable interpretation (see our judgement '?', not '#') suggests that their factivity presupposition has a soft trigger and is easily cancelled (see [2,3]).

(6)   [?]John remembers a woman dancing, but there was no such woman./
                         ..., but no woman was dancing.

(7)   a. [?]I do not know whether a woman was dancing (in @), but John remembers a woman dancing.

    b. *Contrast:* ✓I don't know whether a woman is dancing (in @), but Mary imagines a woman dancing.

(8)   A: A woman was dancing in the park.
    i. B: ✓I remember a woman dancing (in @).
    ii. B: #I imagine a woman dancing (in @).

In contrast to *remember that*-reports, the validity of the factivity inference in episodic memory reports seems to vary with the context.[3] In particular, while this inference is valid in cases (e.g. (5)) where the remembering targets the object of a past (veridical) perception, it is <u>in</u>valid in cases (e.g. (9)) where the remembering targets the object of a past counterfactual experience (in (9): of a dream):

(9)   *Context:* After the picnic, John dozed off and dreamt of a hippo singing.

    a. John remembers a hippo singing.
        $\overset{\text{presup}}{\not\Rightarrow}$ 'A hippo was singing (in @).'
  BUT: $\overset{\text{presup}}{\Rightarrow}$ 'A hippo was singing in John's dream.'

    b. John does not remember a hippo singing.
        $\overset{\text{presup}}{\not\Rightarrow}$ 'A hippo was singing (in @).'

The non-factivity of the memory report in (9a) is evidenced by the fact that – unlike the truth of the complement in (5a) (see (6)) – the truth of the complement in (9a) <u>can</u> be denied without requiring a charitable interpretation (see (10)):

(10)   ✓John remembers a hippo singing, but there was no such hippo (who was singing in @). It all – and only (!) – happened in his dream ...

---

[2] Since *know* and *think* do not accept gerundive complements, we only consider the *remember*-case of (4) in (8), and replace *think* in the 'vacuous' case with *imagine*.

[3] We will show below that the factivity inference can also vary with the report's linguistic context. This is the case when the complement contains a fictional predicate (e.g. *dream(ing)*; see (26) and Sect. 3) or when the embedded content is saliently counterfactual (as in the case of singing hippos or squared circles).

The report in (9a) further <u>fails</u>(!) the speaker's ignorance test (see (11)), and the vacuous dialogue test (see (12)):

(11)   ✓I do not know whether a hippo was singing (in @), but John remembers a hippo singing (viz. in his dream).

(12)   A: A hippo was singing in John's dream.

    a. B: ✓I remember a hippo singing.

    b. B: ✓I imagine a hippo singing.

Note: To apply the speaker's ignorance test to (9a), we evaluate the occurrences of *singing* from (11) w.r.t. different indices (viz. at the actual world, @, resp. at John's oneiric [= dream-] scene). If we had not done this, (11) would be straightforwardly false, due to the falsity of 'John remembers a hippo singing in @'.

Our paper seeks to explain the difference in factivity between (5a) and (9a). To motivate the need for a designated account of factivity variation in episodic memory reports, we first review leading semantic accounts of factivity and factivity variation, and show that they are unable to account for the observed variation (Sect. 2). We then introduce the core idea of our account, viz. the parasitic dependence of memory content on the content of a personal past experience (see Sect. 3). Section 4 provides a compositional semantics for gerundively complemented occurrences of *remember* that has built-in the notion of experiential parasitism. It uses this semantics to account for factivity variation in (5) and (9). The paper closes by suggesting how this semantics can explain the observation that the factivity of some (!) *remember that*-reports (e.g. (13a)) also varies with the context:

(13)   *Context:* After his picnic in the park, John dreamt of a hippo singing.

    a. (Now, John remembers very little about his dream in the park. But)

       He still remembers that a hippo was singing.

       $\overset{\text{presup}}{\nRightarrow}$ 'A hippo was singing (in @).'

2   Existing Accounts

The difference in validity between the factivity inferences in (5a) and (9a) poses a challenge for existing semantic accounts of factivity. Most of these accounts explain factivity inferences like (5a) through the lexical-compositional semantics of the embedding occurrence of *remember* (e.g. (14a); see [13,34]) or through the semantics of the complementizer *that* (e.g. (15a); see [18,19,21]). In (14a) and (15a), the factivity presupposition (i.e. 'p is true at the actual world, @') is underlined.

(14)   a. $[\![\text{remember}_1]\!]^@ = \lambda p^{\langle s,t \rangle} : \underline{p_@}. \lambda z^e. \textit{remember}'_@(z, p)$ (factive)

    b. $[\![\text{remember}_2]\!]^@ = \lambda p^{\langle s,t \rangle}. \lambda z^e. \textit{remember}'_@(z, p)$ (non-factive)

(15)   a. $[\![\text{that}_F]\!] = \lambda p^{\langle s,t \rangle} : \underline{p_@}. \lambda w. p_w$ (factive)

    b. $[\![\text{that}_T]\!] = \lambda p^{\langle s,t \rangle}. \lambda w. p_w$ (non-factive)

In their simplest form, the above accounts straightforwardly capture the factivity inference in (1b) (see (16) resp. (17)):

(16) $[\![(1b)]\!]^@ \equiv [\![not]\!]([\![remember_1]\!]^@([\![John]\!], [\![(that)\ a\ woman\ danced]\!]))$
$= \underline{(\exists x)[woman_@(x) \wedge dance_@(x)]}.$
$\qquad\qquad \neg remember'_@(john, \lambda w\,\exists y.\ woman_w(y) \wedge dance_w(y))$
$\Rightarrow \exists x.\ woman_@(x) \wedge dance_@(x)$

(17) $[\![(1b)]\!]^@ \equiv [\![not]\!]([\![remember_2]\!]^@([\![John]\!], [\![that_F]\!]([\![a\ woman\ danced]\!])))$
$= \neg remember'_@(john, \underline{\exists x.\ woman_@(x) \wedge dance_@(x)}.$
$\qquad\qquad\qquad\qquad \lambda w\,\exists x.\ woman_w(x) \wedge dance_w(x))$
$\equiv (\exists y.\ woman_@(y) \wedge dance_@(y)) \wedge$
$\qquad\qquad \neg remember'_@(john, \lambda w\,\exists y.\ woman_w(y) \wedge dance_w(y))$
$\Rightarrow \exists x.\ woman_@(x) \wedge dance_@(x)$

Assuming Stephenson's [41] semantics for episodic uses of *remember* (see (18)), 'verb-based' accounts (i.e. accounts like (16) that explain factivity inferences through the semantics of the embedding verb) can also capture the gerundive variant of (1a), i.e. (5a). In (18), s is a Kratzer-style situation (see [20]). Since (18) interprets 'remember' as a relation to a situation rather than to a proposition, we use a different non-logical constant for 'remember' in (18), viz. *remember''*:

(18) $[\![remember_3]\!]^@ = \lambda p^{\langle s,t\rangle} \lambda z^e\, \exists s : \underline{p_s \wedge p_@}.\ remember''_@(z, s)$

The need for a different semantics for the interpretation of (5a) (*vis-à-vis* of (1a)) is apparent from the observation that (5a) has different truth-conditions from (1a): to be true, (5a) requires that John has personally (here: visually/perceptually) experienced a woman dancing. The truth of (1a) does not make such requirement. In particular, only (1a) – but not (5a) – is true in a scenario in which Mary told John that a woman had been dancing in the park.

Its merits notwithstanding, the above accounts fail to capture the nonfactivity of (9a): To explain the non-validity of factivity inferences, verb-based accounts could employ Karttunen-style [17] 'plugs' (which block presuppositions from projecting) or could assume that the verb *remember* is ambiguous between two homophonous lexical entries, viz. a factive *remember_1* and a non-factive *remember_2* (see (14)).[4] The non-factivity of (9a) could then be captured by analyzing the matrix verb in this report as *remember_2* (see (14b)):

(19)   a. $[\![(9a)]\!]^@ \equiv [\![remember_2]\!]^@([\![John]\!], [\![a\ hippo\ sang]\!])$
$= remember'_@(john, \lambda w\,\exists x.\ hippo_w(x) \wedge sing_w(x))$
$\not\Rightarrow \exists x.\ hippo_@(x) \wedge sing_@(x)$

However, since plugs typically take the form of lexical material (e.g. a counterfactual attitude verb like *dream*; see (20)) – and since such material is absent in (9a) –, Karttunen's strategy cannot be used to explain the non-factivity of (9a).

---

[4] These two alternatives are given – and rejected – as explanatory options in [8].

(20)   John remembers a hippo singing in his dream.

Analogously to the above, 'complement-based' accounts (i.e. accounts like (17) that explain factivity inferences through the semantics of the complement; see [18,21]) could try to locate the difference between (5a) and (9a) instead in the complement of the matrix verb. The difference in factivity of these reports could then be explained through the use of two different (silent) complementizers, $\emptyset_1$ (our earlier $that_F$; see (21a)) and $\emptyset_2$ (our earlier $that_T$; see (21b)), or of two different silent determiners, Δ_1 and Δ_2, (see (22), where s is a variable over events or scenes). The former strategy follows Kratzer's [21] distinction between a factive and a 'trivial' complementizer $that$. The latter strategy follows Kastner's [18] assumption of a covert presuppositional determiner, Δ.

(21)   a. $[\![\emptyset_1]\!] = \lambda p \colon \underline{p_@}. \lambda w. p_w$ (factive)   b. $[\![\emptyset_2]\!] = \lambda p. \lambda w. p_w$ (non-factive)

(22)   a. $[\![\Delta_1]\!] = \lambda p \colon \underline{p_@}. \eta s. p_s$ (factive)   b. $[\![\Delta_2]\!] = \lambda p. \eta s. p_s$ (non-factive)

The possibility of rephrasing (1a) – but not the $that$-clause variant, (24a), of (9a) – through a $fact$-DP (see (23) vis-$\grave{a}$-vis (24b)) makes the Kastner-style route promising.

(23)   John remembers *the fact* that a woman was dancing (in the real world).

(24)   a.   John remembers that a hippo was singing (in his dream).
       b.   ??John remembers *the fact* that a hippo was singing.

This route has further appeal since the complement in (5a) behaves syntactically very much like a definite DP (see [12]). However, this appeal is weakened by the observation that (5a) and (9a) display the same syntactic behavior. As a result, it seems implausible to analyze them through different silent determiners. The use of Δ_1 and Δ_2 is further challenged by the difficulty of integrating them into existing semantics for the verb *remember*.

Strategy

We propose to explain the difference in factivity between (5a) and (9a) through the observation that the content of the reported remembering depends on the content of an underlying experience.[5] In the context for (5a) (i.e. (5)), this experience is John's (visual) perceiving. In the context for (9a) (i.e. (9)), the relevant experience is John's dreaming. To capture this dependence, we call remembering the *parasite attitude* (following Maier [28]; see [5,6,29]). We dub the experience the *host attitude* (or the *host experience*) and describe the dependence between the two as *experiential parasitism* (see [25]). The different veridicality properties of these experiences (typically: the veridicality of (visual) perception and

---

[5] This dependency motivates the name *experiential remembering* (see, e.g., [4,25]). In psychology and cognitive science, experiential remembering is often called *episodic remembering*, following the work of Endel Tulving (see e.g. [10,43]).

the non-veridicality, or counterfactuality, of dreaming) then explain the different inference behavior of (5a) and (9a): since perception is typically veridical, the factivity inference arises in (5a). Since dreaming is typically counterfactual [= non-veridical], the factivity inference does not arise in (9a).

3   Background: Experiential Parasitism

Our examples in (5) and (9) have explicitly introduced a visual, respectively an oneiric [= dream-]experience on which John's remembering is parasitic. The parasitic dependence of remembering on these primary experiences is supported by the observation that, in the contexts from (5) and (9), (5a) and (9a) can be paraphrased by reports, i.e. (25) resp. (26), that explicitly refer to the target of this experience (here: to the visual scene that features a dancing woman resp. to the oneiric scene that features a singing hippo). In the paraphrases below, the parasite attitude [= remembering] is given a grey frame. The host experience [= visual perception resp. dreaming] is highlighted in grey.

(25)   a. John ⟨remembers⟩ a (particular) visual scene in which a woman was dancing.

    b. John ⟨remembers⟩ the woman whom he saw at the park last week dancing in the park.

(26)   a. John ⟨remembers⟩ an oneiric scene in which a hippo was singing.

    b. John ⟨remembers⟩ the hippo from his dream singing in his dream.

Other examples of experiential parasitism are given in (27) and (28). Example (27) is due to Ninan [32, ex. (18)]. Example (28) is inspired by Blum-berg [6, ex. (102)]:

(27)   Ralph is ⟨imagining⟩ the man whom he sees sneaking around on the flying a kite in an alpine meadow (in his imagination.)

(28)   Ida is ⟨imagining⟩ the unicorn of which she dreamt last night basking in the sun (in her imagination).

In (25)–(28), the parasitic behavior of the reported attitude (there: remembering resp. imagining) is made explicit by the presence of a predicate for the host experience (there: *visual/saw* resp. *oneiric/dreamt*). However, the experience-dependence of episodic memory reports is also evidenced when the experience is not made explicit. This evidence includes intuitively valid inferences from episodic memory reports to reports of the remembering agent's experience of the scene described in the memory report [41] (see (29)–(30)). In what follows, we will call such inferences *experientiality inferences*.

(29)   a. John ⟨remembers⟩ a woman dancing.   (see (5a))

⇒ b. 'John has (seen/perceptually) experienced a woman dancing.'

(30) a. John remembers a hippo singing.   (see (9a))

⇒ b. 'John has (mentally/counterfactually) experienced a hippo singing.'

Support for experiential parasitism further comes from the observation that false memory reports (esp. *misremember*-reports like (31a)) only have intuitive truth-conditions on a reading that evaluates the topic of the complement (i.e. what the statement expressed by the complement is about [22,37]) directly at the experienced scene. The relevant reading still evaluates the comment of the complement (i.e. what is said about the topic) at Bill's mnemonic scenario [= at a designated member of the set of his 'false memory'-alternatives]. In the complement of (31a), the topic expression is the embedded subject pronoun *her*; the comment expression is the embedded predicate *have clear, untattooed skin*. The example in (31) is modelled on Blumberg's [6] 'burgled Bill'-case:

(31) *Context:* Last night, Bill dreamt of a woman with tattoos (no one in particular whom he has come across in real life).

 a. Now, he misremembers her having clear, untattooed skin.

 ≢ i.   *de re:* There exists a tattooed woman whom Bill mis-   (✗) remembers (as) having clear, untattooed skin.

 ≢ ii. *de dicto:* Bill remembers (wrongly) an inconsistent   (✗) situation in which a woman simultaneously did and did not have tattoos.

 ≡ b. Bill misremembers the tattooed woman from his dream   (✓) having clear, untattooed skin.

To capture parasitic dependencies like the above, Blumberg [5] has proposed to parametrize the familiar semantic values of attitude complements (i.e. sets of possible 'parasite' worlds; above: Bill's misremembering-alternatives) by the respective 'host' worlds (here: Bill's oneiric alternatives). This parametrization yields sets of ordered pairs of worlds [= Blumberg's *paired propositions*] (see also [25], [31, Ch. 2]). The first element in these pairs is a 'host' world. The second element is a 'parasite' world that depends on the host alternative.

The syntactic analyses of (31a) in (32) capture this parametrization by positing distinct variables for the alternatives that are introduced by the matrix/parasite attitude (in (31): Bill's misremembering), i.e. w_2, and for the alternatives that are introduced by the host experience (there: Bill's dreaming), i.e. w_1 (see [5,6]; following [33,35]). The readings from (31a-i), (31a-ii), and (31b) are given by the LFs in (32). The relevant LF – on which (31a) is true – is given in (32c).

(32) a. [a woman-in-@] [$\lambda t.$ Bill misremembers in @

$[\lambda w_1 [\lambda w_2. \ t$ has clear skin in $w_2]$]]

b. Bill $\boxed{\text{misremembers}}$ in @

$[\lambda w_1 \, [\lambda w_2. \, \text{a woman-in-}w_2 \text{ has clear skin in } w_2]]$

c. Bill $\boxed{\text{misremembers}}$ in @

$[\lambda w_1 \, [\lambda w_2. \, \text{a woman-in-}w_1 \text{ has clear skin in } w_2]]$

$\underbrace{\qquad\qquad\qquad\qquad\qquad\qquad\qquad\qquad\qquad\qquad}$

(the designator of) a paired proposition

Above, the hyphens in the analysis of *a woman* (see 'woman-in-w') indicate that the topic expression *a woman* has a rigid use w.r.t. the world w. On this use, the semantic value of *a woman* [= the salient female individual in s_1] is constant across all worlds. This individual is then imported in the interpretation of the complement (at w_2, where interpretation is indicated without hyphens). This import can proceed through a rigidifying operator (e.g. through a variant of Kaplan's [15] '*dthat*' that can fix the topic's reference at any world).

Using Blumberg's 'double indexing'-approach, the most plausible readings of (5a) and (9a) are given in (33) respectively in (34):

(33)   John $\boxed{\text{remembers}}$ in @ $[\lambda w_1 \, [\lambda w_2. \, \text{a woman-in-}w_1 \text{ dances in } w_2]]$

(34)   John $\boxed{\text{remembers}}$ in @ $[\lambda w_1 \, [\lambda w_2. \, \text{a hippo-in-}w_1 \text{ sings in } w_2]]$

Note that – analogously to (32c) – the comment expression in (33)/(34) (here: the predicate, *dances* resp. *sings*) is evaluated at the parasite [= memory-] alternative, w_2, while the topic expression (i.e. the embedded subject, *a woman* resp. *a hippo*) is evaluated at the host alternative, w_1. The evaluation of the topic expression at w_1 is needed to 'anchor' the actual referent of *a woman* resp. *a hippo* to the host experience. The evaluation of the comment at w_2 is required by Percus' *Generalization X*. The latter demands that the situation variable that a predicate selects for must be co-indexed with the nearest lambda above it [33, p. 41].

Admittedly, the interpretation of the topic and the comment in (5a) at different alternatives goes against the intuition from (25) (which interprets both *a woman* and *dance* w.r.t. John's visual scene from the park).[6] Our interpretation of episodic uses of *remember* solves this problem, as we will show below.

4   A Uniform Semantics for Episodic *Remember*

To capture the parasitic dependence of remembering on a personally experienced event, we give episodic uses of *remember* the semantics in (35). The latter is a uniform semantics that is used in the interpretation of the factive (5a) [*John remembers a woman dancing*] and of the non-factive (9a) [*John remembers a hippo singing*]:

---

[6] An analogous observation holds w.r.t. and (9a) and (26).

$$\overbrace{\qquad\qquad\qquad}^{\text{experientiality requirement}}$$

(35) $[\![\text{remember}_{\text{EXP}}]\!]^{@} = \lambda R \lambda z \lambda e \,(\exists e')\,[\,exp_{w_{@}}(e', z) \wedge (\exists s_1 \colon \underline{s_1 < w_{@}}.\, s_1 < \omega(e')$

$\wedge \, remember_{@}(e, z, \eta_e s_2 \colon \underline{s_2 = s_1}.\, R(s_1, s_2)))\,]$

$$\underbrace{\qquad\qquad\qquad}_{\text{the object of remembering: a situation}}$$

Above, $exp_{w_{@}}(e', z)$ expresses that, in (some specific spatio-temporal location of) the world, $w_{@}$, of which @ is part, the agent z has had an experience e'. ω is a function that maps the event of z's experiencing, e', to the situation (or scene) that serves as the object of z's experience. For John's seeing event from (5), this object is the scene (perceived from John's particular visual perspective in the park) in which a woman is dancing. The partiality of the inclusion between the memory object, s_1, and the experience object, $\omega(e')$, i.e. $s_1 < \omega(e')$, is motivated by the observation that agents typically only remember a part of the experienced scene.

The semantics in (35) construes episodic remembering as a relation to a situation (i.e. an event or scene, $\eta_e s_2.\, R(s_1, s_2)$) whose content z has previously experienced with their own senses (see [10,41]). Since the situation that serves as the object of episodic remembering intuitively varies with the remembering event, e, we identify it through a choice function, η_e, that is dependent on e. This function selects a situation from the 'classical' proposition (viz. the set of situations, $\lambda s_2.\, R(s_1, s_2)$) that results from filling the first argument slot of a paired proposition (R) with the 'host' situation, s_1 (in (5a): with John's perceived visual scene in which a woman is dancing). For the semantic value of the complement in (33) (see (36a)), this classical proposition is the set of possible worlds in which the woman from s_1 dances, i.e. $\{w : \text{a woman-in-}s_1 \text{ dances in } w\}$ (see (36b)). To enable the identification of memory objects with (partial) situations (rather than total worlds), we generalize possible worlds to possible situations, s.

(36) a. $[\![\lambda s'\,[\lambda s.\ \text{a woman-in-}\boldsymbol{s'}\ \text{dances in } s]]\!]\,(s_1)$

$$\underbrace{\qquad\qquad\qquad}_{\text{a paired proposition}}$$

$= $ b. $\lambda s' \lambda s\,(\exists x)\,[\,dthat\,(\iota y.\, woman_{\boldsymbol{s'}}(y)) = x \wedge dance_s(x)]\,(s_1)$

$\equiv \lambda s\,(\exists x)\,[\,dthat\,(\iota y.\, woman_{\boldsymbol{s_1}}(y)) = x \wedge dance_s(x)]$

$$\underbrace{\qquad\qquad\qquad}_{\text{a 'classical' proposition}}$$

In (36b), $dthat$ is a situation-general variant of Kaplan's 'dthat'-operator. To obtain an easy translation of *a woman* in (5a), we use Russell's iota operator [38,39]. Our use of this operator (esp. of its uniqueness requirement) is warranted by the observation that John's misremembering in (31a) concerns a specific woman (viz. the woman whom he has seen at the park).

4.1 Capturing Experientiality Inferences

We have already pointed out that episodic memory reports give rise to experientiality inferences (see (29)–(30); the former is copied in (37)):

(37) a. John │remembers│ a woman dancing.

⇒ b. 'John has (seen/perceptually) experienced a woman dancing.'

To capture the validity of these inferences, we place an 'experientiality requirement' on episodic uses of *remember*. This requirement demands that, in (some specific spatio-temporal location of) the world, $w_@$, of which @ is part, the agent has had[7] an experience, e' (see $\exists e'.\, exp_{w_@}(e', z)$), whose object, $\omega(e')$ [= the experienced situation], is informationally included in the object of their remembering, $[s_1 =]\, \eta_e\, s_2.\, R(s_1, s_2)$ (i.e. $s_1 \leq \omega(e')$).[8]

The required inclusion relation between the objects of memory and experience ensures that the agent's experience is relevant to the reported remembering. This relation e.g. excludes the use of episodic *remember* for the description of vicarious memories (see (38)). The latter are non-actual mental experiences (typically: the product of another agent's vivid description of an emotionally intense event) that have the same phenomenological qualities (e.g. imagery, perspectivity, emotional intensity) as an actual, real-world experience [27,30,36] (see [47]).

(38) *Context:* Paul has never seen a woman dancing in the park, but John has. In fact, John has told Paul about the woman and her dancing in meticulous detail on so many occasions that Paul has come to believe that he has himself witnessed the event.

a. #Paul remembers a woman dancing.

Our semantics for episodic *remember* straightforwardly captures the inference in (37)/(29).[9] This is so since, given $s_2 = s_1$, the situation (i.e. s_2) in which the woman-in-s_1 dances will be part of the object, $\omega(e')$, of John's experience. (Since the unique (!) referent of *a woman* is determined <u>at</u> $\omega(e')$ – and since (29b) does not require exporting the referent-at-s_1 of *a woman* to another situation –, we can safely replace '$\exists x.\, dthat\,(\iota y.\, woman_{s_1}(y)) = x$' by '$\exists x.\, woman_{\omega(e')}(x)$' in (39b).)

(39) a. $[\![$John remembers$_{\text{EXP}}$ $[\lambda s'\,[\lambda s.\, \text{a woman-in-}s'\ \text{dances in}\ s]]]\!]^@$

$= [\![\text{remember}_{\text{EXP}}]\!]([\![\text{John}]\!], [\lambda s'\,[\lambda s.\, \text{a woman-in-}\boldsymbol{s'}\ \text{dances in}\ s]])$

$= [\![\text{remember}_{\text{EXP}}]\!](john,$ \hfill ($\downarrow$ see (36b))

$\lambda s'\lambda s\,(\exists x)\big[dthat\,(\iota y.\, woman_{s'}(y)) = x \wedge dance_s(x)\big])$

---

[7] To keep our semantics as simple as possible, we assume that the 'past-directedness' of remembering (i.e. that the point in time at which the experience event e' occurred precedes the point in time of the remembering event e, i.e. $t_{e'} \prec t_e$) is built into *exp*.

[8] Following [24, p. 659], we assume that a situation, s_1, includes a situation s_2, i.e. $s_2 \leq s_1$), if the location l_1 and time t_1 of the world-part about which s_1 contains contextually salient information includes the location l_2 and time t_2 of the world-part about which s_2 contains contextually salient information (s.t. l_1 maintains or expands the perimeters of l_2 and t_1 starts before or simultaneously with t_2 and ends after or simultaneously with t_2.

[9] In the final compositional step in (39), we introduce existential closure over the remembering event e, as is common in Neo-Davidsonian semantics (see e.g. [9]).

$$\begin{aligned}= (\exists e)\,(\exists e')\,\overbrace{[exp_{w_@}(e',john) \wedge (\exists s_1\colon \underline{s_1 < w_@}\,.\,s_1 < \omega(e')\,\wedge}^{\text{experientiality requirement}}\\remember_@\,(e, john, \eta_e\,s_2\colon \underline{s_2 = s_1}.\\\exists x.\,dthat\,(\iota y.\,woman_{s_1}(y)) = x \wedge dance_{s_2}(x)))]\end{aligned}$$

$$\Rightarrow \text{ b. } (\exists e')\,[exp_{w_@}(e',john) \wedge (\exists s_1\colon \underline{s_1 < w_@}\,.\,s_1 < \omega(e')\,\wedge\\(\exists x.\,dthat\,(\iota y.\,woman_{s_1}(y)) = x \wedge dance_{s_2}(x)))]$$

$$\equiv (\exists e'\colon \underline{\omega(e') < w_@})\,[exp_{w_@}(e',john) \wedge (\exists x.\,woman_{\omega(e')}(x) \wedge dance_{\omega(e')}(x))]$$

$$= [\![\text{John has experienced a woman dancing}]\!]^@$$

The modelling of the inference in (30) is fully analogous.

Note that, in the semantics for *remember* in (35), the experientiality requirement contributes primary [= at issue-]content, rather than just secondary (e.g. presuppositional) content. The at-issue status of the experience is apparent from the fact that the experience is entailed by positive episodic *remember*-reports like (5a) (see (5)), but does not project through negation (see (40)). It is further supported by the observation that the agent's having had the experience can be directly targeted by negation (see (41)):

(40)   John does not remember a woman dancing.
       $\not\Rightarrow$ 'John has witnessed [= experienced/seen] a woman dancing.'

(41)   a.   Paul: I remember a woman dancing in the park yesterday.
       b.   John: $^\checkmark$That can't be true. You weren't even there – I told you about
            it/her over dinner after I returned.

Note that (39) leaves the particular mode of the experience (expectedly: visual perception) unspecified. In (5), this mode is provided by the situational, real-world context. Alternatively, the mode of the experience could be specified linguistically (e.g. by an overt predicate for this mode; see (25b), copied in (42)) or by a default assumption about the identity of this mode (e.g. visual perception [47]).

(42)   John $\boxed{\text{remembers}}$ the woman $\boxed{\text{whom he saw at the park}}$ ... dancing.

4.2   Capturing Factivity Inferences

Intuitively, different modes of experience (here: visual perception vs. dreaming) have different veridicality properties. For example, visual perception is typically taken to be veridical, in the sense that it validates inferences of the form of (43). Imagination, hallucination, and dreaming are often taken to be non-veridical, in the sense that they do <u>not</u> validate such inferences (see (44)).[10]

---

[10] Much of the contemporary semantics literature treats fiction verbs like *imagine* and *dream* as anti-veridical (or anti-factive) predicates (see e.g. [11,44]). The latter are predicates that entail (resp. presuppose) the falsity of their complement (see (†)):

(43) a. John has seen [= visually perceived] a woman dance(ing).
  $\Rightarrow$ b. 'A woman was dancing (in @).'

(44) a. John has dreamt of a hippo singing.
  $\not\Rightarrow$ b. 'A hippo was singing (in @).'

Our semantics for episodic uses of *remember* treats <u>veridical</u> experience-based memory as the default case. It implements this default by presupposing that the object of the agent's remembering (in (35): $[s_1 =] \, \eta_e \, s_2. \, R(s_1, s_2)$) is informationally included in the world, $w_@$, in which the remembering event e is located (i.e. $s_1 < w_@$). On its global interpretation, this presupposition validates the factivity inference from (5a) (see (45)):

(45) a. global: $[\![$John has experienced a woman dancing$]\!]^@$
  $= (\exists e')\big[\underline{\omega(e') < w_@} \wedge exp_{w_@}(e', john) \wedge$
  $\qquad\qquad\qquad (\exists x. \, woman_{\omega(e')}(x) \wedge dance_{\omega(e')}(x))\big]$
  $\equiv (\exists e')\big[exp_{w_@}(e', john) \wedge (\exists x)\big[(woman_{\omega(e')}(x) \wedge dance_{\omega(e')}(x)) \wedge$
  $\qquad\qquad\qquad\qquad (woman_{\boldsymbol{w_@}}(x) \wedge dance_{\boldsymbol{w_@}}(x))\big] \quad \big]$
  $\Rightarrow$ b. $(\exists x)[woman_{w_@}(x) \wedge dance_{w_@}(x)]$
  $= [\![$A woman is dancing$]\!]^{\boldsymbol{w_@}} \; = \; [\![$A woman was dancing$]\!]^@$

It is well-known that embedded presuppositions can be cancelled (or *suspended*; see e.g. [1, 16, 40]). This holds in particular for for the presuppositions of so- called 'soft' triggers [3] (incl. cognitive factives like *recognize* and *remember*; see [1]). Abrusán [2] has proposed that the complements of factive verbs are only presupposed in the absence of additional contextual information. When such information is present (as is the case in our 'John dreaming' example, see (46a)), the presupposition may not even be triggered in the first place (see [3, p. 182]). Given our semantics for episodic uses of *remember*, Abrusán's account straightforwardly explains both the validity of the factivity inference in (5a) (see (45)) and the non-validity of this inference in (9a) (see (46a)):

(46) *Note:* Below, the ///-strikeout of '$\omega(e') < w_@$' expresses that the context in (9) (or equivalently, the preposition *from his dream* in (26b)) blocks the triggering of the presupposition that $\omega(e') < w_@$.

  a. $[\![$John has experienced a hippo singing$]\!]^@$
  $= [\![$A hippo is singing in John's (non-veridical) experience$]\!]^@$
  $= (\exists e' \; : \; \cancel{\psi(e')} \cancel{<} \cancel{w_@})\big[exp_{w_@}(e', john) \wedge (\exists x. \, hippo_{\omega(e')}(x) \wedge$
  $sing_{\omega(e')}(x))\big]$

($\dagger$) a. John has dreamt of a hippo singing.
  $\Rightarrow$ b. 'It is not the case that a hippo was singing (in @).'

Since non-veridicality is a weaker property than anti-veridicality, we here treat *dream* as a non-veridical predicate.

$\not\Rightarrow$ b. $(\exists x)[hippo_{w_@}(x) \land sing_{w_@}(x)]$

$\quad = [\![\text{A hippo is singing}]\!]^{w_@} = [\![\text{A hippo was singing}]\!]^{@}$

We close this section by applying our proposed semantics to reports of false memories. Since these reports can also contain episodic uses of *remember*, they have an interesting effect on the validity of factivity inferences in reports of memories of veridical experiences.

4.3   Reports of False Episodic Memories

We have observed in (38) that episodic memory reports can<u>not</u> be used to report vicarious memories. However, such reports are often felicitously used to report *false* memories (see (47)):

(47)   *Context:* During last week's picnic, John saw a woman dancing.

     a. John remembers the woman wearing sneakers. ✓But in fact, she was dancing barefoot.

$\equiv$ b. John { falsely remembers, misremembers} a woman wearing sneakers.

These uses also extend to reports of (false) memories of non-veridical experiences:

(48)   *Context:* After the picnic, John dozed off and dreamt of a hippo singing.

     a. John remembers the hippo tapping its feet. ✓But (in John's dream) it wasn't tapping its feet.

$\equiv$ b. John {falsely remembers, misremembers} a hippo tapping its feet.

Our semantics for episodic uses *remember* can capture these cases. This is so since the identity between the situation s_1 (at which *a woman* resp. *a hippo* is interpreted) and the object of remembering (at which the comment is interpreted) is also encoded as a presupposition. The possibility of cancelling this presupposition then captures cases of misremembering (see, e.g., (49)):

(49)   a. $[\![\text{John remembers}_{\text{EXP}} [\lambda s' [\lambda s. \text{ a woman-in-}s' \text{ wears sneakers in } s]]]\!]^{@}$

$\quad = (\exists e)(\exists e')\big[exp_{w_@}(e', john) \land (\exists s_1\colon \underline{s_1 < w_@}. \, s_1 < \omega(e') \land remember_@(e, john,$

$\quad \eta_e \, s_2 \colon \underline{\not{s_2} \neq \not{s_1}}. \, \exists x. \, dthat \, (\iota y. \, woman_{s_1}(y)) = x \land wears \; sneakers_{s_2}(x)))\big]$

$\Rightarrow$ b. $(\exists e')\big[exp_{w_@}(e', john) \land (\exists x)[(woman_{\omega(e')}(x)) \land (woman_{w_@}(x))]\big]$

$\quad = [\![\text{John has experienced (there being) a woman}]\!]^{w_@}$

$\Rightarrow$ c. $[\![\text{There is a woman}]\!]^{w_@} = (\exists x)[woman_{w_@}(x)]$

$\not\Rightarrow$ d. $[\![\text{A woman is wearing sneakers}]\!]^{w_@}$

(49) is consistent with cases where the woman from the park is only wearing sneakers in John's memory, but not in John's veridical perception (from the park). The satisfaction of the presupposition '$s_2 = s_1$' is thus a criterion for the accuracy of the episodic memory.

Since inaccurate remembering introduces memory content that was not part of the original experience (in (47a): that the woman was wearing sneakers), it is another source (next to the experience's non-veridicality) for the invalidity of factivity inferences in episodic memory reports (see (49b–d)).

The observation that s_1 and s_2 come apart in misremembering justifies our use of Blumberg-style paired propositions as inputs to the compositional machinery in (35): Without this observation – and the attendant co-evaluation of the topic and the comment expression in all cases –, it would suffice to stick to 'classical' [= one-dimensional] propositions. We have shown in [25] that, since Blumberg's framework is required for the interpretation of episodic misremembering and imagistic imagining, only *it* enables the systematic discussion and treatment of different experiential attitude verbs.

5 Outlook

Our discussion in this paper has focused on episodic memory reports that are expressed by embedded gerundives. Recent work on clausal selection suggests that episodic memory recall can also be expressed through *remember that*-constructions (e.g. (50a); see [23,41]). This especially holds for languages (e.g. German) where 'remember' rejects gerundive complements: while German can report episodic recall through a non-manner *how-* [*wie-*]clause DP (in (51a); see [46]), *that-* [*dass-*]clause reports like (51b) are much more frequently used for this purpose.

(50) *Context:* After his picnic in the park, John dreamt of a hippo singing.

   a. (Today,) John still remembers that a hippo was singing.
      $\overset{\text{presup}}{\not\Rrightarrow}$ 'A hippo was singing (in @).'

(51) a. John {erinnert sich, weiß noch}, <u>wie</u> ein Nilpferd gesungen hat.
      [*gloss:* John {remembers-REFL, knows still}, how a hippo sung has.]

   b. John {erinnert sich, weiß noch}, <u>dass</u> ein Nilpferd gesungen hat.

In future work, we will study whether factivity variation also arises in reports like (50a) and (51b), and – if this should turn out to be the case – how our account can capture factivity variation in these reports. This work will also identify markers and diagnostics that help distinguish episodic uses of *remember that*-reports (e.g. (50a); which we expect will be subject to factivity variation) from 'propositional' *remember that*-reports (e.g. (52); which we expect will always be factive); see [26]).

(52) John remembers {[✓]that kumquats are fruit, [#]kumquats being fruit}.

References

1. Abbott, B.: Where have some of the presuppositions gone? In: Birner, B., Ward, G. (eds.) Drawing the Boundaries of Meaning, pp. 1–20. John Benjamins (2006)
2. Abrusán, M.: Predicting the presuppositions of soft triggers. Linguist. Philos. **34**(6), 491–535 (2011). https://doi.org/10.1007/s10988-012-9108-y
3. Abrusán, M.: Presupposition cancellation: explaining the 'soft-hard' trigger distinction. Nat. Lang. Semant. **24**, 165–202 (2016). https://doi.org/10.1007/s11050-016-9122-7
4. Bernecker, S.: Memory: A Philosophical Study. Oxford University Press, Oxford (2010)
5. Blumberg, K.: Counterfactual attitudes and the relational analysis. Mind **127**(506), 521–546 (2018)
6. Blumberg, K.: Desire, imagination, and the many-layered mind. Ph.D. thesis, New York University (2019)
7. Bondarenko, T.: Factivity alternation due to semantic composition: *think* and *remember* in Barguzin Buryat. Master's thesis, Massachusetts Institute of Technology, March 2019
8. Bondarenko, T.: Factivity from pre-existence. Glossa **109**, 1–35 (2020)
9. Champollion, L.: The interaction of compositional semantics and event semantics. Linguist. Philos. **38**, 31–66 (2016). https://doi.org/10.1007/s10988-014-9162-8
10. Cheng, S., Werning, M., Suddendorf, T.: Dissociating memory traces and scenario construction in mental time travel. Neurosci. Biobehav. Rev. **60**, 82–89 (2016)
11. Giannakidou, A., Mari, A.: Truth and Veridicality in Grammar and Thought. The University of Chicago Press, Chicago (2021)
12. Grimm, S., McNally, L.: The -*ing* dynasty. Semant. Linguist. Theory (SALT) **25**, 82–102 (2015)
13. Hintikka, J.: Semantics for propositional attitudes. In: Hintikka, J. (ed.) Models for Modalities. SYLI, vol. 23, pp. 87–111. Springer, Dordrecht (1969). https://doi.org/10.1007/978-94-010-1711-4_6
14. Jeong, S.: The effect of prosody on veridicality inferences in Korean. In: Sakamoto, M., Okazaki, N., Mineshima, K., Satoh, K. (eds.) JSAI-isAI 2019. LNCS (LNAI), vol. 12331, pp. 133–147. Springer, Cham (2020). https://doi.org/10.1007/978-3-030-58790-1_9
15. Kaplan, D.: Demonstratives: an essay on the semantics, logic, metaphysics, and epistemology of demonstratives and other indexicals. In: Almog, J., Perry, J., Wettstein, H. (eds.) Themes from Kaplan, pp. 489–563. Oxford University Press (1989)
16. Karttunen, L.: Some observations on factivity. Res. Lang. Soc. Interact. **4**(1), 55–69 (1971)
17. Karttunen, L.: Presuppositions of compound sentences. Linguist. Inquiry **4**(2), 169–193 (1973)
18. Kastner, I.: Factivity mirrors interpretation. Lingua **164**, 156–188 (2015)
19. Kiparsky, P., Kiparsky, C.: Fact. In: Bierwisch, M., Heidolph, K.E. (eds.) Progress in Linguistics, pp. 143–173. De Gruyter Mouton (1970)
20. Kratzer, A.: Facts: particulars or information units? Linguist. Philos. **5–6**(25), 655–670 (2002)
21. Kratzer, A.: Decomposing attitude verbs. Manuscript (2006)
22. Krifka, M.: Basic notions of information structure. Acta Linguistica Hungarica **55**(3–4), 243–276 (2008)

23. Liefke, K.: Two kinds of English non-interrogative, non-manner *how*-complements. In: Jędrzejowski, L., Umbach, C. (eds.) Non-Interrogative Subordinate Wh-Clauses. Oxford Studies in Theoretical Linguistics, Oxford University Press (to appear)

24. Liefke, K., Werning, M.: Evidence for single-type semantics: an alternative to *e/t*-based dual-type semantics. J. Semant. **35**(4), 639–685 (2018)

25. Liefke, K., Werning, M.: Experiential imagination and the inside/outside-distinction. In: Okazaki, N., Yada, K., Satoh, K., Mineshima, K. (eds.) JSAI-isAI 2020. LNCS (LNAI), vol. 12758, pp. 96–112. Springer, Cham (2021). https://doi.org/10.1007/978-3-030-79942-7_7

26. Liefke, K.: Experiential attitude reports. Philos. Compass, e12913 (2023). https://doi.org/10.1111/phc3.12913

27. Loftus, E.F.: The reality of repressed memories. Am. Psychol. **48**(5), 518–537 (1993)

28. Maier, E.: Parasitic attitudes. Linguist. Philos. **38**(3), 205–236 (2015). https://doi.org/10.1007/s10988-015-9174-z

29. Maier, E.: Referential dependencies between conflicting attitudes. J. Philos. Log. **46**(2), 141–167 (2017). https://doi.org/10.1007/s10992-016-9397-7

30. McCarroll, C.J.: Remembering the personal past: beyond the boundaries of imagination. Front. Psychol. **11**, 26–52 (2020)

31. Ninan, D.: Imagination, content, and the self. Ph.D. thesis, Massachusetts Institute of Technology (2008)

32. Ninan, D.: Counterfactual attitudes and multi-centered worlds. Semant. Pragmatics **5**(5), 1–57 (2012)

33. Percus, O.: Constraints on some other variables in syntax. Nat. Lang. Semant. **8**, 173–229 (2000). https://doi.org/10.1023/A:1011298526791

34. Percus, O.: Antipresuppositions. In: Studies of Reference and Anaphora, pp. 52–73 (2006)

35. Percus, O.: Index-dependence and embedding. In: Gutzmann, D., Matthewson, L., Meier, C., Rullmann, H., Zimmermann, T.E. (eds.) The Companion to Semantics. Wiley, Oxford (2020)

36. Pillemer, D.B., Steiner, K.L., Kuwabara, K.J., Kirkegaard Thomsen, D., Svob, C.: Vicarious memories. Conscious. Cogn. **36**, 233–245 (2015)

37. Reinhart, T.: Pragmatics and linguistics: an analysis of sentence topics. Philosophica **27**, 53–94 (1982)

38. Russell, B.: On denoting. Mind **14**(56), 479–493 (1905)

39. Russell, B.: Introduction to Mathematical Philosophy. Allen & Unwin, London (1919)

40. Simons, M.: On the conversational basis of some presuppositions. Semant. Linguist. Theory (SALT) **11**, 431–448 (2001)

41. Stephenson, T.: Vivid attitudes: centered situations in the semantics of *remember* and *imagine*. Semant. Linguist. Theory (SALT) **20**, 147–160 (2010)

42. Tulving, E.: Memory and consciousness. Can. J. Psychol. **26**, 1–26 (1985)

43. Tulving, E.: Episodic memory and autonoesis: uniquely human? In: Terrace, H.S., Metcalfe, J. (eds.) The Missing Link in Cognition: Origins of Self-Reflective Consciousness, pp. 3–56. Oxford University Press, Oxford (2005)

44. Uegaki, W.: Content nouns and the semantics of question-embedding. J. Semant. **33**(4), 623–660 (2016)

45. Uegaki, W.: The existential/uniqueness presupposition of *wh*-complements projects from the answers. Linguist. Philos. **44**, 911–951 (2021). https://doi.org/10.1007/s10988-020-09309-4

46. Umbach, C., Hinterwimmer, S., Gust, H.: German *wie*-complements: manners, methods and events in progress. Nat. Lang. Linguist. Theory **40**, 307–343 (2022). https://doi.org/10.1007/s11049-021-09508-z
47. Vendler, Z.: Vicarious experience. Revue de Métaphysique et de Morale **84**(2), 161–173 (1979)
48. White, A.S.: Lexically triggered veridicality inferences. In: Östman, J.O., Verschueren, J. (eds.) Handbook of Pragmatics, pp. 115–148. John Benjamins Publishing Co. (2019)

The Duality of Negative Attitudes in Japanese Conditionals

Shun Ihara[1]([⊠])(iD) and Yuta Tatsumi[2]

[1] Graduate School of Intercultural Studies, Kobe University, Kobe, Japan
iharashun0@gmail.com
[2] Department of English, Meikai University, Urayasu, Japan
ytats0074@meikai.ac.jp

Abstract. This study investigates semantic properties of Japanese *mono-nara* conditionals that obligatorily encode subjunctivity of the antecedent. Considering the existence of two distinct negative meanings conveyed by *mono-nara* conditionals, we attempt to explain this flexible negativity from the semantics of *mono-nara* and the associated modal in a compositional manner. The analysis contributes to providing a cross-linguistically interesting strategy for deriving negativity of conditional antecedents.

Keywords: Conditionals · Negative attitude · Modality · Japanese

1 Introduction

Japanese has several expressions for conditionals. As shown in (1), the *nara* conditional, one of the most frequently appeared conditional constructions in Japanese, can appear with tensed clauses (both present and past tenses) [2,12].

(1) **Nara conditional**
    mosi Taro-ga   {kuru | kita} nara, minna-ga   odoroku daroo.
    if   Taro-NOM comes came COND everyone-NOM surprise MOD

    Lit. 'If Taro {comes|came}, everyone will be surprised.'

The conditional morpheme *nara* can form another conditional statement. As exemplified in (2), the antecedent clause includes the conditional form *nara* with the light noun *mono* 'thing'. We refer to this construction as *mono-nara* conditionals. A notable feature of these conditionals is that they generally require that

The paper has profited from discussions with Muyi Yang. Financial support was provided by JSPS KAKENHI (Grant Number 21K13000) to the first author. All errors are of course our own.

K. Yada et al. (Eds.): JSAI-isAI 2021 Workshops, LNAI 13856, pp. 128–144, 2023.
https://doi.org/10.1007/978-3-031-36190-6_9

the predicate be marked by the subjunctive expression $[y]oo$ while disallowing a tense marking.[1]

(2)   ***Mono-nara* conditional**
   mosi Taro-ga   {**kuru* | **kita* | *ko-yoo*}   *mono-nara,*
   if   Taro-NOM   come   came   come-MOD   MONO-COND
   minna-ga   *odoroku daroo.*
   everyone-NOM surprise MOD

   Lit. 'If Taro comes, everyone will be surprised.'

In what ways does this particular type of conditional differ from the ordinary conditionals, and how does the difference arise? In this study, we observe that *mono-nara* conditionals are conditionals that induce negativity of the antecedent, and the flavor of the negativity is 'flexible' in that it can be epistemic or deontic. We attempt to capture the fact from the semantics of *mono-nara* and the associated modal in a compositional manner.

2   Negative Attitudes of *Mono-nara* Conditionals

This section observes semantic properties of *mono-nara* conditionals that have not been reported in the literature. First, *mono-nara* conditionals, as exemplified in (3b), always signal the subjunctive mood, in the sense that they are always associated with a negative possibility (or desirability, as we will observe later) toward the antecedent.[2]

(3)   **Context**: before the toss of the coin, the speaker says ...

   a.   *mosi koin-no   omote-ga deta   nara,*
       if   coin-GEN   head-NOM came.out   COND
       kare-wa ooyorokobi-suru daroo.
       he-TOP   big.pleasure-do   MOD

       'If the coin comes up heads, he will be very happy.'

   b.   *mosi koin-no   omote-ga de-yoo   mono-nara,*
       if   coin-GEN   head-NOM come.out-MOD   MONO-COND
       kare-wa ooyorokobi-suru daroo.
       he-TOP   big.pleasure-do   MOD

       'If the coin came up heads, he would be very happy.'

---

[1] We represent the subjunctive marker as "$[y]oo$" throughout this paper. The form *-oo* occurs when the marker attaches to verbal bases ending a consonant, whereas *yoo* is used when it follows verbal bases ending a vowel. Note also that the conditional morpheme *nara* cannot follow $[y]oo$ without the intervening light noun *mono* 'thing' (e.g., "*Taro-ga ko-yoo* *(*mono*) *nara,* ..." 'If Taro comes, ...').

[2] The example is similar to what [6] refers to as the *future less vivid* conditionals, which have the implicature that the actual world is more likely to become a $\neg p$-world than a p-world.

In the given context, we do not yet know whether the coin comes up heads or tails, and (3a, b) are interpreted as non-counterfactual conditionals. (3a) is an ordinary indicative conditional that signals that it is an open possibility that the coin comes up heads. On the other hand, even though the actual probability of a coin coming up heads or tails is the same, 50%, the intuition that we obtain from (3b) is that the speaker believes the propositional content expressed by the antecedent (i.e., *the coin comes up heads*) to be unlikely.

This unlikelihood conveyed by *mono-nara* conditionals can be seen in the contrast in (4). While the standard *nara* conditional in (4a) is compatible with the utterance expressing a high probability of the antecedent (as underlined in the translation), the *mono-nara* conditional in (4b) cannot be compatible with the very same utterance. (The English translations in (4a, b) are excerpted from [6] who argues that the *future less vivid* conveys unlikelihood.)

(4) **Context**: the speaker would like John to come to the party today.

    a. *mosi John-ga   kuru   nara,*
       if   John-NOM come.PRES MONO-COND
       watasi-wa kuru to omou   kedo, paatii-wa   moriagaru daroo.
       I-TOP   come C think.PRES but party-TOP excite   MOD

       'If John comes to the party, <u>and I think he will</u>, we will have a great time.'

    b.# *mosi John-ga   ko-yoo   mono-nara,*
       if   John-NOM come-MOD MONO-COND
       watasi-wa kuru to omou   kedo, paatii-wa   moriagaru daroo.
       I-TOP   come C think.PRES but party-TOP excite   MOD
       #
       'If John came to the party, <u>and I think he will</u>, we would have a great time.'

Another notable feature of *mono-nara* conditionals is that they induce the *undesirability* of the antecedent. For instance, the speaker in (5b) is not committed to an unlikelihood of [*p*: *the addressee climbs the mountain*] but to the preference of ¬*p* over *p*.

(5) **Context**: the addressee, who likes to climb mountains, is about to climb a mountain where there is much danger from bears.

    a. *sono yama-ni   nobot tara   kuma-ga   deru   zo.*
       that mountain-to climb COND bear-NOM appear DP
       dakara {nobor-e | noboru-na}.
       so   climb-IMP   climb-IMP.NEG

       Lit. 'If you climb that mountain, you will see a bear. So {climb | don't climb}.'

   b. *sono yama-ni   nobor-oo   mono-nara   kuma-ga   deru   zo.*
      that mountain-to climb-MOD MONO-COND bear-NOM appear DP
      dakara {#nobor-e | noboru-na}.
      so   climb-IMP   climb-IMP.NEG

      Lit. 'If you climb that mountain, you will see a bear. So {#climb | don't climb}.'

The undesirability of the conditional antecedent is indicated by the positive and negative imperatives. We assume that imperatives $Imp(p)$ encode a preference to p [3]. (5b) is unacceptable because of the conflict between the undesirability expressed by the *mono-nara* conditional and the imperative continuation. In contrast, the effect of undesirability is not mandatory in ordinary conditionals, (5a); the positive imperative in (5a) is natural in a situation where, for example, the addressee wants to hunt a bear.[3]

It is worth noting that the observation here is consistent with [1]'s *desirability table* in (6a) (cf. the classical truth table in (6b)). [1] argues that natural language conditionals are devices for encoding the speaker's affective stance where the relevant notions are (un)desirable rather than truth values, and proposes the desirability logic for conditionals: in ⌜$p \rightarrow q$⌝, p and q must not conflict in the value of desirability. That is, a combination of ⌜DESIRABLE → DESIRABLE⌝ and ⌜UNDESIRABLE → UNDESIRABLE⌝ are possible, while ⌜DESIRABLE → UNDESIRABLE⌝ and ⌜UNDESIRABLE → DESIRABLE⌝ are impossible (where "(UN)DESIRABLE" stands for a proposition encoding the speaker's (un)desirability).

(6)   a.   [1]'s Desirability Table   b.   Classical Truth Table

p	q	$p \rightarrow q$
desirable	desirable	desirable
desirable	undesirable	#
undesirable	desirable	#
undesirable	undesirable	undesirable

p	q	$p \rightarrow q$
T	T	T
T	F	F
F	T	T
F	F	T

The desirability table predicts that for the case of *mono-nara* conditionals, the consequent must encode undesirability when *mono-nara* takes an undesirable antecedent. This prediction is borne out as can be seen in (7).

(7) # *sono yama-ni   nobor-oo   mono-nara,*
    that mountain-to climb-MOD MONO-COND
    zekkei-ga   mi-eru   zo.
    amazing.view-NOM see-can DP

    Lit. 'If you climb that mountain, you will get an amazing view.

---

[3] Using the conditional morpheme *tara* is more preferable than *nara* in (5a), which would be due to the difference in what [7] calls the notion of "settledness", i.e. the determinedness of the truth-value of a proposition at the time of utterance. Refer to [2] for details on the differences between the two.

Contrary to the felicitous example (5b) where the consequent expresses a negative event (i.e., to see a bear), (7) is infelicitous since the consequent encodes a positive encouragement (i.e., to get an amazing view).

To sum up, *mono-nara* conditionals are clearly different from the standard conditionals in Japanese; the properties of *mono-nara* conditionals that we must give an account for are that (i) they are always subjunctive, and (ii) the antecedent can yield the two distinct negative attitudes of the speaker: unlikelihood and undesirability. Note that *mono-nara* conditionals do not need to satisfy the two contextual requirements at the same time. This is already indicated by the examples above: the context in (4) represents a situation where the speaker favors John's coming, which ensures that the speaker's undesirability toward the antecedent proposition is not met; in (5), since the speaker believes that the addressee is likely to climb the mountain, the context is incompatible with an unlikelihood of the antecedent.

3 Proposal and Analysis

3.1 The Meaning of *Mono-nara*

We define the at-issue meaning of *mono-nara* conditionals as standard Kratzer-style conditionals [11]. The definition in (8) amounts to saying that in all the worlds according to the conversational backgrounds in a context c (i.e., the modal base f_c and the ordering source o_c) in which the antecedent p is true, the consequent q is true. For simplicity, we assume that the conversational backgrounds f_c and o_c are supplied by c.

(8) $[\![$ mono-nara $]\!]^{c,w} = \lambda P.\lambda q.\forall w' \in f_c^*(w) : q(w')$, where $P = \lhd p$, $\lhd$ is a modal (i.e., P is a modalized proposition) and $f_c^*(w) = f_c(w) \cup \{[\![p]\!]\}$
    presupposes: $\mathcal{B}el_{spkr_c}(\lhd \neg p)$ (i.e., the speaker in c believes $\lhd \neg p$)

(v.1, to be reformulated)

What is important here is that the speaker's negative attitude toward the prejacent (i.e., $\mathcal{B}el_{spkr_c}(\lhd \neg p)$) is encoded as a presupposition, which is motivated by the earlier examples in (4b) and (5b), where the unlikelihood and undesirability conveyed by *mono-nara* conditionals are not cancelable.

The core of our proposal which will be represented in the next section is that the two negative attitudes in (4b) and (5b) are derived compositionally by the interaction of the semantics of the lexical items that appear in the antecedent clause, i.e., *mono-nara* and the modal [y]*oo*.

3.2 [Y]*oo* as a Weak Necessity Modal with a Flexible Flavor

Before moving on to see how it goes, let us introduce the semantics of [y]*oo*. The sub-proposal of our work is that [y]*oo* is characterized as a weak necessity modal with a flexible modal flavor.[4] The examples in (9) indicate that $[y]oo$ expresses a weak necessity modal-like meaning while having two modal flavors, similar to the English weak necessity modal *should* (as the translations show).[5]

(9)   a.   *asu-niwa*   *yuki-mo*   *toke-yoo.*
          tomorrow-in snow-ADD melt-YOO

          'The snow should melt tomorrow.'   [epistemic ($\approx$ *hazu* '$should_{epi}$')]

   b.   *kenka-wa*   *yame-yoo.*
          fighting-TOP stop-YOO

          'We should stop fighting.'   [prioritizing/deontic ($\approx$ *beki* '$should_{deon}$')]

To test whether $[y]oo$ encodes the weak necessity force (i.e., whether $[y]oo$ is both (i) semantically weaker than strong necessity modals and (ii) stronger than possibility modals), we use the diagnosis of weak necessity proposed by [22]. [22] characterizes weak necessity modals as below.

(10) α is a weak necessity modal if (a) to (c) hold, for any proposition p: (a) The conjunction of $\alpha(p)$ and $\alpha(\neg p)$ is a contradiction; (b) There is a necessity modal β such that $\beta(p)$ entails $\alpha(p)$; (c) There is a possibility modal γ such that $\alpha(p)$ entails $\gamma(p)$.

The first part of the definition above ensures that weak necessity modals are necessity modals, not possibility modals. While possibility modals allow the conjunction of two mutually exclusive propositions, strong necessity modals disallows the similar conjunction.[6] (11) shows that $[y]oo$ patterns with the latter.

---

[4] This may be a surprising and interesting fact from a typological perspective of modals, given that almost all the modal expressions in Japanese (e.g., *nitigainai* '(epistemic) must', *nakerebanaranai* '(deontic) must', *kamosirenai* '(epistemic) may', *temoii* '(deontic) may', etc.) have a fixed modal flavors. See [16] and [9] for properties of Japanese modals and [8] and [15] for possible explanations for the obligatory fixed flavor.

[5] It is worth noting that sentences with the prioritizing/deontic use of $[y]oo$ generally requires the speech act (or illocutionary force) of the utterance to be PROMISSIVE or EXHORTATIVE, both of which includes the speaker as the first-person subject [18]. However, we are hesitant to regard $[y]oo$ itself as a marker of PROMISSIVE or EXHORTATIVE force since sentences with $[y]oo$ can also be used as imperatives with the second-person subject (even though the examples are relatively few). We will thus focus only on the semantic (i.e., the modal) aspect of $[y]oo$ and put aside the question of how the use of $[y]oo$ affects the discourse effect of the utterance.

[6] The relevant examples are shown below.

(i)   a.   *asu-ni-wa*   *yuki-wa*   *tokeru-kamosirenai. mata, toke-nai*   *kamosirenai.*
          tomorrow-in snow-TOP melt-may   also   melt-NEG may

          'The snow may melt tomorrow and may not melt.'

   b. # *asu-ni-wa*   *yuki-wa*   *tokeru-nitigainai. mata toke-nai*   *nitigainai.*
          tomorrow-in snow-TOP melt-must   also   melt-NEG must

          'The snow must melt tomorrow and must not melt.'

(11) # *asu-ni-wa   yuki-wa   toke-yoo.   mata, toke-nakar-oo.*
tomorrow-in snow-TOP melt-YOO also   melt-NEG-YOO
'The snow should melt tomorrow and should not melt.'

The latter parts of the definition, namely the characteristics (b, c) in (10), say that weak necessity modals are different from both strong necessity and possibility modals in terms of entailment relations. In (12), the modal claim of [*y*]*oo* can be reinforced by the strong necessity.

(12)   *yasumu-koto naku   hatarai-te   Taroo-wa tukeretei-yoo.*
take.a.rest-C without work-because Taro-TOP be.tired-YOO
toiuyori, tukareteiru {nitigainai | #kamosirenai}.
rather   be.tired   must   may

'Taro should be tired after working without a break.
Or rather, he {must/#may} be tired.'

In contrast, the meaning of [*y*]*oo* cannot be reinforced by the possibility modal as shown by the oddness in (13a), but the reverse is possible, (13b).[7]

(13)   a.   *yasumu-koto naku   hatarai-te   Taroo-wa tukereteru nitigainai.*
take.a.rest-C without work-because Taro-TOP be.tired   must
toiuyori, tukaretei-yoo.
rather   be.tired-YOO

'Taro must be tired after working without a break. #Or rather, he should be tired.'

    b.   *yasumu-koto naku   hatarai-te Taroo-wa tukereteru kamosirenai.*
take.a.rest-C without work-and Taro-TOP be.tired   may
toiuyori, tukaretei-yoo.
rather   be.tired-YOO

'Taro may be tired after working without a break. Or rather he may be tired.'

---

[7] The definition in (10) also holds in the case of deontic [*y*]*oo*:

(i)   a.   *kenka-o yame-yoo. #soreto, kenka-o si-yoo.*
'We should stop fighting. #Also, we should fight.'

    b.   *kenka-o yame-yoo. #toiuyori, yame-teii.*
'We should stop fighting. #In fact, we can stop fighting.'

    c.   *kenka-o yame-yoo. toiuyori, yame-nakerebanaranai.*
'We should stop fighting. In fact, we must stop fighting.'

The inconsistency in (ia, b) indicates that deontic [*y*]*oo* encodes some sort of necessity, and the contrast found in (ib) and (ic) shows that the necessity is relatively weak.

Given the diagnosis above, we can now safely treat $[y]oo$ as a weak necessity modal. In this paper, we define the meaning of $[y]oo$ by using the domain restriction approach to weak necessity modals in line with [5]. According to [5], what makes weak necessity modals weaker than strong necessity modals is that they have a smaller domain of quantification. That is, strong necessity modals claim that the prejacent is true in all of the favored worlds whereas weak necessity modals say that the prejacent is true in all of the very best among the favored worlds (i.e., in all the best of best worlds).[8]

(14) $[\![\,[y]oo\,]\!]^{c,w} = \lambda p_{\langle s,t \rangle}.\forall w' \in \text{BEST}(o2_{c,w}, \text{BEST}(o1_{c,w}, f_{c,w})) : p(w') = 1$

The point of the semantics for $[y]oo$ as a weak necessity modal is that it accommodates the additional (or secondary) ordering source $o2$. The set of favored worlds $\text{BEST}(o1, f)$ is re-ranked according to this additional ordering source, and the highest ranked worlds are selected as the domain of quantification.

Importantly, in the definition above, there are no constraints on propositions in the conversational backgrounds (i.e. the ordering sources and the modal base), which allows the modal flavor of $[y]oo$ to be flexible, just like *must* or *should* in English. That is, whether the modal flavor of $[y]oo$ will be epistemic or prioritizing depends purely on the contexts uttered. Building on [10], we assume that $[y]oo$ in epistemic readings uses the 'epistemic' modal base (i.e., a set of propositions p s.t. p is *known* in w) and the 'stereotypical' ordering source (i.e., a set of p

---

[8] We could also define the meaning of $[y]oo$ under other frameworks for modals. For instance, if we adopt [23]'s version of weak necessity, $[y]oo(p)$ is true iff p follows from the relevant considerations f_c at every $w' \in h_c(w)$, as represented below. h_c is a contextually supplied function that selects a set of relevant (closest) worlds that are preferred in c—most normal, expected, desirable, etc.

(i) $[\![\,[y]oo(p)\,]\!]^{c,w} = 1$ iff $\forall w' \in h_c(w) : \bigcap f_c(w') \subseteq [\![p]\!]^c$

On the other hand, under degree-based approaches including [13] and [21], the meaning of weak necessity $[y]oo$ is not quantification over possible worlds, but is certain degrees, as in (ii).

(ii) $[\![\,[y]oo(p)\,]\!]^{c,w} = \lambda d.\mu_w(p) \geq d$

The underlying scale that the measure function μ in (ii) operates on includes measures of probability of achieving a certain goal or priority. We leave closer exploration of the issue as to which approach is preferable for the analysis of $[y]oo$ for future research.

s.t. p is a *reasonable expectation* in w) as its conversational backgrounds.[9] $[Y]oo$ in deontic readings, on the other hand, employs the 'circumstantial' modal base (i.e., a set of p s.t. p is true in w) and the 'teleological/bouletic' ordering source (i.e., a set of p s.t. p is the law/goal in w). Figure 1 illustrates in a step-wise fashion how a modal quantificational domain of $[y]oo$ is determined.

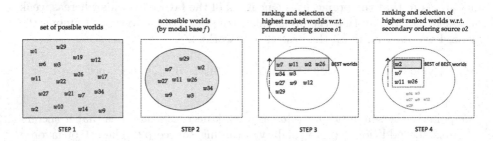

Fig. 1. Quantificational domain for weak necessity (adapted from [24])

3.3 Composing the Negative Attitudes

Given the semantic ingredients introduced above, we are now in a position to illustrate the compositional meaning of *mono-nara* conditionals. As shown in (15), the example in (2) conveys that in all the worlds in which the antecedent p is true, the consequent q is true, while presupposing the speaker's negative attitude toward p.

(15)   a.   LF of (2): mono-nara [yoo $(p$: Taro comes)], [q : everyone will be surprised]

   b. $[\![(2)]\!]^{c,w} = \forall w' \in f_c^*(w)$: everyone will be surprised in w',
       where $f_c^*(w) = f_c(w) \cup \{[\![\,yoo([p : \text{Taro comes}])]\!]\}$

   c.   <u>presupposes</u>: $\mathcal{B}el_{spkr_c}(\text{yoo}(\neg p))$

Then, as schematized below, the presupposition (15c) will be interpreted either as (i) *¬p would happen* (= *p would not happen*) or as (ii) *¬p is desirable* (= *p is undesirable*), depending on the context uttered. In (16), yoo$_{epis}$ stands for $[y]oo$ with an epistemic (or doxastic) flavor (cf. (9a)) and yoo$_{pri}$ for $[y]oo$ with a prioritizing (or deontic) flavor (cf. (9b)). Consequently, the interpretations (16a) and (16b) express unlikelihood and undesirability, respectively.

---

[9] Note that $[y]oo$ seems to allow what [25] calls "pseudo-epistemic" readings where the speaker knows that a prejacent is false:

(i)   *Reizooko-no   biiru-ga   hiete-nai. Hutuu-wa   imagoro   hie-tei   yoo.*
   refrigerator-GEN beer-NOM cool-NEG normal-TOP now.about cool-ASP MOD
   'The beer in the refrigerator isn't cold. Normally it should be cold by now.'

In this case, we assume that the associated modal base is circumstantial rather than epistemic (cf. [5]). See [25], however, for the criticism of this idea.

(16) a. $\mathcal{B}el_{spkr_c}(\text{yoo}(\neg p))$ in EPI contexts $\rightsquigarrow$ $\mathcal{B}el_{spkr_c}(\text{yoo}_{epis}\neg p)$

   b. $\mathcal{B}el_{spkr_c}(\text{yoo}(\neg p))$ in PRI contexts $\rightsquigarrow$ $\mathcal{B}el_{spkr_c}(\text{yoo}_{pri}\neg p)$

Let us see how the proposal explains the behaviors of *mono-nara*-conditionals, starting with the derivation of the negative attitudes. In (4), by using the combination of *mono-nara* and $[y]oo_{epis}$, the speaker presupposes the unlikelihood of John's coming to the party, and this presupposition is incompatible with her attitude report that he would come to the party, thereby inducing the oddness of the entire utterance. The weirdness found in (5b) receives almost the same explanation as the unacceptability of (4b). Here, assuming that $[y]oo$ is interpreted as $[y]oo_{pri}$, the presupposition of *mono-nara* would be like *climbing the mountain is undesirable (because of the risk of being attacked by bears)*. Then, the imperative continuation which encodes the preference over the addressee's climbing the mountain is compatible since this preference clashes with the undesirable presupposition of *mono-nara*.

The remaining fact to be explained is the obligatory modal marking of the antecedent clause. As we have shown in (2), *mono-nara* conditionals require that the antecedent be modalized. In our definition of *mono-nara*, the propositional argument must be modalized in order to associate the modal flavor with the negative attitude as a presupposition. That is, without being modalized, the negative presupposition (i.e. epistemic, prioritizing or other modal meanings, as we will observe in the next section) cannot be determined, thereby yielding presupposition failure.

4 Predictions and Implications

4.1 Interaction with Possibility Modals

Our proposal predicts that modals other than $[y]oo$ can also be used in the antecedent of *mono-nara*-conditionals. This prediction is true for certain modals: Japanese possibility modals such as *eru* 'can' and *teii* 'may' can appear in the conditional antecedent, expressing a negative attitude of the speaker, although this type of *mono-nara* conditional is less productive than the one with $[y]oo$.

(17) *yar-eru mono-nara   yat-temi-na!*
    do-can   MONO-COND do-try-IMP
    (*zettai   {#dekiru | deki-nai}   kara.*)
     definitely   able.to.do   able.to.do-NEG because

   Lit. 'Do it if you can! (I'm sure you {#can | can't} do it.)'

(18) **Context**: the speaker has given her personal number to a client and gets calls all day long asking for business advice. She was totally tired of answering the phone.

tyakusinkyohi-si-teii   *mono-nara*   *suru*   *yo.*
blocking.phone.calls-do-may   MONO-COND   do.PRES   DP
(*sore-wa*   *jissai*   {#*yurusareteru* | *yurusarete-nai*} *kedo.*)
that-TOP   actually   permitted   permitted-NEG   but

Lit. 'If I was allowed to block his calls, I would. (I'm {#allowed | not allowed} to do that.)'

We get the following intuitions from the above two examples respectively. In (17), the speaker is convinced that the addressee will never be able to do a certain action expressed in the conditional antecedent, as suggested by the contrast between the subsequent utterances. The sentence in (18) expresses a negative attitude that the action in the antecedent (i.e., rejecting the call) is prohibited, which is also confirmed by the (in)felicity of the follow-up sentences.

Our proposal for the semantics of *mono-nara* in (8) fails to capture the data above; a desirable prediction that we want in (17) and (18) is that the antecedent *mono-nara*($P_{eru/teii}$) yields a presupposition like $\mathcal{B}el(\neg \lhd_{eru/teii} p)$, namely *the speaker believes that p is impossible/prohibited*. However, if we follow (8), *mono-nara*($P_{eru/teii}$) will express $\mathcal{B}el(\lhd_{eru/teii} \neg p)$, namely *the speaker believes that $\neg p$ is possible/permitted*, contrary to our intuition. To avoid this problem, the original proposal is elaborated as (19) by adding the branching condition to the presupposition.

(19)   The presupposition of $[\![\text{mono-nara}(P)]\!]^{c,w}$:

$$\begin{cases} \mathcal{B}el_{spkr_c}(\lhd \neg p) & \text{if } \lhd = \lhd_\square \\ \mathcal{B}el_{spkr_c}(\neg \lhd p) & \text{otherwise (i.e., if } \lhd = \lhd_\Diamond) \end{cases} \quad (\text{v.2})$$

The above condition simply specifies whether the scope of the negation in the presupposition is inner or outer, depending on whether the modal of P is necessity ($\lhd_\square$) or possibility ($\lhd_\Diamond$). This refinement may seem arbitrary, but it reflects a well-known empirical fact of the scopal interaction between modals and negation. That is, as attested in many languages including English, universal modals such as *must, should, ought*, etc. must be interpreted as having a higher scope than the negation, while existential modals such as *may* or *can* are neutral modals that can scope under negation.[10]

It is also worth noting that *mono-nara* conditionals are selective about the modal marker in the antecedent clause. Japanese has various modal markers. Among them, *mono-nara* conditionals can co-occur with deontic modals such as [y]*oo* 'should' and *teii* 'may' and dynamic modals, but not with other modal markers. (The modal markers in Table 1 are taken from [16].)

---

[10] To the best of our knowledge, this scopal relation between modals and negation has not been attested in Japanese. The situation in Japanese with respect to the scopal relation would be more complex than English because most modal expressions in Japanese have a complex structure consisting of multiple lexical items (cf. [8]) and thus leaving a possibility of having different syntactic/semantic properties than modals that are defined as a single lexical item.

Table 1. Modal expressions and their compatibility with *nara/mono-nara* conditionals

modal markers	category	*nara* cond.	*mono-nara* cond.
-tai 'want'	boulomaic	OK	BAD
-soo	evidential	OK	BAD
-rasii	evidential	OK	BAD
nitigainai 'must'	epistemic	OK	BAD
daroo 'will'	epistemic	OK	BAD
kamosirenai 'may'	epistemic	OK	BAD
-[y]oo 'should'	epistemic/deontic	OK	OK
-te ii 'may'	deontic	OK	OK
beki 'should'	deontic	OK	BAD (cf. fn.11)
-(a)nakereba naranai 'must'	deontic	OK	BAD
-(r)eru/-(r)areru 'can'	dynamic	OK	OK
kotoga dekiru 'can'	dynamic	OK	OK

In our sample, we found that (i) all dynamic (potential/possibility) modals and (ii) some modals that can have a deontic flavor can appear in the antecedent of *mono-nara* conditionals.[11] The selectional restriction of *mono-nara* conditionals is not expected under the current semantic analysis. It might be a matter of syntax and/or morphology, and we leave this for future research.

---

[11] One caveat here is that as shown in (i), the deontic modal *beki* 'should' seems to able to occur with *mono-nara* in Old Japanese.

(i)   Old Japanese
       mosi sessyoo kanpaku-su-beki   *mono-nara-ba, kono ya   atare.*
       if   regent chief.advisor-do-should MONO-IF-if   this arrow hit.IMP
       'If I should be a regent and the chief advisor, this arrow hits.'   [*Ookagami*]

It is unclear whether (i) was uttered in the context where it was unlikely that the speaker would be a regent or the chief advisor. (Undesirability should be irrelevant here because it would be desirable for the speaker (i.e. *Fujiwara-no Michinaga*, the Japanese statesman who reigned the Imperial capital in Kyoto) to obtain the high rank positions.) Further investigation of *mono-nara* conditionals in Old Japanese is an interesting topic, but it is beyond the scope of this article.

4.2 Compatibility with Counterfactuals

Mono-nara-conditionals allow the counterfactual reading as with the standard *nara*-conditionals with a past tense morpheme *ta*. In (20), both (20a) and (20b) require that the antecedent 'it rained' is false.

(20) a. *mosi ame-ga   hut-ta   nara, siai-wa   tyuushi-ni nat-ta   daroo.*
         if   rain-NOM fall-PAST COND game-TOP cancel-to   be-PAST   MOD

   'If it had been raining, the game would have been canceled.'

   b. *mosi ame-ga   hur-oo   mono-nara, siai-wa   tyuushi-ni nat-ta*
      if   rain-NOM fall-MOD MONO-COND   game-TOP   cancel-to   be-PAST
      daroo.
      MOD

   'If it had been raining, the game would have been canceled.'

[20] suggests that *ta* in counterfactual antecedents in (20a) plays a role as excluding the actual world $w_@$ (i.e., the proposition conveyed by the antecedent is compatible with $w_@$). According to [20], counterfactual conditionals with past tense obtain the falsity meaning from the contribution of *ta* in the consequent part, assuming that *ta* scopes over the entire sentence.

What about the case of *mono-nara*, then? Does the falsity in (20b) arise from the negative meaning of *mono-nara*, or does it emerge from the general mechanism of Japanese conditionals as suggested by [20]? Here, we pursue the latter view, and argue that the falsity of the antecedent in (20b) is not derived by the semantic contribution of *mono-nara* itself, but by the past tense marking in the consequent. This seems to be evident from the fact that *mono-nara* conditionals cannot convey the counterfactuality without *ta* in the consequent.

(21) **Context**: the weather cleared up and the game was played as scheduled.
      #*mosi ame-ga   hur-oo   mono-nara, siai-wa   tyuushi-ni na-ru*
       if   rain-NOM fall-MOD MONO-COND   game-TOP   cancel-P   be-PRET
       (*daroo*).
       MOD

   Int. 'If it had been raining, the game would have been canceled.'

How is it possible for the antecedent of *mono-nara*-conditionals to be compatible with counterfactuals without marking a past tense in the antecedent? In our analysis, since *mono-nara* is a conditional morpheme that obligatorily takes a modalized antecedent, the antecedent is always compatible with a situation where the truth value of a proposition is false. That is, a set of circumstantial worlds at which the modal claim (either necessity or possibility) of the prejacent is evaluated can exclude the actual world, thus accepting counterfactual situations. (See also fn.9 for $[y]oo(p)$ in counterfactual-like contexts.)

4.3 Negation and Licensing of Minimizers

Under the current proposal, the speaker's negative attitude toward the prejacent $(\mathcal{B}el_{spkr_c}(\lhd\neg p))$ is encoded in *mono-nara* as a presupposition. In this section, we argue that minimizer expressions in Japanese provide support for the presence of negation in the *mono-nara* conditional.

As shown in (22b), the idiomatic phrase *yubi ip-pon ugokasu* 'move one finger' is interpreted as a minimizer expression when it appears with negation.

(22) a. *Taro-wa   yubi   ip-pon   ugokasi-ta.*
          Taro-TOP finger one-CLS move-PAST

          'Taro moved one finger.'

    b. *Taro-wa   yubi   ip-pon   ugokasa-nakat-ta.*
          Taro-TOP finger one-CLS move-NEG-PAST

          'Taro did nothing.' [MNMZ (minimizer)-interpretation]

Importantly, the minimizer interpretation is unavailable when the phrase appears in the antecedent of conditionals, as shown in (23).[12]

(23) [*yubi   ip-pon   ugokase-ba/ugokasu-to/ugokasu-nara,*] *koukaisuru-daroo.*
     finger one-CLS move-COND   regret-will

     'If you move one finger, you will regret it.'
    # 'If you do anything, you will regret it.'

                       [*ba/to/nara*-cond.: *MNMZ-inter.]

What is important for the current discussion is that the *mono-nara* conditional, unlike the *nara* conditional, can license the minimizer interpretation as in (24).

(24) [*yubi   ip-pon   ugokas-oo   mono-nara,*] *koukaisuru-daroo.*
     finger one-CLS move-MOD MONO-COND regret-will

     'If you do anything, you will regret it.' [*mono-nara* cond.: ✓MNMZ-inter.]

---

[12] [19] reported that the minimizer expression *yubi ip-pon ugokasu* 'move a finger' is licensed in the antecedent of the *tara*-conditional, as in (i).

(i) [*yubi   ip-pon(-demo)   ugokasi-tara,*] *koukaisuru-daroo.*
    finger one-CLS-even   move-COND   regret-will

    'If you move (even) a finger, you will be sorry.'   [*tara*-conditional: ([19]:104)]

The availability of the minimizer interpretation in (i) indicates that the *tara*-conditional, unlike other Japanese conditionals, behaves like the *if*-conditional in English regarding licensing of minimizers. This peculiarity of the *tara*-conditional needs to be explained, but it is beyond the scope of the current paper.

Our proposal can provide an explanation of the acceptability of (24). As shown in (22b), the minimizer expression is licensed by negation. Under the current analysis of the *mono-nara* conditional, the conditional antecedent is associated with negation at the presuppositional level, and this is the main difference between the *mono-nara* conditional and the other conditionals in (23). Given this, we would like to suggest that the negation at the presuppositional level may play an important role in the licensing of the minimizers in (24).[13]

In this connection, it is also worth noting that *mono* appears in another subjunctive construction expressing the speaker's negative attitude. In (25), the light noun *mono* is followed by the particle *ka* with a falling intonation. (25) is interpreted as a rhetorical question rather than an answer-seeking question.

(25)   *Taro-ga   kuru   mono-ka.*
        Taro-NOM   come   MONO-Q

    'Taro will <u>not</u> come.' (#'Will Taro come?')

By using *mono-ka*, the speaker claims that the uttered proposition should be false. What *mono-ka* constructions and *mono-nara* conditionals have in common is that the speaker has a negative attitude toward the proposition associated with the *mono-X* forms (i.e. *mono-ka* and *mono-nara*). Given this, it is not unreasonable to assume that the speaker's negative attitude stems from *mono*. Importantly, the *mono-ka* construction can license the minimizer interpretation of *yubi ip-pon ugokasu*, as in (26).

(26)   *Taro-ga   yubi   ip-pon   ugokasu   mono-ka.*
        Taro-NOM   finger   one-CLS   move.PRET   MONO-Q

    'Taro will not do anything.'   [*mono-ka-Q*: ✓MNMZ-inter.]

The availability of the minimizer interpretation in (26) can be seen as supporting evidence that the *mono-ka* construction includes negation at the non-at-issue level, similarly to the *mono-nara* conditional.

---

[13] Notice also that [4] report that English conditional threats can license minimizers more naturally than conditional promises, as shown in (i).

(i)   a.   *If you lift a finger to hurt him, I will punish you!*

    b.   ?*If you lift a finger to help him, I will buy you an ice-cream cone!*

The contrast in (i) can be captured under the proposed analysis in the current paper. Conditional threats are similar to the *mono-nara* conditional in the sense that in both cases the speaker expresses a negative attitude toward the proposition in the antecedent clause. In (ia), the speaker believes that it is unacceptable that the hearer hurts him. Under the current analysis, it may be possible to hypothesize that the minimizer expression *lift a finger* in (ia) is licensed by negation at the presuppositional level, like the *mono-nara* conditional.

5   Conclusion

Our analysis of Japanese *mono-nara* conditionals contributes to providing an interesting strategy for deriving negativity of conditional antecedents. [17] reports that Slovenian, Hebrew, and Turkish use special morphemes or word orders to express negativity, and Mandarin Chinese and Tagalog employ it by utilizing complementizers that morphologically contain negations. In *mono-nara* conditionals, the negative attitude is not encoded in a particular element or word order but is derived compositionally by the meanings of the special conditional morpheme and the modal embedded in the antecedent. It is noteworthy that potentially decomposable conditional expressions are not limited to *mono-nara*. [14] argues that Korean negative conditional marker *esstakanun* can be decomposed into the perfect aspect marker *ess* and *takanun*, and attempts to explain various speaker attitudes conveyed by *esstakanun* conditionals (although a compositional account is not given). Our next step will thus be to investigate what and why variants of decomposition exist for conditional expressions in natural languages.

References

1. Akatsuka, N.: Dracula conditionals and discourse. In: Georgopolous, C., Ishihara, R. (eds.) Interdisciplinary Approaches to Language: Essays in Honour of S. Kuroda, pp. 25–37. Kluwer Academic Publishers, London (1991)
2. Arita, S.: Nihongo zyookenbun to ziseisetusei [Japanese Conditionals and Tensedness]. Kurosio Publishers, Tokyo (2007)
3. Condoravdi, C., Lauer, S.: Imperatives: meaning and illocutionary force. In: Empirical Issues in Syntax and Semantics, vol. 9, pp. 37–58 (2012)
4. Eckardt, R., Csipak, E.: Minimizers: towards pragmatic licensing. In: Csipak, E., Liu, M., Eckardt, R., Sailer, M. (eds.) Beyond änyänd ëver. New Explorations in Negative Polarity Sensitivity, 267–298. De Gruyter, Berlin (2013)
5. von Fintel, K., Iatridou, S.: How to say ought in foreign: the composition of weak necessity modals. In: Guéron, J., Lecarme, J. (eds.) Time and Modality. SNLT, vol. 75, pp. 115–141. Springer, Berlin (2008). https://doi.org/10.1007/978-1-4020-8354-9_6
6. Iatridou, S.: The grammatical ingredients of counterfactuality. Linguist. Inquiry **31**(2), 231–270 (2000)
7. Kaufmann, S.: Conditional truth and future reference. J. Semant. **22**(3), 231–280 (2005)
8. Kaufmann, M.: What 'may' and 'must' may be in Japanese. In: Funakoshi, K., Kawahara, S., Tancredi, C.D. (eds.) Japanese/Korean Linguistics, p. 24. CSLI Publications, Stanford (2017)
9. Kaufmann, M., Tamura, S.: Japanese modality-possibility and necessity: prioritizing, epistemic, and dynamic. In: Jacobsen, W.M., Takubo, Y. (eds.) Handbook of Japanese Semantics and Pragmatics, pp. 537–585. de Gruyter, Berlin (2020)
10. Kratzer, A.: The notional category of modality. In: Eikmeyer, H.J., Rieser, H. (eds.) Words, Worlds, and Context, pp. 38–74. de Gruyter, Berlin (1981)
11. Kratzer, A.: Conditionals. Chicago Linguist. Soc. **22**(2), 1–15 (1986)
12. Kuno, S.: The Structure of the Japanese Language. MIT Press, Cambridge (1973)

13. Lassiter, D.: Graded Modality: Qualitative and Quantitative Perspectives. Oxford University Press, Oxford (2017)
14. Lee, C.-B.: A study of negative conditionals in Korean: -*takanun* and *esstakanun*. Lang. Res. **44**(2), 299–318 (2008)
15. Mizutani, K., Ihara, S.: Decomposing the Japanese deontic modal hoo ga ii. In: Jeon, H.-S. (ed.) Japanese/Korean Linguistics 28 Online Proceedings. CSLI Publications, Stanford (2021)
16. Narrog, H.: Modality in Japanese: The Layered Structure of the Clause and Hierarchies of Functional Categories. John Benjamins, Amsterdam (2009)
17. Nevins, A.: Counterfactuality without past tense. In: Proceedings of the North East Linguistic Society, vol. 32, pp. 441–451 (2002)
18. Kenkyuukai, N.K.B.: Gendai nihongo bunpoo [Contemporary Japanese Grammar], vol. 4. Kurosio Publishers, Tokyo (2003)
19. Oda, T.: Degree constructions in Japanese. Doctoral dissertations, University of Connecticut (2008)
20. Ogihara, T.: The semantics of -ta in Japanese counterfactual conditionals. In: Crnic, L., Sauerland, U. (eds.) The Art and Craft of Semantics: A Festschrift for Irene Heim, vol. 2, pp. 1–21. MITWPL, Cambridge (2014)
21. Portner, P., Rubinstein, A.: Extreme and non-extreme deontic modals. In: Charlow, N., Chrisman, M. (eds.) Deontic Modality, pp. 256–282. Oxford University Press, Oxford (2016)
22. Rubinstein, A.: Weak necessity. Ms, The Hebrew University of Jerusalem (2017)
23. Silk, A.: Weak and strong necessity modals: on linguistic means of expressing "a primitive concept OUGHT". In: Dunaway, B., Plunkett, D. (eds.) Meaning, Decision, and Norms: Themes from the Work of Allan Gibbard. Michigan Publishing Services, to appear
24. Vander Klok, J., Hohaus, V.: Weak necessity without weak possibility: the composition of modal strength distinctions in Javanese. Semant. Pragmatics **13**(12) (2020)
25. Yalcin, S.: Modalities of normality. In: Charlow, N., Chrisman, M. (eds.) Deontic Modality, pp. 230–55. Oxford University Press, Oxford (2016)

Interpretations of Sense-Based Minimizers in Japanese and English: Direct and Indirect Sense-Based Measurements

Osamu Sawada[✉]

Department of Linguistics, Kobe University, 1-1 Rokkodai-cho, Nada-ku Kobe 657-8501, Japan
sawadao@lit.kobe-u.ac.jp

Abstract. The Japanese degree adverb *kasukani* can be combined with a sense-related gradable predicate, such as *amai* 'sweet' or *kaoru* 'smell', but it cannot usually co-occur with an emotive predicate, such as *odoroi-teiru* 'surprised'. However, if there is a sense-related expression that is structurally placed at a higher position, *kasukani* can combine with an emotive predicate. Building on the idea of Sawada (2021), I will first show that *kasukani* is mixed content (McCready 2010; Gutzmann 2011) in that it not only denotes a low scalar meaning in the at-issue component, but also implies that the judge (typically the speaker) has measured its degree based on their own senses (e.g., vision, smell, taste, or hearing) at the level of conventional implicature (CI)(e.g., Grice 1975; Potts 2005). I will then argue that the projective property of the CI meaning of *kasukani* allows *kasukani* to be used to measure the degree of emotion through a sense-based expression, such as *mie-ru* 'look'. I will also compare *kasukani* to English *faintly*, which can be used to measure the degree of emotion directly or measure the degree of emotion indirectly via a sense-based expression and explain the differences between the two by positing different CI components. This study demonstrates that the multidimensional approach to meaning can successfully explain the concord relationship between a sense-based minimizer and sense-related expression.

Keywords: sense-based minimizers · local measurement · global (indirect) measurement · experience · sense · emotion · multidimensionality

1 Introduction

The Japanese minimizer *kasukani*, which approximately means 'faintly', is sense-based in that it measures the degree based on a judge's (typically the speaker's) senses of taste, vision, smell, or hearing (see also Sawada 2021) as shown in (1) (the examples

I am grateful to Daisuke Bekki, Ikumi Imani, Chris Kennedy, Hideki Kishimoto, Kenta Mizutani, David Oshima, Harumi Sawada, Jun Sawada, Koji Sugisaki, Eri Tanaka, and the reviewers of LENLS 18 for their valuable comments and suggestions. Parts of this paper were presented at the seminar at Kwansei Gakuin University and the ICU Linguistics Colloquium, and I also thank the audiences for their valuable discussions. This study is based on work supported by the JSPS KAKENHI Grant (21K00525, 22K00554) and the NINJAL collaborative research project "Evidence-based Theoretical and Typological Linguistics" All remaining errors are, of course, my own.

K. Yada et al. (Eds.): JSAI-isAI 2021 Workshops, LNAI 13856, pp. 145–160, 2023.
https://doi.org/10.1007/978-3-031-36190-6_10

with *sukoshi* 'a bit' are also natural, but as we will see below, *sukoshi* does not have a sense-related restriction):[1]

(1)   a.   Kono sake-wa   {kasukani / sukoshi} amai.
             This sake-TOP faintly   / a bit   sweet

       'This sake is {faintly/a bit} sweet.' (sense of taste)

       b.   Minto-ga   {kasukani / sukoshi} kao-ru.
             Mint-NOM faintly   / a bit   smell-Non.PST

       'It smells {faintly/a bit} of mint.' (sense of smell)

       c.   Fujisan-ga   {kasukani / sukoshi} mie-ru.
             Mt. Fuji-NOM faintly   / a bit   can.see-Non.PST

       'Mt Fuji is {faintly/a bit} visible.' (sense of sight)

       d.   Oto-ga   {kasukani / sukoshi} kikoe-ru.
             Sound-NOM faintly   / a bit   can.hear-Non.PST

       'I can hear the sound faintly/I can hear a little sound.' (sense of hearing)

       e.   Totte-ga   mada {kasukani / sukoshi} atatakai.
             Handle-NOM still   faintly   / a bit   warm

       'The handle is still {faintly/a bit} warm.' (sense of touch)

As *kasukani* is sense-based, unlike the regular minimizer *sukoshi* 'a bit', *kasukani* cannot combine with non-sense-based adjectives such as *takai* 'expensive' or *ookii* 'big':

(2)   Kono hon-wa   {??kasukani / sukoshi} takai.
       This book-TOP faintly   / a bit   expensive

       'This book is {??faintly/a bit} expensive.'

(3)   Kono T-shatsu-wa {??kasukani / sukoshi} ookii.
       This T-shirt-TOP faintly   / a bit   big

       'This T-shirt is {??faintly/a bit} big.'

One important feature of *kasukani* is that while it cannot directly combine with an emotive predicate (similar to the case of non-sense-based adjectives), as seen in (4a) and (5a), in an embedded context, *kasukani* can combine with an emotive predicate if there is a sense-related expression in a main clause, as in (4b) and (5b):

(4)   a.   Hanako-wa   {??kasukani / sukoshi} odoroi-ta.
             Hanako-TOP faintly   / a bit   surprise-PST

       'Hanako was {faintly/a bit} surprised.'

---

[1] Furthermore, *kasukani* can also be used to measure the degree of memory:

(i)   Ano hi-no   koto-o   {kasukani / sukoshi} oboe-teiru.
       That day-GEN thing-ACC faintly   / a bit   remember-STATE

       'I faintly remember that day./I remember a little bit about that day.' (sense of memory)

    b. Hanako-wa {kasukani / sukoshi} odoroi-ta   hyoujou-o ukabe-ta.
       Hanako-TOP faintly   / a bit   surprise-PST look-ACC express-PST
       'Hanako looked {faintly/a bit} surprised.'

(5) a. Taro-wa   sonokoto-de   {??kasukani / sukoshi} kanashin-dei-ta.
       Taro-TOP that thing-with faintly   / a bit   sad-STATE-PST
       'Taro was {faintly/a bit} sad about that.'

    b. Taro-wa   sono koto-de   {kasukani / sukoshi} kanashin-deiru-yooni
       Taro-TOP that thing-with faintly   / a bit   sad-STATE-like
       mie-ta.
       look-PST
       'Taro looked {faintly/a bit} sad about that.'

Kasukani in (4b) and (5b) syntactically and semantically modifies an emotive predicate, denoting that the degree of surprise/sadness is slightly greater than zero, but the measurement is made through the speaker's perception (sense of sight). How can we explain the asymmetry in (4) and (5) and the dependency of *kasukani* on a sense-related expression? In this study, building on Sawada's (2021) idea, I will first show that *kasukani* has a non-at-issue component/conventional implicature (CI) that the judge (typically the speaker) has measured degree based on their own senses (e.g., vision, smell, taste, hearing), which is logically independent of "what is said" (Grice 1975; Potts 2005). I will then argue that the projective property of the CI meaning of *kasukani* allows *kasukani* to be used to measure the degree of emotion through a sense-based expression, such as *mie-ru* 'look'. I will also compare *kasukani* to English *faintly*, which can measure the degree of emotion directly or indirectly via sense-based expressions, such as *look*, and explain their differences by positing different non-at-issue CI components.

2 The Meaning of Japanese *kasukani* 'faintly'

Let us first consider the meaning and distribution of Japanese *kasukani* 'faintly'.

2.1 The Experiential Component of *kasukani*

As we observed in the Introduction, the Japanese minimizer *kasukani* 'faintly' is sense-based in that it measures degree based on a judge's (typically the speaker's) sense of taste, vision, smell, or hearing. As Sawada (2021) points out, this implies that if a speaker does not have direct experience via a sense, (s)he cannot use *kasukani*. This is evidenced by the following examples. (6) is natural because the speaker measures the degree of sweetness based on their own senses:

(6) (Context: The speaker is drinking coffee.)

    Kono koohii-wa {kasukani / sukoshi} amai.
    This coffee-TOP faintly   / a bit   sweet

    'This coffee is faintly/a bit sweet.'

In contrast, (7) with *kasukani* sounds odd because the speaker has not measured the degree of sweetness of the coffee through their own senses:

(7)   (Context: The speaker is looking at a label. According to the label, on a scale of 1 to 5, the sweetness of the coffee is 1.)

Kono koohii-wa   {#kasukani / sukoshi} amai.
This   coffee-TOP faintly   / a bit   sweet

'This coffee is #faintly/a bit sweet.'

The above discussion suggests that *kasukani* is very similar to predicates of personal taste, which require direct experience (e.g., Pearson 2013; Ninan 2014; Kennedy and Willer 2019; Willer and Kennedy 2020), particularly a sense-related predicate of personal taste, such as *tasty*:

(8)   a. This coffee is tasty.
       b. This sushi is delicious.

For example, Pearson (2013) describes the requirement of direct sensory experience in the predicates of personal taste as follows:

(9)   In order to assert that x is P for some taste predicate P, one typically must have direct sensory experience of the relevant kind on the basis of which to judge whether x is P. [...] To assert that *shortbread is tasty*, I must have tasted shortbread. If I have good reason to believe that shortbread is tasty, say because a reliable expert has told me so, I might say, *Apparently, shortbread is tasty*, but not, *Shortbread is tasty*. (Pearson2013: 117)

However, note that *kasukani* cannot co-occur with a predicate of personal taste, such as *oishii* 'delicious':

(10)   ?? Kono keeki-wa   kasukani oishii.
           This cake-TOP faintly   delicious
           'This cake is faintly delicious.'

We will discuss this point in Sect. 2.4.

2.2   The Barely-Component of *kasukani*

Another important feature of *kasukani* is that it is used in situations where the speaker barely recognizes the given degree. *Nihon kokugo Daijiten* describes that *kasukani* represents the degree of a thing such that it can barely be recognized through the exercise of perception or memory. In other words, the word *kasukani* 'faintly' means not only a small degree, but also a degree that is not clear.

In this sense, *kasukani* is semantically similar to *bonyari* 'dimly'.

(11)   Fujisan-ga   {kasukani/bonyari} mie-ru.
        Mt. Fuji-NOM faintly/dimly   can.see-NON.PST
        'Mt. Fuji is faintly/dimly visible.'

However, *kasukani* and *bonyari* 'dimly' are not semantically the same. *Kasukani* has a low degree meaning but *bonyari* does not have a low degree meaning.

2.3   The Non-at-issue (CI) Property of *kasukani*

Let us now consider the status of the meaning of *kasukani*. I argue that *kasukani* induces a conventional implicature (Grice 1975; Potts 2005) that the judge (typically the speaker) measures the degree based on their own senses (e.g., sight, smell, taste, or hearing). More specifically, I assume that *kasukani* 'faintly' is mixed content in that it has an at-issue scalar meaning and the CI (McCready 2010; Gutzmann 2011) inside the lexical item (cf. Sawada 2021):

(12)   **Descriptive definition of the meaning of *kasukani*:**
       In the at-issue component of *kasukani*, *kasukani* denotes that the degree of a target x is slightly greater than zero (= a minimum standard) on the scale of G and that the given degree is barely recognizable in the at-issue component. Simultaneously, *kasukani* conventionally implicates that the judge (typically the speaker) is measuring or has measured the degree based on their own sense of sight, smell, taste, or hearing.

In Gricean pragmatics, CIs are considered a part of the meaning of words, but they are independent of "what is said" (at-issue meaning; e.g., Grice 1975; Potts 2005; McCready 2010; Gutzmann 2011; Sawada 2010, Sawada 2018). Furthermore, it is often assumed that CIs are speaker-oriented by default (Potts 2007).

The experiential component is a CI because it is independent of "what is said" (at-issue meaning). This is supported by a denial test. First, as (13) and (14) show, the low-degree component can be deniable:

(13)   A: Fujisan-ga   kasukani mie-ru.
            Mt. Fuji-NOM faintly   can.see-Non.PST
            Mt. Fuji is faintly visible.
            CI: I have measured the degree of visibility based on my sense of sight.

       B: Iya sore-wa   uso-da.   Mattaku mie-nai-yo.
            No that-TOP false-PRED At all   see.can-NEG-Prt
            'No, that is false. I can't see it at all.'

(14)   A: Kono koohii-wa   kasukani amai.
            This   coffee-TOP faintly   sweet
            At-issue: The degree of sweetness of this coffee is slightly greater than zero.
            CI: I have measured the degree of sweetness based on my sense of taste.

       B: Iya sore-wa   uso-da.   Mattaku amaku-nai-yo.
            No that-TOP false-PRED At all   sweet-NEG-Prt
            'No, that is false. It is not sweet at all.'

Furthermore, the vague-component is also deniable:

(15)   A: Fujisan-ga   kasukani mie-ru.
            Mt. Fuji-NOM faintly   can.see-Non.PST
            Mt. Fuji is faintly visible.
            CI: I have measured the degree of visibility based on my sense of sight.

B: Iya, bokuj-ni-wa hakkiri mie-ru-yo.
Well I-to-TOP   clearly see.can-Non.PST-Prt
'Well, I can see it clearly.'

(16) A: Oto-ga   kasukani kikoe-ru.
Sound-NOM faintly   can.hear-Non.PST

'I can hear a sound faintly.'
CI: I have measured the degree of sound based on my sense of hearing.

B: Sou? Boku-ni-wa hakkiri kikoe-ru-yo.
Really I-to-TOP   clearly can.hear-Non.PST-Prt

'Really? I can hear it clearly.'

However, it is impossible to reject the experiential meaning by saying, "No, that's false."

(17) A: Kono koohii-wa   kasukani amai.
This coffee-TOP faintly   sweet

At-issue: The degree of sweetness of this coffee is slightly greater than zero.
CI: I have measured the degree of sweetness based on my sense of taste.

B: Iya sore-wa   uso-da.   # Anta-wa mikaku-de kanjite i-nai.
No that-TOP false-PRED   You-TOP taste-with feel   be-NEG
'No, that is false. You are not feeling it with your own mouth.'

Further evidence for the assertion that *kasukani* has a CI and is logically independent of "what is said" comes from the fact that the experiential meaning semantically projects even if *kasukani* is embedded under the verb *omou* 'think' or the modal *kamoshirenai* 'may':

(18) (Context: The speaker is drinking coffee.)

a. Kono koohii-wa   kasukani amai-to   omo-u.
This coffee-TOP faintly   sweet-that think-Non.PST

'I think that this coffee is faintly sweet.'
(CI: I have measured the degree of sweetness based on my sense of taste.)

b. Kono koohii-wa   kasukani amai-kamoshirenai.
This coffee-TOP faintly   sweet-may

'This coffee may be faintly sweet.'
(CI: I have measured the degree of sweetness based on my sense of taste.)

The CI components of (18) are not within the semantic scope of *omou* 'think' or *kamoshirenai* 'may'.

The fact that the experiential component of *kasukani* cannot be within the semantic scope of a logical operator also supports the idea that it is a CI (non-at-issue). For example, the experiential component does not fall within the semantic scope of a confirmation question:

(19) Kono sake kasukani amai-yo-ne?
      This sake faintly   sweet-Prt-Confirm.Q
      'This sake is faintly sweet, right?' (CI: I have measured the degree of sweetness
      based on my sense of taste.)

I assume that the experiential component is not a presupposition in the usual sense
because it is not taken for granted in the utterance of a sentence. However, I will not go
into detail about the difference between a presupposition and a CI; what is important
here is that it has the property of non-at-issueness.

Note that although *kasukani* is typically speaker-oriented, the perspective can shift.
For example, if it is embedded under an attitude predicate and the subject of the sentence
is a third person, the judge of *kasukani* is the subject (i.e., the attitude holder):

(20) Hanako-wa   kono wain-wa   kasukani amai-to   omo-ttei-ru.
      Hanako-TOP this   wine-TOP faintly   sweet-that think-STATE-Non.PST
      'Hanako thinks that this wine is faintly sweet.'

Furthermore, if *kasukani* co-occurs with a hearsay evidential, such as *rashii* 'I hear',
then the judge of *kasukani* is someone who reported that the wine is faintly sweet, as
shown in:

(21) Kono wain-wa   kasukani amai-rashii.
      This wine-TOP faintly   sweet-EVID
      'I heard that this wine is faintly sweet.'

Although Potts (2005) claims that CIs are always speaker-oriented, several scholars
have claimed that CI expressions, such as expressives, can have a non-speaker orienta-
tion (e.g., Amaral et al. 2007; Potts 2007; Harris and Potts 2009). I consider that this
also applies to *kasukani*.[2]

2.4 Formal Analysis of *kasukani*

Let us now consider how the meaning of *kasukani* can be analyzed formally using the
following example:

(22) Kono sake-wa   kasukani amai.
      This sake-TOP faintly   sweet
      'This sake is faintly sweet.'

In this study, I will analyze the meaning of sense-based minimizers based on multidimensional semantics (Potts 2005) in which both an at-issue meaning and a CI meaning are compositional but are interpreted along different dimensions (i.e., an at-issue
dimension and a CI dimension). More specifically, I use the logic of mixed content
(McCready 2010; Gutzmann 2012) to analyze the meaning of *kasukani*. In this system,
the meaning of mixed content is computed via a mixed application as follows:

---

[2] In this study, I do not consider the experiential component of *kasukani* a presupposition. It is
the judge's personal experience (typically a speaker's experience), not something that is shared
between a speaker and a hearer.

(23)   Mixed application

$$\alpha(\gamma) \blacklozenge \beta(\gamma) : \tau^a \times \upsilon^s$$

$$\alpha \blacklozenge \beta : \langle \sigma^a, \tau^a \rangle \times \langle \sigma^a, \upsilon^s \rangle \quad \gamma : \sigma^a$$

(Based on McCready 2010)

The at-issue component is to the left of $\blacklozenge$, and the non-at-issue component/CI is to the right. Superscript a stands for an at-issue type, and superscript s stands for a shunting type, which is used for the semantic interpretation of a CI involving an operation of shunting.[3]

When the derivation of the CI component of mixed content completes, the following rule applies for the final interpretation of the CI part:

(24)   Final interpretation rule: Interpret $\alpha \blacklozenge \beta: \sigma^a \times t^s$ as follows: $\alpha : \sigma^a \bullet \beta : t^s$
        (Based on McCready 2010)

Based on the above setup, I propose that *kasukani* has the following meaning (the variable G is an abbreviated variable for a gradable predicate (measure function) of type $\langle d^a, \langle e^a, t^a \rangle \rangle$ and j stands for a judge and "$\gtrapprox \mathrm{STND}_{MIN.G}$" stands for slightly greater than a minimum standard of G):

(25)   [[kasukani]] : $\langle \langle d^a, \langle e^a, t^a \rangle \rangle, \langle e^a, t^a \rangle \rangle \times \langle \langle d^a, \langle e^a, t^a \rangle \rangle, t^s \rangle =$
        $\lambda G \lambda x. \; \exists d[d \gtrapprox \mathrm{STND}_{MIN.G} \; \wedge G(d)(x) \wedge$ barely-recognizable$(d)] \blacklozenge \; \lambda G.$ have-measured $(j,$ the degree of $G)$ based on j's sense of {vision (color)/smell/taste/hearing/touch/ memory}

In the at-issue dimension, *kasukani* takes a gradable predicate G and an individual x and denotes that there is some degree d such that d is slightly greater than a minimum standard of G and d is barely-recognizable. In the CI component, it takes G and con-

---

[3] The following figure shows the shunting application:
    (i) The shunting application (Based on McCready 2010)

$$\alpha(\beta) : \tau^s$$

$$\alpha : \langle \sigma^a, \tau^s \rangle \quad \beta : \sigma^a$$

The shunting application is different from Potts' (2005) CI application, where it is resource-sensitive. Potts's CI application is resource-insensitive, as shown in (ii):

(ii) CI application (Potts 2005)

$$\beta : \sigma^a$$
$$\bullet$$
$$\alpha(\beta) : \tau^c$$

$$\alpha : \langle \sigma^a, \tau^c \rangle \quad \beta : \sigma^a$$

The superscript c represents the CI type, which is used for CI application. Here, the α of $\langle \sigma^a, \tau^c \rangle$ takes a β of type σ^a and returns τ^c. Simultaneously, a β is passed on to the mother node.

ventionally implies that the judge j (typically the speaker) has measured the degree of G based on their senses of vision, smell, taste, hearing, touch, or memory.[4]

As for the meaning of gradable predicates, I assume that they represent relations between individuals and degrees (e.g., Seuren 1973; Cresswell 1976; von Stechow 1984; Klein 1991; Kennedy and McNally 2005):[5]

(26) [[sweet/amai]]: $\langle d^a, \langle e^a, t^a \rangle \rangle = \lambda d \lambda x.\ \text{sweet}(x) = d$

Kasukani and *amai* are combined via mixed application. Note that as the CI component of *kasukani* is complete (i.e., its denotation is of type t^s), *kasukani* takes the argument *amai* only at the at-issue component. Figure (27) shows the logical structure of sentence (22) (the information on tense and world has been omitted for the sake of simplicity):

(27) The logical structure of (22)

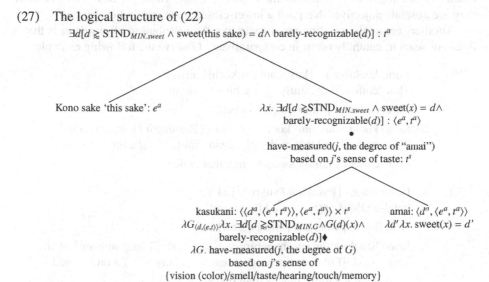

One seemingly puzzling point is that *kasukani* cannot co-occur with a gradable predicate, such as *oishii* 'delicious' and *urusai* 'noisy' despite the fact that they are related to sense (taste/hearing):

---

[4] Here, the CI of *kasukani* is taken as information related to the act of how the judge is weighing the degree in question. *Kasukani* is not evaluative in the sense that it does not express the speaker's attitude toward the degree of the at-issue. Rather, the act of measurement based on the sense and measurement at the at-issue level are taking place simultaneously. This point is different from the mixed content *Kraut*, which denotes German in the at-issue domain and additionally conveys that the speaker has a negative attitude toward German people (McCready 2010; Gutzmann 2011).

[5] Here, I consider that the unmodified adjective *sweet/amai* is of the same type as the usual gradable adjective, and no judge variable (j) is assumed. In positive adjective sentences, *sweet/amai* is evaluated in relation to the speaker's minimum standard, and I assume that the standard is introduced by a positive form (pos) or a degree modifier. This is where the judgment is made. In comparative sentences, the unmodified adjective is attached to the comparative morpheme.

(28) a. ?? Kono keeki-wa kasukani oishii.
          This cake-TOP faintly   delicious
          'This cake is faintly delicious.'

      b. ?? Kono heya-wa   kasukani urusai.
          This room-TOP faintly   noisy

          'This room is faintly noisy.' (cf., *Oto-ga kasukani kiko-e-ru* 'the sound is faintly heard'.)

In Sawada (2021), I claimed that *kasukani* cannot be combined with *oishii* 'delicious' or *urusai* 'noisy' because these adjectives are relative gradable adjectives that posit a contextual standard (norm) and cannot measure degrees from a minimum point. Whether something is tasty or noisy is determined by a contextually determined norm. Contrariwise, *kasukani* is fine with the adjective *amai* 'sweet' or *akai* 'red', because they are absolute adjectives that posit a lower-closed scale (minimum degree).[6]

Another seemingly puzzling point regarding the distribution of *kasukani* is that it does not seem to naturally occur in comparatives.[7] Observe the following examples:

(29) a. Kono koohii-wa {kasukani / sukoshi} amai.
          This coffee-TOP faintly   / a bit   sweet

          'This coffee is {faintly/a bit} sweet.'

      b. Kono koohii-wa ano koohii-yori-mo {?kasukani / sukoshi} amai.
          This coffee-TOP that coffee-than-*mo* faintly   / a bit   sweet

          'This coffee is faintly sweeter than that coffee.'

(30) a. Hanabira-ga {kasukani / sukoshi} akai.
          Petal-NOM faintly   / a bit   red

          'The flower petals are {faintly/a bit} red.'

      b. Kono hanabira-wa ano hanabira-yori-mo {?kasukani / sukoshi} akai.
          This petal-TOP   that petal-than-*mo*   faintly   / a bit   red

          'This petal is faintly redder than that petal.'

In (29b) and (30b) *kasukani/sukoshi* measures the difference between the target and standard degrees and only the sentences with *sukoshi* are natural. The sentences with *kasukani* sound unnatural because in this situation *kasukani* cannot measure degrees from an absolute zero point. *Kasukani* needs to signal that the speaker is aware through their senses that the degree in question is "not zero", but such an awareness is not possible in the environment of differential comparison. Although, theoretically, the standard

---

[6] It seems that the minimum standard of *amai* 'sweet' is context-dependent (person-dependent), and is different in nature from the minimum standard of typical absolute gradable predicates, such as English *bent* and Japanese *magat-teiru* 'bent'. Whether something is sweet is judged based on whether the degree of sweetness exceeds the minimum standard of sweetness, but as people have different senses of taste, the minimum standard is not absolute in a physical sense. It may be that sense-related adjectives belong to a new type of gradable predicate (i.e., possessing the features of both relative and absolute adjectives).

[7] I thank Kenta Mizutani for the valuable discussion regarding this point.

of comparison can be taken as "derived zero point", sensuously it is not a zero point. In contrast, as *sukoshi* does not specify that the judge is measuring degrees from a zero point (minimum degree) based on their sense, the standard of comparison can be of any degree.

However, note that in the context where the standard of comparison happens to be a zero point, *kasukani* seems to be usable in comparative sentences:

(31) a. Higashi-no sora-ga   {kasukani / sukoshi} akarui.
          East-GEN sky-NOM faintly   / a bit   bright
          'The sky is faintly bright.'

     b. (Context: The sky was completely dark a short time ago.)
         Higashi-no sora-ga   sakki-yori-mo {kasukani / sukoshi} akarui.
         EastGEN   sky-NOM before-than-*mo* faintly   / a bit   bright
         'Lit. The eastern sky is faintly brighter than before.'

It seems to me that both (31a) and (31b) are natural. If we assume a context in which the sky was completely dark a short time ago, then the comparative sentence (also) sounds natural. In this context, the speaker feels that the sky is faintly brighter than before, which is completely dark, and *kasukani* is in effect measuring degrees from a zero point. Thus, a comparative sentence with *kasukani* would be natural. However, this seems to be a special case.

3   Indirect Measurement: Measuring the Degree of Emotion via Perception

Let us now consider the case of indirect measurement. As we observed in the Introduction, *kasukani* cannot directly combine with an emotive predicate, but if there is a sense-related expression in the main clause, it can co-occur with an emotive predicate:[8]

(32) a. Hanako-wa   {??kasukani / sukoshi} odoroi-ta.
          Hanako-TOP faintly   / a bit   surprise-PST
          'Hanako was {faintly/a bit} surprised.'

     b. Hanako-wa   {kasukani / sukoshi} odoroi-ta   hyoujou-o ukabe-ta.
         Hanako-TOP faintly   / a bit   surprise-PST look-ACC express-PST
         'Hanako looked {faintly/a bit} surprised.'

(33) a. Taro-wa   {??kasukani / sukoshi} kanashin-deiru.
          Taro-TOP faintly   / a bit   sad-STATE
          'Taro is {faintly/a bit} sad.'

---

[8] Even if the subject is in the first person, *kasukani* 'faintly' cannot modify an emotive predicate:

(i) Watashi-wa {??kasukani / chotto} {kanashii-desu / odorki-mashi-ta}.
     I-TOP   faintly   / a bit   sad-POLITE   / surprise-POLITE-PST
     'I am {faintly/a bit} sad./I was {faintly/a bit} surprised.'

b. Taro-wa   {kasukani / sukoshi} kanashin-deiru-yooni mie-ru.
   Taro-TOP faintly   / a bit   sad-STATE-like   look-Non.PST
   'Taro looks {faintly/a bit} sad.'

In (32b) and (33b) *kasukani* syntactically and semantically modifies an emotive predicate, denoting that the degree of surprise/sadness is slightly greater than zero, but the measurement is made through the speaker's perception (sense of sight).[9]

Intuitively, examples (32a) and (33a) with *kasukani* are odd because of the lack of a perception-related expression, whereas (32b) and (33b) appear natural because *kasukani* interacts with *mie-ru* 'look' or *ukaberu* 'express', which are related to perception.

Note that if we replace the perception verb *mie-ru* 'look' into the evidential *yooda* or the evidential *mitai-da*, the sentence sounds less natural:

(34)   Taro-wa   (sono koto-de)   {??/? kasukani / sukoshi} kanashin-deiru-yooda.
       Taro-TOP that   thing-with   faintly   / a bit   sad-STATE-seem

       'Taro seems to be {faintly/a bit} sad about that.'

(35)   Hanako-wa   (sono koto-de)   {??/? kasukani / sukoshi}
       Hanako-TOP that   thing-with   faintly   / a bit
       kanashin-deiru-mitai-da.
       sad-STATE-seem-PRED

       'Hanako seems to be {faintly/a bit} sad about that.'

Here *yooda* and *mitai-da* behave as hearsay evidentials and are not construed as sense-related expressions.

The proposed multidimensional approach can successfully capture this. The key point is that although *kasukani* directly modifies an emotive predicate, its CI is interpreted (satisfied) at a root level. In the Potts/McCready system, we can capture this using the parsetree interpretation.

(36)   Parsetree interpretation (McCready 2010; cf. Potts 2005)
       Let $\mathcal{T}$ be a semantic parsetree with the at-issue term $\alpha : \sigma^a$ on its root node, and distinct terms $\beta_1 : t^{\{c,s\}}, ..., \beta_n : t^{\{c,s\}}$ on nodes in it. Then, the interpretation of $\mathcal{T}$ is the $\langle [[\alpha : \sigma^a]], [[\beta_1 : t^{\{c,s\}}]], ..., [[\beta_n : t^{\{c,s\}}]] \rangle$
       (Based on McCready 2010: 32)

---

[9] Note that if we place *kasukani* before the main predicate, the sentences become odd:

(i)   a.   ?? Hanako-wa   odoroi-ta   hyoujou-o kasukani ukabe-ta.
           Hanako-TOP surprise-PST look-ACC faintly   express-PST
           'Hanako faintly looked surprised.'

      b.   ?? Taro-wa   kanashin-deiru-yooni kasukani mie-ru.
           Taro-TOP sad-STATE-like   faintly   look-Non.PST
           'Taro faintly looked sad about that.'

For example, in (33b) the CI component of *kasukani* is embedded (situated below the bullet) as shown in (37), but if we apply this rule, we can see both the at-issue and CI meanings on the root node as shown in (38):

(37)

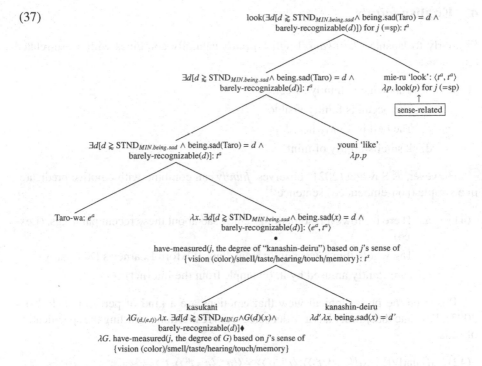

(38)   **After parseetree interpretation**

⟨look($\exists d[d \gtrless$STND$_{MIN.being.sad}$ ∧ being.sad(Taro) = d ∧ barely-recognizable (d)]) for j (=sp): t^a, have-measured(j, the degree of "kanashin-deiru'') based on j's sense of {vision/smell/taste/ hearing/touch/memory}: t^s⟩

In this approach, (32b) and (33b) present natural uses of *kasukani* because the sense-related component of *kasukani* is true in these sentences. Contrariwise, *kasukani* in (32a) and (33a) sounds odd because the sentences do not ensure that the CI component of *kasukani* is true.

One might wonder whether *kasukani* can combine with a regular adjective, such as *furui* 'old' (not an emotive adjective), if we add a sense-related expression, such as *mie-ru* 'look'. While such pattern seems to be theoretically possible, as shown by the following example, it is odd:

(39)   Kono shashin-wa {??kasukani / sukoshi} furuku mie-ru.
     This picture-TOP faintly   / a bit   old   look-Non.PST
     'This picture looks {faintly/a bit} old.'

I consider that this combination is odd because of the scale structure of *furui* 'old'. Just like the example of *oishii* 'delicious' (see Sect. 2.4), *furui* is a relative adjective that posits a contextually determined standard, and this conflicts with the restriction of *kasukani* in that it measures degree from a minimum standard.[10]

4   English *faintly*

Similarly to Japanese *kasukani*, English *faintly* naturally combines with sense-related adjectives:

(40)   a. This wine is faintly sweet.

      b. The ocean is faintly visible.

      c. The bell is faintly heard.

      d. It smells faintly of mint.

However, as Sawada (2021) observes, *faintly* can combine with emotive predicates in a simple (non-embedded) sentence:[11]

(41)   a. There is, however, something faintly sad about these recent paintings. (Lexico)

      b. The whole thing was faintly ridiculous. (Oxford Learner's Dictionary)

      c. I am faintly amused by it. (example from the Internet)

Based on the philosophical view that emotions are a kind of perception (Roberts 2003), I assume that *faintly* has a wider selectional restriction regarding the specification of sense:

(42) $[[\text{faintly}]] : \langle\langle d^a, \langle e^a, t^a \rangle\rangle, \langle e^a, t^a \rangle\rangle \times \langle\langle d^a, \langle e^a, t^a \rangle\rangle, t^s \rangle =$
$\lambda G \lambda x.\ \exists d[d \gtrsim \text{STND}_{MIN.G}\ \wedge G(d)(x)\wedge$ barely-recognizable$(d)] \blacklozenge\ \lambda G.$ have-measured (j, the degree of G) based on j's sense of {vision (color)/smell/taste/hearing/touch/ memory/emotion}

---

[10] A reviewer provided me with the following example, which does not include a perception verb in the main clause:

(i)   Kono koto-o   omoidasu-to   {?kasukani / sukoshi} kanashiku na-ru.
    This thing-ACC remember-when faintly   / a bit   feel.sad   become-Non.PST
    'When I remember this, I feel {faintly/a bit} sad.'

This sentence seems to be relatively natural because the verb *omoidasu* 'remember' is present in the when-clause, which is concerned with memory and experience. However, the sentence may still sound a bit unnatural because it is not clear how the speaker relates the degree of sadness and memory. A more detailed investigation will be necessary to clarify the possible patterns of indirect measurement.

[11] *Faintly* basically cannot combine with non-sense/emotion-related adjectives (i.e., #*faintly expensive*, #*faintly tall*).

The examples in (41) are natural because *faintly* can directly measure the degree of emotion through *j*'s sense of emotion (without the aid of another sense-related expression). This is different from Japanese *kasukani*, which does not allow *j* to measure degree through *j*'s sense of emotion.

The proposed analysis can also explain the judge-dependency of (43a) and (43b):

(43)   a.   Bill found himself faintly embarrassed. (*faintly* = subject-oriented, direct measurement)

       b.   Bill looked faintly amused. (*faintly* = speaker-oriented, indirect measurement)

In (43a), the judge (*j*) of *faintly* corresponds to the subject Bill (not the speaker) and measures degree of embarrassment through his emotion. In this case, the judge cannot be the speaker: The subject Bill directly measures his emotion. Contrariwise, (43b) is a case of indirect measurement. In (43b), the judge of *faintly* is the speaker, who cannot directly measure the degree of amusement. The only possible reading of (43b) is that the judge measures the degree of emotion through their sense of sight. The interpretation in (43b) is similar to that of (32b) and (33b) in Japanese. Therefore, English *faintly* can also measure the degree of emotion through other senses.

5   Conclusion

This study shows that unlike typical minimizers, such as Japanese *sukoshi* and English *a bit*, Japanese *kasukani* and English *faintly* have sense-related experiential components (i.e., they require a judge to measure degrees based on the judge's senses), and their experiential requirements can be satisfied both locally and globally. In the local case, *kasukani/faintly* combines with a gradable predicate *P*, and the experiential component is satisfied in relation to the gradable predicate, which is sense-based (e.g., *This sake is faintly sweet*). In the global case, *kasukani/faintly* combines with a gradable predicate *P* and denotes that the degree of *P* is very small, but its experiential requirement is satisfied based on the predicate, which is placed higher (e.g., *He looks faintly amused*). These points are theoretically significant because they suggest that there can be a mismatch between the at-issue and CI levels in the modification structure. This study presents the ways in which a multidimensional approach can successfully and uniformly capture the local (non-mismatch) and global (mismatch) cases.

This study also clarifies the similarities and differences between a sense-based degree adverb and a predicate of personal taste. Previous studies have argued that predicates of personal taste, such as *tasty*, require direct experience (e.g., Pearson 2013; Ninan 2014; Kennedy and Willer 2020). *Kasukani* and *faintly* are both similar to a predicate of personal taste in that they have an experiential component, but unlike a predicate of personal taste, the experiential component is satisfied via their interaction with other experience-related elements in the sentence, suggesting that they are a type of concord phenomenon.

References

Amaral, P., Roberts, C., Smith., A.E.: Review of the logic of conventional implicatures by Chris Potts. Linguist. Philos. **30**(6), 707–749 (2007). https://doi.org/10.1007/s10988-008-9025-2

Cresswell, M.J.: The semantics of degree. In: Partee, B. (ed.) Montague Grammar, pp. 261–292. Academic Press, New York (1976)

Grice, P.H.: Logic and conversation. In: Cole, P., Morgan, J. (eds.) Syntax and Semantics III: Speech Acts, pp. 43–58. Academic Press, New York (1975)

Gutzmann, D.: Expressive modifiers & mixed expressives. In: Bonami, O., Hofherr, P. (eds.) Empirical Issues in Syntax and Semantics 8, pp. 123–141 (2011)

Harris, J.A., Potts, C.: Perspective-shifting with appositives and expressives. Linguist. Philos. **32**(6), 523–552 (2009). https://doi.org/10.1007/s10988-010-9070-5

Kennedy, C., McNally, L.: Scale structure, degree modification, and the semantics of gradable predicates. Language **81**(2), 345–381 (2005). https://doi.org/10.1353/lan.2005.0071

Kennedy, C., Willer, M.: Evidence, attitudes, and counterstance contingency: Toward a pragmatic theory of subjective meaning, manuscript, University of Chicago (2019)

Klein, E.: Comparatives. In: von Stechow, A., Wunderlich, D. (eds.) Semantik: Ein Internationales Handbuch der Zeitgenossischen Forschung, pp. 673–691. Walter de Gruyter, Berlin (1991)

McCready, E.: Varieties of conventional implicature. Semant. Pragmat. **3**, 1–57 (2010). https://doi.org/10.3765/sp.3.8

Ninan, D.: Taste predicates and the acquaintance inference. In: Snider, T., D'Antonio, S., Weigand, M. (eds.) Proceedings of SALT 24, pp. 290–304 (2014). https://doi.org/10.3765/salt.v24i0.2413

Pearson, H.: A judge-free semantics for predicates of personal taste. J. Semant. **30**(1), 103–154 (2013). https://doi.org/10.1093/jos/ffs001

Potts, C.: The Logic of Conventional Implicatures. Oxford University Press, Oxford (2005). https://doi.org/10.1093/acprof:oso/9780199273829.001.0001

Potts, C.: The expressive dimension. Theoret. Linguist. **33**, 165–197 (2007). https://doi.org/10.1515/TL.2007.011

Roberts, R.C.: Emotions: An Essay in Aid of Moral Psychology. Cambridge University Press, Cambridge (2003)

Sawada, O.: Pragmatic aspects of scalar modifiers. Ph.D. Dissertation, University of Chicago (2010)

Sawada, O.: Pragmatic Aspects of Scalar Modifiers: The Semantics-Pragmatics Interface. Oxford University Press, Oxford (2018). https://doi.org/10.1093/oso/9780198714224.001.0001

Sawada, O.: Scalar properties of Japanese and English sense-based minimizers. Proc. Linguist. Soc. Am. **6**(1), pp. 433–447 (2021). https://doi.org/10.3765/plsa.v6i1.4979

Seuren, P.: The comparative. In: Kiefer, F., Ruwet, N. (eds.) Generative Grammar in Europe, pp. 528–64. Reidel, Dordrecht (1973)

von Stechow, A.: Comparing semantic theories of comparison. J. Semant. **3**, 1–77 (1984). https://doi.org/10.1093/jos/3.1-2.1

Willer, M., Kennedy, C.: Assertion, expression, experience. Inquiry, 1–37 (2020). https://doi.org/10.1080/0020174X.2020.1850338

Presuppositions and Comparison Classes in Japanese *hodo*-equatives

Eri Tanaka[1](✉) and Kenta Mizutani[2]

[1] Osaka University, Toyonaka, Osaka, Japan
`eri-tana@let.osaka-u.ac.jp`
[2] Aichi Prefectural University, Nagakute, Aichi, Japan
`kmizutani@for.aichi-pu.ac.jp`

Abstract. This paper proposes an analysis of a Japanese equative marker *hodo* in terms of a delineation theory of gradable adjectives. *Hodo*-equatives are associated with a norm-related presupposition where the complement of *hodo* exceeds a degree of standard, but the norm-relatedness is flipped when *mo* "even" is appended to *hodo*. We propose that *hodo* takes a comparison class as one of its arguments and argue that this delineation-based analysis of *hodo* successfully captures the flipped norm-related implication.

Keywords: equatives · *mo* "even" · norm-relatedness · presupposition · comparison classes

1 Introduction

This paper deals with an intriguing interaction between a lexical presupposition of Japanese equative marker *hodo* and a focus-related presupposition induced by *mo* "even/also". We propose that the behavior of this interaction is better dealt with if we assume that equative *hodo* is analyzed in terms of delineation approach to gradable adjectives and comparatives in the sense of [8].

2 Quandary

It has been acknowledged that explicit comparatives and equatives do not entail positive form sentences, or they are not **norm-related**.[1] Japanese *yori*-comparatives as in (1b), for example, do not imply that Taro or Jiro is tall.

This project has been supported by "On Development of Logical Language and Mathematical Concepts", Osaka University International Joint Research Program (A), (Principal Investigator: Yoichi Miyamoto) and JSPS KAKENHI Grant Number 21K00525 (Principal Investigator: Eri Tanaka).

[1] Comparatives are classified into explicit and implicit varieties [7]. Explicit comparatives, in contrast to implicit comparatives, do not produce a norm-relatedness. In Japanese, *yori*-comparatives are considered to be an explicit one [15].

© Springer Nature Switzerland AG 2023
K. Yada et al. (Eds.): JSAI-isAI 2021 Workshops, LNAI 13856, pp. 161–171, 2023.
https://doi.org/10.1007/978-3-031-36190-6_11

Japanese *hodo*-equatives, such as the one in (1c), on the other hand, convey that the *hodo*-complement (= Jiro), as well as the subject (=Taro), is tall. Thus in the context in (1a), the *yori*-comparative sounds OK while the *hodo*-equative is found weird. The norm-relatedness is context dependent, in the sense that if we are talking about a set of short people (say jockeys) and Taro and Jiro count as tall in that set, the *hodo*-sentence in (1c) becomes felicitous.

(1)   a.   **Context**: Taro and Jiro are both short.

b.   Taro-wa   Jiro-yori se-ga   takai.
Taro-TOP Jiro-than height-NOM tall.
"Taro is taller than Jiro."

c. #Taro-wa   Jiro-hodo se-ga   takaku-nai.
Taro-TOP Jiro-hodo   height-NOM tall-NEG
"Taro is not as tall as Jiro." (IMPLIES Jiro and Taro are tall.)

The norm-relatedness of the *hodo*-complement is considered to be a lexical property of *hodo*, i.e. its presupposition [16], while the one observed in the subject of the *hodo*-equative sentence is a derived implicature. The former survives in *if*-clauses, for example, and cannot be cancelled (note that a phrasal *hodo* phrase behaves as an NPI. See Sect. 3.), as evidenced by the fact that (2a) is not felicitously followed by (2c). (2b), on the other hand, is compatible with (2c), which suggests that the norm-relatedness on the subject is an implicature.

(2)   a.   I know that Jiro is not tall, and ...

b.   I know that Taro is not tall, and ...

c.

Moshi Taro-ga   Jiro-hodo se-ga   takake-reba, rooraa
if   Taro-NOM Jiro-hodo height-NOM tall-if   roller
coostaa-ni noreta-noni
coaster-DAT rode-COUNTERFACTUAL
"If Taro were as tall as Jiro, he could ride on a roller-coaster."

In spite of this, when focus particle *mo* "even/also" is appended to *hodo*-sentences, the presupposition can be flipped and the sentence implies that Jiro is not tall. Thus in the context in (1a), you can felicitously utter (3):

(3)   Taro-wa   Jiro-hodo-**mo**   se-ga   takaku-nai.
Taro-TOP Jiro-hodo-even/also height-NOM tall-NEG
"Taro is even not as tall as Jiro." (IMPLIES Jiro and Taro are not tall.)

The question is: how can we explain **the flipped norm-relatedness effect** associated with *mo*, when the "tall" norm-relatedness is the presupposition of *hodo*?

3   The Semantics of *hodo* and *mo*

3.1   The Semantics of *hodo*

In addition to the norm-relatedness presupposition, equative *hodo* has been known to be polarity sensitive in that it requires a DE-expression when it takes a phrasal element, as in (4). [16] claim that this is due to the weak existential semantics of *hodo*, per (5).

(4)   Taro-wa   Jiro-hodo ...
      Taro-TOP Jiro-hodo

    a.   *se-ga   takai.   b.   se-ga   takaku-nai.
        height-NOM tall   height-NOM tall-NEG
        "Taro is as tall as Jiro."   "Taro is not as tall as Jiro."

(5) $[\![\text{hodo}]\!]^c = \lambda D_{\langle d,t\rangle}: \theta \geq \theta_c \wedge D(\theta). \lambda P_{\langle d,et\rangle}. \lambda x. P(x)(\theta)$
      (θ is to be existentially closed at the end, and θ_c is a contextually determined degree of standard.)

This analysis captures the two properties of *hodo*: θ_c takes care of the norm-relatedness of the the *hodo*-complement, and the existential quantification without a maximality operator ensures that it requires negation. If an equative is interpreted with the maximality operator as in English *as ... as* equatives, we get a legitimate interpretation whether it is affirmative or negative, as in (6b)-(6c).

(6)   a.   John { is/isn't } as tall as Bill is.

    b. $\exists d. \text{HEIGHT}(j) \geq d \wedge d \geq \mathbf{max}(\lambda d. \text{HEIGHT}(b) \geq d)$

    c. $\neg \exists d.[\text{HEIGHT}(j) \geq d \wedge d \geq \mathbf{max}(\lambda d. \text{HEIGHT}(b) \geq d)]$

Following [16], if we assume that the *hodo*-complement includes an operator movement which abstracts degrees, we get the interpretations of affirmative and negative *hodo*-sentences as in (7a)-(7b).[2] With the semantics of *hodo* in (5), the polarity sensitivity follows because the affirmative *hodo* sentence (=(4a)) yields just an interpretation where both Taro and Jiro are tall relative to θ_c (=(7a)), which competes with a simpler positive sentence (i.e. Taro and Bill are tall), and fails to prevail in terms of the maxim of manner. (4b), on the other hand, has a legitimate interpretation, where both Taro and Jiro are tall, and Jiro is still taller than Taro, as shown in (7b). It is important to note that the negation has to take a narrow scope than the existential quantifier to yield a legitimate interpretation,

---

[2] One could argue against this analysis based on [1]. Alternatively we could utilize the analysis by [6] to produce the same effect.

as the wider negation (=(7c)) leads to an interpretation equivalent to "Taro and Jiro are not tall", which again competes with a simpler positive sentence (i.e. Taro and Jiro are not tall).

(7) a. ⟦ [[Taro is tall][hodo [Op_1 Jiro is d_1-tall]]] ⟧
         = $\exists\theta$. HEIGHT(taro)$\geq \theta \wedge$ HEIGHT(jiro)$\geq \theta$, where $\theta > \theta_c$ (after $\exists$-closure)   **vacuously true**

     b. ⟦ [Taro is not tall][hodo [Op_1 Jiro is d_1-tall]] ⟧
         = $\exists\theta$. ¬HEIGHT(taro)$\geq \theta \wedge$ HEIGHT(jiro)$\geq \theta$, where $\theta > \theta_c$ (after $\exists$-closure)   **not vacuous**

     c. = $\neg\exists\theta$. HEIGHT(taro)$\geq \theta \wedge$ HEIGHT(jiro)$\geq \theta$, where $\theta > \theta_c$ (after $\exists$-closure)   **vacuously false**

3.2 The Semantics of *mo* "even/also"

Let us now turn to what *mo* "even/also" does. Following [11,12], we assume that *mo* introduces a **scalar presupposition**, requiring its prejacent be the least likely among its alternative propositions (i.e. the prejacent asymmetrically entails the other propositions), as in (8).

(8) ⟦ mo ⟧^{w} = $\lambda p_{\langle s,t\rangle}$. p(w)
         + @ $\forall q \in$ ALT$_{\langle st,t\rangle}$[q $\neq$ p $\rightarrow$ p is less likely than q]
                                                           (@ denotes a presupposition.)

[11] endorses a scope theory of *mo*, under which the ambiguity observed in (9a) is explained by the ambiguity in scopal interaction between *mo* and negation, as shown in (9b)-(9c).

(9) a. Ambiguous between 100 yen is a large vs. small amount of money:
         Taro-wa 100 yen-mo mottei-nai.
         Taro-TOP 100 yen-even have-NEG
         "Taro doesn't have even 100 yen."

     b. **not > *mo*:**
         "Taro has 100 yen." ⇒ "Taro has 90 yen, 80 yen, ..."
                                          100 yen is a large amount of money.

     c. *mo* > **not:**
         "Taro doesn't have 100 yen."
                              ⇒ "Taro doesn't have 110 yen, 120 yen, ... "
                              100 yen is a small amount of money.

If we apply this analysis to *hodo-mo* in (3), we would get the LFs in (10a)-(10b). The configuration in (10a) produces no interpretation, because what *mo* takes is an affirmative proposition, which leads to the vacuous interpretation for *hodo* (cf. (7a) above). (10b), on the other hand, creates a non-vacuous interpretation: To satisfy the presupposition of *mo* in (10b), Jiro has to be the shortest among his alternatives, because only in that case, "Taro is not Jiro-hodo tall" asymmetrically entails "Taro is not x-hodo tall" (where x is an alternative to Jiro). Thus (10b) yields the interpretation given in (11):

(10)   a.   **not** [mo [Taro is Jiro$_F$-hodo tall]]   **vacuous**

       b.   mo [Taro is **not** Jiro$_F$-hodo tall]

(11)   (10b) yields ...

       a.   The prejacent: Taro $<_{\text{HEIGHT}}$ Jiro

       b.   The presupposition of *hodo*: Taro and Jiro $>_{\text{HEIGHT}} \theta_c$

       c.   The presupposition of *mo*: Jiro is the shortest among its alternatives.

(11) fails to capture the interpretation of (3), because (11) would make it infelicitous in the context of (1a), due to the presupposition of *hodo*. Furthermore, *mo* introduces a presupposition that Jiro is the shortest, but that does not ensure that Jiro is not tall/short (i.e. *John is the shortest of all.* does not entail *John is short.*)

In sum, the degree-based analysis does not explain the observed implicature.

4   Proposal

We propose the semantics of *hodo* in terms of a delineation theory of gradable adjectives and comparatives/equatives, based on [8]. In this type of theory, positive forms of adjectives are functions that partition a comparison class C ($\subseteq$D) into positive and negative extensions (12) [2].

(12)   For all models M and C $\subseteq$ D, all predicates P, and individuals a $\in$ C,

$$[\![P(a)]\!]_{C,M} = \begin{cases} 1, \text{if} [\![a]\!] \in [\![P]\!]_{C,M} \\ 0 \text{ if} [\![a]\!] \in C - [\![P]\!]_{C,M} \\ i, \text{otherwise} \end{cases}$$

slightly adapted from [2], p.15

Under this analysis, the norm-relatedness is just that an individual is mapped to a positive extension of P.

We assume that comparatives and equatives denote quantification over degree functions [4,13]. Degree functions are ways that divide relevant comparison classes (CCs) into P and not-P. Under this approach, a comparative sentence "a > b" is true iff there is at least one such degree function f that maps a to the positive extension but maps b to the negative extension with respect to a relevant CC. To exclude a degree function that randomly makes (13a) true, we assume the Consistency Postulate in (13b) [9]. The Consistency Postulate ensures that once x is greater than y with respect to P and a comparison class X, then y cannot be greater than x with respect to that predicate and the comparison class. We further assume following [8] that a comparison class has to have both positive and negative extensions as in (14).

(13) a. $\llbracket a > b \rrbracket = \exists f. \, f(P)(C)(a) \wedge \neg f(P)(C)(b)$

b.   Consistency Postulate (based on [9])
Let C be a comparison class such that $C \subseteq D$.
$\forall x. \forall y. \; \forall P. \; [\exists f. \, f(P)(C)(x) \wedge \neg f(P)(C)(y)]$
$$\Rightarrow [\forall f. f(P)(C)(y) \Rightarrow f(P)(C)(x)]$$

(14)   Let C be a comparison class such that $C \subseteq D$:
$\forall C. \, |C| \geq 2 \rightarrow \exists f. \exists x. \; \exists y. \; x, y \in C \wedge f(P)(C)(x) \wedge \neg f(P)(C)(y)$

We propose *hodo* has the semantics in (16). We confine ourselves to *hodo*-sentences with a phrasal complement here.[3] The semantics of *hodo* is dependent on two comparison classes, C and C*. C* is resolved anaphorically, and is responsible for the context dependent interpretation of *hodo*. C is a comparison class that is relevant for the comparison between the subject and the *hodo*-complement. Under this analysis, (4a) and (4b) have the interpretations in (17) and (18), respectively:[4]

(16) $\llbracket \text{hodo}_{\text{phrasal}} \rrbracket = \lambda x. \; \lambda C_{\langle e,t \rangle}. \; \lambda P_{\langle k,et \rangle}. \; \lambda y. \; \exists f. \; f(P)(C)(y)$, where $f(P)(C)(x) + @ \, P(C^*)(x) = 1 \wedge C = \{ \, x, y \, \}$.
(f is a degree function, k is a type for comparison classes, i.e. $\langle e, t \rangle$)

(17) * *Taro is tall [Jiro-hodo]* (=(4a))

a. $\llbracket C_1 \, [\text{Jiro-hodo}] \rrbracket = \lambda P_{\langle k,et \rangle}. \; \lambda y. \; \exists f. \, f(P)(C_1)(y)$, where $f(P)(C_1)(\text{jiro}) + @ \, P(\text{jiro})(C^*) = 1 \wedge \text{jiro}, y \in C_1$.

b. $\llbracket \, [[\text{tall}][C_1 \, [\text{Jiro-hodo}]]] \, \rrbracket = \lambda y. \; \exists f. \, f(\text{tall})(C_1)(y)$, where $f(\text{tall})(C_1)(\text{jiro}) + @ \, \text{tall}(\text{jiro})(C^*)(\text{jiro}) = 1 \wedge \text{jiro}, y \in C_1$.

---

[3] See [16–18] for the properties of clausal *hodo*.

[4] A reviewer inquired whether the comparison class may be linguistically realized. Our tentative answer would be positive, because a possible candidate for an expression of an explicit comparison class, *-nisitewa* "for X" could co-occur with *hodo*-sentences.

(15)   basukettobooru senshu-nisitewa, Taro-wa   Jiro-hodo se-ga   takaku-nai.
Basketball   player-for,   Taro-TOP Jiro-hodo height-NOM tall-NEG.
"(lit.) Taro is not as tall as Jiro for a basketball player."

    c. $\llbracket$ Taro is tall $[C_1[\text{Jiro-hodo}]]\,\rrbracket$ = $\exists$f. f(tall)(C_1)(taro), where f(tall)(C_1)(jiro) + @ tall(C^*)(jiro) = 1 $\wedge$ taro, jiro $\in C_1$.

(18)   *Taro is not tall [Jiro-hodo]* (=(4b))

    a. $\llbracket C_1$ [Jiro-hodo] $\rrbracket$ = $\lambda P_{\langle k, et \rangle}$. λy. $\exists$f. f(P)(C_1)(y), where f(P)(C_1)(jiro) + @ P(jiro)(C^*) = 1 $\wedge$ jiro, y $\in C_1$.

    b. $\llbracket\,[[\text{tall}][C_1$ [Jiro-hodo]]]$\,\rrbracket$ = λy. $\exists$f. f(tall)(C_1)(y), where f(tall)(C_1)(jiro) + @ tall(jiro)(C^*)(jiro) = 1 $\wedge$ jiro, y $\in C_1$.

    c. $\llbracket$ Taro is not tall $[C_1[\text{Jiro-hodo}]]\,\rrbracket$ = $\exists$f. $\neg$f(tall)(C_1)(taro), where f(tall)(C_1)(jiro) + @ tall(C^*)(jiro) = 1 $\wedge$ taro, jiro $\in C_1$.

Let us assume that Jiro, the *hodo*-complement in (4a)-(4b), is 165 cm tall. If C^* is identified by { x: x is a Japanese adult male }, Jiro would not be considered to be a member of tall(C^*), and thus the presupposition fails to be satisfied. If $C^* = \{$ x: x is a jockey $\}$, on the other hand, the presupposition is satisfied.

The explanation of the unacceptability of (17) is carried over to this analysis: (17) is true iff there is a degree function that makes Taro and Jiro tall in comparison class C_1, and Jiro's being tall in C^* is presupposed. If Jiro is in the positive extension in C^* and a degree function in C_1 puts Taro and Jiro to the same extension, that means that Taro and Jiro are both tall in C^*. This competes with a simpler positive sentence, and thus the unacceptability results.[5]

(18), on the other hand, does make sense: that Jiro (the complement of *hodo*) is tall in C^* is presupposed and Taro and Jiro are differentiated in C_1 with respect to a degree function.

Note further that in this analysis, the norm-related implication about the subject is not lexically encoded but derived: If the *hodo*-complement (Jiro) is tall relative to C^* and the subject (Taro) is not tall in C^*, it automatically follows that the latter is shorter than the former, which entails the asserted proposition, but at the same time you can use a simpler positive sentence "Taro is not tall". If the subject (Taro) is tall in C^*, on the other hand, no competition with a positive form arises. Thus, the implication that the subject is tall in C^* is derived.

When *mo* is appended as in (3), the LF will be (19). As in the analysis in (5) and (10) above, negation has to take scope below *mo* with this analysis too.

(19)   **mo** [Taro is not tall [[C [Jiro$_F$-hodo]]]]

Let us now assume that the alternative individuals ALT$_{jiro}$ = { Shiro, Jiro, Ken, Saburo }. Following [5], we compute the scalar presupposition of *mo* when the presupposition of *hodo* in the non-prejacent alternative propositions are accommodated.

---

[5] In other words, to assert that there is a degree function that violates (14) does not make much meaning.

(20)   A set of alternative propositions
$\mathrm{ALT_{prejacent}} = \{\ p \mid \exists x \in \mathrm{ALT_{jiro}}.\ p = \exists f(\mathrm{tall})(C)(x) \wedge \neg f(\mathrm{tall})(C)(\mathrm{taro})$
$@\mathrm{tall}(C^*)(x) = 1\ \}$

Each of the non-prejacent alternative propositions is thus associated with an accommodated presupposition where tall(x)(C*)=1. The scalar presupposition of *mo* requires the prejacent be the least likely one among its alternative propositions in (20), and this amounts to saying that Jiro (=the *hodo*-complement) is the shortest among $\mathrm{ALT_{jiro}}$, as discussed above. We assume that this is carried out by truncation of alternative propositions that include shorter individuals than Jiro (cf. [3,14]).

(21)   a.   Alternative propositions with its presupposition accommodated:
$\exists f.\ \neg f(\mathrm{tall})(C)(\mathrm{taro})$, where $f(\mathrm{tall})(C)(\mathrm{jiro})$
@ $\mathrm{tall}(C^*)(\mathrm{jiro}) = 1$
$\exists f.\ \neg f(\mathrm{tall})(C)(\mathrm{taro})$, where $f(\mathrm{tall})(C)(\mathrm{saburo})$
@ $\mathrm{tall}(C^*)(\mathrm{saburo}) = 1$
$\exists f.\ \neg f(\mathrm{tall})(C)(\mathrm{taro})$, where $f(\mathrm{tall})(C)(\mathrm{ken})$
@ $\mathrm{tall}(C^*)(\mathrm{ken}) = 1$
. . .

b.   A scalar presupposition satisfied through truncation
If a non-prejacent $p \in \mathrm{ALT_{prejacent}}$ entails the prejacent, it is stricken out from the $\mathrm{ALT_{prejacent}}$.

(22a)-(22b) illustrate how the relevant comparison classes are formed in the computation of presuppositions of *hodo* and *mo*. (22a) shows the accommodated presupposition of *hodo*, where C* is assumed to be a relevant comparison class that holds $\mathrm{ALT_{jiro}}$ as its subset. Each of the alternative propositions includes Taro and individual from $\mathrm{ALT_{jiro}}$ as its comparison class (=C in (21)). To satisfy the scalar presupposition of *mo*, it has to be known that Jiro is shorter than his alternatives, which means that there is a comparison class that includes $\mathrm{ALT_{jiro}}$. The comparison class is truncated so that it only allows Jiro to be not-tall, as in (22b).

(22)   a. $\{\underbrace{a, b, c, d, e, shiro,}_{\neg tall(C*)}\ \overbrace{jiro, ken, saburo, \ldots,}^{tall(C*)}\}$

b.   After truncation
$C' = \{\ \underbrace{jiro}_{\neg tall(C')}, \overbrace{ken, saburo, \ldots,}^{tall(C')}\}$

The Consistency Postulate in (13b) ensures that if Jiro is the shortest in C', there will be no degree function f such that it maps Jiro to the positive extension (=(23a)). We also assume the constraint on comparison classes in (14), which requires a comparison class to have both non-empty positive and negative extensions. From these, that Jiro always has to be in a negative extension in C' follows:

(23)   a. $\neg \exists f.\ f(\text{tall})(\text{C'})(\text{jiro})$

     b.   For any comparison classes, there is always a way to partition a comparison class into a positive and a negative extensions. (=(14))

     c.   From (a), (b): Jiro is not tall in C'. => the implicature in (3)

Notice that after the truncation, the relevant comparison class for the interpretation is confined to C', which sets Jiro is the shortest and always puts him onto a negative extension. In other words, the truncation leads to the nullification of presuppositional effect of *hodo*.[6]

Since the presuppositional effect of *hodo* is nullified via truncation when it is associated with *mo*, both contexts A and B are now consonant with (24c).

(24)   a.   Context A: Jiro, Ken, Saburo are all not tall for adult male persons, and Jiro is the shortest among them.

     b.   Context B: Jiro, Ken, Saburo are all tall for adult male persons, and Jiro is the shortest among them.

     c.   What about Taro? Is he taller than Jiro?
        –Iya, Taro-wa Jiro-hodo-mo se-ga takaku-nai.
        –No, Taro-TOP Jiro-hodo-even height-NOM tall-NEG
        "–No, Taro is not even as tall as Jiro."

This analysis makes prediction about the implication on the subject. Recall that the subject of *hodo*-equatives (without *mo*) is associated with a norm-related implication, which is derived from the presupposition on the complement of *hodo* and the asserted proposition (see (1c)). With *hodo* + *mo* sentences, on the other hand, the implication is obscured: The subject may or may not be norm-related. Rather, the subject is *asserted* to be placed lower than the lowest element. (24c), for example, conveys that Taro is extremely short, because he does not exceed Jiro in height, who is known to be short among Jiro, Ken and Saburo. In other words, the implication on the subject is also nullified because of the truncation of the (original) comparison class (=C*).

---

[6] Alternatively, we could explain the elided presuppositional effects of *hodo* by the adjustment of the anaphoric comparison class C*: C* is constrained to be the one that induces no conflict with the presupposition of *mo*. We could accommodate C* such that C* makes Jiro tall but he is not tall in C'. Thus as far as we can supply C* that makes 165-cm tall Jiro tall, the presupposition of *hodo* is satisfied. In other words, C' that makes Jiro not-tall coerces C* to be identified by such comparison class.

To recap, our proposal makes a crucial reference to a comparison class in the semantics of *hodo*. This analysis can capture why the superlative meaning induced by the scalar presupposition of *mo* leads to a flipped norm-relateness implication. We also claim that the satisfaction of a scalar presupposition via truncation of a comparison class is responsible for the apparent lack of the presuppositional effect of *hodo*.

5   Conclusion

We claim that Japanese equative *hodo* should be analyzed under the delineation theory of gradable adjectives and comparative/equatives, rather than a degree-based analysis such as [17]. Our proposal is motivated by the implication that arises when focus sensitive particle *mo* is appended to *hodo*. Comparison classes play a crucial role in explaining the produced implication. We hope to extend our analysis to other focus-related particles such as contrastive topic *wa*, such as the one in (25), when associated with comparative constructions, because *yori*-comparatives also induce a norm-related implication (= the *yori*-complement is *not tall*)(cf. [10]).

(25)   Taro-wa   Jiro-yori-wa se-ga   takai.
        Taro-TOP Jiro-than-CT height-NOM tall
        "Taro is taller at least than Jiro."

References

1. Beck, S., Oda, T., Sugisaki, K.: Parameteric variation in the semantics of comparison: Japanese vs English. J. East Asian Linguist. **13**, 289–344 (2004)
2. Burnett, H.: A delineation solution to the puzzles of absolute adjectives. Linguist. Philos. **37**, 1–39 (2014)
3. Chen, Y.H.: Superlative Modifiers: Ignorance and Concession. Ph.D. thesis, Rutgers, The State University of New Jersey (2018)
4. Doetjes, J., Constantinescu, C., Součková, K.: A neo-Kleinian approach to comparatives. Proc. SALT **19**, 124–141 (2009)
5. Erlewine, M.Y.: Movement out of Focus. Ph.D. thesis, MIT (2014)
6. Hayashishita, J.R.: Yori-comparatives: A reply to Beck et al. (2004). J. East Asian Linguist. **18**, 65–100 (2009)
7. Kennedy, C.: Vagueness and grammar: the semantics of relative and absolute gradable adjective. Linguist. Philos. **30**, 1–45 (2007)
8. Klein, E.: A semantics for positive and comparative adjectives. Linguist. Philos. **4**(1), 1–46 (1980)
9. Klein, E.: The interpretation of adjectival comparatives. J. Linguist. **18**, 113–136 (1982)
10. Mizutani, K., Tanaka, E.: Yori-comparatives revisited. In: Proceedings of the 163rd Linguistic Society of Japan, pp. 164–170 (2021)

11. Nakanishi, K.: Even, only, and negative polarity in Japanese. Proc. SALT **16**, 138–155 (2006)
12. Nakanishi, K.: Scope of even: a cross-linguistic perspective. Proc. NELS **38**, 179–192 (2009)
13. van Rooij, R.: Implicit versus explicit comparatives. In: Paul Egré, N.K. (ed.) Vagueness and Language Use, pp. 51–72. Springer, London (2011). https://doi.org/10.1057/9780230299313_3
14. Sawada, O.: The Japanese contrastive WA: a mirror image of EVEN. Proc. Berkeley Linguist. Soc. **34**, 281–292 (2008)
15. Sawada, O.: Pragmatic aspects of implicit comparison: an economy-based approach. J. Pragmat. **41**, 1079–1103 (2009)
16. Tanaka, E., Kenta, M., Solt, S.: Equative semantics and polarity sensitivity. In: Workshop on Degree Expressions and Polarity Effects. ZAS, Berlin, 9 March 2020
17. Tanaka, E., Mizutani, K., Solt, S.: Existential semantics in equatives in Japanese and German. In: Schlöder, J.J., McHugh, D., Roelofsen, F. (eds.) Proceedings of the 22nd Amsterdam Colloquium, pp. 377–386 (2019)
18. Tanaka, E., Mizutani, K., Solt, S.: Equative hodo and the polarity effects of existential semantics. In: New Frontiers in Artificial Intelligence: JSAI-isAI International Workshops, JURISIN, AI-Biz, LENLS, Kansei-AI Yokohama, Japan, November 10–12, 2019 Revised Selected Papers, pp. 341–353 (2020)

The Semantics and Pragmatics
of the Japanese Honorific Titles *San*, *Kun*,
and *Chan*

David Y. Oshima[(✉)] [iD]

Graduate School of Humanities, Nagoya University, Nagoya 464-8601, Japan
davidyo@nagoya-u.jp
http://www.hum.nagoya-u.ac.jp/~oshima

Abstract. This work discusses the semantics, pragmatic effects, and
usage of the three "honorific titles" (honorific expressions typically
attached to a name) in Japanese: *san*, *kun*, and *chan*. It will be argued
that *kun* and *chan* convey a lower degree of respect than *san* does, and
that due to this feature, they (i) often signal intimacy and endearment
(without conventionally encoding such information) and (ii) are usually
preferentially applied, instead of *san*, to children. It will also be proposed
that there are two variants each of *kun* and *chan*, one unmarked and one
marked. While the unmarked variety of *kun* is applied exclusively to male
referents, the marked variety is neutral as to the referent's gender but
instead conveys that the speaker and the referent stand in the relation of
colleagueship in a broad sense. As for *chan*, while its unmarked variety
indicates that the referent is a child or a female, the marked variety is
not subject to this constraint.

Keywords: honorification · intimacy · not-at-issue meaning · affixal
designation terms · Japanese

1 Introduction

This work discusses the semantics, pragmatic effects, and usage of the three
"honorific titles" in Japanese: *san*, *kun*, and *chan*.

While these expressions constitute a major component of the social-deictic
system of the language, they have been discussed rather scarcely in previous
theoretically-oriented studies. A likely cause of this marginalization is that their
meanings are complex in having both honorific and gender/age-related facets,
and furthermore that the latter exhibits a good deal of interspeaker and stylistic
variation. The three items are abundantly mentioned in reference works, but
there are considerable discrepancies in the descriptions given there as to what
types of individuals each of them is applied to with what sociopragmatic effects.
I will develop a formal-semantic analysis of the three items, paying special attention to (i) the variation in their usage and (ii) the distinction between the coded
and inferred aspects of what their use may convey.

© Springer Nature Switzerland AG 2023
K. Yada et al. (Eds.): JSAI-isAI 2021 Workshops, LNAI 13856, pp. 172–187, 2023.
https://doi.org/10.1007/978-3-031-36190-6_12

2   Affixal Designation Terms

The Japanese language has a class of expressions which follow a name and convey information concerning the referent's social status, gender, age, and/or relation with the speaker. Some instances are illustrated in (1).[1] *San* conveys the speaker's respect toward the referent, much like English *Mr.* and *Ms.* do. *Sensei* likewise conveys respect, but unlike *san*, it is applied exclusively to teachers and experts in certain fields such as medicine and art. *Kyooju* and *hikoku* indicate the status of the referent as a professor and a defendant in court, respectively.

(1) a. {Sato$_s$/Hiroshi$_m$} **san** ga   toochaku shita.
         Sn/M   *san* Nom arrive   do.Pst
         '{(Mr./Ms.) Sato$_s$/Hiroshi$_m$} arrived.'

     b. Yamada$_s$ **sensei** ga   tegami o   kakareta.
         Sn   *sensei* Nom letter Acc write.ARG1Hon.Pst
         '(Dr.) Yamada$_s$ wrote a letter.'

     c. Kojima$_s$ **kyooju** ga   pasokon o   kawareta.
         Sn   professor Nom PC   Acc buy.ARG1Hon.Pst
         'Professor Kojima$_s$ bought a PC.'

     d. Murakami$_s$ **hikoku** wa muzai   o   shuchoo shite
         Sn   defendant Th innocence Acc claim   do.Ger
         iru.
         NpfvAux.Prs
         'Murakami$_s$, the defendant, claims his innocence.'

Expressions like *san*, and their analogs in other languages (such as English *Mr./Ms.* and *Dr.*), have been given various labels, including "(honorific) titles", "(honorific) suffixes/prefixes", and "role terms". This work adopts "affixal designation terms (ADTs)" as a label for the general-linguistic category that includes the Japanese expressions illustrated in (1), as well as English *Mr./Ms., Dr.*, etc., Mandarin Chinese *xiansheng, laoshi*, etc., and so on.

In Japanese the use of an ADT on a name is highly common but not obligatory. In conversations, reference to acquaintances by their surname or given name only—called *yobisute* (lit. 'calling-renouncing') in Japanese—is usually made when the speaker is very close to them, or openly looks down on them.

---

[1] Subscript *s* indicates a surname, *m* indicates a given name referring to a male, and *f* indicates a given name referring to a female. The abbreviations in glosses are: Acc = accusative, AddrHon = addressee(-oriented) honorific, ARG1Hon = ARG1 (subject-oriented) honorific, Attr = attributive, BenAux = benefactive auxiliary, Cop = copula, Dat = dative, DAux = discourse auxiliary, DP = discourse particle, EvidP = evidential particle, F = given name of a female, Gen = genitive, Ger = gerund, Imp = imperative, Inf = infinitive, Intj = interjection, M = given name of a male, NegAux = negative auxiliary, Nom = nominative, NpfvAux = non-perfective auxiliary, Prs = present, Pst = past, Psup = presumptive, Psv = passive, Sn = surname, Th = thematic *wa* (topic/ground marker), Top = topic marker, Vol = volitional.

People who the speaker knows only indirectly (e.g., famous artists, historical figures) too tend to be referred to without an ADT. It is also worth noting that in Japanese, a name with or without an ADT is commonly used not only for third-person reference but also for (vocative or non-vocative) second-person reference, as in (2) (Takubo 1997:21–23).

(2)   (addressing Sato$_s$)

    a.   Sato$_s$ **san**, nanji   ni   toochaku shita no?
       Sn   *san* what.time Dat arrive   do.Pst DAux

       'Sato$_s$, what time did (you) arrive?'

    b.   Sato$_s$ **san** wa nanji   ni   toochaku shita no?
       Sn   *san* Th what.time Dat arrive   do.Pst DAux

       lit. 'What time did Sato$_s$ arrive?'

Japanese ADTs may be classified by various criteria. First, while some forms, including *san*, *kun*, and *chan*, are used exclusively as ADTs, some others, such as *kyooju* 'professor' and *yoogisha* 'suspect', may function either as a common noun or as an ADT, the latter use derivative of the former. A parallel contrast is exhibited by English *Mr.*, *Ms.*, etc. on the one hand and *doctor* (*Dr.*), *professor* (*Prof.*), etc. on the other.

Second, some ADTs encode honorific meaning while some others do not. *San* and *sensei* belong to the first type, and *kyooju* 'professor' and *hikoku* 'defendant' to the second. ADTs like *kyooju* and *keibu* 'police inspector', which represent social statuses of prestige, are often used in consideration of politeness and respectfulness. They are not to be regarded as honorifics per se, however, in view of the fact that they can be used in contexts and registers where the use of honorifics toward the referent would be unnatural (Kikuchi 1997:245), as in (3).

(3)   (in a book or article on the history of physics)

    1895-nen, Würzburg daigaku   no   Wilhelm Röntgen
    1895-year W.   university Gen W.   R.
    {∅/kyooju/#sensei} ga   X-sen o   hakken shita.
    {∅/professor/*sensei*} Nom X-ray Acc discover do.Pst

    'In 1895, (Professor) Wilhelm Röntgen at University of Würzburg discovered the X-ray.'

Third, different ADTs contrast as to the possible range of application in terms of age and gender. (*O*)*joo*(*sama*), *oo*, and *toji* are examples of ADTs that are used only for relatively small age/gender groups, applied respectively to young women, elderly men, and elderly women.

Fourth, different ADTs contrast as to what types of host they are attached to. Occupation- and rank-based ones, such as *kyooju* and *keibu*, generally are attached to a surname or a full name (of the form "Surname + Given Name", in the case of the legal names of Japanese nationals), while kinship-based ones such as *oji*(*san*) 'uncle' are usually attached to a given name. *San* and *kun* may be used on a surname, a given name, or a full name, while the use of *chan* on a surname is relatively rare.[2]

3 *San*, *Kun*, and *Chan*: Basic Facts

San, *kun*, and *chan* are high-frequency ADTs that (i) encode honorific meaning and (ii) are used in a wide range of registers including colloquial conversations and news reports.

In reference works on the Japanese language, it is widely noted that the use of *kun* and *chan* is subject to constraints concerning gender and age of the referent. In the textbook series *Japanese for Busy People* (Association for Japanese-Language Teaching 2006a, 2006b), *san*, *kun*, and *chan* are described as follows:

(4)   *San*: a title of respect that may be used with both male and female names
       Kun: a title of courtesy used among friends or toward people who rank beneath you
       Chan: an informal title of courtesy used mainly toward women younger than oneself, or toward children

Makino & Tsutsui (1986) describe *kun* as "a suffix attached to the first or last name of a male equal or to the first or last name of a person whose status or rank is lower than the speaker's" (p.211), and remark that *chan* "is used with children's names or in child-like language" (p.386).

Contemporary newspapers and news programs generally adopt the guidelines in (5) (NHK Broadcasting Culture Research Institute 2005:68–69; Kyodo News 2016:536–537), although the details may differ from organization to organization and from context to context:

(5)   a.   *Chan* is applied to preschool children.
       b.   *Kun* is applied to male elementary schoolers.
       c.   *San* is applied to males in middle school and older, and females in elementary school and older.
       d.   Other ADTs, such as *shushoo* 'prime minister', *kaichoo* 'president', and *hikoku* 'defendant', may be preferentially applied, where relevant.

---

[2] *San*, *kun*, and *chan* may also be used with a common noun or the name of an organization, as in (i), or form a nickname with an abbreviation of a (family or given) name, as in (ii).

(i) [bengoshi 'lawyer' + san] 'Mr./Ms. Lawyer'; [megane 'glasses' + kun] 'the guy with glasses' (somewhat pejorative); [wan 'bowwow' + chan] 'doggie'
(ii) Yanagiba$_s$ + san ⇒ Gibasan; Atsushi$_m$ + kun ⇒ Akkun; Noriko$_f$ + chan ⇒ Norichan, Nonchan

This work will not discuss further *san*/*kun*/*chan* occurring with an item other than a (complete) name.

The three ADTs' ranges of application overlap in a rather intricate way. To list some points of interest: (i) in formal settings, *san* may be applied to preschool children, (ii) some speakers apply *kun* to females in company or school settings, and (iii) in informal settings, *chan* may be applied to adult females, as well as, though less commonly, to adult males. A full account of *san*, *kun*, and *chan* must be able to deal with such intricacies.

An additional noteworthy feature of *kun* and *chan* is that they tend to signal intimacy and endearment. Remarks to this effect are common in reference works including dictionaries (e.g., 3A Corporation 2000:15; Kikuchi 2010:25; Shogakukan Daijisen Henshuubu (ed.) 2012). It will be argued below that the indication of intimacy is not part of the coded meanings of *kun* and *chan*, but pragmatically arises from their conveying a mild degree of respect.

The semantics of *san*, *kun*, and *chan* has been scarcely discussed in the existing formal literature. McCready (2019) does discuss (though in passing) *san* along with some other ADTs from Japanese and English, but not *kun* or *chan* (her treatment of *san* will be mentioned in Sect. 5).

4   Formal Semantics of Honorification

This section introduces some background assumptions as to the semantics and pragmatics of honorifics (honorific expressions).

Japanese honorifics can roughly be divided into (i) referent(-oriented) honorifics and (ii) addressee(-oriented) honorifics. The first type, which includes ARG1 (subject-oriented) honorific predicates like *kakareta* and *kawareta* in (1b,c) and honorific ADTs like *san*, conveys respect toward one of the referents mentioned or evoked in the utterance. The second type conveys respect toward the addressee, and is exemplified by the predicates *arimasu* and *gozaimasu* in (6b,c).

(6)   Resutoran wa kyuukai ni {a. **aru**   / b. **arimasu**   /
       restaurant Th 9th.floor Dat {a. exist.Prs / b. exist.AddrHon.Prs /
       c. **gozaimasu**   }.
       c. exist.AddrHon.Prs }
       'The restaurant is on the 9th floor.'

(6a) does not encode any honorific meaning. (6b) and (6c) convey respect toward the addressee, the latter's honorific meaning being stronger.

By and large building on Oshima (2019, 2021; cf. McCready 2019, Yamada 2019), I represent the range of respectfulness expressible with honorifics as the interval of real numbers 0 and 1, and assume (i) that each honorific expression conveys, as a not-at-issue content, that its target is at least as "honorable" as some value within this range and (ii) that the indexical (context-sensitive) function **HON** assigns honorific values to individuals, thereby representing who the speaker honors to what extent in the utterance context. (6b) and (6c)'s honorific meanings can be formulated as in (7a) and (7b), with the tentative minimum honorific values of 0.3 and 0.7.

(7) a. **HON(Addressee)** ≥ 0.3 b. **HON(Addressee)** ≥ 0.7

For a Japanese conversation to be felicitous, it is required that "due respect" be expressed toward the individuals mentioned or evoked in the utterance as well as toward the addressee, and also that none of these individuals be excessively elevated ("overhonorified"). To account for this, Oshima (2019, 2021) introduces the following pragmatic principle, which henceforth will be referred to as the RMC principle (it is conceivable that this principle can be reduced to a general pragmatic principle along the lines of *Maximize Presupposition*; I remain agnostic on this matter here):[3]

(8) **Reverence Maximization (Content)**: For any utterance u, each lexical item (word or multi-word unit) i involved in u must be chosen in such a way that i, among its honorific variants, expresses the highest degrees of reverence toward (i) the addressee of u and (ii) the referents mentioned or evoked in u that do not exceed what these individuals deserve.

Aru, arimasu, and *gozaimasu* in (6) are honorific variants of each other. The RMC principle dictates that (6a), (6b), and (6c) be the appropriate choice when the addressee's honorific value is within (i) [0, 0.3), (ii) [0.3, 0.7), and (iii) [0.7, 1], respectively. When the addressee is the speaker's child, sibling, or parent, (6a) will be the only natural option; this implies that the Japanese social norms are such that one does not attribute an honorific value of 0.3 or greater to their close blood relatives. When the speaker is a receptionist of a luxury hotel and is talking to a guest, (6c) will be the most natural option; this implies that in this setting the speaker is expected to assign an honorific value of 0.7 or greater to the addressee.

It will be discussed below the RMC principle plays a key role in the use and choice of an ADT, too.

5 The Semantics and Pragmatics of *San*

San can sensibly be regarded as a referent honorific targeting the referent of its host (the name). *San* is associated with a lower degree of respect than an addressee-oriented honorific verb with *mas* (so-called "polite verb") is. This can be confirmed by observing that one may use a plain (non-honorific) verb while applying *san* to the addressee, as in (9a).

(9) Sato$_s$ **san,** reizooko no keeki { a. **tabeta** / b. **tabemashita** }?
    Sn   *san* refrigerator Gen cake { a. eat.Pst / b. eat.AddrHon.Pst }
    'Sato$_s$, did you eat the cake in the fridge?'

---

[3] In Oshima (2019, 2021), (8) is paired with another principle complementing it, called Reverence Maximization (Form). This second principle amounts to saying that when respect toward a certain party can be expressed within a single lexical item with more than one type of honorific expression (e.g., an addressee honorific and an ARG1 honorific), it must. It is not of relevance to the current paper, which focuses on one type of honorific expression (i.e. honorific ADTs).

The alternative patterns where the speaker uses a verb with *mas* while leaving out *san*, or using *kun* or *chan* instead, sound disharmonious.

(10) a.   #{Sato$_s$/Hiroshi$_m$} (**kun**), reizooko   no   keeki
            Sn/M   *kun*   refrigerator Gen cake
            tabemashita?
            eat.AddrHon.Pst
            '{Sato$_s$/Hiroshi$_m$}, did you eat the cake in the fridge?'

      b.   #Hiroko$_f$ **chan**, reizooko   no   keeki **tabemashita**?
            F   *chan*   refrigerator Gen cake eat.AddrHon.Pst
            'Hiroko$_f$, did you eat the cake in the fridge?'

Note that this does not imply that *san* indicates that its target is *only* mildly honorable; it, instead, indicates that its target is *at least* mildly honorable.

The (not-at-issue) meaning contributed by *san* can be represented as in (11), with the tentative minimum value of 0.2; α is the slot for the (logical translation of the) host of *san*.

(11)   **HON**$(\alpha) \geq 0.2$

The honorific meaning of *san* posited here is quite similar to the one proposed by McCready (2019:76–77), but differs in not constraining the upper limit of the honorific value of the host's referent (under McCready's treatment, *san* conventionally indicates that its target is honorable but not extremely so). The choice of *san* may be deemed "not respectful enough" in some contexts, but I take this to be an effect arising from the non-use of some other more appropriate ADT, such as *sensei* and *sama* (a formal ADT more respectful than *san*). In the setting specified in (12), (12a) is much less plausible than (12b), the choice of *san* likely perceived as disrespectful.

(12)   (Kojima$_s$ is a university professor, and the interlocutors work in administration at her department.)

      a.   Kojima$_s$ **san** ga   pasokon o   kawareta.
            Sn   *san* Nom PC   Acc buy.ARG1Hon.Pst
            '(Ms.) Kojima$_s$ bought a PC.'

      b.   Kojima$_s$ **sensei** ga   pasokon o   kawareta.
            Sn   *sensei* Nom PC   Acc buy.ARG1Hon.Pst
            '(Dr.) Kojima$_s$ bought a PC.'

Assuming that *sensei* conveys a meaning along the lines of (13), the choice of *san* indicates, due to the RMC principle, that the speaker assigns to Kojima an honorific value smaller than 0.35; this explains why (12a) sounds less respectful than (12b).[4]

(13)   **HON**$(\alpha) \geq 0.35$ & [**teacher**$(\alpha) \vee$ **expert**(α)]

---

[4] (i) sounds more respectful than (12a), and more or less as respectful as (12b).

As mentioned above, in typical settings *san* is not applied to young children. I suggest that this is not because *san* encodes information concerning the referent's age, but because the standard norms are such that generally children are not considered "honorable enough" to deserve the application of *san*—that is, they tend to be assigned an honorific value smaller than 0.2.

This supposition is corroborated by the fact that honorifics, including verbs with *mas* that convey a relatively mild degree of respect (in comparison to other honorifics), are generally not used toward children.

(14)   (The speaker, an adult, is at a train station and standing near the ticket machines. {i. A man about her age/ii. a boy around eight years old} passes by, and she notices a glove fall off from his bag.)

    a.   A, tebukuro otoshita yo.

         Intj glove   drop.Pst DP

         'Hey, you dropped a glove.' (man: #, boy: √)

    b.   A, tebukuro otoshimashita   yo.

         Intj glove   drop.AddrHon.Pst DP

         'idem' (man: √, boy: ??)

    c.   A, tebukuro otosaremashita   yo.

         Intj glove   drop.ARG1Hon.AddrHon.Pst DP

         'idem' (man: √, boy: #)

As illustrated in (14), when one talks to an adult stranger, it is the norm to use polite verbs with *mas* rather than plain verbs. The speaker may also apply a referent-oriented honorific feature such as (*r*)*are* (an ARG1 honorific suffix) to show a higher degree of respect toward the addressee. When the addressee is a young child, on the other hand, polite forms are generally not used, implying that children are usually assigned an honorific value smaller than 0.3. By the same reasoning, that *san* is usually not applied to young children can be taken to mean that they are usually assigned an honorific value smaller than 0.2.

In some settings, however, *san* may be applied to young children. Some kindergarten teachers, for example, address and refer to the kindergartners with *san*. Ones who usually do not, too, may do so on some formal occasions, such as a graduation ceremony of their kindergarten. As discussed in works such as Iwasaki

---

(i) Kojima*s* **kyooju** ga   pasokon o   kawareta.

    Sn   professor Nom PC   Acc buy.ARG1Hon.Pst

    '(Professor) Kojima*s* bought a PC.'

This cannot be attributed to the RMC principle, as *kyooju* does not directly encode honorific meaning (see Sect. 2) and conveys (as a not-at-issue content) merely that the referent is a professor. This implies that some additional discourse principle, which (i) favors an occupation-based ADT and (ii) is potentially at odds with the RMC principle, needs to be postulated to account for why some non-honorific— or quasi-honorific—ADTs such as *kyooju* may "win over", or "tie with", honorific ones. A full discussion of the competition between honorific and non-honorific ADTs, however, is beyond the scope of the current work.

& Ingkaphirom Horie (1995), Kikuchi (1997, 2010), and McCready (2019), the use of honorifics is affected not only by the relative social rank (vertical interpersonal relation) between the speaker and the potential targets of honorification, but also by the closeness (horizontal interpersonal relation) and the formality of the setting.

(15)   **Three major factors affecting who the speaker linguistically honorify to what extent**
Other things being equal:

a.   The higher-ranked an individual is relative to the speaker, the higher honorific value the speaker tends to assign to him/her.

b.   The more intimate two individuals are, the lower honorific values they tend to assign to each other.

c.   The more formal the situation is, the higher honorific values the speaker tends to assign to the addressee and the referents mentioned or evoked.

I suggest that some kindergarten teachers consider the kindergarten activities to be fairly formal settings, and this leads them to assign honorific values exceeding 0.2 to the kindergartners, and thus to apply *san* to them.

6   The Semantics and Pragmatics of *kun*

6.1   *Kun* applied to males

As noted above, *kun* is as a rule applied to (i) a male (ii) who is socially equal to or ranked beneath the speaker. Feature (i) can be accounted for by postulating that *kun* conventionally encodes the [+male] feature of the referent, like English *he* and *Mr.* do. Feature (ii), I propose, arises from $(\alpha\text{-})kun$'s conveying a lower degree of respect than its honorific variant $(\alpha\text{-})san$. I put forth (16) as the (not-at-issue) meaning contributed by *kun*.

(16) $\mathbf{HON}(\alpha) \geq 0.1$ & $\mathbf{male}(\alpha)$

When the referent satisfies the maleness condition, the selection of *kun* implies, due to the RMC principle, the non-applicability of *san*, and thus the referent's being assigned an honorific value smaller than 0.2. The standard norms dictate that a speaker constantly uses polite verbs with *mas* when talking with a socially higher-ranked individual (outside her family[5]), and this implies that a speaker assigns honorific values at least as high as 0.3 to socially higher-ranked

---

[5] As mentioned above, contemporary speakers generally do not apply honorifics to members of their families, including elderly ones. This pattern seems open to two interpretations. The first is that members of the same family perceive each other as more or less equally ranked. The second is that, although family members may perceive of each other as differently ranked, the extreme intimacy between them leads them to assign very low honorific values to each other.

individuals. As such, the use of *kun* is invariably blocked when the referent is a higher-ranked individual.

When the referent is equally- or lower-ranked, the speaker may assign to him a relatively high honorific value or a value as low as 0, a major determining factor being the intimacy. Adult strangers are, even if they are younger than the speaker, likely assigned the value of 0.3 or higher. Childhood friends, on the other hand, are likely assigned a very low value—possibly 0—so that the use of any honorific targeting them is deemed inappropriate.

Kun, consequently, may signal either a high or low degree or intimacy, depending on the standard of comparison. One who addresses his or her male work colleague Sato$_s$ as *Sato san* (in both work and private settings) may switch to *Sato kun* (at least in private settings) after they start a romantic relationship. In this case, *kun* can be said to indicate the increased intimacy. A high-school student may address closer male classmates without an ADT (i.e. apply *yobisute*-reference to them), while applying *kun* to less close ones, as in (17):

(17)   (The interlocutors are high-school students, and talking about a plan to go to the bowling alley together.)

Okada$_s$ mo kuru   tte.   Komatsu$_s$ **kun** mo sasotte   miyoo
Sn   also come.Prs EvidP Sn   *kun* also invite.Ger try.Vol
ka? Hora, tenkoosei   no.
DP Intj   transfer.student Cop.Attr

'Okada$_s$ says he is joining us too. How about asking Komatsu$_s$ to come too? You know, the transfer student.'

In such cases, *kun* can be said to indicate a lower degree of intimacy.

As mentioned above, in newspapers and news programs, reference with *kun* is generally limited to (male) elementary schoolers. This can be taken to imply that, in these registers, boys in middle school or older are assigned the honorific value of 0.2 or higher (so that they "deserve" *san*), while male elementary schoolers are assigned a value smaller than 0.2 but not smaller than 0.1.

It is interesting to note that in some settings *kun* functions as a "masculine counterpart" of *san*.[6] In the context of (18), the two people mentioned, one male and one female, are expected to have comparable honorific values, given that they stand in by and large the same interpersonal relation with the speaker. As such, this *kun/san* pattern, which implies here that Yumi's honorific value is 0.2 or greater but Kenta's is below 0.2, is intriguing.

(18)   (The interlocutors are a married couple, and are talking about their neighbors' twin children, Kenta$_m$ and Yumi$_f$, who have recently taken the entrance exam of the local university. The interlocutors are not particularly close to the neighbors, and have hardly spoken to the two children.)

---

[6] This practice has been questioned by some, considered to go against the principle of gender equality/inclusivity (Hayashi & Oshima 2021).

Kenta$_m$ *kun* wa gookaku shita   kedo, Yumi$_f$ *san* wa dame
M   *kun* Th pass   do.Pst but   F   *san* Th unsuccessful
datta   n   da   tte.
Cop.Pst DAux Cop.Prs EvidP
'I heard that Kenta$_m$ passed the exam, but Yumi$_f$ did not.'

Recall also that, in news articles and news programs, it is a common custom to apply this *kun/san* pattern to elementary schoolers.

One possible way to account for this asymmetric pattern is to suppose that *san* is not entirely gender-neutral after all, and specifies different minimum honorific values for a male and female referent—e.g., 0.2 for males and 0.1 or 0.15 for females. An alternative account, which I find more appealing, is that the gender asymmetry in question arises from Japanese speakers' general inclination *not* to assign very low honorific values—values smaller than 0.2, to be more specific—to females who they are not intimate with. This implies that the utterer of (18) does assign a higher honorific value to Yumi, a girl, than to Kenta, a boy.

6.2   Gender-neutral *kun*

Kun is sometimes applied to females, implying that the semantic formulation given in (16) cannot be the whole story. Makino & Tsutsui (1986:211) note: "A male may address females of lower rank by -*kun*. [...] Such addresses are commonly used in situations such as schools and companies". (19) is an example from nonfiction writing; (20) and (21) are examples from manga (comics; Figs. 1 and 2).

(19)   (In reference to an old song with the lyric: "*Ten ni kawarite fugi o utsu* (On behalf of Heaven, we shall defeat the unrighteous)", the author, a columnist-publishing editor in his 60s, talks about how young people nowadays are unfamiliar with this song and cannot even answer the question "What comes after 'On behalf of Heaven, we shall ...'?")
        [...] "'Aku o   utsu',   desho"   nante   kotaeru   uchi
                evil   Acc defeat.Prs Cop.Psup such.a.thing.as answer.Prs we
        no   jimusho no   Kasahara$_s$ Chiaki$_f$ **kun** (gen   30 sai)
        Gen office   Gen Sn   F   *kun*   currently 30 year.old
        nanka   wa, mada   sukuwareru. Motto tanoshii   no
        and.the.like Th in.comparison save.Psv.Prs more   amusing.Prs Pro
        wa Mihara$_s$ Chika$_f$ **kun** (25 sai)   de,   "'Fue o   fuku',
        Th Sn   F   *kun*   25 year.old Cop.Inf   flute Acc blow
        ja   nai   n   desu   kaa" nante
        Cop.Inf NegAux.Prs DAux Cop.AddrHon.Prs DP   such.a.thing.as
        kotaeru   n   desu   ne.
        answer.Prs DAux Cop.AddrHon.Prs DP
        '[...] my office colleague Kasahara$_s$ Chiaki$_f$ (currently 30 years old), whose answer was: "'Defeat the evil', right?", is not too bad. More

amusing is Mihara*s* Chika*f* (25 years old), who says: "Is it not 'play the flute'?""
(from *Uso happyaku, kore demo ka!!!!* by Yukichi Amano, published by Bungei Shunjuu in 1994)

(20)   (The speaker is a male employee of a newspaper company and is working in his office. Yamaoka, a 27 year-old male, and Kurita, a 22 year-old female, are his colleagues.)

Oi Kurita*s* **kun** denwa, Yamaoka*s* kara da.
hey Sn   *kun* phone Sn   from Cop.Prs
'Hey Kurita*s*, you've got a phone call from Yamaoka*s*.'
(from *Oishinbo*, vol.1 by Tetsu Kariya and Akira Hanasaki, published by Shogakukan in 1984)

Fig. 1. the graphic panels involving (20) (to be seen from right to left)

(21)   (The speaker is a male professor of veterinary medicine. He is talking with a group of students including Hishinuma, a female doctoral student.)

Sooka, sengetsu no   chuusha wa Hishinuma*s* **kun** ni   tetsudatte
Intj   last.month Gen injection Th Sn   *kun* Dat help.Ger
moratta   n   da   na.
BenAux.Pst DAux Cop.Prs DP
'Oh right, Ms. Hishinuma helped me vaccinate [the pigs] last month.'
(from *Doobutsu no oishasan*, vol.1 by Noriko Sasaki, published by Kodansha in 1988)

One may hypothesize that, some speakers use, in certain registers, *kun* as a gender-neutral ADT like *san* but with a lower degree of deference. This simple analysis is hard to maintain, however, in view of the fact that application of *kun* to young female children is highly marked, and is much less common than that to adult females. Given that *kun* is commonly applied to male preschoolers and elementary schoolers, its gender-neutral version should be applicable to girls in the same age range.

Fig. 2. the graphic panels involving (21) (to be seen from right to left)

Reference to women with *kun* is not common, and appears (i) to be made typically by male rather than female speakers and (ii) to generally require that there be some professional or intellectual community—such as a company and a university—to which both the speaker and the referent belong (The National Language Research Institute 1982; Ozaki 2001; Hayashi & Oshima 2021). The National Language Research Institute (1982) reports that, in a survey administered to employees of Hitachi, Ltd. in 1975–1977, only eight among the 191 male participants, and none of the 66 female participants, reported that there were some female co-workers who they, at least sometimes, addressed as "Surname + *kun*". Ozaki (2001) reports that, in a questionnaire-based survey administered to students of public middle schools in Tokyo (1,285 males, 1,171 females) in 1990, (i) 5.2% of male students and 7.5% of female students reported that they sometimes use "Surname + *kun*" to address their female classmates, and (ii) 5.8% of male students and 4.6% of female students reported that they sometimes use "Given Name + *kun*" to address their female classmates.

I suggest that there is a stylistically constrained variant of *kun* with the meaning in (22) and characteristic to (but not entirely confined to) men's speech. The logical predicate **Col**, standing for "colleague", is meant to cover not only co-workership but also a wider range relations including ones between professors and their students, senior graduate students and junior ones in the same lab, an artist and his assistants, a politician and her secretaries, etc.

(22) $\mathbf{HON}(\alpha) \geq 0.1$ & $\mathbf{Col}(\mathbf{Speaker}, \alpha)$

7   The Semantics and Pragmatics of *chan*

7.1   *Chan* applied to children and females

Application of *chan* signals that the referent is a young child or a female, and exhibits a strong tendency to follow a given name or a full name rather than a surname. For example, a female elementary schooler Sato$_s$ Emi$_f$ is much more likely to be referred to as *Emi chan* than *Sato chan*. In this respect *chan* sharply contrasts with *kun*; reference to a male elementary schooler as "Surname + *kun*" is quite common. I propose that *chan* typically conveys the (not-at-issue) meaning shown in (23).

(23)   **HON**($\alpha_{[+\text{GN}]}$) ≥ 0.1 & [**child**(α) $\vee$ **female**(α)]

Feature "+GN" indicates that the host has to be a given name ([−Sn, +GN]) or full name ([+Sn, +GN]).

Chan may signal either intimacy or distance, in the same way as *kun*. A college student who refers to his or her senior female friend Akemi$_f$ as *Akemi san* may swich to *Akemi chan* after they start a romantic relationship, in which case *chan* can be said to indicate a higher degree of intimacy. A female high-schooler may address the transfer student Miki$_f$ as *Miki chan*, but switch to *yobisute*-reference (start dropping *chan*) as they get closer; in this case, the use of *chan* in the initial stage can be taken to have been motivated by her desire to avoid being too intrusive.

7.2   Gender/age-neutral *chan*

Chan sometimes occurs on a surname, rather than a given name. It is, further-more, sometimes applied to adult males, as well as to adult females. (24) is an example from a magazine article based on a conversation, and (25) from a manga (Fig. 3).

(24)   (The speaker is a male automobile critic in his 40s, and Arai$_s$ is a male car dealer. They are test driving a Volkswagen.)

Sooiya   Arai$_s$ **chan**, Roorusu   no   bampaa no   natto tte   doo
by.the.way Sn   *chan* Rolls-Royce Gen bumper Gen nut   Top how
natta?
become.Pst

'Oh, by the way, what happened with the bumper nuts for the Rolls-Royce, Arai$_s$?'

(from *Saigo no jidoosha ron* by Reiichiro Fukuno, published by Soyosha in 2005)

(25)   (Kogure and Shima, both males in their 30s, are colleagues at a major company.)

K: Ja,   Shima$_s$ **chan**, anta mo yabai   yo.
     then Sn   *chan* you also dangerous.Prs DP

'Then, you're in trouble too, Shima$_s$.'

S: Dakara Kogure$_s$ **chan** ni   tanonde n   da   yo! Ore wa
     so   Sn   *chan* Dat ask.Ger DAux Cop.Prs DP I   Th
     umaku   riyoo sareta   n   da!!
     good.Inf use   do.Psv.Pst DAux Cop.Prs

'That's why I'm asking for your help, Kogure$_s$! They used me!'
(from *Kachoo Shima Koosaku*, vol.1 by Kenshi Hirokane, published
by Shogakukan in 1985)

Fig. 3. the graphic panels involving (25) (to be seen from right to left)

This gender/age-neutral variant of *chan* occurs only in informal registers,
and may be used between private friends and relatives (e.g., a man and his
brother-in-law), as well as between work-related acquaintances. I thus propose
that its meaning is simply as in (26).

(26)   **HON**(α) ≥ 0.1

8   Conclusion

A semantic analysis of the three high-frequency affixal designation terms in
Japanese, *san*, *kun* and *chan*, was put forth. It was argued that although *kun*
and *chan* have been commonly characterized as markers of intimacy and endearment, they do not lexically encode such information. Rather, the affectionate
tone pragmatically arises from *kun* and *chan*'s implying a relatively low degree
of "honorability" of the referent.

San does not encode any information concerning the gender or age of the
referent. It is generally not applied to children, because children tend to be considered "not honorable enough" to be addressed with *san*. *Kun* has two varieties,
one indicating the maleness of the referent and the other being gender-neutral.
The latter is used by a relatively small number of speakers, and indicates that
the speaker and the referent are in a colleague-like relation. *Chan* too has two
varieties. One indicates that the referent is a child or a female, while the other
does not convey such information. The latter is used relatively infrequently and
only in colloquial registers.

The proposed analysis accounts for how the ranges of application of the three
ADTs overlap, while distinguishing their typical and marked usage. The findings
of this work hopefully contribute to a better understanding of the category of
ADTs in Japanese and across languages.

References

3A Corporation: Minna no nihongo, Elementary I: Translation and Grammar Notes-Romanized (English) (2nd edition). 3A Corporation, Tokyo (2000)

Association for Japanese-Language Teaching: Japanese for Busy People I: Kana Version (revised 3rd edition). Kodansha International, Tokyo (2006a)

Association for Japanese-Language Teaching: Japanese for Busy People II: Kana Version (revised 3rd edition). Kodansha International, Tokyo (2006b)

Hayashi, M., Oshima, D.Y.: Fukateki koshooshi "san" "kun" no shiyooto jendaa chuuritsusei: Jittai to kihan o megutte. Kotoba **42**, 72–89 (2021). https://doi.org/10.20741/kotoba.42.0_72

Iwasaki, S., Ingkaphirom Horie, P.: Creating speech register in Thai conversation. Lang. Soc. **29**, 519–554 (1995)

Kikuchi, Y.: Keigo. Kodansha, Tokyo (1997)

Kikuchi, Y.: Keigo sainyuumon. Kodansha, Tokyo (2010)

Kyodo News (ed.): Kisha handobukku: Shinbun yooji yoogo shuu (13th edition). Kyodo News, Tokyo (2016)

Makino, S., Tsutsui, M.: A Dictionary of Basic Japanese Grammar. The Japan Times, Tokyo (1986)

McCready, E.: The Semantics and Pragmatics of Honorification: Register and Social Meaning. Oxford University Press, Oxford (2019)

National Language Research Institute: Kigyoo no naka no keigo. Sanseido (1982)

NHK Broadcasting Culture Research Institute (ed.): NHK kotoba no handobukku (2nd edition). NHK Publishing, Tokyo (2005)

Oshima, D.Y.: The logical principles of honorification and dishonorification in Japanese. In: Kojima, K., Sakamoto, M., Mineshima, K., Satoh, K. (eds.) New Frontiers in Artificial Intelligence: JSAI-ISAI 2018 Workshops, JURISIN, AI-Biz, SKL, LENLS, IDAA, Yokohama, Japan, November 12–14, 2018, Revised Selected Papers, pp. 325–340. Springer, Heidelberg (2019)

Oshima, D.Y.: Against the multidimensional approach to honorific meaning: A solution to the binding problem of conventional implicature. In: Okazaki, N., Yada, K., Satoh, K., Mineshima, K. (eds.) New Frontiers in Artificial Intelligence: JSAI-ISAI 2020 Workshops, JURISIN, LENLS 2020 Workshops, Virtual Event, November 15–17, 2020, Revised Selected Papers, pp. 113–128. Springer, Heidelberg (2021)

Ozaki, Y.: Gakkoo no naka de no chuugakusei no koshoo. In: Endo, O. (ed.) Onna to kotoba, pp. 145–152. Akashi Shoten, Tokyo (2001)

Shogakukan Daijisen Henshuubu (ed.): Daijisen (2nd edition). Shogakukan, Tokyo (2012)

Takubo, Y.: Nihongo no ninshoo hyoogen. In: Takubo, Y. (ed.) Shiten to gengo koodoo, pp. 13–44. Kurosio Publishers, Tokyo (1997)

Yamada, A.: The syntax, semantics and pragmatics of Japanese addressee-honorific markers. Ph.D. thesis, Georgetown University, Washington, DC (2019)

Honorifics, Grounds and Ideologies

Elin McCready(⊠)

Aoyama Gakuin University, Tokyo, Japan
mccready@cl.aoyama.ac.jp

Abstract. This paper discusses the notion of *grounds* using honorifics as a main example case. Grounds are 'global' assumptions that are essential for the use of particular linguistic items or constructions. They differ from other meaning categories in various ways, for example differing from presupposition in that they are sufficiently large, complex, and even ineffable as to be essentially unaccommodatable. Certain grounds of honorifics are presented together with several other examples and some implications of the analysis discussed.

1 Introduction

Honorifics and honorification are receiving increasing attention in formal semantics and pragmatics (e.g. McCready 2014, 2019; Portner et al. 2019, i.a.). Most of this literature focuses on the semantics of particular honorific expressions and on proposing frameworks for expressing such meanings. Such meanings necessarily involve social relations – formality of speech situation, social hierarchies, and so on – and thus are one kind of social meaning. The precise semantics and pragmatics of honorifics is an area of lively discussion in the field, but this paper aims to instead consider honorifics as bearers of social meaning in a different sense.

This paper proposes that honorifics, as part of their meaning, express a range of assumptions about society and social interaction: in a word, a complex of social fact. If these assumptions don't hold, it makes no sense to even use an honorific. I call foundational assumptions of this kind *grounds*. §2 introduces the notion of honorifics and presents one approach to their semantics and pragmatics (my own), which already makes clear some of the necessary grounds for making sense of them. The paper then provides a treatment of this phenomenon in §3 based on recent work of Henderson and McCready on enriching dogwhistles as a starting point (Henderson and McCready, 2021b, 2021a). In that work, enrichment is treated as a kind of invited inference which is mediated by the recognition of a social persona communicated by the speaker, which is in turn associated with an ideology: a way of valuing things in the world and a set of beliefs or background assumptions about it. The paper then shows that the grounds introduced by honorifics can be treated as an ideology in Henderson and McCready's sense, after indicating in some detail what features of a social environment ground the use of honorific expressions, in §4.

Thanks to the audience of LENLS 2022 for interesting and helpful discussion, and to audiences at the 2022 Deutschen Gesellschaft für Sprachwissenschaft and the 22nd Szklarska Poreba Workshop on the Roots of Pragmasemantics.

K. Yada et al. (Eds.): JSAI-isAI 2021 Workshops, LNAI 13856, pp. 188–197, 2023.
https://doi.org/10.1007/978-3-031-36190-6_13

The paper concludes with more general discussion of grounds. I first show in Sect. 5 how they can be distinguished from other classes of meaning such as presuppositions, and then turn to comparisons to other, related proposals about perspectives and invocations in the literature on slurs (Camp, 2013; Davis and McCready, 2020), and to the *hinge propositions* of Wittgenstein (1991). Finally, I show several other domains in which grounds can be observed in Sect. 6, taking as exemplars classifiers, gendered speech, and nonanthropomorphic narrative.

2   Honorifics and Their Semantics

Honorific expressions are, roughly, terms lexically specified for formality or used to indicate the social standing of one individual with respect to another, usually but not always the speaker (see Agha 1994 for an overview). It's not entirely straightforward to paraphrase their precise meaning, which is one motivation for treating their meanings as expressive, but one possible view is that their primary use is roughly to indicate a formal (or informal) attitude toward an individual, possibly the addressee, or to indicate that the discourse situation is one requiring formality; this is the approach of McCready (2019). Pragmatically, such meanings naturally extend to interpretation as respect for an addressee or as an indication of social distance from them, though genuine, sincere respect is in no sense a precondition for the use of an honorific, as with the case of a teacher one hates, or a boss one thinks is incompetent, but still must use honorific forms with because of relative social positioning.

McCready (2019), extending and refining the work of Potts (2007), treats honorifics as interacting with a register which forms part of a discourse model. Registers are real-numbered subintervals of $[0, 1]$, and honorifics also have such subintervals as part of their lexical meanings (which we might call 'honorific denotations'): they are mixed expressive items (McCready, 2010), where in general the subinterval forms the expressive component of the denotation. For instance, consider the denotation of the Japanese honorific verbal suffix -*mas*-, which indicates a high degree of formality of the discourse situation:

(1) $[[-mas-]] = \lambda P \lambda x [P(x)] \blacklozenge (Hon = [.6, 1)) : \langle\langle e, t\rangle, \langle e, t\rangle\rangle^a \times t^s$

Here, on the right-hand side of the diamond in the denotation, we see an expressive-typed object of type t, which picks out the interval $[.6, 1]$. Taken together with a rule for determining the appropriateness of the use of honorific expressions (see McCready 2019), if the register and honorific denotation of a discourse segment have a nonempty intersection, use of that segment (and its honorifics) is felicitous; here, that's just to say that the discourse register must share a nonempty interval with $[.6, 1]$, which is a fairly formal context. There are complications involving multiple honorifics and expressions where the honorific denotation is derived from inferential processes, but this is the basic picture of the semantics and pragmatic effect of pure honorifics.

We might ask the question: does this exhaust the effects of honorifics on the discourse context, and on epistemic states of interpreters? As with many other kinds of expressions, it seems clear that the simple semantics, and the simple method of determining felicity in the sense familiar from eg. the analysis of presuppositions (e.g. Beaver

1997, 2001) does not. When honorifics are used, certain kinds of assumptions are unavoidably introduced about social situations: what they are, the kinds of relations that hold between the people involved in them, and how one should behave in them. Without these assumptions, it wouldn't make sense to use honorifics; more, their semantics would be left unsupported by social reality. These kinds of things are in no sense part of the lexical entries of the honorifics. How should we understand them in terms of our semantic and pragmatic theories? How should they be introduced to formal models? And do other examples exist?

3   Ideologies

This paper suggests that two elements are needed for a better understanding of how the kind of honorific grounding sketched in the previous paragraph works. The first involves a manner of formulating the grounds themselves, and the second involves the manner in which they are introduced. For the first, the topic of this section and the next, I adopt aspects of the strategy of Henderson and McCready (2021a), an extended work on the semantics and pragmatics of dogwhistles, expressions which convey one piece of content to an outgroup and other, or additional, content to an ingroup which is 'in-the-know' about the covert meaning of the dogwhistle. Henderson and McCready separate dogwhistles into two types, *identifying* and *enriching* dogwhistles: the latter are a subtype of the former which, in addition to indicating something about the social persona of the speaker to the interpreter, also induce an enrichment of the content of the dogwhistle expression.

   Consider, for an example, the dogwhistle 'inner city,' which has as standard denotational meaning the set of urban neighborhoods (in a framework taking 'common nouns' to denote sets of individuals a la Montague 1974 or Heim and Kratzer 1998), but which is also a dogwhistle for (racialized views of) Black neighborhoods in such urban areas. To slightly simplify the analysis of H&M, this dogwhistle conveys a quasi-racist social persona; recognition of this persona entails recognition that the speaker is willing to, or even intends to, be associated with this persona and the ideological commitments that come along with it (this last point guaranteed by an axiom about commitment for social personas called *Social Sincerity* analogous to Gricean Quality: see Henderson and McCready 2021b for details). Supposing that one of these ideological commitments is that most people living in US urban neighborhoods are Black, the expression 'inner city' together with that commitment allow the interpreter to infer that the speaker means to say something about Black people. This is a kind of invited inference mediated by the recognition of a social persona by a savvy listener.

   What do ideologies look like in this framework? They are pairs $\iota = \langle \rho, \mathcal{B} \rangle$. Here, ρ is a function yielding affective values: the speaker's attitudes toward various individuals (e.g. particular politicians) and also toward certain kinds of actions, attitudes, properties or groups of people. The latter are also modeled as individuals via the kind-mapping function '$\cap$' employed by employed by Chierchia (1998) to map properties to kinds in the denotation of bare nominals, but here used more generally to create individuals from sets. ρ thus maps individuals – or individual objects derived from properties (being antiauthoritarian, being a member of a social group, being of a particular gender or ethnicity, etc) to real numbers corresponding to the affective attitudes of those who subscribe to the ideology ι. The second element of ideologies, $\mathcal{B}$, is the *basis* of an ideology: a set of propositions corresponding to the beliefs about the world that comprise those things that people subscribing to the ideology take to be true. Given the *Social Sincerity* principle, a speaker projecting a persona associated with an ideology licenses the inference that the speaker accepts a significant subset of $\mathcal{B}$. It's these properties which induce the kind of inferences discussed in connection with enriching dogwhistles like 'inner city' above, and which can be used to model the grounds introduced by honorifics.

4   Honorific Grounds via Ideologies

The main claim of the present paper is that a similar method to that employed by Henderson and McCready for ideologies can be used to make sense of the kind of grounding assumptions introduced by honorifics. The basic idea is that the use of honorifics 'projects' a set of assumptions $\mathcal{H}$ about social situations and the social world that can be codified in a similar way to ideologies, i.e. via a pair consisting of an affective value-assigning expression and a set of propositions. The precise manner in which this projection takes place will be addressed in the next section.

The grounds of honorifics include at least the following assumptions about the social world: that social situations differ in their formality (F), that the speaker's behavior should be conditioned by the formality of the social situation in which they are speaking (A), that there are social hierarchies (H), that the speaker has a well-defined position in those hierarchies (P), and that it is appropriate to let one's speech behavior be conditioned by those hierarchies (D). All these assumptions are appropriate candidates for inclusion in the grounding set for honorifics $\mathcal{H}$.[1] These things, taken together, are required for the use of honorifics to even be sensible.

(F) Social situations involve various levels of formality.
(A) One should behave differently in social situations of differing formality.
(H) Society involves hierarchies and relations of social superiority between people.
(P) Each person in a social situation has a position in social hierarchies relative to each other person in the situation.
(D) It is appropriate to exhibit deference when speaking to a social superior.

The impetus to use honorifics at all can also be tied to aspects of affective function: an individual who assigns a positive valuation to following social norms related to formality and politeness has a reason to use honorifics where others might not. The upshot here is that the statements (A) and (D) can be restated in terms of the affective function ρ if desired, where, as with the ideologies of Henderson and McCready, the properties *adjusts behavior to suit (in)formality of situation* and *exhibits deference to superiors*

---

[1] The last principle, (D), seems extendable to a converse position, ie. that one need not exhibit any kind of politeness behavior to perceived social inferiors, but this is a kind of behavior idiosyncratic to badly behaved individuals and probably doesn't ground the actual use of honorifics.

are transformed into individuals via application of Chierchia's (1998) $^\cap$-function. In general, the roughly similar result of employing *should*-statements in $\mathcal{B}$ codifying particular kinds of linguistic behavior B and assigning high affective values to the result of applying ρ to $^\cap B$ will be quite similar : this speaks to the generally complex relationship between belief and assignment of affective values, and further shows that ρ and $\mathcal{B}$ cannot be completely independent, a fact already clear from political ideologies.

Several interesting questions arise from this basic picture. Let me consider three here.

The first question is whether all honorifics are created equal in terms of the grounds they introduce. I think the answer here is negative. One key difference in the semantics of honorifics is whether they pertain to the formality of the speech situation or to the relationship between the speaker and some individual in an argument position in the sentence. McCready (2019) calls the former *utterance honorifics* and the latter *argument honorifics* and I will follow this terminology here. It seems to me that the former require (F) and (A) to hold in order to be sensibly used, and the latter require (H) and (D), and also perhaps (P), or at least a weakened version thereof which requires only there to be a hierarchical relationship between the speaker and whatever individual is named by the argument in question. Thus, for utterance honorifics, $(F), (A) \in \mathcal{H}$, and for argument honorifics, $(H), (D), (P) \in \mathcal{H}$. This is one way to cash out the kinds of differences between particular honorifics noted by e.g. Yamada (2019), Yamada and Donatelli (2020) and Oshima (2021), while retaining a maximally simple set of use-conditions on them of the kind proposed by McCready (2019), where felicitous use in a particular context requires only checking a register or subregister.

It seems plausible that other kinds of honorifics should come with different kinds of grounds. McCready, for example, discusses what she calls *role honorifics* which have honorific effects because of shared knowledge about the prestige of whatever social role is named; an example is the Japanese *sensei* 'teacher', which has an honorific function because teachers are respected within Japanese social structures. Here, if the social role in question fails to have a well-defined status, it can't be successfully used in an honorific manner; this idea can be schematized as follows, for the social role S denoted by role honorific RH. This grounding rules out the honorific use of random occupations like 'dogcatcher' or 'grout specialist.'

(S) S has a well-defined place in social structures.

Second, we can ask if these grounding conditions tell us anything about the history of honorifics in the history of linguistic development. If these are the grounding conditions for honorifics, it follows that social structures which fail to verify the conditions will not support the existence of honorifics, for the grounds for their use will not exist, and consequently they won't make any sense. According to Morton (2021), the kinds of hierarchies and social structures that ground honorifics are a result of the development of agriculture and consequent social changes involving the development of different classes of people, some engaged in the labor of food production and others in religious activity, war, and so forth; previous to agricultural societies the requisite kind of stratification wasn't present, and so, if this is right, we can pinpoint the development of linguistic honorifics to a time period no earlier than the development of agriculture.

The third question pertains to how grounds are introduced. Are they presuppositional, in a more standard sense? Are they closer to conventional implicatures or expressives? How in general should we think of preconditions so fundamental to the use of particular expressions that using those expressions is nonsensical unless the preconditions are satisfied? This is a more complex question, and is the topic of the next section.

5 Grounds as Category

To begin answering this question, we can start by observing an intriguing difference from dogwhistles and social personas in general: $\mathcal{H}$ is necessarily in play after use of an honorific. With dogwhistles, the speaker might or might not have the persona in question: this deniability is essential to these items. Compare slurs or pejoratives, which also put forward certain kinds of ideologies, for instance racist ones: these social personas, and the ideologies they come with, are conventional content expressed by the slur and cannot be negated or denied, unlike what is seen with dogwhistles (Henderson and McCready, 2021a). In this sense, the assumptions introduced by honorifics, $\mathcal{H}$, are similar. They differ in that the content isn't associated with an ideology which makes claims about the world, but instead is in a nontechnical sense presupposed, in that without it the honorific just isn't sensible.

The upshot of this is that the grounds of honorifics are purely conventional. This already rules out an analysis in terms of conversational implicature: for example, one might take Gricean Manner or even Quality to require certain things of the world (or, more technically, to place constraints on the model, cf. Zimmermann 1999) for honorifics to be properly used; but this would imply that these constraints are defeasible, and, for the sorts of grounds under discussion, they are not.

Can we view grounds as presuppositions in the technical sense? I don't think so. Like presuppositions, they aren't asserted content, but they don't seem to exhibit other well-known traits of presuppositions. For example, they don't seem to be accommodatable, which is unexpected for most presuppositions (Beaver and Zeevat, 2007), though not all (e.g. *too*, which also can't be accommodated). Because some presuppositions don't admit accommodation, this is only weak evidence. However, grounds also can't be bound in conditional antecedents, which is more unexpected.[2]

(2) ?? moshi kono gyookai ni joogekankei-ga atta-ra
     if   this field   in hierarchy-Nom have-Cond
    Tanaka-san-ga irasshaima-shi-ta
    Tanaka-Mx-Nom come.Hon-UttHon-Pst

    'If this field had a hierarchy, then Mx Tanaka came + speaker
    expresses formal relation toward Tanaka'

This is just bizarre on the intended reading (where the ground of the honorific is bound by the conditional antecedent). One might worry that the reason for this is just that the honorific has too many separate grounds for this kind of binding to work; but

---

[2] Here 'Mx' indicates an ungendered honorific suffix.

consider related discourse-structural methods of putting multiple assumptions into the interpretative context for a claim. Specifically, suppose that $\mathcal{H}$ contains four grounds, A, B, C and D, and consider the following discourse, constructed along the lines of a modal or generic subordination structure (Roberts, 1989; Carlson and Spejewski, 1997):

(3)   Suppose that A. Suppose further that B, and C, and D. Then

      ?? Tanaka-san-ga   irasshaima-shi-ta
      Tanaka-Mx-Nom come.Hon-UttHon-Pst

      'Mx Tanaka came + speaker expresses formal relation toward Tanaka'

I conclude that we can't really think of grounds as standardly presuppositional, because they don't interact in the expected way with discourse content and context. It has become standard in recent years to throw meanings like this into the 'new waste-basket' of expressive content (or conventional implicature, together CIE). Can we think of grounds in this way? Again, I think not: there is a clear conceptual problem from the outset, because both conventional implicatures and expressive items introduce new information to the context, but this is precisely what grounds don't do; rather, they provide a basis for the communication itself, and for the semantics of whatever terms are requiring them. Trying to shoehorn them into the CIE category would be taking the wastebasket metaphor one step too far.

The observation about the current pragmatic-wastebasket status of expressivity was one impetus for the development of the theory of invocational meaning of Davis and McCready (2020). Invocational meanings can be thought of as semantic objects which, by their use, 'invoke' content of various kinds. Slurs, for instance, are taken to conjure up complexes of historical fact and stereotypical attitudes which bear some resemblance to the ideologies of Henderson and McCready (2021b). Above I claimed that at least the grounds associated with honorifics also have this form. Can we then think of hinges as instances of this kind of invocational meaning? I don't think so: in Davis and McCready's sense, invocational meanings call to awareness existing objects. But for the case of grounds, awareness isn't even implicated; one can certainly use honorifics without being aware of the requirements they impose on the model (/the world/thought). This disanalogy makes invocations look like a different kind of phenomenon entirely.

I conclude that grounds are a singular kind of meaning and one which essentially has not received any attention within linguistic theory up to the present. In general, these kinds of assumptions are closer to Wittgensteinian *hinge propositions* than any kind of meaning that has been looked at in detail in linguistics, in the sense that they don't require, or even admit, epistemic defense in order to be active, but instead form the basis for inquiry and conversation (Wittgenstein, 1991). As Wittgenstein puts it, hinge propositions form the "scaffolding" to our thought, and thus aren't subject to rational doubt or the need for justification. The parallel with linguistic grounds is clear; the difference is that hinge propositions form the scaffolding of inquiry and belief, and grounds the scaffolding of the use of particular pieces of language. I leave a more detailed examination of how the two kinds of phenomena relate to each other for another occasion.

6 Other Examples

Up to this point, this paper has exclusively considered the grounds of honorifics, arguing that they look very much like ideologies in the sense formalized by Henderson and McCready: sets of propositions combined with ways of assigning affective values. But do all grounds look like this, or are there other kinds of assumptions that might be built into our language use? This section discusses two other kinds of grounds (or what I will claim are grounds), with an eye toward comparison with the grounds of honorifics.

A second example of grounds comes from classifiers in languages like Chinese and Japanese. In this kind of language, numeral quantification requires that the numeral appear with a classifier, which itself picks out a particular kind of object (or group of objects): in Japanese, for instance, we find -*hiki* 'animal', -*hon* 'long, thin object', and -*zen* 'pair of chopsticks'. McCready (2012) takes these kinds of restrictions to be conventionally implicated due to their inability to be bound (among other reasons), but also discusses another 'presupposition' of classifiers: that objects can in fact be individuated. This 'presupposition' is more of a metaphysical assumption required for classifier use than anything else. McCready herself concludes that it is inappropriate to treat this kind of thing as conventional implicature, but leaves open the question of what sort of meaning it might be. The present discussion makes available a new answer: that the possibility of individuating objects forms at least part of the grounds for the use of classifiers (and perhaps for quantification itself).

One lesson that can be drawn from the above is that ideologies are not always going to be the proper tool to capture the grounds of linguistic expressions. Classifier grounding requires the possibility of individuating objects, which is not something that can be naturally captured via propositional content. Rather, these grounds put conditions directly on the kind of models that are appropriate for the interpretation and use of classifiers; the same can be said for some honorifics, in that they require the existence of interpersonal hierarchies and so models lacking such structures will be unable to ground honorific use. It seems to me that conditions on models is the most promising avenue for the general analysis of grounds, in a sense a return to the currently unfashionable practice of using meaning postulates in semantic theory, though space considerations here preclude a giving a fuller picture.

A final example comes from another kind of invisible assumption made by language. McCready and Ottosson (2021) consider narrative for nonhuman agents, particularly plants, which are different from human agents in extreme ways. Many of these center around the fact that these two kinds of organisms, while broadly parallel in the sense of being physically embodied in the world, differ so greatly in the manner of their embodiment as to be in certain respects incommensurable. McCready and Ottosson consider the possibility of narratives which genuinely center botanical agents in a nonanthropomorphic manner (i.e. without 'humanizing' the plant), and conclude that doing so requires a departure from language-based narrative into embodied pattern. They take one reason for this to be the way in which human language has as its foundation human embodiment: it is difficult or impossible to parse linguistic narrative without recourse to the human sensory apparatus and experience of the physical world. If this view is right, we can conclude that experience in a certain kind of body forms a ground for natural language, at the very least in descriptions of physical phenomena. This observation seems to call for a different kind of formalization of grounds: rather than placing constraints on the models in which language is interpreted, they place constraints on the kind of semantics we must have for language itself, pointing up the need to give space to the physical in our theoretical representations.

7   Conclusion and Prospects

In this paper, I have proposed the existence of a previously unstudied category of linguistic meaning: the grounds of utterance, those things that must hold for the use of an expression to make sense. The main evidence adduced for this meaning type is from honorifics: while particular honorifics have meanings indicating the formality of the speech situation or the kind of relationships holding between the speaker and other individuals, it doesn't make sense to proffer these kinds of meanings in the absence of social hierarchies and certain kinds of normative expectations about polite linguistic behavior. The paper proceeded to distinguish grounds from more familiar meaning categories like standard presuppositions and expressive meanings, and closed with two additional examples of grounding from numeral classifiers and anthropomorphism in narrative.

What this paper has not done is to propose a unified technique for formalizing grounds. The sorts of preconditions introduced by honorifics, I argued, can be stated in terms of ideologies, but not all grounds can be: the grounds of numeral classifiers require certain kinds of individuation, and the lesson of nonanthropomorphic narrative is that the semantics of many parts of natural language must incorporate representations of the body. Neither of these latter points was explored in any detail in this paper, mostly for reasons of space. But the rather various nature of the grounds of these three phenomena might call into question whether this is really a unified category at all, or at least whether it admits a uniform kind of semantic treatment. Alternatively, are grounds a more heterogeneous category by their very nature? I believe that a more detailed formal investigation would shed light on these questions, as would a close comparison with Wittgensteinian hinges. Both of these tasks are left for future work.

References

Agha, A.: Honorification. Annu. Rev. Anthropol. **23**, 277–302 (1994)

Beaver, D.: Presupposition. In: Handbook of Logic and Language, pp. 939–1008. Elsevier (1997)

Beaver, D.: Presupposition and Assertion in Dynamic Semantics. Number 16 in Studies in Logic, Language and Information. CSLI/FoLLI, Stanford, CA (2001)

Beaver, D., Zeevat, H.: Accommodation. In: Ramchand, G., Reiss, C., (eds.), Oxford Handbook of Linguistic Interfaces. Oxford (2007)

Camp, E.: Slurring perspectives. Anal. Philos. **54**(3), 330–349 (2013)

Carlson, G., Spejewski, B.: Generic passages. Nat. Lang. Seman. **5**, 101–165 (1997)

Chierchia, G.: Reference to kinds across language. Nat. Lang. Seman. **6**, 339–405 (1998). https://doi.org/10.1023/A:1008324218506

Davis, C., McCready, E.: The instability of slurs. Grazer Philosophische Studien **97**, 63–85 (2020)

Heim, I., Kratzer, A.: Semantics in Generative Grammar. Number 13 in Blackwell Textbooks in Linguistics. Blackwell, Oxford, England (1998)

Henderson, R., McCready, E.: Signaling without Saying: The Semantics and Pragmatics of Dog-whistles. Oxford University Press (2021a to appear)

Henderson, R., McCready, E.: Dogwhistles: Persona and ideology. To appear in Semantics and Linguistic Theory 31 (2021b)

McCready, E.: Classification without assertion. In: Tucker, M., Thompson, A., Northup, O., Bennett, R. (eds.), Proceedings of FAJL 5, MITWPL, pp. 141–154. MIT (2012)

McCready, E.: A semantics for honorifics with reference to Thai. In: Aroonmanakun, W., Boonkwan, P., Supnithi, T., (eds.), Proceedings of PACLIC 28, pp. 513–521. Chulalongkorn University (2014)

McCready, E.: Varieties of conventional implicature. Semant. Pragmat. 3, 1–57 (2010)

McCready, E.: The Semantics and Pragmatics of Honorification: Register and Social Meaning. Oxford University Press (2019)

McCready, E., Ottosson, E.: Pattern as narrative: the structure of botanical stories. ANEST International Workshop, National Chung-Hsing University, Taichung, Taiwan, Paper presented at Narrating Nature (2021)

Montague, R.: The proper treatment of quantification in ordinary English. In: Thomason, R.H. (ed.) Formal Philosophy: Selected papers of Richard Montague, pp. 188–221. Yale University Press, New Haven, CO, 1974. Originally published in Approaches to Natural Language (1973)

Morton, T.: All Art is Ecological. Penguin (2021)

Oshima, D.Y.: Against the multidimensional approach to honorific meaning: a solution to the binding problem of conventional implicature. In: Okazaki, N., Yada, K., Satoh, K., Mineshima, K. (eds.) JSAI-isAI 2020. LNCS (LNAI), vol. 12758, pp. 113–128. Springer, Cham (2021). https://doi.org/10.1007/978-3-030-79942-7_8

Portner, P., Pak, M., Zanuttini, R.: The speaker-addressee relation at the syntax-semantics interface. Language 95(1), 1–36 (2019)

Potts, C.: The expressive dimension. Theoret. Linguist. 33, 165–198 (2007). https://doi.org/10.1515/TL.2007.011

Roberts, C.: Modal subordination and pronominal anaphora in discourse. Linguist. Philos. 12(6), 683–721 (1989)

Wittgenstein, L.: On Certainty. Wiley-Blackwell (1991). Originally published 1969

Yamada, A.: The syntax, semantics and pragmatics of Japanese addressee-honorific markers. Ph.D. thesis, Georgetown University (2019)

Yamada, A., Donatelli, L.: A persona-based analysis of politeness in Japanese and Spanish. In: Proceedings of Logic and Engineering of Natural Language Semantics, vol. 17. JSAI (2020)

Zimmermann, T.E.: Meaning postulates and the model-theoretic approach to natural language semantics. Linguist. Philos. 22, 529–561 (1999)

QNP Textual Entailment with Polynomial Event Semantics

Oleg Kiselyov[✉] and Haruki Watanabe

Tohoku University, Sendai, Japan
oleg@okmij.org

Abstract. FraCaS textual entailment corpus has become the standard benchmark for semantics theories, in particular, theories of quantification (Sect. 1 of FraCaS). Here we apply it to polynomial event semantics: the latest approach to combining quantification and Neo-Davidsonian event semantics, maintaining compositionality and the in situ analysis of quantifiers. Although several FraCaS problems look custom-made for the polynomial events semantics, there are challenges: the variety of generalized quantifiers (including 'many', 'most' and 'few'); copula, existence, and relative clauses. We address them in this paper.

1 Introduction

The strong point of (Neo-)Davidsonian event semantics [9] (see [8] for a survey) is explaining entailments among sentences without ad hoc meaning postulates. It seems just the right tool to apply to the FraCaS textual inference problem set [2,7]. However, FraCaS starts with quantifier entailment problems – the weakest point of event semantics. The latest approach to address this weakness (viz., the event quantification problem: see [1] for extensive discussion) is polynomial event semantics [5,6]. FraCaS however features not only the familiar 'some', 'all' and 'no' quantifiers, but also 'many', 'most', 'at most 10' and 'few' – rarely dealt with in the event quantification problem literature. In this paper we show that the polynomial event semantics surprisingly easily handles the full spectrum of generalized quantifiers – in situ and compositionally. We extend and systematically apply the algebraic approach started in [6]. Section 1 of FraCaS also contains a number of copula and existential clauses, which, to the authors knowledge, are rarely if at all being dealt with in the event semantics literature. Although they are emphatically not 'action sentences', they can still be analyzed in the event semantics framework and used in entailments, we argue.

Applying event semantics to (mechanically) solve text entailment problems in FraCaS was the primary motivation for developing the polynomial event semantics [5]. That first paper laid the foundation and introduced the model of variable-free event semantics, which not only gets around the event quantification problem but also accounts for quantifier ambiguity. [6] extended the framework to negative quantification – and also introduced the algebraic approach.

The present paper extends the algebraic approach and casts it to what amounts to a deductive system for deciding entailments. The next section, after

K. Yada et al. (Eds.): JSAI-isAI 2021 Workshops, LNAI 13856, pp. 198–211, 2023.
https://doi.org/10.1007/978-3-031-36190-6_14

a brief introduction to the polynomial event semantics, extends the earlier work to all sorts of generalized quantifiers appearing in Sect. 1 of FraCaS. In particular, Sect. 2.1 discusses negative and downward-monotone quantifiers such as 'at most ten'; Sect. 2.2 deals with proportional quantifiers such as 'most' and 'few'. Formally the polynomial event semantics, with its algebra and deduction system, is presented in Sect. 3. As an example, Sect. 3.1 describes in detail the treatment of negation. We then deal with further challenges of event semantics: copular clauses in Sect. 4, and subject relative clauses, often appearing in existential sentences, in Sect. 5. Related work is discussed in Sect. 6.

2   Generalized Quantifiers

This section introduces both the polynomial event semantics and FraCaS, using the examples from FraCaS to bring up denotations and entailments. Unlike the earlier work, we discuss here truly generalized quantifiers, and in a simpler way.

The poster problem for event semantics is FraCaS problem 023:

(1)   Some delegates finished the survey on time.

(2)   Some delegates finished the survey.

As with all other problems in the FraCaS corpus, the goal is to check if the last sentence (in our case, (2)) is entailed from the others (that is, (1)).

In polynomial event semantics, these sentences have the following denotations (whose form closely matches the structure of the original sentences):[1]

(3) $(\text{subj}'/(\mathcal{G}_{N>1}\ \text{Delegate})) \sqcap \text{finished} \sqcap$

                              $(\text{ob1}'/\text{theSurvey}) \sqcap \text{onTime}$

(4) $\text{subj}'/\mathcal{G}_{N>1}\ \text{Delegate} \sqcap \text{finished} \sqcap \text{ob1}'/\text{theSurvey}$

Polynomial event semantics deals with individuals and event sets, which are collectively called atoms and denoted by uncapitalized san-serif identifiers: theSurvey is the particular salient survey,[2] finished is a set of finished events, onTime is the set of events on time.[3] Capitalized san-serif identifiers stand for sets of individuals, called concepts: Delegate.

The characteristic of the polynomial event semantics is polyconcepts, which are atoms, and also groups.[4] The latter are formed by the operator $\mathcal{G}_n$: whereas

---

[1] (3) shows how the denotations are supposed to be parenthesized. We drop the parentheses from now on.

[2] More generally, definite descriptions can analyzed as $\mathcal{I}$Survey, see Sect. 3. Our example works either way, so we proceed with the simpler analysis.

[3] We suppose there are thematic functions occursAt$'$ and deadline$'$. that tell the time of occurrence and the deadline, resp., for an event. Then onTime = $\{e \mid \text{occursAt}'(e) \leq \text{deadline}'(e)\}$. One may analyze 'on time' differently (e.g., with the deadline being taken from the context). However, that does not matter for entailment, which is decided for our example solely from the property of $\sqcap$, see (5).

[4] By group, here and in the following, we mean any unorderded collection: something like a roster.

Delegate is a set of delegates, $\mathcal{G}_5$ Delegate is a group of 5 delegates (if there are that many delegates; otherwise, $\mathcal{G}_5$ Delegate is $\bot$: the empty polyconcept). $\mathcal{G}_{N>1}$ in (3) and (4) means a group of N delegates where N is a positive number that should be clear from the context. The vagueness is inherent in the meaning of 'several' and plural 'some'.

If x is a polyconcept of individuals and subj$'$ is a relation between events and individuals (viz., between events and their agents), subj$'/x$ is the polyconcept of events whose agents are x. Likewise, obl$'/x$. for themes. The symmetric and commutative polyconcept intersection $\sqcap$ is akin to set intersection. We will see in Sect. 3 that this overloaded operator is indeed set intersection when applied to event sets.

Unlike Montagovian or the ordinary (Neo-) Davidsonian semantics, the denotations (3) and (4) are not (first- or higher-order) logic formulas. In particular, they have no variables, even the event variable, and no quantifiers. Rather, our denotations are queries, of a database of events. The result of a query is the set of events which witness the corresponding sentence. If we imagine a record of delegates, surveys and their status of completion, then (4) is the query for events, i.e., records of survey completion by at least N delegates.

One query entails another just in case whenever the result of the former is non-empty, so is the result of the latter – for any event database. The entailment may be decided algebraically, keeping in mind that $\sqcap$, like the ordinary set intersection, is upward-monotone in both arguments, as we discuss in more detail in Sect. 3:

$$(5) \qquad\qquad x \sqcap y \Longrightarrow x$$

The entailment of (4) from (3) (that is, (2) from (1)) is hence decided by the application of (5), without needing to know what exactly $\mathcal{G}_N\, c$ means. (It is still instructive to know: see Sect. 3.)

Many other FraCaS generalized quantifier problems are solved analogously: for example,

017   An Irishman won the Nobel prize for literature.
        An Irishman won a Nobel prize.

024   Many delegates obtained interesting results from the survey.
        Many delegates obtained results from the survey.

025   Several delegates got the results published in
                                            major national newspapers.
        Several delegates got the results published.

031   At least three commissioners spend a lot of time at home.
        At least three commissioners spend time at home.

We do not even need to know how exactly these quantifiers are defined beyond them grouping witnesses somehow. (We describe the analysis of 'many' later.)

2.1   Negative Quantification and Downward Monotonicity

Negation of all kinds – negative quantification, sentential and clausal (VP) negation – is, on our account, about counter-examples. Whereas an affirmative sentence affirms certain events, a sentence with any sort of negation denies certain events – and whose appearance would thus cause contradiction. Therefore, negative sentences mean is what they deny.

As an example, consider problem 022:

(6)   No delegate finished the report on time.

(7)   No delegate finished the report.

whose denotations are

(8) $\mathsf{subj'/\neg Delegate \sqcap finished \sqcap ob1'/theReport \sqcap onTime}$
         $= \neg\,(\mathsf{subj'/Delegate \sqcap finished \sqcap ob1'/theReport \sqcap onTime})$

(9) $\mathsf{subj'/\neg Delegate \sqcap finished \sqcap ob1'/theReport}$
         $= \neg\,(\mathsf{subj'/Delegate \sqcap finished \sqcap ob1'/theReport})$

(shown after the equal sign are the results of applying algebraic laws in Sect. 3.) (8) and (9) are also queries – searching, however, not for witnesses for the original sentences but for their refutations: counter-evidence, whose polyconcept is denoted $\neg x$. According to (5), (8) entails (9), like with problem 023 before. However, this is the entailment of counter-evidence: The refutation of (6) entailing the refutation of (7) does lead to the emptiness of (8) (i.e., non-refutation of (6)) entailing the emptiness of (9). Thus (7) cannot be concluded from (6). (In fact, the opposite is true.)

Similar is problem 032:

(10)   At most ten commissioners spend a lot of time at home.

(11)   At most ten commissioners spend time at home.

A refutation for (11) is the existence of at least 11 commissioners who spend time at home. Therefore, the denotation for 'at most ten commissioners' is $\neg\mathcal{G}_{11}$ Commissioner and we proceed similarly to problem 022 just above. There are many more similar FraCaS problems:

038   No delegate finished the report.
      Some delegate finished the report on time.

070   No delegate finished the report on time.
      Some Scandinavian delegate finished the report on time.

2.2 Many, Most, Few

More interesting, and controversial, is problem 056:

(12)   Many British delegates obtained interesting results
                                                    from the survey.

(13)   Many delegates obtained interesting results from the survey.

for which the original FraCaS report gives the answer "Don't know". Bill Mac-Cartney [7] comments that apparently FraCaS editors interpret 'many' as a large proportion. He, among others, however, take 'many' to mean a large absolute number. Polynomial event semantics supports both alternatives. The polyconcept *Many* c (where c is a concept) can be defined in two ways:

(14) $Many\ c = \mathcal{G}_N\ c$ $Many\ c = \mathcal{G}_{\alpha|c|}\ c$

where N is a large absolute number and $0 < \alpha \leq 1$. Upon the first reading, we apply (5) to obtain the entailment of (13) from (12). On the 'large proportion' reading of 'many', the entailment fails because (13) has generally different, and larger, group cardinality than (12). *Most* c is analyzed then as $\mathcal{G}_{\alpha|c|}\ c$, where α is at least 0.5. Few is handled as the negation of 'many':

060   Few female committee members are from southern Europe.
       Few committee members are from southern Europe.

3   Algebra of Polynomial Event Semantics

This section presents the polynomial event semantics formally, emphasizing its algebra and deductive system.

At its basis, the polynomial event semantics deals with individuals (notated by metavariable i), events (notated by e) and relations among them, written as rel$'$. Often-used relations are

$$\mathsf{subj}' = \{(e,i) \mid \mathsf{ag}(e) = i\} \qquad \mathsf{action}' = \{(e,i) \mid \mathsf{action}(e) = i\}$$
$$\mathsf{ob1}' = \{(e,i) \mid \mathsf{th}(e) = i\} \qquad \mathsf{mode}' = \{(e,i) \mid \mathsf{mode}(e) = i\}$$

where ag, th, action and mode are thematic functions. If rel$'$ is a relation of events to individuals, rel$'/i = \{e \mid (e,i) \in \mathsf{rel}'\}$ is the set of events related to i. We call individuals and nonempty event sets atoms, denoted by metavariable j.

The subject of polynomial event semantics is polyconcepts, denoted by metavariables x, y and z, which are atoms and applications of operations described below. Technically, the collection of operations acting on polyconcepts is an algebra. Strictly speaking, polynomial event semantics deals with two algebras: the algebra of individuals and the algebra of event sets. They are very similar and have the same operations. The unary operation is negation (or, marking as counter-evidence) $\neg$. Binary operations, which are commutative and associative, and the correspondent zero-arity operations (units) are as follows.

$\otimes$	unit: 1	grouping/conjunction
$\sqcup$	unit: $\perp$	internal choice, union
$\sqcap$	unit: $\top$	intersection
$\oplus$	unit: 0	external choice

The often-occurring $\perp$ is the empty polyconcept; it being the unit of $\sqcup$ means $x \sqcup \perp = x$. In the algebra of individuals, $\sqcap$ is defined as

$$i_1 \sqcap i_2 = \begin{cases} i_1 & \text{if } i_1 = i_2 \\ \perp & \text{otherwise} \end{cases}$$

In the algebra of event sets, $\perp$ is identical to the empty set. When applied to atoms (i.e., event sets), $\sqcap$ is set intersection.

The operations satisfy the following additional identities:

$$x \oplus x = x \qquad x \sqcap x = x \qquad x \sqcup x = x$$
$$x \sqcap \perp = \perp \qquad x \otimes \perp = \perp$$

$$\neg x \sqcap \neg y = \neg(x \sqcap y)$$
$$(x \oplus y) \sqcup z = (x \sqcup z) \oplus (y \sqcup z) \qquad (x \oplus y) \sqcap z = (x \sqcap z) \oplus (y \sqcap z)$$
$$(x \oplus y) \otimes z = (x \otimes z) \oplus (y \otimes z)$$

Thus the external choice $\oplus$ distributes over all other binary operations, and can be 'pulled out', so to speak. The negation of $\perp$, notated as $\neg\perp$ or $\bar{\perp}$, is different from $\perp$. In particular, $x \otimes \bar{\perp} \neq \bar{\perp}$. There are further, more specific identities (distribution laws) which holds only for atoms or negated polyconcepts:

$$j \sqcap (x \otimes y) = (j \sqcap x) \otimes (j \sqcap y) \qquad j \sqcap (x \sqcup y) = (j \sqcap x) \sqcup (j \sqcap y)$$
$$j \sqcap \neg y = \neg(j \sqcap y) \qquad \neg z \sqcap (x \sqcup y) = (\neg z \sqcap x) \sqcup (\neg z \sqcap y)$$

Relations rel$'$ bridge the algebras of individuals and of event sets. Technically, rel$'$ act as algebra homomorphisms from the former to the latter:

$$\text{rel}'/(\neg x) = \neg\text{rel}'/x \qquad \text{rel}'/(x \sqcap y) = \text{rel}'/x \sqcap \text{rel}'/y$$

and similarly for other binary operations.

Typically we deal not with individuals but with sets of individuals, called concepts – and with sets of non-empty event sets, called e-concepts. Since the operations apply uniformly to concepts and e-concepts, we often call them just concepts and use metavariable c.[5] Relations extend to concepts straightforwardly: If c is a set of individuals then rel$'/c = \{$nonempty rel$'/i \mid i \in c\}$ is the set of

---

[5] One may hence say that a concept is a set of atoms – however, we never mix individuals and event sets in the same set.

non-empty event sets related to each individual in c. Often we build polyconcepts by applying a binary operation $\sqcup$, $\oplus$ or $\otimes$ to all elements of a concept. We introduce a special notation for such cases:

$$\mathcal{E}c = \sqcup_{j \in c}\, j \qquad \mathcal{I}c = \oplus_{j \in c}\, j \qquad \mathcal{A}c = \otimes_{j \in c}\, j$$

One immediately notices that for singleton concepts:

$$\mathcal{E}\{j\} = \mathcal{I}\{j\} = \mathcal{A}\{j\} = j$$

Specifically for the $\mathcal{E}$ operation, we notice that $\mathcal{E}c = \bot$ iff $c = \varnothing$.

The operation $\sqcap$ extends to concepts as

$$c_1 \sqcap c_2 = \{j_1 \sqcap j_2 \mid j_1 \in c_1, j_2 \in c_2, j_1 \sqcap j_2 \neq \bot\}$$

That is, on sets of individuals, $\sqcap$ is set intersection. The distributivity of $\oplus$ over $\sqcap$ gives $\mathcal{I}c_1 \sqcap \mathcal{I}c_2 = \mathcal{I}(c_1 \sqcap c_2)$.

The grouping $\mathcal{G}_N\, c$ mentioned earlier – the collection of all N-element groups out of c – is defined as

$$\mathcal{G}_N\, c = \sqcup\, \mathcal{A}c' \text{ for all } c' \subset c \text{ such that } |c'| = N$$

Clearly,

$$\mathcal{G}_1 = \mathcal{E} \qquad\qquad \mathcal{G}_N\, c = \bot \quad \text{iff } |c| < N$$

where $|c|$ is the cardinality of c. From the distributivity laws above, we obtain useful identities:

$$(\mathcal{G}_N\, c) \sqcap j = \mathcal{G}_N(c \sqcap j) \qquad (\mathcal{G}_N\, c_1) \sqcap \mathcal{E}c_2 = \mathcal{G}_N(c_1 \sqcap \{\sqcup c_2\})$$

Since a relation rel' is the algebra homomorphism,

$$\mathsf{rel}'/\mathcal{E}c = \mathcal{E}\mathsf{rel}'/c \qquad \mathsf{rel}'/\mathcal{I}c = \mathcal{I}\mathsf{rel}'/c \qquad \mathsf{rel}'/\mathcal{A}c = \mathcal{A}\mathsf{rel}'/c$$
$$\mathsf{rel}'/\mathcal{G}_N\, c = \mathcal{G}_N\, \mathsf{rel}'/c$$

The reader has no doubt noticed the similarity of the presented algebra with linear logic (and that our $\sqcup$ behaves like & and $\sqcap$ as par). We are currently trying to understand this connection.

As an example of using the algebras and its identities, consider (15) below

(15)　　　　　The delegate finished the report.

(16)　　　　　$\mathsf{subj}'/\mathsf{theDelegate} \sqcap \mathsf{finished} \sqcap \mathsf{ob1}'/\mathsf{theReport}$

whose denotation (16) is the intersection of three event sets: events whose agent is theDelegate, finished events, and events whose theme is theReport. The denotation is hence the set of events that witness (15).

The second example is (2) from the problem 023 analyzed in Sect. 2, and its denotation (4), repeated below with an insignificant modification:

Some delegates finished the report.

$\mathsf{subj'} / \mathcal{G}_{\mathsf{N}>1} \, \mathsf{Delegate} \sqcap \mathsf{finished} \sqcap \mathsf{ob1'} / \mathsf{theReport}$

Applying the algebraic identities to the denotation, we derive

$$\mathcal{G}_{N>1}(\mathsf{subj'} / \, \mathsf{Delegate} \sqcap \mathsf{finished} \sqcap \mathsf{ob1'} / \mathsf{theReport})$$
$$= \mathcal{G}_{N>1}\{\mathsf{nonempty} \, \mathsf{subj'} / \, i \cap \mathsf{finished} \cap \mathsf{ob1'} / \mathsf{theReport} \mid i \in \mathsf{Delegate}\}$$

which is non-$\perp$ just in case there are records in the event database of at least $N>1$ delegates having finished the report.

3.1 Negation

A more extensive example of applying algebraic identities and semantic calculations is negation. In addition to negative quantification we also consider VP negation, although it is hardly present in FraCaS (certainly not in Sect. 1). We hence expand the account of [6], which, although touched upon the clausal (VP) negation, did not describe it in detail for the lack of space.

Recall that negation of all kinds is, on our account, about counter-examples. Whereas an affirmative sentence affirms certain events, a sentence with any sort of negation denies certain events – and whose appearance would thus cause contradiction.

The following sample illustrates the variety of negation.

(17)   The delegate didn't finish the report.

(18)   No delegate finished the report.

(19)   The delegate finished no report.

(20)   A delegate didn't finish the report.

Sentence (17) looks like the negation of (15). Its compositional denotation

$$\mathsf{subj'} / \mathsf{theDelegate} \sqcap \neg \, \mathsf{finished} \sqcap \mathsf{ob1'} / \mathsf{theReport}$$
$$= \neg \, (\mathsf{subj'} / \mathsf{theDelegate} \sqcap \mathsf{finished} \sqcap \mathsf{ob1'} / \mathsf{theReport})$$

(where we applied the algebraic identities to pull $\neg$ out) is indeed the negation of the denotation (16). What is a witness for (15) is a counter-example for (17): the two sentences are contradictory, as expected.

The compositional denotation for (18) is

$$\mathsf{subj'} / \neg \mathcal{E} \mathsf{Delegate} \sqcap \mathsf{finished} \sqcap \mathsf{ob1'} / \mathsf{theReport}$$
$$= \neg \mathcal{E}(\mathsf{subj'} / \, \mathsf{Delegate}) \sqcap \mathsf{finished} \sqcap \mathsf{ob1'} / \mathsf{theReport}$$
$$= \neg(\mathcal{E} \mathsf{subj'} / \, \mathsf{Delegate} \sqcap \mathsf{finished} \sqcap \mathsf{ob1'} / \mathsf{theReport})$$

Once again we are able to pull $\neg$ out, relying on the fact that finished and ob1′/theReport are atomic. The denotation is the negation of the denotation for

A delegate finished the report.

which is hence the contradictory with (18). Furthermore, since theDelegate is included in the set Delegate, we obtain the entailment of (17) from (18). Sentence (19) is analyzed similarly to (18).

However, (20) is different. Its denotation

$$\mathsf{subj}'/\,\mathcal{E}\mathsf{Delegate} \sqcap \neg\,\mathsf{finished} \sqcap \mathsf{ob1}'/\,\mathsf{theReport}$$
$$= \mathcal{E}(\mathsf{subj}'/\,\mathsf{Delegate}) \sqcap \neg(\mathsf{finished} \sqcap \mathsf{ob1}'/\,\mathsf{theReport})$$

but then we cannot pull $\neg$ further up, because $\mathcal{E}(\mathsf{subj}'/\,\mathsf{Delegate})$ is neither atomic nor negated. The key point is that

$$x \sqcap \neg y = \neg(x \sqcap y)$$

(the negation marker propagating up) holds only when x is atomic or negated. We may apply the distributive law however:

$$(x \sqcup y) \sqcap z = (x \sqcap z) \sqcup (y \sqcap z)$$

where z is atomic or negated, obtaining

$$= \mathcal{E}(\mathsf{subj}'/\,\mathsf{Delegate} \sqcap \neg(\mathsf{finished} \sqcap \mathsf{ob1}'/\,\mathsf{theReport}))$$
$$= \sqcup_{i \in \mathsf{Delegate}} \neg(\mathsf{subj}'/\,i \sqcap \mathsf{finished} \sqcap \mathsf{ob1}'/\,\mathsf{theReport})$$

Whereas any delegate finishing the report would be a counter-example for (18), the counter-example for (20) is every delegate finishing the report.

Here are more examples of negation and quantification:

(21)   A delegate finished no report.

(22)   A delegate didn't finish a report.

(23)   A delegate didn't finish any report.

(24)   A delegate didn't FINISH a report.

(25)   Some delegate finished a report not on time.

Sentence (21) with the negative quantifier has as its denotation

(26) $\mathsf{subj}'/\,\mathcal{E}\mathsf{Delegate} \sqcap \mathsf{finished} \sqcap \mathsf{ob1}'/\,\neg\mathcal{E}\mathsf{Report}$

(27) $= \bigsqcup_{i \in \mathsf{Delegate}} \neg \bigsqcup_{j \in \mathsf{Report}} \mathsf{subj}'/\,i \cap \mathsf{finished} \cap \mathsf{ob1}'/\,j$

with (27) derived using the laws of Sect. 3. The sentence is non-contradicted if there is a delegate for which the set of counter-examples (events of this delegate finishing any report) is empty.

The sentence (22) with VP negation has, on the other hand

(28) $\qquad$ subj$'$/ $\mathcal{E}$Delegate $\sqcap \neg$ finished $\sqcap$ ob1$'$/ $\mathcal{E}$Report

$$= \bigsqcup\nolimits_{i \in \text{Delegate}} \bigsqcup\nolimits_{j \in \text{Report}} \neg(\text{subj}'/i \cap \text{finished} \cap \text{ob1}'/j)$$

The sentence is non-contradicted if there is a delegate-report pair such that the set of counter-examples (having finished events for that agent, theme pair) is empty. If for every delegate-report pair, either there is a finished event, or failed to finish event, then "A delegate failed to finish a report" (the existence of of the failed-to-finish event) implies an empty counter-example to (22).

For (23), we have

$$\text{subj}'/ \mathcal{E}\text{Delegate} \sqcap \neg \text{finished} \sqcap \text{ob1}'/ \neg\mathcal{E}\text{Report}$$

$$= \bigsqcup\nolimits_{i \in \text{Delegate}} \neg \bigsqcup\nolimits_{j \in \text{Report}} \text{subj}'/i \cap \text{finished} \cap \text{ob1}'/j$$

which turns out identical to (21).

In the sentence with the stressed negation (24), the negated VP has the mixed denotation action$'$/$\mathcal{E}$Action $\otimes \neg$ action$'$/finished. The sentence is true if there is a delegate who did something with a report, but that action was not the finishing action. (25) is similar.

4 Copula Clauses

Having introduced the polynomial event semantic in full in Sect. 3, we are set to tackle further challenges. This section deals with copular clauses; existence and subject relative clauses are considered in Sect. 5.

Copular clauses are frequent in FraCaS (in Sect. 1 and others); for example, problem 049:

(29) $\qquad$ A Swede won a Nobel prize.

(30) $\qquad$ Every Swede is a Scandinavian.

(31) $\qquad$ A Scandinavian won a Nobel prize.

Copular clauses are not 'action sentences'; one may wonder if the event semantics even applies. We argue it does: Just as 'it', on Davidson's analysis, in "John died. I did not know it until yesterday" refers to the event of John's death, so should 'it' in "John is tall. I did not know it until I saw him" refer to an event: an event of being tall whose 'agent' is John.

Formally, for each individual i we introduce the event of being that individual, to be denoted as be(i), of which i is an agent. The function be may also be regarded as the relation be$'$, so that be$'/i$ is the singleton event set, of the event of i existence. The e-concept of all existence events (in the current 'world') is then

(32) $\qquad\qquad\qquad$ Be = be$'$/ AllIndividuals

If Tall is a set of all tall (by some standard) things and people, the corresponding BeingTall e-concept is $\mathsf{be}'/\,\mathsf{Tall} \subset \mathsf{Be}$. Since i is an agent of its being, $\mathsf{ag}(\mathsf{be}(i)) = i$, which can be written as

$$(33) \qquad\qquad \mathsf{be}'/\,c = \mathsf{subj}'/\,c \sqcap \mathsf{Be}$$

for any concept c, from which it immediately follows that

$$(34) \qquad \mathsf{subj}'/\,c_1 \sqcap \mathsf{be}'/\,c_2 = \mathsf{be}'/\,c_1 \sqcap \mathsf{be}/\,c_2 = \mathsf{be}'/\,(c_1 \cap c_2)$$

This is *not* a meaning postulate, but a logical consequence of (33) and the algebraic identities.

Returning to problem 049, the denotation of (30) then takes the form:

$$(35) \qquad\quad \mathsf{subj}'/\,\mathcal{G}_{|\mathsf{Swede}|}\,\mathsf{Swede} \sqcap \mathsf{be}'/\,\mathcal{E}\mathsf{Scandinavian}.$$

$$= \mathcal{G}_{|\mathsf{Swede}|}\,\mathsf{subj}'/\,\mathsf{Swede} \sqcap \mathcal{E}\,\mathsf{be}'/\,\mathsf{Scandinavian}$$

$$= \mathcal{G}_{|\mathsf{Swede}|}\,(\mathsf{subj}'/\,\mathsf{Swede} \sqcap \{\cup\,\mathsf{be}'/\,\mathsf{Scandinavian}\})$$

$$(36) \qquad\qquad = \mathsf{be}'/\,\mathcal{G}_{|\mathsf{Swede}|}\,(\mathsf{Swede} \cap \mathsf{Scandinavian})$$

by applying identities of Sect. 3 and (34). Thus the denotation (36) is non-$\perp$ just in case $|\mathsf{Swede} \cap \mathsf{Scandinavian}| \geq |\mathsf{Swede}|$, that is, $\mathsf{Swede} \subseteq \mathsf{Scandinavian}$. With this premise, the entailment of (31) from (29) follows by monotonicity of $\mathcal{E}$. We must stress that we have used only the ordinary set theory (and the properties of polyconcept operators justified from set theory [6]), without any extra-logical meaning postulates.

5   Existence and Subject Relative Clauses

FraCaS also contains a number of existential sentences many of which include subject relative clauses, such as (38) of problem 001:

(37)   An Italian became the world's greatest tenor.

(38)   There was an Italian who became the world's greatest tenor.

We take the existential sentence (38) to be a surface variant of

(39)   An Italian who became the world's greatest tenor existed.

Let wgt be the 'world's greatest tenor'. Then $\mathsf{became} \sqcap \mathsf{obl}'/\,\mathsf{wgt}$ is a poly-concept of events of having become the world's greatest tenor, and "who became the world's greatest tenor" is the agent of those events:

$$(40) \qquad\qquad \overline{\mathsf{subj}}'/\,(\mathsf{became} \sqcap \mathsf{obl}'/\,\mathsf{wgt})$$

where the overline denotes an inverse relation. Recall, subj' relates events with their agents. The inverse relation $\overline{\mathsf{subj}}'$ then relates individuals with the events they are agents of. We thus have

$$(41) \qquad (a) \;\; \overline{\mathsf{subj}}'/\,\mathsf{subj}'/\,c = c \qquad\qquad (b) \;\; d \Longrightarrow \mathsf{subj}'/\,\overline{\mathsf{subj}}'/\,d$$

as the composition of a relation with its inverse includes the identity relation. Since thematic functions are functions, (41)(a) is stronger.

Overall, the denotation of (39) becomes

$$\mathsf{subj'}/(\mathcal{E}\mathsf{Italian} \sqcap (\overline{\mathsf{subj}}'/(\mathsf{became} \sqcap \mathsf{ob1'}/\mathsf{wgt}))) \sqcap \mathcal{E}\,\mathsf{Be}$$

(42) $= \mathsf{subj'}/(\overline{\mathsf{subj}}'/\mathsf{subj'}/\mathcal{E}\mathsf{Italian} \sqcap$

$$(\overline{\mathsf{subj}}'/(\mathsf{became} \sqcap \mathsf{ob1'}/\mathsf{wgt}))) \sqcap \mathcal{E}\,\mathsf{Be}$$

(43) $= \mathsf{subj'}/\overline{\mathsf{subj}}'/(\mathsf{subj'}/\mathcal{E}\mathsf{Italian} \sqcap \mathsf{became} \sqcap \mathsf{ob1'}/\mathsf{wgt})$

$$\sqcap \mathcal{E}\,\mathsf{Be}$$

where (42) is obtained by applying (41)(a), and (43) by distributing relation application over intersection. Be is the set of 'being an individual', i.e., the existence events. The expression in parentheses in (43) is exactly the denotation of (37). Thus entailment is immediate, if we overlook the existence claim. The past tense of 'became' does presuppose the existence of such Italian, so the entailment of (39) from (37) is justified. At present we do not account for tense and related presuppositions however.

Many of subject relative clauses in FraCaS are copular clauses, e.g., (45) of problem 007:

(44)   Some great tenors are Swedish.

(45)   There are great tenors who are Swedish.

which also exhibits a bare plural. In the context of an existential clause, it seems justified to treat is as existentially quantified; therefore, as explained earlier, we treat the whole (45) as a surface realization of

(46)   Several great tenors who are Swedish exist.

Applying the just outlined approach to subject relative clauses, coupled with the analysis of copular clauses in Sect. 4 gives as the denotation for (46):

$$\mathsf{subj'}/(\mathcal{G}_{N>1}\,\mathsf{GreatTenor} \sqcap (\overline{\mathsf{subj}}'/\mathsf{be'}/\mathcal{E}\mathsf{Swedish})) \sqcap \mathcal{E}\,\mathsf{Be}$$

$$= \mathsf{subj'}/(\mathcal{G}_{N>1}(\overline{\mathsf{subj}}'/\mathsf{subj'}/\mathsf{GreatTenor}) \sqcap (\overline{\mathsf{subj}}'/\mathsf{be'}/\mathcal{E}\mathsf{Swedish})) \sqcap \mathcal{E}\,\mathsf{Be}$$

$$= \mathsf{subj'}/\overline{\mathsf{subj}}'/(\mathsf{subj'}/\mathcal{G}_{N>1}\,\mathsf{GreatTenor} \sqcap \mathsf{be'}/\mathcal{E}\mathsf{Swedish}) \sqcap \mathcal{E}\,\mathsf{Be}$$

$$= \mathsf{subj'}/\mathcal{G}_{N>1}\,\mathsf{GreatTenor} \sqcap \mathsf{be'}/\mathcal{E}\mathsf{Swedish}$$

(note that $\mathsf{be'}/\mathcal{E}\mathsf{Swedish}$ are existence events). The result is exactly the denotation of (44), which is thus equivalent on our analysis to (46).

6   Related Work

Treating denotations as queries and considering the entailment of queries is rather rare, although one may say it is fully in the spirit of Heim and Kratzer

[4]. The (only) closest related work is that of Tian et al. [3,10] on abstract Dependency-based Compositional Semantics (DCS). It also appeals to the intuition of database queries, uses relational algebra and algebraic entailments, and also Sect. 1 of FraCaS. For example, "students read books" gets the abstract denotation

$$\mathbf{read} \cup (\mathbf{student}_{SUBJ} \times \mathbf{book}_{OBJ})$$

"It is not hard to see the abstract denotation denotes the intersection of the 'reading' set (as illustrated by the 'read' table in Table 1) with the product of 'student' set and 'book' set." [10, §2.2] The meaning of the declarative sentence is the statement about the denotation: its non-emptiness [10, §2.4.2].

The above reads quite like the opening sections of [5]. Then the differences emerge: our denotations are not (queries for) simple sets of events: rather, they are more complicated polyconcepts, capable of explaining all sorts of quantifier ambiguities (including those due to negative quantification and negation). Although [10] mentions negation, it is only 'atomic' (that is, antonym) and 'root' (sentential).

Tian et al. do not actually use event semantics, and do not consider denotations to be witnesses of the truth of the sentence. Denotations in the abstract DCS are rather coarse: the meaning of "Mary loves every dog" is a one-point set (trivial database relation). Therefore, "mary loves every dog" and "John likes every cat" (if true) have the identical truth value. In contrast, our semantics is 'hyperfine': true sentences have distinct truth value: their own witnesses of the truth.

Finally, there are also methodological differences. Tian et al. work is in the context of NLP rather than theoretical linguistics, and widely uses approximate paraphrasing, word sense similarity and other NLP techniques.

For critical analysis of other approaches to event quantification problem, see [6].

7   Conclusions

We have presented, on paper for now, the application of the polynomial event semantics to textual entailment problems in Sect. 1 of FraCaS. This required extending the prior work to the whole set of generalized quantifiers (including proportional ones), as well as copula and existential clauses and subject relative clauses. The mechanical implementation of this approach is pending.

Also the subject of future work is the treatment of tense and the presuppositions of existence.

Acknowledgments. We are very grateful to the reviewers and Daisuke Bekki for their insightful comments and questions. This work was partially supported by a JSPS KAKENHI Grant Number 17K00091.

References

1. Champollion, L.: The interaction of compositional semantics and event semantics. Linguist. Philos. **38**(1), 31–66 (2015)
2. Cooper, R., et al.: Using the framework. Deliverable D16, FraCaS Project (1996)
3. Dong, Y., Tian, R., Miyao, Y.: Encoding generalized quantifiers in dependency-based compositional semantics. In: Proceedings of the 28th Pacific Asia Conference on Language, Information and Computation, PACLIC 28, Cape Panwa Hotel, Phuket, Thailand, 12–14 December 2014, pp. 585–594 (2014). http://aclweb.org/anthology/Y/Y14/Y14-1067.pdf
4. Heim, I., Kratzer, A.: Semantics in Generative Grammar. Blackwell Publishers, Oxford (1997)
5. Kiselyov, O.: Polynomial event semantics. In: Kojima, K., Sakamoto, M., Mineshima, K., Satoh, K. (eds.) JSAI-isAI 2018. LNCS (LNAI), vol. 11717, pp. 313–324. Springer, Cham (2019). https://doi.org/10.1007/978-3-030-31605-1_23
6. Kiselyov, O.: Polynomial event semantics: negation. In: Okazaki, N., Yada, K., Satoh, K., Mineshima, K. (eds.) JSAI-isAI 2020. LNCS (LNAI), vol. 12758, pp. 82–95. Springer, Cham (2021). https://doi.org/10.1007/978-3-030-79942-7_6
7. MacCartney, B.: The FRACAS textual inference problem set. https://nlp.stanford.edu/wcmac/downloads/fracas.xml
8. Maienborn, C.: Event semantics, chap. 8, pp. 232–266. Semantics - Theories, De Gruyter Mouton (2019). https://doi.org/10.1515/9783110589245-008
9. Parsons, T.: Events in the Semantics of English: a Study in Subatomic Semantics. The MIT Press, Cambridge (1990)
10. Tian, R., Miyao, Y., Matsuzaki, T.: Logical inference on dependency-based compositional semantics. In: ACL (1), pp. 79–89. The Association for Computer Linguistics (2014). http://aclweb.org/anthology/P/P14/

Parsed Corpus Development with a Quick Access Interface

Alastair Butler[✉]

Faculty of Humanities and Social Sciences, Hirosaki University,
Bunkyo-cho 1, Hirosaki-shi 036-8560, Japan
ajb129@hirosaki-u.ac.jp

Abstract. This paper introduces a web browser based quick access interface for the Treebank Semantics Parsed Corpus (TSPC) as a demonstration of corpus development. The TSPC is a corpus of English with hand worked tree analysis for approaching half-a-million words. The interface provides a 'live' view of the corpus as it is worked on, with search functionality and visualisations of the analysis from three different perspectives: Tree, Word, and Graph. The Graph view is especially notable for displaying semantic level relationships to make visually apparent a wider range of the connections that the design of the annotation captures.

Keywords: parsed corpus development · analysis visualisation · semantic dependencies · data format · annotation scheme

1 Introduction

This paper introduces the TSPC quick access interface as a demonstration of corpus development.[1] This interface aims to give quick and simple access to the content of the Treebank Semantics Parsed Corpus (TSPC), a corpus of English with hand worked tree analysis for approaching half-a-million words. The corpus was started as a testing ground for the Treebank Semantics method (Butler 2021) of processing constituency tree annotations to return logic based meaning representations, but has grown into a corpus resource of general use. Highlights include:

- labelled constituent structure,
- assignments of grammatical role and function,
- grammatical codes for verbs, and
- witness information to resolve anaphoric dependencies.

---

[1] The interface is accessed as the "search interface" of http://entrees.github.io.

This paper benefited from the comments of two anonymous reviewers who are gratefully acknowledged. This research was supported by the Japan Society for the Promotion of Science (JSPS), Research Project Number: 19K00541.

K. Yada et al. (Eds.): JSAI-isAI 2021 Workshops, LNAI 13856, pp. 212–227, 2023.
https://doi.org/10.1007/978-3-031-36190-6_15

While on a smaller scale, the annotation approach is comparable to the resources of the Penn Treebank (Marcus, Santorini, and Marcinkiewicz 1993), ICE Corpora (Nelson, Wallis and Aarts 2002), and the Penn Historical Parsed Corpora (Santorini 2010). The annotation content is most relatable to the SUSANNE Corpus and Analytic Scheme (Sampson 1995), and a large percentage (nearly three quarters) exists as data that was converted from annotation that had been following the SUSANNE scheme. Differentiating factors of the current resource are the richness of disambiguation information contained, and the high degree of normalised structure present. Both of these properties assist the automatic creation of meaning representations, seen through the interface as dependency graphs.

The interface described in this paper is useful for:

 (i) browsing the corpus,
 (ii) accessing content by providing ID information,
 (iii) searching the corpus, and
 (iv) seeing visualisations of the parse analysis from three different perspectives: Tree, Word, and Graph.

The interface provides a 'live' view of the corpus as it is being built. Indeed, the principle reason for the interface development has been to provide quick and simple access to visualisations of the corpus analysis as it is worked on. The interface also has a secondary role of offering an active way to explore the parsed data over the internet, with its querying functions being useful for linguistic research and English grammar teaching purposes.

2 The Corpus Overview Page and Interface Map

The corpus overview page is the default entry point to the interface and is also reached by clicking the 'Corpus overview' link of any of the other pages. Other possible navigations through the interface are illustrated in Fig. 1. Notably, the search pages and context page are intermediate steps for reaching a tree page. From a tree page, you can toggle between the other visualisation pages, or visit/return to the context page.

The corpus overview page contains links for reaching the Grep and TGrep2 pages. There is also an ID field box with the functionality described in Sect. 3 below. Finally, there are grouped listings of all the corpus files, with each list item serving as a clickable link to a context page for the corresponding file. If the ID text box field has content, then the listing of files will be restricted to those files with names that contain the given content, ignoring case distinctions. With the corpus consisting of over four hundred files, this provides a useful way to zoom in on file collections, especially as related files have related names. If there is no match for the content of the ID text box, then the overview page is left with no listed files.

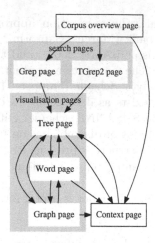

Fig. 1. Map of the interface

3   Accessing Content by Providing ID Information

The corpus overview page, context page, and visualisation pages all contain an ID text field box. When the corpus overview page is open, the ID box is blank by default. With the context page, the ID box contains the name of the shown file. With a visualisation page, the ID box contains the full ID name of the shown parse analysis. Multiple full ID names can be entered into the ID box when they are space separated, in which case a visualisation for all the referenced parse analysis is shown.

A full ID name for a given instance of parse analysis takes the form of a number followed by an underscore character ('_') and then the name of the file that contains the parse analysis.

The user is free to edit the content of the ID box, and then, by pressing the [ENTER] key, will jump to the corresponding page for the edited ID information.

4   The Underlying Data Format

To understand the functionality of the interface, particularly the options for search, it is helpful to know about the underlying data format used by the TSPC. Each corpus file is a text file containing instances of parse analysis separated by blank lines. Each analysis instance begins with a line that presents the overall word yield for the analysis, where a word yield is the extraction of the terminal nodes of the tree, but without zero elements like relative clause traces. The yield is presented between opening and closing brackets with the form: '=N(" ' and '")'. Following this opening line comes the parse analysis itself, with each word of the analysis placed at the end of its own line and accompanied by lemma information between curly braces with an initial semi-colon ('; {', '}'). Furthermore, each analysis line presents the path information from the root layer of the parse through to the word layer. The last line of a parse analysis instance is the ID node for the instance.

As examples, (1) shows the two opening instances of parse analysis from the file `classics_POTTER_1902.txt`:

(1)
```
=N(" THE TALE OF PETER RABBIT BY BEATRIX POTTER ")
"FRAG","NP","D","THE;{the}"
"FRAG","NP","N","TALE;{tale}"
"FRAG","NP","PP","P-ROLE","OF;{of}"
"FRAG","NP","PP","NP","NPR","PETER;{PETER}"
"FRAG","NP","PP","NP","N","RABBIT;{rabbit}"
"FRAG","PP","P-ROLE","BY;{by}"
"FRAG","PP","NP","NPR","BEATRIX;{BEATRIX}"
"FRAG","PP","NP","NPR","POTTER;{POTTER}"
"ID","1_classics_POTTER_1902"
```

```
=N(" Once upon a time there were four little Rabbits <comma> and their names were <mdash> Flopsy
<comma> Mopsy <comma> Cotton-tail <comma> and Peter . ")
"IP-MAT","IML","IML","ADVP-TMP","ADV","Once;{once}"
"IP-MAT","IML","IML","ADVP-TMP","PP","P-ROLE","upon;{upon}"
"IP-MAT","IML","IML","ADVP-TMP","PP","NP","D","a;{a}"
"IP-MAT","IML","IML","ADVP-TMP","PP","NP","N","time;{time}"
"IP-MAT","IML","IML","EX","there;{there}"
"IP-MAT","IML","IML","BED;~I","were;{be}"
"IP-MAT","IML","IML","NP-ESBJ;{RABBITS}","NUM","four;{four}"
"IP-MAT","IML","IML","NP-ESBJ;{RABBITS}","ADJP","ADJ","little;{little}"
"IP-MAT","IML","IML","NP-ESBJ;{RABBITS}","NS","Rabbits;{rabbit}"
"IP-MAT","IML","PU","<comma>"
"IP-MAT","IML","CONJP","CONJ","and;{and}"
"IP-MAT","IML","CONJP","IML","NP-SBJ","NP-GENV;{RABBITS}","PRO","their;{their}"
"IP-MAT","IML","CONJP","IML","NP-SBJ","NS","names;{name}"
"IP-MAT","IML","CONJP","IML","BED;~Ln","were;{be}"
"IP-MAT","IML","CONJP","IML","PU","<mdash>"
"IP-MAT","IML","CONJP","IML","NP-PRD2","NML","NP","NPR","Flopsy;{Flopsy}"
"IP-MAT","IML","CONJP","IML","NP-PRD2","NML","PU","<comma>"
"IP-MAT","IML","CONJP","IML","NP-PRD2","NML","CONJP;@3","NP","NPR","Mopsy;{Mopsy}"
"IP-MAT","IML","CONJP","IML","NP-PRD2","NML","PU","<comma>"
"IP-MAT","IML","CONJP","IML","NP-PRD2","NML","CONJP;@5","NP","NPR","Cotton-tail;{Cotton_tail}"
"IP-MAT","IML","CONJP","IML","NP-PRD2","NML","PU","<comma>"
"IP-MAT","IML","CONJP","IML","NP-PRD2","NML","CONJP;@7","CONJ","and;{and}"
"IP-MAT","IML","CONJP","IML","NP-PRD2","NML","CONJP;@7","NP","NPR","Peter;{Peter}"
"IP-MAT","PU","."
"ID","2_classics_POTTER_1902"
```

Note that some nodes in (1) have extra markings: `"CONJP;@3"`, `"CONJP;@5"`, and `"CONJP;@7"` of 2_classics_POTTER_1902. If there are distinct nodes that are non-terminal with the same tag and the same preceding path, then extra marking is required to ensure these nodes are uniquely distinguished when considering multiple paths. The convention followed for extra marking includes ';@n' for the n-th sister node of a shared preceding path.

The analysis of (1) demonstrates some key aspects of the annotation scheme:

- words project word class nodes (D=determiner, N=noun, P-ROLE=role marking preposition, NPR=proper noun, BED=past tense BE, PU=punctuation, etc.),
- clauses are typed (IP-MAT=declarative main clause, FRAG=sentence fragment),

216   A. Butler

- coordination involves CONJP projections and intermediate layers of structure (IML=clause intermediate level, NML=nominal intermediate level),
- clause level constituents are function marked (-ESBJ=subject of an existential construction, -SBJ=subject, -PRD2=subject predicative role, etc.),
- constituents contributing discourse referents have witness information (for the collection of rabbits named Flopsy, Mopsy, Cotton-tail, and Peter, there is {RABBITS}),
- pronouns with antecedents have resolved witness information ({RABBITS} appearing with their), and
- verbs have grammar pattern information (~I=selection of clause structure where there is an intransitive verb with no selected adverbial elements, ~Ln=selection of clause structure where there is a linking verb with a subject predicative that is a noun phrase).

The data format of (1) is easy to edit, especially with a text editor capable of multi-line editing. It is notable that edits will always maintain balanced regularised tree structure. But what is most significant is that the format allows for quick and simple line and table based post-processing. As a case in point, an overview can be returned for items that have a particular word class. Figure 2 shows the result for all words in the corpus that are tagged RPRO (relative pronoun). This information is presented with the lemma of the word serving as a link to a Grep search for the lemma followed by a list within brackets of the particular attestations of the lemma with a count of instances after a colon.

Fig. 2. Words marked as relative pronouns (RPRO)

As an example of a line extracted overview which requires information beyond the word class layer of structure, Fig. 3 gives a table with function markings (ABS=absolute, BNF=benefactive, CNT=contingency, etc.) and the lemmas of adverbs that realise the particular function, all with counts, and also serving as clickable links to Grep searches for probing deeper into how the adverb lemma with the particular referenced function occurs in the data (demonstrated below in Sect. 5.1 with (3)).

Corpus overview

Functions	Lemmas with occurrence counts	Total
ABS	as(18) at(1) in(3) include(2) with(51) without(8)	83
BNF	at(2) before(2) for(279) in(2) in_behalf_of(2) on(4) on_behalf_of(4) to(7)	302
CNT	against(19) along_with(1) amid(1) as(41) at(20) because(3) because_of(83) by(24) by_virtue_of(1) considering(2) contrary_to(1) cos_of(1) despite(41) except_for(1) follow(1) following(1) for(532) from(28) in(125) in_accordance_with(1) in_case_of(4) in_connection_with(1) in_favour_of(1) in_or_in_connection_with(1) in_pursuance_of(1) in_return_for(1) in_spite_of(8) instead_of(1) into(1) in_view_of(2) irrespective_of(3) nor(1) notwithstanding(6) of(1) on(39) on_account_of(1) out_of(1) over(1) round_about(1) so(1) subject_to(1) thanks_to(9) through(16) to(13) toward(1) under(24) upon(4) with(36) within(1) with_or_without(1) without(44)	1156
COM	alongside(3) along_with(10) by(2) in(6) in_conjunction_with(2) on(1) to(8) together_with(1) with(494) within(1) with_or_without(1) without(25)	554

Fig. 3. Function marking with prepositions (P-ROLE)

To support TGrep2 search, the TSPC native format of (1) is converted into bracketed trees with a TOP node, as in (2).

(2)
```
(TOP (FRAG (NP (D THE;{the})
               (N TALE;{tale})
               (PP (P-ROLE OF;{of})
                   (NP (NPR PETER;{PETER})
                       (N RABBIT;{rabbit}))))
           (PP (P-ROLE BY;{by})
               (NP (NPR BEATRIX;{BEATRIX})
                   (NPR POTTER;{POTTER}))))
     (ID 1_classics_POTTER_1902))
```

With conversion to bracketed trees, ';@n' markings of nodes are removed, since nodes appear only once within the bracketed structure and so are always distinct.

5   Search Pages

The interface provides two different methods for searching the corpus: the Grep page (Sect. 5.1) and the TGrep2 page (Sect. 5.2).

5.1   Grep Page

The Grep page gives a link for returning to the corpus overview page, and a text field box for entering a grep search pattern. There is a second field box for entering a start number (explained below). If the search text box is blank, then there are tables listing the full tag set used in the corpus. A search begins when the 'Search' button is clicked, or after a search pattern is entered into the text field box and the [ENTER] key is pressed.

Search is made using the `grep` command (Magloire et al. 2021) under a recursive call (`grep -nr`) in a directory that contains the corpus data in the native corpus format described in Sect. 4, and illustrated with (1). Aside from making changes to the search pattern, there is no other way to restrict the searched data.

Figure 4 illustrates using the Grep page to find instances of the string `against` in the corpus. The results page tells us the number of lines found to match the search expression. This is followed by a display of the results in a tabled format with three columns. The first column is the hit number following corpus order, that is, with line matches taken from files following an alphanumeric sort of the corpus filenames. The second column consists of possibly coloured cells that contain the full content of a matched line from the corpus data. The third column contains information about the line number followed by an underscore character ('_') and then the filename for the reported content. This line number and filename serve as a link to a tree page for the overall linked instance of parse analysis, with the terminal node for line content highlighted in the resulting tree of the reached tree page.

Corpus overview	Grep pattern:	against		Search

There were 395 line matches.

1	There were waves on the water <apos>s top and the water was lashing against the edge of the swimming pool .	99_age_10_K60
2	"IP-MAT","IML","CONJP","IML","IP-PPL-CAT","PP-DIR","P-ROLE","against; {against}"	113_age_10_K60
3	The girls have netball matches against other schools in the winter .	91_age_11_H21
4	"IP-MAT","NP-OB1","PP","P-ROLE","against; {against}"	97_age_11_H21

Fig. 4. Grep search for `against`

The colouring of cells is a notable aid for being able to easily pick up on differences in the annotation, especially as a search can bring together lines from throughout the corpus.

As Fig. 4 demonstrates, a Grep search is useful for searching through the yield lines of the annotation. Any search that involves a space character will automatically be restricted to finding its matches from only yield lines. When the matched line is a yield line from the corpus data which (as seen with (1) above) consists of a line with opening and closing brackets with the form: '=N("' and '")', these opening and closing brackets are removed from the shown result and the segment of the line that matches the search expression is highlighted.

Search pattern (3) will find instances of the lemma {against} restricted to having the `P-ROLE` (preposition) word class that occurs in a preposition phrase with `-CNT` (contingency) function.

(3) `PP-CNT[^-,]*,.P-ROLE[^,]*,[^,]*{against}`

Note that the double quotes character (") cannot be used in grep search patterns made with the interface. In pattern (3), mention of double quote characters is avoided with use of the dot ('.') character, which matches any single character.

Figure 5 shows the top of the results page from searching with (3), with the number of matched lines now restricted to nineteen lines.

Corpus overview	Grep pattern:	PP-CNT[^.]*,P-ROLE[^.]*,[^.]*(against)			Search	Toggle

There were 19 line matches. See all results

1	"IP-MAT","PP-CNT","P-ROLE","against;{against}"	729_bnc_B05
2	"IP-MAT","IML","CONJP","IML","PP-SCON-TMP","IP-ADV","IP-PPL-CAT","PP-CNT","P-ROLE","against;{against}"	1979_bnc_B22
3	"IP-MAT","CP-QUE-OB1","IP-SUB","IP-PPL-CAT","PP-CNT","P-ROLE","against;{against}"	2699_bnc_C05
4	"IP-MAT","PP-CNT","P-ROLE","against;{against}"	714_christine_T07

Fig. 5. Grep search for lemma {against} occuring as a preposition with contingency function

If there are no yield results and the number of matched lines is less than 100 (as in Fig. 5), then a 'See all results' link is provided for opening in a tree page a display of all results as trees.

Up to 2500 matched lines are returned following corpus order. That returned matches follow a set order is important because this allows for the potential of contextual information being seen across returned lines. Quite where in the corpus order the search results start from is established either (i) by a start number entered into the number field that is adjacent to the text field box for entering a grep search pattern, or, (ii) when the start number field is empty, through the random creation of a start number. If there are more than 2500 results, you can see a different batch of 2500 results by re-running the search with a different start number.

With returned line results following corpus order, full constituents appear as adjacent lines when the search expression matches constituent level nodes. This is demonstrated in Fig. 6, with its search expression finding IP-REL (relative clause) nodes. Results start from line match 43606.

Corpus overview	Grep pattern:	IP-REL		43606	Search	Toggle

There were 45725 line matches.

43606	"IP-MAT","NP-CNT","IP-REL","ADJP-PRD2","ADVP","RADV","however;{however}"	371_young_adult_E15
43607	"IP-MAT","NP-CNT","IP-REL","ADJP-PRD2","ADJ","crazy;{crazy}"	372_young_adult_E15
43608	"IP-MAT","NP-CNT","IP-REL","MD","may;{may}"	373_young_adult_E15
43609	"IP-MAT","NP-CNT","IP-REL","VB;~La","seem;{seem}"	374_young_adult_E15
43610	"IP-MAT","NP-OB1","IP-REL","NP-SBJ","RPRO","that;{that}"	395_young_adult_E15
43611	"IP-MAT","NP-OB1","IP-REL","VBP","cause;{cause}"	396_young_adult_E15
43612	"IP-MAT","NP-OB1","IP-REL","NP-OB1","D","that;{that}"	397_young_adult_E15
43613	"IP-MAT","NP-OB1","IP-REL","NP-OB1","N","disease;{disease}"	398_young_adult_E15

Fig. 6. Search for IP-REL (relative clause)

When there are no yield line matches, a 'Toggle' link appears. Clicking 'Toggle' of Fig. 6 opens the page of Fig. 7. Clicking 'Toggle' again returns back to Fig. 6.

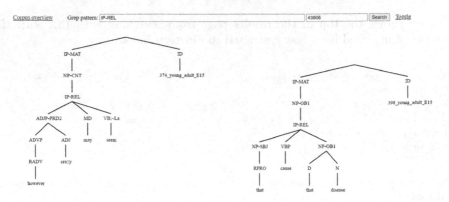

Fig. 7. Search for `IP-REL` (relative clause) after toggle

The page of Fig. 7 shows the same results as Fig. 6 only as tree fragments. Tree fragments are given an ID node that consists of a line number corresponding to the last line that goes into making up the tree fragment and its filename. These ID nodes serve as a link to a tree page for the overall linked instance of parse analysis, with the terminal node for the numbered line content highlighted. Other nodes serve as links to trigger a Grep search for the node label that opens to a page displaying tree fragment results. All this functionality assists finding related examples including inconsistencies and errors in the annotation. Because the underlying search is performed with Grep, results are gathered from the source data files almost instantly.

5.2   TGrep2 Page

The TGrep2 page gives a link for returning to the corpus overview page, and a text field box for entering a TGrep2 search pattern. There is a second field box for entering a start number. There is also a pull-down-selector for choosing between two methods for displaying results:

– The default 'basic' display provides a listing of **up to five hundred** tree yields from matched trees in corpus order. A part of each yield is highlighted as the match of the query.
– Choosing 'graphical' display provides a listing of **up to fifty** graphical trees in corpus order with one highlighted node per tree.

If the search text box is blank, then there are tables listing the full tag set used in the corpus. A search begins when the 'Search' button is clicked, or after a search pattern is entered into the text field box and the [ENTER] key is pressed.

Search is made using the `tgrep2` command (Rohde 2005) over all the corpus data in a binary database built from data that was first converted into the bracketed format described in Sect. 4, and illustrated with (2). Aside from making changes to the search pattern, there is no other way to restrict the searched data.

TGrep2 search patterns consist of expressions to match nodes and relationships defining links or negated links to other nodes. Nodes of searched trees are matched either with simple character strings, or OR'd character strings, or extended regular expressions. A complex node expression consists of a node expression (the master node) which is followed by relationships. Also, nodes can be assigned labels and may be referred to elsewhere in the pattern by those labels.

As an example, consider pattern (4) which finds free relatives.

(4) /^NP\b/ <: (/^IP-REL/=i << (/^(RPRO|RD|RADV)\b/ < _ !>> (/^IP\b/ >> =i)))

The tree relation '<:' of (4) states that a matched IP-REL node is the only daughter of a matched NP node. The NP node is the master node found by the overall pattern. Brackets ensure that other conditions of the pattern concern the need for the matched IP-REL node to contain a relative word (that is, a word tagged as either RPRO, RD, or RADV) without there being a distinct intervening IP layer.

After a query is made, at the top of the page, the search reports the number of hits found, and the number of texts that contain hits. There will also be a button near the top of the page for downloading the search results.

6   Visualisation Pages

The interface provides three different modes for visualising consequences of parse analysis: the tree page (Sect. 6.1), the word page (Sect. 6.2), and the graph page (Sect. 6.3). These pages all have an ID text field box that will contain the full name(s) for the analysis being shown. The content of the ID box can be edited, as described in Sect. 3.

6.1   Tree Page

The tree page shows a tree visualisation of an instance of parse analysis. If multiple parse analysis IDs appear in the ID text field box, then a tree for each ID is shown. In the case of multiple trees being shown, each tree is preceded by an ID heading that works as a link for opening the same tree in a new tree view page. Nodes of a tree can be clicked and will take you to a Grep search for the clicked node element.

6.2   Word Page

The word page shows the word analysis of an instance of parse analysis. If multiple parse analysis IDs appear in the ID text field box, then word analysis for each ID is shown. Figure 8 illustrates the word page.

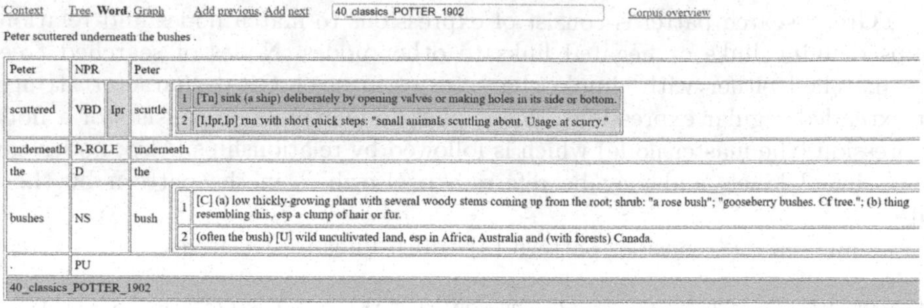

Context   Tree, **Word**, Graph   Add previous, Add next | 40_classics_POTTER_1902 | Corpus overview

Peter scuttered underneath the bushes .

Peter	NPR	Peter		
scuttered	VBD	Ipr	scuttle	1 [Tn] sink (a ship) deliberately by opening valves or making holes in its side or bottom.
				2 [I,Ipr,Ip] run with short quick steps: "small animals scuttling about. Usage at scurry."
underneath	P-ROLE	underneath		
the	D	the		
bushes	NS	bush	1	[C] (a) low thickly-growing plant with several woody stems coming up from the root; shrub: "a rose bush"; "gooseberry bushes. Cf tree."; (b) thing resembling this, esp a clump of hair or fur.
			2	(often the bush) [U] wild uncultivated land, esp in Africa, Australia and (with forests) Canada.
.	PU			

40_classics_POTTER_1902

Fig. 8. Example word page

As Fig. 8 shows, word analysis is presented in a tabled format with three main columns for words. The first column is for a word as it occurs in the source sentence(s). The second column presents the word class of the word from the first column. If the word is a verb associated with a grammar pattern, then this pattern information is also presented and highlighted with yellow. The third column presents information about the word of the first column with minimally a word lemma. If the word is a lexical word then it is also given sense definitions from a dictionary database. Moreover, if the word is a verb then the grammar pattern information is used to highlight compatible sense definitions with yellow, and leave other sense definitions shaded grey. Sense definitions with grammar codes are sourced from Cowie (1989). If the word is a verb without a grammar pattern, then all the cells containing sense numbers for the associated sense definitions are coloured red (reflecting outstanding annotation work).

6.3   Graph Page

The graph page shows a graph visualisation of semantic dependencies for parse analysis produced by the Treebank Semantics evaluation system (Butler 2021). This evaluation system works as an ordered collection of discourse referents from input expressions and then their subsequent release over the input expressions, that is, across the span of the input discourse. Nodes of displayed graphs correspond to the collected discourse referents, including event referents, with dependencies cashing out the relationships that are calculated to hold from the dispersal of the referents as the derived information content of the discourse.

This amounts to an implementation and visualisation of the 'accessibility' relation from Dynamic Semantics. The particular implementation generalises the approach of the system of Predicate Logic with Anaphora (PLA; Dekker 2002, 2012), with a revised version of the formal language of Scope Control Theory (SCT; Butler 2007, 2015) as an intermediate component. (Note the generalisation is not as general as the related Sequence Semantics of Vermeulen (1993); also PLA is close to being the inverse of Incremental Dynamics (van Eijck 2001).)

Besides Sequence Semantics, Incremental Semantics, PLA and SCT, there are many other ways to achieve the relevant notion of accessibility, as seen from the diverse range of systems that fall under the wider Dynamic Semantics umbrella. Most notably, there are the founding systems of Discourse Representation Theory (DRT; Kamp and Reyle 1993) and File Change Semantics (FCS; Heim 1982) that set the standard for empirical results.

The standout virtue of the current approach over its alternatives is its nature of self-regulation that enables the system to calculate results from a minimum of explicit lexical input. This holds not only at the level of discourse accessibility but also feeds through to controlling the (un)availability of bindings for expression internal layers.

For the interface, the result is that if multiple parse analysis IDs appear in the ID text field box, then a single graph is calculated from all the parse analysis of the given IDs. Figure 9 illustrates the graph page.

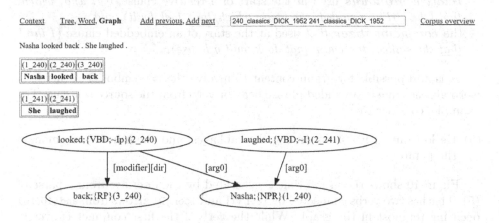

Fig. 9. Example graph page

In a graph, word content for source sentences is found outside of square brackets ('[', ']') and is always accompanied by (i) content between curly braces ('{', '}') to say the word class of the word, and (ii) numbering inside round brackets ('(', ')') to say the word position within the source sentence(s). Word position numbering involves two numbers separated by an underscore character ('_'). The second number says which source sentence the word belongs to. The first number says the position of the word within its source sentence.

Square bracket content tells us about how words function, e.g. [ARGO]=logical subject, [DIR]=direction role. It is most typical for square bracket content to be part of the label for a directed arrow that connects graph nodes.

Most words from source sentences have a presence within the corresponding graph, however some words make a contribution that has to be seen in terms of consequences for graph nodes and their dependencies. Missing words include words that are used to make reference to what is talked about, with node presence capturing the reference contribution. These words can be either:

- **indefinites** (e.g. *a*, *an*, *some*) used to introduce new items for discussion (discourse referents),
- **definites** (e.g. *the*, *these*, *this*) used for a familiar or unique referent of the discourse, or
- **sentence/discourse bound pronouns** (e.g. *he*, *her*, *themselves*) that are links to already established referents.

Note that unbound pronouns do have graph presence, as seen with *He* in Fig. 10 below.

Other words with no graph presence are:

- **relative pronouns** used at the start of a relative clause, e.g. *who*, *which*, *that* (*the girl who smiled*, *the house which/that Jack built*), and
- the **complementizer** *that* used at the start of an embedded clause (*I think that she smiled*, *the claim that Jack built a house*).

It is also possible for graph content to involve the '#' symbol. This marks a word absence due to an elided phrase head or verb from the source sentence. For example, consider (5).

(5) He lost one of his shoes among the cabbages, and the other shoe amongst the potatoes.

Figure 10 shows the graph that is generated by the interface from a parse of (5). This has two verbs connected by [conj1] and [conj2] arrows from and(10_15) occuring topmost in the graph. While the verb of the first conjunct is overtly realised with lost(2_15), the content for the verb of the second conjunct is shown as #1002_15 to indicate the licensed absence of a verb (a lost *lost*!). One further instance of '#' occurs in the graph (referenced as #1001_15) to indicate a nominal head absence that has [num] (numeral modifier) and 'of' (role preposition) links. Note that the indexing with '#' involves two numbers without round brackets. The second number says which solution sentence the elided content belongs to. The first number follows a count of the number of elided instances that occur within the sentence, initialised at 1000. This gives indexing that is distinct from the word location indexing within round brackets that accompanies each word.

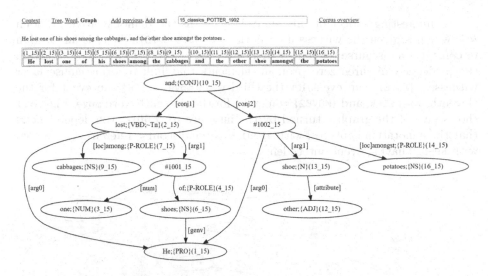

Fig. 10. An example with elided content

7   A Final Example

As a final example to illustrate annotation facilitated by the interface, consider the analysis of (6).

(6)

```
=N(" You then move your legs and arms forward <comma> and then kick your legs out and move your hands round
<comma> and then do this again  ")
"IP-MAT","NP-SBJ;{YOU}","PRO","You;{you}"
"IP-MAT","IML","ADVP-CNT","ADV","then;{then}"
"IP-MAT","IML","IML","IML","IML;{MOVE1}","VBP;~Tn.p","move;{move}"
"IP-MAT","IML","IML","IML","IML;{MOVE1}","NP-OB1","NP-GENV;{YOU}","PRO","your;{your}"
"IP-MAT","IML","IML","IML","IML;{MOVE1}","NP-OB1","NML","NP","NS","legs;{leg}"
"IP-MAT","IML","IML","IML","IML;{MOVE1}","NP-OB1","NML","CONJP","CONJ","and;{and}"
"IP-MAT","IML","IML","IML","IML;{MOVE1}","NP-OB1","NML","CONJP","NP","NS","arms;{arm}"
"IP-MAT","IML","IML","IML","IML;{MOVE1}","ADVP-DIR","ADV","forward;{forward}"
"IP-MAT","IML","IML","IML","PU","<comma>"
"IP-MAT","IML","IML","IML","CONJP","CONJ","and;{and}"
"IP-MAT","IML","IML","IML","CONJP","ADVP-CNT","ADV","then;{then}"
"IP-MAT","IML","IML","IML","CONJP","IML","IML","IML;{KICK}","VBP;~Tn.p","kick;{kick}"
"IP-MAT","IML","IML","IML","CONJP","IML","IML","IML;{KICK}","NP-OB1","NP-GENV;{YOU}","PRO","your;{your}"
"IP-MAT","IML","IML","IML","CONJP","IML","IML","IML;{KICK}","NP-OB1","NS","legs;{leg}"
"IP-MAT","IML","IML","IML","CONJP","IML","IML","IML;{KICK}","ADVP-DIR","RP","out;{out}"
"IP-MAT","IML","IML","IML","CONJP","IML","IML","CONJP","CONJ","and;{and}"
"IP-MAT","IML","IML","IML","CONJP","IML","IML","CONJP","IML;{MOVE2}","VBP;~Tn.p","move;{move}"
"IP-MAT","IML","IML","IML","CONJP","IML","IML","CONJP","IML;{MOVE2}","NP-OB1","NP-GENV;{YOU}","PRO","your;{your}"
"IP-MAT","IML","IML","IML","CONJP","IML","IML","CONJP","IML;{MOVE2}","NP-OB1","NS","hands;{hand}"
"IP-MAT","IML","IML","IML","CONJP","IML","IML","CONJP","IML;{MOVE2}","ADVP-DIR","ADV","round;{round}"
"IP-MAT","IML","PU","<comma>"
"IP-MAT","IML","CONJP","CONJ","and;{and}"
"IP-MAT","IML","CONJP","ADVP-CNT","ADV","then;{then}"
"IP-MAT","IML","CONJP","IML","NP-DSC;{MOVEMENTS}","NML","NP;{MOVE1}","PRO","*"
"IP-MAT","IML","CONJP","IML","NP-DSC;{MOVEMENTS}","NML","CONJP;@2","NP;{KICK}","PRO","*"
"IP-MAT","IML","CONJP","IML","NP-DSC;{MOVEMENTS}","NML","CONJP;@3","NP;{MOVE2}","PRO","*"
"IP-MAT","IML","CONJP","IML","DOP;~Tn","do;{do}"
"IP-MAT","IML","CONJP","IML","NP-OB1;{MOVEMENTS}","D","this;{this}"
"IP-MAT","IML","CONJP","IML","ADVP-TMP","ADV","again;{again}"
"IP-MAT","PU","."
"ID","5_stories_09_M14"
```

An interesting aspect of this analysis concerns the demonstrative pronoun *this* which is given the witness information of {MOVEMENTS}. There is annotation to construct a discourse referent with NP-DSC (DSC=discourse element) built from the projection of three zero pronoun elements that link to prior clause layer witnesses: {MOVE1}=an event for the third word move, {KICK}=an event for the eleventh word kick, and {MOVE2}=an event for the sixteenth word move. Figure 11 shows part of the graph returned by the interface to confirm the dependencies that the annotation captures, with #1001_5 as the discourse referent constructed with NP-DSC having event antecedents.

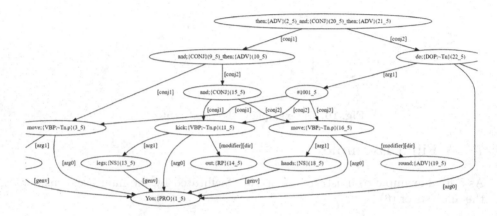

Fig. 11. Part of the graph for (11), an example with a constructed discourse referent

8   Closing Remarks

The search options of Grep (line based search over data in the format discussed in Sect. 4) and TGrep2 (pattern based search over compiled trees) allow for the quick location of sentences with related properties (lemmas, grammar patterns, tree relationships, etc.). Parse analysis can be modified and the consequences for the Tree, Word and Graph views seen instantly. In this way, annotators can ensure that their interpretation of a text is consistently represented in its annotation.

Corrections that have an impact on the tree and graph view typically include changing attachment sites for constituents, changing the specifications of function information, the addition or subtraction of zero elements such as traces for relative clauses, and the addition of 'witness' information to force the resolution of pronominal links and links established with definites. Overt indices are rarely used in the annotation, the structural assignments given are usually common patterns, and exceptions are typically listed in the annotation documentation. The predictable behaviour of the interface and its visualisations allows annotators to use a finite set of strategies to capture dependencies involved in the interpretation of sentence meaning from discourse context down to the granularity of word sense.

References

Butler, A.: Scope control and grammatical dependencies. J. Logic Lang. Inform. **16**, 241–264 (2007)

Butler, A.: Linguistic Expressions and Semantic Processing: A Practical Approach. Springer, Heidelberg (2015). https://doi.org/10.1007/978-3-319-18830-0

Butler, A.: Meaning representations from treebanks. The Treebank Semantics Web Site (2021). http://www.compling.jp/ajb129/ts.html

Cowie, A.P.: Oxford Advanced Learner's Dictionary, 4th edn. Oxford University Press, Oxford (1989)

Dekker, P.: Meaning and use of indefinite expressions. J. Logic Lang. Inform. **11**, 141–194 (2002)

Dekker, P.: Dynamic Semantics. Studies in Linguistics and Philosophy, vol. 91. Springer, Dordrecht (2012). https://doi.org/10.1007/978-94-007-4869-9

van Eijck, J.: Incremental dynamics. J. Logic Lang. Inform. **10**, 319–351 (2001)

Heim, I.: The Semantics of Definite and Indefinite Noun Phrases. Ph.D. thesis, University of Massachusetts, Amherst (1982)

Kamp, H., Reyle, U.: From Discourse to Logic: Introduction to Model-theoretic Semantics of Natural Language, Formal Logic and Discourse Representation Theory. Kluwer, Dordrecht (1993)

Magloire, A., et al.: GNU Grep: Print lines that match patterns, version 3.7. Free Software Foundation (2021)

Marcus, M., Santorini, B., Marcinkiewicz, M.A.: Building a large annotated corpus of English: The Penn Treebank. Comput. Linguist. **19**(2), 313–330 (1993)

Nelson, G., Wallis, S., Aarts, B.: Exploring Natural Language: Working with the British Component of the International Corpus of English. John Benjamins, Amsterdam (2002)

Randall, B.: CorpusSearch 2 Users Guide (2009). http://corpussearch.sourceforge.net/CS-manual/Contents.html

Rohde, D.: TGrep2 User Manual version 1.15 (2005). http://tedlab.mit.edu/~dr/Tgrep2

Sampson, G.R.: English for the Computer: The SUSANNE Corpus and Analytic Scheme. Clarendon Press (Oxford University Press), Oxford (1995)

Santorini, B.: Annotation manual for the Penn Historical Corpora and the PCEEC (Release 2). Technical report, Department of Computer and Information Science, University of Pennsylvania, Philadelphia (2010). http://www.ling.upenn.edu/histcorpora/annotation

Vermeulen, C.F.M.: Sequence semantics for dynamic predicate logic. J. Logic Lang. Inform. **2**, 217–254 (1993)

A Proof-Theoretic Analysis of Weak Crossover

Daisuke Bekki[✉]

Ochanomizu University, Faculty of Core Research, 2-1-1 Ohtsuka, Bunkyo-ku, Tokyo 112-8610, Japan
bekki@is.ocha.ac.jp

Abstract. Dependent type semantics (DTS) is a framework for proof-theoretic semantics of natural language based on Martin-Löf type theory. In this paper, I first show that DTS has an empirical problem regarding the quantificational weak crossover. I then suggest that the definition of underspecified terms in DTS shall be replaced by the *underspecified types*. Finally, I claim that the suggested setting not only successfully solves the problem, but also allows us to naturally define the mechanism of local accommodation in DTS.

1 Quantificational Weak Crossover

1.1 Background

The quantificational variant of the weak crossover (WCO) effect, discussed in Wasow (1972), Chomsky (1976), and Reinhart (1983), among others, is exemplified by its asymmetrical status[1] of the pair of sentences in (1) regarding their acceptability under the bound variable anaphora (BVA) reading between the quantifier every boy and the pronoun his.[2]

(1)   a.   **Every boy praised his father.** (under BVA(every boy, his))

Daisuke Bekki: I sincerely thank the anonymous reviewers of LENLS18 for their insightful comments. This work was partially supported by Japan Science and Technology Agency (JST) CREST Grant Number JPMJCR20D2.22 and Japan Society for the Promotion of Science (JSPS) KAKENHI Grant Number JP18H03284.

[1] Much of the literature reports that (1b) is not completely unacceptable under the specified BVA reading and judges its acceptability as "??" or even "?", rather than "*", as in (1b). I assume, however, that the status of (1b) is unacceptable for carefully controlled informants, especially those who do not allow the quantifier chosen for the experiment (every, in the case of (1)) to take the inverse scope over the subject. See See Hoji (2015), in which chapter 6 is devoted to the interpretation and the controls of experiments on the acceptability of (1).

[2] Another construction in the WCO paradigm is the *wh-question* variant of WCO, originating from Postal (1971), for which I do not provide analysis here. Because the analysis of WCO in DTS is purely semantic, we also need a purely semantic analysis of wh-questions prior to the analysis of the wh-question variant of WCO, which I prefer to leave as an open issue.

K. Yada et al. (Eds.): JSAI-isAI 2021 Workshops, LNAI 13856, pp. 228–241, 2023.
https://doi.org/10.1007/978-3-031-36190-6_16

b.   *His father praised every boy. (under BVA(every boy, his))

The conventional analysis of this paradigm in generative grammar since Reinhart (1983) is that the QR-trace of every boy must c-command his in LF in order to license the above BVA readings. Under the assumption that the subject asymmetrically c-commands the object in English, (1a) satisfies this condition but (1b) does not. This is a purely syntactic analysis that assumes that the availability of the BVA reading is a matter of licensing co-indexations, namely, whether every boy and his can share the same index, which is assumed to be a syntactic object.

Now, the question arises as to whether a purely semantic analysis of the WCO effect can be performed. Dependent type semantics (DTS; Bekki and Mineshima (2017))[3], which is a proof-theoretic framework for natural language semantics, provides a compositional account for the availability of anaphoric links and their interpretations, including the BVA reading, and is therefore a good candidate for investigating the question. However, I will point out that, although DTS correctly predicts the availability of the BVA reading in (1a), it wrongly predicts that the BVA reading in (1b) is also available, which is one of the empirical problems of DTS that has not yet been discussed in the literature.

1.2   The Right Prediction

How are these predictions borne out in DTS? First, let us demonstrate the process by which the BVA reading of (1a) is predicted as acceptable in DTS. Suppose that we assume combinatory categorial grammar (CCG) (Steedman, 1996) as our syntactic theory,[4] then the canonical syntactic structures of (1a)(1b) are (2a)(2b), respectively.

(2)   a. $[_S [_{S/(S\backslash NP)} [_{S/(S\backslash NP)/N} \text{ every}] [_N \text{ boy}]] [_{S\backslash NP} [_{S\backslash NP/NP} \text{ praised}]$
$[_{NP} [_{NP/N} \text{ his}] [_N \text{ father}]]]]$

b. $[_S [_{NP} [_{NP/N} \text{ his}] [_N \text{ father}]] [_{S\backslash NP} [_{S\backslash NP/NP} \text{ praised}]$
$[_{S\backslash NP\backslash(S\backslash NP/NP)} [_{S\backslash NP\backslash(S\backslash NP/NP)/N} \text{ every}] [_N \text{ boy}]]]]$

We also assume the following lexical items that map CCG words to semantic representations in DTS.[5]

(3)   every $\mapsto \lambda n.\lambda p.\lambda x. (u: (x : e) \times n(x)) \to px(\pi_1 u)$

boy $\mapsto$ **boy**   father $\mapsto$ **father**   praised $\mapsto \lambda y.\lambda x.\mathbf{praise}(x, y)$

---

[3] By DTS, I refer to the version of DTS adopted in Yana et al. (2019), Kubota et al. (2019), and Tanaka (2021), which is slightly different from the one adopted in Bekki and Mineshima (2017) that uses the *context-passing* mechanism.

[4] The particular choice of a syntactic theory does not affect the following discussion; we may adopt any lexical grammar assuming it is homomorphic to the type system of DTS.

[5] The abbreviation e stands for entity, the type for entities. Tense information is omitted for the sake of simplicity.

$$\text{his} \mapsto \lambda n.\pi_1@((y:\mathbf{e}) \times n(y) \times \mathbf{of}(y, \pi_1@((z:\mathbf{e}) \times \mathbf{male}(z))))$$

When the lexical items are fully specified, they uniquely determine the homomorphic map from syntactic structures in CCG to semantic compositions in DTS, which sends (2a)(2b) to the preterms (4a)(4b).

(4)   a. $(u\colon(x:\mathbf{e}) \times \mathbf{boy}(x)) \;\rightarrow\; \mathbf{praise}(\pi_1 u, \pi_1@((y:\mathbf{e}) \times \mathbf{father}(y) \times \mathbf{of}(y, \pi_1@((z:\mathbf{e}) \times \mathbf{male}(z)))))$

  b. $(u\colon(x:\mathbf{e}) \times \mathbf{boy}(x)) \;\rightarrow\; \mathbf{praise}(\pi_1@((y:\mathbf{e}) \times \mathbf{father}(y) \times \mathbf{of}(y, \pi_1@((z:\mathbf{e}) \times \mathbf{male}(z)))), \pi_1 u)$

The *semantic felicity condition* of DTS requires each of (4a) and (4b) to be a *type* under a given context Γ (a type-theoretic context representing the preceding discourse); more formally, the judgment $\Gamma \vdash (4a) : \mathsf{type}$ and $\Gamma \vdash (4b) : \mathsf{type}$ must hold, reflecting the assumption that a semantic representation of a sentence in DTS is a type and therefore a collection of proofs.

The underlying type theory adopted in DTS is underspecified dependent type theory (UDTT: Bekki and Sato (2015)), which extends Martin-Löf type theory (or dependent type theory; DTT) with *underspecified terms* (Bekki, 2014), namely, terms of the form $@A$ (pronounced as *asperand* A) for some type A. Underspecified terms are the key devices by which DTS represents the meanings of pronouns and presupposition triggers while keeping the semantic theory compositional.

Intuitively, a term $@A$ is an *open proof* of A, which behaves as a term of type A without any actual proof, assuming the existence of a proof of A. In (4a), $@((z:\mathbf{e}) \times \mathbf{male}(z))$ is an example of an underspecified term, which behaves as a term of type $(z:\mathbf{e}) \times \mathbf{male}(z)$, assuming that it has a proof, that is, a pair of some entity and a proof of its being a male, which is a witness of the presupposition triggered by the use of the pronoun his.

Theoretically, $@A$ is defined as a *control operator* in the type inference and type checking algorithms of DTT.[6] Bekki and Sato (2015) defined and implemented the type inference and the type checking of DTT as algorithms that respectively take a DTT query $\Gamma \vdash M : ?$ and a DTT judgment $\Gamma \vdash M : A$, and return a set of proof diagrams for $\Gamma \vdash M : A$ for some A (which we denote $[\![\Gamma \vdash M : ?]\!]$) and a set of proof diagrams for $\Gamma \vdash M : A$ (which we denote $[\![\Gamma \vdash M : A]\!]$). Then, the behavior of $@A$ is determined by the type inference rule (5).

(5)   Type inference rule for underspecified terms:

$$[\![\Gamma \vdash @A : ?]\!] = \left\{ \begin{array}{c} \Gamma \\ \mathcal{D}_M \\ M : A' \end{array} \middle| \begin{array}{l} \quad\vdots \qquad\qquad \in [\![\Gamma \vdash A : \mathsf{type}]\!] \\ \Gamma \vdash A' : \mathsf{type} \\ \mathcal{D}_M \in [\![\Gamma \vdash ? : A']\!] \end{array} \right\}$$

---

[6] In this paper, I adopt a slightly different definition of UDTT (for the sake of simplicity) to that presented in Bekki and Sato (2015), where UDTT has its own type system that consists of a set of typing rules and a set of @-elimination rules, which are defined in a mutually recursive manner. See the Appendix for details.

where $[\![\Gamma \vdash ? : A']\!]$ is a proof search in DTT.

The rule (5) requires that the type checking for $\Gamma \vdash A :$ type returns proof diagrams for $\Gamma \vdash A' :$ type (notation $\mathcal{D}_A$), where A' is the "@-eliminated" version of A, and A' inhabits some proof M. As a whole, $[\![\Gamma \vdash @A : ?]\!]$ returns a set of proof diagrams for $\Gamma \vdash M : A'$ for such M and A'.

Therefore, the semantic felicity condition for (4a) and (4b) is ensured when each of $[\![\Gamma \vdash (4a) : \text{type}]\!]$ and $[\![\Gamma \vdash (4b) : \text{type}]\!]$ is a non-empty set. The type checking in UDTT is a decidable process when the given preterm contains no underspecified term, but otherwise encounters the rule (5) at some point and launches *proof search* $\Gamma \vdash ? : A'$ to check whether A' has a proof.[7] Since both (4a) and (4b) contain underspecified terms, the type checking of (4a) and (4b) factor through the type inference for (6).

(6) Γ, u : $(x : \mathbf{e}) \times \mathbf{boy}(x) \vdash @((y : \mathbf{e}) \times \mathbf{father}(y) \times \mathbf{of}(y, \pi_1@((z : \mathbf{e}) \times \mathbf{male}(z)))) : ?$

According to (5), it calls for the following type check. In words, it checks whether the proposition he has a father is a well-formed type.

(7) Γ, u : $(x : \mathbf{e}) \times \mathbf{boy}(x) \vdash (y : \mathbf{e}) \times \mathbf{father}(y) \times \mathbf{of}(y, \pi_1@((z : \mathbf{e}) \times \mathbf{male}(z))) : \text{type}$

Because the term in (7) contains another underspecified term $@((z : \mathbf{e}) \times \mathbf{male}(z))$ (in words, he), it invokes the following type inference in the type-checking process of (7).

(8) Γ, $u : (x : \mathbf{e}) \times \mathbf{boy}(x)$, $y : \mathbf{e}$, $v : \mathbf{father}(y) \vdash @((z : \mathbf{e}) \times \mathbf{male}(z)) : ?$

The rule (5) is called again and type checks (9a), which is straightforward. Then it launches the proof search (9b).

(9) a. Γ, $u : (x : \mathbf{e}) \times \mathbf{boy}(x)$, $y : \mathbf{e}$, $v : \mathbf{father}(y) \vdash (z : \mathbf{e}) \times \mathbf{male}(z) : \text{type}$

 b. Γ, $u : (x : \mathbf{e}) \times \mathbf{boy}(x)$, $y : \mathbf{e}$, $v : \mathbf{father}(y) \vdash ? : (z : \mathbf{e}) \times \mathbf{male}(z)$

In words, it searches for a male under the assumption that there exists a boy. By assuming the world knowledge that every boy is male (i.e., the signature contains a constant term $\mathbf{bm}$: $(x{:}\mathbf{e}) \to \mathbf{boy}(x) \to \mathbf{male}(x)$), this proof search finds a solution $(\pi_1 u, \mathbf{bm}(\pi_1 u)(\pi_2 u))$ corresponding to the BVA reading of this pronoun, among other solutions.[8] Therefore, the type checking for (7) returns a set of proof diagrams containing a proof diagram for (10) (since $\pi_1(\pi_1 u, \mathbf{bm}(\pi_1 u)(\pi_2 u)) =_\beta \pi_1 u$).

---

[7] Proof search in DTT is undecidable; therefore, anaphora resolution in DTS is undecidable. This may not be a useful result from the computational perspective, but it does not constitute an empirical problem either since there is no evidence that human anaphora resolution is a decidable process.

[8] This is not a unique solution—the signature may provide proof constructions of other male persons as well.

(10) $\Gamma,\ u : (x : \mathbf{e}) \times \mathbf{boy}(x) \vdash (y : \mathbf{e}) \times \mathbf{father}(y) \times \mathbf{of}(y, \pi_1 u) : \mathsf{type}$

The type checker then launches the following proof search, which in turn is the proof construction for the presupposed content by the use of the possessive, in words, he has a father.

(11) $\Gamma,\ u : (x : \mathbf{e}) \times \mathbf{boy}(x) \vdash ? : (y : \mathbf{e}) \times \mathbf{father}(y) \times \mathbf{of}(y, \pi_1 u)$

If we further assume the world knowledge that every boy has a father, that is, a constant term $\mathbf{fatherOf} : (u : (x : \mathbf{e}) \times \mathbf{boy}(x)) \to (y : \mathbf{e}) \times \mathbf{father}(y) \times \mathbf{of}(y, \pi_1 u)$, then (11) finds a proof term $\mathbf{fatherOf}(u)$. Thus, the type inference for (6) returns a set of proof diagrams containing a proof diagram for (12).

(12) $\Gamma \vdash (u : (x : \mathbf{e}) \times \mathbf{boy}(x)) \to \mathbf{praise}(\pi_1 u, \pi_1 \mathbf{fatherOf}(u)) : \mathsf{type}$

In this way, we end up with, as one of the semantic representations for (1a), $(u : (x : \mathbf{e}) \times \mathbf{boy}(x)) \to \mathbf{praise}(\pi_1 u, \pi_1 \mathbf{fatherOf}(u))$, which is a type in DTT that corresponds to every boy praised his own father. Therefore, DTS correctly predicts the acceptability of (1a) under the specified BVA reading.

1.3 The Wrong Prediction

However, DTS wrongly predicts that (1b) is also acceptable under the specified BVA reading. The reason is that, because the two semantic representations (4a) and (4b) are almost the same except for the order of arguments of **praise**, the type checking of (4b) goes in the same way as the one we demonstrated for (4a), boiling down to (13), which corresponds to the specified BVA reading of (1b).[9]

(13) $\Gamma \vdash (u : (x : \mathbf{e}) \times \mathbf{boy}(x)) \to \mathbf{praise}(\pi_1 \mathbf{fatherOf}(u), \pi_1 u) : \mathsf{type}$

Therefore, DTS has an empirical problem, namely, the lack of subject–object asymmetry in the quantificational variant of WCO constructions.

2 Proposal: Underspecified Types in DTS

The source of this problem lies in the fact that, given a semantic representation that contains (a projection of) an underspecified term @A as an argument of a predicate, the proof search of A' takes place within the scopes of both the subject and the object quantifiers, that is, in its semantic argument positions, where hierarchical subject–object asymmetry is lost. The position at which the proof search takes place should reflect the syntactic position in the structural hierarchy of the lexical item that triggers @A. For this reason, I suggest replacing the definition of underspecified terms in DTS with the definition of *underspecified types*, which is defined by the rules (14).[10]

---

[9] I thank Kenichi Asai for pointing out this problem (p.c. July 19th, 2015).
[10] See Appendix A for a formal presentation.

(14)   Type inference rule for underspecified types (@-Rule)

$$\left[\!\left[\Gamma \vdash \begin{bmatrix} x @ A \\ B \end{bmatrix} : ?\right]\!\right] = \left\{ \begin{array}{l|l} & \begin{array}{l} \vdots \qquad\qquad \in [\![\Gamma \vdash A : \mathsf{type}]\!] \\ A' : \mathsf{type} \end{array} \\ \begin{array}{c} \Gamma \\ \mathcal{D}_B \\ B'' : \mathsf{type} \end{array} & \begin{array}{l} \vdots \qquad \in [\![\Gamma \vdash ? : A']\!] \\ M : A' \\ B[M/x] \twoheadrightarrow_\beta B' \\ \mathcal{D}_B \in [\![\Gamma \vdash B' : \mathsf{type}]\!] \end{array} \end{array} \right\}$$

where $[\![\Gamma \vdash ? : A']\!]$ is a proof search in DTT.

In the update, the proof search result substitutes the variable x in B, thereby ensuring that the proof search is launched outside B. With underspecified types, the lexical item for **his** (in the object position) in the lexicon is revised as follows.[11]

(15)   **his** $\mapsto (S\backslash NP)\backslash(S\backslash NP/NP)/N : \lambda n.\lambda p.\lambda x. \begin{bmatrix} u@ (x : \mathbf{e}) \times \mathbf{male}(x) \\ v@ (y : \mathbf{e}) \times n(y) \times \mathbf{of}(y, \pi_1 u) \\ px(\pi_1 v) \end{bmatrix}$

The syntactic structures of (1a) and (1b) need a slight revision according to the change in syntactic category for **his**; then, they can be mapped to the semantic representations (16a) and (16b), respectively.

(16)   a. $(w\colon (x : \mathbf{e}) \times \mathbf{boy}(x)) \rightarrow \begin{bmatrix} u@ (x : \mathbf{e}) \times \mathbf{male}(x) \\ v@ (y : \mathbf{e}) \times \mathbf{father}(y) \times \mathbf{of}(y, \pi_1 u) \\ \mathbf{praise}(\pi_1 w, \pi_1 v) \end{bmatrix}$

   b. $\begin{bmatrix} u@ (x : \mathbf{e}) \times \mathbf{male}(x) \\ v@ (y : \mathbf{e}) \times \mathbf{father}(y) \times \mathbf{of}(y, \pi_1 u) \\ (w\colon (x : \mathbf{e}) \times \mathbf{boy}(x)) \rightarrow \mathbf{praise}(\pi_1 v, \pi_1 w) \end{bmatrix}$

In (16a), u appears within the scope of w and can be resolved by $(\pi_1 w, \mathbf{bm}(\pi_1 w)(\pi_2 w))$, while in (16b), u appears outside the scope of w and has no such option. Let us look at the process more closely. First, the semantic felicity condition for (16a) calls for the type checking (17):

(17) $\Gamma, \; w : (x : \mathbf{e}) \times \mathbf{boy}(x) \vdash \begin{bmatrix} u@ (x : \mathbf{e}) \times \mathbf{male}(x) \\ v@ (y : \mathbf{e}) \times \mathbf{father}(y) \times \mathbf{of}(y, \pi_1 u) \\ \mathbf{praise}(\pi_1 w, \pi_1 v) \end{bmatrix} : \mathsf{type}$

which calls for the rule (14) and therefore checks the following.

---

[11] The square brackets for underspecified types are syntactically distinguished from those of the Σ-type notation, but when these square brackets nest, they may be omitted except for the outermost ones in the same way as brackets used in Σ-type notation.

(18)   a. $\Gamma,\ w : (x : \mathbf{e}) \times \mathbf{boy}(x) \vdash (x : \mathbf{e}) \times \mathbf{male}(x) : \mathsf{type}$

       b. $\Gamma,\ w : (x : \mathbf{e}) \times \mathbf{boy}(x) \vdash ? : (x : \mathbf{e}) \times \mathbf{male}(x)$

The type checking (18a) is a routine. The proof search for (18b) will find a proof $(\pi_1 u, \mathbf{bm}(\pi_1 u)(\pi_2 u))$ that corresponds to the BVA reading of (1a), after which (19) will be checked.

(19) $\Gamma,\ w : (x : \mathbf{e}) \times \mathbf{boy}(x) \vdash \begin{bmatrix} v@\,(y : \mathbf{e}) \times \mathbf{father}(y) \times \mathbf{of}(y, \pi_1 w) \\ \mathbf{praise}(\pi_1 w, \pi_1 v) \end{bmatrix} : \mathsf{type}$

This calls for the rule (14) again, and checks the following.

(20)   a. $\Gamma,\ w : (x : \mathbf{e}) \times \mathbf{boy}(x) \vdash (y : \mathbf{e}) \times \mathbf{father}(y) \times \mathbf{of}(y, \pi_1 w) : \mathsf{type}$

       b. $\Gamma,\ w : (x : \mathbf{e}) \times \mathbf{boy}(x) \vdash ? : (y : \mathbf{e}) \times \mathbf{father}(y) \times \mathbf{of}(y, \pi_1 w)$

The type checking (20a) is also a routine. As in (12), the proof search for (20b) will find $\mathbf{fatherOf}(w)$, thus the type checking $[\![\Gamma \vdash (16a) : \mathsf{type}]\!]$ ends up in a set of proof diagrams whose conclusion is (21), the term part of which serves as a semantic representation for (1a) .

(21) $\Gamma \vdash (w : (x : \mathbf{e}) \times \mathbf{boy}(x)) \to \mathbf{praise}(\pi_1 w, \pi_1 \mathbf{fatherOf}(w)) : \mathsf{type}$

Secondly, the type checking of (16b), via the rule (14), checks (22a) and (22b).

(22)   a. $\Gamma \vdash (x : \mathbf{e}) \times \mathbf{male}(x) : \mathsf{type}$

       b. $\Gamma \vdash ? : (x : \mathbf{e}) \times \mathbf{male}(x)$

The type checking (22a) is also a routine under the standard signature, but the proof search (22b) requires one to construct a proof of a *male person* from only the signature and the context Γ, which means that we have to find a male antecedent from only the world knowledge and the preceding context. Thus, the specified BVA reading for (1b) is not available, since the variable w introduced by **every boy** is not available for the proof search (22b).

This is how the revised semantic theory correctly explains the fact that the specified BVA reading is available in (1a) but not in (1b), relying on only the basic-concepts of DTS and not any extra or ad hoc mechanisms. Now the subject–object asymmetry is reflected in the scopes of underspecified types by their syntactic positions.

3   Global and Local Accommodations

Another benefit of employing the underspecified types is that it allows us to define the operation of local accommodation in a straightforward way. This is due to their definition that takes a closer form to that of the Σ-formation rule: when the proof search $[\![\Gamma \vdash ? : A]\!]$ fails in the type checking $\left[\!\left[\Gamma \vdash \begin{bmatrix} x@A \\ B \end{bmatrix} : \mathsf{type}\right]\!\right]$, the semantic system may optionally replace $\begin{bmatrix} x@A \\ B \end{bmatrix}$ with $(x : A) \times B$ and re-run the type checking. Note that this transformation is safe owing to the similarity between the verification conditions of the @-rule and Σ-formation rule. Consider (23), taken from Heim (1983).[12]

(23)   No nation cherishes its king.

The sentence (23) is interpreted in two distinct ways regarding its presupposition, as described in Heim (1983, p. 403) as follows:

> What about quantifiers other than universal? Concerning "no," we find conflicting factual claims in the literature. According to Cooper (1983), (24) [=our (23)] should presuppose that every nation (in the relevant domain of discourse) has a king; for Lerner and Zimmermann (1981), it presuppose that some nation does.

One reading of (23) that implies **every nation has a king** is obtained via the *global accommodation*, whereas another reading of (23) implying **Some nation has a king** is obtained via the *local accommodation*.

We assume that the lexical item of **its** is defined as (24) in almost the same way as **his** in (15) except for its presuppositional content:

(24)   its $\mapsto (S\backslash NP)\backslash(S\backslash NP/NP)/N : \lambda n.\lambda p.\lambda x. \begin{bmatrix} u@\,(x : \mathbf{e}) \times \neg\mathbf{human}(x) \\ v@\,(y : \mathbf{e}) \times n(y) \times \mathbf{of}(y, \pi_1 u) \\ px(\pi_1 v) \end{bmatrix}$

Since the syntactic structure of (23) is almost the same as (1a), we obtain its semantic representation via the homomorphic semantic composition, which is (25) corresponding to the BVA reading for (23).

(25) $(w : (x : \mathbf{e}) \times \mathbf{nation}(x)) \rightarrow \neg \begin{bmatrix} u@\,(x : \mathbf{e}) \times \neg\mathbf{human}(x) \\ v@\,(y : \mathbf{e}) \times \mathbf{king}(y) \times \mathbf{of}(y, \pi_1 u) \\ \mathbf{cherish}(\pi_1 v, \pi_1 w) \end{bmatrix}$

The type checking for (25) factors through (26).

(26) $\Gamma,\ w : (x : \mathbf{e}) \times \mathbf{nation}(x) \vdash \begin{bmatrix} u@\,(x : \mathbf{e}) \times \neg\mathbf{human}(x) \\ v@\,(y : \mathbf{e}) \times \mathbf{king}(y) \times \mathbf{of}(y, \pi_1 u) \\ \mathbf{cherish}(\pi_1 v, \pi_1 w) \end{bmatrix} : \mathsf{type}$

which will invoke the @-rule (14) and call for the type checking (27a), which obviously succeeds, and then the proof search (27b).

(27)   a. $\Gamma,\ w : (x : \mathbf{e}) \times \mathbf{nation}(x) \vdash (x : \mathbf{e}) \times \neg\mathbf{human}(x) : \mathsf{type}$

   b. $\Gamma,\ w : (x : \mathbf{e}) \times \mathbf{nation}(x) \vdash ? : (x : \mathbf{e}) \times \neg\mathbf{human}(x)$

---

[12] Sentence (24) on p. 403.

If we assume world knowledge that every nation is non-human (i.e., the constant term **nnh**: $(x{:}\mathbf{e}) \to \mathbf{nation}(x) \to \neg\mathbf{human}(x)$), the proof search for (27b) will find the term $(\pi_1 w, \mathbf{nnh}(\pi_1 w)(\pi_2 w))$ that corresponds to the BVA reading of (23). The next step is the type checking (28), which breaks down to the type checking (29a) and the proof search (29b).

(28) $\Gamma, \; w : (x : \mathbf{e}) \times \mathbf{nation}(x) \vdash \begin{bmatrix} v@ (y : \mathbf{e}) \times \mathbf{king}(y) \times \mathbf{of}(y, \pi_1 w) \\ \mathbf{cherish}(\pi_1 v, \pi_1 w) \end{bmatrix} : \mathsf{type}$

(29)   a. $\Gamma, \; w : (x : \mathbf{e}) \times \mathbf{nation}(x) \vdash (y : \mathbf{e}) \times \mathbf{king}(y) \times \mathbf{of}(y, \pi_1 w) : \mathsf{type}$

        b. $\Gamma, \; w : (x : \mathbf{e}) \times \mathbf{nation}(x) \vdash ? : (y : \mathbf{e}) \times \mathbf{king}(y) \times \mathbf{of}(y, \pi_1 w)$

Again, (29a) is a routine, and the proof search for (29b) is a search for the king of y. Remember that, in the case of (12) and (20b), we assumed that there exists a world knowledge **fatherOf**, that is, every boy has a father. The question here is what happens if we do not have a knowledge that every nation has a king, and thus the proof searching for (29b) fails.

The first strategy for our type checker is global accommodation, defined in Bekki (2014), which can be restated as the following instruction.

Definition 1 (Global accommodation).   *When the proof search*

$$[\![x_1 : A_1, \ldots, x_n : A_n \vdash ? : A]\!]$$

fails, the type checker may add the constant term of type $(x_1 : A_1) \to \cdots \to (x_n : A_n) \to A$ *to the signature and re-run the type checking.*

Applying Definition 1 to the case of (29b), the constant term added to the signature is $(w{:}(x : \mathbf{e}) \times \mathbf{nation}(x)) \to (y : \mathbf{e}) \times \mathbf{king}(y) \times \mathbf{of}(y, \pi_1 w)$, which is exactly the knowledge that every nation has a king.

The second strategy for our type checker is local accommodation, which, under the definition of underspecified types, is given the following definition.

Definition 2 (Local accommodation).   *When the proof search* $[\![\Gamma \vdash ? : A']\!]$ *required for the type checking* $[\![\Gamma \vdash (x@A) \times B : \mathsf{type}]\!]$ *fails, the type checker may replace the result of* $[\![\Gamma \vdash (x@A) \times B : \mathsf{type}]\!]$ *with the result of type checking* $[\![\Gamma \vdash (x : A) \times B : \mathsf{type}]\!]$.[13]

In other words, the local accommodation in DTS is understood as accommodating the presupposed content of an underspecified type by existentially quantifying it. Applying Definition 2 to (29b), replacing the type checking for (28) with the following:

---

[13] This operation should not be applied to all types of anaphora and presupposition: for example, it is known that pronouns in general do not undergo local accommodation when their antecedents are missing. For this purpose, we may want to add a binary feature to underspecified types that tells us whether local accommodation is applicable to them. Alternatively, we may argue that the prohibition of local accommodation for pronouns is based rather on pragmatic factors. This is a controversial issue and I would like to leave it open. I thank the anonymous reviewer of LENLS18 for pointing it out.

$$(30) \quad \Gamma, \ w : (x : \mathbf{e}) \times \mathbf{nation}(x) \vdash \begin{bmatrix} v : (y : \mathbf{e}) \times \mathbf{king}(y) \times \mathbf{of}(y, \pi_1 w) \\ \mathbf{cherish}(\pi_1 v, \pi_1 w) \end{bmatrix} : \mathsf{type}$$

thus the whole semantic representation for (23) turns into (31).

$$(31) \quad \Gamma \vdash (w : (x : \mathbf{e}) \times \mathbf{nation}(x)) \ \rightarrow \ \neg \begin{bmatrix} v : (y : \mathbf{e}) \times \mathbf{king}(y) \times \mathbf{of}(y, \pi_1 w) \\ \mathbf{cherish}(\pi_1 v, \pi_1 w) \end{bmatrix} :$$
$$\mathsf{type}$$

In words, (31) claims that No nation has a king and cherishes it, which exactly corresponds to the locally accommodated reading of (23).

4   Conclusion

I have demonstrated that the revision of DTS proposed in this paper in which underspecified terms are replaced by underspecified types successfully eliminates the empirical challenges for DTS regarding the quantificational WCO. I have also shown that the notion of underspecified type allows us to define the operation of local accommodation in a straightforward way. This extension, together with the global accommodation operation provided in Bekki (2014), furnishes the presuppositional theory of DTS. Their conceptual and empirical consequences are now open issues that await further examination.

Appendix

A   Dependent Type Theory

A.1   Syntax

Definition 3 (Preterms, Inferable terms and checkable terms). *The collection of preterms (notation Λ) are defined by the following BNF grammar, where $x \in Var$ and $c \in Con$.*

$$\Lambda ::= x \mid c \mid \mathsf{type} \mid (x : \Lambda) \rightarrow \Lambda \mid \lambda x.\Lambda \mid \Lambda\Lambda \mid (x : \Lambda) \times \Lambda \mid (\Lambda, \Lambda) \mid \pi_1(\Lambda) \mid \pi_2(\Lambda)$$

The collection of inferable terms (notation $\Lambda_\uparrow$) and the collection of checkable terms (notation $\Lambda_\downarrow$) are simultaneously defined by the following BNF grammar where $x \in Var$ and $c \in Con$.

$$\Lambda_\uparrow ::= x \mid c \mid \mathsf{type} \mid (x : \Lambda_\downarrow) \rightarrow \Lambda_\downarrow \mid \Lambda_\uparrow \Lambda_\downarrow \mid \begin{bmatrix} x : \Lambda_\downarrow \\ \Lambda_\downarrow \end{bmatrix} \mid \pi_1 \Lambda_\uparrow \mid \pi_2 \Lambda_\uparrow \mid \begin{bmatrix} x @ \Lambda_\downarrow \\ \Lambda_\downarrow \end{bmatrix} \mid \Lambda_\downarrow : \Lambda_\uparrow$$
$$\Lambda_\downarrow ::= \Lambda_\uparrow \mid \lambda x.\Lambda_\downarrow \mid (\Lambda_\downarrow, \Lambda_\downarrow)$$

Free variables, substitutions, β-reductions are defined in the standard way. The full version of DTT also employs such types as enumeration types, disjoint union types, intensional equality types, natural number types, wellordering types, and universes. See Martin-Löf (1984) for details.

Definition 4 (Vertical/box notation for Σ-type). $\begin{bmatrix} x{:}A \\ B \end{bmatrix} \overset{def}{\equiv} (x : A) \times B$

Definition 5 (Implication, conjunction, and negation).[14]

$$A \to B \overset{def}{\equiv} (x{:}A) \to B \quad \text{where } x \notin fv(B). \quad \bot \overset{def}{\equiv} \{\}$$

$$\begin{bmatrix} A \\ B \end{bmatrix} \overset{def}{\equiv} \begin{bmatrix} x{:}A \\ B \end{bmatrix} \quad \text{where } x \notin fv(B). \qquad \neg A \overset{def}{\equiv} A \to \bot$$

A.2   Type System

Definition 6 (Signature). *A collection of signatures (notation σ) for an alphabet (Var, Con) is defined by the following BNF grammar:*

$$\sigma ::= () \mid \sigma, c : A,$$

where $()$ is an empty signature, $c \in Con$, and $\sigma \vdash A :$ type.

Definition 7 (Context). *A collection of contexts under a signature σ (notation Γ) is defined by the following BNF grammar:*

$$\Gamma ::= () \mid \Gamma, x : A,$$

where $()$ is an empty context, $x \in Var$, and $\Gamma \vdash_\sigma$ type.

Definition 8 (Judgment). *A judgment of DTT is the following form*

$$\Gamma \vdash_\sigma M : A,$$

where Γ is a context under a signature σ and M and A are preterms, which states that there exists a proof diagram of DTT from the context Γ to the type assignment $M : A$. The subscript σ may be omitted when no confusion arises.

Definition 9 (Truth). *The judgment of the form Γ' true states that there exists a term M that satisfies $\Gamma \vdash M : A$.*

Definition 10 (Structural rules).

$$\frac{A : \text{type}}{x : A} \, (VAR) \qquad\qquad \frac{}{c : A} \, (CON) \quad \text{where } \sigma \vdash c : A.$$

$$\frac{M : A \quad N : B}{M : A} \, (WK) \qquad \frac{M : A}{M : B} \, (CONV) \quad \text{where } A =_\beta B.$$

Definition 11 (Π-types).

---

[14] $\{\}$ is the enumeration type with no constructor.

$$\cfrac{\overline{x:A}^{\ i} \atop \vdots}{\cfrac{A:\text{type} \quad B:\text{type}}{(x{:}A) \to B : \text{type}}} \ (\Pi F),i \qquad \cfrac{\overline{x:A}^{\ i} \atop \vdots}{\cfrac{A:\text{type} \quad M:B}{\lambda x.M : (x{:}A) \to B}} \ (\Pi I),i \qquad \cfrac{M:(x{:}A) \to B \quad N:A}{MN : B[N/x]} \ (\Pi E)$$

Definition 12 (Σ-types).

$$\cfrac{\overline{x:A}^{\ i} \atop \vdots}{\cfrac{A:\text{type} \quad B:\text{type}}{(x:A) \times B : \text{type}}} \ (\Sigma F),i \qquad \cfrac{M:A \quad N:B[M/x]}{(M,N):(x:A) \times B} \ (\Sigma I)$$

$$\cfrac{M:(x:A) \times B}{\pi_1(M):A} \ (\Sigma E) \qquad \cfrac{M:(x:A) \times B}{\pi_2(M):B[\pi_1(M)/x]} \ (\Sigma E)$$

A.3 Type Checking

A type checking of UDTT, which has the form

$$[\![\Gamma \vdash_\sigma M : A]\!],$$

where Γ is a context of DTT under a signature σ, M is a checkable term of UDTT, and A is a term of DTT, denotes a (possibly empty) set of proof diagrams of DTT, recursively defined by the following set of rules.

Definition 13 (Type checking rules for checkable terms).

$$[\![\Gamma \vdash M : A]\!] = \left\{ \left. \begin{array}{c} \Gamma \\ \mathcal{D}_M \\ M:A' \end{array} \right| \begin{array}{l} \mathcal{D}_M \in [\![\Gamma \vdash M : ?]\!] \\ A =_\beta A' \end{array} \right\} \qquad \text{where } M \text{ inferable.}$$

$$[\![\Gamma \vdash \lambda x.M : (x{:}A) \to B]\!] = \left\{ \left. \cfrac{\begin{array}{cc} \Gamma & \Gamma, x:A' \\ \mathcal{D}_A & \mathcal{D}_M \\ A':\text{type} & M':B' \end{array}}{\lambda x.M' : (x{:}A') \to B'} \ (\Pi I) \right| \begin{array}{l} \mathcal{D}_A \in [\![\Gamma \vdash A : \text{type}]\!] \\ \mathcal{D}_M \in [\![\Gamma, x:A' \vdash M : B]\!] \end{array} \right\}$$

$$\left[\!\!\left[\Gamma \vdash (M,N) : \begin{bmatrix} x{:}A \\ B \end{bmatrix}\right]\!\!\right] = \left\{ \left. \cfrac{\begin{array}{cc} \Gamma & \Gamma \\ \mathcal{D}_M & \mathcal{D}_N \\ M':A' & N':B' \end{array}}{(M',N') : \begin{bmatrix} x{:}A' \\ B' \end{bmatrix}} \ (\Sigma I) \right| \begin{array}{l} \mathcal{D}_M \in [\![\Gamma \vdash M : A]\!] \\ B[M'/x] \twoheadrightarrow_\beta B' \\ \mathcal{D}_N \in [\![\Gamma \vdash N : B']\!] \end{array} \right\}$$

A.4 Type Inference

A type inference of UDTT, which has the form

$$[\![\Gamma \vdash_\sigma M : ?]\!],$$

where Γ is a context of DTT under a signature σ and M is a inferable term of UDTT, denotes a (possibly empty) set of proof diagrams of DTT, recursively defined by the following set of rules.[15]

Definition 14 (Structural rules).

$$\llbracket \Gamma, x : A, \Delta \vdash x : ? \rrbracket = \left\{ x : A' \;\middle|\; \begin{array}{c} \vdots \\ A' : \text{type} \end{array} \in \llbracket \Gamma \vdash A : \text{type} \rrbracket \right\}$$

$$\llbracket \Gamma \vdash c : ? \rrbracket = \left\{ \dfrac{}{c : A} \, (CON) \;\middle|\; \sigma \vdash c : A \right\}$$

Definition 15 (Π-types).

$$\llbracket \Gamma \vdash (x{:}A) \to B : ? \rrbracket = \left\{ \dfrac{\begin{array}{cc} \begin{array}{c} \Gamma \\ \mathcal{D}_A \\ A' : \text{type} \end{array} & \begin{array}{c} \Gamma, x : A' \\ \mathcal{D}_B \\ B' : \text{type} \end{array} \end{array}}{(x{:}A') \to B' : \text{type}} \, (\Pi F) \;\middle|\; \begin{array}{c} \mathcal{D}_A \in \llbracket \Gamma \vdash A : \text{type} \rrbracket \\ \mathcal{D}_B \in \llbracket \Gamma, x : A' \vdash B : \text{type} \rrbracket \end{array} \right\}$$

$$\llbracket \Gamma \vdash MN : ? \rrbracket = \left\{ \dfrac{\dfrac{\begin{array}{cc} \begin{array}{c} \Gamma \\ \mathcal{D}_M \\ M' : (x{:}A) \to B \end{array} & \begin{array}{c} \Gamma \\ \mathcal{D}_N \\ N' : A \end{array} \end{array}}{M'N' : B[N'/x]} \, (\Pi E)}{M'N' : B'} \, (CONV) \;\middle|\; \begin{array}{c} \mathcal{D}_M \in \llbracket \Gamma \vdash M : ? \rrbracket \\ \mathcal{D}_N \in \llbracket \Gamma \vdash N : A \rrbracket \\ B[N'/x] \twoheadrightarrow_\beta B' \end{array} \right\}$$

Definition 16 (Σ-types).

$$\left\llbracket \Gamma \vdash \begin{bmatrix} x{:}A \\ B \end{bmatrix} : ? \right\rrbracket = \left\{ \dfrac{\begin{array}{cc} \begin{array}{c} \Gamma \\ \mathcal{D}_A \\ A' : \text{type} \end{array} & \begin{array}{c} \Gamma, x : A' \\ \mathcal{D}_B \\ B' : \text{type} \end{array} \end{array}}{\begin{bmatrix} x{:}A' \\ B' \end{bmatrix} : \text{type}} \, (\Sigma F) \;\middle|\; \begin{array}{c} \mathcal{D}_A \in \llbracket \Gamma \vdash A : \text{type} \rrbracket \\ \mathcal{D}_B \in \llbracket \Gamma, x : A' \vdash B : \text{type} \rrbracket \end{array} \right\}$$

$$\llbracket \Gamma \vdash \pi_1(M) : ? \rrbracket = \left\{ \dfrac{\begin{array}{c} \Gamma \\ \mathcal{D}_M \\ M' : \begin{bmatrix} x{:}A \\ B \end{bmatrix} \end{array}}{\pi_1(M) : A} \, (\Sigma E) \;\middle|\; \mathcal{D}_M \in \llbracket \Gamma \vdash M : ? \rrbracket \right\}$$

$$\llbracket \Gamma \vdash \pi_2(M) : ? \rrbracket = \left\{ \dfrac{\dfrac{\begin{array}{c} \Gamma \\ \mathcal{D}_M \\ M' : \begin{bmatrix} x{:}A \\ B \end{bmatrix} \end{array}}{\pi_2(M) : B[\pi_1 M'/x]} \, (\Sigma E)}{\pi_2(M) : B'} \, (CONV) \;\middle|\; \begin{array}{c} \mathcal{D}_M \in \llbracket \Gamma \vdash M : ? \rrbracket \\ B[\pi_1 M'/x] \twoheadrightarrow_\beta B' \end{array} \right\}$$

---

[15] The type inference and type checking rules for enumeration types, disjoint union types, intensional equality types, natural number types, wellordering types, and universes are omitted for brevity.

Definition 17 (Underspecified types).

$$\left[\!\left[\Gamma \vdash \begin{bmatrix} x@A \\ B \end{bmatrix} : ?\right]\!\right] = \left\{ \begin{array}{c|c} & \begin{array}{c} \vdots \\ A' : \text{type} \end{array} \in [\![\Gamma \vdash A : \text{type}]\!] \\ \begin{array}{c} \Gamma \\ \mathcal{D}_B \\ B'' : \text{type} \end{array} & \begin{array}{c} \vdots \\ M : A' \end{array} \in [\![\Gamma \vdash ? : A']\!] \\ & B[M/x] \twoheadrightarrow_\beta B' \\ & \mathcal{D}_B \in [\![\Gamma \vdash B' : \text{type}]\!] \end{array} \right\},$$

where $[\![\Gamma \vdash ? : A']\!]$ is a proof search in DTT.

Definition 18 (Annotated terms).

$$[\![\Gamma \vdash (M : A) : ?]\!] = [\![\Gamma \vdash M : A]\!]$$

References

Bekki, D.: Representing anaphora with dependent types. In: Asher, N., Soloviev, S. (eds.) LACL 2014. LNCS, vol. 8535, pp. 14–29. Springer, Heidelberg (2014). https://doi.org/10.1007/978-3-662-43742-1_2

Bekki, D., Mineshima, K.: Context-passing and Underspecification in dependent type semantics. In: Chatzikyriakidis, S., Luo, Z. (eds.) Modern Perspectives in Type-Theoretical Semantics. SLP, vol. 98, pp. 11–41. Springer, Cham (2017). https://doi.org/10.1007/978-3-319-50422-3_2

Bekki, D., Sato, M.: Calculating Projections via type checking. In: Proceedings of TYpe Theory and LExical Semantics (TYTLES), ESSLLI2015 Workshop (2015)

Chomsky, N.: Conditions on rule of grammar. Linguist. Anal. **2**(4), 303–351 (1976)

Cooper, R.: Quantification and Syntactic Theory. Reidel, Dordrecht (1983)

Heim, I.: On the projection problem for presuppositions. In: Proceedings of the West Coast Conference of Formal. Linguistics II, pp. 114–126 (1983)

Hoji, H.: Language Faculty Science. Cambridge University Press, Cambridge (2015)

Kubota, Y., Mineshima, K., Bekki, D., Levine. R.: Underspecification and interpretive parallelism in dependent type semantics. In: Proceedings of IWCS 2019 Workshop on Computing Semantics with Types, Frames and Related Structures (CSTFRS). pp. 1–9 (2019)

Lerner, J., Zimmermann, T.: Mehrdimensionale Semantik: Die Präsupposition und die Kontextabhängigkeit von 'nur.. Report (1981)

Martin-Löf, P.: Intuitionistic Type Theory, vol. 17. Bibliopolis, Naples (1984)

Postal, P.: Cross-over Phenomena. Holt, Reinhart and Winston, New York (1971)

Reinhart, T.: Anaphora and Semantic Interpretation. The University of Chicago, Chicago (1983)

Steedman, M.J.: Surface Structure and Interpretation. The MIT Press, Cambridge (1996)

Tanaka, R.: natural language quantification and dependent types. Doctoral dissertation (2021)

Wasow, T.: Anaphoric relations in English. Doctoral dissertation (1972)

Yana, Y., Mineshima, K., Bekki, D.: Variable handling and compositionality: comparing DRT and DTS. J. Logic Lang. Inform. **28**(2), 261–285 (2019). https://doi.org/10.1007/s10849-019-09294-3

Probabilistic Compositional Semantics, Purely

Julian Grove[✉] and Jean-Philippe Bernardy

Centre for Linguistic Theory and Studies in Probability, Department of Philosophy,
Linguistics and Theory of Science, University of Gothenburg, Gothenburg, Sweden
julian.grove@gmail.com, jean-philippe.bernardy@gu.se

Abstract. We provide a general framework for the integration of formal semantics with probabilistic reasoning. This framework is conservative, in the sense that it relies only on typed λ-calculus and is thus compatible with logical systems already in use. The framework is also presented modularly, in that it regards probabilistic effects (i.e., sampling and marginalization) as *side effects*, using continuations. We show how our framework may be used to build probabilistic programs compositionally within typed λ-calculus and then illustrate its use on two applications: semantic learning and pragmatic inference within the Rational Speech Act framework.

1 Introduction

Formal semantics in the tradition of Montague characterizes linguistic meaning in terms of either a logic or a model, constructed set-theoretically. By exploiting an already well understood formalism, a logical characterization of meaning allows one to reason about it in terms of notions like entailment. Indeed, while the formal description such a characterization provides is necessarily abstract, it can be assembled compositionally, in terms of rules that combine the meanings of syntactic constituents. It is this feature of formal semantics that makes it such an attractive approach to meaning, and one which has persisted throughout the development of the field.

There has been much effort in the last decade to connect formal semantics to mathematically explicit models of pragmatic reasoning, with Rational Speech Act (RSA) models providing a paradigmatic case. RSA models consider utterance interpretation to be a process of updating probability distributions over logically characterized meanings [7,10,14,15]. In doing so, they aim to capture a central feature of discourse known since the work of Grice [11]; namely, that it is constrained by principles of appropriate social behavior, which, through the reasoning of interlocutors, serve to enrich the very meanings which are communicated.

The present work provides a general approach to the integration of formal semantics with probabilistic reasoning—one which is both modular and conservative. Past efforts to consider linguistic meaning probabilistically (including the

© Springer Nature Switzerland AG 2023
K. Yada et al. (Eds.): JSAI-isAI 2021 Workshops, LNAI 13856, pp. 242–256, 2023.
https://doi.org/10.1007/978-3-031-36190-6_17

formative work of Goodman and Lassiter) have drastically modified the underlying logic to express it, typically in a way that freely mixes a logical semantics with probabilities. Goodman and Lassiter [8], for example, encode meanings using the probabilistic programming language Church [9], a decision which constitutes a radical departure from formal semantics in the style of Montague: while the latter uses a pure λ-calculus, Church programs can invoke probabilistic effects, i.e., by sampling from or updating a distribution at any point in a given program.

In contrast to this and similar approaches to probabilistic semantics, ours allows for the usual approach to compositional semantics, in terms of a *pure* logical language. Moreover, we expect that our approach will be quite general: it in principle allows for any simply typed language with products, but it should also be compatible with more expressive systems, e.g., System F [6] and dependent type theory (we defer an investigation of the generality of our approach, however). Our trick is to treat probabilistic computation modularly, as a side effect, using continuations. Doing so allows logical meanings to be viewed as values computed by probabilistic programs. Even so, as we shall see, our semantics does not overstep the tight bounds of typed λ-calculus: probabilistic programs are *themselves* expressed using the same logic. We can thus provide an expressive probabilistic compositional semantics without the use of radically novel tools.

2 Formal Semantics

To illustrate, we provide a schematic English fragment, which we translate into a higher-order language with types for individuals (e), truth values (t), and real numbers (r). In addition to function types ($\alpha \to \beta$), we assume access to products ($\alpha \times \beta$ and unit type $\diamond$), along with their associated constructors $\langle M, N \rangle : \alpha \times \beta$ (for $M : \alpha$ and $N : \beta$), destructors $\pi_1 M : \alpha$ and $\pi_2 M : \beta$ (for $M : \alpha \times \beta$), and unit $\diamond : \diamond$, as well as n-ary generalizations of these. Notably, we employ an indicator function $\mathbb{1} : t \to r$ taking $\top$ ('true') and $\bot$ ('false') onto 1 and 0, respectively. We additionally assume the existence of a family d_i of subtypes of r corresponding to degree types. For instance d_{tall} represents degrees of height, d_{happy} degrees of happiness, etc.

In general, we assume the language to have, among the non-logical constants, a finite number to be assigned probabilistic interpretations. We call such constants "special" constants. For our example, we employ the following:

$$\text{person} : e \to t \qquad \text{height} : e \to d_{tall} \qquad \theta_{tall} : d_{tall} \qquad (\geq) : r \to r \to t$$

In terms of these, the following meanings can be given for *someone, is,* and *tall*, in order to derive the meaning of *someone is tall* via functional application:

$$[\![someone]\!] = \lambda k.\exists x : \text{person}(x) \wedge k(x)$$
$$[\![is]\!] = \lambda x.x$$
$$[\![tall]\!] = \lambda x.\text{height}(x) \geq \theta_{tall}$$

The meaning of *someone is tall*, $[\![someone]\!]([\![is]\!]([\![tall]\!]))$, can then be computed to be $\exists x : \text{person}(x) \wedge \text{height}(x) \geq \theta_{tall}$.

3   The Traditional Interpretation

For completeness, we spell out the "traditional" interpretation of the logical language illustrated above, in terms of an interpretation function, $(\!|\cdot|\!)$, which is given by a λ-homomorphism:[1]

$$(\!|x|\!) = x \qquad\qquad (x \text{ is a variable})$$
$$(\!|\lambda x.M|\!) = \lambda x.(\!|M|\!)$$
$$(\!|M(N)|\!) = (\!|M|\!)((\!|N|\!))$$
$$(\!|\langle M, N\rangle|\!) = \langle (\!|M|\!), (\!|N|\!)\rangle$$
$$(\!|\pi_i M|\!) = \pi_i(\!|M|\!)$$
$$(\!|\theta_{tall}|\!) = d$$
$$(\!|\text{height}|\!) = height$$
$$(\!|\text{person}|\!) = person$$
$$(\!|(\geq)|\!) = (\geq)$$

Here, $d : d_{tall}$ is some real number representing the contextual standard of height used by the adjective *tall*, $height : e \to d_{tall}$ is some function from individuals to real numbers, and $person : e \to t$ is some function from individuals to truth values. The constant $(\geq) : r \to r \to r$ is intended to be the "greater-than-or-equal-to" relation on real numbers. To save space, we have left implicit the interpretation of the other constants, such as $\top$, $\bot$, and $\exists$, which is standard. One can now compose $(\!|\cdot|\!)$ with $[\![\cdot]\!]$ and map *someone is tall* onto $\exists x : person(x) \wedge height(x) \geq d$, i.e., a (formula representing a) truth value.

4   The Probabilistic Interpretation

We provide the probabilistic interpretation in two steps. First, we parameterize our interpretation function, $(\!|\cdot|\!)^{\kappa}$, by a tuple κ of values, which we call a *context*. The idea is to use such a tuple to provide an interpretation for the special constants. In particular, we assume that the n special constants of the language are ordered, such that, if constant c_i has type α_i, then $\kappa : \alpha_1 \times \ldots \times \alpha_n$. For any such κ, $(\!|\cdot|\!)^{\kappa}$ is the following λ-homomorphism:

---

[1] The λ-homomorphisms that we employ map one higher-order language into another, preserving variables, abstractions, applications, pairing, and projection. They are accompanied by type-homomorphisms $\overline{\alpha}$ which, for us, preserve implication and products (i.e., $\overline{\alpha \to \beta} = \overline{\alpha} \to \overline{\beta}$ and $\overline{\alpha \times \beta} = \overline{\alpha} \times \overline{\beta}$), but which may in principle affect base types. In general, if $M : \alpha$, then $(\!|M|\!) : \overline{\alpha}$. The motivation for these constraints is that they provide meanings to the constants of the source language, leaving the surrounding λ-calculus unaffected (as analogous to a traditional model-theoretic interpretation). In this case, both $(\!|\cdot|\!)$ and its associated type homomorphism are trivial, mapping both constants and base types onto themselves.

$$(\![x]\!)^{\kappa} = x \qquad\qquad\qquad (x \text{ is a variable})$$

$$(\![\lambda x.M]\!)^{\kappa} = \lambda x.(\![M]\!)^{\kappa}$$

$$(\![M(N)]\!)^{\kappa} = (\![M]\!)^{\kappa}((\![N]\!)^{\kappa})$$

$$(\![\langle M, N\rangle]\!)^{\kappa} = \langle(\![M]\!)^{\kappa}, (\![N]\!)^{\kappa}\rangle$$

$$(\![\pi_i M]\!)^{\kappa} = \pi_i(\![M]\!)^{\kappa}$$

$$(\![c_i]\!)^{\kappa} = \pi_i \kappa \qquad\qquad\qquad (c_i \text{ is the } i^{th} \text{ special constant})$$

Thus if c_i is one of θ_{tall}, height, person, or $\geq$, then its interpretation is determined by the context κ. (Again, we have omitted the interpretation of other constants to save space.) Obviously, if c_i is of type α_i, then so is $\pi_i \kappa$. We assume that all probabilistic semantic knowledge resides in the interpretation of special constants, and thus ultimately in the context κ. It remains to be shown how to evaluate the above expressions when κ is a random variable.

5   Probabilistic Programs

In general, we consider something a random variable if it is the value returned by a probabilistic program. In our framework, a probabilistic program returning values of type α is a function of type $(\alpha \rightarrow r) \rightarrow r$; that is, one which consumes a *projection* function (from values of type α to real numbers), in order to return a real number.[2] The intent is that if p is a probabilistic program and f is a projection function, then $p(f)$ is the sum of $f(x)$, for all possible values of x returned by the program, weighted in proportion to their probabilities.

Given this setup, probabilistic programs form a *monad*. A monad, as stated in Fig. 1, is a functor M from types to types, associated with two operators, η ('return') and $\star$ ('bind'), satisfying certain laws. In general, implementing a monad in a pure setting, such as the λ-calculus, allows one to simulate various notions of side effect, including probabilistic computation, as we shall see. The role of η is to inject an ordinary value into the monad, while that of $\star$ is to compose *computations*. More precisely, $\star$ runs a computation of type $M\alpha$, and then binds the returned value to a variable in the next computation (something of type $\alpha \rightarrow M\beta$). In the case of probabilistic programs, $M\alpha = (\alpha \rightarrow r) \rightarrow r$, and the return η and bind operator $\star$ are inherited from the continuation monad:

---

[2] There is some precedent for this representation of probabilistic programs, by Mohammed Ismail and Shan [17], who describe a small typed probabilistic programming language and provide a denotational semantics for it in terms of continuations. Our formulation is chiefly inspired by the dependently typed language of Bernardy et al. [3]. See also Jansson et al. [13].

Operators

$$\eta : \alpha \to M\alpha$$
$$(\star) : M\alpha \to (\alpha \to M\beta) \to M\beta$$

Laws on terms

$\eta(v) \star k = k(v)$	(Left Identity)
$m \star \eta = m$	(Right Identity)
$(m \star n) \star o = m \star (\lambda x.n(x) \star o)$	(Associativity)

Fig. 1. Definition of a monad

$$\eta : \alpha \to (\alpha \to r) \to r$$
$$\eta(a) = \lambda c.c(a)$$

$$(\star) : ((\alpha \to r) \to r) \to$$
$$(\alpha \to (\beta \to r) \to r) \to$$
$$(\beta \to r) \to r$$
$$m \star k = \lambda c.m(\lambda x.k(x)(c))$$

By employing the monadic operators, one may sequence a probabilistic program $p : (\alpha \to r) \to r$ with some projection function $f : \alpha \to r$ by binding the value returned by p to a variable x and returning $f(x)$ (via η):

$$p \star \lambda x.\eta(f(x)) : (r \to r) \to r$$

Indeed, feeding the identity function of type $r \to r$ to the result obtains $p(f) : r$.

The encoding of probabilistic programs in terms of continuations may at first appear somewhat opaque and indirect. In general, one can see a continuation (here, of type $\alpha \to r$) as a question to ask a program. The result type r restricts the sorts of questions one may ask, i.e., to those having real numbers as answers. As if responding with a riddle, moreover, the probabilistic program returns the weighted sum of the answers for its possible values. This means, for instance, that given a probabilistic program p, one may feed it the question $(\lambda x.1)$, which asks how much mass it assigns to any given value x, in order to get the answer $p(\lambda x.1)$, which is just the total mass assigned by p.

If p returns truth values (i.e., if it is of type $(t \to r) \to r$), we can ask for the mass it assigns to $\top$ by passing the indicator function as a continuation: $p(\mathbb{1})$. Consequently, we may compute a *probability* for p as the expected value of $\mathbb{1}$, in terms of a function $P : ((t \to r) \to r) \to r$:

$$P(p) = \frac{p(\mathbb{1})}{p(\lambda b.1)}$$

The denominator (the total mass assigned by p) normalizes the result.

Now, let K be a probabilistic program representing the distribution of contexts; that is, if $\alpha_1 \times \ldots \times \alpha_n$ is the type of contexts, K is of type $(\alpha_1 \times \ldots \times \alpha_n \to r) \to r$. Given a term ϕ of type t, we encode its interpretation in the context of K as the following probabilistic program:

$$K \star \lambda \kappa. \eta((\!|\phi|\!)^\kappa)$$

Like all probabilistic programs returning truth values, the above is of type $(t \to r) \to r$. Operationally, it reads in the random context returned by K and computes from it a truth value for ϕ in this context. As such, one can determine a probability for it, as outlined above.

To illustrate, consider our running example, *someone is tall*, to which we assigned the interpretation $\exists x : \mathsf{person}(x) \wedge \mathsf{height}(x) \geq \theta_{tall}$. Let us assume a probabilistic program K returning contexts where the interpretation of θ_{tall} is a random variable having a normal distribution with a mean of 72 in. and a standard deviation of 3 in. Moreover, we assume that the interpretations of the other special constants are fixed as the functions *height*, *person*, and $\geq$, as above. Then, assuming that the order of the constants is height, person, $\geq$, θ_{tall}, we have the following definition of K:

$$K : (((e \to d_{tall}) \times (e \to t) \times (r \to r \to t) \times d_{tall}) \to r) \to r$$
$$K = \mathcal{N}(72, 3) \star \lambda d. \eta(height, person, (\geq), d)$$

Here, $\mathcal{N}(72, 3)$ is a probabilistic program (of type $(d_{tall} \to r) \to r$) representing a normal distribution with the relevant mean and standard deviation. If fed a projection function f of type $d_{tall} \to r$, this program results in a real number which is gotten by integrating f over the real line, weighting each $f(d)$ by the probability of d.[3]

Our strategy allows us to associate a probabilistic program with the sentence *someone is tall*, as follows:

$$K \star \lambda \kappa. \eta((\!|\exists x : \mathsf{person}(x) \wedge \mathsf{height}(x) \geq \theta_{tall}|\!)^\kappa)$$
$$= K \star \lambda \kappa. \eta(\exists x : (\!|\mathsf{person}|\!)^\kappa(x) \wedge (\!|(\geq)|\!)^\kappa((\!|\mathsf{height}|\!)^\kappa(x))((\!|\theta_{tall}|\!)^\kappa))$$
$$= \mathcal{N}(72, 3) \star \lambda d. (\eta(height, person, (\geq), d) \qquad \text{(by Assoc.)}$$
$$\star \lambda \kappa. \eta(\exists x : (\pi_2 \kappa)(x) \wedge (\pi_3 \kappa)((\pi_1 \kappa)(x))(\pi_4 \kappa)))$$
$$= \mathcal{N}(72, 3) \star \lambda d. \eta(\exists x : person(x) \wedge height(x) \geq d) \qquad \text{(by Left Id.)}$$
$$= \lambda c. \mathcal{N}(72, 3)(\lambda d. c(\exists x : person(x) \wedge height(x) \geq d))$$

---

[3] Here, we leave $\mathcal{N} : d_{tall} \times d_{tall} \to (d_{tall} \to r) \to r$ unanalyzed. In general, computing a continuous distribution $\mathcal{D} : p_1 \times \ldots \times p_n \to (d \to r) \to r$ over d amounts to computing

$$\lambda \langle p_1, \ldots, p_n \rangle, f. \int_{-\infty}^{\infty} \mathrm{PDF}_{\mathcal{D}(p_1, \ldots, p_n)}(x) * f(x) dx$$

where $\mathrm{PDF}_{\mathcal{D}(p_1, \ldots, p_n)}$ provides the probability density function associated with $\mathcal{D}$ (given parameters $p_1, \ldots, p_n$). Such integrals don't in general admit closed-form solutions, and so one must resort to approximations. We implement this via Markov chain Monte Carlo sampling in our Haskell implementation, using the library at https://github.com/jyp/ProbProg.

As expected, we have a program of type $(t \to r) \to r$. We may therefore compute a probability for it as:

$$\frac{(\lambda c.\mathcal{N}(72,3)(\lambda d.c(\exists x : person(x) \wedge height(x) \geq d)))(\mathbb{1})}{(\lambda c.\mathcal{N}(72,3)(\lambda d.c(\exists x : person(x) \wedge height(x) \geq d)))(\lambda b.1)}$$

$$= \frac{\mathcal{N}(72,3)(\lambda d.\mathbb{1}(\exists x : person(x) \wedge height(x) \geq d))}{\mathcal{N}(72,3)(\lambda d.1)}$$

Because $\mathcal{N}$ represents a genuine probability distribution, its total mass is 1, and we can simply ignore the denominator:

$$\mathcal{N}(72,3)(\lambda d.\mathbb{1}(\exists x : person(x) \wedge height(x) \geq d))$$

The value of this expression is determined by computing the truth (i.e., either 1 or 0) of the proposition that someone's height exceeds the height threshold d at every possible value of d, and weighting it by d's probability. This model of the uncertainty associated with *someone is tall* locates it in the meaning of *tall*; in particular, how tall one must be, in order to be considered tall.

For example, consider a case in which someone is 72 in. tall and no one is taller. Then the condition imposed by the meaning of *someone is tall* will be met by all $d \leq 72$, and the sentence will be assigned the probability 0.5. In general, the probability assigned will be equal to the mass of $\mathcal{N}(72,3)$ that is less than or equal to the height of the tallest person.

6   Bayesian Inference

One of the main interests of a probabilistic semantics such as the one we have proposed is that it can be used to characterize Bayesian update. For this purpose, we define the following function *observe*:

$$observe : t \to (\diamond \to r) \to r$$
$$observe(\phi)(f) = \mathbb{1}(\phi) * f(\diamond)$$

Given a proposition ϕ, *observe* either keeps or throws out its continuation, depending on whether ϕ is true or false; hence, the resulting program retains only values from the part of the distribution it represents compatible with ϕ being true.[4] This function thus allows us to condition the probability of ϕ on a premise ψ as follows, exploiting the monadic structure of probabilistic programs:

$$K \star \lambda\kappa.observe((\!(\psi)\!)^{\kappa}) \star \lambda\diamond.\eta((\!(\phi)\!)^{\kappa})$$

Such a conditioning process can be used for several purposes: for probabilistic inference (as suggested by our running example), but also to refine the probability distributions associated with constants; that is, for semantic learning. We briefly suggest how each of these tasks can be accomplished in our framework, starting with semantic learning.

---

[4] Some may recognize it as akin to the *guard* function of Haskell's MonadPlus and Alternative classes.

6.1   Semantic Learning

Semantic learning in our framework is matter of updating (distributions of) contexts. Given a program K_0 returning contexts which represents the initial state of one's semantic knowledge, one may observe a number of propositions to be true or false, thus obtaining a new program, K_1:

$$K_1 = K_0 \star \lambda\kappa.observe(\phi_1) \star \lambda\diamond. \ldots observe(\phi_n) \star \lambda\diamond.\eta(\kappa)$$

The effect of sequencing K_0 with such a series of observations is to zero out the portion of its distribution in which $\phi_1, ..., \phi_n$ are false, returning the values that survive.

Let us say that a learner is attempting to learn the meaning of *tall*, and they start out with a distribution of contexts such that the height threshold that the adjective makes use of ranges over a normal distribution with a mean of 68 in. and a standard deviation of 3 in. (we will deal here with the constants height, $\geq$, and θ_{tall}, along with the four names for individuals c, m, a, and v):

$$K_0 : ((e \times e \times e \times e \times (e \rightarrow d_{tall}) \times (r \rightarrow r \rightarrow t) \times d_{tall}) \rightarrow r) \rightarrow r$$
$$K_0 = \mathcal{N}(68,3) \star \lambda d.\eta(c,m,a,v,height,(\geq),d)$$

In addition, this learner happens to know the following three facts: that Camilla is 65 in. tall, that Matt is 67 in. tall, and that Anna is 72 in. tall:

$$height(c) = 65 \qquad height(m) = 67 \qquad height(a) = 72$$

One day, someone this learner trusts utters the following three sentences, in sequence: (1) *Camilla isn't tall*, (2) *Matt isn't tall*, (3) *Anna is tall*. Upon hearing these utterances, the learner updates K_0, in order to obtain K_1:

$$K_1 = K_0$$
$$\star \lambda\kappa.observe((\!|\neg height(c) \geq \theta_{tall}|\!)^\kappa)$$
$$\star \lambda\diamond.observe((\!|\neg height(m) \geq \theta_{tall}|\!)^\kappa)$$
$$\star \lambda\diamond.observe((\!|height(a) \geq \theta_{tall}|\!)^\kappa)$$
$$\star \lambda\diamond.\eta(\kappa)$$

$$= \mathcal{N}(68,3)$$
$$\star \lambda d.observe(\neg 65 \geq d) \qquad \text{(by Associativity and Left Identity)}$$
$$\star \lambda\diamond.observe(\neg 67 \geq d)$$
$$\star \lambda\diamond.observe(72 \geq d)$$
$$\star \lambda\diamond.\eta(c,m,a,v,height,(\geq),d)$$

This may in turn be simplified to:

$$\mathcal{N}(68,3) \star \lambda d.observe(72 \geq d \wedge d > 67) \star \lambda\diamond.\eta(c,m,a,v,height,(\geq),d)$$

Thus K_1 is just like K_0, but for the fact that the distribution associated with θ_{tall} has been pared down to only include the mass of $\mathcal{N}(68, 3)$ in the interval $(67, 72]$. If Vlad is 68 in. tall ($height(v) = 68$), then the sentence *Vlad is tall* would have been associated with the probability 0.5 in K_0, while it is associated with a probability of around 0.24 in K_1:

$$\frac{K_0(\lambda \kappa. \mathbb{1}((\!|height(v) \geq \theta_{tall}|\!)^{\kappa}))}{K_0(\lambda \kappa. 1)} = 0.5$$

$$\frac{K_1(\lambda \kappa. \mathbb{1}((\!|height(v) \geq \theta_{tall}|\!)^{\kappa}))}{K_1(\lambda \kappa. 1)} \approx 0.24$$

6.2   RSA: Background

In the case of probabilistic inference, our framework can serve as the basis for complex pragmatic reasoning, as in RSA models. For example, Lassiter and Goodman [14] present an RSA model of the inference made when someone utters a sentence such as *Vlad is tall*. This model consists of a pragmatic listener (L_1), who reasons about probable meanings based on the expected behavior of a pragmatic speaker (S_1), who, in turn, reasons about a literal listener (L_0). These agents' behaviors are modeled in terms of the following equations (adapted to the current example):

$$P_{L_1}(h, d_{tall} \mid \text{'Vlad is tall'}) \propto P_{S_1}(\text{'Vlad is tall'} \mid h, d_{tall}) * P_{L_1}(h) \qquad (L_1)$$

$$P_{S_1}(u \mid h, d_{tall}) \propto (P_{L_0}(h \mid u, d_{tall}) * e^{-C(u)})^{\alpha} \qquad (S_1)$$

$$P_{L_0}(h \mid u, d_{tall}) = P_{L_0}(h \mid [\![u]\!]^{d_{tall}} = \top) \qquad (L_0)$$

Each of these statements defines a probability distribution for the random variables of interest. L_1, in particular, infers a joint probability distribution for h and d_{tall}, the values of the random variables representing Vlad's height and the height threshold for the adjective *tall*, respectively. The function C in the S_1 model is utterance cost. The parameter α is the "temperature" of the S_1 model: it controls the extent to which the speaker behaves rationally, i.e., by taking the expected behavior of the literal listener L_0, as well as utterance cost, into account in designing their distribution over utterances.

Given the more general notions of a world state w and a parameter θ, (h and d_{tall}, respectively, in the example above), these equations may be presented more perspicuously as follows, given some utterance u_0:

$$P_{L_1}(w, \theta \mid u_0) = \frac{P_{S_1}(u_0 \mid w, \theta) * P_{L_1}(w, \theta)}{\int_{w' \in W} \int_{\theta' \in \Theta} P_{S_1}(u_0 \mid w', \theta') * P_{L_1}(w', \theta') d\theta' dw'} \qquad (L_1)$$

$$P_{S_1}(u \mid w, \theta) = \frac{(P_{L_0}(w \mid u, \theta) * e^{-C(u)})^{\alpha}}{\Sigma_{u' \in U}(P_{L_0}(w \mid u', \theta) * e^{-C(u')})^{\alpha}} \qquad (S_1)$$

$$P_{L_0}(w \mid u, \theta) = P_{L_0}(w \mid [\![u]\!]^{\theta} = \top) \qquad (L_0)$$

Thus abstractly, pragmatic listeners provide a joint posterior distribution over world states w and parameters θ, given an utterance u_0.[5] Pragmatic speakers provide a distribution of utterances, given the particular world state w (and parameter θ) they wish to communicate. These utterances, moreover, are taken from an antecedently chosen set U of possible utterances, which is generally assumed to be finite, thus justifying the use of summation in the normalizing factor for S_1. Finally, linguistic uncertainty is represented by the parameter θ, which is passed from the pragmatic listener L_1 down to the literal listener L_0, through the speaker model S_1. Note, therefore, that L_1 differs from L_0 in a crucial respect: while L_1 samples both world states and parameters, L_0 samples only world states, relying on a parameter which has been fixed by S_1 (and L_1, in turn).

6.3 RSA: Implementation

Our purpose is to illustrate how the RSA framework may be realized in the vocabulary of probabilistic programs. Taking u to be the type of utterances, s the type of world states, and θ the type of linguistic parameters, we aim to find a program L_1 of type $u \to (s \times \theta \to r) \to r$, which, given an utterance, provides a joint distribution over world states and parameters, and which satisfies the desiderata laid out above. In order to do so, it is useful to introduce the following generalization of *observe* to fuzzy conditions:

$$factor : r \to (\diamond \to r) \to r$$
$$factor(x)(f) = x * f(\diamond)$$

Instead of a truth value, *factor* takes a real number and applies it as a weight to the result of its continuation. Thus *observe* may be viewed as the specific case of *factor* in which the relevant weight is either 1 or 0.[6]

Now, we may formulate L_1 as follows. Say that S_1 provides a probabilistic program returning *utterances*, given a world state and a parameter; i.e., it is of type $s \times \theta \to (u \to r) \to r$. Then given some w and θ, we would like access to the probability mass function corresponding to $S_1(w, \theta)$ — $\mathrm{PMF}_{S_1(w,\theta)}$ — of type $u \to r$, so that we may appropriately factor the probability of $\langle w, \theta \rangle$ in L_1, given an utterance. (We will come back to how we obtain the PMFs of probabilistic programs shortly. For now, we simply take them for granted.) Moreover, let us assume that world states and parameters take prior distributions $W : (s \to r) \to r$ and $\Theta : (\theta \to r) \to r$, respectively. These assumptions leave us with the following definition of L_1:

$$L_1 : u \to (s \times \theta \to r) \to r$$
$$L_1(u_0) = W \star \lambda w.\Theta \star \lambda\theta.factor(\mathrm{PMF}_{S_1(w,\theta)}(u_0)) \star \lambda\diamond.\eta(w, \theta)$$

---

[5] Note that we define this posterior in terms of a joint prior distribution $P_{L_1}(w, \theta)$. Lassiter and Goodman [14] assume the prior distributions over world states and linguistic parameters to be independent, with an effectively uniform prior over parameters.

[6] That is, $observe(\phi)(f) = factor(\mathbb{1}(\phi))(f)$.

Now, given some prior distribution U over utterances (i.e., of type $(u \to r) \to r$), we may similarly provide definitions of S_1 and L_0, where PDF_p is the probability density function associated with p, i.e., when the value p returns is continuous:

$$S_1 : s \times \theta \to (u \to r) \to r$$

$$S_1(w, \theta) = U \star \lambda u.factor((\text{PDF}_{L_0(u,\theta)}(w) * e^{-C(u)})^\alpha) \star \lambda \diamond. \eta(u)$$

$$L_0 : u \times \theta \to (s \to r) \to r$$

$$L_0(u, \theta) = W \star \lambda w.observe(\llbracket u \rrbracket^{\langle w, \theta \rangle}) \star \lambda \diamond. \eta(w)$$

Note our use of notation in the definition of L_0. Here, the pair $\langle w, \theta \rangle$ provides a context in terms of which we can interpret the utterance u, which we assume is translated, via $\llbracket \cdot \rrbracket^{\langle w, \theta \rangle}$, into a formula of type t. Moreover, such a formula may be obtained by first providing a traditional Montague-style semantics to obtain a meaning of type t, and then applying the λ-homomorphism $(\!| \cdot |\!)^{\langle w, \theta \rangle}$, which replaces any special constants with w or θ, as appropriate.

Having stated our formulation of RSA somewhat abstractly, let us now turn to the problem of PMFs (and PDFs); that is, of obtaining a function of type $\alpha \to r$ from a probabilistic program of type $(\alpha \to r) \to r$. If α is discrete, we may construct its PMF as follows (recall that P takes a probabilistic program of type $(t \to r) \to r$ onto a probability):

$$\text{PMF}_{(\cdot)} : ((\alpha \to r) \to r) \to \alpha \to r$$

$$\text{PMF}_p = \lambda x.P(p \star \lambda y.\eta(y = x))$$

That is, for every $x : \alpha$, $\text{PMF}_p(x)$ evaluates the probability that p returns x.

If α is continuous, however, we have a problem: the probability that any two values x and y are equal is zero, and the above definition (but for a PDF) would have it return zero everywhere! Fortunately, there are sound remedies which we may adopt for the continuous case. For instance, we may take the derivative of the cumulative mass of a given distribution p with respect to the argument:

$$\text{PDF}_p = \lambda x.\frac{d}{dx}[P(p \star \lambda y.\eta(y \le x))]$$

Indeed, these two definitions may be plugged into the descriptions of L_1, S_1, and L_0 above, in order to provide them with fuller specifications.[7] One need only determine what the distributions U, W, and Θ are. To realize the model of Lassiter and Goodman [14], we would take U to be a small finite set, W to be

---

[7] An alternative, syntactically closer to the discrete case, relies on the Dirac δ distribution, whose value is zero everywhere except when its argument is zero, and whose total mass sums to one. Thus we recover a non-zero result after integration:

$$\text{PDF}_p = \lambda x.p(\lambda y.\delta(x - y))$$

a normal distribution, and Θ to be, effectively, uniform.[8] The resulting probabilistic program can be computed approximately using Monte Carlo methods; in this case, one will typically evaluate a probabilistic program to an approximate, finite PDF.

We close out this section by observing a noteworthy feature of the foregoing formulation of RSA: it highlights an odd lack of symmetry between the L_1 model and the L_0 model. Why does L_1 sample both world states from W and linguistic parameters from Θ, while L_0 samples only the former? Indeed, this fact is now reflected in their types! L_1 is of type $u \to (s \times \theta \to r) \to r$: it takes an utterance and returns a distribution over pairs of world states and parameters. Meanwhile, L_0 is of type $u \times \theta \to (s \to r) \to r$: it takes a pair of an utterance *and* a parameter and returns a distribution over world states. Thus L_0 considers a linguistic parameter which has been *fixed* by L_1 and S_1. Put differently, S_1 reasons about an L_0 that knows θ ahead of time, when determining what to say. Yet more vividly, the pragmatic listener assumes that the speaker is under the impression that the two have already (telepathically, perhaps) coordinated on linguistic parameters.

Maybe, it is more realistic not to assume that S_1 imagines such an omniscient L_0. In fact, relaxing this assumption restores the symmetry of the model. At the same time, it conveniently allows us not to explicitly split the context κ into two parts w and θ. As in previous sections, we assume that the context has some type $\kappa = \alpha_1 \times \ldots \times \alpha_n$:

$$L_1 : u \to (\kappa \to r) \to r$$
$$L_1(u) = K \star \lambda\kappa.\mathit{factor}(\mathrm{PMF}_{S_1(\kappa)}(u)) \star \lambda\diamond.\eta(\kappa)$$

$$S_1 : \kappa \to (u \to r) \to r$$
$$S_1(\kappa) = U^* \star \lambda u.\mathit{factor}(\mathrm{PDF}_{L_0(u)}(\kappa)^\alpha) \star \lambda\diamond.\eta(u)$$

$$L_0 : u \to (\kappa \to r) \to r$$
$$L_0(u) = K \star \lambda\kappa.\mathit{observe}(\llbracket u \rrbracket^\kappa) \star \lambda\diamond.\eta(\kappa)$$

To simplify the presentation, we have used the notation U^* to stand for a distribution over utterances which has already incorporated a notion of cost.[9] In our final formulation, both L_1 and L_0 have the same type. There is thus a more general notion of "listener", corresponding to a family of maps from utterances to distributions over contexts (or, equivalently, joint distributions over world states and linguistic parameters).[10] Such listeners differ only in how they update the prior—the literal listener uses a literal interpretation, while the pragmatic listener uses a pragmatic interpretation. Such pragmatic interpretations arise from

---

[8] More accurately, we would take U to be uniform over a finite set, S_U. Thus we would define it as $U = \lambda k.\Sigma_{u \in S_U} k(u)$.

[9] To implement the definition of cost employed by RSA models, for example, U^* could be $U \star \lambda u.\mathit{factor}(e^{-\alpha*C(u)}) \star \lambda\diamond.\eta(u)$, given some uniform distribution U.

[10] Emerson [5] advocates yet a third approach to RSA, in which linguistic parameters are marginalized out in the listener model altogether.

the speaker model, which chooses utterances which best fit the state of the world and linguistic parameters that it wishes to communicate.[11]

In summary, we have a realization of RSA that is highly compositional, in two senses. First, the models themselves are assembled compositionally in terms of probabilistic programs and monadic combinators. Second, utterances, represented by logical formulae, are interpreted compositionally, and such formulae may be obtained from natural language sentences using standard compositional techniques. At the same time, the mathematical vocabulary for describing RSA models is one and the same as that for describing linguistic meanings.

7   Conclusion

Our aim has been to lay a strong foundation for compositional probabilistic semantics. Many details have been left out, including about how one might represent prior knowledge, concretely. Many possibilities arise here. For instance, one may follow machine-learning methods and use vectors to represent individuals [3], while predicates are represented by hyperplanes in the relevant space [2]. An alternative would encode prior knowledge in terms of the same logic used to represent meanings, i.e., as sets of formulae. One may then constrain distributions over contexts in terms of such formulae [12]. Following this route, one may obtain a seamless integration of Bayesian and logical representations of knowledge.

We should note that, while the logical fragments provided here are rudimentary, they are also merely expository: there is no deep reason that we did not provide a richer semantics for natural language expressions, e.g., incorporating dynamism (following a tradition of combining dynamic semantics with typed λ-calculus). Indeed, one could combine the framework we have illustrated with a logical semantics that *itself* uses continuations [1,4,16].

Finally, while our contribution is chiefly a theoretical one, the core aspects of the system described in this paper has been implemented using the Haskell programming language.[12] The mathematical vocabulary that we have employed here to assemble expressions of type r is closely mirrored by the implementation in terms of a domain-specific language for characterizing Markov chain Monte Carlo sampling procedures. Thus while many probabilistic programs cannot be evaluated to closed-form solutions, they may generally be finitely approximated, given sufficiently many samples. Most important, however, the modular representation of logical meaning and probabilistic side effects is straightforward to encode in Haskell, given the pure functional setting it provides.

We have shown how a probabilistic semantics of natural language is amenable to a fully formal treatment—one which remains squarely within the realm of pure typed λ-calculi. The key idea is to use an effect system to capture probabilistic operations (i.e., sampling and marginalization). Our approach fits the general

---

[11] Systematically, if α tends to ∞; probabilistically, otherwise.

[12] Available at https://github.com/juliangrove/grove-bernardy-lenls18.

framework of monadic semantics, and, as such, augments a literature that has grown in many exciting ways since the work of Shan [18].

References

1. Barker, C., Shan, C.C.: Continuations and Natural Language, vol. 53. Oxford Studies in Theoretical Linguistics (2014)
2. Bernardy, J.P., Blanck, R., Chatzikyriakidis, S., Lappin, S., Maskharashvili, A.: Predicates as boxes in Bayesian semantics for natural language. In: Proceedings of the 22nd Nordic Conference on Computational Linguistics, Turku, Finland, pp. 333–337. Linköping University Electronic Press (2019). https://www.aclweb.org/anthology/W19-6137
3. Bernardy, J.P., Blanck, R., Chatzikyriakidis, S., Maskharashvili, A.: Bayesian natural language semantics and pragmatics. In: Bernardy, J.P., Blanck, R., Chatzikyriakidis, S., Lappin, S., Maskharashvili, A. (eds.) Probabilistic Approaches to Linguistic Theory. CSLI Publications (2022)
4. Charlow, S.: On the semantics of exceptional scope. Ph.D. thesis, NYU, New York (2014). https://semanticsarchive.net/Archive/2JmMWRjY
5. Emerson, G.: Probabilistic lexical semantics: from gaussian embeddings to bernoulli fields. In: Bernardy, J.P., Blanck, R., Chatzikyriakidis, S., Lappin, S., Maskharashvili, A. (eds.) Probabilistic Approaches to Linguistic Theory. CSLI Publications (2022)
6. Girard, J.Y.: Interprétation fonctionnelle et élimination des coupures de l'arithmétique d'ordre supérieur. Ph.D. thesis, Université Paris 7 (1972)
7. Goodman, N.D., Frank, M.C.: Pragmatic language interpretation as probabilistic inference. Trends Cogn. Sci. **20**(11), 818–829 (2016). ISSN 1364-6613. https://doi.org/10.1016/j.tics.2016.08.005. https://www.sciencedirect.com/science/article/pii/S136466131630122X
8. Goodman, N.D., Lassiter, D.: Probabilistic semantics and pragmatics uncertainty in language and thought. In: Lappin, S., Fox, C. (eds.) The Handbook of Contemporary Semantic Theory, pp. 655–686. Wiley (2015). ISBN 978-1-118-88213-9. https://doi.org/10.1002/9781118882139.ch21. http://onlinelibrary.wiley.com/doi/abs/10.1002/9781118882139.ch21, section: 21 _eprint: https://onlinelibrary.wiley.com/doi/pdf/10.1002/9781118882139.ch21
9. Goodman, N.D., Mansinghka, V.K., Roy, D., Bonawitz, K., Tenenbaum, J.B.: Church: a language for generative models. In: Proceedings of the Twenty-Fourth Conference on Uncertainty in Artificial Intelligence, UAI 2008, Arlington, Virginia, USA, pp. 220–229. AUAI Press (2008). ISBN 978-0-9749039-4-1
10. Goodman, N.D., Stuhlmüller, A.: Knowledge and implicature: modeling language understanding as social cognition. Top. Cogn. Sci. **5**(1), 173–184 (2013). ISSN 1756-8765. https://doi.org/10.1111/tops.12007. https://onlinelibrary.wiley.com/doi/abs/10.1111/tops.12007
11. Grice, H.P.: Logic and conversation. In: Cole, P., Morgan, J.L. (eds.) Syntax and Semantics. Speech Acts, vol. 3, pp. 41–58. Academic Press, New York (1975)
12. Grove, J., Bernardy, J.P., Chatzikyriakidis, S.: From compositional semantics to Bayesian pragmatics via logical inference. In: Proceedings of the 1st and 2nd Workshops on Natural Logic Meets Machine Learning (NALOMA), Groningen, The Netherlands, pp. 60–70. Association for Computational Linguistics (2021). https://aclanthology.org/2021.naloma-1.8

13. Jansson, P., Ionescu, C., Bernardy, J.P.: Probability theory. In: Domain Specific Languages of Mathematics. Texts in Computing, no. 24, pp. 223–246 (2022)
14. Lassiter, D., Goodman, N.D.: Context, scale structure, and statistics in the interpretation of positive-form adjectives. Semant. Linguist. Theory **23**(0), 587–610 (2013). ISSN 2163-5951. https://doi.org/10.3765/salt.v23i0.2658. https://journals.linguisticsociety.org/proceedings/index.php/SALT/article/view/2658
15. Lassiter, D., Goodman, N.D.: Adjectival vagueness in a Bayesian model of interpretation. Synthese **194**(10), 3801–3836 (2015). https://doi.org/10.1007/s11229-015-0786-1
16. Lebedeva, E.: Expressing discourse dynamics through continuations. phdthesis, Université de Lorraine (2012). https://tel.archives-ouvertes.fr/tel-01749193
17. Mohammed Ismail, W., Shan, C.C.: Deriving a probability density calculator (functional pearl). In: Proceedings of the 21st ACM SIGPLAN International Conference on Functional Programming, ICFP 2016, pp. 47–59. Association for Computing Machinery, New York (2016). ISBN 978-1-4503-4219-3. https://doi.org/10.1145/2951913.2951922. https://doi.org/10.1145/2951913.2951922
18. Shan, C.C.: Monads for natural language semantics. arXiv:cs/0205026 (2002). http://arxiv.org/abs/cs/0205026. arXiv: cs/0205026

Pluralism for Relativists: A New Framework for Context Dependence

Ahmad Jabbar[✉]

Stanford University, Stanford, USA
jabbar@stanford.edu

Abstract. There are several semantic accounts of context-sensitive expressions. Broadly, while contextualism claims that a context-sensitive expression's interpretation is sensitive to some feature of the context of utterance, relativism considers judgment or assessment to play a significant role in the expression's context-sensitivity. The main motivation for relativism comes from consideration of retraction data. Given variance in retraction data, we argue that the best move is to espouse a pluralism of the following sort. Take an expression E to be such that its interpretation is sensitive to a feature f. Then, given a context of use c_1 and a context of assessment c_2, we allow the interpretation of E to be sensitive to f in c_1 or f in c_2. In other words, there's no need to choose between a contextualist or relativist postsemantics. The proposed theory welcomes more generality in formalism.

Keywords: context-sensitivity · contextualism · relativism · assessment-sensitivity · pluralism · generality · initialization

1 Introduction

Relativism about truth can take various forms. The interesting relativism, according to MacFarlane, is what he calls *assessment-sensitivity*. To show that usual forms of relativism in semantics don't enter the interesting territory of relativism and thus to motivate assessment-sensitivity, MacFarlane puts considerable time distinguishing assessment-sensitivity from non-indexical contextualism. The difference is brought about by considering retraction data. For this paper, by considering retraction data, we argue that whether speakers think that they should retract a taste utterance they made in the past does not have

This is part of an ongoing project. Many thanks to Éno Agolli, Mitch Green, Magdalena Kaufmann, Stefan Kaufmann, Zhiyu Luo, Dilip Ninan, and Lionel Shapiro for comments and discussion. Thanks also to two anonymous reviewers for *LENLS*. All mistakes are my own.

K. Yada et al. (Eds.): JSAI-isAI 2021 Workshops, LNAI 13856, pp. 257–270, 2023.
https://doi.org/10.1007/978-3-031-36190-6_18

a clear answer.[1] The intuition and the data suggest that some people do think it appropriate to retract a previously made taste utterance and some people don't. Given this variance, we suggest a framework for context-dependence, which makes room for both assessment-sensitivity and non-indexical contextualism. Whether a given utterance is relativist in the assessment-sensitive way or in the non-indexical contextualist way, we think, depends on the interpreter of the utterance. This accounts for the variance in the judgments concerning whether one should retract a past taste utterance or not. In this paper, we spend more time in sketching a workable formalism for the proposal, and less time on philosophical underpinnings and implications of such a relativized relativism, so to speak.

In the process of cashing out the proposed formalism, we pay significant attention to what Belnap, Perloff, and Xu (2001) call *initialization*.[2] *Initialization* may be thought of as another word for determination of a parameter in the index of evaluation by the context. However, it highlights an important feature of the Kaplanian context-dependence picture: that before any shifting (of a parameter) occurs, there's an initial value of the parameter in the index of evaluation set by the context of utterance. We propose a formalization of initialization. Obviously, it doesn't hurt to make the theory more precise by formalizing an important step of meaning composition. In addition however we also present reasons to think that initialization is not just a way of speaking, but a process that requires formalization. We also highlight methodological reasons. Let's explicitly state the two aims of this paper:

(1) Formalizing initialization

(2) Proposing a formal model that makes space for both assessment-sensitivity and non-indexical contextualism in an overall semantic theory

If (1) and (2) were unrelated, then it would be strategically poor to discuss both in a short paper. We think that (2) crucially relies on (1). It is in our choice of model that we use for (1) that makes it amenable to the sort aims associated with (2).

Plan for Rest of the Paper: In Sect. 2, we explain the basic Kaplanian picture of context-sensitivity in which both assessment-sensitivity (R) and non-indexical contextualism (C) are couched. In Sect. 3, we explain the difference between R and C. Here, we discuss the significance of retraction data. In Sect. 4, after reflecting on some retraction data, we suggest a pluralism that makes space for both R and C; here we also motivate formalizing initialization. In Sect. 5, we sketch a formal model that achieves the aims outlined in Sect. 4.

---

[1] Although we expand on what sort of utterances we take to be taste utterances, we have in mind the usual utterances of personal taste like *Licorice is tasty*. Also note that although we primarily consider retraction data about predicates of personal taste and epistemic modals, the scope of this paper extends to all language for which a relativism of the two sorts can be argued for.

[2] Also see Belnap and Green 1994.

2   Context-Sensitivity

The usual story with Kaplan's two-dimensional framework starts with interpreting each expression in language relative to a context and an index. What are contexts and indices? For Kaplan, context models the actual context of speech. Then, accordingly, a context is taken to include a speaker/author, a world, a time, a location, etc. More formally, a context c is taken to be a sequence of such parameters. Relativizing interpretation of each expression to a context formally amounts to relativizing the standard interpretation function $[\![.]\!]$ to c, as in $[\![.]\!]_c$. This increases the expressive power of our semantic theory, as we can easily define a single unambiguous rule that determines reference of indexicals such as I and now.[3] However, modal and temporal displacements are key features of natural language. In easier terminology: we can use language to talk about what can be, what was, etc. instead of strictly talking about what actually obtains at present. Then, there should be some way of shifting the parameters of the context, which models the actual context of speech, to parameters which are relevant for interpreting a given utterance. Then, one can suggest that there are operators in language that change a context c in such a way that the changed c' differs from c in its value for one of its parameters. In other words, one can simply suggest shifting say the time parameter of c to an earlier time for interpreting past utterances.

There are principled reasons to resist the above move. Let's consider two such reasons briefly. It is argued (cf. Rabern and Ball 2019) that context for Kaplan has a theoretical role – that of generating content, where content is what one believes and asserts. Then a semantic theory must make space for a step in meaning composition where we obtain what we take to be the object of belief and speech acts. Secondly, Lewis (1980) notes that context is just not the sort of thing that one can shift. John can talk about matters before John was born, but if we were to shift the time parameter of such a context, we would get a context with a time before John was born with John in it. So, we come far away from the independent motivations of modeling the actual context of speech for which we posited c in the first place.

The more reasonable move to incorporate temporal and modal displacement in a semantic theory is to keep c as it is, but posit an artificial object, call it *index* (i for short), such that it is a sequence of those parameters of c that are shiftable. Now, we have two objects to relativize $[\![.]\!]$ to, as in $[\![.]\!]_c^i$. Accordingly, we also get a division of labour between c and i, and a two step procedure to go from an expression to its extension.[4] To take an example, for a sentence S, at c, first a content is generated. What this content looks like will depend on what you take content to be, but for now, we can take it to be a set of world-time pairs.[5] Once this content is generated, at the time and world coordinate of the index, we get a truth-value; 1 iff the world-time pair that constitutes the index

---

[3] See Pickel et al. 2018.

[4] Obviously, the two step procedure is not essential to context-dependence as Lewis (1980) argues; uncurrying the two functions gives us one function.

[5] cf. Lewis (1979) and Perry (1979).

belongs to the content generated at c for S, 0 otherwise. In other words, some semantic rules (*character* for Kaplan) determine the content at c. Content in turn is a function that takes the index to some extension. Here, we don't spend any more time arguing for why this framework is preferable to other alternatives, but the above considerations serve to show at the very least that the Kaplanian picture is well-founded as a formalism with underlying theoretical and formal considerations.[6]

Both R and C are positions couched in the above framework. Before we shift our discussion to R and C, let us make a brief comment on the importance of initialization in a theory of context-dependence. Note that a compositional semantics for $S^\square$, a sentence with a modal or temporal operator, will require evaluation of the content of $S^\square$ relative to a world or time determined by comparison to the world or time of the context. Thus, the values of the parameters of the index, before any shift, are set by the context. As these are the initial values of the index, we can say that the context initializes the parameter values in the index. This locution of *Initialization* comes from Belnap, Perloff, and Xu (2001). Not only, as we said, we provide a formalization of initialization, the notion is also important in understanding the difference between R and C. The above background on the Kaplanian context-dependence framework suffices to talk about MacFarlane's co-opting of it for assessment-sensitivity.

3   Relativisms

Now, MacFarlane would insist on considering only assessment-sensitivity as the interesting relativism. Although we agree, we don't think it is important for us to convince the reader of that for the purposes of this paper. Therefore, the title of this section *Relativisims* is meant to include both assessment-sensitivity and non-indexical contextualism. Here, we first sketch a picture of non-indexical contextualism, and then introduce assessment-sensitivity. This sets up the stage to bring out the differences in how each handles retraction data.

3.1   Non-indexical Contextualism

Now, it would help to introduce some data about predicates of personal taste. Take for instance, (3) and (4).

(3)   Licorice is tasty.

(4)   Licorice isn't tasty.

Before we dive into the formalism, the conceptual point of non-indexical contextualism can be illustrated by considering a speaker, say John, who likes licorice. Now, *inter alia*, John constitutes a context. Non-indexical contextualist would further say that the context of utterance of (3) or (4) also includes a

---

[6] For a critique, see Santorio (2017). Also see Schlenker 2003, Anand & Nevins (2004), Deal (2020).

taste standard (g (gastronomic) for short) as a parameter. Then, where $\langle w, t, g \rangle$ is an index comprising a world, time, and taste parameter, one can define a compositional semantics for *tasty* as in (5).

(5) $[\![tasty]\!]_c^{\langle w,t,g \rangle} = \lambda x.\ x$ is tasty according to g at t in w

Given the compositional semantics in (5), the content expressed at c is a set of world-time-standard triples. So, in addition to worlds and times, we can let contents be sensitive to taste standards as well. The step that follows is evaluation of this expressed context at c with respect to a set of parameters of a given index, which, without any shift, constitute the world, time, and taste standard of c, the context of utterance. We can call such an index – one containing initial values of a set of parameters – the index of the context. (3) comes out true in c as the taste standard g of c is such that licorice is tasty according to g in w at t. Given the above sketch, we can arrive at a definition of truth of a proposition in such a picture.[7]

(6) A proposition p is true as used at a context c iff p is true at $\langle w, t, g \rangle$.

This looks like a good picture capturing context-sensitivity of contents to taste.[8] Now, we turn to assessment-sensitivity.

3.2 Assessment-Sensitivity

As we see it, what distinguishes assessment-sensitivity from non-indexical contextualism, on a formal level, are (7), (8), and (9).

(7) Positing two contexts relevant for initialization of the index.

(8) Defining the truth of a proposition/sentence w.r.t. two contexts.

(9) Letting the role played by one of the two contexts in (8) to be associated with assessment of the proposition/sentence.

In what follows, we expand on (7)–(9), and then by considering retraction data, bring out the differences in predictions between non-indexical contextualism and assessment-sensitivity. Let's consider (7)–(9) now.

---

[7] This definition of truth of a proposition is stated in the style MacFarlane adopts in his 2014 (cf. MacFarlane 2014, 105).

[8] Note that both non-indexical contextualism and assessment-sensitivity assume contents to be simple in that they are evaluated with respect to taste standards. The more traditional contextualism (cf. Kratzer (1977), DeRose (1996), Soames (2002), Stanley (2004)), which MacFarlane calls *indexical contextualism* would let contents be such that before evaluation occurs, they are already specified with regards to the parameter that the non-indexical contextualist would consider relevant for evaluation of the expressed content. In other words, under the traditional contextualism about taste predicates, the content expressed by (3) would be a set of world-time pairs. Whether contents are complex or not is an interesting question, but one too complicated to be considered for the purposes of this paper. For a comparison between the two positions, see MacFarlane (2009). Also see Cappelen & Hawthorne (2009).

Let's introduce two contexts as being relevant to a given proposition/sentence. One of these contexts is the context of use, where the proposition or sentence is used to make an utterance. The other relevant context is that of assessment, where the utterance is assessed for truth. Now, given that we have two relevant contexts, a natural question about the parameter values in the index arises. Remember that in the Kaplanian framework, a given sentence is interpreted with respect to a context and an index, and we let the index comprise parameters whose values are initialized by the context. Now that we have two posited contexts, it doesn't make sense to say that the parameter values in the index are initialized by *the* context. This is where MacFarlane thinks we enter the interesting territory of relativism; we can now let the parameter values according to which the truth of a content is evaluated be initialized by the context of assessment. Whether one does that or not for a particular parameter σ makes one relativist in the interesting sense for σ. In less loaded terms, we can say that such a decision makes one to propose assessment-sensitivity for σ. For instance, if one lets the taste parameter be initialized by the context of assessment, then one is considered assessment-sensitive about taste. Moreover, one is also considered to propose assessment-sensitivity for an expression if the compositional semantics for that expression makes reference to a parameter for which one lets its value be initialized in the index by the context of assessment. What we have in mind here is epistemic modals like *might* and the parameter information state, to which reference is made in some compositional semantics.[9]

Now that in the assessment-sensitivity framework, two contexts are posited, and a proposition is evaluated with respect to an index that can comprise parameters initialized by either the context of utterance or context of assessment, we need to rethink the definition of truth of a proposition/sentence as in (6). MacFarlane presents an assessment-sensitive definition of truth of a proposition as in (10).

(10)   A proposition p is true as used at a context c_1 and assessed from context c_2 iff p is true at $\langle w_{c_1}, t_{c_1}, g_{c_2} \rangle$.

Given (10), the story from character to extension goes like this: first a compositional semantics as in (5) is proposed which makes reference to some parameter in its right hand side clause. This in turn specifies a content, or a proposition, so to speak. This proposition is then evaluated with respect to an index that comprises parameters s.t. their values can be initialized by either the context of use or context of assessment. Further, note that the non-indexical contextualist can embrace the two contexts, and also embrace that a proposition p's truth is defined at a context of use and context of assessment. All that the non-indexical contextualist about a parameter σ needs to do to keep assessment-sensitivity at bay is to propose that σ gets initialized by the context of use in defining the

---

[9] See Yalcin 2007, MacFarlane 2011, 2014 for such semantic theories. We mention these just as one type of semantic theory for epistemic modals. See Ninan (2018) and Mandelkern (2019) for interesting and independent critiques.

truth of a proposition. For clarity, let's summarize non-indexical contextualism and assessment-sensitivity about taste below.

(11) Non-indexical Contextualism for g: A proposition p is true as used at a context c_1 and assessed from context c_2 iff p is true at $\langle w_{c_1}, t_{c_1}, g_{c_1} \rangle$.

(12) Assessment-sensitivity for g: A proposition p is true as used at a context c_1 and assessed from context c_2 iff p is true at $\langle w_{c_1}, t_{c_1}, g_{c_2} \rangle$.

Now, questions about significance of proposing assessment-sensitivity may arise. The most relevant one for MacFarlane, and for us in this paper, is: do the two positions differ in their predictions about some data? If they do, and Assessment-Sensitivity makes better predictions, then one can see merit in adopting MacFarlane's framework. In the next section, we focus our attention to retraction, where non-indexical contextualism and assessment-sensitivity come apart in the predictions they make.[10]

4 Retraction

4.1 Non-indexical Contextualism vs Assessment-Sensitivity

As we intend to refer to the two theories frequently here, we choose to abbreviate them as C for non-indexical contextualism and R for assessment-sensitivity. For MacFarlane, retraction becomes important in the context of constitutive norms for speech acts. For reasons of space and appropriate audience, we avoid discussion of constitutive norms for assertion and retraction. Instead, we try to make sense of the difference between R and C in the context of retraction, assuming that speakers retract past utterances that they take to be false.

Consider the example of Bano who found licorice tasty when she was 10 years old. She is 25 now, and hates the taste of licorice. Bano had uttered (3), i.e. *Licorice is tasty* in 2005. Asked about it now, she takes it back. Now, take C. If it is the context of use that initializes the taste parameter, g, in the index of evaluation, then there's no reason for Bano to take (3) back. At her context of assessment in the present, (3) is still true, as it is still evaluated w.r.t. g of the context of utterance, whose t is a moment in 2005. That doesn't explain why Bano feels the urge to take back her utterance given her changing tastes.

R has a different story to tell. As g is determined by the context of assessment under R, (3) in the present time is evaluated to be false. As an utterance that was made in 2005 is now taken to be false by Bano, she retracts it. It seems like R has a story to tell about retraction that C misses. We think that although this is a major achievement of the assessment-sensitivity framework, retraction itself isn't that simple.

---

[10] MacFarlane seems committal only about his views on how retraction is handled by assessment-sensitivity. Disagreement takes center stage for MacFarlane, only for him to conclude that it's messy, or at least that's how we interpret him. For discussion on disagreement, see MacFarlane (2014, Sect. 6).

4.2   Variance to Remedy Strength

We think that MacFarlane's views about retraction are too strong. Taken from a descriptive perspective, MacFarlane seems to propose that speakers will retract their past utterances about taste if their tastes change, as in the Bano example above. MacFarlane (2014, 141) comments: "Our account should explain why speakers will retract (rather than stand by) an earlier assertion that something was tasty, if the flavor the thing had at the time of the assertion is not pleasing to their present tastes-even if it was pleasing to the tastes they had then." Note that MacFarlane makes the *a priori* judgment that speakers *will* retract an earlier assertion. This seems like a strong judgment. Taken from a less descriptive, and more normative perspective, as Ninan (2016, 445) notes MacFarlane's "Relativist Retraction Rule obliges A to retract the assertion she made in *c*."

What if one doesn't retract? What if one thinks that one need not retract? Or what if Bano thinks that it isn't appropriate for her to retract (3) in the present? Given its reliance on strong views about retraction, R doesn't seem like the panacea we thought it to be anymore. But what about C? C, as MacFarlane noted, wouldn't make sense of why speakers do retract. The dialectic here might seem confusing, but we are simply noting the fact that some speakers would retract and some wouldn't. In cases where they do, R seems like a good theory, and in cases where they don't, R doesn't seem like a good theory. We propose building a framework that can handle such variance. Our assumption here is simply that whether a speaker retracts an earlier assertion depends on whether that speaker considers it appropriate for her to retract the earlier assertion. Now, there are many questions to be answered here. Firstly, how do we build a space in our formalism for appropriateness judgments, upon which we would take retraction patterns to rely? Second, and more importantly, how should we build a model that can be true to the Kaplanian picture of context-sensitivity that has a plethora of theoretical and formal virtues, while incorporating insights by both R and C. We present a sketch below.

5   Pluralism

5.1   Motivations

Let's state our motivations and assumptions explicitly. What motivates the picture here is the variance in retraction patterns. It is quite clear that there's a speaker, as MacFarlane presents the example of Joey (2014, 109), who would retract an earlier assertion of (3) in the present where his taste standards have changed. It is also true that there's a speaker who would not retract an earlier assertion of (3) in the present where her taste standards have changed. Moreover, we can imagine a speaker standing by their previous assertion of (3), by finding it odd if an interlocutor asks them to take back their previous assertion. Suppose that Bano and Joey are friends who are meeting after ten years. Joey liked licorice so much as a kid that he wrote a document expressing his love for it. On being offered licorice by Bano in the present, the following exchange occurs.

(13)   Joey: I won't have licorice. I can't stand it.
       Bano: Wow! I still remember that document. So, you wrote it, just to
       take back all of it?
       Joey: I don't take it back; after all, I liked licorice.

If the above exchange doesn't qualify as illustrating Joey standing by his
assertion, then we invite the reader to think up of an explicit statement of what
standing by would amount to; we think that there's a speaker who would assert
such a statement, even when their tastes have changed.

By considering examples like (13), we are simply noting that to enforce a
blanket judgment about retraction on behalf of all speakers is not warranted. (13)
is not to be understood as data that suggests that speakers don't retract their
past assertions about taste. We agree with MacFarlane insofar as in thinking
that at least some speakers do retract their past assertions. Our goal is to ignore
neither of the two judgments. We intend to explain more data than R or C
can explain on their own. Let's start with our sketching a way to achieve this
interesting task.

5.2   Pluralism for Variance

We embrace MacFarlane's assessment-sensitivity framework. More specifically,
we make important use of the two contexts to state our thesis. Taking this as
point of departure, we think that there is a choice for the agent of the context
of assessment in how they interpret a taste utterance. We can state this more
systematically as in (14):

(14)   Pluralism: For a proposition p, which is evaluated relative to a parameter
       σ, given c_1, context where the assertion of p is made, and c_2, context
       where the assertion of p is assessed, σ in the index can be initialized by
       either c_1 or c_2.

Note that even MacFarlane's framework allows a parameter to be initialized
by the context of use or context of assessment; but, presenting a complete account
of meanings of context-sensitive expressions requires picking one initialization
option. We think that there's no reason for such austerity. Then, pluralism can be
thought of as a non-austere approach towards the postsemantic stage of meaning
calculation. Pluralism allows a theoretician to think that a given parameter can
be initialized by either the context of use or of assessment, and not be forced
to pick up one initialization function as correct. Now, we want to implement
(14) formally. Two immediate and connected questions that we face are: (i) how
do we build this choice of initialization; (ii) where in the formalism should we
build this choice? In other words, is there any space in the Kaplanian framework,
supplemented with MacFarlane's two contexts, to include a feature underlying
(14)? We think that there is space if we look closely. Note that we don't have
a formalization for initialization in the context-dependence frameworks we work
within. So, we propose to formalize initialization.

5.3   Formalizing Initialization

Let's first motivate our formalization. Why do we think that initialization requires formalization? To answer this, let's first state how we perceive initialization.

(15)   Initialization of σ: the process of populating the index of evaluation with σ where $\sigma \in c_1$ or $\sigma \in c_2$.

There is nothing controversial or new that we have said about initialization so far. Probably, the only thing that we have added is our conception of it as a process. Suppose that c_{u_1} and c_{u_2} are both contexts of utterance that differ in their value for σ, and σ in the index is initialized by the context of utterance. Now, the value of σ in the index for evaluation of a proposition is determined by whether we take c_{u_1} or c_{u_2} to be the context of utterance. What this simple fact motivates is that initialization is to be thought of as a process that populates the index with a parameter, while obeying the constraint that this parameter comes from the context of utterance (if the parameter is initialized by the context of utterance). In other words, the match between the initialized parameters of the index and features of the context is to be obeyed. Moreover, there's independent motivation to formalize initialization in that it would make our theory of context-dependence more precise. The precision is to be valued independently, but if one doesn't lean that way, then the value of precision can be found in its potential benefits. The benefits we have in mind are those that we get when Farkas and Bruce (2010) pay attention to and formalize the proposal bit in Stalnaker's (1978) account of assertion. Then, at the very least, there is some motivation to at least pay a bit more attention to initialization in a theory of context-dependence. So, how should we model it?

5.4   The Model

Here, we build a model for Pluralism as stated in (14). Note that we are building on the Kaplanian framework, supplemented with MacFarlane's two contexts and his definition of truth of a proposition. We conceive the context of utterance and context of assessment together to determine an initialization procedure. We understand *procedure* in a computationally loaded sense (cf. Suppes 1979) and take it to be instantiated by a finite state automaton.

Let M_1 model the initialization procedure at a given context of use and a context of assessment. M_1 is a 5-tuple $(\Sigma, Q, q_0, \{q_3, q_4\}, \delta)$ such that:

(16) Σ: $\{0, 1\}$

(17) Q: $\{q_0, q_1, q_2, q_3, q_4\}$

(18) q_0 is the start state

(19) $\{q_3, q_4\}$ is the set of accept states

(20) δ is the transition function for M_1 which can be read off from the state diagram below:

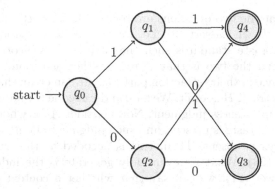

In the above model, we presume that there are two relevant parameters for evaluation of sentences in natural language. This feature is not essential to our model. We choose the number 'two' to not make the model too complex, while illustrating that it works for initialization of more than one parameter. Let's try to make the picture clearer. Formally, there are four sequences that this model generates. Each of these sequences is of length 2. We can pair up these sequences with corresponding indices containing two parameters.

(21)   00: $\langle g_1, s_1 \rangle$

(22)   01: $\langle g_1, s_2 \rangle$

(23)   10: $\langle g_2, s_1 \rangle$

(24)   11: $\langle g_2, s_2 \rangle$

Here, each sequence is paired up with a unique index. Generation of each sequence then corresponds to and models initialization of two parameters. However, note that each sequence is associated with a distinct initialization pattern. For instance, if it is (23) that is generated, then the taste parameter, g, is initialized by the context of assessment, while the information state parameter, s, is initialized by the context of use. Moreover, if it is (23) that is generated, we make sense of why Bano retracts her assertion of (3). (23) also explains why a speaker can retract her previous taste assertions, while not retracting their previous assertions of the form *might p*. As other sequences can be generated as well, say (21), a speaker can stand by an assertion of (3), even if their tastes have changed (see discourse in (13)). We can explicitly state a few facts about the model below.

(25)   For any two parameters σ and τ, σ can be set by c_1, while τ is set by c_2.

(26)   A discrete step in the computation models initialization of a parameter by one of the contexts.

There are two further questions that we intend to answer about the model.

(27)   Does our model explain why the context of assessment (or of utterance for that matter) initializes the parameter it does in a given situation?

(28)   What do 0 and 1 encode?

We think that the two questions are related. Let's start with (28). Take two speakers A and B who assert (3), i.e. *licorice is tasty*. Later both experience changes in their taste standards such that neither likes licorice anymore. The difference between the two is that A retracts her assertion, while B doesn't. Given this variance in their retraction patterns, we can claim that while A finds it appropriate to retract, B doesn't. We let 0 and 1 encode the absence and presence of such an appropriateness judgment. Now consider A for whom such judgment about assertions of taste is present, and such judgment about assertions of *might p*-type utterances is absent. Then, this is encoded as the string 10, which is paired up with (23). What we eventually generate is the index of evaluation, $\langle g_2, s_1 \rangle$. To answer (27), we can say that whether a context of assessment or context of utterance initializes a given parameter depends on the presence or absence of the appropriateness judgment of the speaker talked about above. This concludes our discussion the formal model that captures Pluralism, and comes out to have more empirical coverage than non-indexical contextualism or assessment-sensitivity taken on its own.

6   Taking Stock

What we have presented above is a model that tries to make room for variance as explained above, and relies crucially on a formalization of initialization. Here, we want to stress that this is to be considered a part of the usual Kaplanian context-dependence picture. In other words, we have presented a way to think about what the initial values of the index of evaluation can be. We haven't revolutionized shifting etc. so all the shifting by operators occurs in the usual way.

From the relativist's perspective, the Pluralism and the accompanying model should be a welcome result. If what distinguishes non-indexical contextualism and relativism is retraction, and the jury is still out to judge this difference (cf. Ninan 2016) and there's data like (13), then our model provides respite for the relativist. Furthermore, our model vindicates MacFarlane's positing of a separate context as essential to relativism.[11] We argued that contexts of assessment are essential to a theory of context-dependence more generally, as we build our model on the assumption that there are two relevant contexts for evaluating truth of a given proposition. Although *pluralism* seems like a misnomer for our sketched theory given the usual uses of *pluralism* in the philosophy literature, we have used it nonetheless for sake of familiarity.

The model presented might have implications for issues other than the ones we were concerned with in this paper. To conclude our discussion, we touch on one such issue. Suppes (1979) critiques set-theoretic semantics by stating that the psychology of the speakers is "barely touched" by set-theoretic semantics (cf. Steinhert-Threlkeld & Icard 2013). Psychology of the speakers as in their appropriateness judgments underlying retraction patterns do find a home in our

---

[11] See Lasersohn 2005 and Stephenson 2007 for relativisms without contexts of assessment.

model. Whether this captures the psychology of the speakers in some substantial way, or only barely touches it is a question we haven't explored here. Nonetheless, we do think that we have taken a step in the right direction. However, we should note that our model differs from the sort of models that try to capture psychological processes like verification of quantified sentences more directly, where one sees a direct correspondence between the form of the model and the psychological processing.[12] Our automaton doesn't seem to have any such direct correspondence.

References

Anand, P., Nevins, A.: Shifty operators in changing contexts. Proc. SALT **14**, 20–37 (2004)

Belnap, N., Green, M.: Indeterminism and the thin red line. Philos. Perspect. **8**, 365–88 (1994)

Belnap, N., Perloff, M., Xu, M.: Facing the Future: Agents and Choices in Our Indeterminist World. Oxford University Press, New York (2001)

van Benthem, J.: Essays in Logical Semantics. D Reidel, Dordrecht (1986)

Cappelen, H., Hawthorne, J.: Relativism and Monadic Truth. Oxford University Press, Oxford (2009)

Deal, A.: A Theory of Indexical Shift: Meaning, Grammar, and Crosslinguistic Variation. MIT Press, Cambridge (2020)

DeRose, K.: Relevant alternative and the content of knowledge attributions. Philos. Phenomenol. Res. **56**, 193–97 (1996)

Farkas, D., Bruce, K.: On reacting to assertions and polar questions. J. Semant. **27**, 81–118 (2010)

Kaplan, D.: Demonstratives. In: Almog, J., Perry, J., Wettstein, H. (eds.) Themes from Kaplan, pp. 481–563. Oxford University Press, Oxford (1989)

Kratzer, A.: What must and can must and can mean. Linguist. Philos. **1**, 38–74 (1977)

Lasersohn, P.: Context dependence, disagreement, and predicates of personal taste. Linguist. Philos. **28**, 643–86 (2005)

Lewis, D.: Attitudes De Dicto and De Se. Philos. Rev. **88**, 513–543 (1979)

Lewis, D.: Index, context, and content. In: Kanger, S., Öhman, S. (eds.), Philosophy and Grammar, pp. 79–100. Reidel (1980)

MacFarlane, J.: Nonindexical contextualism. Synthese **166**, 231–50 (2009)

MacFarlane, J.: Epistemic modals are assessment-sensitive. In: Egan, A., Weatherson, B. (eds.) Epistemic Modals, pp. 144–178. Oxford University Press, Oxford (2011)

MacFarlane, J.: Assessment Sensitivity: Relative Truth and its Applications. Oxford University Press, Oxford (2014)

Mandelkern, M.: Bounded modality. Philos. Rev. **128**, 1–61 (2019)

McMillan, C., Clark, R., Moore, P., Devita, C., Grossman, M.: Neural basis for generalized quantifier comprehension. Neuropsychologia **43**, 1729–1737 (2005)

Ninan, D.: Review of John Macfarlane, assessment sensitivity: relative truth and its applications. Philos. Rev. **125**, 439–447 (2016)

---

[12] See van Benthem (1986), Steinhert-Threlkeld & Icard 2013 for such models. See McMillan et al. 2005, Szymanik 2007, and Szymanik and Zajenkowski 2010 for experiments and comments on such experiments.

Ninan, D.: Relational semantics and domain semantics for epistemic modals. J. Philos. Log. **47**, 1–16 (2018)

Perry, J.: The problem of the essential indexical. Noûs **13**, 3–21 (1979)

Pickel, B., Rabern, B., Dever, J.: Reviving the parameter revolution in semantics. In: Ball, D., Rabern, B. (eds.) The Science of Meaning, pp. 138–171. Oxford University Press, Oxford (2018)

Rabern, B., Ball, D.: Monsters and the theoretical role of context. Philos. Phenomenol. Res. **98**, 392–416 (2019)

Santorio, P.: Context-Free Semantics. In: Lepore, E., Sosa, D. (eds.) Oxford Studies in Philosophy of Language, vol. 1, pp. 208–239. Oxford University Press, Oxford (2017)

Schlenker, P.: A plea for monsters. Linguist. Philos. **26**, 29–120 (2003)

Soames, S.: Replies. Philos. Phenomenol. Res. **65**, 429–452 (2002)

Stalnaker, R.: Assertion. In: Cole, P. (ed.) Pragmatics, vol. 9, pp. 315–332. New York Academic Press, New York (1978)

Stanley, J.: On the linguistic basis for contextualism. Philos. Stud. **119**, 119–146 (2004)

Steinert-Threlkeld, S., Icard, T.: Iterating semantic automata. Linguist. Philos. **36**, 151–173 (2013)

Stephenson, T.: Judge dependence, epistemic modals, and predicates of personal taste. Linguist. Philos. **30**, 487–525 (2007)

Suppes, P.: Procedural semantics. In: Haller, R., Grassl, W. (eds.) Language, Logic, and Philosophy Proceedings, pp. 27–35. Hölder-Pichler-Tempsy, Vienna (1980)

Szymanik, J.: A comment on a neuroimaging study of natural language quantifier comprehension. Neuropsychologia **45**, 2158–2160 (2007)

Szymanik, J., Zajenkowski, M.: Comprehension of simple quantifiers: empirical evaluation of a computational model. Cogn. Sci. **34**, 521–532 (2010)

Yalcin, S.: Epistemic modals. Mind **116**, 983–1026 (2007)

Cheap Talk Under Partial Conflicts: A Dynamic Analysis of Pragmatic Meaning

Liping Tang[✉]

School of International Liberal Studies, Waseda University, Tokyo 169-8050, Japan
lipingsysu@gmail.com

Abstract. In natural language, meanings of words often deviate from their literal meanings under pragmatic reasoning. As is shown in game-theoretical pragmatics, when players do not have aligned benefits, communication with non-literal meaning is even more frequent. In these situations, the pragmatic inference under iterated best response plays the essential role for building the pragmatic meaning. The paper provides a systematic analysis of the deviation from literal meaning to pragmatic meaning when the interlocutors have partial conflicts. We apply the classical Cheap Talk game and Iterated Best Response reasoning to demonstrate the result.

Keywords: Game-theoretical pragmatics · Cheap talk game · Partial conflicts · Iterated best response

1 Introduction

Pragmatic meaning often deviates from the literal meaning in natural language communication (i.e. conversational implicature). The context of the conversation and the interlocutors' inferences play the essential role in forming the pragmatic meaning. However, communication context and inference are hard to be formally studied.

Game theory and Bayesian models have been verified as comprehensive quantitive analyses of pragmatic context and inference in language communication. Rational Speech Act (RSA)Theory [6, 9] and Game-theoretical Pragmatics [1, 11] are such quantitive models.

The RSA model focuses on the interlocutors' inferences in language communication through probability analysis. The goal of the RSA model is to predicate the interlocutors' utterance behaviors. Game-theoretical pragmatics, on the other hand, focuses on the rationality analysis of the interlocutors' beliefs and understanding of the language through signaling games. Nevertheless, Both models are embedding with Grice's cooperative principle [10] and Lewis's signaling game [13].

Grice's theory and the classical Lewis's signaling game pre-assume that interlocutors have common interests. In Lewis's signaling game with common interests, there are two kinds of equilibria: pooling equilibrium and separating equilibrium. Under separating equilibrium, truthful communication is induced. In

© Springer Nature Switzerland AG 2023
K. Yada et al. (Eds.): JSAI-isAI 2021 Workshops, LNAI 13856, pp. 271–282, 2023.
https://doi.org/10.1007/978-3-031-36190-6_19

addition, according to the credibility criterion from Farrell [5][1], signals with pre-defined literal meaning in some separating equilibrium are credible. Therefore, the pragmatic meaning is included in the literal meaning in the signaling game with common interests.

However, in application, signaling game or cheap talk game[2] often encounters the situation that interlocutors' have conflicting or partial conflicting interests. For a signaling game with zero-sum utility, it is easy to verify that this game yields no communication. We will not focus on this case. The interesting case is when the game consists of two players with partial conflicts.

Crawford and Sobel [2] established such a game in which the players' utilities are always differ by a certain number. As a result, the truthful communication is never an equilibrium. It is proved that the equilibrium of this game takes the form of the partition equilibrium. Under the partition equilibrium, partial information can be communicated. The signals within such an equilibrium all represent ambiguous meanings.

In the case of cheap talk game with meaningful signals under partial conflicts, the pragmatic meaning of signals could be far apart from the literal meaning. Jäger and Franke provided the iterated best response reasoning for discussing this issue ([7,11]). However, how far and how quickly the pragmatic meaning can deviate from the literal meaning are not fully explored and is worth a systematic analysis.

The goal of the paper is to explore the dynamic change of pragmatic meanings being apart from the literal meanings with respect to how differ the interlocutors' interests is. We construct our result based on Crawford and Sobel's cheap talk game (hereafter we call it the CS game) and the Iterated Best Response (IBR) reasoning.

The rest of the paper is organized as follows. Section 2 reviews the signaling game and how it is applied for pragmatic inference. Section 3 introduces the basic results in CS game, then we extend it to a modified game with an expanded signal structure. In Sect. 4, we apply the IBR model on the modified cheap talk game. We show that how the pragmatic meaning deviates from the literal meaning. The paper ends with a short conclusion.

2   Communication Under Partial Conflicts: Inference and Credibility

Signaling game is a useful tool for studying pragmatic inference and the credibility of signals ([1,14]). A signal is credible if there is a rational reason for using it truthfully. We use the signaling game with meaningful signals for illustrating this point.[3]

---

[1] Farrell [5] defines a novel equilibrium notion called "neologism proofness", under which the number of equilibrium in signaling game is reduced.

[2] In economic literature, signaling game is often called cheap talk game. It is because the cost of the signals is usually not taken into account into the utility function.

[3] The traditional signaling game or cheap talk game does not pre-assume that the signals are meaningful within the game.

The signaling game characterizes a simple communication scenario. A sender S observes the state of the world $t \in T$, then sends a message $I \in \mathcal{I}$ to the receiver (all the messages carry the unique commonly known meaning). The receiver R observes the message and takes an action $r \in \mathcal{R}$. The signaling game with meaningful signals is a tuple $\{\{S, R\}, T, Pr, \mathcal{I}, \llbracket \cdot \rrbracket, \mathcal{R}, U_S, U_R\}$, in which

- Pr is a probability distribution over T;
- $\llbracket \cdot \rrbracket$ is a semantic denotation function: $\llbracket \cdot \rrbracket : \mathcal{I} \to \mathcal{P}(T)$;
- $U_{S,R} : T \times \mathcal{I} \times \mathcal{R} \to R$ are utility function for the sender and the receiver.

In a signaling game, when the players share the same utility, then the cheap talk is beneficial for the players. It is because both players would like to cooperate as much as possible. Communication makes this cooperation more efficient.

On the other hand, if the game is a zero-sum game, then communication is not possible. Hence, we do not consider the zero-sum game. The most interesting case is when the players have partial conflicts. We use the following two examples to illustrate players' inferences about the use of the message under partial conflicts. Intuitively speaking, the pragmatic inference represents how each player conducts the best response upon his beliefs about his opponent. The examples are from Franke [8].

Table 1. Signaling inference

	r_1	r_2	r_3	I_1	I_2
t_1	2,2	0,0	1,1	✓	-
t_2	2,0	0,2	1,1	-	✓

(a) Case 1

	r_1	r_2	r_3	r_4	I_{12}	I_{23}	I_{13}
t_1	4,5	5,4	0,0	1,4	✓	-	✓
t_2	0,0	4,5	5,4	1,4	✓	✓	-
t_3	5,4	0,0	4,5	1,4	-	✓	✓

(b) Case 2

In Table 1, there are two games with different payoffs and actions. In each game, the row represents the state of the world. The first part of the column represents the receiver's actions. The second part of the column represents the literal meaning of each signal. For instance, in Case 1, $\llbracket I_1 \rrbracket = \{t_1\}$ and in Case 2, $\llbracket I_{12} \rrbracket = \{t_1, t_2\}$. The first number in the cell is the sender's payoff while the second one is the receiver's payoff. It is obvious that two games are neither zero-sum nor common-interest.

In Case 1, if only state t_1 is considered, then the sender would like to send the truthful message I_1 and the receiver would like to trust it since they both prefer the truth telling message. However, when state t_2 occurs, the players face conflicts. The sender prefers action r_1 while the receiver prefers r_2. If the receiver thinks the sender's message I_2 is truth telling, then he would choose r_2 which gives the sender the worse outcome. Thus the sender would not send I_2 but I_1 for t_2 if he thinks the receiver takes the literal meaning of the message. Moreover, if the receiver knows that the sender is not truth telling, then he would just ignore the sender's message and take action r_3 all the time. It shows that at each level of inference, meaning of the signals could change based on the players' beliefs.

In Case 2, similar situation occurs involving more layers of inferences. Suppose the receiver interprets the meaning of the message literally that S^{t_1} sends I_{12}, S^{t_2} sends I_{23} and S^{t_3} sends I_{13} truthfully. Then, when the receiver receives I_{12}, he would choose action r_1. But if the sender realized that the message t_{12} triggers the receiver to play r_1, then S^{t_3} wants to send I_{12} untruthfully. Similar inference can go further.

These two examples show that the literal meaning of the message could change as the interlocutors conduct pragmatic inferences, especially when the players have non-aligned payoffs. The inference usually starts with interpreting the meaning of the signals literally. Assuming that players are all rational, then the players take the best response reasonings upon their beliefs about their opponent. This kind of iterated reasonings has been studied for pragmatic inference ([7,11]) in game theory ([3,12]).

To reach a systematic analysis of the change of literal meanings in signaling games, I will explore a modified version of Crawford and Sobel's classical cheap talk game and apply the iterated best response reasoning on the game. There are two reasons that this game is worth more explorations along this line of research.

1. CS game captures a general model of signaling game under partial conflicts. Thus, by exploring this game, we have included a large group of signaling games with partial conflicts.
2. Following the tradition of equilibrium refinement approach, Farrell [5] tries to define an equilibrium with respect to the semantic meaning of the message. Thus, he defines the notion of neologism proof. The intuition under this notion is that given a common language with semantic meanings, within an equilibrium, all the $t \in [\![I]\!]$ prefers the receiver to interpret I literally. However, CS game has no equilibrium with respect to neologism proof. In other word, there is always an out-of-equilibrium best response (none-literal meanings) in this game. For this consideration, a weaker notion than Nash equilibrium is suitable for the analysis of this game. i.e. the iterated best response model with bounded rationality.

3   CS Game with the Expanded Signal Structure

The CS game models that a better informed sender sends a signal which may not exactly convey his private information about the true state to a receiver. Nevertheless, given the received signal, the receiver needs to choose an action that determines the welfare of both players. Formally, there are two players in this game, namely, a sender (S) and a receiver (R). Only S can observe the value of the random variable t which is uniformly distributed on $[0, 1]$. Then S should send a signal to the receiver, which may be random. Based on the signal, R chooses the action r a real number that determines both players' payoffs. Their payoff functions are given as follows.

$$U_S = -(r - (t + b))^2$$
$$U_R = -(r - t)^2$$

where b is a positive real number indicating the conflicts between players. Suppose the set of signals is $\mathcal{I}$. Then the sender's strategy is a function $s : [0, 1] \to \mathcal{I}$. The receiver's strategy is a function $r : \mathcal{I} \to \mathcal{R}$. As the features of the quadratic functions, U_S and U_R both have a unique maximal in r for each t. Hence we let $\bar{r}(t_i, t_j)$ indicate the unique solution for $max_r \int_{t_i}^{t_j} U_R(r, t) Pr(t)$ such that $t \in [t_i, t_j]$ where $0 \leqslant t_i \leqslant 1$ and $0 \leqslant t_j \leqslant 1$. Since we assume that $Pr(t)$ is a uniform distribution, hence $\bar{r}(t_i, t_j) = \frac{1}{2}(t_i + t_j)$.

It is easy to verify that the game has no truthful communication equilibrium because of the interest difference b. Instead, the equilibrium of CS model takes the form of partition equilibrium. They demonstrated the following.

Theorem 1 (Crawford and Sobel). *There exists a positive integer $N(b)$ such that, for every integer N with $1 \leq N \leq N(b)$, there exists one partition equilibrium. The equilibrium is presented by a partition on the state space $t(N) = (t_0(N), t_1(N), \ldots, t_N(N))$, where $0 = t_0(N) < t_1(N) < \cdots < t_N(N) = 1$. Moreover, there are signals I_i, $i = 1, 2, \ldots, N$ such that for all $N = 1, 2, \ldots, N(b)$,*

1. $U_S(\bar{r}(t_i, t_{i+1}), t_i) - U_S(\bar{r}(t_{i-1}, t_i), t_i) = 0$ *in which* $\bar{r}(t_i, t_j) = \frac{1}{2}(t_i + t_j)$;
2. $s(t_i) = I_i$ *for* $t_i \in [t_{i-1}, t_i]$
3. $r(I_i) = \bar{r}(t_{i-1}, t_i)$

Condition 1 states that the sender is indifference between sending a signal I_i or I_{i+1} on all the boundaries in the partition. Condition 2 states that the sender sends the same signal for all the states in the same partition element. Condition 3 says that the receiver best responds to the sender's strategy.

The variable b plays the essential role in generating the key features of this game. Intuitively, b measures the conflicting interests between the two players. Formally, it decides the size of the partition equilibrium $N(b)$. By solving the equations $U_S(\bar{r}(t_i, t_{i+1}), t_i) - U_S(\bar{r}(t_{i-1}, t_i), t_i) = 0$ for $i = 1, 2, \ldots, N$, we can get the inequality $2N(N - 1)b < 1$. Then $N(b)$ is defined as the largest integer that satisfies the inequality. Hence, the smaller the b is, the larger the $N(b)$ is. In other words, the smaller b yields a finer partition for the partition equilibrium such that more information can be communicated.

Moreover, CS model has proved that the partition equilibrium with the size $N(b)$ is the *ex ante* pareto superior equilibrium among all the partition equilibria. However, a different analysis is required for this game when examining from the *ex post* perspective (after the true value of t has been observed).

An example would be helpful for illustrating the equilibrium in CS game. Suppose $b = 1/20$, then $N(b) = 3$. All the partition equilibria and their corresponding signals and the sender's utility functions are listed as follows.

Example 1.

$N = 1 \quad I_{11}[0,1]$
$$U_S = -(\tfrac{27}{60} - t)^2$$

$N = 2 \quad I_{21}[0, \tfrac{24}{60}] \quad I_{22}[\tfrac{24}{60}, 1]$
$$U_S = -(\tfrac{9}{60} - t)^2 \quad U_S = -(\tfrac{39}{60} - t)^2$$

$N = 3 \quad I_{31}[0, \tfrac{8}{60}] \quad I_{32}[\tfrac{8}{60}, \tfrac{28}{60}] \qquad I_{33}[\tfrac{28}{60}, 1]$
$$U_S = -(\tfrac{1}{60} - t)^2 \quad U_S = -(\tfrac{15}{60} - t)^2 \quad U_S = -(\tfrac{41}{60} - t)^2$$

When $N = 1$, there is only one element in the partition, namely, for any state, the sender always sends the same signal. When $N = 2$, there are two elements in the partition equilibrium. Hence, if $t \in [0, \tfrac{24}{60}]$, the sender sends the signal I_{21}. When the receiver receives I_{21}, his best response is to solve $max_r Pr(t|I_{21})U_R$, which equals to $r=$"midpoint of the internal corresponding to I_{21}". Similarly, if $t \in [\tfrac{24}{60}, 1]$, the sender sends I_{22} and the receiver takes $r = \tfrac{1}{2}(\tfrac{24}{60} + 1)$.

Moreover, the finest equilibrium ($N = 3$ in Example 1) is the *ex ante* pareto superior equilibrium . Intuitively, most information is communicated in this equilibrium. In addition, as b decreases, $N(b)$ increases. There are many partition equilibria, and the finest partition equilibrium communicates more information. Thus, from the *ex ante* point of view, the finest partition equilibrium should be selected.

However, following Farrell's credibility analysis, the CS game is not neologism proof. It is because there is always a pre-defined signal which deviates from the equilibrium signals. Therefore, from the *ex post* point of view, there is no informative equilibrium and none of the partition equilibrium is ex post superior.

Since no *ex ante* partition equilibrium in CS game is superior than any others in the *ex post* play of the game, therefore, we just consider all of the partition equilibria together. Then we define a signal structure based on all the partition equilibria in Definition 1.

Definition 1. *The CS game with an expanded signal structure I is denoted as G_I, in which $I = \{I_{11}\} \cup \{I_{21}, I_{22}\} \cup \cdots \cup \{I_{i1}, I_{i2}, \ldots, I_{ii}\} \cup \cdots \cup \{I_{Nb1}, I_{N(b)2}, \ldots, I_{N(b)N(b)}\}$ with the following features as in Fig. 1. P_i is a partition equilibrium in CS game. For each signal I_{ij}, the literal meaning of the signal is the corresponding interval in the equilibrium.*

Considering all the partition equilibria, if we assume the full rationality of the players. There will be no equilibrium for this game, since there is always an out-of-equilibrium strategy forming a best response for the players. Hence, the following section applies the iterated best response reasoning to the modified CS game within which the full rationality assumption of the players is dropped.

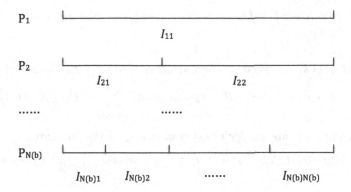

Fig. 1. Expanded signal structure

4 Iterated Best Response (IBR) Under the Expanded Signal Structure

Based on the CS game with the expanded signal structure, we define the iterated best response model I^k as follows. At each level of the reasoning, the players' strategies are best responses to that level of beliefs about the meanings of signals. The iterated best response model can be defined recursively from the sender's point of view.

Definition 2. *Given a game G_I, the IBR model I^k is defined recursively as follows.*

- $I_R^0 = I$, *Let $r_0 \in \mathcal{R}$ be the receiver's strategy, $Pr(t|I_R^0)$ is his posterior probability of the state according to his belief about the literal meaning of the signals.*

$$r_0 \in BR(Pr(t|I_R^0))$$

(r_0 is the best response of the receiver to his belief $Pr(t|I_R^0)$ iff

$$r_0 \in argmax \sum_{t \in [0,1]} Pr(t|I_R^0)U_R(t, I_R^0, r_0)$$

- *Let $s_0 \in S$ be the sender's strategy, $p(r|I_R^0)^4$ a probability distribution over the receiver's strategy space with respect to the literal meaning of the signal structure I_R^0,*

$$s_0 \in BR(p(r|I_R^0)) \quad iff \quad for\ each\ \ t_i \in T, s_0 \in argmax_{s_0(t_i) \in I_S^0} U_S(t_i, r_0, s_0(t_i), b)$$

After the sender's best response to the receiver's belief on the literal meaning of the signals. The meaning of the signals have already changed. The new meaning of the signals deduced under s_0 is denoted as I_S^0.

---

[4] We use $p(\cdot|\cdot)$ representing the sender's conditional belief about the receiver's strategy, and $q(\cdot|\cdot)$ reprenting the receiver's conditional belief about the sender's strategy.

- Since the receiver's belief is always one level lower than the sender's, therefore, we can define

$$I_R^k = I_S^{k-1}$$

Thus, at level k, the receiver's best strategy is to solve the following problem.[5]

$$r_k \in BR(q(s|I_S^{k-1})) \quad \textit{iff} \quad r_k \in argmax \sum_{t \in [0,1]} Pr(t|I_R^k) U_R(t, I_R^k, r_k)$$

- Correspondingly, the sender's best response s_k is the following.

$$s_k \in BR(p(r|I_R^k)) \quad \textit{iff} \quad \textit{for each } t_i \in T, s_k \in argmax_{s_k(t_i) \in I_S^k} U_S(t_i, r_k, s_k(t_i), b)$$

The new meaning of the signals deduced under s_k is denoted as I_S^k.

It is easy to prove that the player's best response strategies in G_I are pure strategies taking the following forms in Proposition 1.

Proposition 1. *Given the game G_I, and I^k, for any level k, the sender's best response s_k and the receiver's best response r_k take the following forms.*

- *s_k is induced from the signal structure I_S^k, that is, for any $t \in [t_{Si(j-1)}^k, t_{Sij}^k]$, where $I_{Sij}^k \in I_S^k$, and $[t_{Si(j-1)}^k, t_{Sij}^k]$ is the interval meaning of the signal I_{Sij}^k.*
- *$r_k = \frac{1}{2}(t_{Ri(j-1)}^k + t_{Rij}^k)$*

Applying the IBR model I^k in Example 1, the change of the signal meaning can be listed as follows. We omit the subscript S in I^k in the following expressions.

I^1 : $[0, \frac{5}{60})$ $(\frac{5}{60}, \frac{12}{60})$ $(\frac{12}{60}, \frac{21}{60})$ $(\frac{21}{60}, \frac{33}{60})$ $(\frac{33}{60}, \frac{40}{60})$ $(\frac{40}{60}, 1]$
$\quad\quad\quad I_{31}^1 \quad\quad\quad I_{21}^1 \quad\quad\quad I_{32}^1 \quad\quad\quad I_{11}^1 \quad\quad\quad I_{22}^1 \quad\quad\quad I_{33}^1$

I^2 : $[0, \frac{2.5}{60})$ $(\frac{2.5}{60}, \frac{9.5}{60})$ $(\frac{9.5}{60}, \frac{18.75}{60})$ $(\frac{18.75}{60}, \frac{28.75}{60})$ $(\frac{28.75}{60}, \frac{40.25}{60})$ $(\frac{40.25}{60}, 1]$
$\quad\quad\quad I_{31}^2 \quad\quad\quad I_{21}^2 \quad\quad\quad I_{32}^2 \quad\quad\quad I_{11}^2 \quad\quad\quad I_{22}^2 \quad\quad\quad I_{33}^2$

H I^3 : $[0, \frac{0.38}{60})$ $(\frac{0.38}{60}, \frac{7.06}{60})$ $(\frac{7.06}{60}, \frac{15.94}{60})$ $(\frac{15.94}{60}, \frac{26.13}{60})$ $(\frac{26.13}{60}, \frac{39.31}{60})$ $(\frac{39.31}{60}, 1]$
$\quad\quad\quad\quad I_{31}^3 \quad\quad\quad I_{21}^3 \quad\quad\quad I_{32}^3 \quad\quad\quad I_{11}^3 \quad\quad\quad I_{22}^3 \quad\quad\quad I_{33}^3$

I^4 : $[0, \frac{4.61}{60})$ $(\frac{4.61}{60}, \frac{13.27}{60})$ $(\frac{13.27}{60}, \frac{23.88}{60})$ $(\frac{23.88}{60}, \frac{38.19}{60})$ $(\frac{38.19}{60}, 1]$
$\quad\quad\quad I_{21}^4 \quad\quad\quad I_{32}^4 \quad\quad\quad I_{11}^4 \quad\quad\quad I_{22}^4 \quad\quad\quad I_{33}^4$

$\cdots \quad \cdots$

The dynamic is that the meaning of the signals change at each level. The signals on the left side loose the meaning of positive numbers one by one as k goes up. Eventually, only the right most signal remains which represents the most ambiguous meaning $[0, 1]$. This dynamic holds in general. We state the general result in Theorem 2.

---

[5] We use I^k in the utility function to indicate the sender's choice of the signals are within the signal structure I_k. Since the meaning of the signals are assumed as common knowledge at each epistemic level, we can omit to specify the signals.

Theorem 2. *Given a game G_I and the IBR model I^k, there exists a natural number n such that for any natural number $m \geqslant n$, $I_S^m = I_R^m = [0,1]$, and (s_m, r_m) yields the pooling equilibrium.*

Proof. See Appendix.

The converging speed depends on the number b in the cheap talk game. As b decreases, the number of partition equilibria increases. Then, it takes deeper level for the occurrence of the convergence result. For example, if $b = 1/20$, at I^{14}, the convergence result occurs. If $b = 1/50$, at I^{42}, the convergence result occurs. This result matches with our intuition that fewer conflicts lead to more communication.

The IBR model does not yield an equilibrium result but provides a rationalizability analysis for the CS game. Each player's behavior is rational with respect to their limited and current beliefs. Although the settle point is always pooling equilibrium in this analysis, but at each level of reasoning, the players are best responses to certain level of beliefs to each other.

5 Conclusion

It is often the case in natural language that words carry non-literal meanings, especially when the interlocutors do not have aligned benefits. We use a canonical model of signaling game under partial conflicts to show how the literal meaning can change under the pragmatic inference, i.e. everyone conducts the best response to their current beliefs. The main contribution of this work is that we can systematically show how the literal meaning changes as the players' conflicts increase and the iterated inference goes deeper.

Acknowledgements. The author is an international research fellow of Japan Society for the Promotion of Science.This research is supported by Grant-in-Aid for JSPS Fellows (No. 20F20012), Chinese National Funding of Social Science (No. 18CZX064) and the Key Project of National Social Science Foundation of China (No. 16AZX017).

Appendix

Theorem 2 *Given a game G_I and the IBR model I^k, there exists a natural number n such that for any natural number $m \geqslant n$, $I_S^m = I_R^m = [0,1]$, and (s_m, r_m) yields a pooling equilibrium.*

Proof

Case 1: Suppose that $b >= 1/4$, $N(b) = 1$, the required result holds trivially.

Case 2: Suppose that $0 < b < 1/4$.

The idea is to find the connection of the sender's inutility functions and the changes of the meanings between different levels. Then construct the convergence result of the dynamic.

First, given any $b \in (0, \frac{1}{4})$, we can calculate $N(b) = N$ which is the largest number of the partitions for the partition equilibrium, then the total number of the signals are $M = \frac{(N+1)N}{2}$.

From the constructions of the IBR model, for any signal I_{ij}^k, the sender's utility function has the form $U_S = -(r^k - t)^2$, where $r^k = r - b$. List all these functions as r increases as $U_S = -(r_1^k - t)^2, U_S = -(r_2^k - t)^2, \ldots, U_S = -(r_M^k - t)^2$ where $r_1^k < r_2^k < \cdots < r_M^k$.

All the interval meanings of the signals at each level are derived from those utility functions, as we illustrated in Fig. 2.

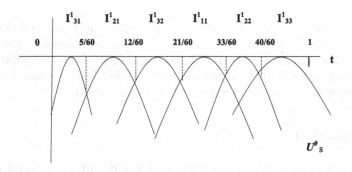

Fig. 2. Expanded signal structure for b = 1/20

p_j^k is used to indicate those interval points. And for any level k, assume that $p_0^k = 0$ and $p_M^k = 1$. And for any $0 < i < j < M$, $p_i < p_j$. Then by the structure of the game, r and p has the following relationships.

$$p_1^0 = \tfrac{1}{2}(r_1^0 + r_2^0)$$
$$p_2^0 = \tfrac{1}{2}(r_2^0 + r_3^0)$$
$$\cdots$$
$$p_{M-1}^0 = \tfrac{1}{2}(r_{M-1}^0 + r_M^0)$$

Moreover, we have that

$$r_1^{k+1} = \tfrac{1}{2}(0 + p_1^k) - b$$
$$r_2^{k+1} = \tfrac{1}{2}(p_1^k + p_2^k) - b \qquad [1]$$
$$\cdots$$
$$r_M^{k+1} = \tfrac{1}{2}(p_{M-1}^k + 1) - b$$

In addition, we have the following equations:

$$p_1^{k+1} = \tfrac{1}{2}(r_1^{k+1} + r_2^{k+1})$$
$$p_2^{k+1} = \tfrac{1}{2}(r_2^{k+1} + r_3^{k+1}) \qquad [2]$$
$$\cdots$$
$$p_{M-1}^{k+1} = \tfrac{1}{2}(r_{M-1}^{k+1} + r_M^{k+1})$$

By substituting all the r_i^{k+1}s in formula series [2] with all the formulas in [1], we can obtain the following equations:

$$p_1^{k+1} = \tfrac{1}{4}p_0^k + \tfrac{1}{2}p_{1(n)} + \tfrac{1}{4}p_{2^k} - b$$
$$p_2^{k+1} = \tfrac{1}{4}p_1^k + \tfrac{1}{2}p_{2(n)} + \tfrac{1}{4}p_{3^k} - b$$
$$p_3^{k+1} = \tfrac{1}{4}p_2^k + \tfrac{1}{2}p_{3(n)} + \tfrac{1}{4}p_4^k - b \qquad [3]$$
$$\cdots$$
$$p_{M-1}^{k+1} = \tfrac{1}{4}p_{M-2}^k + \tfrac{1}{2}p_{M-1}^k + \tfrac{1}{4}p_M^k - b$$

Therefore, the formulas in [3] can be rewritten in the metric form as follows:

$$p(n+1) = Ap(n) - B$$

where

$$A = \begin{pmatrix} \tfrac{1}{2} & \tfrac{1}{4} & 0 & \cdots & 0 & 0 \\ \tfrac{1}{4} & \tfrac{1}{2} & \tfrac{1}{4} & 0 & \cdots & 0 \\ 0 & \tfrac{1}{4} & \tfrac{1}{2} & \tfrac{1}{4} & \cdots & 0 \\ \vdots & & \ddots & \ddots & \ddots & \vdots \\ 0 & 0 & \cdots & \tfrac{1}{4} & \tfrac{1}{2} & \tfrac{1}{4} \\ 0 & 0 & \cdots & 0 & \tfrac{1}{4} & \tfrac{1}{2} \end{pmatrix}$$

$$B = \begin{pmatrix} b \\ \cdots \\ b \\ \cdots \\ \tfrac{1}{4} - b \end{pmatrix}$$

Observe that A has the exact form as the matrix known as Toeplitz Matrix. Thus its eigenvalues are given by

$$\lambda_n = \frac{1}{2} + \frac{1}{4}\cos(\frac{n\pi}{k+1}), n = 1, 2, \cdots, M - 1$$

Therefore, $|\lambda| < 1$ for all n. According to the following mathematical result: *Assuming that A is any $k \times k$ matrix, then $\lim_{n \to \infty} A^n = 0$ iff $|\lambda| < 1$ for all* *eigenvalues* λ *of* A,[6] we thus have that $\lim_{n \to \infty} A^n = 0$. It follows that $p_{n+1} < 0$ as $n \to \infty$. As all the p_is are becoming negative, there will be no divided point in the interval $[0, 1]$. That is to say, there is only one signal that is considered from the sender's point of view for $t \in [0, 1]$. Thus, the babbling equilibrium eventually occurs.

References

1. Benz, A., Jäger, G., Van Rooij, R., Van Rooij, R.: Game Theory and Pragmatics. Springer, Cham (2005)
2. Crawford, V.P., Sobel, J.: Strategic information transmission. Econometrica: J. Econometr. Soc., 1431–1451 (1982)
3. Crawford, V.P., et al.: Let's talk it over: Coordination via preplay communication with level-k thinking. Unpublished Manuscript (2007)
4. Elaydi, S.: An Introduction to Difference Equations. Springer Science and Business Media, Cham (2005)
5. Farrell, J.: Meaning and credibility in cheap-talk games. Games Econom. Behav. **5**(4), 514–531 (1993)
6. Frank, M.C., Goodman, N.D.: Predicting pragmatic reasoning in language games. Science **336**(6084), 998–998 (2012)
7. Franke, M.: Game theoretic pragmatics. Philos Compass **8**(3), 269–284 (2013)
8. Franke, M., et al.: Meaning and inference in case of conflict. In: Proceedings of the 13th ESSLLI student session, pp. 65–74 (2008)
9. Goodman, N.D., Frank, M.C.: Pragmatic language interpretation as probabilistic inference. Trends Cogn. Sci. **20**(11), 818–829 (2016)
10. Grice, H.P.: Logic and conversation. In: Speech acts, pp. 41–58. Brill (1975)
11. Jäger, G.: Rationalizable signaling. Erkenntnis **79**(4), 673–706 (2014)
12. Kawagoe, T., Takizawa, H.: Equilibrium refinement vs. level-k analysis: an experimental study of cheap-talk games with private information. Games Econ. Behav. **66**(1), 238–255 (2009)
13. Lewis, D.: Convention: A Philosophical Study. John Wiley & Sons, Hoboken (2008)
14. Stalnaker, R.: Saying and meaning, cheap talk and credibility. In: Benz, A., Jager, G., van Rooji, R. (eds.) Game theory and pragmatics, pp. 83–100. Springer, Cham (2006)

---

[6] See for instance [4], p. 145 for a detailed proof of this result.

SCIDOCA 2021

Fifth International Workshop on SCIentific DOCument Analysis (SCIDOCA2021)

Le-Minh Nguyen (ID)

Japan Advanced Institute of Science and Technology, Japan
nguyenml@jaist.ac.jp

1 The Workshop

The Fifth International Workshop on SCIentific DOCument Analysis (SCIDOCA2021) took online on November 11–13. This is the first time we have organized SCIDOCA online due to the COVID-19 pandemic. SCIDOCA was held as a workshop of the thirteen JSAI International Symposia on AI (JSAI-isAI 2021), sponsored by The Japan Society for Artificial Intelligence (JSAI).

SCIDOCA is an annual international workshop focusing on the topic on natural language processing for scientific papers and technical documents. Dealing with such data has become an obstacle to efficient information acquisition of new information in various fields. It is almost impossible for individual researchers to check and read all related documents. Even retrieving relevant documents is becoming harder and harder. This workshop gathers all the researchers and experts aiming at scientific document analysis from various perspectives and invites technical paper presentations and system demonstrations that cover any aspects of scientific document analysis.

This year the workshop featured invited talks by Prof. Iryna Gurevych, UKP Lab at the Technical University, Germany. This invited talk mainly brings us to a study dealing with peer reviews. The invited talk draws a general picture for exploiting NLP techniques to enhance the quality of peer reviews and reduce the human efforts in dealing with a large number of paper submissions.

In addition, there were nine presentations of talks selected by the program committee. Most papers performs a research of using advanced deep learning models for dealing with scientific papers and beyond. The workshop demonstrates that it is an interesting forum which have meaningful discussions on various issues of natural language processing methods for scientific papers and beyond.

The remainder of this introduction will briefly indicate the content of the papers selected to appear in the present volume.

2 The Papers

The first paper, entitled "Investigating the Effects of Pre-trained BERT to Improve Sparse Data Recommender Systems," presents a method of text recommendation using transformer models. The authors investigate the effect of utilizing BERT models to represent item reviews to enhance matrix factorization-based recommender systems, especially in sparse data settings. Instead of using conventional pre-trained word embeddings as some previous models, the author utilizes BERT for item review representations. The technology presented in the paper can be applied to scientific papers in the recommendation.

The second paper entitles "A Novel Pipeline to Enhance Question-Answering Model by Identifying Relevant Information." proposes a novel model-agnostic pipeline to remove distracting information from the contexts of the span-extraction QA task. In addition, the paper also presents a delegate process to extract the training dataset for Potential Sentence Classification Model (PSCM) from the original QA resources. The experimental results show that the proposed method remarkably enhances existing QA models and can be applied to a wide range of models and datasets. The paper also shows that the pipeline is especially useful in QA in scientific documents, which have massive and complex contexts.

Acknowledgements. We would like to thank the PC committee and organization who help organzing the workshop successfully. Nguyen Le Minh, Noriki Nishida, Vu Tran, Yusuke Miyao Yuji Matsumoto, Yoshinobu Kano, Akiko Aizawa, Ken Satoh, Junichiro Mori, Kentaro Inui.

We also would like to thank the financial support from JSAI for giving us the opportunity to hold the workshop.

Investigating the Effects of Pre-trained BERT to Improve Sparse Data Recommender Systems

Xuan Huy Nguyen[1]($^{(\boxtimes)}$), Long H. Trieu[2], and Le Minh Nguyen[1]

[1] Japan Advanced Institute of Science and Technology, Nomi, Japan
{nguyenhx,nguyenml}@jaist.ac.jp
[2] Thai Nguyen University of Education, Thai Nguyen, Vietnam
longth@tnue.edu.vn

Abstract. Recommender systems play an important role with many applications in natural language processing such as in e-commerce services. Matrix factorization (MF) is a powerful method in recommender systems, but a main issue is the sparse data problem. In order to overcome the problem, some previous models use neural networks to represent additional information such as product item reviews to enhance MF-based methods, and obtain improvement in recommender systems. However, these models use conventional pre-trained word embeddings, which raise a question whether recent powerful models such as BERT can improve these MF-based methods enhanced by item reviews. In this work, we investigate the effect of utilizing BERT model to improve some previous models, especially focusing on several specific sparse data settings. Experimental results on the MovieLens dataset show that our model has successfully utilized BERT to represent item reviews and outperformed the previous probabilistic MF-based model which does not use item reviews. We also conducted intensive analyses on several settings related to sparse data and obtained some promising findings related to the lengths of review texts, which may open directions to improve this on-going model to solve the problem of sparse data in MF-based recommender systems.

1 Introduction

Recommendation systems play an important role in natural language processing applications such as e-commerce, e-learning, e-business services which cover various domains such as recommending books, movies, documents, etc. [1,3]. One of the most effective methods for recommendation systems is called *collaborative filtering (CF)* [6,13]. Given users and product items and the relationships among users and items such as ratings (for instance a score from 1 to 5 a user gives to a product), CF models identify new relationships among users and items based on existing relationships. In CF methods, *matrix factorization (MF)* [8] is a powerful method and commonly used recently, which tries to explain the ratings

© Springer Nature Switzerland AG 2023
K. Yada et al. (Eds.): JSAI-isAI 2021 Workshops, LNAI 13856, pp. 287–295, 2023.
https://doi.org/10.1007/978-3-031-36190-6_20

by characterizing items and users by vectors of latent *factors* inferred from the ratings patterns (for instance, drama versus comedy, amount of action, etc. in discovered *factors* of movie domain). One of the main issues of CF methods is the sparseness data problem when majority of items may lack the feedback(or ratings) from users [4,9].

In order to overcome the sparseness issue in CF methods, external information can be utilized to enhance new rating prediction such as item reviews (textual comments that a user gives to product items) [7,8]. Item reviews can be represented by convolutional neural networks (CNNs) then combined with a probabilistic matrix factorization model [7] (ConvMF). Instead of using CNNs, a recent model called AMF [11] improves the ConvMF based on an attention mechanism with genre information of product items. However, these models are based on conventional pre-trained word embeddings such as Glove [12] while recent proposed pre-trained models such as BERT [2] are still yet investigated.

In this work, we propose a model for recommender system which combines the probabilistic matrix factorization enhanced by contextual information of item reviews represented by utilizing BERT models. Our goal is to investigate the effect of BERT models to improve the previous document-enhanced matrix factorization based model [11]. In this model, we utilize BERT models [2] for item review representations instead of the pre-trained word embeddings such as Glove [12] used in the AMF model [11]. We evaluate our model on the widely used the MovieLens-1m dataset and compare with the baseline AMF model [11] as well as with some other previous models including the ConvMF [7]. In addition, we conduct intensive analyses to investigate our models on different aspects of sparse data, a challenge which is still remaining for recommender systems. Experimental results show that our model obtains better performance than the ConvMF, but still lower than the AMF model. However, our findings from the analyses are that our model improves the baseline AMF model with the data setting where review text lengths are in a specific range (less than 200 words), which may open a direction for our model to deal with sparse data issues.

2   Our Model

We name our proposed model BMF, which stands for **B**ERT-based item review representation enhancing for **M**atrix **F**actorization recommender systems. The overall architecture of our model is presented in Fig. 1. The model consists of two components: the probabilistic matrix factorization (PMF) and the item review representations based on BERT.

2.1   Probabilistic Matrix Factorization (PMF)

Matrix factorization is one of the most popular methods in collaborative filtering-based (CF) for recommender systems [8]. In MF models, users and items are represented based on vectors of latent features, in which users and items are projected into a shared latent space. PMF methods [14] use a probabilistic model

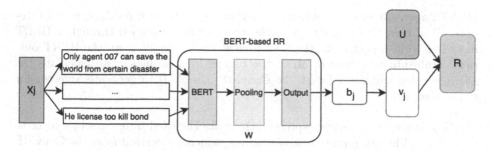

Fig. 1. The overall architecture of our model. The probabilistic matrix factorization (PMF) is in the right, and the item review representations are in the left. An user u_i of the user set U gives a rating to a product item v_j of the product item set V, which results in the ratings matrix R. A product item in V may have reviews X which are comments from users about this product. We represent these reviews X by using BERT models to enhance the prediction of new ratings for items in V based on the $BERT-based\ RR$ architecture with three layers: BERT, pooling, and output layers to generate the item review representation b_j.

with matrix factorization, which assume that observations (observed ratings) are generated from a Gaussian distribution. PMF models can learn low-rank representations (latent factors) of users and items from the user-item matrix, which is then used to predict new ratings between users and items. Given N is the set of users, M is the set of items, and R is a rating matrix of users for items ($R \in \mathbb{R}^{N \times M}$). PMF discovers the k-dimensional models, which are the latent models of user u_i ($u_i \in \mathbb{R}^k$) and item v_j ($v_j \in \mathbb{R}^k$). The rating r_{ij} of user i on item j can be approximated by equation: $r_{ij} \approx \hat{r}_{ij} = u_i{}^T v_j$.

2.2 Representations of Item Reviews

In this section, we present the representations of item reviews based on BERT models in our BMF model. In the previous work AMF model [11], pre-trained word embeddings such as Glove [12] are used to represent item reviews. Instead of that, in this BMF model, we represent item reviews based on a BERT model [2]. In recent years, BERT models have shown to be effective when they are integrated into neural architectures in many NLP applications. In addition, some previous works have utilized pre-trained BERT for sparse data problems such as in language understanding, inference, or information extraction [5,17]. Therefore, we aim at investigating whether we can improve the AMF baseline model by using the BERT model to address the sparse data issue in recommendation task.

We follow the same representation approach in previous works [7], but we replace the convolutional layer in [7] by the BERT. Specifically, we named this representation architecture as $BERT\_based\ RR$ (which stands for BERT-based review representation). The architecture contains three layers: a BERT layer, a pooling layer, and an output layer.

BERT Layer. Given a list of reviews corresponding to each product, we concatenate all of these reviews into a single sequence to be passed through a BERT model to form a vector for the item review.[1] Specifically, from the BERT outputs' embedding vectors of all of the tokens in a sequence, we calculate the average value which we follow the ConvMF model [7] to generate a vector for the sequence.

Pooling Layer. The review representations are then fed into a pooling layer to extract fixed-length representative features, which we derived from the ConvMF model [7]. The pooling layer uses a max-pooling approach to produce fixed-length feature vector so that it can deal with variable lengths of review texts.

Output Layer. Finally, an output layer receives the extracted features from the pooling layer to form latent vectors of each review. In summary, given review texts (X_j), this process extracts latent vectors (b_j) for each product $(v_j$ of $V)$, in which the weights of the *BERT_based RR* (W) are learned.

Optimization. We directly use the optimization method of [7], which is a maximum posteriori (MAP) estimation as presented in Eq. 1.

$$
\mathcal{L}(\mathcal{U}, \mathcal{V}, \mathcal{W}) = \sum_i^N \sum_j^M I_{ij}(r_{ij} - u_i^T v_j)_2 + \frac{\lambda_U}{2} \sum_i^N \| u_i \|_2
$$

$$
+ \frac{\lambda_V}{2} \sum_j^M \| v_j - b_j \|_2 + \frac{\lambda_W}{2} \sum_k^{|w_k|} \| w_k \|_2, \tag{1}
$$

where: U, V, R denote the vectors of users, items, and ratings, respectively; I is a diagonal matrix; $\lambda_U, \lambda_V, \lambda_W$ are balancing parameters. By optimizing the latent variable (the b_j review representation via *BERT_based RR*'s W learnable parameters) and the user U and items v in V, unknown ratings can be predicted.

3 Experiments

3.1 Data

We evaluate our models on the MovieLens dataset[2] (MovieLen-1M), which is widely used in this task. For item review information, we extracted from the IMDB.[3] For genre information, we extracted from item files (*_movies.dat). For evaluation, we randomly divided each dataset into three sets: training (80%), validation (10%), and test sets (10%), which we followed the previous work [11]. The training set contains at least one rating on each user and each item so that all users and items are included in PMF.

---

[1] We set the maximum length of the concatenated sequences as 300, which we followed [7].

[2] https://grouplens.org/datasets/movielens/.

[3] http://www.imdb.com/.

3.2   Baseline

We compared our proposed BMF with previous models:

- **PMF** [14]: Probabilistic Matrix Factorization uses only user ratings for CF. This is a standard rating prediction model.
- **CTR** [15]: Collaborative Topic Regression combines collaborative filtering (PMF) and topic modeling (LDA) to use both ratings and documents.
- **CDL** [16]: Collaborative Deep Learning improves rating prediction by analyzing documents.
- **ConvMF** [7]: Convolutional Matrix Factorization uses convolutional neural networks to represent item reviews to enhance rating prediction accuracy.
- **AMF** [11]: This model uses an Attention mechanism into Matrix Factorization. It employed the item genre information in attention neural network to find out attended features from item reviews. This is the main baseline of our model.

For our BMF model, we used different BERT models in the BMF model, which result in the three different variants of our BMF model.

- **BMF(bert-base-uncased)**: we used the bert-base-uncased model[4] to represent item reviews and combine with a PMF framework.
- **BMF(robeta-bert)**: this is the same as the BMF(bert-base-uncased) model but we use another BERT model, i.e. the robeta-bert [10].
- **BMF(albert-base-v1)**: this is the same as the BMF(bert-base-uncased) but we use another BERT model, i.e. the albert-base-v1.[5]

3.3   Metrics

The models are evaluated based on the widely used root mean squared error (RMSE), which we followed the previous work [7,11].

$$RMSE = \sqrt{\frac{\sum_{i,j}^{N,M}(r_{ij} - \hat{r}_{ij})^2}{\# \; of \; ratings}} \tag{2}$$

3.4   Settings

We implemented our model on Pytorch. We set the latent dimensions (U and V) as 50 according to the previous work in [16] and initialized U, V randomly from 0 to 1. For the BERT-based review representation, BERT's dimension is set as 768 as the pre-trained models', and the output layer is set as 50 which we followed the same setting of [7].

---

[4]   https://huggingface.co/bert-base-uncased.
[5]   https://huggingface.co/albert-base-v1.

3.5 Results

The Contribution of Reviews. We first investigate the contribution of using reviews in our BMF model. Table 1 presents rating prediction error of our BMF model and compare with some baseline models which are relied on only user ratings and do not use reviews, i.e., the PMF, CDL, and CTR models. The results show that our BMF model obtains better performance than these baseline models. In comparison with the PMF model, which is also based on probabilistic matrix factorization similar to out model but without item text reviews, our BMF model achieved a significant improvement with 6.11%. This result shows that our BMF model has successfully utilized item text reviews via BERT.

Table 1. The contribution of reviews on the ML-1m test set (RMSE score: lower is better; the best score is in bold)

Model	RMSE
PMF [14]	0.8961
CTR [15]	0.8968
CDL [16]	0.8876
BMF(bert-base-uncased)	**0.8516**
BMF(robeta-bert)	0.8516
BMF(albert-base-v1)	0.8515

Comparing with Baseline Models. We compare our model with the ConvMF and AMF models, which are also use represent item text reviews in Table 2. Our model improves 0.6% in comparison with the ConvMF. However, our model performance is still lower than the AMF result. We present further analyses to investigate the BMF and AMF models in Sect. 3.6.

Table 2. Comparison of our BMF with baseline models on the ML-1m test set (RMSE score: lower is better; the best score is in bold; the score that is better than the ConvMF baseline is in underline)

Model	RMSE
ConvMF [7]	0.8578
AMF [11]	**0.8350**
BMF(bert-base-uncased)	0.8516
BMF(robeta-bert)	0.8516
BMF(albert-base-v1)	0.8515

3.6 Analyses and Discussions

We conduct analyses on the different aspects to investigate our model on different settings related to sparse data.

The Effect of Genre Information. We added the *item genre information* as additional input for BERT. We used the same representation architecture as described in Sect. 2.2 to represent genre information. The item genres' texts and item reviews are passed through BERT and pooling layers separately. After that, the two vectors of the genres and reviews from the pooling layer are concatenated before going through the output layer to generate the representation. We compare the BMF model with and without using the *item genre information*. The results in Table 3 show that using *item genre information* does not improve the performance. This result indicates that item genre information may not be helpful in combination with the BERT model in our proposed BMF model. It may be because the length of item genre texts is quite short (with several words). In future work, we need to conduct more experiments on other datasets with longer text sequences of item genres to further investigate the contribution of genre information in combination with the powerful BERT model in building recommender systems.

Table 3. The effect of *item genre information (IGI)* (RMSE score: lower is better)

Model	With IGI	Without IGI
BMF(bert-base-uncased)	0.8520	0.8516
BMF(robeta-bert)	0.8515	0.8516
BMF(albert-base-v1)	0.8525	0.8515

The Effect of Training Data Size. We investigate the effect of training data size by setting the training data with different ratios, in which we randomly selected 20%, 40%, 60%, and 80% of training data to train the model. The results presented in Table 4 show that our BMF model outperforms the baseline ConvMF [7] in all of the data ratios. Meanwhile, the AMF model [11] achieves the best performance. The results indicate that our BMF model, which uses BERT, is not better than the baseline AMF [7] using pre-trained word embeddings in the setting of sparse data. We plan to conduct further analyses and investigations in experiments including trying different ratios of number of ratings on each items. In addition, modifications in the BMF model architecture are also needed to better utilize text reviews to improve the model in future work.

The Effect of Review Text Lengths. We investigate the effect of review text length in the MovieLens-1M. We first analyze the lengths of review texts in the MovieLens-1M data. This dataset contains 10,076 reviews, in which the length of a review is in range from 13 to 1,276 words. We calculate the ratios of text lengths (the number of words in each review) in the entire review texts in the data. There are 36.22% of review texts with less than 100 words, and 31.71%

Table 4. Results on using different ratios of training data (RMSE) (the best score is in bold; the score that is better than the ConvMF baseline is in underline)

Model	20%	40%	60%	80%
AMF [11]	**0.9096**	**0.875**	**0.8534**	**0.8359**
ConvMF [7]	0.9477	0.8949	0.8734	0.8578
BMF(robeta-bert)	0.9183	0.8838	0.8674	0.8516

of reviews texts of which the lengths are from 100 to 200 words. The statistics show that there is a large portion of review texts of which the lengths are in the range of less than 200 words. We evaluate the performance of our BMF and the baseline AMF models on such different text lengths to investigate whether the lengths of review texts affect the behavior of our model.

Table 5. Comparison of our model and the baseline AMF model on different ranges of review text lengths (RMSE) (l: the length of review texts;the best scores are in bold)

Model	$l < 100$	$100 < l < 200$
AMF [11]	0.9251	0.9284
BMF(robeta-bert)	**0.9135**	**0.9191**

We present the results in Table 5 to compare our BMF model and the AMF model [11] in the two different ranges of text lengths: less than 100 words, and from 100 to 200 words. The results show that our BMF model outperforms the AMF model in both cases. It confirms that our BMF model is better than the AMF model in this setting, in which the review text lengths should be less than 200 words. The reason may come with the text lengths used in the BERT model, in which using this range of text lengths may be more suitable to leverage the strength of the BERT model. We will conduct more experiments and analyses regarding this setting of text lengths so that we can further take advantages of the power of the BERT model in our recommender systems.

4   Conclusion

In this work we investigate the effect of utilizing BERT models to represent item reviews to enhance matrix factorization-based recommender systems especially in sparse data settings. Instead of using conventional pre-trained word embeddings as some previous models, we utilize BERT for item review representations. We conducted experiments on the Movielens dataset. Although experimental results show that our model is still needed to be further investigated to improve the baseline model, we also achieve some promising findings from the intensive analyses. Our model can improve the baseline model with a specific review text lengths (less than 200 words). We plan to improve this on-going work by conducting other analyses as well as making further modifications in both model architectures and experiment settings in future work.

References

1. Dahdouh, K., Dakkak, A., Oughdir, L., Ibriz, A.: Large-scale e-learning recommender system based on spark and Hadoop. J. Big Data **6**(1), 1–23 (2019)
2. Devlin, J., Chang, M.W., Lee, K., Toutanova, K.: BERT: pre-training of deep bidirectional transformers for language understanding. arXiv preprint: arXiv:1810.04805 (2018)
3. Felfernig, A., Le, V.M., Popescu, A., Uta, M., Tran, T.N.T., Atas, M.: An overview of recommender systems and machine learning in feature modeling and configuration. In: 15th International Working Conference on Variability Modelling of Software-Intensive Systems, pp. 1–8 (2021)
4. Feng, C., Liang, J., Song, P., Wang, Z.: A fusion collaborative filtering method for sparse data in recommender systems. Inf. Sci. **521**, 365–379 (2020)
5. Grießhaber, D., Maucher, J., Vu, N.T.: Fine-tuning BERT for low-resource natural language understanding via active learning. In: Proceedings of the 28th International Conference on Computational Linguistics, pp. 1158–1171 (2020)
6. He, X., Liao, L., Zhang, H., Nie, L., Hu, X., Chua, T.S.: Neural collaborative filtering. In: Proceedings of the 26th International Conference on World Wide Web, pp. 173–182 (2017)
7. Kim, D.H., Park, C., Oh, J., Lee, S., Yu, H.: Convolutional matrix factorization for document context-aware recommendation. In: Sen, S., Geyer, W., Freyne, J., Castells, P. (eds.) RecSys, pp. 233–240. ACM (2016)
8. Koren, Y., Bell, R., Volinsky, C.: Matrix factorization techniques for recommender systems. Computer **42**(8), 30–37 (2009)
9. Lika, B., Kolomvatsos, K., Hadjiefthymiades, S.: Facing the cold start problem in recommender systems. Expert Syst. Appl. **41**(4), 2065–2073 (2014)
10. Liu, Y., et al.: RoBERTa: a robustly optimized BERT pretraining approach. arXiv preprint: arXiv:1907.11692 (2019)
11. Nguyen, H.X., Nguyen, M.L.: Attention mechanism for recommender systems. In: Proceedings of the 33rd Pacific Asia Conference on Language, Information and Computation. Association for Computational Linguistics, Japan (2019)
12. Pennington, J., Socher, R., Manning, C.D.: Glove: global vectors for word representation. In: Proceedings of EMNLP, pp. 1532–1543 (2014)
13. Rendle, S., Krichene, W., Zhang, L., Anderson, J.: Neural collaborative filtering vs. matrix factorization revisited. In: Fourteenth ACM Conference on Recommender Systems, pp. 240–248 (2020)
14. Salakhutdinov, R., Mnih, A.: Probabilistic matrix factorization. In: Advances in Neural Information Processing Systems, vol. 20 (2008)
15. Wang, C., Blei, D.M.: Collaborative topic modeling for recommending scientific articles. In: Apté, C., Ghosh, J., Smyth, P. (eds.) KDD, pp. 448–456. ACM (2011)
16. Wang, H., Wang, N., Yeung, D.Y.: Collaborative deep learning for recommender systems. In: Cao, L., Zhang, C., Joachims, T., Webb, G.I., Margineantu, D.D., Williams, G. (eds.) KDD, pp. 1235–1244. ACM (2015)
17. Wang, Z., Karthikeyan, K., Mayhew, S., Roth, D.: Extending multilingual BERT to low-resource languages. In: Findings of the Association for Computational Linguistics: EMNLP 2020, pp. 2649–2656 (2020)

A Novel Pipeline to Enhance Question-Answering Model by Identifying Relevant Information

Nguyen-Khang Le[1], Dieu-Hien Nguyen[1], Thi-Thu-Trang Nguyen[1],
Minh Phuong Nguyen[1], Tung Le[1,2,3], and Minh Le Nguyen[1(✉)]

[1] Japan Advanced Institute of Science and Technology, Ishikawa, Japan
{lnkhang,ndhien,trangttn,phuongnm,nguyenml}@jaist.ac.jp,
lttung@fit.hcmus.edu.vn
[2] Faculty of Information Technology, University of Science,
Ho Chi Minh city, Vietnam
[3] Vietnam National University, Ho Chi Minh city, Vietnam

Abstract. Question-Answering (QA) systems have increasingly drawn much interest in the research community. A significant number of methods and datasets are proposed for the QA tasks. One of the gold standard QA resources is span-extraction Machine Reading Comprehension datasets, where the system must extract a span of text from the context to answer the question. Although state-of-the-art methods for span-extraction QA are proposed, distracting information in the context can be a significant factor that reduces these methods' performance. Especially, QA in scientific documents has massive contexts whose only a small part contains the relevant information to answer the question. As a result, it is challenging for QA models to arrive at the answer in scientific documents. As an observation, performance can be improved by only considering relevant sentences. This study proposed a novel pipeline to enhance the performance of existing QA methods by identifying and keeping relevant information from the context. The proposed pipeline is model-agnostic, multilingual, and can be flexibly applied to any QA model to increase performance. Our experiments on QA datasets in scientific documents (Qasper) and SQuAD 2.0 show that our approach successfully improves the performance of state-of-the-art QA models. Especially, our detailed comparisons reveal the effectiveness and flexibility of our proposed models in enhancing the current QA systems in low-resource languages such as Vietnamese (UIT-VIQUAD).

Keywords: Question answering · Information Retrieval · Machine Reading Comprehension

1 Introduction

Question Answering (QA) is one of the core disciplines within information retrieval in general and natural language processing in specific. It has lately

---

N.-K. Le and D.-H. Nguyen—These authors contributed equally to this work.

© Springer Nature Switzerland AG 2023
K. Yada et al. (Eds.): JSAI-isAI 2021 Workshops, LNAI 13856, pp. 296–311, 2023.
https://doi.org/10.1007/978-3-031-36190-6_21

gained more attention in the research community as well as the enterprise. The goal of QA systems is to automatically answer human questions in a natural language from the given context. In particular, a sample of a QA model often is a pair of a given sequence and a question. Therefore, QA systems require the text understanding of natural language to find the relationship between contexts and questions. However, inputs often contain a lot of redundant information, which is useless for answering. The key research question in most QA systems is how to determine critical sentences and eliminate redundancy.

Based on the complexity of the input, QA systems can be divided into traditional QA systems and modern QA systems. In traditional QA systems [9,20], the input is a single document or passage and a question. The system aims to extract the answer to the question from the document. Figure 1a illustrates the simple process of a traditional QA system. In modern QA systems [2,15], the input contains a collection of documents and a question. Therefore, a typical modern QA system is usually a 2-step process. The first step is the retrieval phase aiming to find the relevant documents. The second step is text understanding, where the reader's goal is to extract answers from the relevant documents. Figure 1b shows the 2-step process of a typical QA system.

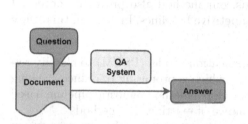 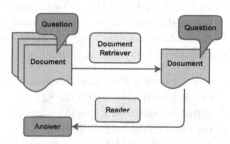

(a) Traditional Question Answering system process. The input is a document containing the answer, and a question. The output is the answer to the question

(b) Modern Question Answering system process. The input is a collection of documents containing the answer, and a question. The output is the answer to the question

Fig. 1. Typical processes of Question Answering systems

One of the core components in QA systems is Machine Reading Comprehension (MRC) as the reader. Machine Reading Comprehension refers to the machine's ability to read, comprehend a given text passage, and answer questions based on it. MRC has increasingly attracted interest in the research community on natural language understanding. The MRC task is proposed as a QA problem where the system automatically extracts answers to questions from a given document. Another essential component that decides a QA system's performance is the Information Retrieval (IR) module. IR refers to the process of retrieving information resources that are relevant to a query from a collection of passages.

In a modern QA system, the input is a list of documents and a question. The length of the input documents is remarkably challenging in modern systems. Therefore, a modern QA system usually has an IR component to extract the relevant documents before extracting the answer via MRC component. In addition, previous works [7,10] have shown that the performance of the machine reading comprehension component can be improved using summarization. It reveals the potential and necessity of IR in modern QA systems where the input information is more massive and diverse.

Distracting information in the context can be a significant factor that reduces the QA model's performance. However, it is still a challenging and ambitious goal in many existing QA approaches. Nguyen et al. [13] proposed ViReader, which employs a phase to select *top-k* sentences in the context that are similar to the question and achieves state-of-the-art performance on Vietnamese QA datasets UIT-ViQuAD [14]. However, this method is constrained by a fixed number k for every context. As a result, it is limited to improve the QA model because different contexts have distracting information with different sizes. Therefore, we propose a flexible Potential Sentence Classification model and pipeline to enhance the performance of current QA systems. Besides, our models are also ideal to be integrated and adapted into most popular QA systems, even in multilingual domains such as Vietnamese documents. Especially to deal with the massive documents in scientific domains, our method also proves its potential and effectiveness against the current competitive baselines. In general, this study makes the following contributions:

- We propose a Potential Sentence Classification Model (PSCM) to classify relevant information from the QA context, which is promising to reduce the long input documents. Especially, we also develop a method-agnostic pipeline based on our PSCM to enhance the performance of existing QA methods.
- Instead of pre-defining a fixed threshold in previous works, we propose an algorithm for adjusting the threshold in our classification model and a delegate process to generate the training dataset for the classification model from the original QA resources.
- We conduct experiments on many kinds of QA datasets, including scientific documents (Qasper), Vietnamese language (ViQuAD), and SQuAD 2.0. The results indicate that our approach successfully improves the performance of existing QA models
- Our pipeline is especially useful in QA on scientific documents, which has massive and complex contexts. Moreover, using the state-of-the-art multilingual model in QA, our pipeline achieves state-of-the-art performance on ViQuAD dataset.

The remainder of this paper is organized as follows: The background and related works are provided in Sect. 2. We also describe the details of our proposed system in Sect. 3. Section 4 presents the results and evaluation of our system. Discussion and analyses of the result are shown in Sect. 5. Finally, Sect. 6 concludes this study and describes directions for future work.

2   Related Works

2.1   Machine Reading Comprehension

MRC is the fundamental component of many proposed QA systems. It plays an important role in extracting the correct answer through understanding the input texts. In previous works, MRC approaches are often divided into two kinds as Traditional Neural Network and Transformer. Firstly, many MRC models based on neural-network are proposed due to the rapid development of high-quality datasets. These models achieve significant results on the common MRC datasets and are more robust than the traditional machine learning approaches utilizing handcrafted features. The typical systems in this kind should be considered such as Match-Long Short Term Memory [22], Bi-directional Attention Flow [21], R-Net [8], DrQA Reader [2], FusionNet [16], FastQA [23], and QANet [25].

On the other hand, the success of the Transformer model in Natural Language Processing is a tremendous inspiration in many areas and MRC. Indeed, many models based on Transformer have been proven to be efficient in various NLP tasks and applications. Recently, BERT [6] and its variants such as XLM-R [4], ALBERT [11] have achieved state-of-the-art performances on MRC datasets. The strength of these approaches comes from pre-trained parameters in the huge datasets. Therefore, to take advantage of these portable language models, we also integrate them into our MRC phase.

2.2   Information Retrieval

In the explosion of text data, IR plays a prominent role in many applications, including QA systems. IR techniques rank information based on its relevance to the query. Based on the type of learning, IR systems are often categorized into supervised and unsupervised learning. At first glance, unsupervised approaches usually employ frequency and probability features such as TF-IDF (term frequency-inverse document frequency), BM25, and TextRank.

On the other hand, approaches based on Transformer perform well on plenty of tasks and are independent of domains. As a result, these algorithms are preferred over previous methods.

2.3   Question-Answering Context Reduction

In previous works, there are some approaches proposed to reduce the QA context to increase the performance as well as decrease the inference times. Min et al. [12] proposed the sentence selector to select the minimal set of sentences to feed into the QA model. However, the coupling between the sentence selector and the QA model in the architecture makes this method inflexible and cannot be applied to any QA model. Our proposed method separates the context reduction module and the QA model, making it model-agnostic. In the Vietnamese language, Nguyen et al. [13] proposed STR as the sentence retrieval component of the ViReader system, a system for QA in the Vietnamese language. By utilizing the advantage of multi-lingual Sentence-BERT [19], STR is useful to extract informative sentences. However, STR performs on ViQuAD and employs the Bi-Encoder architecture of SBERT, while Cross-Encoder achieves better performances than Bi-Encoder [19]. With the context size of the ViQuAD, it is more reasonable to use approaches like the Cross-Encoder to find relevant sentences.

3   The Proposed System

3.1   Overall

Our proposed pipeline consists of two main steps. The first step constructs the reduced context by using a classification model. In particular, the original context is first segmented into sentences. These sentences are then fed to our proposed Potential Sentence Classification Model. A procedure to adjust the threshold of the classification model for each context is applied. Sentences classified as potential are selected to create a new concise context. In the second step, the new context and the question are fed to the QA model to extract the answer span. Figure 2 shows the overall process of our proposed pipeline.

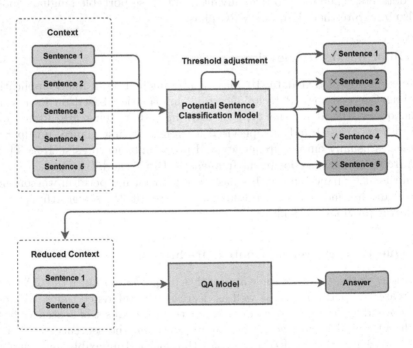

Fig. 2. An overview of proposed system

3.2   Potential Sentence Classification Model

The Potential Sentence Classification Model (PSCM) is the core component of our pipeline. Its input is a pair of sentences: a question and a candidate sentence in the context. The goal of our PSCM is to predict whether the candidate sentence contains the answer to the question or not. We employ the transformer-based approach to build the PSCM. In particular, we utilize RoBERTa [26], XLM-RoBERTa [4], and Sentence-BERT [19] depending on the dataset.

Data Generation and Model Fine-Tuning. We build the PSCM model by employing transfer learning to adapt the pre-trained transformer-based classification model (RoBERTa) to the target QA dataset. To do this, we propose a method for generating the sentence-pair dataset for PSCM training from the QA resources. Particularly, the generation rule is as follows: For a context and a question in the QA training set, if a sentence in the context contains the answer to the question, the classification label for that sentence and the question will be 1. Otherwise, it will be 0. We described the generated dataset for PSCM from SQuAD 2.0 in Sect. 4.

Threshold Adjustment. A fixed threshold can not work well for every question and context. Therefore, we propose a procedure to adjust the threshold for each context and question. Our constraint is that the length of the target context (reduced context) has to be in the range $(minLength, maxLength)$. The $minLength$ and $maxLength$ are hyperparameters and are determined based on the dataset and task. A binary-search technique is employed to find a suitable threshold that satisfies this constraint. Algorithm 1 describes in detail the method to determine the threshold for each context and question. Particularly, the number of sentences or tokens is decided by the threshold of $minLength$ and $maxLength$. The sentences are selected by the relevant score of sentence and question from $PSCM()$ and concatenated by $makeContext()$ to create the new concise context.

3.3   Answer Extraction

The second step of the pipeline uses a QA model to extract the answer span from the context. The QA model concerns only the reduced context. Naturally, our pipeline is model-agnostic and can work with any QA model because the second step is independent of the first step. Because many state-of-the-art models in span-extraction QA are transformer-based, we conduct experiments on our pipeline with various state-of-the-art transformer-based QA models. To extract the answer span from the passage, we follow the implementation of Transformers [24]. In this implementation, we add a span classification head on top of the transformer model. The span classification head is a linear layer on top of the hidden-states output to compute the span start and end logits. The final answer is calculated using the span start logits and the span end logits. The valid pair

---

Algorithm 1. Threshold adjustment algorithm

Require: $minLength, maxLength, question, context$
Ensure: $minLength < maxLength$
  $minThreshold \leftarrow 0$
  $maxThreshold \leftarrow 1$
  while $minThreshold < maxThreshold$ **do**
    $threshold \leftarrow (minThreshold + maxThreshold)/2$
    $sentences \leftarrow sentenceSegment(context)$
    $potentialSentences \leftarrow PSCM(sentences, question)$
    $reducedContext \leftarrow makeContext(potentialSentences)$
    if length of $reducedContext <= minLength$ **then**
      $maxThreshold \leftarrow threshold$
    else if length of $reducedContext >= maxLength$ **then**
      $minThreshold \leftarrow threshold$
    else
      return $threshold$
    end if
  end while

---

of start and end logit with the highest sum of the two values is chosen. The answer start and end position are the positions of the tokens with the selected start logit and end logit, respectively.

4 Experiments and Results

4.1 Dataset

To prove the effectiveness and flexibility of our model, we train and evaluate our model on three different datasets and some existing and popular QA models. The detail of these datasets are introduced as follows:

- **Qasper** [5] is a QA dataset on Natural Language Processing (NLP) papers where questions and answers are provided by NLP practitioners. The context for each question is an entire scientific research paper whose size is massive compared to other QA datasets. Qasper is shown to be challenging for existing state-of-the-art models.
- **UIT-ViQuAD** [14] is one of the first span-extraction datasets for Vietnamese MRC systems, created manually through crowd-sourcing based on the Vietnamese Wikipedia. It contains over 23,000 question-answer pairs created manually by humans. These question-answer pairs come from about 5,000 passages. It is considered one of a few large-scale Wikipedia-based datasets available for evaluating Vietnamese QA systems.
- **SQuAD 2.0** [17] is a reading comprehension dataset, consisting of questions posed by crowd-workers on a set of Wikipedia articles, where the answer to every question is a segment of text, or span, from the corresponding reading passage. SQuAD 2.0 combines the 100,000 questions in SQuAD1.1 [18] with over 50,000 unanswerable questions written adversarially by crowd-workers to look similar to answerable ones.

The data analyses of three datasets are shown in Table 1. There are three main points in our comparison. Firstly, it is valuable to prove the effectiveness of our model in the general domain via SQuAD 2.0 against the most popular QA systems. Secondly, we also emphasize the potential of our pipeline in multilingual adaption via the Vietnamese UIT-ViQuAD dataset. It reveals the novelty of our model in this language, where we propose the flexible threshold in context filtering. Finally, we also point out the promising results of our models in scientific documents whose contexts are highly huge in length.

Table 1. The detailed analysis of the datasets in the experiments.

Dataset	Detail	All	Train	Dev	Test
Qasper	#questions	5,049	2,593	1,005	1,451
SQuAD 2.0	#articles	505	442	35	28
	#questions	151,051	130,319	11,873	8,862
UIT-ViQuAD	#articles	174	138	18	18
	#passages	5,109	4,101	515	493
	#questions	23,074	18,579	2,285	2,210
	Average passage length	153.4	153.9	147.9	155.0
	Average question length	12.2	12.2	11.9	12.2
	Average answer length	8.2	8.1	8.4	8.9
	Vocabulary size (words)	41,773	36,174	9,184	9,792

As we mentioned above, we also propose a process to generate the dataset for the PSCM module. We apply the proposed method to generate the dataset for training the PSCM module from UIT-ViQuAD and SQuAD 2.0. The detail of our extracted dataset is presented in Table 2. For Qasper dataset, a context for a question is an entire paper, and the negative sentences (sentences that do not contain the answer) are dominant compared to positive sentences (sentences containing the answer). As a result, the process of generating training data for PSCM for Qasper is not trivial and requires more research. Therefore, we do not fine-tune the PSCM module in our experiments on Qasper dataset.

Table 2. Overview of the generated datasets for PSCM.

Source Dataset	Detail	All	Train	Validation
UIT-ViQuAD	Number of samples	116,038	102,972	13,066
	Number of label 1	20,865	18,579	2,286
	Number of label 0	95,173	84,393	10,780
SQuAD	Number of samples	718,295	655,404	62,891
	Number of label 1	106,113	98,439	7,674
	Number of label 0	612,182	556,965	55,217

4.2   Models

Models for Qasper Dataset. For the PSCM module, we employ SBERT [19] and the pre-trained SBERT model **all-mpnet-base-v2** to get the embedding of sentences. The cosine-similarity score between the sentence in the context and the question is calculated and compared with the threshold to choose the potential sentences. For answer extraction, we employ the implementation of **Qasper-LED** model proposed by [5], which is based on Longformer-Encoder-Decoder (LED) [1]. We conduct experiments to evaluate the improvement of Qasper-LED when applying our pipeline.

Models for UIT-ViQuAD Dataset. For the PSCM, the multilingual model XLM-RoBERTa$_{Large}$ with a sequence regression head on top is used. We utilize the implementation of XLMRobertaForSequenceClassification from Wolf et al. [24]. For answer extraction, the following state-of-the-art multilingual QA models are applied.

- **Multilingual BERT (mBERT)** [6]: The multilingual version of BERT, one of the most popular models in many NLP tasks. mBERT is pre-trained in 104 languages, including Vietnamese.
- **XLM-RoBERTa** [4]: A state-of-the-art multilingual model that has significant performance for a variety of cross-lingual transfer tasks. In our experiments, we evaluate two versions of this model, XLM-RoBERTa$_{Base}$ and XLM-RoBERTa$_{Large}$.

We also conducted experiments to compare our method with the ViReader system, one of the state-of-the-art MRC systems trained and evaluated in Vietnamese. For comparison, we take the ViReader API and training source codes from the original paper and reproduce the result in our experiment environment.

Models for SQuAD 2.0 Dataset. For the PSCM, we use RoBERTa$_{Large}$ with a sequence regression head on top is used. We utilize the implementation of RobertaForSequenceClassification from Wolf et al. [24]. For answer extraction, the following methods are used.

- **RoBERTa**: The model was proposed by Zhuang et al. [26]. It improves BERT by adjusting key hyperparameters, removing the next-sentence pretraining objective, and training with much larger mini-batches and learning rates. For the QA task, RoBERTa achieves remarkable results in SQuAD 2.0 dataset. We conduct experiments on two versions of RoBERTa (Base and Large).
- **ELECTRA**: The model was proposed by Clark et al. [3]. It employs a new pretraining approach that trains two transformer models: the generator and the discriminator. ELECTRA achieves noticeable results on QA benchmarks like SQuAD and HotpotQA. We conduct experiments on the Base version of ELECTRA

– **BERT**: The model was proposed by Devlin et al. [6] as a bidirectional transformer pre-trained using a mixture of masked language modeling objective and next sentence prediction. We conduct experiments on the Base-Case version BERT.

4.3 Experimental Results

We first conduct an experiment to evaluate the performance of the PSCM module. The PSCM module is trained using the train set and evaluated using the validation set in the dataset described above. Table 3 shows the result of the PSCM module evaluation.

Table 3. Result of the PSCM module evaluation on the generated dataset

Source Dataset	Accuracy (%)	AUPRC (%)	AUROC (%)	Precision (%)	Recall (%)	F1 (%)
SQuAD 2.0	94.36	81.18	94.19	84.47	65.90	74.04
UIT-ViQuAD	91.47	87.23	94.46	89.36	66.49	76.25

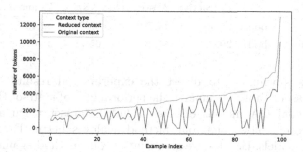

(a) Lengths of original and reduced contexts in 100 examples in Qasper

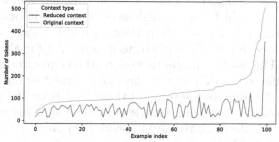

(b) Lengths of original and reduced contexts in 100 examples in SQuAD 2.0

Fig. 3. Comparing the number of tokens in the original and reduced contexts

To visualize how much our method reduced the context in the SQuAD dataset. We randomly sample several examples from the SQuAD dataset and plot the lengths of the original contexts and the contexts reduced by our method. We sort the examples based on the original context lengths to make them easy to interpret. Figure 3 visualizes the amount of distracting information removed by employing our method. The space between the "Original context" line and the "Reduced context" line denotes the portion of the context reduced by our method.

After proving the strength of our proposed module to reduce the context, we also present the effectiveness of our pipeline in general QA systems. Firstly, Table 4 shows the overall results of Qasper-LED model on the Qasper test set when applying our pipeline to improve the performance. The result is shown with the performance breakdown on the different answer types. The result reveals that our pipeline successfully enhances the overall performance of Qasper-LED, especially in Extractive and Yes/No questions. The other types of questions, including Abstractive and Unanswerable are not suitable for context reduction. The reason for this phenomenon comes from its requirement of the general relationship in content to find out the abstract answer as well as conflict between input documents and questions.

Table 4. Result on Qasper dataset of single model and our method

Method	Extractive	Abstractive	Yes/No	Unanswerable	Overall
Qasper-LED (Single Model)	27.53	14.78	60.87	49.49	30.58
Qasper-LED (Our Method)	29.69	14.31	65.78	41.67	**31.30**

Secondly, it is valuable to digest the experimental results in the Vietnamese QA dataset. Table 5 compares the performance of state-of-the-art methods in multilingual QA models on the ViQuAD dataset when applying our pipeline. The result shows that our method achieves better F1 scores in all three evaluated models. Besides, we also compare our method against the SOTA QA system in UIT-ViQuAD named ViReader. Table 6 presents the details of our comparison. In particular, we use the version of our method applying on XLM-RoBERTa$_{Large}$, which has the highest performance in our experiment on ViQuAD. It is easily noticed that the performance of ViReader depends on the number of sentences (K) which is pre-defined and fixed for all samples in the retrieval module. The result indicates that our method outperforms the ViReader on the ViQuAD dataset with a flexible threshold learned by our Algorithm 1.

Finally, Table 7 compares the result of these models on the general domain via SQuAD 2.0 dataset when using a single model and applying our pipeline. We use the metric Exact Match (EM), and F1 score (F1) proposed by Rajpurkar et al. [18] for evaluation. The result shows that our method produces better results when applied to any of the four models. In the RoBERTa Large model, our method successfully increases the EM to 82.69% (almost 1.0 point improvement) and the F1 score to 85.78% (over 1.0 point improvement).

Table 5. Result on UIT-ViQuAD dataset of single model and our method

Model	Single Model		Our Method	
	EM	F1	EM	F1
XLM-RoBERTa $_{Large}$	**73.59**	88.74	73.27	**89.06**
XLM-RoBERTa $_{Base}$	63.72	81.54	**64.08**	**82.56**
mBERT	58.83	77.72	**59.82**	**78.98**

Table 6. Compares our method(applying on XLM-RoBERTa) and the ViReader. The ViReader depends on the numbers of sentences (K) in the retrieval step

K-sentences retrieved	ViReader		Our Method (with XLM-RoBERTa$_{Large}$)	
	EM	F1	EM	F1
1	55.20	67.94	73.27	**89.06**
2	63.90	78.92		
3	69.29	84.57		
4	71.37	86.83		
5	72.19	87.70		
6	73.41	88.52		
7	73.46	88.50		
8	73.55	88.60		
9	73.59	88.74		
10	73.59	88.80		

Table 7. Result on SQuAD dataset of single model and our method

Model	Single Model		Our Method	
	EM	F1	EM	F1
RoBERTa $_{Large}$	81.75	84.57	**82.69**	**85.78**
RoBERTa $_{Base}$	76.48	79.48	**78.94**	**82.02**
ELECTRA $_{Base}$	64.64	69.15	**65.01**	**69.46**
BERT	71.47	74.98	**71.78**	**75.25**

5   Discussion

To provide a better understanding of the improvements and the limits of our proposed methods for the sentence retrieval module, we discuss two examples in this section.

Table 8. Example in SQuAD 2.0 where distracting information affects the model decision. The correct answer is highlight in red

Question: Who was the duke in the battle of Hastings?
Answer: William the Conqueror
The Reduced Context: Norman adventurers founded the Kingdom of Sicily under Roger II after conquering southern Italy on the Saracens and Byzantines, and an expedition on behalf of their duke, William the Conqueror, led to the Norman conquest of England at the Battle of Hastings in 1066.
RoBERTa answer: "William the Conqueror"
Score: $EM = 1, F1 = 1$
The Original Context: The Norman dynasty had a major political, cultural and military impact on medieval Europe and even the Near East. The Normans were famed for their martial spirit and eventually for their Christian piety, becoming exponents of the Catholic orthodoxy into which they assimilated. They adopted the Gallo-Romance language of the Frankish land they settled, their dialect becoming known as Norman, Normaund or Norman French, an important literary language. The Duchy of Normandy, which they formed by treaty with the French crown, was a great fief of medieval France, and under Richard I of Normandy was forged into a cohesive and formidable principality in feudal tenure. The Normans are noted both for their culture, such as their unique Romanesque architecture and musical traditions, and for their significant military accomplishments and innovations. Norman adventurers founded the Kingdom of Sicily under Roger II after conquering southern Italy on the Saracens and Byzantines, and an expedition on behalf of their duke, William the Conqueror, led to the Norman conquest of England at the Battle of Hastings in 1066. Norman cultural and military influence spread from these new European centres to the Crusader states of the Near East, where their prince Bohemond I founded the Principality of Antioch in the Levant, to Scotland and Wales in Great Britain, to Ireland, and to the coasts of north Africa and the Canary Islands.
RoBERTa answer: "" (empty string)
Score: $EM = 0, F1 = 0$

Table 8 shows the first example where distracting information affects the model decision in SQuAD 2.0. The highlighted text is the exact answer to the question in this example. With the reduced context, RoBERTa model can answer with F1 score $= 1$ and Exact Match $= 1$. With the original context, the same RoBERTa model can not identify the answer span and arrive at the empty string answer, with the F1 score $= 0$ and Exact Match $= 0$. This example indicates that our pipeline selects the sentences that contain the answer span and successfully removes distracting information. In addition, it also shows that too many distracting details can hurt the QA model's performance noticeably.

Table 9. Compares the context reduced using our pipeline and using ViReader retrieval module. The correct answer is highlight in red

Question: Hơn phân nửa số người Đức nhưng không có quyền công dân Đức là sống ở đâu? (*Where do more than half of Germans without German citizenship live?*)
Answer: miền tây của liên bang và hầu hết là tại các khu vực đô thị (*western part of the federation and mostly in urban areas*)
Our retrieved passage: Có khoảng 5 triệu người có quốc tịch Đức cư trú tại nước ngoài (2012). Năm 2014, có khoảng bảy triệu người trong số 81 triệu cư dân Đức không có quyền công dân Đức. Sáu mươi chín phần trăm trong số đó sống tại miền tây của liên bang và hầu hết là tại các khu vực đô thị. Đức xếp hạng bảy trong EU và thứ 37 toàn cầu về tỷ lệ người nhập cư so với tổng dân số. Từ năm 1987, có khoảng 3 triệu người dân tộc Đức, hầu hết từ các quốc gia Khối phía Đông, đã thực hiện quyền trở về của mình và di cư đến Đức. (*There are about 5 million German nationals residing abroad (2012). In 2014, about seven million of Germany's 81 million residents did not have German citizenship. Sixty-nine percent of them live in the western part of the federation and most are in urban areas. Germany ranks seventh in the EU and 37th globally in terms of immigration to total population. Since 1987, about 3 million ethnic Germans, mostly from Eastern Bloc countries, have exercised their right to return and emigrate to Germany*)
Our answer: miền tây của liên bang và hầu hết là tại các khu vực đô thị (*western part of the federation and mostly in urban areas*)   **Score:** $EM = 1, F1 = 1$
The STR retrieved passage: Có khoảng 5 triệu người có quốc tịch Đức cư trú tại nước ngoài (2012). Năm 2014, có khoảng bảy triệu người trong số 81 triệu cư dân Đức không có quyền công dân Đức. Năm 2015, Đức là quốc gia có số lượng di dân quốc tế cao thứ hai thế giới, với khoảng 5% hay 12 triệu người. Đức xếp hạng bảy trong EU và thứ 37 toàn cầu về tỷ lệ người nhập cư so với tổng dân số. Từ năm 1987, có khoảng 3 triệu người dân tộc Đức, hầu hết từ các quốc gia Khối phía Đông, đã thực hiện quyền trở về của mình và di cư đến Đức. (*There are about 5 million German nationals residing abroad (2012). In 2014, about seven million of Germany's 81 million residents did not have German citizenship. In 2015, Germany was the country with the second highest number of international migrants in the world, with about 5 % or 12 million people. Germany ranks seventh in the EU and 37th globally in terms of immigration to total population. Since 1987, about 3 million ethnic Germans, mostly from Eastern Bloc countries, have exercised their right to return and emigrate to Germany.*)
The reproduced ViReader's answer: nước ngoài (*foreign country*)   **Score:** $EM = 0, F1 = 0$

Table 9 shows the contexts reduced using our pipeline and using ViReader retrieval module. In this example, the highlighted text is the exact answer to the question. Our system has the correct answer with F1 score = 1 and Exact Match = 1 while the ViReader's answer has F1 score = 0 and Exact Match = 0. It is clear that our system successfully retrieves the sentence that contains the answer span. This enables the answer extracting model to find the correct answer. In contrast, the ViReader retrieval module cannot retrieve the sentence with the answer span. This leads to poor results in the answer extraction module.

6 Conclusion

In this paper, we propose a novel model-agnostic pipeline to remove distracting information from the contexts of the span-extraction QA task. The proposed method successfully improves existing QA models ' performance through the Potential Sentence Classification Model (PSCM) and the Threshold Adjustment algorithm. In addition, we also propose a delegate process to extract the training dataset for PSCM from the original QA resources. The experimental results show that our method remarkably enhances existing QA models and can be applied to a wide range of models and datasets. Our pipeline is especially useful in QA in scientific documents, which have massive and complex contexts. In addition, using the state-of-the-art multilingual model in QA, our pipeline achieve state-of-the-art performance on ViQuAD dataset in Vietnamese. Our detailed discussion reveals how distracting information affects the model's decision and the necessity of our method.

References

1. Beltagy, I., Peters, M.E., Cohan, A.: Longformer: the long-document transformer. ArXiv abs/2004.05150 (2020)
2. Chen, D., Fisch, A., Weston, J., Bordes, A.: Reading Wikipedia to answer open-domain questions. In: ACL (2017)
3. Clark, K., Luong, M.T., Le, Q.V., Manning, C.D.: ELECTRA: pre-training text encoders as discriminators rather than generators. In: ICLR (2020)
4. Conneau, A., et al.: Unsupervised cross-lingual representation learning at scale. In: Proceedings of the 58th Annual Meeting of the Association for Computational Linguistics, pp. 8440–8451 (Jnaury 2020)
5. Dasigi, P., Lo, K., Beltagy, I., Cohan, A., Smith, N.A., Gardner, M.: A dataset of information-seeking questions and answers anchored in research papers. In: NAACL (2021)
6. Devlin, J., Chang, M., Lee, K., Toutanova, K.: BERT: pre-training of deep bidirectional transformers for language understanding. In: Burstein, J., Doran, C., Solorio, T. (eds.) Proceedings of the 2019 Conference of the North American Chapter of the Association for Computational Linguistics: Human Language Technologies, NAACL-HLT 2019, Minneapolis, MN, USA, 2–7 June 2019, Volume 1 (Long and Short Papers), pp. 4171–4186. Association for Computational Linguistics (2019)
7. Duke, N.K., Pearson, P.D.: Effective practices for developing reading comprehension. J. Educ. **1–2**, 107–122 (2009)
8. Group, N.L.C.: R-Net: machine reading comprehension with self-matching networks (May 2017)
9. Harabagiu, S., Moldovan, D., Clark, C., Bowden, M., Williams, J., Bensley, J.: Answer mining by combining extraction techniques with abductive reasoning. pp. 375–382 (January 2003)
10. Khoshsima, H., Tiyar, F.: The effect of summarizing strategy on reading comprehension of Iranian intermediate EFL learners. Int. J. Lang. Linguist. **2**, 134–139 (Jnaury 2014)
11. Lan, Z., Chen, M., Goodman, S., Gimpel, K., Sharma, P., Soricut, R.: ALBERT: a lite BERT for self-supervised learning of language representations (2020)

12. Min, S., Zhong, V., Socher, R., Xiong, C.: Efficient and robust question answering from minimal context over documents. In: Proceedings of the 56th Annual Meeting of the Association for Computational Linguistics (Volume 1: Long Papers). pp. 1725–1735. Association for Computational Linguistics, Melbourne, Australia (July 2018). https://doi.org/10.18653/v1/P18-1160
13. Nguyen, K., Nguyen, N., Do, P., Nguyen, A., Nguyen, N.: ViReader: a Wikipedia-based Vietnamese reading comprehension system using transfer learning. J. Intell. Fuzzy Syst. **41**, 1–19 (2021)
14. Nguyen, K., Nguyen, V., Nguyen, A., Nguyen, N.: A Vietnamese dataset for evaluating machine reading comprehension. In: Proceedings of the 28th International Conference on Computational Linguistics, pp. 2595–2605. International Committee on Computational Linguistics, Barcelona, Spain (Online) (December 2020)
15. Noraset, T., Lowphansirikul, L., Tuarob, S.: WabiQA: a Wikipedia-based Thai question-answering system. Inf. Process. Manag. **41**, 102431 (2021)
16. Quan, T.M., Hildebrand, D.G.C., Jeong, W.K.: FusionNet: a deep fully residual convolutional neural network for image segmentation in connectomics. Front. Comput. Sci. **3** (May 2021)
17. Rajpurkar, P., Jia, R., Liang, P.: Know what you don't know: Unanswerable questions for SQuAD. In: Proceedings of the 56th Annual Meeting of the Association for Computational Linguistics (Volume 2: Short Papers), pp. 784–789. Association for Computational Linguistics, Melbourne, Australia (July 2018)
18. Rajpurkar, P., Zhang, J., Lopyrev, K., Liang, P.: SQuAD: 100,000+ questions for machine comprehension of text. In: Proceedings of the 2016 Conference on Empirical Methods in Natural Language Processing, pp. 2383–2392. Association for Computational Linguistics, Austin, Texas (November 2016)
19. Reimers, N., Gurevych, I.: Sentence-BERT: Sentence embeddings using siamese BERT-networks, pp. 3973–3983 (January 2019)
20. Ryu, P.M., Jang, M.G., Kim, H.: Open domain question answering using Wikipedia-based knowledge model. Inf. Process. Manag. **50**, pp. 683–692 (2014)
21. Seo, M., Kembhavi, A., Farhadi, A., Hajishirzi, H.: Bidirectional attention flow for machine comprehension. In: ICLR (November 2016)
22. Wang, S., Jiang, J.: Learning natural language inference with LSTM. In; Proceedings of the 2016 Conference of the North American Chapter of the Association for Computational Linguistics: Human Language Technologies (December 2015)
23. Weissenborn, D., Wiese, G., Seiffe, L.:FastQA: a simple and efficient neural architecture for question answering (2017)
24. Wolf, T., et al.: Transformers: State-of-the-art natural language processing. In: Proceedings of the 2020 Conference on Empirical Methods in Natural Language Processing: System Demonstrations, pp. 38–45. Association for Computational Linguistics, Online (October 2020)
25. Yu, A., et al.: QANet: combining local convolution with global self-attention for reading comprehension. In; ICLR (April 2018)
26. Zhuang, L., Wayne, L., Ya, S., Jun, Z.: A robustly optimized BERT pre-training approach with post-training. In: Proceedings of the 20th Chinese National Conference on Computational Linguistics, pp. 1218–1227. Chinese Information Processing Society of China, Huhhot, China (August 2021)

KANSEIAI 2021

Kansei and Artificial Intelligence 2021

Koichi Yamagata(iD)

The University of Electro-Communication, 1-5-1 Chofugaoka, Tokyo 182-8285,
Japan
koichi.yamagata@uec.ac.jp

1 The Workshop

On November 14, 2021, a workshop of Kansei and Artificial Intelligence (KANSEI-AI) took place online. It was one of workshops of the JSAI International Symposia on AI (JSAI-isAI 2021), sponsored by The Japan Society for Artificial Intelligence (JSAI),

The purpose of this workshop was to share the progress of research and to share methodology by researchers studying the five senses. Various perceptions through the five senses are used in our decision making and executions. Our level of understanding and methodology differ in each of the five senses. Researches in visual-texture perception are said to be the most developed among all. However, the neural mechanism of visual-texture perception remains unclear for the most part. Thus, there is no established way to reproduce the mechanism with artificial intelligence. The scope of this workshop was research of science and engineering related to value judgements made through the five senses, such as image processing, tactile engineering, acoustics, machine learning, sensitivity engineering, and natural language processing.

There were two speakers giving talks on texture and kansei. The first lecture was "Ketchup GAN: A New Dataset for Realistic Synthesis of Letters on Food" by Dr. Gibran Benitez-Garcia (The University of Electro-Communications). The second one is "The influence of visual context on the naturalness impression of auditory stimuli" by Dr. Watanabe (The University of Electro-Communications). Both of these studies were challenging and unique. From them, one research was selected by the committee for this volume.

2 Paper

There is one paper by Dr. Watanabe et al. in the KANSEI-AI part of the present volume. The title of this paper is "The influence of visual context on the naturalness impression of auditory stimuli". This study is a fundamental research of kansei. The authors investigate in detail the influence of visual information on kansei. This research topic is very challenging since kansei is mostly a mystery and unknown field. The evaluation method using onomatopoeia adopted in the subject experiments is very unique.

Acknowledgements. Let me acknowledge those who helped with the workshop. The program committee and organisers were Yuji Nozaki and myself. The organisers would like to thank JSAI for giving us the opportunity to hold the workshop.

The Influence of Visual Context on the Naturalness Impression of Auditory Stimuli

Ryo Watanabe[1](✉), Takuya Koumura[2], Hiroki Terashima[2], Shigeto Furukawa[2], and Maki Sakamoto[1]

[1] Department of Informatics, The University of Electro-Communications, 1-5-1 Chofugaoka, Chofu 182-8585, Tokyo, Japan
rwatanabe@mail.dendai.ac.jp

[2] NTT Communication Science Laboratories, Nippon Telegraph and Telephone Corporation, 3-1 Morinosato Wakamiya, Atsugi-Shi, Kanagawa 243-0198, Japan

Abstract. We conducted two experiments that investigated the effect of visual context on the naturalness of auditory stimuli. The visual context was provided by two images with different natural senses in Experiment 1. In Experiment 2, participants evaluated auditory stimuli presented in two rooms that would give a different sense of nature. The participants' evaluations were done by the SD method and onomatopoeic responses. Onomatopoeia is considered to represent multiple sensory information and has the advantage that it is easy to obtain intuitive impressions. The results showed that the visual context influenced the impressions of auditory stimuli. The naturalness of the visual context influenced the phonology of the answered onomatopoeia.

Keywords: Naturalness · Cross-modal perception · Audio-Visual · Onomatopoeia

1 Introduction

In the field of texture perception, the importance of "naturalness" has been discussed. It is known that humans tend to prefer natural things to artificial ones, and naturalness influences human choices such as purchasing behavior [1–3]. The perception of naturalness is characterized by single or multiple sensory information [4, 5]. For example, the sense of temperature and the sense of hardness and softness are related to the perception of natural sensation as tactile information, and the sense of color and gloss are related to the perception of naturalness as visual information [6]. In the case of different types of sensory information as cues, the perceived naturalness also differs. Overvliet & Soto-Faraco conducted an experiment to evaluate the perceived naturalness of an object, and found different ratings among visual information only, tactile information only, and both visual and tactile information [1]. In their experiment, they evaluated the naturalness of an object using both visual and tactile information. This indicates that there is a difference in the evaluation of the sense of nature depending on the type of sensory

© Springer Nature Switzerland AG 2023
K. Yada et al. (Eds.): JSAI-isAI 2021 Workshops, LNAI 13856, pp. 317–329, 2023.
https://doi.org/10.1007/978-3-031-36190-6_22

information, and that when multiple sensory information is obtained simultaneously, they affect each other. For the evaluation of the sense of naturalness, there is a possibility that vision influences hearing, as in the example above. It is well known that there is a close interrelationship between human vision and hearing. In particular, many studies on spatial localization of stimuli have been conducted over the years, and it has been shown that when audiovisual stimuli are presented simultaneously, auditory stimuli are mislocalized closer to visual stimuli than they actually are [7, 8]. Similarly, it is known that when there is a temporal difference in the presentation of audiovisual stimuli, the temporal localization of audio stimuli is mislocalized closer to the visual stimuli [9, 10]. These spatiotemporal mislocalizations have been shown to become less effective as the spatiotemporal distance between stimuli increases [11, 12]. On the other hand, the effect of visual stimuli on the impression of auditory stimuli has also been studied. For example, it has been reported that visual stimuli affect the perceived reverberation of room sounds [12, 13]. In addition, from the perspective of urban environment development, it has been shown that visual factors affect the sensory evaluation of sound [14–16].

Many studies, including those mentioned above, have used the semantic differential (SD) technique method as an evaluation method to quantify sensation, including the sense of naturalness. On the other hand, onomatopoeia (a general term for onomatopoeic and mimetic words) has also been employed in recent years for sensitivity evaluation. Onomatopoeias are mainly onomatopoeic words that imitate physical sounds perceived through the sense of hearing with verbal sounds, but they can also be used as mimetic words that imitate sensations other than sound, such as sight and touch, with verbal sounds. It has been conventionally indicated that the phonemes that make up onomatopoeia have sound symbolism [17–19]. Sound symbolism means that the sound itself is associated with some image. In psychology, many studies on sound symbolism have been conducted since early times. The Bouba/Kiki Effect, which showed that differences in visual impressions are associated with speech sounds, is a famous example [20, 21]. In this study, we focus on onomatopoeia, which is known to associate not only visual impressions other than sound with linguistic sounds, but also impressions from multiple sensory modalities such as touch and taste, and investigate whether vision affects sound impressions [24, 25]. Onomatopoeia is cross-modal in that it reflects multiple sensory impressions and is associated with higher-order sensory impressions such as pleasure and displeasure. Sakamoto have developed a system to quantify the impressions of an arbitrary onomatopoeia, which can be reflected on a total of 43 sensory scales including tactile-related scales, such as "bright-dark," "smooth-sticky," "natural-artificial" and "luxurious-cheap" [22]. In the output results of the system shown in Fig. 1, it can be seen that when the onomatopoeia "huho-huho," which can be used to express impressions of physical sounds, is input, not only is the impression of "soft" the strongest, but impressions such as naturalness are also strong.

In this study, we also use this system to investigate whether vision influences auditory impressions in different ways of perceiving "naturalness".

By using onomatopoeia to evaluate the influence of vision on sound impressions, we expect to be able to obtain the sound impressions themselves. If the onomatopoeia reflects a sense of nature, we can analyze the unconscious influence of vision on sound impressions.

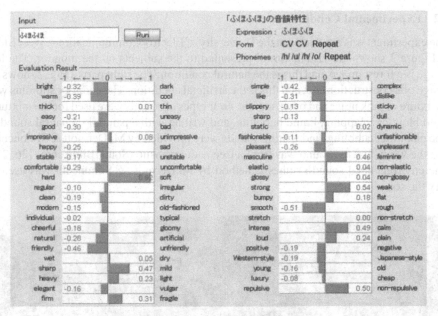

Fig. 1. Evaluation system for onomatopoeia [22, 23]

In this study, we investigate the effect of visual stimuli on the evaluation of sound impressions, especially naturalness, by means of two kinds of experiments. In Experiment 1, we used two types of landscape images as visual stimuli, and subjects gazed at the images on a flat display. Subjects were asked to evaluate their impressions of the auditory stimuli presented simultaneously with the images. In Experiment 2, the room environment was used as a visual stimulus. The subjects enter one of the two rooms with different interior styles and evaluate the impression of the auditory stimuli presented in the room. In the case of viewing images on the monitor, the visual stimuli occupy only a part of the field of view, while in the case of evaluating in the room environment, the visual stimuli cover the entire field of view. In addition to the 7-point SD method, onomatopoeic responses were used in the evaluation. The two experiments were conducted under the approval of the Ethics Committee of the University of Electro-Communications.

2 Evaluation Experiment 1: Influence of Images on the Monitor on Sound Evaluation

Subjects were asked to evaluate their impressions of sound when they listened to a sound while viewing an image that was considered to be highly natural (natural condition) and viewing an image that was considered to be less natural (artificial condition).

2.1 Subjects

Thirty subjects (15 males and 15 females, mean age 21.5 years, standard deviation 1.09 years) participated in the study.

2.2 Experimental Conditions

The experiment was conducted at the University of Electro-Communications, West Bldg. 6. Figure 2 shows the visual stimuli presented to the subjects on the monitor. The left image is a forest image, and this is the natural condition. The right part of Fig. 2 shows an image of a construction site, and this is the artificial condition. The auditory stimulus was a mixture of pink noise and other sounds. Four types of sounds were used for the mixture: wind blowing, clapping, liquid bubbling, and writing with a pen (all monaural sounds). The clapping, bubbling, and writing sounds were provided by McDermott & Simoncelli, and the wind blowing sound was from a free audio website (SoundBible.com) [26, 27]. The environmental sound synthesis method by McDermott & Simoncelli was used to mix the sounds.

Fig. 2. Visual stimuli (left: natural condition, right: artificial condition)

2.3 Experimental Procedure

Subjects were seated in a chair in front of the experimental desk and wore headphones. In each trial, while the subject was gazing at either of the visual stimuli on a monitor, an auditory stimulus was presented through headphones. After the end of the stimulus, the subjects rated their impressions of the audio using onomatopoeia. The subjects then rated their impressions of the sounds on a 7-point scale from -3 to $+3$ for four adjective pairs for SD method: natural-artificial, luxurious-cheap, modern-old-fashioned, and comfortable-uncomfortable. Negative values were given to "natural," "luxurious," "modern," and "comfortable" in each scale. Of the four scales, the main focus was on "natural-artificial" and the remaining three scales were dummies. Subjects performed the above procedure once for each condition, in a random order, a total of 18 times (2 conditions for visual stimuli × 9 conditions for auditory stimuli).

3 Evaluation Experiment 2: Influence of Indoor Environment on Sound Evaluation

While Experiment 1 used images on a monitor as visual stimuli, Experiment 2 uses a more environmental context, the space around the subject. Specifically, we used a Japanese-style room and an inorganic room (Fig. 3) as visual stimuli, and subjects evaluated the impressions of auditory stimuli in the same way as in Experiment 1.

3.1 Subjects

The same 30 subjects as in Experiment 1 participated.

3.2 Experimental Conditions

The environment of the visual stimulus is shown in Fig. 3. The Japanese room in the left part of Fig. 3 is the natural condition, and the room in the right part of Fig. 3 is the artificial condition. The Japanese room in the natural condition consists of tatami mats, shoji screens, and wood-grained pillars, while the room in the artificial condition has a flat floor and walls without any undulations. In both conditions, no furniture is placed in the room except for a monitor and a desk.

Fig. 3. Experimental environment (left: natural conditions, right: artificial conditions)

3.3 Experimental Procedure

The subject was seated in the center of the room and wore headphones. The subject faced the front of the monitor and the auditory stimulus was presented through the headphones. After the end of the stimulus, the subjects completed the scale evaluation and onomatopoeic response as in the evaluation experiment 1. The subjects performed the above procedures once for each condition, for a total of 18 times (9 times for each of the two visual conditions).

4 Experimental Results

4.1 Analysis of Scale and Response Results by SD Method

The response values for each adjective pair and each visual condition were tabulated, and the differences between the natural and artificial conditions were tested by t-test. Figure 4 shows the scale response results for Evaluation Experiment 1 and Evaluation Experiment 2. For each of the four adjective pairs, the mean values of the natural and artificial conditions are shown (the error bars on the following graphs indicate the standard error, with "natural," "luxurious," "modern," and "comfortable" of each scale being negative values). There was a significant difference at p < 0.1 between the natural and artificial conditions for each of the four scales in both experiments. In the following, when the term "significant difference" is used, it means those with p < 0.001. In this paper, multiple tests were conducted, including the analysis described below, but no correction was made for these comparisons.

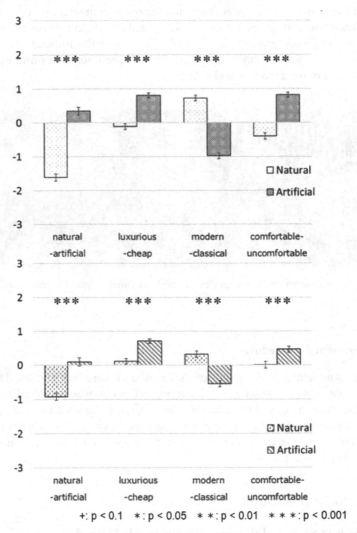

+: p < 0.1   *: p < 0.05   * *: p < 0.01   * * *: p < 0.001

Fig. 4. Results of responses using the SD method (upper: Experiment 1, lower: Experiment 2)

4.2 Analysis of the Results of Quantifying Onomatopoeia with the System

In order to analyze the onomatopoeia answered by the subjects, we used the evaluation system for onomatopoeia [22]. This system can quantify the impression of any onomatopoeia input by the user. The system is based on a set of data on the effects of phonemes on texture impressions, which were quantified by psychological experiments on the sounds that make up the onomatopoeia. The system can quantify 43 sensory scales selected based on Japanese dictionaries and previous studies.

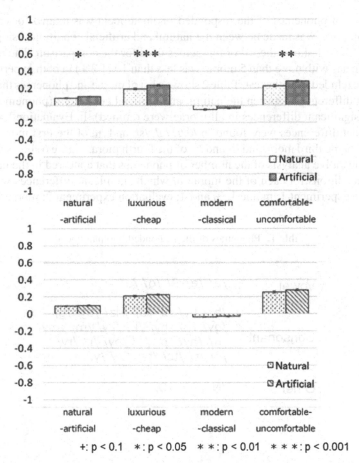

+ : p < 0.1   * : p < 0.05   * * : p < 0.01   * * * : p < 0.001

Fig. 5. Onomatopoeia analysis results (upper: evaluation experiment 1, lower: evaluation experiment 2)

In this experiment, we focused on the four scales that are common to the ones used in the SD method among the 43 scales. The advantage of this system is that it can acquire dozens of sensory information from a single onomatopoeia, but in this paper, since the items to be evaluated have already been decided, we limit ourselves to the above four scales.

Figure 5 shows the results of the first evaluation experiment and the second evaluation experiment. For each of the four scales, the average values for natural and artificial conditions are shown. There were significant differences between the natural and artificial conditions for the three scales of "natural-artificial," "luxurious-cheap," and "comfortable-uncomfortable" in Evaluation Experiment 1, while there were no significant differences for all scales in Evaluation Experiment 2.

4.3   Analysis of the Number of Phonemes of the Onomatopoeia that Appeared

The number of phonemes of the responded onomatopoeia was totaled for each mora, and a comparison was made between the natural and artificial conditions using Fisher's exact test. Table 1 shows the list of phonemes used for the comparison. The number of onomatopoeias with more than 5 morae was less than 10 (1.2%) in both experiments, so they were excluded from the test. Table 2 shows a list of morae and phonemes that showed significant differences between the natural and artificial conditions (phonemes that did not show significant differences in all morae were omitted). In Evaluation Experiment 1, significant differences were found in /dz/, /g/, /s/, and /tɕ/of the first mora, /a/, /dz/, /g/, and /s/ of the third mora, and /r/ and /s/ of the fourth mora. Figure 6 shows the results of the comparative analysis of the number of phonemes that appeared in the natural and artificial conditions for each of the morae in which significant differences were found (evaluation experiment 1: morae 1, 3, and 4; evaluation experiment 2: morae 1 and 3).

Table 1. Phonemes of the responded onomatopoeia.

Vowel	/a/ /e/ /i/ /o/ /u/
Consonant	/b/ /by/ /ɕ/ /d/ /dz/ /dʒ/ /g/ /gy/ /h/ /hy/ /k/ /ky/ /m/ /my/ /n/ /ny/ /p/ /ɸ/ /py/ /r/ /ry/ /s/ /t/ /tɕ/ /ts/ /w/ /y/
Other	/N/ /-/ /Q/

Table 2. List of morae and phonemes that showed significant differences between conditions.

Expt. 1	a	u	dz	g	r	s	tɕ
First Mora			+	**		***	+
Second Mora							
Third Mora	+		*	**		***	
Fourth Mora					*	***	
Expt. 2	a	u	dz	g	r	s	tɕ
First Mora		+		+		*	
Second Mora							
Third Mora		+				*	
Fourth Mora							

+: p < 0.1 *: p < 0.05 **: p < 0.01 ***: p < 0.001

5 Discussion

5.1 Differences in Ratings Between Adjective-Scale and Onomatopoeic Responses

The results of the analysis of the subjects' adjective scale responses showed that the difference between the natural and artificial conditions was large in both experiments, with a significant difference of 0.1% for all scales. On the other hand, the results of the onomatopoeia analysis did not show a clear difference as in the case of the adjective scale. In Evaluation Experiment 1, significant differences were found for the three scales of "natural - artificial," "luxurious - cheap," and "comfortable - uncomfortable," but in Evaluation Experiment 2, no significant differences were found for all scales.

The differences due to the evaluation method indicate that it is easier to detect differences when the participants are asked to respond to an adjective scale than when they are asked to respond to onomatopoeia when performing sensitivity evaluation on a specific adjective. The advantage of using a system to analyze onomatopoeia is that as many as 43 sensory scales can be obtained from a single onomatopoeia, and unconscious sensibility values that are not expected by the experimenter or subject can be evaluated. In cases such as this study, which the items to be evaluated are determined, the adjective scale should be used.

In both the adjective scale and the onomatopoeic analysis, the differences between conditions were smaller in Evaluation Experiment 2 than in Evaluation Experiment 1, making it difficult to detect significant differences. This may be due to the fact that the Japanese-style room used in Evaluation Experiment 2, even though it was made of wood and other materials that reminded us of nature, was much less natural than the image in Evaluation Experiment 1, which captured the natural environment itself.

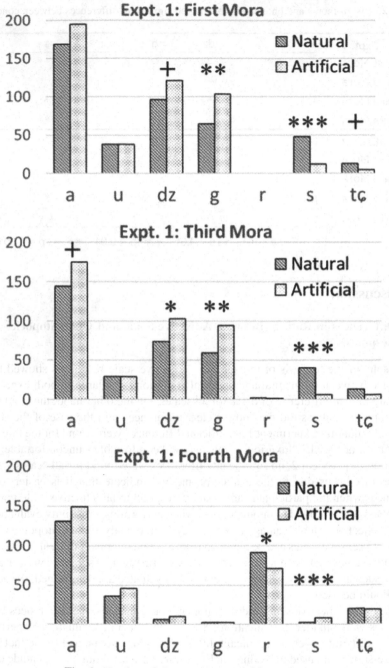

Fig. 6. Number of phonemes answered for each mora

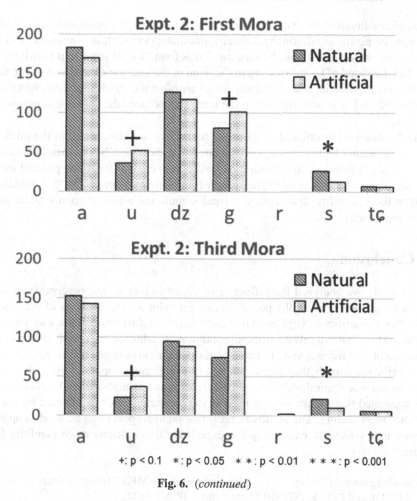

Fig. 6. (continued)

5.2 Phonology of the Onomatopoeia Responses

The results described in previous section suggest that the system's method of quantifying onomatopoeia may not be able to detect significant differences, and that the influence of visual stimuli may not be reflected in the onomatopoeia that represents sound. Therefore, instead of analyzing the results of the system, we analyzed the phonetics of the onomatopoeia that appeared. The results are shown in Table 2. It can be seen from this table that the number of phonemes that showed a significant difference in Evaluation Experiment 2 was smaller than in Evaluation Experiment 1. It is possible that the difference in the spatial environment in which the subject participates in the experiment does not have a direct effect on the perception of sound, while the effect on onomatopoeia is more pronounced when natural or artificial images are presented directly on the monitor as visual stimuli.

However, this does not mean that there is no effect at all. In the two evaluation experiments, there were significant differences in phonation between the natural and artificial conditions. In both experiments, /s/ was found to be significantly more likely to occur in the natural condition. Specifically, onomatopoeia such as "sara-sara" and "sah-sah-" were answered. Although "sara-sara" was found for all stimuli, it may have been heard as the sound of leaves rustling in the wind or the murmur of a stream under natural conditions. In addition, since voiceless sound are often used to describe pleasant sensory stimuli [22, 24], it is possible that in the natural condition, the sound was perceived as pleasant.

In Evaluation Experiment 1, /g/ in the first mora and /dz/ and /g/ in the third mora were significantly higher in the artificial condition. Specifically, onomatopoeia such as "zara-zara", "zah-zah-", and "gata-gata" were answered. It has been pointed out that dull sounds is often used to express unpleasant sensory stimuli [24, 25], which may suggest the possibility that artificial visual stimuli and artificial rooms make sounds more unpleasant.

6   Conclusion

In this study, we analyzed the influence of visual factors on the perception of sound, with a particular focus on the perception of naturalness. The analysis of the adjective scale "natural-artificial" suggested that there may be a difference in the way sounds are perceived between natural and artificial conditions. In addition, we tried to understand the influence of unconscious visual factors on the perception of sound by asking participants to describe the sounds they heard intuitively using onomatopoeia, rather than asking them to evaluate them directly using a scale such as "natural-artificial". As a result, it was suggested that the phonology used in the onomatopoeia was affected by the level of naturalness feeling. The results suggest that onomatopoeia can be used to approach unconscious senses by examining the experimental conditions more carefully in the future.

Acknowledgments. Funding: This work was supported by MEXT [grant numbers JP23135510, JP25135713]; and JSPS KAKENHI [grant number JP15H05922].

References

1. Overvliet, K.E., Soto-Faraco, S.: I can't believe this isn't wood! Acta Psychologia **136**, 95–111 (2011)
2. Overvliet, K.E., Karana, E., Soto-Faraco, S.: Perception of naturalness in textiles. Mater. Des. **90**, 1192–1199 (2016)
3. Rozin, P.: The meaning of natural: process more important than content. Psychol. Sci. **16**, 652–658 (2005)
4. Soto-Faraco, S., Deco, G.: Multisensory contributions to the perception of vibrotactile events. Behav. Brain Res. **196**, 145–154 (2009)
5. Tiest, W.M.B., Kappers, A.M.L.: Haptic and visual perception of roughness. Acta Physiol. (Oxf.) **124**, 177–189 (2007)
6. Ho, H.N., Jones, L.A.: Contribution of thermal cues to material discrimination and localization. Atten. Percept. Psychophys. **68**, 118–128 (2006)

7. Thomas, G.J.: Experimental study of the influence of vision on sound localization. J. Exp. Psychol. **28**(2), 163–177 (1941)
8. Bertelson, P., De Gelder, B.: The psychology of multimodal perception. Crossmodal Space Crossmodal Attention, 141–177 (2004)
9. Vroomen, J., Keetels, M.: The spatial constraint in intersensory pairing: no role in temporal ventriloquism. J. Exp. Psychol. Hum. Percept. Perform. **32**(4), 1063–1071 (2006)
10. Slutsky, D.A., Recanzone, G.H.: Temporal and spatial dependency of the ventriloquism effect. NeuroReport **12**(1), 7–10 (2001)
11. Alais, D., Burr, D.: The ventriloquist effect results from near-optimal bimodal integration. Curr. Biol. **14**(3), 257–262 (2004)
12. Valente, D.L., Braasch, J.: Subjective scaling of spatial room acoustic parameters influenced by visual environmental cues. J. Acoust. Soc. Am. **128**(4), 1952–1964 (2010)
13. Wani, Y., Terashima, T., Tokunaga, Y.: Effect of visual information on subjective impression for sound field in architectural space. In: Proceedings of Meetings on Acoustics ICA2013, vol. 19, no. 1, p. 040102 (2013)
14. Kuwano, S., Namba, S., Hayashi, Y., Komatsu, M., Kato, T.: Auditory and visual interaction in the aesthetic evaluation of environment. Empir. Stud. Arts **19**(2), 191–200 (2001)
15. Preis, A., Kociński, J., Hafke-Dys, H., Wrzosek, M.: Audio-visual interactions in environment assessment. Sci. Total Environ. **523**, 191–200 (2015)
16. Szychowska, M., Hafke-Dys, H., Preis, A., Kociński, J., Kleka, P.: The influence of audio-visual interactions on the annoyance ratings for wind turbines. Appl. Acoust. **129**, 190–203 (2018)
17. Parise, C.V., Spence, C.: Audiovisual crossmodal correspondences and sound symbolism: a study using the implicit association test. Exp. Brain Res. **220**, 319–333 (2012)
18. Spence, C.: Crossmodal correspondences: a tutorial review. Atten. Percept. Psychophys. **73**, 971–995 (2011)
19. Sucevic, J., Jankovic, D., Kovic, V.: When the sound-symbolism effect disappears: the differential role of order and timing in presenting visual and auditory stimuli. Psychology **4**, 11–18 (2013)
20. Ramachandran, V.S., Hubbard, E.M.: Synaesthesia–a window into perception, thought and language. J. Conscious. Stud. **8**(12), 3–34 (2001)
21. Ramachandran, V.S., Hubbard, E.M.: Hearing colors, tasting shapes. Sci. Am. **288**(5), 52–59 (2003)
22. Sakamoto, M.: System to quantify the impression of sounds expressed by onomatopoeias. Acoust. Sci. Technol. **41**(1), 229–232 (2020)
23. Doizaki, R., Watanabe, J., Sakamoto, M.: Automatic estimation of multidimensional ratings from a single sound-symbolic word and word-based visualization of tactile perceptual space. IEEE Trans. Haptics **10**(2), 173–182 (2017)
24. Sakamoto, M., Watanabe, J.: Cross-modal associations between sounds and drink tastes/textures: a study with spontaneous production of sound-symbolic words. Chem. Senses **4**, 197–203 (2016)
25. Sakamoto, M., Watanabe, J.: Bouba/Kiki in touch: associations between tactile perceptual qualities and japanese phonemes. Front. Psychol. **9**, 295 (2018)
26. McDermott, J.H., Simoncelli, E.P.: Sound texture perception via statistics of the auditory periphery: evidence from sound synthesis. Neuron **71**, 926–940 (2011)
27. Free Sound Clips I SoundBible.com, SoundBible.com

AI-Biz 2021

Artificial Intelligence of and for Business (AI-Biz2021)

Takao Terano[1], Setsuya Kurahashi[2], and Hiroshi Takahashi[3]

[1] Chiba University of Commerce
[2] University of Tsukuba
[3] Keio University

1 The Workshop

In AI-Biz 2021, held on November 15, two excellent invited lectures and twelve cutting-edge research papers were presented with a total of 23 participants. The workshop theme focused on various recent issues in business activities and the application technologies of Artificial Intelligence to them.

The first invited lecture was "Building an Agent-based Network Model for Simulating Epidemic Outbreaks and Epidemic-induced Medical Demand" by Prof. Tzai-Hung Wen of National Taiwan University, Department of Geography. In his presentation, he discussed a methodological framework for generating geospatial agent-based networks and a spatially explicit model for simulating epidemic outbreaks and epidemic-induced medical demand.

The second invited lecture was "Empirical inference for agent-based models, where are we going next?" by Research Officer Dr Ernesto Carrella of Oxford University Centre for the Environment. In his presentation, he explained agent-based models to answer empirical questions and provide actionable insights. This can only be done if the agent-based models can be informed by the large amount of data the world collects.

The AI-Biz2021 was the fifth workshop hosted by the SIG-BI (Business Informatics) of JSAI. We believe the workshop was held successfully because of the vast fields of business and AI technology. It includes Investment Strategy, Stock Market, Mergers and Acquisitions, Online Advertisement, Knowledge Extraction, Power Market, Collaborative Multi-agent, Visualization, COVID-19 Infections, Classification, Fake News, Wide and Deep Learning, and so on.

2 Papers

Fourteen papers were submitted for the workshop, and twelve of them were selected for oral presentation in the workshop (86% acceptance rate). After the workshop, they were reviewed by PC members again, and four papers were finally selected (29% acceptance rate). Followings are their synopses.

Satoshi Kawamoto, Toshio Akimitsu, and Kikuo Asai implemented the model of a documentary feature based on the discrete Fourier transform(DFT) of word vectors weighted using an index. They demonstrated that the proposed model outperformed previous models in terms of discriminative performance of the F-measure. They found that the proposed index emphasizes word vectors of specific nouns and verbs in Japanese advertisements. Kazuya Morimatsu and Hiroshi Takahashi used an agent-based model to elucidate the strategies of firms that had achieved superior performance even in an environment of market shakeout due to innovation. They analyzed the specific actions of the company regarding investment strategy from the viewpoint of decision-making and found that it quantitatively provided valid suggestions regarding investment strategies for businesses. Nozomi Tamagawa and Hiroshi Takahashi analyzed the impact of mergers and acquisitions (M&A) on innovation activities in companies. The analysis classified M&A according to the trend of innovation output through their index clustering. In addition, they measured the technological distances among companies using patent document data and then applied the distances to the evaluation of M&A. Setsuya Kurahashi proposed a new SEIR model for COVID-19 infection prediction using mobile statistics and evolutionary optimization, which took into account the risk of influx. The model was able to predict the number of infected people in a region with high accuracy, and the results of estimation in Sapporo City and Tokyo Metropolitan showed high prediction accuracy.

3 Acknowledgment

As the organizing committee chair, I would like to thank the steering committee members. The members are leading researchers in various fields:

Chang-Won Ahn, VAIV Company, Korea
Ernesto Carella, University of Oxford, UK
Reiko Hishiyama, Waseda University, Japan
Manabu Ichikawa, Shibaura Institute of Technology, Japan
Yoko Ishino, Yamaguchi University, Japan
Hajime Kita, Kyoto University, Japan
Hajime Mizuyama, Aoyama Gakuin University, Japan
Matthias Raddant, Kiel University, Gemany
Chathura Rajapaksha, University of Kelaniya, Sri Lanka
Masakazu Takahashi, Yamaguchi University, Japan
Shingo Takahashi, Waseda University, Japan
Alfred Taudes, Vienna University, Austria
Takashi Yamada, Yamaguchi University, Japan
Chao Yang, Hunan University, China

The organizers would like to thank JSAI for its financial support. Finally, we wish to express our gratitude to all those who submitted papers, steering committee members, reviewers, discussants and the attentive audience. We are extremely grateful to all the reviewers. We would like to thank everybody involved in the sympodia organization that helped us in making this event successful.

Legality Identification of Japanese Online Advertisements Using Complex-Valued Support Vector Machines with DFT-Coded Document Vectors

Satoshi Kawamoto[1,2(✉)], Toshio Akimitsu[1], and Kikuo Asai[1]

[1] The Graduate School of Arts and Sciences, The Open University of Japan, Chiba, Japan
[2] Engineering Div. i-mobile Co., Ltd., Tokyo, Japan
kawamoto@i-mobile.co.jp
https://www.i-mobile.co.jp/

Abstract. As the Internet advertising market expands, the number of advertisements containing inappropriate language is increasing. Advertisements that exaggerate the efficacy of products may contravene the Pharmaceutical Affairs Law and the Act against Unjustifiable Premiums and Misleading Representations. Therefore, a system that can detect problematic expressions is required. Some advertisements cannot be classified using only the statistics of words. Therefore, embedding other information, such as word order and word period in the features, is effective to categorize documents. However, the number of labeled data in advertising documents is limited; consequently, models with complex structures tend to overlearn. In addition, features and discriminant models with high generalization performance must be found even if the number of data is small. To address these severe issues, we propose a document feature based on the discrete Fourier transform (DFT) of word vectors weighted using an index previously proposed in a study that attempted to categorize Chinese online advertisements. We also propose a document discriminant model based on a complex-valued support vector machine.

We demonstrate that the proposed model outperforms previous models in terms of discriminative performance of F-measure. We found that the proposed index emphasizes word vectors of specific nouns and verbs in Japanese advertisements. In addition, we found that certain words appeared periodically, and such words are highlighted by the discrete Fourier transform. These factors contributed to the better performance of the proposed model.

Keywords: Discrete Fourier Transform · Natural Language Processing · Internet Advertisement · Complex-valued Support Vector Machine

1 Introduction

To enhance their appeal, online advertisements often contain text as well as images and videos. Textual information makes it easier to convey the appeal of

© Springer Nature Switzerland AG 2023
K. Yada et al. (Eds.): JSAI-isAI 2021 Workshops, LNAI 13856, pp. 335–350, 2023.
https://doi.org/10.1007/978-3-031-36190-6_23

a product. However, although text can increase the effectiveness of an advertisement, the text may include legally or ethically inappropriate expressions. Advertising service providers exclude inappropriate advertisements through manual screening; however, as the Internet advertising market expands, the cost of the screening process is increasing. Therefore, to reduce the workload, a method that automatically identifies inappropriate advertising expressions is required. Such an automatic identification system can reduce the risk of unintentional delivery of inappropriate advertisements.

As shown in Table 1, there is a finite number of advertising documents that are labeled legal or illegal. In addition, as Huang et al. [5] pointed out, determininig the legality of advertisements requires legal training. Consequently, it is impractical to prepare annotation data using methods that do not involve legally trained annotators, such as crowdsourcing. In addition, as shown in Sect. 4.3, some documents cannot be identified only based on simple statistics of the words that appear in the document. Therefore, it is necessary to maintain the simplicity of the discriminant models and features while embedding word order and other information into the features.

In this study, we first define inappropriate advertising expressions and describe the characteristics of problematic documents. Then, we propose a document embedding method based on the index proposed by Tang et al. [16] and discrete Fourier transform (DFT) to identify illegal advertisements effectively. We conducted simulations using complex-valued support vector machines to obtain accuracy, precision, recall, and F-measure values. The results demonstrate that, in terms of discriminative performance(evaluated by F-measure), the proposed model outperformed models proposed in previous studies [5, 16].

2   Relatated Work

Since 2014, many studies have investigated document identification in web content, such as determining whether an advertisement is legal or whether a news article is fake news.

Tang et al. [16] proposed a method to determine the legality of Chinese advertisements using unigram and support vector machines. They showed that word weightings using Eq. (1)(Sect. 4.1) improved accuracy.

Huang et al. [5] proposed a model to discriminate the legality of Chinese advertisements using a dependency-based CNN [12]. They showed that additional inputs of syntactic structures into the CNN improves the discriminative performance compared to only inputting the word vectors. The overall structure of the CNN is based on a previous model [15]. In their study, accuracy, precision, recall, and F-measure values were evaluated. Their proposed model showed overall high discriminative performance.

Zhang et al. [10] proposed a model based on neural networks to detect fake news, and Kaurr et al. [14] proposed a method to detect fake news by majority vote using multiple features, such as TF-IDF and BOW, and multiple discriminative models, such as support vector machine and logistic regression.

Mahajan et al. [2] proposed using wavelet coefficients to reduce the dimensionality of a document vector represented as a bag of words. In their model, a document vector is considered a one-dimensional sequence of signals, and its dimensionality reduction is performed by wavelet transform. Mahajan et al. showed that detection performance does not degrade in the SMS spam detection task.

Wieting et al. [9] devised BOREP, which multiplies a sequence of word vectors by a random matrix and creates a document vector using a pooling function. Despite its simplicity, BOREP exhibited high performance.

Devlin et al. [7] employed a neural network-based technique, i.e. BERT, and demonstrated that their proposed method achieved high performance on various tasks related to natural language processing, suggesting the effectiveness of the attention mechanism.

Although the Self-attention mechanism of BERT is highly effective, the computational cost is very high. Lee-Thorp et al. [8] proposed FNet, which replaces the Self-Attention layer of BERT with a discrete Fourier transform layer and uses the real part of the encoded features. In the large model, FNet was shown to have better learning stability than BERT, and comparable performance to BERT (about 97% accuracy). In addition, the computational cost of FNet was much smaller than BERT.

3   Legality of Advertising Documents

3.1   Definition of Problematic Documents

Occasionally, Internet advertisements contain inappropriate materials from legal and ethical perspectives. It is necessary to clearly define inappropriate advertisements to create a system to detect such documents.

In this study, we defined problematic advertisements based on the Pharmaceutical Affairs Law. Advertising expressions for cosmetics are regulated by Article 66 of the Pharmaceutical Affairs Law, which prohibits false and exaggerated advertising. In addition, the Ministry of Health, Labour and Welfare's Standards for Proper Advertising of Drugs and Other Products [11] provides specific standards. In the following, we define problematic expressions and present concrete examples.

Restrictions on Expressions Related to Efficacy and Safety. The possible range of expressions regarding efficacy for cosmetics is given in the Pharmaceutical Affairs Law No. 0721-1. Expressions such as "eliminates fine lines and wrinkles," "has an anti-aging effect," and "improves wrinkles and sagging skin," are prohibited in cosmetics advertisements. In addition, there are strong restrictions on the use of efficacy and safety claims for pharmaceuticals and quasi-drugs, including cosmetics. Specifically, it is prohibited to use historical expressions, e.g., "effective based on evidence from the past 100 years" and give examples of clinical or experimental data. Expressions that guarantee efficacy, e.g., "few side effects," are also not permitted. Note that testimonials about the impressions of using a product are permitted; however, testimonials regarding efficacy and safety are not permitted. Relative to efficacy and safety, statements that claim a maximum level of efficacy or productivity, e.g., "the best efficacy" or "the ace of gastrointestinal drugs" are also not permitted.

Restrictions on Expressions About Ingredients and Raw Materials. Restrictions on special labeling for cosmetics are outlined in the Standards for Proper Advertising of Drugs and Other Products. In the case of special labeling of raw materials, the purpose of their inclusion (within the range of efficacy approved for cosmetics) should be stated clearly.

Restrictions on Slanderous Advertising of Other Companies' Products. Defamatory expressions, e.g., "this works better than other companies' products" are not permitted.

Recommendations from Pharmaceutical Professionals, Etc. Advertisements that contain expressions that convey endorsements or recommendations by pharmaceutical professionals, clinics, universities, or other institutions are prohibited. This type of expression is not permitted even if they are true, which means that strong restrictions are placed on advertisements that may have substantial impacts on people's decisions. In addition, expressions regarding patents are also inappropriate even if true.

4 Features of Inappropriate Advertising Documents

4.1 Frequency Features of Words

In the previous section, we described the definitions of inappropriate advertising documents. In Sects. 4.1 and 4.2, we discuss the statistical characteristics of problematic documents. Tang et al. [16] identified that there were differences in the frequency of word occurrence between normal and inappropriate advertisements. In addition, they proposed to use Eq. (1) to weight word vectors. Their simulation using an SVM demonstrated that the weighting of word vectors improves discrimination accuracy.

$$U_w = \log\left(\frac{\left(\frac{l_w}{L}\right)}{\left(\frac{k_w}{K}\right)}\right) \tag{1}$$

Here, w is a word in advertising documents, l_w is the number of occurrences of w in problematic advertisements, and k_w is the number of occurrences of w in nonproblematic advertisements. L is the total number of words (i.e., tokens) in problematic advertisements, and K is the number of tokens in the nonproblematic advertisements.

In this section, we describe the features of the top-level words of U_w in advertisements provided by i-mobile Co., Ltd. As shown in Table 1, the advertisements include documents about cosmetics, health foods, and other products. In addition, the advertisements for cosmetics and health food are labeled to identify whether there are problems relative to the Pharmaceutical Affairs Law. Here, positive and negative labels are applied by the holder of a pharmaceutical law administrator license.

Table 1. Number of advertisements

Total number of advertisements	78581
Cosmetics (nonproblematic documents)	8103
Cosmetics (problematic documents)	3008
Health Foods (nonproblematic documents)	12999
Health Foods (problematic documents)	1487

As shown in Tables 2, and 3, words related to medicine, e.g., "medicine" and "pharmaceutical" appear more frequently in problematic advertisements. As described in Sect. 3.1, recommendation expressions in advertisements by pharmaceutical professionals are not permitted; therefore, U_w tends to be higher for words related to pharmaceuticals.

In this study, we used MeCab (version 0.996) for morphological analysis, and the default IPA dictionary was used.

4.2 Part-of-Speech Features

It is necessary to identify effective features to determine the legality of advertisements. Table 4 shows the percentage of occurrence of the parts of speech in each document type. Unfortunately, there is no characteristic that a particular part of speech is more likely to appear in problematic documents. In other words, the expressions in problematic advertisements do not deviate from the Japanese grammar.

However, if we plot the distribution of U_w in parts-of-speech units, we can observe large differences in their distribution. Figure 1 plots the distribution of U_w for each part of speech in cosmetic advertisements. As shown in Fig. 1, the variance of U_w is large for nouns and verbs. In particular, U_w for nouns shows many outliers, which means that there are nouns and verbs that are likely to appear in illegal advertisements. For prefixes, particles, auxiliaries, and symbols, the variance of U_w is small (although there are some outliers), and the influence of the legality of documents is small.

4.3 Documents that Cannot Be Discriminated by Words Only

As described in Sects. 4.1, and 4.2, the frequency of nouns related to medical field (e.g., "medicine" and "drug") is high in problematic advertisements. In

Table 2. High U_w words (cosmetics)

Word	U_w	POS
極限(limit)	4.309	Noun
認める(admit)	3.884	Verb
ウチ(inner)	4.053	Noun
綿棒(cotton swab)	3.871	Noun
大学(university)	3.697	Noun
(company name)	3.648	Noun
家庭(family)	3.583	Noun
誌(magazine)	3.471	Noun
監修(supervision)	3.438	Noun
医学(medical science)	3.401	Noun
放っ(leave)	3.360	Verb
医薬品(pharmaceuticals)	3.332	Noun
83	3.273	Noun
地肌(skin)	3.273	Noun
フサ(full hair)	3.127	Noun

Table 3. High U_w words(health foods)

Word	U_w	POS
医学(medical science)	4.893	Noun
誌(magazine)	4.794	Noun
すすめる(recommend)	4.519	Verb
作り方(how to make)	4.519	Noun
排便(bowel movement)	4.505	Noun
医師(medical doctor)	4.359	Noun
掲載(publication)	4.118	Noun
歯医者(dentist)	3.949	Noun
?!?	3.949	Noun
断言(affirm)	3.949	Noun
医者(medical doctor)	3.906	Noun
スッ(smoothly)	3.558	Noun
共同(cooperation)	3.463	Noun
単品(single item)	3.463	Noun
(name of the celebrity)	3.463	Noun

addition, the frequency of verbs that appear in contexts where medical professionals recommend products (e.g., "can" and "recommend") is high. However, we cannot judge a document as problematic simply because it contains words with large U_w. In the following, we present examples where legality cannot be determined using only the occurrence of words.

Documents in Which Subjects Are Not Medical Professionals. As discussed in Sect. 3.1, texts in which medical professionals recommend products are not permitted; however, there are cases where the subjects are not medical professional, as in the following example.

> 皮膚科医の妻「毛穴汚れはこれ」簡単すぎて話題に(in Japanese)
> Dermatologist's wife said, "Here's how to clean your pores." It's too easy and went viral.

In this case, the subject is the "dermatologist's wife," which does not correspond to the expression of the doctor's personal recommendation.

Items that Do Not Express Efficacy Explicitly. There are strong restrictions on advertising expressions about efficacy. For example, the statement, "the effects of the cosmetics will make your skin beautiful" is not permitted. However, some advertising expressions do not explicitly state the existence of efficacy, as in the following example.

Table 4. Occurrence of each part of speech in advertising documents

	Cosmetics (illegal)	Cosmetics (legal)	Foods (illegal)	Foods (legal)
Particle	23.2720%	23.2153%	22.6153%	21.3215%
Auxiliary verb	3.8632%	4.3906%	4.0897%	4.9718%
Adjective	1.2968%	1.6053%	0.9073%	1.2065%
Symbol	12.2399%	12.9804%	12.0993%	13.0527%
Interjection	0.0972%	0.1196%	0.0228%	0.0601%
Filler	0.0145%	0.0378%	0.0105%	0.0252%
Conjunction	0.1235%	0.1446%	0.1033%	0.1258%
Prefix	1.1261%	1.3446%	0.9949%	1.0684%
Verb	9.5028%	10.3234%	10.8663%	11.7316%
Adverb	1.7118%	2.6067%	1.8969%	3.1471%
Adnominal adjective	0.3324%	0.5450%	0.1769%	0.3245%
Noun	46.4197%	42.6848%	46.2168%	42.9647%
Others	0.0000%	0.0019%	0.0000%	0.0000%

> 20代に見える40代女医さんの透明感の秘密！(in Japanese)
> The secret to the beautiful skin of a forty-something female doctor who looks like she's in her twenties!

5   Features to Discriminate Advertising Documents

5.1   Properties of Effective Features for Discrimination

As discussed in Sect. 4.3, we cannot detect all the illegal advertisement documents accurately using only the statistics of the words. However, if the positional information of words is embedded in the document vector, it is possible to determine whether the subject is a medical professional. In addition, document vectors embedded with the periodic features of words are effective relative to discriminating contrastive expressions, e.g., "40-something who looks like a 20-something" or "I lost 60 kg to 45 kg."

In addition, as shown in Fig. 1, certain nouns and verbs are used at high frequency in problematic documents, and it is expected that weighting the word vectors will improve the discrimination performance of advertisement documents.

Therefore, we propose a document vector that combines the weighting of word vectors by the log frequency ratio(U_w) and DFT.

5.2   Document Vector Combining U_w and DFT

When a document D comprises a sequence of words $(l_0, l_1, ..., l_{N-1})$, D has a sequence of word vectors $(\mathbf{v}_{l_0}, \mathbf{v}_{l_1}, ..., \mathbf{v}_{l_{N-1}})$. Here, $\mathbf{v}_{l_t} (t = 0, 1, 2, ., N-1)$ are 200-dimensional word vectors created by word2vec (skip-gram; window size: 10). Then, we define $(\mathbf{u}_{l_0}, \mathbf{u}_{l_1}, ..., \mathbf{u}_{l_{N-1}})$ as follows.

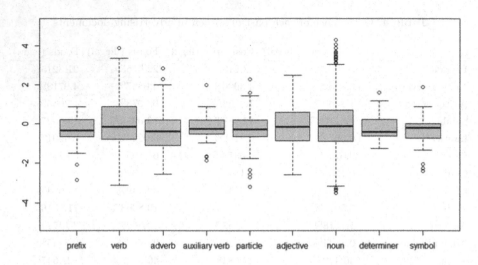

Fig. 1. Distribution of U_w of words in each part of speech

$$(\mathbf{u}_{l_0}, \mathbf{u}_{l_1}, ..., \mathbf{u}_{l_{N-1}}) = (U_{l_0}\mathbf{v}_{l_0}, U_{l_1}\mathbf{v}_{l_1}, ..., U_{l_{N-1}}\mathbf{v}_{l_{N-1}}) \tag{2}$$

The DFT of this sequence is expressed as follows.

$$\mathbf{F}(\theta) = \frac{1}{N} \sum_{t=0}^{N-1} \mathbf{u}_{l_t} \exp\left(-i\frac{2\pi(\theta - 1)}{N}t\right) \tag{3}$$

Here, t is the position at which the word appears. The document vector $\mathbf{x}_D$ is obtained by multiplying $\mathbf{F}(\theta)$ by a random matrix $\mathbf{W}_\theta$ as follows.

$$\mathbf{x}_D = \sum_{\theta=1}^{\Theta} \mathbf{F}(\theta)\mathbf{W}_\theta \tag{4}$$

Here, $\Theta \in \{1, 2, 3, 4, 5\}$. We also evaluate the performance of F-measure when the word vectors are not weighted, which is discussed in Sect. 7.3(see Equation (3), where $\mathbf{v}_{l_t}$ is used rather than $\mathbf{u}_{l_t}$). $\mathbf{W}_\theta$ is a random matrix obtained via sparse random projection [3] as follows.

$$W_{\theta_{kl}} = \begin{cases} -1 & \text{(with probability } \frac{1}{6}) \\ 0 & \text{(with probability } \frac{2}{3}) \\ 1 & \text{(with probability } \frac{1}{6}) \end{cases} \tag{5}$$

Here, $W_{\theta_{kl}}$ is the kth row and lth column element of the matrix (where $1 \leq k, l \leq 200$).

6 Discriminating Documents Using Complex-Valued Support Vector Machine

As shown in Table 1, the number of positive examples of the data used in this study is in the order of thousands. Therefore, to determine whether advertising document D is problematic document, we must use a discriminant model with high generalization performance. Thus, we employed the complex-valued support vector machine(CV-SVM) [6] as a discriminant model with high generalization performance. The discriminant function of CV-SVM is expressed as $f(\mathbf{x}_D) = \mathbf{w}\phi(\mathbf{x}_D^*) - b$. Here, $\mathbf{w}$ is a complex-valued weight vector, and $\mathbf{x}_D^*$ is the vector in which each element of $\mathbf{x}_D$ is conjugated. In addition, $\phi(\mathbf{x})$ is the basis function, and b is the bias term of the complex number.

The objective function E is expressed as follows, where the problem is to minimize E. Here, Γ is the document set and α_D, β_D are the Lagrange coefficients. If D is a problematic advertising document, y_D is labeled $y_D = 1$; otherwise, $y_D = -1$. Note that ξ_D, ζ_D are the relaxation parameters of the constraints.

$$E = \frac{1}{2}|\mathbf{w}|^2 - \sum_{D \in \Gamma} \alpha_D \left(\mathrm{Re}\left(y_D(\mathbf{w}\phi(\mathbf{x}_D^*) - b)\right) - 1 + \xi_D\right)$$

$$- \sum_{D \in \Gamma} \beta_D \left(\mathrm{Im}\left(y_D(\mathbf{w}\phi(\mathbf{x}_D^*) - b)\right) - 1 + \zeta_D\right) \tag{6}$$

$$+ C \sum_{D \in \Gamma} \xi_D + C \sum_{D \in \Gamma} \zeta_D$$

However, it is easier to solve the dual problem than solve Eq. (6). The dual problem was proved to be derived using the Wiltinger derivative by Bouboulis [13]. Specifically, $\frac{\partial E}{\partial \mathbf{w}^*}, \frac{\partial E}{\partial b^*}, \frac{\partial E}{\partial \xi_D}, \frac{\partial E}{\partial \zeta_D}$ are calculated and the dual problem is expressed as follows.

$$E = -\frac{1}{2} \sum_{D_1 \in \Gamma} \sum_{D_2 \in \Gamma} \psi_{D_1} \cdot \psi_{D_2}^* \cdot y_{D_1} \cdot y_{D_2} \cdot K\left(\mathbf{x}_{D_1}, \mathbf{x}_{D_2}\right) + \sum_{D \in \Gamma} (\alpha_D + \beta_D) \tag{7}$$

where $\psi_D = \alpha_D + i\beta_D$. In addition, the following conditions must be satisfied as constraints.

$$\sum_{D \in \Gamma} \alpha_D \cdot y_D = 0, \sum_{D \in \Gamma} \beta_D \cdot y_D = 0, 0 \le \alpha_D, \beta_D \le C \tag{8}$$

The discriminant function is obtained by finding α_D, β_D that maximizes E while satisfying the constraints. When $\mathrm{Re}(f(\mathbf{x}_D)) + \mathrm{Im}(f(\mathbf{x}_D)) \ge 0$, D is considered a problematic document; otherwise, D is a nonproblematic document. In this study, we use the RBF kernel function $K(\mathbf{x}_1, \mathbf{x}_2)$, which is defined as follows.

$$K(\mathbf{x}_1, \mathbf{x}_2) = \exp\left(-\frac{(\mathbf{x}_1 - \mathbf{x}_2) \cdot (\mathbf{x}_1 - \mathbf{x}_2)^*}{\sigma^2}\right) \tag{9}$$

where $\mathbf{x}_1$ and $\mathbf{x}_2$ are complex-valued vectors. In addition, $(\mathbf{x}_1 - \mathbf{x}_2)^*$ is a complex-valued vector in which each element of $(\mathbf{x}_1 - \mathbf{x}_2)$ is conjugated.

7   Discrimination Simulation of Cosmetic Advertisements

7.1   Performance Indicators of Discriminant Model

We conducted a numerical evaluation of a model to discriminate the legality of cosmetic advertisements. We found relatively few positive examples, as shown in Table 1. Therefore, it is desirable to evaluate the performance of the discriminant model using a metric other than accuracy.

It is desirable to have high recall and precision with a discrimination model. Therefore, we evaluated model performance using the F-measure as an index.

7.2   Simulation Using Holdout Method

Here, we used the holdout method in the simulation to compare F-measure. Specifically, we split the data in Table 1 into training data, validation data, and test data at ratio of 2:1:1, respectively. In other words, the model was trained using the training data, the parameters with high F-measure were searched using the validation data, and the actual performance of the model was evaluated using the test data.

The C parameters of the SVM and CV-SVM were fixed at $C = 256$, and the σ^2 parameters were selected from $\sigma^2 \in \{0.001, 0.01, 0.1, 1, 10, 100, 1000, 10000\}$ using the grid search method.

7.3   Discriminant Models and Document Vectors to Compare

The word vectors in this simulation involve two patterns, i.e., word2vec word vectors weighted by U_w and unweighted word vectors.

In addition, SWEM-Aver [4] and the document vector defined by Eq. (4) were compared in the simulation, which was performed with five patterns of $\Theta(\in \{1, 2, 3, 4, 5\})$.

Here, we compared Tang's SVM method [16], Huang's CNN method [5], and the proposed CV-SVM method. Huang showed that adding word vectors and clause structures to the input vectors improved the discriminative performance of the CNN method; however, the improvement was limited. Therefore, to simplify implementation, in this simulation, the comparison was performed without adding the clause structure to the input vector.

The patterns of the simulation are shown in Table 5. Here, the weighted word vectors are denoted word2vec(U_w), and the unweighted word vectors are denoted as word2vec.

The configuration of the CNN used for comparison is shown in Table 6. Here, the dropout rate was set to 0%. N is the total number of words in the document, and the labels used for training are $y = 1$ for problematic advertisements and $y = -1$ for nonproblematic advertisements.

Table 5. Simulation Patterns

Discriminant model	Word vector	Document vector
SVM	word2vec	SWEM-Aver
CNN	word2vec	-
CV-SVM	word2vec	SWEM-Aver
CV-SVM	word2vec	DFT($\Theta \in \{1,2,3,4,5\}$)
SVM	word2vec(U_w)	SWEM-Aver
CV-SVM	word2vec(U_w)	SWEM-Aver
CNN	word2vec(U_w)	-
CV-SVM	word2vec(U_w)	DFT($\Theta \in \{1,2,3,4,5\}$)

Table 6. CNN configuration

Unit	Detail
input layer	200(Dimensionality of word vectors)$\times N$
convolutional layer(ReLU)	200 $\times$ 3 : 100channels 200 $\times$ 4 : 100channels 200 $\times$ 5 : 100channels
pooling layer	Max Pooling
fully-connected layer	activation function : ReLU
output layer	activation function : y=x

7.4 Simulation Results

Effectiveness of Word Weighting. We simulated the discrimination of problematic advertisements using the patterns given in Table 5, and the results are shown in Table 7. As can be seen from Table 7, the overall accuracy and F-measure values tended to be improved when using word vectors weighted by U_w. This result means that it is effective to emphasize nouns and verbs that tend to appear in problematic documents.

Discrimination Results by the SVM and CNN. Discrimination using SWEM-Aver by the SVM did not result in the best F-measure values. However, overall good discrimination results were obtained. This result means that most of the documents, except for some documents, are characterized by the statistics of the words that appear in them.

The CNN achieved high levels of recall values, but the precision values were very low; therefore, the overall discriminant results were not excellent. This result was because the number of data was insufficient for the neural networks to acquire sufficient generalization performance.

Discrimination Results by the CV-SVM. When $\Theta = 1$, the phase is zero even if the word position t changes, as shown in Eqs. (3) and (4). In addition, the document vector $\mathbf{x}_D$ is the same as BOREP [9] using average pooling. The difference between SWEM-Aver [4] and $\mathbf{x}_D$ is the presence of a random matrix. Wieting et al. [9] showed that BOREP is more effective than BOE (Bag of Embeddings) in the performance evaluation of features using SentEval [1]. However, in this simulation, the F-measure values decreased by small amounts as a result of using the sparse random projection.

This result does not mean that simply multiplying by a random matrix will improve the effectiveness of the features. Finding the conditions under which the random matrix works effectively for the discriminant model is a future challenge.

When $\Theta = 2$, the document vector $\mathbf{x}_D$ is BOREP (average pooling) with additional word order information. In addition, for $\Theta = n(n \geq 3)$, words that occur $n-1$ times in the document are highlighted and embedded in the document vector. As a result, as Θ increases, the word statistics, word order, and period information are embedded in sequence.

In this simulation, the combination of weighting by U_w and the discrete Fourier transform achieved high F-measure values, with the highest discriminant performance when $\Theta = 3$. In addition, when $\Theta = 3$, the highest accuracy value was also obtained. However, when $\Theta \geq 4$, precision and recall values decreased and discrimination performance declined. Next, we discuss the reason for the high F-measure value obtained when $\Theta = 3$.

Figure 2(a) shows the histogram of relative positions of words with $2.261 < U_w$ (upper 2.5%) in the inappropriate documents. The horizontal axis in the figure is the relative position of the word. The relative position of the word is calculated by $\frac{t}{N}$. Here, N is the number of tokens in a document, and $t(\in 1, 2, ..., N-1)$ is the position of the word. The histogram shows that the distribution is bimodal with peaks near 0.0 and 0.6 on the horizontal axis. In other words, the frequency of words satisfying $2.261 < U_w$ is biased toward the beginning and middle of the sentence, and the interval between them is slightly larger than 0.5. Therefore, if a word occurs twice in a document, its period is likely to be slightly larger than $0.5N$. With the period close to $0.5N$, $\mathbf{F}(\theta)$ is emphasized as a feature when θ is 3 in Eq. (3).

Figure 3(a) shows the histogram of relative positions of words with $2.261 < U_w$ in the non-problematic documents. The distribution is very different from that of Fig. 2(a), and cannot be said to be bimodal. The difference in distribution between Fig. 2(a) and Fig. 3(a) was emphasized by the Discrete Fourier Transform, leading to improved discrimination results.

Figure 2(c) shows the histogram of relative positions of words with $-1.897 < U_w \leq 1.791$(upper 5.0% to 95.0%) in the inappropriate documents. Figure 3(c) shows the same histogram in the non-problematic documents. Both distributions are close to a uniform distribution, and there is no clear bias in the word positions, nor do they have cyclic occurrence characteristics. Therefore, the word order information $\mathbf{F}(2)$ and the period information $\mathbf{F}(3)$ might not have significant effects. However, word statistics are represented by $\mathbf{F}(1)$, and $\mathbf{F}(1)$ works effectively in the document discrimination task.

From the above discussions, a situation arises where at least one of $\mathbf{F}(1)$, $\mathbf{F}(2)$, and $\mathbf{F}(3)$ is valid for discrimination even if U_w in a document has various values. Therefore, when $\Theta = 3$, document vectors effective for discrimination were created; consequently, the simulation results showed high discrimination performance.

Table 7. Simulation results

	σ^2	WordVector	DocumentVector	TP	TN	FP	FN	Accuracy	Precision	Recall	F-measure
SVM	10	word2vec	SWEM-Aver	303	1974	51	449	0.8199	**0.8559**	0.4029	0.5479
CNN	-	word2vec	-	616	859	1166	136	0.5311	0.3457	0.8191	0.4862
CV-SVM	10	word2vec	SWEM-Aver	638	1753	272	114	0.8610	0.7011	0.8484	0.7677
CV-SVM	10^3	word2vec	DFT($\Theta=1$)	646	1608	417	106	0.8117	0.6077	0.8590	0.7118
CV-SVM	10^3	word2vec	DFT($\Theta=2$)	469	1931	94	283	0.8642	0.8330	0.6237	0.7133
CV-SVM	10^3	word2vec	DFT($\Theta=3$)	529	1846	179	223	0.8552	0.7472	0.7035	0.7247
CV-SVM	10^3	word2vec	DFT($\Theta=4$)	473	1899	126	279	0.8542	0.7896	0.6290	0.7002
CV-SVM	10^4	word2vec	DFT($\Theta=5$)	448	1854	171	304	0.8290	0.7237	0.5957	0.6535
SVM	1.0	word2vec(U_w)	SWEM-Aver	567	1807	218	185	0.8549	0.7223	0.7540	0.7378
CNN	-	word2vec(U_w)	-	684	435	1590	68	0.4030	0.3008	**0.9096**	0.4521
CV-SVM	10	word2vec(U_w)	SWEM-Aver	579	1846	179	173	0.8732	0.7639	0.7699	0.7669
CV-SVM	10^3	word2vec(U_w)	DFT($\Theta=1$)	596	1801	224	156	0.8632	0.7268	0.7926	0.7583
CV-SVM	10^3	word2vec(U_w)	DFT($\Theta=2$)	650	1770	255	102	0.8714	0.7182	0.8644	0.7846
CV-SVM	10^3	word2vec(U_w)	DFT($\Theta=3$)	590	1890	135	162	**0.8931**	0.8138	0.7846	**0.7989**
CV-SVM	10^3	word2vec(U_w)	DFT($\Theta=4$)	568	1874	151	184	0.8794	0.7900	0.7553	0.7723
CV-SVM	10^4	word2vec(U_w)	DFT($\Theta=5$)	554	1753	272	198	0.8308	0.6707	0.7367	0.7022

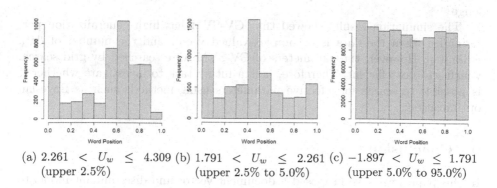

(a) $2.261 < U_w \le 4.309$ (b) $1.791 < U_w \le 2.261$ (c) $-1.897 < U_w \le 1.791$
    (upper 2.5%)   (upper 2.5% to 5.0%)   (upper 5.0% to 95.0%)

Fig. 2. Histogram of the word positions in illegal documents

8   Discussion

This study has shown that a document vector that combines the weighting of word vectors by U_w and DFT is effective in discriminating cosmetic advertisement documents. As mentioned in Sect. 7.4, the words with large U_w have strong

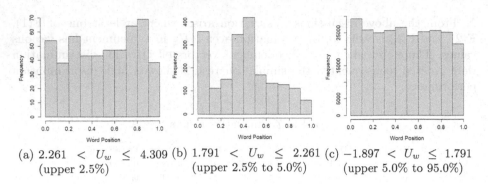

(a) $2.261 < U_w \le 4.309$ (b) $1.791 < U_w \le 2.261$ (c) $-1.897 < U_w \le 1.791$
(upper 2.5%)   (upper 2.5% to 5.0%)   (upper 5.0% to 95.0%)

Fig. 3. Histogram of the word positions in legal documents

positional biases in the cosmetics advertisements, and these words have periodic occurrence characteristics. These characteristics of the words in the cosmetic advertisements were highlighted by DFT and contributed to the improvement of the discrimination performance.

This method (i.e., combining word weighting and DFT) is also expected to be highly effective in the task of categorizing other types of advertisements than cosmetics, but it is necessary to be verified through further investigation.

In addition, we found that by searching for appropriate Θ values, effective document features for document discrimination can be obtained. However, the appropriate Θ value may depend on the type of document set; consequently, finding an efficient way to explore optimal Θ values is needed as a future challenge.

The simulation results showed that CV-SVM has high generalization performance when the data is a complex-valued vector and the number of data is limited. However, the parameters of CV-SVM were searched by grid search, which was not efficient. Therefore, it is a future task to investigate whether it is possible to search for effective parameters using methods such as Bayesian optimization.

9   Conclusion

In this paper, we have proposed a document vector and discriminant model to discriminate the legality of Japanese advertisement documents for cosmetics. In addition, we evaluated and compared their performance to exsisting models.

In the proposed model, word vectors are weighted by the index of Tang [16], and DFT is embedded in the document vectors. Such document features are utilized effectively in the proposed CV-SVM. The experimental results denmostrate the proposed CV-SVM can provide high generalizability even with limited data; the F-measure value has improved from 0.7378 to 0.7989 compared to the model of Tang et al. In addition, we have demonstrated that Tang's index has the effect of highlighting nouns and verbs that are likely to appear in problematic Japanese advertisements.

There are not many studies on natural language processing that utilize complex values. Mahajan et al. [2] proposed a method for feature selection using wavelet coefficients, but their goal was dimensionality reduction, and the features given to the discriminant model were assumed to be real numbers. FNet [8] is a model in which the Self-Attention layer of BERT is replaced by a Discrete Fourier Transform layer, and its learning stability has also been shown; however, the imaginary parts of the features have been removed, and the discussion on the effect of the imaginary parts remain pending. However, as shown in this study, by extending the document features to complex numbers, it is now possible to embed word order information and periodic features of words into document vectors in a simple way.

The result of this study demonstrated that features combining word vector weighting and DFT are effective in terms of discriminating advertisements. In addition, the proposed method in this study is expected to be applicable to general document classification tasks such as document topic classification, spam estimation, and analysis of movie review documents.

The ability to create flexible document features with a small computational load is a key feature of complex-valued models, and clarifying tasks for which complex-valued features are effective compared to language models, e.g., BERT, is also a future task.

References

1. Conneau, A., Kiela, D.: Senteval: an evaluation toolkit for universal sentence representations. In: Proceedings of the Eleventh International Conference on Language Resources and Evaluation (LREC 2018) (2018))
2. Mahajan, A., Jat, S., Roy, S.: Feature selection for short text classification using wavelet packet transform. In: Proceedings of the 19th Conference on Computational Language Learning, pp. 321–326 (2015)
3. Achlioptas, D.: Database-friendly random projections: Johnson-lindenstrauss with bi-nary coins. J. Comput. Syst. Sci. **66**(4), 671–687 (2003)
4. Shen, D., et al.: Baseline needs more love: on simple word-embedding-based models and associated pooling mechanisms. In: Proceedings of the 56th Annual Meeting of the Association for Computational Linguistics, pp. 440–450 (2018)
5. Huang, H., Wen, Y., Chen, H.: Detection of false online advertisements with DCNN. In: Proceedings of the International Conference on World Wide Web Companion. International World Wide Web Conferences Steering Committee, pp. 795–796 (2017)
6. Shinoda, H., Hattori, M., Kobayashi, M.: [Complex-valued Support Vector Machine] Hukuso Support Vector Machine(in Japanese). In: The 73rd National Convention of IPSJ, pp. 315–316 (2011)
7. Devlin, J., Chang, M.-W., Lee, K., Toutanova, K.: BERT: pre-training of deep bidirectional transformers for language understanding. In: arXiv preprint, arXiv:1810.04805 (2018)
8. Lee-Thorp, J., Ainslie, J., Eckstein, L., Ontanon, S.: FNet: mixing tokens with fourier transforms. In: arXiv preprint, arXiv:2105.03824 (2021)
9. Wieting, J., Kiela, D.: No training required: Exploring random encoders for sentence classification. In: arXiv preprint, arXiv:1901.10444 (2019)

10. Zhang, J., Dong, B., Philip, S.: Fakedetector: Effective fake news detection with deep diffusive neural network. In: 2020 IEEE 36th International Conference on Data Engineering (ICDE), pp. 1826–1829 (2020)
11. Ministry of Health, Labour and Welfare: [Standard for Adequate Advertisement of Pharmaceutical Products]Iyakuhin tou tekisei koukoku kijun (in Japanese). https://www.mhlw.go.jp/file/06-Seisakujouhou-11120000-Iyakushokuhinkyoku/0000179263.pdf
12. Ma, M., Huang, L., Xiang, B., Zhou, B.: Dependency-based convolutional neural networks for sentence embedding. In: Proceedings of the 53rd Annual Meeting of the Association for Computational Linguistics and the 7th International Joint Conference on Natural Language Processing, pp. 174–179 (2015)
13. Bouboulis, P., Theodoridis, S., Mavroforakis, C., Evaggelatou-Dalla, L.: Complex support vector machines for regression and quaternary classification. IEEE Trans. Neural Netw. Learn. Syst. **26**(6), 1260–1274 (2014)
14. Kaur, S., Kumar, P., Kumaraguru, P.: Automating fake news detection system using multilevel voting model. Soft. Comput. **24**(12), 9049–9069 (2020)
15. Kim, Y.: Convolutional neural networks for sentence classification. In: Proceedings of the 2014 Conference on Empirical Methods in Natural Language Processing (EMNLP), pp. 1746–1751 (2014)
16. Tang, Y., Chen, H.: FAdR: a system for recognizing false online advertisements. In: Proceedings of 52nd Annual Meeting of the Association for Computational Linguistics: System Demonstrations. ACL, pp. 103–108 (2014)

What is the Investment Strategy to Overcome the Severe Business Environment?
Perspectives on the Relationship Between Business and Human Resources Management

Kazuya Morimatsu(✉) and Hiroshi Takahashi

Keio University Graduate School of Business Administration, 4-1-1 Hiyoshi, Kohoku-Ku, Yokohama City 223-8526, Kanagawa, Japan
{kazuya.morimatsu,htaka}@keio.jp

Abstract. We use an agent-based model to elucidate the strategies of firms that have achieved superior performance even in an environment of market shakeout due to innovation. Assuming that a company's sales consist only of intangible assets, we analyze the specific actions of the company regarding investment strategy from the viewpoint of decision-making and found that (1) it is important to invest more than competitors even at the expense of efficiency in the early stage of a business, and (2) business growth by investing talented human resources ahead of competitors is the most important factor in the (3) If it is difficult to secure human resources, it is important to make investment decisions for further new business development ahead of competitors. One of the novelties of this study is that it quantitatively provides valid suggestions regarding investment strategies for businesses.

Keywords: Decision-making · Intellectual capital · Agent-based model

1 Introduction

To overcome this severe business environment, where the pace of innovation is increasing and former excellent companies are in decline, is clear that appropriate business diversification must be addressed. Numerous studies have been conducted on diversification. For example, Christensen (1992) suggests that companies experiencing further growth need to focus on new markets positioned as substitutes [1, 2], and Kim et al. (1996) suggests that there is a strong relationship between knowledge accumulation and related diversification based on trends in patent applications [3]. Studies have also been conducted on related diversification strategies. For example, Mishina (2007) found that companies that we're able to change their core business through diversification in response to market conditions were able to sustain their operations, suggesting that even if short-term profitability is low, there are companies whose diversification makes sense from a long-term perspective [4, 5]. Konno (2017) focuses on the business of a Japanese auto parts company and suggests a link between customer relationships and the success of related diversification [6].

© Springer Nature Switzerland AG 2023
K. Yada et al. (Eds.): JSAI-isAI 2021 Workshops, LNAI 13856, pp. 351–364, 2023.
https://doi.org/10.1007/978-3-031-36190-6_24

A variety of useful suggestions have been derived from previous research findings. Unfortunately, no recommendations have been made regarding the actions of specific strategies, such as when and how decisions should be made. We infer that it is difficult to extract strategies inductively because the actual business environment is complicated by a variety of factors. However, there are still excellent managers who have successfully diversified their businesses, and we believe that there are still some generalizations that can be made about diversification strategies. What do excellent managers see and what kind of decisions do they make?

We address this issue with a primary focus on analyzing the specific actions of firms with respect to their investment strategies for business diversification from a decision-making perspective.

2 Setting the Condition

To extract general implications for decision-making from complex business environments, the approach proposed in this study (1) assumes a company that operates only with Intellectual Capital (e.g., a fabless company) to simplify causal inference, and (2) uses an agent-based model to derive general perspectives even among complex events in practice.

(1) Intellectual capital is a field that studies intangible assets related to economic activities, and these assets include "Human Capital," "Structural Capital" and "Relational Capital" [7, 8]. Bontis (1998) attempted to see if there is a relationship with industry data for the above three classifications [9], and Chen et al. (2004) examined the above three classifications with the "Innovation Capital "is added to the four models to attempt an analysis [10]. The basic approach in this field is to analyze the relationship between elements of intellectual capital and performance through multiple regression analysis, and few studies use agent-based models to derive a general perspective on strategic theories such as decision-making.

(2) The agent-based model described is a method in which an agent acting autonomously and an environment surrounding the agent are prepared to simulate complex phenomena by having the agents interfere with each other while repeating certain rules, and the results can be analyzed [11]. Studies that utilize the NK model to examine the performance of centralizing or decentralizing authority under the granularity of decision-making within an organization and its complex dependencies [12, 13], and studies that utilize economic models and cite the findings of economics to examine them in models aimed at maximizing utility [14], and its applications are wide-ranging. Due to its versatility, this field has been developed in various ways for strategic and organizational theories. However, few studies have focused on intangible assets and their utilization.

There is little prior research that combines (1) and (2). In recent years, Morimatsu et al. (2021) have focused on the relationship between decision-makers and performance using Intellectual Capital based on an economic model [15], but there is no perspective on the important issue of human resource recruitment. Given the current situation in which intangible assets are increasingly in the spotlight, as some fabless companies have gained high market value in recent years, we see value in the area that this study will open.

3 Modeling

3.1 Composition of the Decision-Making Model in the Agent

To analyze a company's specific actions regarding investment strategies for business diversification from a decision-making perspective, it is desirable to have a model in which the decisions made are reflected directly in sales as much as possible. Therefore, the basic model structure is based on Morimatsu et al. (2021) and adopts an economic model, especially an econometric approach [15]. Figure 1 shows an overview of the model. The model uses the amount available for investment, which is defined as sales minus costs, minus savings, to invest in the elements represented by intellectual capital. The effect of the investment is returned to sales, creating a loop structure. The model also assumes that the decision maker's strategy is involved in the allocation of the investment.

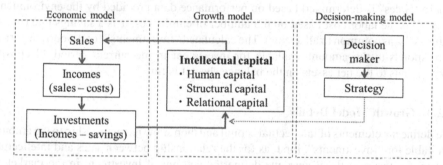

Fig. 1. Defining relationships in a model

3.2 Agent Details

3.2.1 Overview

We model firms that have no tangible or intangible assets. Therefore, since all sources of cash flow will be human resources, each agent will own human resources, which is employees. The agents decide how much to invest in existing markets and new markets based on the assets (employees), market conditions, and investment strategy. Agents strive to maximize their own utility using market conditions information in addition to the code of conduct (initial values), just as they make decisions in real business activities, even with imperfect information. Therefore, it is limited to partial optimization problems. The variable parameter that can be varied when striving for maximization is the amount of increase in labor due to the hiring of new human resources. This is set based on the definition of labor as capital in this simulation setting. And valuation function is assumed to be the firm value. Thus, the agent will act to maximize the firm value. Equity financing and borrowing are excluded from the implementation in this model for the sake of simplicity. Therefore, the corporate value will depend entirely on the cash flows generated by its agents. In this model, only the "research-driven" type, which always conducts a certain amount of research and invests in new markets, is implemented. This unifies the types to simulate the situation of related diversification as well as to compare the situation across simulations.

3.2.2 Economic Model Details

The economic model is defined with simple content, as shown in the model in Fig. 1.

$$Incomes = Sales - costs \tag{1}$$

$$Investments = Incomes \times (1 - \alpha) \tag{2}$$

$$Deposit_{t+1} = Deposit_t + Incomes \times \alpha \tag{3}$$

where "Sales" is determined based on performance data provided by the environment. "Costs" is the labor cost based on the number of employees. α is a savings rate (initial value is 0.2 as common to all agents). The calculated "Investments" for the current period corresponds to the amount available for investment in the current period. "Deposit" corresponds to the net assets on the balance sheet. t is time.

3.2.3 Growth Model Details

We define the elements of intellectual capital and then show its relationship to the amount available for "Investments". First, as for the relationship between sales and intellectual capital for the next fiscal year, we define the amount of investment in the market as the amount that will lead directly to sales if market saturation is not observed. The amount of investment is based on the field of Intellectual Capital [7] and is calculated as follows: the internal "human resource capability" corresponding to Human Capital and the "organizational capability" corresponding to Structural Capital. We define it as the multiplication of both. In other words, the economic impact of a company is measured by two contributions, one from its human resources and the other from its corporate brand and track record. Note, we will follow the structural model that all Customer Capital will be included in Structural Capital this time [16].

$$R_t = \sum_{i=1}^{n} I_{i,t} \tag{4}$$

$$I_{i,t} = \alpha_{i,t} \times \beta_{i,t} \tag{5}$$

where R_t is the agent's total investment (which would be sales as is if the constraint is not violated), $I_{i,t}$ is the amount of investment in the relevant market, n is the number of businesses owned, $\alpha_{i,t}$ is human resource capability, $\beta_{i,t}$ is organizational capability, and t is time.

The definition of human resource capability is the multiplication of each employee's capability by the time he or she is engaged. The model is based on the learning curve proposed in the field of psychology and is defined simply as a natural logarithmic function. The time spent on the project will be determined by the decision maker's adoption. Organizational capability is defined as the growth or decline in sales of all businesses, to express the accumulation of performance.

$$\alpha_{i,t} = \sum_{j=1}^{m} \left(c_{j,t} \times h_{j,t} \right)$$
$$s.t. 0 \leq h_{j,t} \leq 1 \tag{6}$$

$$c_{j,t} = \log E_{j,t}$$
$$E_{j,t} = E_{j,t-1} + Investments_{j,t} \tag{7}$$
$$s.t. 0 < c_{i,t}$$

$$\beta_{i,t} = \beta_{i,t-1} + \left(\frac{R_t}{R_{t-1}} - 1 \right)$$
$$s.t. \beta_0 = 1 \# \tag{8}$$

where $\alpha_{i,t}$ is human resource capacity, $\beta_{i,t}$ is organizational capacity, m is the number of employees engaged, $C_{j,t}$ is employee capacity, $h_{j,t}$ is time spent in the relevant business, $E_{j,t}$ is the amount of cumulative investment in the employee, $Investments_{j,t}$ is the amount invested in the relevant employee for the current period, and t is time.

3.2.4 Details of the Decision-Making Model

The decision-making model implements (1) a method for defining decisions as variables (parameters) and (2) optimization of actions by a dynamic discrete choice model, to simulate the behavior of a company.

(1) Each company has parameters that correspond to its culture according to its characteristics at the time of creation. Strategies are formulated based on these values, and the behavior of each agent will differ. In addition to the factors of (a) the number of prospective years, (b) the criteria for allocation of investment, (c) the amount of investment in new markets, and (d) the employment rate. (a) means the number of years a company considers when forecasting the future of a market for and, the criteria for (b) are used to choose which business to allocate the in-vestment amount to, in order of contribution to sales or expected growth rate of the market. (c) is the previous study used a constant amount, but we are verifying the results when the amount is varied in this study. (d) is newly added in this study and represents an internal indicator of the extent to which the return on investment is expected when hiring human resources. All of these are defined at the time of generation and are defined as being independent of external conditions.

(2) Before optimization by dynamic discrete choice model, the amount of investment in the new market is defined first to implement a "research-driven" model. The amount of investment is calculated using Eq. (5) by assigning the employee hours $h_{j,t}$ from the parameters in above (c). Note that the target employees for development are selected at random. Next, regarding the amount of investment in the existing

market, we consider maximizing the efficiency of each project based on the dynamic discrete choice model [17, 18]. Here, as an important setting in this model, the parameter that can be varied when striving to optimize actions in the dynamic discrete choice model is the amount of increase in the labor force due to the hiring of new human resources. While two actions exist to increase sales, training employees and hiring new employees, there is a limit to how much an employee can improve his or her abilities, so hiring new employees is necessary to significantly increase sales. However, since the company will be in the red at the time of hiring, its policy will vary greatly depending on whether it is seeking short-term or long-term profits. Activities are directed toward the expected state of business environment at the time of hiring, even if the future employment status of the employee is uncertain. And we define a firm's decision to move toward employment activity if the amount of incremental profit per person employed that can be expected in the future is greater than or equal to the firm's expected rate. By incorporating this formula into the optimization process using a dynamic discrete choice model, if the expected rate is less than or equal to the expected rate, the firm will choose not to hire.

$$Rate_a = \frac{\sum_{i=1}^{n} I_{(i,t|a)}}{a} \tag{9}$$

where $Rate$ is the amount of profit increase per employee, $\sum_{i=1}^{n} I_{(i,t|a)}$ is the expected sales, and a is the number of people to be hired (since the cost is set to 1 per employee, it is assumed to be the cost).

The following is defined as a dynamic discrete choice model method based on above condition. The algorithm of the details is also shown in Fig. 2. Based on the updated employee list, the expected sales are calculated using Eqs. (1) through (8). Once the expected sales can be calculated, the expected profit for the next fiscal year can also be calculated and based on this, training is conducted again, and the employee list is continuously updated for the expected number of years. Finally, the state that will yield the greatest profit after the expected number of years is selected and adopted as the action to be taken in the current fiscal year to achieve it.

$$V(x_t) = \max_{a \in A} \left\{ u(x_t, \alpha) + \beta \sum_{m=1}^{M} V(x_t, Rate_a) f(x_t | (x_t, a, g, s, o, h, El) \right\} \tag{10}$$

$$s.t. Rate_a \geq Target$$

where V is the value function (expected state), x_t is the state in period t, a is the number of employees, $u(x_{it,\alpha})$ is the state in the current period, β is the discount rate, M is the number of forecast years, g is the market growth rate, s is the market share, o is organizational capability, h is human resource capability, El is the employee list, $Target$ is the number of employees a firm needs to hire for one employee The expected rate of profit improvement (initial value at the time of company creation). The parameters fixed at the time of forecasting are β, M, g, s, o, and o. However, if there are multiple states in which similar profits can be expected due to market saturation, the state with the fewest number of employees is selected.

The actual cost is defined as the cost per person employed at the time of hiring and firing. Because external capital is excluded from the model, incorporating this cost into

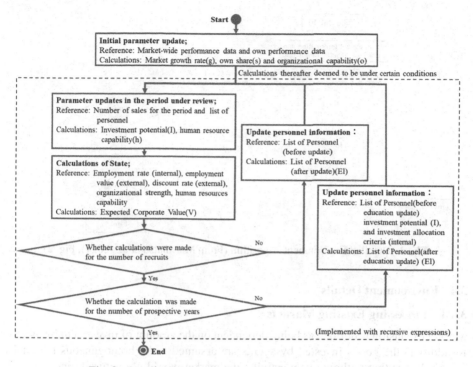

Fig. 2. Details of Dynamic discrete choice model Algorithm

the above dynamic discrete choice model method would result in a shortfall of funds in the short term, and the agent would not be able to operate. Therefore, although it is a strong assumption here, this cost is directly subtracted from the Balance Sheet, and the valuation is verified by substituting the enterprise value in the final period. In other words, the updated formula for the Balance Sheet is as follows.

$$BS_t = BS_{t-1} + D - \sum_{k=1}^{l} E_l \tag{11}$$

where BS_t is the net assets of the current period, BS_{t-1} is the net assets of the previous period, D is the savings of the current period, E is the cost of hiring or firing, l is the number of people employed.

3.3 Defining the Relationship Between the Environment and the Agent

The environment settings are taken from Morimatsu et al. (2021). Figure 3 shows the algorithmic flow of the cited environment. A life cycle is set up for the market to represent market selection through innovation. The existing market is defined as receiving investment from agents, managing the growth or contraction of the overall market, and providing feedback of results to each agent. New markets are defined by receiving investments from agents, making decisions on whether the creation of new markets will be successful, and providing feedback on the results to each agent.

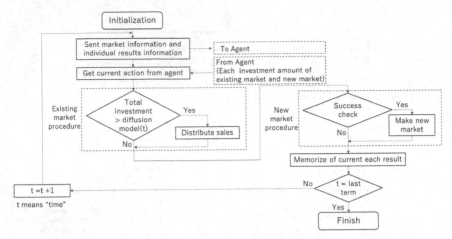

Fig. 3. Detailed Environment Algorithm (From Morimatsu et al. (2021), Fig. 2)

3.4 Environment Details

3.4.1 Processing Existing Markets

Market expansion is defined as being dependent on the amount of investment by agents. In addition, the goods invested by agents are assumed to be homogeneous materials. This indicates that without agent activity, the market would not naturally increase. On the other hand, since there is a limit to the needs of the market, as a constraint in the expansion of the market, we manage that market based on the output value of the diffusion model of new products by Mahajan et al. (1990) [19].

$$f(t) = \frac{p(p+q)^2 e^{-(p+q)t}}{(p+qe^{-(p+q)t})^2} \times bias \qquad (12)$$

where p is the innovator and defines the speed of product diffusion. t is time and *bias* is an adjustment term.

Numerical values and ratios for p and q in Eq. (12) have been proposed for various markets through empirical studies. We will operate with p and q as 0.03 and 0.38, respectively, to get an indication of the severity of the semiconductor industry, as described in the hypothesis. Note that we multiply by 1,000 as a bias for the sake of readability. If there are multiple agents when the constraint is violated, sales are assumed to be distributed to each agent according to its percentage of the respective investment amount. Based on Eqs. (1), (4), and (12), we define.

$$\begin{cases} Sales_k = R_k, & f(t) \geq \sum_{k=1}^{l} R_k \\ Sales_k = f(t) \times \frac{R_k}{\sum_{k=1}^{A} R_k}, & f(t) < \sum_{k=1}^{l} R_k \end{cases} \qquad (13)$$

where *Sales* is the actual sales for the next period, k is the corresponding agent number, R_k is the investment of the corresponding agent, $f(t)$ is the limiting quantity for the current period, and A is the total number of agents.

3.4.2 Processing New Markets

The conditions for their creation need to be defined. To facilitate the analysis of the strategy, the new markets should not be disrupted but should be adjusted so that there are a total of three large market life cycles. The definition of its generation is given below.

$$F(t) = \frac{1-e^{-(p+q)I}}{1+\left(\frac{q}{p}\right)e^{-(p+q)I}} \times bias$$

$$I = \sum_{t=1}^{N} I_{i,t} \tag{14}$$

$$\begin{cases} Success_k, F(t) \geq Random\,value \\ Failure_k, F(t) < Random\,value \end{cases}$$

where $F(t)$ is the threshold for generation, p is the innovator, q is the imitator, I is the agent's cumulative investment, bias is the adjustment term, k is the agent's number, N is the cumulative number of years, and *Randomvalue* is a random value in period t.

The specification is based on the accumulation of investment over the past five years (N = 5) for each agent, and then a lottery is used for each agent to determine whether it is successful in creating or entering the market. The probability density function is based on the diffusion model described above. The parameters defined in Eq. (1) are used for the variables p and q in this equation. Substituting each variable at time t, a proxy generation probability can be calculated, and then a random number is used to determine whether the new market has been successfully generated by checking whether it is within that probability or not.

3.5 Simulation Overview

We summarize the overall simulation setup. The evaluation shall be the final phase of the simulation. The final period should be set up so that the environment is such that the results will be those of a stage in which the agent's activities are generally completed. This is because the results cannot be compared from simulation to simulation unless the growth has converged. Simulation period is set the 30 years based on the analysis of Mishina (2004) [4, 5]. This is to avoid the possibility that a shorter period would result in an evaluation at a stray or tactical level rather than a strategic one. Information management is defined that the only information provided to all agents as public information is the size of the overall market and the establishment status (presence or absence) of new markets. Other nonpublic information, such as the actual sales of each agent or the amount of investment in a new business, for example, is not disclosed to the public.

The processing flow of actions that are necessary and common to all agents in the simulation operation is shown in Fig. 4.

A new market generation check is performed (number 1). If successful, the process is to transfer all employees who were engaged in new business development in the previous period to the newly created business unit. Note that upon transfer, the employees shall be transferred to the new division with half the capacity of the original division. If that is less than the initial value, it will be the initial value. The restructuring process is then carried out when the company has a surplus of labor (number 2). The order of processing here

Algorithm 1: Processing on simulation operation

Input:
  I : amount of Investments
  Nm: New Market Generation Flag
  Np :Number of projects
  Ta: Transfer authority
  El: Employee List (before update)
  Tv: Target value
  Gr: Growth rate focus flag
  Mg: Market growth rate
Output:
  D: Savings for the current term
  El: Employee List (after update)

```
1   IF Nm is applicable THEN
      Np + 1
      El = Transfer_target(El)
    ENDIF
    FOR Np
2     IF Excessive labor force THEN
        IF Ta is applicable THEN
          Target_list = Transfer_target(El, Tv)
        ENDIF
        El = Dissmissal_target(El, Tv, Target_list)
      ENDIF
3     IF Gr is applicable THEN
        value = growth_rate_standard(Np, I, Np, Mg)
      ELSE
        value = sales_standard(Np, I, Np, S)
4     El = Education(value, El)
    ENDFOR
```

Fig. 4. Processing on simulation operation

is done before the previous study. Next, the amount available for investment is allocated based on the allocation criteria (number 3). The allocation criteria are defined at the time the agents are generated. Two allocation criteria are established: a sales criterion and a market growth rate criterion. Finally, the allocated amount and the personnel assigned to the project are trained (number 4).

These situations are described in python and simulations are performed.

4 Verification Results

To analyze the specific behavior of firms concerning their investment strategy for business diversification from a decision-making perspective, we examine (1) the observed changes in strategy due to hiring and firing rates and (2) the observed changes in strategy due to changes in investment rates and initial headcount skills.

Unless otherwise noted, each sample size is 200, the number of agents is 2, β is 0.9 savings ratio is 0.2, the number of employees initially assigned is 7, and the total initial skill value is 10. The initial value of BS is 0. Even if BS becomes negative, the company will not go bankrupt, and its activities can continue.

4.1 Hiring Rates and Firing Rates

We analyze the change in firm value when reflecting on the decision to hire and fire personnel as an extension of the previous study. Figure 5 shows the results for agents that reflect hiring rates and those that do not. The horizontal axis is the employment rate, and the left vertical axis shows the average firm value in the last period, while the right side shows the investment efficiency in the transition period between periods 5 and 10, respectively. It can be read that the employment rate is reflected in agent 1, and as the rate increases, investment efficiency also increases but is not linked to firm value. This same trend was observed in the test conditions for all agents.[1]

Figure 6 shows the results for agents that reflect the cost of hiring/firing and those that do not. The horizontal axis shows the hiring/firing rate, and the left vertical axis shows the average firm value in the last period, while the right side shows the average number of employees hired. At a hiring/firing cost of 3, the performance of agents is flat between agents, but the cost of employees is set at 1 per period, which would be a niche industry example since the labor market case is based on a projected cost of six times annual revenue. As can be seen in the increase in investment efficiency discussed earlier, Agent 1 can mitigate the impact of rising costs, but the difference between Agent 1 and Agent 2 is difficult to close because of the relatively low performance in the core business in the first place.[2]

Fig. 5 Adoption rate and investment efficiency vs enterprise value

---

[1] The details of this test condition do not reflect employment costs for both agents; Agent 1 has a 2-year outlook year and a growth rate allocation, and Agent 2 has a 3-year outlook year and a growth rate allocation. The amount of investment in new markets is uniformly 10%.

[2] The details of this test condition are as follows: agent 1 has a 2-year outlook year and a growth rate allocation; agent 2 has a 3-year outlook year and a growth rate allocation. The amount of investment in new markets is uniformly 10%.

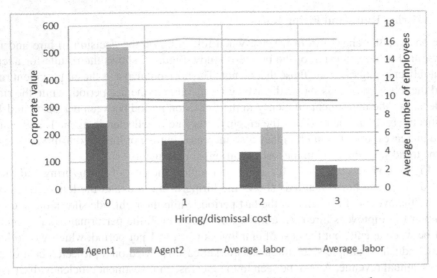

Fig. 6 Average recruitment cost and several hires vs company value

4.2 Change in Investment Rate and Skills of Initial Number of People

Test whether the strategy should be changed depending on the allocation of investment to new businesses and the skills of the employees deployed during the start-up phase (t = 0). Table 1 summarizes the test results. The horizontal axis of the table shows the differences in the test conditions, with the skills of the employees initially assigned to the new business set at a lower level as one move to the right. The vertical axis of the table sets the conditions under which the investment ratio for new business was varied. Note that all changes in the test conditions are reflected only in Agent 1, while Agent 2 remains in the initial conditions. The results show that under the original conditions, the firm that increased its investment in new businesses and successfully diversified ahead of its competitors was ahead of the pack. However, we also see that over-investment without adapting to the market environment, as in the 30% result, results in lower final corporate value. Even in the case where the skills of the initially deployed employees deteriorated, the company was able to gain an advantage in the next market, even if it could not gain an advantage in the first market, by being ahead of its competitors in developing new businesses, indicating that the final corporate value is higher for Agent 1. However, it can also be seen that in the case of an investment volume that does not match the market, a lot of losses are wasted.[3]

---

[3] The details of the conditions of this study are as follows: both Agents 1 and 2 have a 3-year outlook period, a growth rate allocation, and an employment rate of 0.5.

Table 1. Experimental results from all conditions

Average of coporate value in the last period		Original		Condition 1		Condition 2	
		Agent 1	Agent 2	Agent 1	Agent 2	Agent 1	Agent 2
Investment Ratio	10%	32.7	30.3	−54.2	38.2	−163.6	−27.5
	20%	256.7	1.8	8.6	−9.7	−18.6	−44.8
	30%	42.9	−18.0	−86.7	−40.6	−178.8	−49.2

Note: All changes in test conditions are reflected only in Agent 1. The total skill value of the original condition is 10.0, Condition 1 is 8.8, Condition 2 is 7.4

4.3 Discussion

To analyze the specific behavior of firms regarding investment strategies for business diversification from a decision-making perspective, two tests were conducted: (1) observation of changes in strategies by hiring and firing rates, and (2) observation of changes in strategies by investment rates and an initial number of skills.

(1) The results agree with the suggestion of the previous study that "companies that invest human resources equal to or better than their competitors at the dawn of the market, even at the expense of some efficiency, achieve superior performance" [15]. This suggests that establishing a position in the early stage of the market and quickly building a growth loop is the most important factor in overcoming the severe business environment.
(2) When the above is unattainable, rather than forcing firms to compete with strong competitors, firms should invest in new businesses and innovate ahead of their competitors, which will ultimately lead to higher corporate value.

However, it is important to note that this life cycle simulates a very difficult situation, as exemplified by semiconductors. Therefore, while there is value in fighting for market share in the short term, it should be noted that in the case of a gradual life cycle, it may be better to change the range of strategies based on the market.

5 Conclusions and Further Work

We use an agent-based model to elucidate the strategies of firms that have achieved superior performance even in an environment of market shakeout due to innovation. Assuming that a company's sales consist only of intangible assets, we analyze the specific actions of the company regarding investment strategy from the viewpoint of decision-making and found that (1) it is important to invest more than competitors even at the expense of efficiency in the early stage of a business, and (2) business growth by investing talented human resources ahead of competitors is the most important factor in the (3) If it is difficult to secure human resources, it is important to make investment decisions for further new business development ahead of competitors. One of the novelties of this study is that it quantitatively provides valid suggestions regarding investment strategies for businesses.

Future work includes increasing the number of decision-making options to better project the real environment. For example, each employee may have a different learning curve and more investment options. In addition, although we used a single parameter of organizational strength in this study it should be possible to subdivide it into various factors such as brand, channel, culture, etc. We should be able to examine the details of these factors, including the validation of the model. We will expand the model to provide more specific suggestions in the future.

References

1. Christensen, C.M.: Exploring the limits of the technology s-curve. Part I Comp. Technol. Prod. Oper. Manage. **1**(4), 334–357 (1992)
2. Christensen, C.M.: Exploring the limits of the technology s-curve. Part II Arch. Technol. Prod. Oper. Manage. **1**(4), 358–366 (1992)
3. Kim, D., Kogut, B.: Technological platforms and diversification. Organ. Sci. **7**(3), 283–301 (1996)
4. Mishina, K.: The Logic of Strategic Failure, TOYO KEIZAI INC, Japan (2004) (in Japanese)
5. Mishina, K.: Causes and effects of Strategic Failure, TOYO KEIZAI INC, Japan (2007) (in Japanese)
6. Konno, Y.: Impact of "product scope" and "customer scope": suppliers' diversification strategy and performance. Ann. Bus. Administrative Sci. **16**(1), 15–28 (2017)
7. Edvinsson, L.: Developing a model for managing intellectual capital. Eur. Manage. J. **14**(4), 356–364 (1996)
8. Petty, R., Guthrie, J.: Intellectual capital literature review measurement, reporting, and management. J. Intellect. Cap. **1**(2), 155–176 (2000)
9. Bontis, N.: Intellectual capital an exploratory study that develops measures and models. Manag. Decis. **36**(2), 63–76 (1998)
10. Chen, J., Zhu, Z., Xie, H.Y.: Measuring intellectual capital: a new model and empirical study. J. Intellectual Capital **5**(1), 195–212 (2004)
11. Tesfatsion, L.: Agent-Based Computational Economics_ Overview and Brief History. Iowa State University Working, Paper Number 21004 (2021)
12. Kollman, K., Miller, J.H., Page, S.E.: Decentralization and the search for policy solutions. J. Law Econ. Organ. **16**, 102–128 (2000)
13. Rivkin, J.W., Siggelkow, N.: Balancing search and stability: interdependencies among elements of organizational design. Manage. Sci. **49**, 290–311 (2003)
14. Chang, M.-H., Harrington, J.E., Jr.: Centralization vs decentralization in a multi-unit organization: a computational model of a retail chain as a multi-agent adaptive system. Manage. Sci. **46**(11), 1427–1440 (2000)
15. Morimatsu, K., Takahashi, H.: What is the investment strategy to overcome the severe business environment? - Perspectives on decision makers competencies and institutional designs -. In: International Workshop: Artificial Intelligence of and for Business (2021)
16. Lovingsson, F., Dell'Orto, S., Baladi, P.: Navigating with new managerial tools. J. Intellect. Cap. **1**(2), 147–154 (2000)
17. Rust, J.: Structural estimation of markov decision processes. Handb. Econ. **4**, 3081–3143 (1994)
18. Aguirregabiria, V., Mira, P.: Dynamic discrete choice structural models: a survey. J. Econometrics **156**, 38–67 (2010)
19. Mahajan, V, Muller, E., bass, F.M.: New product diffusion models in marketing: a review and directions for research. J. Market. **54**(1), 1–26 (1990)

Empirical Analysis of the Impact of Mergers and Acquisitions on Innovation Activities Through Clustering

Nozomi Tamagawa$^{(\boxtimes)}$ and Hiroshi Takahashi

Graduate School of Business Administration, Keio University, 4-1-1 Hiyoshi, Kohoku-Ku, Yokohama 223-8526, Kanagawa, Japan
{tmrevo1996,htaka}@keio.jp

Abstract. Using large-scale patent data, we analyze the impact of mergers and acquisitions (M&A) on innovation activities in companies. The analysis classifies M&A according to the trend of innovation output through their index clustering. In addition, we measure the technological distances among companies using patent document data, then apply the distances to the evaluation of M&A. As a result, we find two types of clusters: 1) one with the tendency to increase the postmerger innovation outputs; 2) the other with a trend to decrease innovation output around M&A deals. The former cluster tends to have a smaller innovation output scale around deals than the other clusters. Furthermore, compared to the other groups, the group whose postmerger innovation output decreases has the largest increase in stock price return after the deal announcement. This study's major findings indicate that the combination of unstructured text data and machine learning methods applies to M&A and innovation.

Keywords: M&A · Innovation · Natural Language Processing · Patent Document Vector

1 Introduction

This paper empirically analyzes the impact of mergers and acquisitions (M&A) on subsequent innovation activities in a company. Previous studies have discussed the relationship between M&A and innovation activities [1–3]; however, there is a problem with the number of patent applications, the International Patent Classification (IPC), and the industry classification used in these analyses, which cannot consider the details of the technology owned by companies. Simultaneously, with the recent development of information technology, new methods and unstructured data have been applied in many research fields. With this background, this paper refers to Tamagawa and Takahashi (2021) to analyze the index of innovation output for M&A in the Japanese market by using clustering, a machine learning method [4]. We also quantitatively measure the technological similarity between companies by analyzing the patent document data using the natural language processing method. Furthermore, we add to the extant literature by

© Springer Nature Switzerland AG 2023
K. Yada et al. (Eds.): JSAI-isAI 2021 Workshops, LNAI 13856, pp. 365–379, 2023.
https://doi.org/10.1007/978-3-031-36190-6_25

refining the data extraction method, comparing stock returns, and validating the analysis results using tests [4]. In this way, we attempt to apply information technology methods to finance while considering the details of the company's technology in the analysis.

Previous studies conducted various discussions on M&A and innovation, and their importance can be seen. First, concerning the relationship between corporate activities and innovation, it is widely recognized that innovation improves corporate value [5]. In addition, Kaplan (2001) argues that many M&A deals were conducted for technological reasons [6]. However, it is also claimed that M&A harms companies' innovation output through considerable costs incurred by M&A and delays in daily technical decisions because the management's time and effort are directed to tasks generated by M&A [7, 8]. However, M&A many companies still conduct M&A, and this conclusion fails to explain the situation. For example, it is possible to gain economies of scale and scope in R&D through M&A, create new combinations of technologies, and increase innovation output [9, 10]. Therefore, factors and conditions that increase or decrease innovation output through M&A have been widely discussed. In their analysis of the chemical industry, Ahuja and Katila (2001) show that in technological acquisitions, the absolute size of the acquired knowledge base increases the innovation output, while the relative size of the acquired knowledge base decreases output [3]. In addition, Bena and Li (2014) use a large dataset of patents, finding that technological overlap among firms positively affects the probability of M&A deals occurring, and pairs with technological overlap produce more innovation output after the deal [1].

These previous studies analyze indicators based on the criteria, such as Financial Indexes, Industrial Classifications, IPC, and other indicators. Patent data has been widely utilized in analyzing firms' technological characteristics and innovation output; however, one issue with focusing on the number of patent applications or the IPC used in previous research is that it may be challenging to consider the technology's detailed content or differences in product information or technology may be overlooked. Conversely, recent advances in information technology have made it possible to handle unstructured data. For example, large-scale textual information, which was previously challenging to analyze, is now being examined and applied for research in various fields. Specifically, Hoberg and Phillips (2010) analyze unstructured data of product descriptions for research in corporate finance [11], and Nishi et al. (2019) improve the accuracy of classification models through GPT-2 to analyze the impact of news articles on stock prices [12]. There is also a discussion, using computer simulation analysis, on the impact of central banking and financial risk management on markets [13, 14]. Matsumoto et al. (2019) use the patent document vector to quantitatively measure firms' degree of technological diversification [15].

Based on these previous studies, we apply unstructured data and machine learning methods to the research field of M&A and innovation activities. Specifically, to analyze the trend of M&A's impact on innovation activities, we measure the index of innovation output, use clustering to classify M&A, and compare each cluster. The advantage of using clustering is that it is easy to eliminate an analyst's arbitrariness. For example, Matsumoto et al. (2019) proposed an industry classification of companies using Fuzzy Clustering [16]. Regarding the technological similarity, the patent document vector is calculated by analyzing the patent document data from the acquirer and the target company in M&A through natural language processing; the technological distance between the companies is quantitatively measured. This method considers the details of the technologies possessed by the companies, making it possible to analyze document information, such as patent abstracts, which was difficult in previous studies. This approach allows us to analyze the impact of M&A on innovation output while applying the methods of unstructured data and machine learning.

2 Sample and Data

This paper uses patent data, M&A deals, and corporate stock data. First, we use the Derwent World Patent Index (DWPI) for patent data[1] from Japan, the U.S., and Germany, where patents were published between 1970 and 2015. The DWPI is a secondary patent database provided by Clarivate, which contains abstracts by technical experts and their titles and technical classifications. The advantage of using DWPI is that it allows us to examine the patent document objectively without depending on the patent applicant [17]. In addition, a patent's publication refers to the patent office releasing information regarding the application after about 18 months have passed from the submission [18]. Next, we obtain data on M&A deals from Refinitiv Eikon, a database provided by Refinitiv. The following shows the extraction method of M&A deals for analysis, divided into three major steps.

First, in Step 1, we extract M&A deals announced between 1988 and 2012 between Japanese public companies. Among those M&A deals, we exclude the deals classified as "Exchange Offer," "Buyback," or "Recapitalization" and extract only the deals classified as "Completed" in the Refinitiv Eikon database. Second, in Step 2, from the M&A data extracted above, we select deals in which both the acquirer and the target are assigned a standard code[2] in DWPI; the code comprises four unique letters that Clarivate Analytics assigns to the companies with a particularly large number of patents (usually 500 or more) among the applicants [19]. In addition, among the extracted M&A deals, we extract only companies in which the acquirer and the target company have applied for at least one patent from the year of the deal announcement to three years prior. Finally, in Step 3, we eliminate deals in which the ratio of shares acquired in M&A is less than 50%, leaving 75 M&A deals for analysis. Figure 1 shows the extraction method of M&A to be analyzed.

Finally, we obtain the companies' stock data from Nikkei NEEDS. Specifically, we take the acquirer's monthly ex-rights adjusted closing prices in the M&A deals to be analyzed from January 1985 to December 2015. Since there are cases where the target company's corporate name changed around the M&A announcement, we identify such deals by examining the corporate history from each company's website. Then, we analyze the acquirer's stock price by using the stock data of the company name[3] after the change.

---

[1] Some of the patents in the data used include patents that the applicant does not yet license.

[2] The standard code is assigned to the subsidiaries as well.

[3] If both the closing price of the company name before and after the change exists in the database, we use the new company name to conduct the analysis.

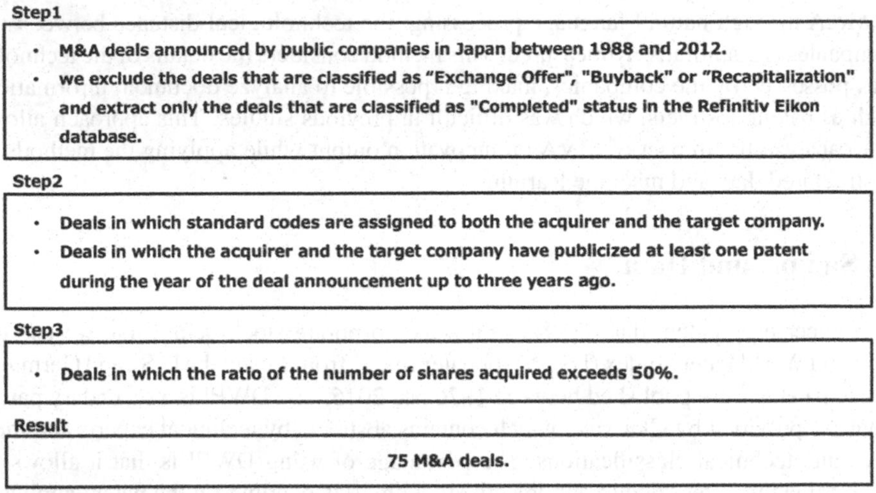

Step1

> • **M&A deals announced by public companies in Japan between 1988 and 2012.**
> • **we exclude the deals that are classified as "Exchange Offer", "Buyback" or "Recapitalization" and extract only the deals that are classified as "Completed" status in the Refinitiv Eikon database.**

Step2

> • **Deals in which standard codes are assigned to both the acquirer and the target company.**
> • **Deals in which the acquirer and the target company have publicized at least one patent during the year of the deal announcement up to three years ago.**

Step3

> • **Deals in which the ratio of the number of shares acquired exceeds 50%.**

Result

> **75 M&A deals.**

Fig. 1. Extraction of M&A deals for analysis.

3 Methodology

This chapter shows the analysis methodology: Sect. 3.1 describes the measurement of innovation output; Sect. 3.2 provides the classification method through clustering; Sect. 3.3 describes the measurement of stock price return; Sect. 3.4 provides the calculation method of patent document vector; Sect. 3.5 describes the measurement of technological distance.

3.1 Measurement of Innovation Output

We calculate *Patent Index* for each M&A deal concerning Bena and Li (2014) and utilize it as an index of innovation output [1]. To compare the change of innovation output around M&A, we measure *Patent Index* for each year, in the seven years from three years before (ayr-3) to three years after (ayr+3), based on the year when each M&A deal was announced (ayr).

There are three steps in calculating the *Patent Index*. First, we compute the median value of the number of published patents in technology class k with year t across all firms that published at least one patent in technology class k in year t in Japan. This paper uses the classification code assigned to patents in IPC as the technology class k. IPC classifies patents in four levels—section, class, subclass, and group—assigning a classification code to each level [20]. This analysis treats the classification codes up to class in IPC as the technology class k. In addition, if multiple classes are assigned to a single patent, the combination of classes is treated as one unique technology class k. In addition, we measure the number of applicants using each patent's applicant code in the DWPI and the company name in English. If a patent has multiple applicants, we count one patent for each company. Second, we measure the acquirer's and target firm's total number of published patents in each technology class k with the year t in Japan, scaled by the median value from the second step. This process excludes patents jointly applied by the acquirer and the target company to avoid duplicate counting. Third, we calculate *Patent Index* by summing the scaled value from the second step across all technology classes k and year t for each M&A deal. Using the above method, the acquirer's and target firm's combined innovation output is the *Patent Index* for each M&A deal.

We then show the method for extracting the acquirer's and target firm's patents from DWPI in this analysis. We use the applicant standard code of DWPI from Tamagawa and Takahashi (2021) [4] to search the patent data from DWPI. However, the previous study's search methods indicate a possibility that patent data may contain subsidiaries that are unrelated to the analysis target or companies that are not directly related to M&A. Therefore, we include the name of the analyzed company in addition to the standard code to provide more accurate and reliable data. Finally, we examine each company's history using its website and identify cases where the company name changed after M&A and established its name after the change. Then, the company's patent data and the new English name after the change are also searched using the standard or non-standard code in the DWPI applicant code to analyze patent data in the M&A.

3.2 Classification Method Through Clustering

We show the method to classify M&A through the clustering method for the innovation output calculated above. Referring to Tamagawa and Takahashi (2021), based on the *Patent Index*'s seven values for each deal from $ayr-3$ to $ayr+3$, calculated by the above method, we classify the 75 M&A deals through clustering [4], as described below. First, for each M&A deal, we calculate the sum of the seven-year *Patent Index* values from $ayr-3$ to $ayr+3$. We use the sum of these values to divide the *Patent Index*'s value for each M&A deal each year. In this way, we obtain the percentage of *Patent Index* for each year ($ayr-3$ to $ayr+3$) against the total value of *Patent Index* for seven years in each deal. When this value is summed from $ayr-3$ to $ayr+3$ for each M&A, it takes the value of 1. This value shows the percentage of innovation output each year to the total *Patent Index* from $ayr-3$ to $ayr+3$. This process makes it possible to eliminate the scale factor from each M&A's value of the *Patent Index*, making it possible to classify by the characteristics of the change in *Patent Index* in clustering. Finally, we classify the M&A by utilizing the k-means method for the seven values calculated above. We set the number of clusters to 3.[4]

3.3 Measurement of Stock Price Return

We show the method to calculate the acquirer's annual average stock price return in M&A. The acquirer's monthly closing prices from Nikkei NEEDS are used. For each acquirer, the period for measuring the average stock price return is seven years, from three years before ($ayr-3$) to three years after ($ayr+3$), based on the year when each M&A deal was announced (ayr). First, we calculate the stock price return for each month based on the acquirer's monthly closing price. To calculate the monthly stock price return, we

---

[4] Among the analyses using other numbers of clusters, we describe the results when the number of clusters is set to 3 for interpretability reasons.

measure the difference between the acquirer's closing price S_t in month t and the closing price S_{t-1} in the previous month $t-1$, divided by the closing price in month $t-1$, shown in Eq. (1) below.

$$Stock\ Price\ Return_t = \frac{S_t - S_{t-1}}{S_t - 1}$$ (1)

Finally, the annual average stock return is measured by averaging the stock returns for each month in the analysis year. The closing price data before 1985 is not available from Nikkei NEEDS. Therefore, because we could not measure the stock price return in January 1985, we treated the average value of the stock price return for 11 months from February to December as the average stock price return for the year. In addition, one M&A[5] is excluded from the average stock price return analysis because there is a period when the stock price cannot be obtained.

3.4 Calculation Method of Patent Document Vector

We use Sparse Composite Document Vector (SCDV), concerning Mekala et al. (2017), to vectorize the patent document [21], and the analysis objects of SCDV and the settings of various parameters are determined following the analysis of Matsumoto et al. (2019) [15]. We analyze four items of textual information in DWPI's abstract as the objects of SCDV: novelty, detailed description, use, and advantage of the patent. First, the word vectors are obtained using the Skip-Gram model with dimensionality d set to 200 after stemming. Next, utilizing the gaussian mixture model, we classify the entire word vector into clusters, with the number of clusters k at 60 and the weight of each cluster with a probability ($w\vec{cv}_{ik}$). Then, we obtain the word vector of the $d \times k$ dimension by combining ($\oplus_{(1 \sim k)}$) these word vectors k times. The word vector is weighted again by the inverse document frequency IDF to obtain $w\vec{tv}_i$. In the following, the above analysis method of SCDV is shown by Eqs. (2), (3), and (4). N means the total number of documents, and df_t is the number of documents in which a word t appears.

$$w\vec{cv}_{ik} = wv_i \times P(C_k|w_i)$$ (2)

$$IDF_t = log\frac{N}{df_t} + 1$$ (3)

$$w\vec{tv}_i = IDF_t \times \oplus_{(1 \sim k)} w\vec{cv}_{ik}$$ (4)

Finally, we sum, standardize, and make the $w\vec{tv}_i$ sparse at the threshold, which provides a distributed representation of each patent document.

We visualize the patent document vector in two dimensions. Figure 2 shows the result of visualizing the patent vector of Toyota Motor Corporation and Daihatsu Motor Co., Ltd., an acquisition deal announced in 1998 (*ayr*). The visualization covers the

---

[5] In the case of the Komatsu Electronic Metals Co Ltd acquisition by SUMCO Corp announced in 2006, SUMCO Corp became public in 2005, and it was impossible to obtain the closing price data from Nikkei NEEDS from *ayr-3* to *ayr-1* before the deal announcement.

published patents for both firms over three years, from 1995 to 1997 (*ayr-3* to *ayr-1*) premerger. The 12,000-dimensional patent vector is represented by compressing it in two dimensions using the t-SNE method. The points plotted in Fig. 2 represent the patent vectors of both firms.

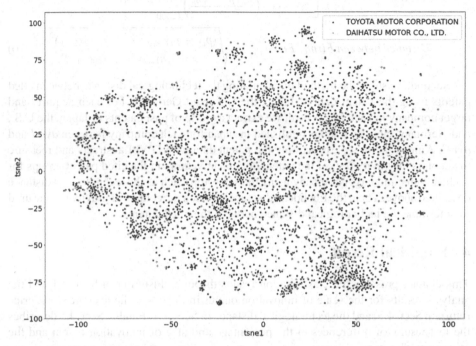

Fig. 2. Visualization of the patent document vector (Toyota, Daihatsu)

3.5 Measurement of Technological Distance

The following section shows the method to measure the technological distance between the acquirer and the target company for each M&A deal. In this paper, we measure two types of technological distance: one is the technological distance using the patents that the acquirer and the target company published before the announcement of M&A, and the other is the technological distance using the patents that those patents cite.

For the former, we calculate the distance between centers of gravity from the patent document vectors of the two companies, which we use as an index of technological distance in each M&A deal. The following method calculates the distance between the centers of gravity between acquirers and target firms for each M&A deal. First, we extract the document vectors of patents obtained by the acquirer and the target firm in each M&A deal, from three years ago to one year ago (*ayr-1* to *ayr-3*), based on the year the deal was announced (*ayr*). Then, we calculate the center of gravity (*cv*) for each acquirer and target firm by averaging the extracted 12,000-dimensional patent document vectors. We then calculate the Euclidean distance between the acquirer and the target firm's centers of gravity (cv) for each deal and use this as the technological distance. We show the above analysis method in Eqs. (5) and (6).

$$cv_i = \left[\left(\frac{p_1+p_2+\cdots+p_n}{n} \right)_1, \left(\frac{p_1+p_2+\cdots+p_n}{n} \right)_2, \cdots, \left(\frac{p_1+p_2+\cdots+p_n}{n} \right)_{12000} \right] \tag{5}$$

$$Distance\ between\ Firm_i,\ Firm_{i+1} = \sqrt{\frac{(p_{i1} - p_{i1+1})^2 + (p_{i2} - p_{i2+1})^2}{\cdots + (p_{i12000} - p_{i12000+1})^2}} \tag{6}$$

Second, we show the method of calculating the technological distance between cited patents using the patent data of Japan, the U.S., and Germany. For each acquirer and target company in each M&A deal, we extract a group of past patents in Japan, the U.S., and Germany, cited by patents published in Japan for each company between *ayr-1* and *ayr-3*. Among them, we extract only the patent data with DWPI abstracts and measure the centers of gravity (cv) of the patent document vectors in the cited patent groups for each acquirer and target company using the same approach as the technological distance described above. Then, the Euclidean distance between the centers of gravity is measured to determine the technological distance between the cited patents.

4 Empirical Result

This chapter presents the classification results through clustering in Sect. 4.1 and the analysis results for the scale of innovation output in Sect. 4.2, the average stock price return in Sect. 4.3, and the technological distance in Sect. 4.4. Finally, Sect. 4.5 describes the test results of differences in the percentage and size of innovation output and the average stock return.

4.1 Classification Results Through Clustering

As a result of clustering analysis, the numbers of deals classified into Clusters 1, 2, and 3 are 38, 22, and 15, respectively. Figure 3 shows the change of the ratio of each year's *Patent Index* to the total of the *Patent Index* of seven years calculated for each M&A deal used for the clustering analysis. The horizontal axis of the figure indicates the seven years from *ayr-3* (three years ago) to *ayr+3* (three years later) based on *ayr*, the year when each M&A deal was announced. The vertical axis in the figure indicates the ratio of the *Patent Index* for each year to the total *Patent Index* for the seven years. The figure shows the average value of the percentage of Patent Index of all M&A classified in each cluster and the average value of the percentage of Patent Index of all analyzed M&A deals.

From Fig. 3, we can confirm the innovation output trend around the announcement of M&A in each cluster. First, Cluster 1 generally follows the same trend as the average of all analyzed M&A deals. In Cluster 2, from *ayr-3* to *ayr+3*, the average value of the *Patent Index* decreases consistently compared to the average of the other clusters. Conversely, Cluster 3 has a trend of increasing the *Patent Index* for three years, from *ayr+1* to *ayr+3*.

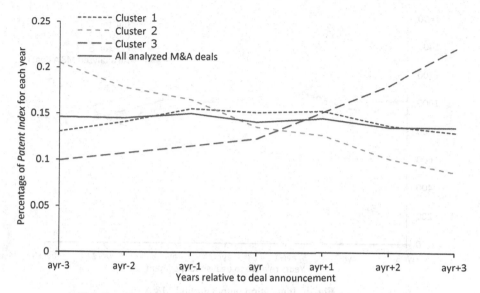

Fig. 3. Percentage of innovation output around M&A in each year.

4.2 Scale of Innovation Output

We next compare the scale of the *Patent Index* in each cluster. Fig. 4 shows the average value of the *Patent Index* for M&A classified in each cluster; the horizontal axis indicates the time around M&A (from *ayr-3* to *ayr+3*), and the vertical axis indicates the average value of each cluster's *Patent Index*. The figure shows the average of the M&A's Patent Index, classified into each cluster, and the average of the Patent Index values of all analyzed M&A deals.

Fig. 4 confirms the tendency of the scale of *Patent Index* in each cluster. Cluster 3, in which the upward trend of innovation output after the announcement of M&A, tends to have a smaller scale of *Patent Index*, from *ayr-3* to *ayr-1*, compared with the average of other clusters. The detailed analysis of these results is a future research subject.

4.3 Average Stock Price Return

Figure 5 shows the average stock price return each year, averaged by M&A, classified into each cluster. The horizontal axis indicates the time before and after M&A (ayr-3 to ayr+3), and the vertical axis indicates each year's average value of average stock return in each cluster.

From Fig. 5, the average stock price return trend for each year in each cluster can be confirmed. First, we can confirm the tendency that the upward average stock price return increases most in *ayr+1*, the year following the announcement year, in the seven years around the deal's announcement in all clusters. Furthermore, Cluster 2's average stock return, which shows a decrease in innovation output around the M&A announcement, increases significantly in *ayr+1*. The average stock price return of Cluster 2, which is confirmed to have increased innovation output after the M&A announcement, is the

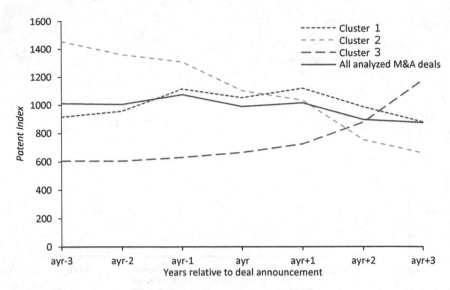

Fig. 4. Innovation output around M&A

smallest value in *ayr+1*. This result is interesting because it indicates that the innovation output and stock return trends after the M&A announcement are not necessarily the same.

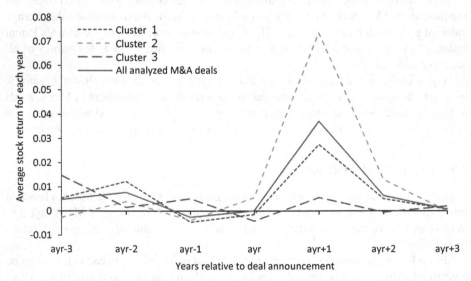

Fig. 5. Annual average stock returns in each cluster.

4.4 Technological Distance

We next compare the values of the technological distance in each cluster. Fig. 6 shows the technological distance between the acquirer and the target company and between the cited patents in each cluster. The technological distance between the cited patents is the value obtained from calculating the centers of gravity of the document vectors of the past patents cited by all patents that were published before the M&A announcement (*ayr-3* to *ayr-1*) in the acquirer and target company and then calculating the distance between the patents' centers of gravity. The vertical axis in the figure indicates the average technological distance between each cluster and the entire analysis target.

Figure 6 confirms that the technological distances in each cluster are almost the same. This analysis cannot confirm the relationship between the technological distance and the innovation output after the M&A announcement. Future research can conduct a detailed analysis by focusing on the industry and period when M&A was conducted, following the extant literature [22].

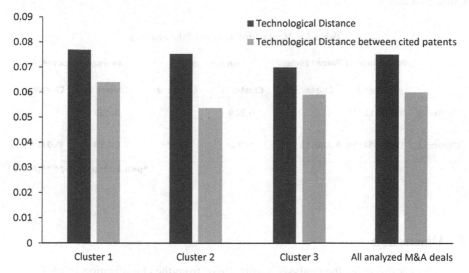

Fig. 6. Premerger technological distance.

4.5 Verification of Analysis Results

Finally, we show the difference tests using *t*-tests for the proportion and size of innovation output and average stock returns. The tests assume that the variances are not equal; the p-values (two-tailed) are shown in Table 1, and the details of each test are described below.

First, to determine the percentage of innovation output, the *t*-test results are shown using the percentage of the *Patent Index* for each year relative to the total of the *Patent Index* for seven years, from *ayr+1* to *ayr+3*, after the announcement of the deals used for clustering analysis. From the test results, we confirm that the difference in the mean value of the percentage of *Patent Index* after the deal announcement in each cluster is statistically significant (***: $p < 0.01$). This finding indicates that the difference in the trend after announcing a deal in each cluster is statistically significant.

Second, to determine the scale of innovation output, the t-test results are shown using the values of the *Patent Index* from *ayr-3* to *ayr*, when the trends among the clusters are observed. The test results confirm that the difference between the mean values of the *Patent Index* of Cluster 3 and the other clusters is statistically significant (**: $p < 0.05$, *: $p < 0.1$). Therefore, the difference in the trend of the size regarding the *Patent Index* before the deal announcement in Cluster 3 is statistically significant.

Finally, the t-test results for the average stock price returns are shown using each group's average stock price returns from *ayr* to *ayr+3*, when the characteristics are observed. From the test results, the difference between the mean values of Cluster 2, which has the largest stock return value in *ayr+1*, and Cluster 3, which has the smallest stock return value, is statistically significant (**: $p < 0.05$). This confirms the statistical result from the average stock return trend difference after the deal announcement between Clusters 2 and 3.

Table 1. Verification results of the analysis.

	Percentage of *Patent Index*		*Patent Index*		Average stock return	
	Cluster 1	Cluster 2	Cluster 1	Cluster 2	Cluster 1	Cluster 2
Cluster 2	3.67E-11***		0.309		0.163	
Cluster 3	1.51E-07***	4.17E-15***	0.072*	0.02**	0.253	0.045**

*p<0.1; **p<0.05; ***p<0.01

5 Discussion

This chapter discusses the analysis results. First, from the classification result by clustering, the clusters are classified into clusters whose innovation output increases and decreases after M&A, in line with the previous study [4]. This indicates that it is possible to classify M&A by the tendency of innovation activities after the announcement of M&A by using clustering as the innovation output indicator. Furthermore, as in the previous study, the cluster in which the innovation output tends to increase after the announcement tends to have a smaller scale of innovation output around M&A [4]. In this regard, the target company that is technologically small enough to allow the acquirer to take the initiative enables the smooth integration of R&D organizations and possibly increases the innovation output after the M&A announcement. In addition, the findings suggest that the trend of innovation output and stock price return after M&A is not necessarily the same.

Regarding the clusters where innovation output decreased, it is possible that R&D activities concerning the same technology were reduced after the M&A announcement or that the large-scale acquisition disrupted the R&D integration. Therefore, when we consider the trend of stock price return, stock prices evaluate the efficiency of R&D by reducing the same technology after M&A and the gains in economy of scale and scope. Another possibility is that stock prices do not immediately evaluate a company's R&D trend and reflect it in the evaluation when the new technology is implemented in products, and the business performance rises.

6 Conclusion

Utilizing large-scale patent data, we classify M&A deals through clustering and analyze the characteristics of each cluster for the innovation output around the announcement of the measured M&A. The analysis measures the innovation output of each M&A using patent data. In addition, we calculate patent document vectors by using natural language processing on patent document data. We also measure the technological distance between the acquirer and target companies in each deal and apply it to the evaluation of M&A. Based on the previous studies, we refine the data extraction method, compare stock price returns, and verify the results of this analysis using statistical tests [4].

The results indicate two types of clusters: 1) a cluster with the tendency to increase the postmerger innovation output; 2) another cluster with a trend to decrease innovation output around M&A deals. The first cluster tends to have a smaller innovation output scale around deals than the other cluster. In addition, the group whose postmerger innovation output decreases tends to have larger stock price return increases after the M&A announcement. One of this study's novelties is that it shows the applicability of unstructured data and machine learning methods to the research field of M&A and innovation. This result is interesting because we extract the deals that positively impact innovation output after the announcement of M&A, while previous studies argue that innovation output generally decreases after the deal.

Finally, we describe the future subjects in this paper's analysis and provide directions for future research. First, this analysis cannot confirm the relationship between the technological distance and the innovation output after the M&A announcement. Thus, future research can conduct a detailed analysis by focusing on the industry and the timing when M&A was conducted, following the previous studies [22]. Additional future topics include studying the utility of patent document vectors, focusing on the factors that cause changes in innovation output, clustering other than k-means, and a detailed analysis of the validity of the number of clusters. The event study method can also analyze the relationship between stock price return and innovation output. Finally, it is assumed that the effect is realized after the organizational integration of R&D. Therefore, the change of innovation output around the M&A integration should be analyzed instead of the deal announcement.

References

1. Bena, J., Li, K.: Corporate innovations and mergers and acquisitions. J. Financ. **69**(5), 1923–1960 (2014)

2. Cassiman, B., Veugelers, R.: In search of complementarity in innovation strategy: internal R&D and external knowledge acquisition. Manage. Sci. **52**, 68–52 (2006)
3. Ahuja, G., Katila, R.: Technological acquisitions and the innovations performance of acquiring firms: a longitudinal study. Strateg. Manag. J. **22**(3), 197–220 (2001)
4. Tamagawa, N., Takahashi, H.: Classifying mergers and acquisitions through clustering method with innovation output. In: International Workshop: Artificial Intelligence of and for Business (2021)
5. Bloom, N., Reenen, J.V.: Patents, real options and firm performance. Econ. J. **112**, 97–116 (2002)
6. Kaplan, S, N.: Mergers and Productivity. University of Chicago Press (2000)
7. Hitt, M.A., Hoskisson, R.E., Ireland, R.D., Harrison, J.S.: Effects of acquisitions on R&D inputs and outputs. Acad. Manag. J. **34**(3), 693–706 (1991)
8. Hitt, M.A., Hoskisson, R.E., Johnson, R.A.: The market for corporate control and firm innovation. Acad. Manag. J. **39**, 1084–1119 (1996)
9. Henderson, R., Cockburn, I.: Scale, scope, and spillovers: the determinants of research productivity in drug discovery. Rand J. Econ. **27**, 32–59 (1996)
10. Fleming, L.: Recombinant uncertainty in technological search. Manage. Sci. **47**(1), 117–132 (2001)
11. Hoberg, G., Phillips, G.: Product market synergies and competition in mergers and acquisitions: a text-based analysis. Rev. Finan. Stud. **23**, 3773–3811 (2010)
12. Nishi, Y., Suge, A., Takahashi, H.: Text analysis on the stock market in the automotive industry through fake news generated by GPT-2. In: Proceedings of the JSAI international symposia on AI 2019 (2019)
13. Kikuchi, T., Kunigami, M., Yamada, T., Takahashi, H. Terano, T.: Analysis of the influences of central bank financing on operative collapses of financial institutions using agent-based simulation. In: 2016 IEEE 40th Annual Computer Software and Applications Conference (COMPSAC), pp. 95–104 (2016)
14. Takahashi, H., Terano, T.: Analysis of micro–macro structure of financial markets via agent-based model: Risk management and dynamics of asset pricing. Electron. Commun. Jpn Part II Electron. **87**(7), 38–48 (2004)
15. Matsumoto, Y., Suge, A., Takahashi, H.: Analysis of the relationship between technological diversification and enterprise value using patent data. In: Nippon Finance Associate 27th Annual Conference Program (2019)
16. Matsumoto, Y., Suge, A., Takahashi, H.: Capturing corporate attributes in a new perspective through fuzzy clustering. In: Kojima, K., Sakamoto, M., Mineshima, K., Satoh, K. (eds.) New Frontiers in Artificial Intelligence. LNCS (LNAI), vol. 11717, pp. 19–33. Springer, Cham (2019). https://doi.org/10.1007/978-3-030-31605-1_2
17. Matsutani, T., Oka, N., Kobayashi, N., Kato, K.: Evaluation of the Derwent World Patents Index (DWPI) abstracts quality using Japanese patent documents. J. Inform. Process. Manage. **56**(4), 208–216 (2013). (in Japanese)
18. JAPAN PATENT OFFICE Homepage. https://www.jpo.go.jp/system/laws/koho/general/kou hou_hakkou_annai.html. Accessed 10 Feb 2022
19. Clarivate Homepage. https://clarivate.com/derwent/dwpi-reference-center/dwpi-patent-ass ignee-codes/. Accessed 10 Feb 2022
20. JAPAN PATENT OFFICE Homepage. https://www.jpo.go.jp/system/patent/gaiyo/bunrui/ipc/ipc8wk.html. Accessed 10 Feb 2022

21. Mekala, D., Gupta, V., Paranjape, B., Karnick, H.: SCDV: Sparse composite document vector using soft clustering over distributional representations. In: Proceedings of the 2017 Conference on Empirical Methods in Natural Language Processing, pp. 659–669. Association for Computational Linguistics (2017)
22. Tamagawa, N., Takahashi, H.: System for analyzing innovation activities in mergers and acquisitions through measuring technological distance. In: International Workshop: KES-AMSTA 2022, (working paper)

Assessment of the Impact of COVID-19 Infections Considering Risk of Infected People Inflow to the Region

Setsuya Kurahashi[✉]

University of Tsukuba, 3-29-1 Otsuka, Bunkyo, Tokyo, Japan
kurahashi.setsuya.gf@u.tsukuba.ac.jp
http://www.springer.com/gp/computer-science/lncs

Abstract. In this paper, we propose a new SEIR model for COVID-19 infection prediction using mobile statistics and evolutionary optimisation, which takes into account the risk of influx. The model is able to predict the number of infected people in a region with high accuracy, and the results of estimation in Sapporo City and Tokyo Metropolitan show high prediction accuracy. Using this model, we analyse the impact of the risk of influx to Sapporo City and show that the spread of infection in November could have been reduced to less than a half if the number of influxes had been limited after the summer. We also examine the preventive measures called for in the emergency declaration of the Tokyo metropolitan area. We found that comprehensive measures are highly effective using the effective reproduction reduction rate of infection control measures obtained from the individual-based model and the SEIR model. We also estimated the effect of vaccination and circuit breakers.

Keywords: COVID-19 · individual-based model · SEIR model · vaccination effect · new coronavirus variants

1 Introduction

In the summer of 2020, a tourism promotion campaign in Japan started while the infection caused by the new coronavirus was about to reach the second wave. In the guide of the project, it was required to comply with various infection control measures for "safe and secure travel". However, without showing the effectiveness of these measures, travellers were asked to agree to comply with the "new travel etiquette", and tourists businesses were required to implement coronavirus infection prevention measures as a condition of participation. However, the number of infected people in rural areas continued to increase. The gap between the strict behavioural restrictions that have no effect and the policies that revitalise the local economy led to various opinions on this project. Amid economic losses such as a decrease in the number of tourists suffering from corona, there was concern that the local health care system would fall into a critical situation

© Springer Nature Switzerland AG 2023
K. Yada et al. (Eds.): JSAI-isAI 2021 Workshops, LNAI 13856, pp. 380–392, 2023.
https://doi.org/10.1007/978-3-031-36190-6_26

between promoting tourism demand that supports the local economy and preventing the spread of infection. Under these circumstances, a rapid spread of infection occurred in Hokkaido from October to December 2020. As a result, a state of emergency unique to the road was issued, and the situation was severely hit, mainly by tourists, the tourism industry, and downtown. It also occurred in tourist cities nationwide such as Okinawa and Hiroshima, and people strongly suspected the relationship between tourism and infection. At the same time, the infection spread in Tokyo, and the second declaration of emergency was issued.

2 Related Work

In March, when the infection began to spread rapidly in the UK, the British government announced that it would adopt a herd immunity strategy. Shortly afterwards, a research report was released by Imperial College London in the UK that questioned the government's policy [Ferguson20]. It was a shocking simulation result showing how tight the hospital was due to the spread of infection. In response, the British Prime Minister suddenly changed his policy to closing all pubs and movie theatres to maintain a strict social distance. This study estimated the number of cases increased sharply without intervention to reduce contact rates, such as by isolating high-risk people at home and so on, eventually requiring more than 400,000 deaths and more than 200,000 ICU beds. It showed that such interventions and alleviations would be repeated for more than a year unless vaccines and antivirals were available. The advantages of this prediction approach are that at a very early stage of interventions, school and university closures, and home quarantine. In this case, the effect of concrete measures, such as all household members stay at home for 14 days and the social distance of the entire people, was quickly shown by an individual-based simulation model.

Researchers at Harvard University published a paper in Science magazine that considered the seasonality and cross-immunity of other coronaviruses [Kissler20]. In order to maintain the medical system, it suggested that surveillance should be maintained because long-term, intermittent social distance is required, and the infectious disease may repeatedly recur even if the infection appears to have disappeared. The method used was a combination of a statistical regression model using coronavirus infection data and a mathematical simulation model. An analysis of COVID-19 infections, reported by the Max Planck Institute in Germany in May, detected the timing of public intervention conducted by the government and the points of change in the spread of the infection [Dehning20]. The model showed that the exponential increase in infections resumed as soon as the intervention, such as going out restrictions and store closures, was released earlier. The model used for the analysis was a combination of an epidemiological simulation model and Bayesian statistical inference. In addition, the model scrutinised the data of infected persons in the UK and analysed the effects of social distance, follow-up survey, PCR test, etc., with an individual-based model attracted attention as a detailed study that integrated the infection data and the information model [Kucharski20].

In this way, in international infection research, combining a data science model using the enormous amount of data accumulated daily and a simulation model using AI and mathematical methods was the first to produce results. This is very different from the current situation in which corona infection research in Japan relies mainly on mathematical (SIR) models of infectious diseases.

On the other hand, the Advisory Council on Countermeasures against COVID-19, established under the Cabinet Secretariat, requested feasible and concrete prevention measures to consider the local economy directly connected to the people's lives, such as tourism in downtown areas. In a study [Kurahashi20a], we compared infection prevention measures for the new coronavirus using an individual-based model and the effectiveness of preventive measures that the general public can take, businesses, schools, etc., was compared and examined. In this model, as a result of an experiment simulating a state in which a virtual resident agent commute to work or visit a store and is exposed to the risk of infection with the new coronavirus, individual infection prevention measures (staggered commuting, telework, class closure, reduction of contact rate, waiting at home after fever) alone or partially combined, but no significant effect can be obtained. On the other hand, it shows if combined measures are implemented, the number of infected patients and severely hospitalised patients can be greatly reduced. However, this study focused on the comparison of various infection prevention measures. It did not focus on predicting the number of infected people in each region or the long-distance movement across local governments, so there was a problem in prediction accuracy [Kurahashi20a,Kurahashi20b].

Therefore, in this study, we constructed a new data-driven coronavirus infection simulation model based on the trends of these international studies, the risk of inflow from other regions, and the financial exhaustion of people working in tourist spots and downtown areas. Then, we will verify the risk of infection spread, considering the risk of influx of infected people into the area.

3   SEIR Infection Model Considering Inflow Risk

It is expected that the infection will spread due to long-distance travel of people such as travel, homecoming, and business trips, but no clear answer has been given as to the extent of the impact. For this reason, discussions have been divided on the travel campaign, which the government has promoted, and it isn't easy to make decisions on when to stop and when to resume. On the other hand, now that many people own smartphones, mobile spatial statistical data using location information such as GPS built into smartphones is available. Therefore, in this study, we analyze the information of people who move across prefectures and use the data that estimates the influx risk of infected people. The estimated calculation of inflow risk is as follows.

$$in\_risk_{j,t} = \sum_{i=1,i\neq j}^{47} \frac{\sum_{k=1}^{14} cp_{i,t-k} * flow_{i,j,t-k}}{pop_i} \tag{1}$$

Here, $in\_risk_{j,t}$ is the inflow risk of the municipality j at the time point t, and $cp_{i,t}$ is the number of infected persons of the municipality i at the time point t. $flow_{i,j,t}$ represents the number of influxes from municipality i to j at time point t, and pop_i represents the population of municipality i.

The general SIR model describes the relationship between an uninfected person without immunity, an affected person, and a recovered person by a differential equation. Still, the new coronavirus has a long incubation period of about six days [CCDC20], so we consider a model that includes the incubation period (period without infectivity) considering the time lag until positive confirmation.

In addition, in local cities, including tourist destinations, it is possible that influxes will promote the spread of infection from large cities such as the Tokyo metropolitan area, where the spread of infection is fast. Therefore, we build an SEIR model that takes the above inflow risk into consideration.

Here, S_i is the number of people without immunity in the age i, E_i is the number of people in the incubation period (non-infectious period) of the age i, and I_i is the infectivity of the age i. The number of people with the disease, R_i is the number of people who have recovered from the age i, N is the total population, t is the time, m is the birth rate $=$ mortality rate, $b_{i,i',t}$ is the infection rate due to contact between ages i, i' at time t, a is the incidence of infection (the inverse of the expected length of the incubation period), g is the recovery rate from infectious diseases, $in\ _risk_{i',t}$ is the inflow risk of age i' at time t (influx of infected people from outside), $\sigma_{i,k}$ is the k per unit time vaccination rate parameter of the age i, and $\lambda_{i,k}$ is the k th vaccine of the age i. represents the immunity acquisition probability parameter.

$$\frac{dS_i}{dt} = mN_i - mS_i - \sum_{i'} \frac{b_{i,i',t}\, S_i(I_{i'} + in\_risk_{i',t})}{N_i}$$
$$- \sum_{k} \sigma_{i,k}\lambda_{i,k}N_i \tag{2}$$

$$\frac{dE_i}{dt} = \sum_{i'} \frac{b_{i,i',t}S_i\,(I_{i'} + in\_risk_{i',t})}{N_i} - (m+a)E_i \tag{3}$$

$$\frac{dI_i}{dt} = aE_i - (m+g)I_i \tag{4}$$

$$\frac{dR_i}{dt} = gI_i - mR_i + \sum_{k} \sigma_{i,k}\lambda_{i,k}N_i \tag{5}$$

These parameter setting values are Table 1.

4   Sapporo Model Construction and Experimental Results

The results of estimating the number of infected people in Sapporo City from June 1st to November 30th, 2020, will be explained. Regarding the inflow risk, we used the inflow data [LocationMind20] and adjusted the composition ratio

Table 1. Model parameters

variable	value	variable	value
S initial value	population	E initial value	Number of initial latent infected people
I initial value	Number of initial infections	R initial value	Number of initial infection recovery
m	0	b	Effective reproduction number * g
a	0.217	g	0.2
N	S + E + I + R		

of the Central Hokkaido area according to the Hokkaido Tourism Incoming Visitors Survey Report [TourismStatistics21]. The effective reproduction number was calculated from the number of infected people in Sapporo City by a simple calculation [ToyoKeizai21].

This makes it possible to estimate the effect of changes in inflow risk on the number of infected people, independent of other factors, and if the number of people visiting Hokkaido after July 20th is "halved" or "0.2". We conducted a what-if analysis on what would happen if the visitors were reduced. This was expressed by reducing the inflow risk by 0.5 times and 0.2 times, respectively. These prediction results are shown in Fig. 1.

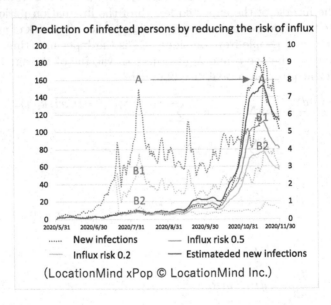

Fig. 1. Prediction results of the number of newly infected people by reducing the risk of inflow

In this figure, the purple dotted line represents the inflow risk 0.5 times, the green dotted line represents the inflow risk 0.2 times, and the orange and yellow solid lines represent the prediction of the number of newly infected persons. As a prediction result, if the inflow risk after July 20th is 0.5 times, the peak number of infected people in November is 0.68 times. If the inflow risk is 0.2 times, it seems that the peak number of infected people in November is reduced up to 0.47 times. Looking at the inflow risk value changes, it does not appear that the number of inflows has increased significantly since October. In addition, the effective reproduction number has increased since October, but almost the same increase can be confirmed in July and September.

From these facts, the inflow risk does not show a short-term effect. On the contrary, the effective reproduction number, which indicates the infection rate, repeatedly rises and falls regularly, and it is particularly relaxed in November. It seems that it always repeats ups and downs. From this, if the inflow risk continues for several months, the number of infected people in the city will gradually increase. If the chances of infection increase due to changes in the behaviour of residents in that city, the number of infected people will be exponential. It is inferred that this will lead to an increase. Although the movement of people across borders does not seem to increase the number of infected people in the short term, the medium- to long-term effect of 2 to 3 months is due to the increase in the regular infection rate. Therefore, it can be expected to cause an infection explosion at once.

5 Construction and Experimental Results of the Individual-Based Model of Tokyo Suburbs

In this section, we explain the infection prediction in Tokyo. In Tokyo and the three prefectures of the metropolitan area, the number of infected people increased sharply from December 2020, leading to a state of emergency from January 8th. Therefore, we constructed an infection prediction model for Tokyo, compared it with the measured values from June 1st, 2020, to January 23rd, 2021, and predicted the number of infected people after January 24th, 2021, for each scenario.

Before constructing the SEIR model, an individual-based model is constructed to estimate the infection control effect of each infection preventive measure. The SEIR model is suitable for predicting the number of infected people in the entire region, but it is difficult to model the effect of specific infection control measures. On the other hand, the individual-based model is a method in which each inhabitant is created as a virtual inhabitant agent on a computer. Various infection prevention measures that this agent can take in daily life can be experimented on.

The model is constructed by 1348 agents composed of two cities based on the household composition of the suburbs of Tokyo. It also refers to the number of infected people in Wuhan and Tokyo in 2020. We extended it using a model [Kurahashi20a], which has been verified as the basic model. The household distribution is shown in Table 2.

In this Tokyo suburban city model, the main infection prevention measures called for in the state of emergency, such as closing restaurants at 20:00, strengthening telework, and limiting the number of large-scale events to 5,000, were set in the model Table 3. The large-scale event limit was set to limit 13 venues with

Table 2. The individual-based model of Tokyo suburbs

Household composition	Number	Household composition	Number
Elderly single	18	Elderly couple	30
3 generations	6	Adult single	40
Adult couple	35	1 parent 1 child	4
2 parents 1 child	21	2 parents 2 children	12

more than 5,000 people in Tokyo to 5,000 people and limit 124 venues with more than 1,000 people to 50% of seats. Regarding telework, the government recommended that the implementation be strengthened by 70%. On the other hand, the decrease of the floating population around Tokyo Station, Shinjuku Station, Shibuya Center Street, and Shinagawa Station, which are the main urban areas in Tokyo, at 15:00 on weekdays from January 20th to 24th was only 26.5% compared with December 21st to 25th. Based on this, we considered that a stepwise strengthening measure was necessary, and in addition to strengthening to 70%, we also conducted an experiment of 50%. In this model, the telework rate is set as the 1-commuting rate to the workplace.

In the experiment, the individual-based model shown in Fig. 2 was constructed, and the expected value of the contact rate was set as the initial value so that the basic reproduction number would be 2.5. Then, as a setting before the declaration of an emergency, the telework rate was 25%, the contact rate between the office and the school was reduced to 1/4 of the normal rate, and an experiment was conducted with Table 3 as a scenario.

Table 3. Infection prevention measures in the state of emergency

Infection prevention measures	Settings
Restaurant closed at 20:00	Half of restaurant visitors
Restaurant closed at 18:00	1/4 of restaurant visitors
Strengthening telework to 50%	Attendance rate 50%
Strengthening telework to 70%	Attendance rate 30%
Large event restrictions	Venue restrictions

The above figure of Fig. 2 is a model of an urban area on the outskirts of Tokyo. The light pink area on the left is a shopping street, the lilac area is an event venue, and there are two towns above and below the centre. The upper part of each represents a single person, an adult couple, and a household with parents and children, and the brown dot at the bottom represents an elderly household. The squares on the right represent workplaces, schools, restaurants, hospitals, and morgues, respectively. The figure on the left below shows the number of effective reproductions (black), and the figure on the right shows the transition of infected people. Based on a detailed analysis of the epidemic of the new coronavirus COVID-19 [CCDC20, WHO20a], the infection process was defined as follows. The incubation period is five days on average after infection, but two days before the onset of infection, it has the ability to infect others even during the incubation period. Fever, cough, etc., appear on the 5th day when the incubation period ends. [Lauer20]. After fever, the base model has a 50% chance of seeing a doctor at the hospital and waiting at home. The remaining 50% of infected people are asymptomatic or have mild symptoms, so they are self-treated with antipyretics and continue to commute to work or school. Those who have had a fever for 4 days or more and have visited the hospital will undergo a PCR test, and the test results will be available the next day, and the infected person will be hospitalised. The PCR test implementation rate was set at 50%. Since the estimated number of infected people is significantly smaller than the number of deaths that have occurred, the supplementary rate of the test was estimated to be about half. Fifteen days after infection, 0.04% for young people, 1.12% for adults, and 9.55% for elderly people became severely infected. Those who did not receive a medical examination in advance are also transported to the hospital. On the 23rd day after infection, 10.14% of young people, 24.38% of adults, and 68.55% of elderly people die. Mildly infected patients recovered 27 to 48 days after infection. Severely hospitalised patients who escaped death recovered in 49 days, and they were supposed to acquire immunity temporarily. This model was designed based on the COVID-19 agent-based model [Kurahashi20a].

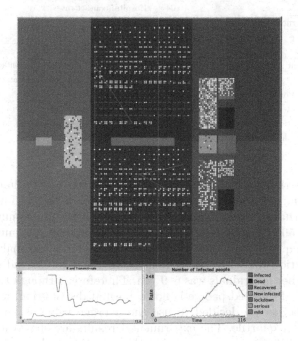

Fig. 2. The individual-based model of Tokyo suburbs

Residents come into contact with others in various aspects of their lives. The basic parameters of the model, such as the contact rate in each situation, such as offices and restaurants and the infection rate per contact, are shown in Table 4. Epidemiological studies have reported that in the case of the new coronavirus, the rate at which one infected person infects another is less than 0.5. The cause has not been clarified, but unlike influenza, it is presumed that one of the factors is that infection does not occur unless close contact continues for a certain period of time. Therefore, assuming that there is a small-world network structure among the inhabitants, we set the degree distribution to follow the power rule with reference to the empirical study of friend networks [Tomochi11]. When eating and drinking at restaurants and pubs, instead of randomly selecting a companion, we chose three people from each family and friend network and set them to be present with four people. In addition, as a measure for restaurants, it was possible to limit the number of people at the table and set diagonal seats. In this experiment, the number of seats is limited to 4 people, and from the droplet diffusion simulation experiment [Tsubokura20], the amount of droplets on the diagonal seats is 1/4. The effect is halved in the diagonal seat arrangement.

Table 4. Basic parameters of the Tokyo suburbs model

Parameter	Value	parameter	Value
Home contact rate	0.46	Workplace contact rate	0.25
School contact rate	0.25	train contact rate	0.07
Store contact rate	0.04	Hospital contact rate	0.01
Restaurant contact rate	0.25	Event contact rate	0.1
Train utilization rate	0.5	commuting rate	0.75
Store utilization rate	0.5	Restaurant utilization rate	0.25
Number of restaurant seats	4	Suppression of diagonal seat contact number	0.5
Local event rate	0.07	Probability of propagation/Contact	0.1
Contact Preference Power Index	0.5	Younger Severity Rate	0.04%
Adult aggravation rate	1.12%	Elderly aggravation rate	9.55%
Case fatality rate of severely ill young people	10.14%	Case fatality rate of severely ill adults	24.38%
Case fatality rate of the elderly severely ill	68.55%		

In the experiment, one adult randomly selected as the initial value was infected with the new coronavirus and shown in Table 3. In each infection prevention measure, the spread of infection was simulated for a maximum of one year. We performed 500 trials each and analysed the maximum, minimum, arithmetic mean, median, quartile, and outlier-removed mean. From the analysis results, no spread of infection was observed in many trials, and the spread of infection to one or more other individuals was 6–9 yen. Therefore, although the distribution of the number of infected people is not a normal distribution, it shows almost the same shape, so we decided to use the average value as an index instead of the median or quartile. The experimental results are shown in Fig. 3. As 10 types of preventive measures, assuming the situation in December 2020, basic preventive measures with office and school contact rate of 20% and telework rate of 25%, the number of restaurant users 50%, 25%, 50% for diagonal seats, 25% for diagonal seats, event limit and accommodation rate of 50% for up to 5000 people, telework rate 50%, 70%, comprehensive measures Eating and drinking 50% diagonal seat limit and telework rate 50% and event limit were set. The blue bar graph shows the number of infected people in the 1348 people model. If there is no more inflow from the outside, the infection will end within about 30 days, which is close to the monthly number of infected people. The orange rhombus represents the average of the effective reproduction number during the infection outbreak period for each countermeasure. It is between 0.14 and 0.08, and this rate of decrease in the number of effective reproductions will be used in subsequent experiments as the effect of each infection prevention measure.

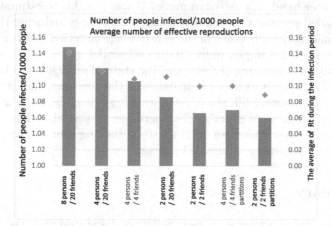

Fig. 3. The result of the Tokyo suburbs model The blue bar graph shows the number of infected people/1000 (left vertical axis), and the orange rhombus shows the average of the effective reproduction number during the infection outbreak period (right vertical axis). (Color figure online)

6   Discussion

While the general SEIR model models the transition of infected people in closed areas, this model considers the influx risk of infected people from other regions. The inflow risk was set by obtaining a highly accurate estimate using mobile spatial statistical data. As a result, we were able to build a highly accurate model. Next, the results of the analysis will be examined using this model. In the Sapporo city model, if the number of influxes from other prefectures after the end of July can be limited, we found that the number of infected people may be reduced up to 0.47 times due to predicting the number of infected people in November.

The increase of infected people is affected by the infection rate associated with behavioural changes one to two weeks ago. Still, when the number of infected people in the city is small, infection explosions rarely occur. On the other hand, with the increase of infected people in the city from September to October in Sapporo City, a huge outbreak of infection has occurred since November, even if the infection rate has increased to the same extent. Although this can be expected to some extent from the fact that the infection phenomenon becomes an exponential function, it was concretely able to show how much the increase in cross-border movement from summer affected the spread of infection in a few months using this model. On the other hand, even if there is almost no risk of inflow, the spread of infection in November will occur to some extent, so it is necessary to take measures to control the number of infected people in the city.

On the other hand, in the Tokyo model, it was possible to estimate the effect of more detailed preventive measures rather than simply reducing the infection rate by estimating the difference in the effective reproduction number of infection preventive measures using an individual-based model.

As a result of estimating the effect of the state of emergency using this estimated value, it is not a measure that damages the economy, such as shortening the time of restaurants. Still, the effect of thorough diagonal seats and shielding plates and telework were effective. Furthermore, it was also shown that comprehensive preventive measures such as strengthening and limiting large-scale events reduce the number of infected people.

7   Summary

In this paper, we constructed a new SEIR model considering the inflow risk, proposed a method that enables highly accurate prediction of infected persons in the region, and analysed the estimation results in Sapporo City. As a result, we were able to show high prediction accuracy. Then, using this model, if the impact of the inflow risk to Sapporo City could be analysed and the number of influxes after the summer could be limited, it is possible that the spread of infection in November could have been reduced to less than half. It was shown that there is. In addition, we will verify the infection preventive measures called for in the state of emergency in the Tokyo metropolitan area. From the reduction rate of the infection rate (effective reproduction number) for each preventive measure in the individual-based model, it was shown that comprehensive measures would have a great effect. Future work is to compare the dynamics of transmission when using GPS travel data in 2019 to evaluate what these self-isolation strategies achieved. And we will try to find a way to translate ABM experimental results back into parameters for the SEIR model.

This research was supported by JSPS Grant-in-Aid for Scientific Research JP21H01561. In addition, we would like to thank the Cabinet Secretariat COVID-19 AI/Simulation Project and LocationMind corp. for their cooperation in mobile spatial statistical data.

References

[Ferguson20] Ferguson, N.M., et al.: Impact of non-pharmaceutical interventions (NPIs) to reduce COVID-19 mortality and healthcare demand. MRC Centre for Global Infectious Disease Analysis, Report 9 (2020)

[Kissler20] Kissler, S.M., et al.: Projecting the transmission dynamics of SARS-CoV-2 through the postpandemic period. Science (2020). https://doi.org/10.1126/science.abb5793

[Dehning20] Dehning, D., et al.: Inferring change points in the spread of COVID-19 reveals the effectiveness of interventions. Science (2020). https://doi.org/10.1126/science.abb9789

[Kucharski20] Kucharski, A.J., et al.: Effectiveness of isolation, testing, contact tracing, and physical distancing on reducing transmission of SARS-CoV-2 in different settings: a mathematical modelling study. The LANCET **20**(10), 1151–1160 (2020)

[Kurahashi20a] Kurahashi, S.: Estimating effectiveness of preventing measures for 2019 novel coronavirus diseases (COVID-19). Jpn. Soc. Artif. Intell. **35**(3), D-K28_1/8 (2020)

[Kurahashi20b] Kurahashi, S.: Estimating effectiveness of preventing measures for 2019 novel coronavirus diseases. In: 9th International Congress on Advanced Applied Informatics, SCAI, vol. 18, pp. 1–6 (2020)

[CCDC20] Zhang, Y. and The Novel Coronavirus Pneumonia Emergency Response Epidemiology Team: The epidemiological characteristics of an outbreak of 2019 novel coronavirus diseases (COVID-19) - China, 2020. China CDC Weekly **41**(2), 145/151 (2020)

[LocationMind20] https://corona.go.jp/dashboard/pdf/inflow_risk_20210125.pdf

[TourismStatistics21] https://www.pref.hokkaido.lg.jp/kz/kkd/irikomi.html

[ToyoKeizai21] https://toyokeizai.net/sp/visual/tko/covid19/

[WHO20a] Aylward, B., et al.: Report of the WHO-China joint mission on coronavirus disease 2019 (COVID-19), WHO-China joint mission members (2020). https://www.who.int/docs/default-source/coronaviruse/who-china-joint-mission-on-covid-19-final-report.pdf

[Lauer20] Lauer, S.A., Grantz, K.H., Bi, Q., Jones, F.K.: The incubation period of coronavirus disease 2019 (COVID-19) from publicly reported confirmed cases: estimation and application. Ann. Internal Med. (2020). https://doi.org/10.7326/M20-0504

[Tomochi11] Tomochi, M., Tanaka, A., Shichijo, T.: Stratification and nested structure of small world in a friendship network - data analysis, modeling, and simulation on a social networking service a.k.a "Tomocom". Sociol. Theory Methods **26**(1), 83/97 (2011)

[Tsubokura20] Tsubokura, M.: Prediction and Countermeasures for Infection by Virus Contaminated Droplet in Indoor Environment, Issue November 20 (2020). https://www.covid19-ai.jp/en-us/presentation/2020_rq1_droplet_infection_simulation/

[Dagan21] Dagan, N., et al.: BNT162b2 mRNA Covid-19 vaccine in a nationwide mass vaccination setting. N. Engl. J. Med. (2021). https://doi.org/10.1056/NEJMoa2101765

[Liu21] Liu, Y., et al.: Neutralizing activity of BNT162b2-elicited serum. N. Engl. J. Med. (2021). https://doi.org/10.1056/NEJMc21020175

Author Index

© Springer Nature Switzerland AG 2023
K. Yada et al. (Eds.): JSAI-isAI 2021 Workshops LNAI 13856, pp. 393–394, 2023.
https://doi.org/10.1007/978-3-031-36190-6

Printed in the United States
by Baker & Taylor Publisher Services